Communion,
Community,
Commonweal

Communion, Community, Commonweal

READINGS FOR SPIRITUAL LEADERSHIP

JOHN S. MOGABGAB

UPPER
ROOM BOOKS
NASHVILLE

The scripture quotations identified in the text are used by permission: NRSV from the New Revised Standard Version Bible, copyright © 1989 by the Division of Christian Education of the National Council of the Churches of Christ in the U.S.A. Used by permission. All rights reserved; KJV from The King James Version of the Bible; NEB from *The New English Bible,* © The Delegates of Oxford University Press and The Syndics of the Cambridge University Press 1961, 1970. Reprinted with permission; RSV from The Revised Standard Version, copyrighted © 1946, 1952, and © 1971 by the Division of Christian Education of the National Council of the Churches of Christ in the United States of America. Used by permission; JB from THE JERUSALEM BIBLE, copyright © 1966 by Darton, Longman & Todd, Ltd. and Doubleday, a division of Bantam, Doubleday, Dell Publishing Group, Inc. Reprinted by permission; NJB from THE NEW JERUSALEM BIBLE, copyright © 1985 by Darton, Longman & Todd, Ltd. and Doubleday, a division of Bantam, Doubleday, Dell Publishing Group, Inc. Reprinted by permission.

Any scripture quotation designated AT is the author's translation.

The publisher gratefully acknowledges permission to reprint the following copyrighted material:

Prayer from *Life Within: Prayers by Brother Roger of Taizé.* Copyright © Ateliers et Presses de Taizé, 71250 Taizé Communauté, France. Used by permission of Ateliers et Presses de Taizé and Westminster/John Knox Press.

"A Hold on the Eternal" adapted from Evelyn Underhill, *The Spiritual Life: Great Spiritual Truths for Everyday Life* (Oxford: Oneworld Publications, Ltd., 1993), pp. 16–19, 27. Used by permission of the publisher.

"Psalm of the Salt Marsh" by Maxwell Corydon Wheat from *Limulus: Poems of the Great Waters* (Virginia Wheat, 333 Bedwell St., Freeport, NY 11520). Used by permission.

"Memory in Congregational Life" by Bruce C. Birch from *Congregations: Their Power to Form and Transform,* edited by C. Ellis Nelson. Used by permission of Westminster/John Knox Press.

Lyrics from "For Musicians" by Erik Routley, copyright © 1977 by Hope Publishing Co., Carol Stream, IL. All rights reserved. Used by permission.

Excerpts from "The Kingdom: God's Domination-Free Order" by Walter Wink are reprinted by permission from *Engaging the Powers* by Walter Wink, copyright © 1992 Augsburg Fortress.

"Power, Powerlessness, and Power" by Henri J. M. Nouwen is published as a separate booklet by Crossroad under the title *The Path of Power.* Copyright © 1995 by Henri J. M. Nouwen. Reprinted by permission of The Crossroad Publishing Co., New York and Darton, Longman & Todd, Ltd.

While every attempt has been made to secure permission, we may have failed in a few cases to trace or contact the copyright holder. We apologize for any inadvertent oversight or error.

Cover Design: Bruce Gore
Interior Design: Nancy Cole
First Printing: September 1995 (5)
Library of Congress Catalog Number: 95-60919
ISBN: 0-8358-0737-1
Printed in the United States of America

To Marjorie J. Thompson,
esteemed spiritual leader, dearest friend,
and beloved partner
in the vocation of Christian marriage

Contents

Commonweal

Acknowledgments

N O BOOK IS THE PRODUCT of only one person's energies, and nowhere is this more evident than in a collection of essays. My deep thanks go to the authors gathered in this volume. Over the years, their generosity of mind and spirit has made my work on *Weavings* a privilege and a joy. I am indebted to Charla Honea, formerly team leader of Upper Room Books, for her enthusiastic reception of the project outline. Robin Philpo Pippin, managing editor of Upper Room Books during the early stages of production, offered timely encouragement when my uncertainties multiplied. Karen Williams deserves special recognition for deftly steering the book through a maze of editorial deadlines. *Weavings* editorial secretary Carol Meyer, whose prowess at the computer keyboard is legendary, has earned sustained applause for fast and error-free entry of the text. Throughout a decade of planning and producing *Weavings*, one person especially has been a source of unwavering support and guidance. To my wife, Marjorie J. Thompson, whose gentle-hearted wisdom has so often shown me the way ahead, I dedicate this book with gratitude beyond words.

Preface

SILENCE SLOWLY PERMEATED the room as retreat participants found their seats and settled themselves for the morning session. A group of spiritual leaders from across the country had gathered in this place apart for several days of personal renewal. We would begin, I suggested, by spending time with a story. My hope was that the questions posed by the story might provide direction for our time together. The story itself, drawn from Father Theophane the Monk's *Tales of a Magic Monastery*, goes like this:

There's a monk there who will never give you advice, but only a question. I was told his questions could be very helpful. I sought him out.

"I am a parish priest," I said. "I'm here on retreat. Could you give me a question?"

"Ah, yes," he answered. "My question is, What do they need?*"*

I came away disappointed. I spent a few hours with the question, writing out answers, but finally I went back to him.

"Excuse me. Perhaps I didn't make myself clear. Your question has been helpful, but I wasn't so much interested in thinking about my apostolate during this retreat. Rather I wanted to think seriously about my own spiritual life. Could you give me a question for my own spiritual life?"

"Ah, I see. Then my question is, What do they REALLY need?*"*[1]

Thomas Merton once observed that the spiritual life is not primarily the domain of the individual. Rather, it is the life of the Holy Spirit unfolding in a particular epoch in and through the lives of a whole people. Father Theophane's wise elder knew this. He knew that spiritual seekers and those called to lead them are bound together in the mystery of the Holy Spirit's life with God's people. This gracious interweaving of listening and leading, of need and provision, of personal, congregational, and societal renewal, forms the substance of this book. Its purpose is to provide a framework for spiritual leaders, whether ordained or lay, to enter more deeply and fruitfully into their

---

[1] Theophane the Monk, *Tales of a Magic Monastery* (New York: Crossroad, 1981), p. 42.

own ministry through the doorway opened by the question, "What do they *really* need?"

The structure of this volume reflects my own initial soundings of this fathomless question. The Introduction by Evelyn Underhill, whose words are as compelling today as when she first wrote them more than fifty years ago, sets the context by inviting us to a life in which "all that we do comes from the centre, where we are anchored in God." What do they *really* need? They need leaders who live without pretense and whose eyes shine with the radiance that comes from spending time with God. They need to taste the hope that comes with knowing that God is real. They need to be ushered into the presence of Christ often enough that a transfiguration of their vision can occur. They need to see God. For this reason Part I, entitled Communion, explores the rhythm of listening and responding that shapes our relationship with God. Behind this choice of starting point lies the ancient conviction expressed in the formula, *contemplata tradere*—we can pass on to others only what we ourselves have contemplated.

What do they *really* need? They need to know they are cared for with unfailing fidelity. They need companions with whom to go deep into life so that they know they are not in it alone. They need time and encouragement to savor the wisdom and beauty of those around them. They need occasions to "be glad in the LORD and rejoice" (Psalm 32:11, NRSV) because they have heard a simple message clearly spoken and received living water from the deepest, freshest part of the well (John 4:5-15). Part II, therefore, focuses on several core disciplines of Christian community: remembering, celebrating, communicating, and guiding. Each of these illuminates Dietrich Bonhoeffer's belief that in Christian community we "meet one another as bringers of the message of salvation."[2]

What do they *really* need? They need to discover the creativity and power of simple availability. They need to witness worldly holiness and holy courage. They need to see joy crest the social horizon of cynicism and chronic despair. They need to recognize that what they seek for themselves is also the heart's desire of thousands around them: to "see the goodness of the LORD in the land of the living" (Psalm 27:13, NRSV). Part III takes up the theme of Commonweal, the general welfare for which God came among us in Jesus Christ and toward which God is drawing all of history. It is this orientation to the

---

[2] Dietrich Bonhoeffer, *Life Together*, trans. and Intro. by John W. Doberstein (New York: Harper & Row, 1954), p. 23.

injured world beyond the congregation that Brother Roger of Taizé evokes in these words of prayer:

Lord Christ, you see us
sometimes strangers on the earth,
taken aback by the violence,
by the harshness of oppositions.

And you come to send out a gentle breeze
on the dry ground of our doubts,
and so prepare us to be bearers
of peace and reconciliation.[3]

May the gentle breeze of the Spirit, astir now all across the Church, prepare us to seek and to find ever more faithful responses to the question, "What do they *really* need?"

John S. Mogabgab

[3] Brother Roger of Taizé, *Life From Within: Prayers by Brother Roger of Taizé* (Louisville, KY: Westminster/John Knox Press, 1990), p. 22.

Introduction

BENEATH THE SURFACE OF LIFE, which generally contents us, there are unsuspected deeps and great spiritual forces that condition and control our small lives. Some people are, or become, sensitive to the pressure of these forces. The rest of us easily ignore the evidence for this whole realm of experience, just because it is all so hidden and interior; and we are so busy responding to obvious and outward things. But no psychology that fails to take account of it can claim to be complete. When we take it seriously, it surely suggests that we are essentially spiritual as well as natural creatures; and that therefore life in its fullness, the life that develops and uses all our capacities and fulfills all our possibilities, must involve correspondence not only with our visible and ever-changing, but also with our invisible and unchanging environment: the Spirit of all spirits, God, in whom we live and move and have our being. The significance, the greatness of humanity, consists in our ability to do this. The meaning of our life is bound up with the meaning of the universe. Even though so far the consciousness of this ability and this meaning is latent in most people, what an enhancement of life, what devotedness, heroism, and capacity for suffering and for love, what a sure hold upon reality it already produces in those who have felt its attraction, and who respond with courage and without reserve to its demands.

When we consider our situation from this point of view, when we lift our eyes from the crowded by-pass to the eternal hills; then, how much the personal and practical things we have to deal with are enriched. What meaning and coherence come into our scattered lives. We mostly spend those lives conjugating three verbs: to *want*, to *have*, and to *do*. Craving, clutching, and fussing, on the material, political, social, emotional, intellectual—even on the religious—plane, we are kept in perpetual unrest: forgetting that none of these verbs has any ultimate significance, except so far as they are transcended by, and included in, the fundamental verb, to *be*: and that *being*, not wanting, having, and doing, is the essence of a spiritual life. But now, with this widening of the horizon, our personal ups and downs, desires,

---

Adapted from Evelyn Underhill, *The Spiritual Life: Great Spiritual Truths for Everyday Life* (Oxford: Oneworld Publications, Ltd., 1993), pp. 16–19, 27. Used by permission of the publisher.

cravings, efforts, are seen in scale; as small and transitory spiritual facts, within a vast, abiding spiritual world, and lit by a steady spiritual light. And at once a new coherence comes into our existence, a new tranquility and release. Like a chalet in the Alps, that homely existence gains atmosphere, dignity, significance from the greatness of the sky above it and the background of the everlasting hills.

THE PEOPLE OF OUR TIME are helpless, distracted and rebellious, unable to interpret what is happening, and full of apprehension about what is to come, largely because they have lost this sure hold on the eternal, which gives to each life meaning and direction, and with meaning and direction gives steadiness. I do not mean by this a mere escape from our problems and dangers, a slinking away from the actual to enjoy the eternal. I mean an acceptance and living out of the actual, in its homeliest details and its utmost demands, in the light of the eternal; and with that peculiar sense of ultimate security that only a hold on the eternal brings. When the vivid reality represented by these rather abstract words is truly possessed by us, when what is unchanging in ourselves is given its chance, and emerges from the stream of succession to recognize its true home and goal, which is God—then, though much suffering may, indeed will remain, apprehension, confusion, instability and despair will cease. . . . For a spiritual life is simply a life in which all that we do comes from the center, where we are anchored in God: a life soaked through and through by a sense of His reality and claim, and self-given to the great movement of His will.

Evelyn Underhill

Evelyn Underhill (1875-1941) was an Anglican, a mystic, and a pioneer among twentieth century women in the church and the spiritual life. She was a worker in the war effort of World War I and a pacifist in World War II. She was the author of about forty books.

Communion

Communion

The Paradox of Prayer

by Roberta C. Bondi

P RAY WITHOUT CEASING" (1 Thess. 5:17, KJV), Paul says to us. What is Paul asking us to do and why or how should we do it? Beyond praying for a specific need in a particular situation, many of us do not know what prayer can be. And yet we know prayer is important.

Indeed, we may even discover that we have a real longing for prayer. Many things may set off this longing—our relationship with people who are who they are because of their prayer, a particularly strong experience of God, an empty restlessness or sense of God's absence, or impenetrable moral ambiguities.

But there is a deeper reason for our longing for prayer. We are so made that we cannot live fully without it. Prayer is central to the Christian life. It joins us to God, and it leads us to ourselves in God. It is the place where we can be completely ourselves. In prayer we can see ourselves as we are and be truthful about what we see. We can enjoy our own gifts and wonder at all we have been given. We can argue with God about who we are and who we have been. We can acknowledge our mistakes and set them aside. Most important, we can learn to love God, ourselves as belonging to God, and other people as images of God, because we are shaped at our very deepest levels by our prayer. The spiritual mothers and fathers of the early church knew all this and much more as well. Their wisdom can guide us in our exploration of prayer. First I want to emphasize that God's love is the foundation of our prayer. Then I would like to focus on the way our manner of prayer must be suited to our unique needs. This will lead us to consider the relation between God's grace and our work in the life of prayer. Finally, I will offer some comments on scripture as a resource for prayer.

GOD'S LOVE FOR US

T HE FIRST and most fundamental truth our Christian ancestors knew about prayer was this: God's love is the starting point and ending point of all prayer. Made in God's image, we are beloved by God who loves us as unwaveringly and responsively as a mother loves her baby. The author of the Macarian homilies, a fifth-century Syrian writer, describes the emotional tone of God's love for us in this way:

> . . . *a baby, even though it is powerless to accomplish anything or with its own feet to go to its mother, still rolls and makes noises and cries as it seeks its mother. . . . And she picks it up and fondles it and feeds it with great love. This is also what God, the Lover of [humankind], does to the person that comes to [God] and ardently desires [God].*[1]

This image of God makes it clear that God's love is not the love of a dispassionate and just king for his distant subjects. It is intimate and tender, a natural response based on the closest ties of kinship, and it takes delight in the object of its love.

The metaphor of mother and baby illustrates the extravagant nature of God's love for us—a love characterized by God's persistence throughout human history in trying to rescue us from our brokenness—a love that does not depend upon our having looked for God first.

In addition to the tender and persistent love of God, each of us has been given God's own image that can never be completely lost. According to our Christian ancestors, though human life may appear hopelessly broken, God's image remains within us—partially erased or covered over but still there. This means that however skewed our vision of God, others, and ourselves becomes, something in us still recognizes God. That image of God which is in us is that part of ourselves that never stops desiring to move toward love. Even if there seems to be no room for human freedom at all, that part of our selves is still always able to choose to cry out for help, to make the tiniest movement toward love. Because of the persistent presence of the image of God, there is a fundamental goodness in every human being that always connects us to God and to each other.

THE UNIQUENESS OF PRAYER

WHENEVER WE PRAY, we pray with the whole people of God, with the people of the old covenant as well as with all the faithful Christians throughout the centuries and in all places. At the same time, with God's enduring love as its starting point, prayer is an expression of each person's relationship with God.

[1] *Intoxicated with God: The Fifty Spiritual Homilies of Macarius*, trans. George Maloney, S.J. (Denville, NJ: Dimension Books, 1978), pp. 212–213.

Therefore, there is no one right way to pray. Even if we think there is nothing distinctive about our individual families of origin, temperaments, gifts, interests, or weaknesses, they are combined in each of us in a special way. Beginning to pray means beginning to find a way of prayer that suits us in a particular way. A friend of Anthony the Great, founder of Christian monasticism, once asked him, "What thing is so good that I may do it and live by it?"

Instead of saying, "Here is what you need to do and here is how you need to pray," Anthony answered:

> *Cannot all works please God equally? Scripture says, Abraham was hospitable and God was with him. And Elijah loved quiet, and God was with him. And David was humble and God was with him. So whatever you find your soul wills in following God's will, do it, and keep your heart.*[2]

No one can tell us what Christian discipline we should adopt; we must find for ourselves what works best for us.

Our prayer is unique. But this does not mean that it can be merely whimsical, without definite patterns and commitment. Whatever time of day we set aside for prayer, whatever place we select, whatever forms of prayer we use, it is important to understand that regularity is more sustaining in prayer than intensity or length. We are spending time with God, learning who God is and who we are, learning to love God and God's world. This happens over a matter of years. If we miss some days, we should simply start again and think small. A brother told an abba that he had gotten away from his monastic disciplines, presumably including his prayer, and he felt too discouraged to begin again. The abba replied by telling him this story:

> *A man had a plot of land. And through his carelessness brambles sprang up and it became a wilderness of thistles and thorns. Then he decided to cultivate it. So he said to his son: "Go and clear that ground." So the son went to clear it, and saw that the thistles and thorns had multiplied. . . . He said: "How much time shall I need to clear and weed all this?" And he lay on the ground and went to sleep. He did this day after day. Later his father came to see what he had done, and found him doing nothing. When his father asked*

---

[2] "The Sayings of the Fathers" in *Western Asceticism*, trans. Owen Chadwick, Library of Christian Classics (Philadelphia: Westminster Press, 1958), pp. 38–39.

21

him about it, the son replied that the job looked so bad that he could never make himself begin. His father replied: "Son, if you had cleared each day the area on which you lay down, your work would have advanced slowly and you would not have lost heart." So the lad did what his father said, and in a short time the plot was cultivated.

So, the abba told the discouraged brother, "Do a little work and do not faint, and God will give you grace."[3] The disheartened brother took up his prayer again with patience without trying to do everything.

We can, too. Prayer is not a test of character, an endurance contest, or a heroic task set before us. If lapses in prayer lead us to self-reproach, we will find it difficult indeed to grow in our prayer life.

GRACE AND WORK

MANY OF US are accustomed to going through our days continually reproaching ourselves for what we perceive to be our failures in all areas of life. If we do this, it will truly hinder our prayer. We are taking on the role of God against ourselves, but not treating ourselves as God, in fact, treats us. We are exercising violence against ourselves while God treats all of us gently, never forcing or bullying us or riding roughshod over us. If we want to pray and learn to love God, we must give up our self-condemnation.

Much self-reproach concerning our prayer life results from some peculiar convictions about prayer that Christians of other periods do not always share with us. Many of us believe that if we are real Christians, love and prayer should flow out of us effortlessly, sincerely, and spontaneously. We also seem to believe that if we are not sure how to pray and if love for God and for others does not flow out of us, then we must not really be Christians. Furthermore, we believe that if we use the words of others in our prayer instead of our own words flowing freely from our hearts, our prayer is not sincere. These convictions can make us feel guilty, frustrated, and embarrassed because we are not more loving and we do not pray more. A lot of energy in church life then is spent trying to keep other people from finding out that we may be Christian frauds. But under the fronts we put up are a lot of truly suffering, truly discouraged, and often very angry hearts.

This pain is not necessary. Our early monastic ancestors would be

---

[3] Chadwick, *Western Asceticism*, p. 94.

baffled to think that we could be so unrealistic about ourselves, our love, and our prayer. They knew that love and prayer, being closely related, must both be learned over a whole lifetime of often very unspontaneous work on our part coupled with the continuous gift of God's grace. Even working at it a long time may not make love come easily or enable us to love everyone in the same way. Abba Evagrius Ponticus, who had very firm notions about what human beings are capable of, described for the members of his monastic community what was realistically possible for them:

> *It is not possible to love all the brethren to the same degree. But it is possible to associate with all in a manner that is . . . free of resentment and hatred.*[4]

Prayer, like love, is also something people learn to do over a lifetime. Furthermore, far from being spontaneous at all times, the sincere prayer of the monastics rested on recitation of and meditation on the psalms, which they believed were given to God's people partly because we often would be at a loss for words in prayer without them.

We must be intentional in our growth in prayer. Anthony uses a helpful metaphor to demonstrate the foolishness of expecting ourselves to be spontaneous in our growth in the Christian virtues, among which he often includes prayer. In order to grow we must make some choices about the kind of people we want to be and the kind of prayer we want to pray:

> *Whoever hammers a lump of iron, first decides what he is going to make of it, a scythe, a sword, or an axe. Even so we ought to make up our minds what kind of virtue we want to forge or we labor in vain.*[5]

This is not to suggest that early monastic prayer or love is simply the result of hard work and determination. Evagrius spoke of prayer as the gift of God, and all of the desert fathers and mothers believed that whenever we are present to God in our prayer and God is present to us, it is always by the gift of God's grace rather than the result of something we do.

---

[4] Evagrius Ponticus, *The Praktikos: Chapters on Prayer*, ed. M. Basil Pennington, O.C.S.O., trans. John Bamburger, O.C.S.O. (Spenser, MA: Cistercian Publications, 1977), p. 41.

[5] *The Sayings of the Desert Fathers: The Alphabetical Collection*, trans. Benedicta Ward, SLG (Oxford: A.R. Mowbray, 1981), Anthony 35, p. 8.

OR MANY PROTESTANTS the notion of *learning* either to pray or to love is startling. The families of Protestantism that have either descended from or been influenced by Luther or Calvin have stressed the insignificance of human work compared to the size of the gift of God's grace. At the same time these traditions have emphasized that anything good we do, such as loving or praying, is a gift of God. All we can contribute is our faith, for "salvation [is] by faith, alone." Talk about learning to love and learning to pray or using the prayers of others for our own prayers suggests a failure to understand that our salvation does indeed spring from faith in God alone.

Our early monastic relatives would be confused. Of course, they would say, salvation is the gift of God to us; it is true that salvation is partly a matter of God loving us and accepting us as we are, but it also has a great deal to do with growing in love and prayer in the Christian life. If we mean by salvation God's love and acceptance of us, then we certainly do nothing to earn it. If we use the term "salvation" to include our Christian growth in God, this growth is not something that is given to us all at once without our doing anything to bring it about. We are given the image of God at our creation, and it is never totally erased. That image remains within us as a need and ability to *respond* to God's saving grace, and to seek out the grace which God has promised will be given to us as we grow in the Christian life.

John Wesley agreed with the monastics. He affirmed as one of his most important theological points that we do not earn God's love or any other part of God's salvation. Nevertheless, he also insisted that we have both the ability and the need to respond to God's grace, for grace never overwhelms us, forcing us to do or to be what we do not choose ourselves.

God's grace and our response come together in prayer as surely as they come together in every other place in our lives. The secret of seeing this grace is found in realizing that the interchange of grace and response do not remain within prayer alone. Prayer and life must be all of a piece. Suppose I am perpetually angry with a neighbor who seems to have nothing better to do than to harass the people who live on her street. I pray for help in forgiving my neighbor and for the ability to treat her, as Evagrius says, "without resentment and hatred." During the course of my prayer I may receive an insight into the neighbor or myself that allows me to see her differently. That insight is a gift of grace. It is not so compelling, however, that I will have to relate differently to her in the future. I can have the insight, continue to nurse a grudge, and end up angrier than ever. Or I may carry my insight out of my prayer, ponder it, and bring myself to begin a friendly conversation with her that may make compassion even more possible toward her. No one who has had this very ordinary experience will have any illusions about gritting the teeth and forgiving as an effort of will. It simply is not possible without grace. And yet when it comes we must be waiting to respond by our actions and by our further prayer.

In the final analysis, prayer is paradoxically both something we learn to do and a gift given to us by God which we must receive, "for [God] it is who gives prayer to the [one] who prays."[6] First and last, prayer is a pursuit of the One who has promised to be with us, not just for the time of the prayer, but for always.

PRAYER AND SCRIPTURE

S CRIPTURE FORMED THE BACKBONE of early monastic prayer. Although the monks did not use scripture every time they prayed, they did pray it several times every day. They considered scripture to be one of God's most precious gifts. It embodied God's truth and love and served as a record of God's self-revelation to us, especially in Jesus. It presented to them both a picture of what they wanted to become in Christ and the way to it.

Our Christian ancestors regarded the psalms, however, as unique in the Bible. They believed that the psalms contained the whole rest of the Bible in miniature. But the real uniqueness of the psalms was that they are themselves prayers given to us by God the Holy Spirit to be spoken as our own words in our own particular situations. Athanasius, the great fourth-century theologian and bishop of Alexandria, who was the special friend of the monks, says about the psalms:

> . . . Each psalm is both spoken and composed by the Spirit so that in these same words . . . the stirring of our souls might be grasped, and all of them be said as concerning us, and [the Psalms] issue from us as our own words.[7]

Very often when we pray, suggests Athanasius, we do not recognize what is going on in our deepest selves. But the words of the psalms, he says, have the power as we pray them to "become like a mirror to the person singing them." By praying a psalm expressing anger, grief, happiness, or guilt, we become able to express our deepest and most

---

[6] Evagrius, *Prayer*, 58, p. 64.

[7] Athanasius, *The Life of Anthony* and *The Letter to Marcellinus*, ed. Robert Gregg. Classics of Western Spirituality (Mahwah, NJ: Paulist Press, 1980), p. 111.

heartfelt emotions and gain insight into our state of mind and heart. In this way, says Athanasius:

> Just as [Christ] provided the model of the earthly and heavenly [person] in [Christ's] own person, so also from the Psalms he [or she] who wants to do so can learn the emotions and dispositions of the soul, finding in them also the therapy and correction suited for each emotion.[8]

When we make the psalms part of our daily prayer, we will find that very often they have the unique ability to help us in very specific ways to recognize ourselves and the self-inflicted distortions with which we live. If we will let them, the psalms can touch us at a very deep level, shaking loose old ways of seeing and relating to God. Praying and meditating on the psalms can have a transforming effect within us as we become capable of hearing, understanding, and taking on, with the help of God's grace, the meaning of new and life-giving images of God, ourselves, and other human beings. Thus do we grow in love.

CONCLUSION

WE BRING our whole life experience to our prayer. In prayer, nothing is ever wasted. Childhood pain, adult humiliation, experiences of joy, our own treacheries, confusion, loss—all of these find their place in our prayer, linking us ever more deeply with the God whom we confess once became like us and lived among us. As our prayer grows more spacious, we will find ourselves praying with the psalmist:

> O [God], you are my portion and cup;
>   it is you who uphold my lot.
> My boundaries enclose a pleasant land;
>   indeed, I have a goodly heritage. . . .
> My heart, therefore, is glad, and my spirit rejoices;
>   my body also shall rest in hope. . . .
> You will show me the path of life;
>   in your presence there is fullness of joy,
>   and in your right hand are pleasures for evermore.
>
> (Psalm 16, *Book of Common Prayer*)

---

[8] Athanasius, *Letter to Marcellinus*, p. 112.

The author deals with the subject of prayer more extensively in her book *To Pray and to Love: Conversations on Prayers with the Early Church* (Minneapolis: Fortress Press, 1991).

Sing *a* New Song

by Elizabeth J. Canham

T HE PSALMS EXPRESS the full range of human emotion, and God is excluded from none of it. They open up a way to pray authentically, to engage in the work of prayer which refuses to take refuge in a domesticated God who smooths life's rough edges. These old prayers and songs are vibrantly alive, new, and inviting. They have sustained Jewish and Christian worshipers through many centuries. In them we hear the expression of joy, hope, lament, rage, fear, oppression, trust, and abandonment that is part of our experience, too. There are moments of triumph in which God is blessed, and there are times of tragedy when life is emptied of meaning and God seems absent. All the extremes of human experience find a place in the prayer of the Psalter.

SEASONS OF EXPERIENCE

O UR DESIRE for equilibrium can become an idolatrous attempt to deny a large part of what life is about. The advertising industry achieves a good deal of its success through the message that if only we opt for this or that product, our needs and longings will be satisfied. We learn that life is not yet perfect, but we can fix it by obtaining the right house, floor polish, insurance policy, or therapy. In other words, we are encouraged to believe that there is something wrong with us if things are out of kilter and that life is meant to be lived on a plateau of happiness. The psalms give the lie to this kind of thinking by encouraging us to robustly deal with life as it really is and to find God in disorientation as well as harmony.

It is both a relief and a challenge to comprehend that there is no place where God is not. Psalm 139 speaks of the attempt to escape the Creator by soaring into the heavens, going into the depths, or sinking into the horizon where sea and sky meet. The sense that God is behind, in front, and above, laying a hand upon the one who feels searched out and known, makes the omnipresence of the Creator into a felt reality. I pray this psalm and I have to ask "Who am I? How can I respond to this all-encompassing presence of God?" In my time and place I am on holy ground, and as I allow myself to be held in that moment of awareness, I must respond with what is truly in my heart. I tell God that I am afraid, relieved, filled with gratitude, or overwhelmed by a sense of being invaded.

The seasons of our life will condition our response to the God who encounters us in the psalms. Again, Psalm 139 is a good example. When I feel that I am in a precarious place, I will be relieved to know that God surrounds me, but when I am caught up in prideful ambition, I may wish that a distance could be placed between us. The psalm raises my awareness of what is going on for me at that moment and, in the process, puts me in touch with the Source of my life. It offers no magic "fix" but sets me to the task of figuring out the most appropriate response to the One who loved me into being. Often that response will be an invitation to change!

Thanksgiving and celebration play a central role in the life of God's people. Many psalms commemorate great redeeming acts and times of triumph when victory over enemies was accomplished. Dancing, music, and festive joy filled the community as they rejoiced together, praising the God of their deliverance. Our own joy resonates with theirs as we recall the giftedness of our lives and the times God has saved us from the enemies of despair, fear, and pain. Sometimes the reading of such psalms as 145–150 serves to remind me of the many reasons I have to offer thanks to God—a reminder I often need when wants and longings seem unfulfilled. Without opting for a Pollyanna style of happiness which denies the troubled aspects of life, I can allow God to call out of me gratitude for all that is good in my experience. "Praise the LORD, O my soul! I will praise the LORD as long as I live; I will sing praises to my God all my life long." (Psalm 146:1-2, NRSV).

Many Christians have difficulty with the psalms of revenge or curse and would banish them from the Psalter. This has the effect of denying a real part of our experience, however. While it is true that we are to forgive our enemies and pray for those who hurt us, we can usually arrive at that place only when we truly acknowledge the vindictive rage we bear toward them. In the expression of our desire for revenge, we tell God who we are—hurting, broken people not yet able to relinquish our pain—and we give the rage to God. Often in the psalms we see a healing taking place and a fresh vision of reality emerging as all the bitterness and disappointment are poured out. Psalm 55 is a good example of this expression of righteous indignation (and some paranoia) leading to healing and hope:

I am panic-stricken at the shouts of my enemies,
at the shrill clamour of the wicked;
for they heap trouble on me
and they revile me in their anger. . . .
May death strike them,
and may they perish in confusion,
may they go down alive into Sheol;
for their homes are haunts of evil!
But I will call upon God;
the LORD will save me.

(Psalm 55:3, 15-16, NEB)

WHEN I FEEL BETRAYED and oppressed, I need to share my longing for vengeance with God. If I choose instead to bury it, the likelihood is that it will erupt inappropriately in a far more destructive form.

The seasons of lament also find a place in the Psalter. There are times when life is sad, when disaster, sickness, and loss overwhelm us and we need to express the anguish to God. The best known of the corporate psalms of lament is 137, where the covenant community languishing in Babylon cry out their hopelessness. "How shall we sing the LORD's song upon alien soil?" (v. 4, *Book of Common Prayer*). Exile had robbed them of the Temple and all other familiar structures that offered security. It was appropriate to wail and mourn as they went through the painful experience of loss; it was appropriate to give God their tears. Here too the psalms can give voice to our own experience of anguish. The parent with Alzheimer's disease, the friend with AIDS, the death of one we love causes us to cry out in our impotence, bewailing the losses of life. The Compassionate One hears and weeps with us and in due time enables us to find redemption even in the void.

Many of the psalms reflect the pilgrim nature of the community. Sometimes these celebrate the gathering in Jerusalem for great festivals and the reenactment of God's interventions in human history which sustain the pilgrims in their present uncertainties. There are also indications of the individual sense of traveling, sometimes securely but often hesitantly, on a precarious journey. The valley of the shadow of death is as much a part of the experience as the green pastures and still waters (Psalm 23), for those in pilgrimage are not static. Our own journey has many contours and leads us through places where specters of fear threaten our willingness to continue. The psalms help us to go on, identifying with those who have run and stumbled before us and

29

finding, as they did, the unseen presence of God in all our wandering.

Feelings of dereliction and abandonment are also a reality for those who commit themselves to honestly follow the Creator God who takes risks again and again. The Word which spoke the universe into being was God's affirmation of risk, and the Word which became flesh embodied risk and knew all our human frailty. When Christ cried out his sense of abandonment in the words of Psalm 22, he was expressing the agonizing experience of an absent God and of a risk that seemed not to have paid off. There are seasons of life when the isolation and abandonment are so great that nothing less than the screaming of our "Why?" to God can be true prayer. Rationalizing, blaming, and explaining would be a hollow attempt to vindicate God by the denial of our experience, and we would fall into the category of Job's "comforters" with their banal platitudes. The death of six million Jews, Mahatma Gandhi, Oscar Romero, or Martin Luther King, Jr., as well as the pointless deaths of those we know more intimately, demand that we pray our feelings of God's absence.

RHYTHMS OF PRAYER AND LIFE

MANY OF THE PSALMS were written for liturgical use and to celebrate God's presence among the people, especially in the Temple. The enthronement of the Davidic king, and his representative position as God's vice-regent, was a cause for great thanksgiving. Psalm 110 expresses the victory of the earthly king who owes his position and success to God whom he serves. God's epiphany happens as human history is enacted in the place of worship; the liturgy reveals the presence of the holy God among a holy people. And so it is still. In both Jewish and Christian worship the Psalter continues to be a vehicle through which the divine presence is manifested. In the personal reading of the psalms also God comes to us.

For many centuries the recitation of the Psalter has provided the primary rhythm of prayer for monastic communities. The psalmist's statement "seven times a day do I praise you" (Psalm 119:164) gave rise to the sevenfold Daily Office, now often reduced to four, in which the psalms were chanted. For some years I have lived in a Benedictine community where this tradition continues, and the psalms, which I have always loved, now take on even richer meaning. Day in and day out we go on singing the familiar words, and, like waves washing on the beach, they form a rhythm out of which our life is expressed. It is not simply a cognitive recitation of ancient words but an experience of being immersed in their acknowledgment of God's reality in all the vicissitudes of life. I feel drawn into their rhythmic flow of sound and into connectedness with all the millions of God's people who have prayed through them across the ages.

Matins happens at 5:30 a.m. I do not always feel very connected, very glad to be called by the bell to worship, very awake at that time in the morning! Yet somehow, as the Psalter begins, I am caught up again into the pattern of ancient worship and the psalms pray for me. A commitment to this kind of recitation of the offices has the advantage of removing prayer from the realm of my moods. Prayer is, as St. Benedict pointed out, the work of God, and sometimes it is very hard work, especially when some new tone or chant is required. So whether I feel like it or not, I say or sing the psalms because they are there to be offered in worship. Sometimes I am bored, sometimes distressed, and sometimes inexplicably thrilled by the words as they become mine and take on fresh meaning.

It is not necessary to live in a monastic community in order to incorporate the psalms into daily worship. For a number of years I served a parish in New York City, and there too the psalms were sustaining. Sitting in my tiny studio apartment with the sound of garbage trucks and sirens far down in the street below, the Psalter provided a beginning to my day (together with a large mug of coffee!). A far cry, maybe, from the Temple in Jerusalem, but a necessary link with the Hebrew scriptures to which I owe so much, and to those unknown pray-ers in vastly different times and contexts who have also been enriched by psalm prayer. Often a phrase or thought, maybe a fresh image of God, would emerge as I read the words, and that would go with me into the day, inserting itself periodically into my frenetic schedule. Speaking the words aloud helped both with awareness of meaning and attentiveness. Journaling with whatever emerged from my reading also served to reinforce what the psalm said to me and often led to further reflection upon it.

AN INVITATION TO CREATIVITY

As WE ALLOW the psalms to provide rhythm for our lives and as we use them to express the various seasons of our experience, it may be that our own creativity is invited; we can begin to write our own psalms! One very simple method for doing this is to choose an existing psalm as a model and change some of the images so that we celebrate our own observation of God's presence in the midst of life. Using verses from Psalm 104, Maxwell Croydon Wheat moves the locus of the psalm from the hills and valleys of Judea to the Long Island salt marsh which he loves:

Psalm of the Salt Marsh

O Lord, my God, you are the Creator
You make the tides rise
*   into the marsh grasses*
bringing sustenance to every
*   quahog in the creeks*
To every mussel on the banks
To every egret stalking
*   yellow tiptoe by yellow tiptoe*
*   plunging its long bill for mummichug*
The salt marsh is flooded with your ecology.[1]

At a workshop on praying our anger, I invited participants to write their own psalms expressing anger, modeling them on some of the imprecatory psalms. Our purpose was to truly acknowledge the angry, vindictive feelings we had and then to offer them in prayer. We asked whether there were ways in which God was asking us to be part of the healing of the situation calling forth the anger. The following psalm is my own effort, based on Psalm 52:

You oppressor,
why do you practice tyranny
against the poor year after year?
You inflame hatred;
your policies promote injustice,
O wrecker of human families.
You love segregation more than unity
and bondage more than freedom.
You cherish superiority
O you twister of the truth.
Oh, that God would destroy your schemes,
thrust you out of your power structure
and incarcerate you on Robins Island.[2]

---

[1] Maxwell Croydon Wheat, *Limulus: Poems of the Great Waters* (Virginia Wheat: 333 Bedell St., Freeport, NY 11520), p. 6. Used by permission.
[2] Robins Island, off the coast of Cape Town, South Africa, is the notorious prison in which many dissidents are incarcerated.

The disenfranchised shall rise and rejoice,
they will dance and sing:
"This is the one who thought God was on his side,
who placed confidence in white supremacy
and relied on apartheid."
But I am like one whose dreams have come true;
I trust in the Gospel of freedom and life.
I will celebrate the wonder of God's compassion
and share liberty with my sisters and brothers for all time.

Often the original context of the psalm is lost to us but not its impact as we discover ourselves in its emotional milieu. I lived for a while in South Africa, and I agonize for those still so cruelly oppressed. At the same time I am called to pray. I pray for courageous leaders like Archbishop Desmond Tutu, for those who have lost their lives in the struggle for justice, and for those who remain incarcerated and silenced. As I pray for the oppressor and the oppressed, I am also challenged to search out my own collusion with oppressive ways of thinking and acting which so insidiously corrupt the environment in which I live.

The psalms are old, yet ever new. I return again and again to the same words, but each time I come from a fresh time and place. T.S. Eliot speaks of our arriving at the same place in our journey and knowing it for the first time. That is often the sense I have with the psalms; I have stood on this rock, been in this pit, known this joy in the company of God's people. It is the same and yet it is not the same, for I am still traveling and still seeing in new ways as God nudges and sometimes drives me along on my human pilgrimage.

Praying *with* Scripture

by Marjorie J. Thompson

ANY OF US have learned to think of prayer and the reading of scripture as wholly distinct from one another. The hearing of scripture and the act of praying are experienced as separate activities in corporate worship and church education, so it should not surprise us if we tend to assume their separation in individual worship as well. The study of scripture in a rigorous, critical sense, or the reading of scripture for biblical "facts and figures" is, indeed, removed from the experience of prayer for most of us. But what of meditative reflection with scripture—that unhurried dwelling with God's word that Benedictine tradition sometimes has likened to a cow chewing its cud? Here the image is one of gradually extracting full nourishment from a source of food. Many of us, perhaps, have experienced meditative reflection with scripture leading *to* prayer; what may strike us as novel is the notion that it can be engaged in *as* prayer.

There is a time-honored tradition in our Christian heritage called "praying the scriptures." It is an approach that may fruitfully be used with almost any type of biblical literature. Underlying this form of prayer rests the assumption that God is personally present in the words of the text through the working of the Holy Spirit and has something to communicate to us in our current circumstances through the ancient yet somehow timeless biblical witness. Scripture, then, is a medium of encounter with the living God of all history. In our listening, we are addressed, challenged, and comforted by One whose will for humankind is not limited to the cultural expressions of previous generations, although it is conveyed to us through them. The divine word seems always ready to be broken open in ways fitting our present capacity, offering fresh bread to sustain our hungry spirits.

It is precisely the expectation of a genuine *encounter* with God that makes this form of scriptural meditation *prayer*. Prayer is above all an encounter and relationship with God.[1] The relationship is brought full circle as we respond to the One who has encountered us. Our

---

[1] An insight from Russian Orthodox Archbishop Anthony Bloom. See *Beginning to Pray* (New York: Paulist Press, 1970), p. 2.

response may be expressed by a range of feelings, words, or actions and becomes most faithful when it encompasses all three.

Praying the scriptures has found particularly colorful expression in practices derived from the Spiritual Exercises of Ignatius of Loyola, founder of the Jesuit order. A hallmark of these exercises is the use of sensory imagination in meditating with the Gospels. (It is worth noting that other narrative portions of scripture are equally adaptable to the Ignatian method.) By entering into the stories and characters of the Gospels imaginatively, we are invited to encounter the living Lord—the Word Incarnate—in a more vivid and personal way.

As prayer, the Ignatian form is contemplative, meaning that it has primarily to do with "seeing" rather than thinking or speaking. It does not represent a passive contemplation, however, since it engages the active use of images and senses. The effect is to elicit more of our experience and bring it into active dialogue with God's word. One could call this "prayer of the heart" in a genuinely biblical sense. According to Hebrew tradition, the heart is the seat of the whole person, including body, intellect, feeling, will, intuition, imagination, and action. This method of prayer has the capacity to draw our memories, hopes, attitudes, and feelings into a context where they can be revealed and transformed by the living Word. Consequently, we discover ourselves more deeply (what kinds of images of God and self we harbor, where our faith and fears lie, how we perceive ourselves and others in particular roles), and we hear the word addressing us more directly.

The Ignatian method may be understood as a holistic form of prayer which encourages us to attend to God with all our heart, mind, soul, and strength. In this respect, it constitutes a prayer path of profound simplicity—one in which our whole being is gathered toward a singular attentiveness. The integration of such an approach contrasts with the scattered and disparate kind of attention we so often offer to God when we bring only our intellect or feelings to prayer.

Questions often arise when people first try this form of prayer: "Isn't this just the product of my own fantasy? How can my imagination illuminate the meaning of scripture?" It is quite true that an *informed* imagination is less susceptible to distorting the original intent of biblical writers. Historical or cultural understanding will shape the content and direction of our imagination. Therefore it is important to bring whatever contextual knowledge we can to praying the scriptures. Modest exegetical preparation is recommended, but not to the point of becoming a distraction or substitute for prayer. We must realize that the purpose here is not to recreate the most accurate biblical scene possible (a goal even the best scholarship can only approximate) but rather to allow the stories to become alive for us by entering into them with all the knowledge, experience, and imagination we possess. It is wise to ask the Spirit to guide the use of our inner resources so that through them we may hear whatever word God wishes to speak. Then we need to trust that the Spirit works through the gift of our informed imagination and that God can reach us where we are and as we are.

The prayer method described here is adapted from one I was taught during a month-long Ignatian retreat. It is based in part on the writings of Armand Nigro, S.J., whose pamphlet rested on each retreatant's desk. I have seen similar descriptions of praying with scripture elsewhere and simply adapt here, in my own words, a tradition which has its origins elsewhere. I believe it provides us with a way of juxtaposing our own experience of faith and God's voice of invitation in scripture.

HOWEVER YOU MAY BE ACCUSTOMED to thinking about prayer, for now try to understand it as your personal response to God's presence. This will mean, first, simply being aware of that presence—allowing yourself to be present to God, and allowing the constant divine presence to be known to you. Only when we are conscious of God's sustaining presence with us can we, in turn, respond with thanksgiving and love. Otherwise it is a bit like opening the door of a dark room and talking into it because someone might be there to hear. Normally we will speak and respond only to a known personal presence.

What can we do to open ourselves to God's communication? How can we listen so as to receive what the Lover of our souls desires to give us?

• Commit yourself to at least fifteen to twenty minutes daily of time specifically given to God in listening prayer. If our relationship with the Spirit is truly a priority, it will deserve "prime time"—good, attentive time, not tired, low-energy time.

• Make this a regular time each day, if at all possible. Establishing a rhythm is important for any discipline. Then try the following steps:

1. *Passage:* Choose a few verses of scripture that you want especially to listen to, taste, and savor. These may be selected to fit your mood and need, or you may elect to follow the lectionary or move through an entire book of the Bible. Put a marker in it and have it available; you may or may not return to it.

2. *Place:* Find a private, quiet space where you can freely respond to God's presence without concern over the attention or reaction of others, and where you will not be disturbed by external distractions.

3. *Posture:* Since we pray as human beings with bodies, posture is important. Experiment with different positions—standing, sitting, kneeling, lying down, hands raised, clasped, palms open—whatever feels comfortable and expresses your inward disposition toward God. Take time to settle yourself peacefully.

4. *Presence:* Gently remind yourself of God's presence in your life, here and now. Allow that presence to become real and affirm it in terms of a "You-I" relationship (not third person). Remember that God is loving life into you at each moment. Let God love you. Do not rush this part of prayer, even if it takes the whole time. If you experience God's presence deeply, stay with it, linger over it, take comfort and joy in it. This in itself is prayer—the prayer of simple communion. You need not react with a rush of words; enjoy the Presence in gratitude and let it carry you. You may want to repeat a simple phrase like "My Lord and my God," or "My Shepherd," or whatever is meaningful to you at this point.

5. *Passage:* When the sense of presence fades, or if you feel nothing and God seems absent, do not worry. Turn back to the marked passage of scripture and begin to listen for what God may be communicating to you through it. Read it slowly (for some, silent reading allows the mind to wander, and reading aloud or whispering the words is preferable). Pause between phrases, let words echo and meanings sink in. If a word or phrase seems significant, remain with it and turn it over in your mind and heart until that sense fades. You need not find applications, implications, conclusions, or

resolutions. This is prayer, not preparation for teaching or preaching. You are not "thinking about" these things so much as communicating with God through them. Be content to listen simply and openly, like a child in a loving parent's lap. Let God speak to your heart.

If the passage is a story with characters, let yourself enter into it imaginatively. Visualize the setting; see where you are, feel the textures, smell the fragrances, hear the sounds, taste whatever you can of the story. Find yourself in this setting as one of the characters, or as an onlooker. You might try becoming each of the characters (or type of characters) in turn, imagining how it feels to be in their place. Engage in dialogue between characters (sometimes it is easier to write dialogues out), then return to the parameters of the storyline in scripture.

When you have lived into the story as fully as you can, or the sense of its significance diminishes, remember that you are still in the loving presence of God. Think back through what was new to you in experiencing the text this way. If some fresh insight or grace of understanding was given, take time to express your gratitude.

REMEMBER THAT WE CANNOT EARN, deserve, or force an experience of God's presence and communion. Our effort in personal prayer does not guarantee what can only be a grace. All we can do is open ourselves to God's mercy and friendship and dispose ourselves to receive divine love in the trust that it is a gift eagerly waiting to be given. God will speak to you in the ways and times most appropriate for you. Experience teaches us that time given faithfully to God is returned immeasurably enriched.

Ways *of* Prayer

DESIGNING A PERSONAL RULE

by William O. Paulsell

HOLINESS IS A GIFT OF GRACE. Its qualities cannot be imitated or faked. If we try to act them out, people will sense our inauthenticity, for such gifts come from deep intimacy with God.

How can we cultivate such gifts in our own lives? It would be nice if we could take a course guaranteed to produce personal holiness or find some exercise or technique that would make us saints. But, of course, it is not that simple. It is not a matter of technique; it is a matter of values, of commitment, and, more than anything else, of love—love for the God who created us and has called us to discipleship.

A study of the great saints of Christian history reveals that an important feature of their lives was discipline. It was this discipline that enabled them to give major attention to the cultivation of intimacy with God. Discipline is a hard, even a harsh word, and our hedonistic society resists it rather rigorously. Yet, in almost any field of endeavor those who accomplish the most are usually those who are the most disciplined. Athletes, musicians, writers, scientists, and others progress in their fields because they are well-disciplined people. Unfortunately, there is a tendency to think that in matters of faith we should pray, meditate, and engage in other spiritual disciplines only when we feel like it.

The great religious orders in church history all developed some kind of rule to live by which formed the lives of their members. Notable among these are the Rule of St. Benedict, the Rule of St. Gregory the Great, and the Rule of St. Francis. But corporate rules are not the only ones offered as models by our Christian heritage. There are many rules written for individuals to provide some structure and direction for daily living. Living these rules seeks to deepen intimacy with God and foster the gifts of the Spirit in personal life.

One of the earliest personal rules in Christian history was a mid-second century document known to us today as the Didache. It may well have been a manual for new converts. It begins by discussing the way of life and the way of death and suggests conduct appropriate to each way. It has some specific suggestions about spiritual disciplines, including fasting two days a week and praying the Lord's Prayer three times a day.

One of the finest examples of a personal rule is a little book that was never intended for publication. We know it by the title *The Private Devotions of Lancelot Andrewes*. Andrewes, who lived from 1555–1626, was educated at Cambridge where he became known as a devoted, hard-working scholar. He mastered fifteen languages, developed strong preaching skills, served as chaplain to Queen Elizabeth and Privy Counselor to James I, and was one of the translators of the King James version of the Bible. He served successively as bishop of Chichester, Ely, and Winchester, and played a major role in the development of Anglican theology.

In the midst of all this work and responsibility, he worked out for himself a personal rule for daily prayer. It is characterized by thoroughness, beauty of language, and faithfulness to the gospel. The book, intended only for Andrewes's personal use, was published after his death. It has five major parts.

First, there is a collection of Bible verses on three themes: the times for prayer, the places of prayer, and the circumstances of prayer.

Second, there is an order for morning prayer. This consists of three standard items. It begins with meditation followed by a lengthy confession. The order ends with a section called "Commendations," which we might call petitions.

The third major section is an order for evening prayer, organized in basically the same way as morning prayer. The longest section is the fourth part which is a collection of prayers for each day of the week. Here are included prayers of confession, prayers for grace, prayers of intercession and praise, and a creed. The final section is simply called "Additional Exercises." It contains more intercessions; meditations on Christian duty, the day of judgment, and human frailness; and a long prayer to be used in preparation for Holy Communion.

Those with a serious interest in developing a personal rule would profit by studying the *Journal of a Soul* by Pope John XXIII. It is a selection of diary entries beginning with his own seminary days in Italy, and the entries are often lists of rules he set down for himself for keeping a devotional life. For example, while a student for the priesthood, he outlined a personal program that included the following:

1. Devote at least a quarter of an hour to silent prayer as soon as you get out of bed in the morning.

2. Devote a quarter of an hour to spiritual reading.

3. In the evening, before going to bed, make a general examination of conscience, followed by confession, and identify issues for the next day's prayer.

4. So as to be constant in your observation of these points, arrange the hours of your day, and set apart special time for prayer, study, and other devotion, for recreation and sleep.

5. Make a habit of frequently turning your mind to God in prayer.

A different style of personal rule is suggested by Catherine de Hueck Doherty, a Russian baroness, who came to Canada in 1920, penniless with a baby son and a husband in poor health. She eventually became an executive with a lecture bureau and had a comfortable life. She was much impressed, however, with the gospel demand to sell one's goods and give to the poor. Eventually, she established Madonna House, a religious community in Combermere, Ontario. Her remarkable book, *Poustinia*, builds on the Russian hermit tradition and suggests periodic retreats into solitude such as twenty-four hours once a month. A poustinia, or hermitage, should be a simple place where one fasts, reads scripture, prays, and listens to God. Doherty describes her own problems with restlessness upon first entering her poustinia, but she always found that eventually the fasting and solitude would lead to some new insight about the will of God for her own life.

Another important twentieth-century woman was Dorothy Day, founder of the *Catholic Worker*, a newspaper published by a group who operate "houses of hospitality" for the poor in the slums of New York. Her own work was devoted to peace and the encouragement of a just economic order. She said that she saw Christ in the faces of the poor. Her social activism was undergirded by a deep spirituality. She called for "practicing the presence of God" which, for her, meant daily Eucharist. She read the Bible daily and kept a journal which she saw as another way of praying.

Personal rules sometimes show up in unexpected places. When Martin Luther King, Jr. began leading nonviolent protests, he attempted to instill within the participants certain spiritual principles.

For his first demonstrations in Birmingham he put together a simple rule to which all protestors had to subscribe. It included the following items:

1. Meditate daily on the teachings and life of Jesus.

2. Remember always that the nonviolent movement in Birmingham seeks justice and reconciliation, not victory.

3. Walk and talk in the manner of love, for God is love.

4. Pray daily to be used by God in order that all might be free.

5. Sacrifice personal wishes in order that all might be free.

6. Observe with both friend and foe the ordinary rules of courtesy.

7. Seek to perform regular service for others and the world.

8. Refrain from violence of fist, tongue, or heart.

9. Strive to be in good spiritual and bodily health.

All of these examples indicate that deeply formed Christian people see the need for self-discipline and regulating the day in order to keep their lives properly oriented toward and focused on God. Many of us find it virtually impossible to set an agenda. Others tend to set them for us. But it is important that we discipline ourselves to withdraw from that situation on some kind of regular basis, even if for the briefest of times. The only way we can hope to do that with any regularity is to plan ahead and have a clear picture of what we wish to do.

The most difficult, but perhaps the most important, discipline is to set times for prayer and reflection. Giving up time may be the twentieth-century form of self-denial demanded of us. It is easier to sacrifice almost anything but time. We need not schedule by the clock, but we do need to commit ourselves to using some time during the day to refocus our attention on God. If once a day is the best we can do, start with that. In fact, it is important that we not plan more than is realistic. If we consistently fail to live by our own rule, the frustration will cause us to give up the whole idea. It is important to begin simply and build as we grow. Five minutes once a day may expand to fifteen, to twice a day, or more.

Many people fail at this sort of thing because they have no clear plan for what to do with the time. There is a long and persistent

Christian tradition of praying the psalms in the Old Testament on a daily basis. Praying a comfortable number each day relieves us of the burden of deciding how we are going to use the time or for what we shall pray. Simply let the psalter make those decisions. What better prayers can we pray than those God has given us in scripture?

Minimally, our daily prayer should include praise and thanksgiving, confession or examination of conscience, and intercession. We should pray for our own calling, our local congregation, our co-workers, our friends, our families, and all with whom we are in regular contact. There are many who will ask us to pray for them if they sense that we are serious about prayer. There are also those larger concerns of peace and justice that should be part of our prayer.

There are other things a personal rule should include. Regular scripture reading nourishes our faith. Reading of the great spiritual classics and writings of contemporary spiritual writers is an important stimulus to growth. It is useful to have a book around to be reading, even if only a few pages a day can be read. The best devotional literature is that written by people who have been through deep struggles of faith. Those that make faith sound easy are of little use in the crises of life.

Also included in a personal rule should be commitment to family time, small efforts of self-denial and penance, and time for silence and solitude. In addition, a rule will be enriched by attention to regular but not necessarily daily disciplines such as retreats, forms of service, corporate worship, and group study.

To be fruitful, any rule must take into account the individual's personality and circumstances in life. Some of us need a more rigid rule to follow; others will flourish with more flexibility. Some of us are morning people, and some of us are night people. Some of us love silence and solitude; others find God's presence in human interaction.

It is unlikely that we will deepen our relationship with God in a casual or haphazard manner. There will be a need for some intentional commitment and some reorganization in our own lives. But there is nothing that will enrich our lives more than a deeper and clearer perception of God's presence in the routine of daily living. From time to time Jesus left the crowds to go apart and pray in solitude. He now calls us to intimacy with the Divine. The development of a personal rule will be the one way to increase our sensitivity to what God is doing and to organize our days to live the gospel.

The Examen
Re-examined

by Deborah Smith Douglas

W HEN I FIRST LEARNED, in my Protestant childhood, how to pray a kind of "examination of conscience," it was a frightening and discouraging experience—a sort of inept, private confession of sin without guidance and without absolution. "Remember your day," my Bible school teachers urged us, "and all the unkind and naughty things you did and said, and ask God to forgive you for them, and promise to try to be better tomorrow." A harmless practice, one would think, and a valuable one in theory: Those good women were attempting to instill in our heedless young hearts the beginnings of compunction and remorse, to hold out for us the ever-renewed possibility of God's patient mercy.

However, the only other bedtime prayer we knew inevitably informed the whole idea of conscience smitten at bedtime: "Now I lay me down to sleep, I pray Thee, Lord, my soul to keep. If I should die before I wake, I pray Thee, Lord, my soul to take." The terrible possibility of "if I should die before I wake" lurked darkly behind the urgent need to have sought and found all the day's sins before "I lay me down to sleep."

So, dutifully and anxiously, I would rummage through the day's events as I would have through a toy chest—but I was training myself to see only the broken toys. I searched diligently through heaps of beloved treasure, blind to everything that was not dented or torn or incomplete. It did not occur to me that God might delight, as I did, in the wholeness of what miraculously remained unspoiled; it certainly never crossed my mind that God might like to be present in my play. I never questioned God's odd preference for my worst, most fretful, selfish moments; naturally I had no idea how deeply I was shaping my image of God or my sense of myself.

So when, many years later, I was making my first individually guided Ignatian retreat,[1] and my director suggested that I "pray the

---

[1] At St. Bueno's College in North Wales. I am deeply grateful to Fr. Paul Edwards, S.J. for his wise direction.

Examen," I thought (with a sinking heart) that I knew just what to do. But by the grace of God, I was wrong.

I discovered that week a whole new way of offering my life to God, one day at a time—a whole new and redemptive way of finding God present in all things. Gradually, I learned to invite God to be with me in the remembering itself: Together we sorted through the day's nets. While I still grieved, as I had as a child, over the precious things I had carelessly or willfully broken, I could also rejoice in discovering gifts received but perhaps not acknowledged—or even noticed—in the busyness of the moment. Most importantly, I was beginning to notice patterns and directions; I was beginning to move from self-scrutiny to discernment.

I learned, in short, that an examination of *conscience*—a single-minded, grim-hearted quest for sins—is not at all the same enterprise as an examination of *consciousness*, in which we look back over the day in order to find where God has been in it.[2]

After my retreat, in my growing appreciation for the Examen[3] as a particularly rich and fruitful form of prayer, I sought to learn more about it. One of the first things one sees, on examining the Examen, is that the purpose is not, as I had vaguely assumed in my childhood, the mere nightly emptying of the day's trash, lest we die "in our sins" before morning. Neither is the Examen primarily concerned with what good or bad actions we have done during the day—not that that lets us off the hook in any way: The broader way of praying is not at all a more shallow way. It is not a bit easier or "nicer"—a sort of watered-down confession of sin with the sting of self-knowledge taken out. Indeed, it is far deeper and more costly, more conducive to profound self-offering and interior transformation, than the mere dis-spirited raking over of refuse that was my childish idea of "examining conscience."

On the contrary, the deep purpose—and effect—of the Examen is to change our way of seeing. The German film director Wim Wenders believes that that is how angels communicate the love of God to humans: "The angel realizes that the goal is not to talk into your ears, but to try and live in your eyes."[4]

---

[2] George A. Aschenbrenner, S.J., "Consciousness Examen," *Review for Religious*, Vol. 31, 1972/1, pp. 14–21.

[3] *The Spiritual Exercises of Saint Ignatius*, trans. and commentary by George E. Ganss, S.J. (St. Louis: The Institute of Jesuit Sources, 1992), p. 38 (SpEx, 43).

[4] An interview in the *Christian Science Monitor*, Dec. 16, 1993.

If we pray the Examen regularly, generously, and courageously, God will come and live in our eyes. Gradually, we will begin to see ourselves, and understand our actions, in a whole new way. Eventually, by the grace of God, we will begin to recognize God in all things, to rejoice in the invitational, relational love of God "unto whom all hearts are open, all desires known, and from whom no secrets are hid."[5]

So how may we avail ourselves of this new way of seeing? We have only to begin.

Usually most helpful if prayed in the quiet just before sleep, the Examen takes about a quarter of an hour, and consists of five parts; first thanksgiving, then a prayer for illumination, next the examination of the day itself, followed by appropriate sorrow or delight, and finally, hope for the morrow.

The First Point Is to Give Thanks to God Our Lord For the Benefits I Have Received (SpEx, 43.2)

IN THE FIRST PART of the prayer, one simply remembers that all we have and are belong to God, who has loved us into being and will love us forever. It may well be, as the liturgy of the Episcopal Church reminds us, "right, and a good and joyful thing, always and everywhere to give thanks to [God],"[6] but always and everywhere have a way of rushing past unrecognized: It is good to pause in our vulnerability on the rim of sleep, to rest into the amazing grace that surrounds us eternally. Specifically, we can give thanks for particular events or encounters or insights the day has brought us as gift. I have often been surprised to see what memories rise spontaneously to the surface of my mind in this first stage of the prayer—many times I have found myself delightedly saluting as pure gift a moment I otherwise probably would have completely forgotten.

The Second Is to Ask Grace to Know My Sins And Rid Myself of Them (SpEx, 43.3)

As preparation for the general overview of the whole day, one next prays simply for light, that God will enlighten our hearts. We ask for "grace to know"—and part of what that illuminating grace will

---

[5] From the Collect for Purity, Holy Eucharist II, *Book of Common Prayer*, (New York: The Church Hymnal Corporation and The Seabury Press, 1979), p. 355.

[6] *Book of Common Prayer*, p. 361.

reveal is, of course, the ways we have sinned. But we want to be open as well to an appreciation of the grace itself, an awareness of God authentically at work (and, perhaps at play) in the day's events. Jesus promises that "The Holy Spirit, whom the Father will send in my name, will teach you everything, and remind you of all that I have said to you" (John 14:26, NRSV). Day by day, if we consent to it, the Spirit will teach us more and more about God, and about the ways we use God's gifts. I often imagine this teaching as what Julian of Norwich called "showings"—it is as though God directs the beam of a flashlight to reveal what otherwise might remain hidden from us. This part of the prayer is simply asking for that light.

The Third Is to Ask an Account of My Soul from the Hour of Rising to the Present Examen, Hour by Hour Or Period by Period. . . . (SpEx, 43.4, 5)

THIS THIRD PART is the heart of the prayer, the examination of the day in the light of Christ, grounded in thankfulness for all that God has done for us. In my experience this is a bit as though God and I were sitting side by side, watching clips of the day on videotape, from the moment I first woke up in the morning. It may be important to keep that somewhat detached view: As memories unwind, we are invited simply to watch them, not to leap in with judgments about ourselves or others. Too scrupulous or self-preoccupied an attention to our own failures and victories can miss the point as well: Remember, we are not seeking so much to identify good and bad actions (to sort, label, and dismiss them as though taking an inventory in a shop), as to look beneath the actions to the desires and feelings that lie underneath (to discern how we have responded to God's loving presence in our lives).

For example, one might ask: In what I read today, or overheard on the bus, or saw in the evening news, was I drawn to God? Did I meet God in the joy or pain of others? Did I in some way bring Christ into my world? Did anyone bring God to me? Did I reach out to someone in trouble or sorrow? Did I fail or refuse to do so? Did something that happened to me today give me a keener sense of being loved, or being angry or tired, or needing God in some special way? Is there any concrete event of the day which revealed some part of my life that I am withholding from God? George Aschenbrenner, S.J. has pointed out, "In this third element of the Examen we ordinarily rush to review, in some specific detail, our actions . . . so we can catalogue them as good or bad. Just what we shouldn't do! . . . *The operative questions are: What has been happening in us? How has the Lord been working in us? What has [God] been asking us?* And only secondarily are our own actions to be considered."[7]

Clearly, this form of prayer involves carefully and lovingly examining *everything* in the treasure chest, everything that's been caught in the nets. This is no compelled or compulsive search for broken places to be rejected. Rather, it is but a prayerful exploration of *all* of our day, in order to discover not only what is in need of healing, but also what may have been neglected or ignored, or what might be celebrated.

The Fourth Is to Ask Pardon of God Our Lord For My Faults (SpEx, 43.6)

A quiet, honest look at the day from this perspective will lead naturally into both gratitude and sorrow. Particular memories of how we have responded (or failed to respond) to opportunities to see or to serve God may fill us with regret, and we will want to express to God how sorry we are. True awareness of our brokenness and blindness is in itself, of course, a gift granted in love, so at the same time we can give thanks for that. We can also—and this is very important—learn to see and be grateful for the ways in which we *were* able to rejoice in or witness to the love of God. Perhaps something marvelous has happened: We heard from an old friend; we reconciled with an old enemy; the kindness of a stranger reminded us of goodness alive in the world; a line in a song half-heard on the radio suddenly spoke to our heart.

There *will* be something in your day, a Jesuit friend of mine gently insists to people under his direction, that you can be proud of. "There will be things," he promises. "If you can't think of anything, then you haven't looked hard enough: Don't move on before you think of what it might be. Then give thanks for this."[8]

Even in the painful light of real sins named and offered to God's forgiving grace, we can marvel at the way God constantly brings us home and steadily leads us closer to becoming the people God means for us to be. The English poet Elizabeth Jennings muses:

---

[7] Aschenbrenner, "Consciousness Examen," p. 18. Emphasis added.

[8] Fr. Dermot Preston, S.J., in a booklet on the Examen prepared for use at Loyola Hall, Merseyside, U.K.

Prayer yet could be a dance
But still a cross. I offer small heartbreak,
Catch grace almost by chance.[9]

"Almost by chance"—but not quite, of course, not really. The grace we "catch" is steadily poured out for us in the clear and unshakable divine intention that we participate ever more fully in the very life of God.

For this reason, we need never lose hope.

The Fifth Is to Resolve, with [God's] Grace, to Amend Them (SpEx, 43.7)

THE FINAL PART of the Examen is to rest in that hope for the future. Tomorrow, like yesterday and today, is in God's hands. We can end our review of the day just past, our examination of our consciousness of God's activity in the ordinary events of our daily lives, by looking ahead to the next day. Sometimes I end this final part of the prayer by recalling Paul's declaration: "One thing I do: forgetting what lies behind and straining forward to what lies ahead, I press on toward the goal for the prize of the upward call of God in Christ Jesus" (Phil. 3:13, 14, NRSV). Sometimes, I pray the prayer of St. Richard of Chichester: "May I know Thee more clearly, love Thee more dearly, and follow Thee more nearly, day by day."

Thomas Keating, the Cistercian monk who has introduced thousands to the method of "centering prayer," suggests that "our ordinary thoughts are like boats sitting on a river so closely packed together that we cannot see the river that is holding them up." The boats are not only crowded together, but they also pass by us quickly, and we become confused and distracted in our efforts to pay attention to the boats and what is on them. But the really important thing to see and understand is not the boats at all, but the river. When we enter deeply and quietly into prayer, Keating suggests, "Space begins to appear between the boats. Up comes the reality on which they are floating."[10]

Very much the same dynamic is operative, I believe, in the

---

[9] Elizabeth Jennings, "Prayer yet could be a dance," from *Praying with the English Poets*, compiled and introduced by Ruth Etchells (London: Triangle Books, 1990), p. 45.

[10] Thomas Keating, *Open Mind, Open Heart: The Contemplative Dimension of the Gospel* (Rockport, MA: Element Books, 1986), p. 110.

Examen. As we allow God to draw our attention below the surface busyness (the color and activity of the boats) to the river itself, our hearts will be more and more deeply drawn into the fathomless reality of God. The purpose of the Examen is not simply to count the boats, or to judge either their condition or their cargo, but to get to know the river. The Examen, prayed deeply and faithfully, will enable us to take soundings, to learn the currents, to discern why the boats behave as they do. As we get to know the river, we will learn from experience that, for instance, staying too long in the shallows can be stagnating, that the ripples on the surface on a certain stretch warn of dangerous snags below, that if we go too fast in certain places, the boats will collide.

The better we come to know the river, the easier it will be to see the subtle movement of God in our lives, and the more joyfully and fully we can cooperate with God's plans for us. The more authentically we "offer small heartbreak," the more grace we will "catch."

The more we pray the Examen, the more we will allow ourselves to be "transformed by the renewing of [our] minds, so that [we] may discern what is the will of God—what is good and acceptable and perfect" (Rom. 12:2, NRSV).

Conditioning *the* Spiritual Eye

ICONS AS A WAY TO DIVINE PRESENCE

by Tilden Edwards

HOW DOES YOUR SIGHT affect your awareness of God? Think for a minute of the myriad images that pass through your mind during the day, stimulated by exterior sights and internal memories and dispositions. More than likely you will sense that many of your images have a way of drawing you away from God, dividing you moment by moment from the direct Presence that is our true home. Thus in effect we often find ourselves living in exile from God, even when at least part of us desires otherwise. We wander in a confusing swamp of temptations and fears that easily lead us astray, or our sight is simply dulled in a way that misses the radiant Presence.

This situation expresses our deepest human dilemma. We want the intimacy of home, the oneness in God through Christ that he prays for us (John 17:21). We know somewhere deep in our hearts that nothing short of this will leave us or our world with real peace, freedom, joy, wisdom, and all the other words we have for fulfillment. And yet a confused, ignorant, and sometimes willful part of us whispers that our real happiness lies in our ultimate separateness, in whatever we can do to enhance our sense of control, power, and security apart from God. This whisper rises to an overwhelming shout in most of contemporary culture.

Spiritual discipline is whatever we can do to help turn aside from this divisive tendency in and around us and dispose ourselves for the One who declares in Christ that God and humanity are more one than two. This mutual indwelling is not meant to be embraced through conceptual assent alone. God yearns for us to truly realize this fundamental truth through every dimension of our being: our body, mind, senses, feelings, imagination, subconscious, will, and intuitive awareness. That is a lifetime process of ongoing conversion: the transformation of all that wanders outside of God into that which truly proceeds from God's Spirit.

SEEING AS SPIRITUAL DISCIPLINE

OUR VISUAL SENSE is a neglected arena of spiritual discipline. There was a time when the Western church shared with the Eastern church a deep concern for the formation of the spiritual eye through what is seen. The relative neglect of this discipline in recent centuries has left our sight easy prey to certain commercial and political interests. They recognize the power of sight and try to satisfy our longing for home without an understanding of the depth to which we are really called to find our home.[1] People who have critical theological minds may be delivered from such seduction because their training or knowledge alerts them to the subtle manipulations of the culture. Such people can usually avoid the idolatrous tendency to let finite visual forms (including written ones) become substitutes for God's presence. But they can be impoverished in another way. They can become overly dependent on an analytical way of seeing that separates them too radically from what they see.

HOLY ICONS

HOW CAN WE DISCIPLINE our sight to lead us to God and our true nature? How can what we see draw our affections, will, and unguarded presence to their true Source? One historic discipline is prayer before a holy icon (the Greek word for "image"): a reverently painted image of Jesus, Mary, or other biblical and saintly figures. Apart from the cross, the Gospels, and living encounters with Spirit-filled people, probably nothing has conditioned the Christian eye historically as much as icons. St. Basil in the early church declared them to be equal to scripture in their capacity to reveal God's presence. Probably the most famous recorded example of the influence of a painted image in the West was the instrumentality of an icon cross, combined with scripture, in the conversion of Francis of Assisi.

An icon is not simply any religious painting. To be an icon, a piece must authentically reveal God (as agreed upon by the early

---

[1] See Margaret Miles, *Image as Insight* (Boston: Beacon Press, 1985), especially chapters 5, 6, 7, for seminal historical and contemporary insights on the place of religious images in forming the spiritual heart. See also John Dillenberger, *A Theology of Artistic Sensibilities* (New York: Crossroad, 1986).

church). This does not mean that other paintings can have no spiritual value, just as the Bible does not invalidate the potential spiritual value of other books, nor the Eucharist of other meals. It means rather that authentic icons in Eastern Orthodox tradition, like the Bible and the Eucharist, are meant to express a divine-human reality that is collectively recognized in the heart of the church's tradition of experience and interpretation.

Over time, certain guidelines emerged for painting an authentic icon. For example, it should not emerge simply from the artist's own subjectivity but from the artist's first-hand contemplation and knowledge of the gospel (gained, in part, through a process of prayer and fasting). The icon is not meant to be a personal creation but rather a description of what is contemplated, a vital communion with the mysterious truth of the tradition.[2]

Painting an icon requires that the artist listen deeply to the Holy Spirit's expression in existing icons and draw upon this same Spirit. It is not a matter of imitation but of the artist's interiorized spiritual knowledge of "God becoming human, so that we might become God," as St. Athanasius put it. Thus the artist shows forth the transfigured human state to which we are called, the body's participation in divine life. The artist is charged with portraying this good news in a way that draws all our faculties into its realization. The icon needs to be a transparency for reality in God, not a form that draws attention to itself. The highly stylized form of icons assists the icon's transparency for reality in God. The stylized form is not meant to be inhuman. On the contrary, it is meant to show us our fullest humanity illuminated in the Spirit.

The icon will have the effect of drawing us into this divine-human reality through the use of a reverse perspective, where the vanishing point is behind the viewer rather than in the icon. This effect emphasizes the invitation to a *participative* way of knowing God's presence with the icon. Thus, the icon discourages an objective, observing, analytical way of knowing, which has never been sufficient

---

[2] Leonid Ouspensky and Vladimir Lossky, *The Meaning of Icons* (Crestwood, New York: St. Vladimir's Press, 1983), pp. 40–41. This book provides an excellent, if scholarly, history and theology of icons, as well as an excellent collection of color reproductions of icons, carefully interpreted. A more detailed and personal interpretation of four particular icons can be found in Henri Nouwen, *Behold the Beauty of the Lord: Praying with Icons* (Notre Dame: Ave Maria Press, 1987).

for realizing spiritual truth. The icon requires our participation; it is not complete without our faith-filled, engaged presence.

The icon is meant to complement other means of exposing the gospel. As St. Basil put it, "What the word transmits through the ear, the painting silently shows through the image." In Eastern Orthodox understanding, the divine liturgy enacts what the icons show and the words say. Thus action, word, and image are brought together as reinforcing dimensions of a single liturgical whole.

In the Eastern Orthodox world icons are placed everywhere. They are in churches, homes, and buses; people carry small icons in their pockets. They serve as "revelation of the future sanctification of the world and its coming transfiguration, as pattern of its realization, and as promulgation of its grace and presence."[3] The saintly figures in the icons are considered to participate in the divine energies to which they point. They draw us to an intimate, living spiritual reality, to the incomprehensible commingling of body and spirit, of time and eternity. Icons help to extend the mystery of the Incarnation into our midst.

CHOOSING AN ICON

WHAT KIND OF ICON is best for use in prayer and meditation? There is no one right answer. We need to heed our sense of being drawn to a particular icon at a given time in our lives. I have found that the icon should have a capacity to draw you into the mystery of God's Spirit illumining human form. This will likely be more obvious in an icon with only one or two figures, probably one of Jesus or of Jesus and Mary. The eyes of one or more of these sacred personages should be particularly apparent, and looking directly toward you. An icon pre-dating the late seventeenth century, or a later one clearly made with the intent and style of such an early icon, will probably be best. Post-seventeenth century icons often were not created according to the earlier orthodox standards and lost their power to testify to the transfigured state.

---

[3] *The Meaning of Icons*, p. 44.

PRAYING BEFORE AN ICON

H ERE IS ONE WAY for individuals or groups to pray with an icon:

1. Light a candle before the icon.

2. Sit (or stand) close to the icon, with it at eye level.

3. Offer a prayer that expresses your desire to touch God's presence through this icon and to relinquish whatever may distance you from that intent.

4. Rest your eyes on the eyes of the icon. Resist the normal impulse to grasp for some kind of knowledge. Instead, keep your eyes still and let yourself be known by God through the icon's eyes. Gently release any sense of judgment, distance, hardness, curiosity, mistrust, self-image, or withheld love, as these may arise. Simply let yourself be "hollowed out," letting nothing remain hidden. Let nothing remain outside receptive exposure to God's severe love that can melt your insulating sense of self and so free your true being in God. Let yourself be sanctified by God's penetrating visioning of you. This in turn helps to free the sanctification of our vision in the world, wherein we see God's living Spirit at work.

5. After however many minutes seem right to you, close your eyes, but try to retain in your mind a sense of God's presence through the icon. Visualize the eyes of the icon reappearing as *your* eyes, God seeing the world through you. Thus you may find yourself *becoming* the icon. You realize yourself to be an image/icon of God through whom the world is loved into the fullness of being.[4]

SACRED AND SECULAR VISION

S UCH SANCTIFICATION of our vision can save us from the secularization of our sight. By secularization I mean the myopic vision that develops apart from God. This vision leaves us prone to

---

[4] This discussion of icons is elaborated in my book *Living in the Presence: Disciplines for the Spiritual Heart* (San Francisco: Harper & Row, 1987), chapter 4.

embrace uncritically the finite commercial, social, economic, and political images of reality frequently offered us in contemporary culture. We are caught up in the collective narrowness, blindness, and delusions of secular vision, especially its desire to control life and center it on the enhancement of the individual or collective ego with no sense of belonging to a larger, transcendent reality.

Sanctified vision frees our capacity to discern this larger reality and its divine energies subtly alive in our midst. The world becomes more sacramental. Then people, trees, stones, forms of every kind can become icons, transparencies for God's presence—indeed for the presence of the whole company of heaven. Such vision enables us to sense what is of God and what is not amidst the many visions swirling around us. Our calling to collaborate with this reality in every sphere of life also becomes clearer. We notice a growing liberation from the great human problem of separating ourselves from God and narrowing reality down to a grasping, fearing, spiritually dulled ego-centeredness. We become more available for and at home in the One closer to us than our breath, closer to us than any external or internal image. Each response to this calling finds us participating in the sanctification of our age. Icons are visible and constant reminders of this transforming depth to which our vision is called. They are not meant to remove us from the many concrete realities of our daily individual and collective lives. Indeed, they can help give us courage to face these realities with compassion and a discerning eye.

Asceticism Reconsidered

by Elizabeth A. Dreyer

E VERYWHERE WE TURN people are trying to get in touch with their roots. Popular television series, children in search of their birth parents, religious communities and churches examining anew the initial élan of their founders, individuals coming to terms with childhood experience—all this activity points to a hunger to rediscover the past, to negotiate with it, to see how it can contribute to identity and new life today.

The ascetic tradition is one of the many objects of this search. We can propose various reasons for the recent interest in ascetic practices. Most of us are all too aware of the abundance of wealth in this country and of our penchant toward consumerism. Many have also experienced a sense of loss of the character-enhancing rigors of earlier times.

Christians approach asceticism from a variety of perspectives. One popular approach is to begin with the traditional categories, such as fasting or sexual abstinence, and then to articulate the meaning these practices might have within a contemporary spiritual framework. Another approach is to begin with the everyday experience of modern persons as the primary resource for a fresh understanding of asceticism. Although those who have written about asceticism have as a goal the presentation of a relevant understanding of asceticism, in my judgment few take with adequate seriousness life's experiences in the modern world.

One obvious benefit of taking human experience as the starting point for our understanding of asceticism is that it makes room for the whole range of human experience. The ascetic life will look different in poor or war-torn countries and affluent or peaceful nations. It will be different for women and men, for persons of various ages, colors, belief systems, and economic status. This vision of asceticism is also more directly communal in its orientation. Authentic, private ascetic practices do rebound to the welfare of the community, but a true asceticism of everyday life, by its vary nature, directly enhances our life together. In either case, and one does not exclude the other, the fruit is the same: tender compassion, freedom, joy, courage, and fullness of life.

ASCETICISM: GENERAL COMMENTS

A SCETIC PRACTICE is a universal phenomenon. Nearly all religions have encouraged believers to engage in behavior that is characterized by some renunciation of the social and physical world. Christianity inherited two important traditions—those of the Jewish and Greek communities. In the Greek world, *ascesis* referred to training, exercise, or practice. At first it referred to the achievement of bodily excellence; later it was applied to the training of the mind in the acquisition of wisdom and to training in virtue, disciplining the will to turn away from all forms of self-indulgence, especially wine, food, and sexual expression.[1] In the Hebrew community periodic fasting was a custom enjoined on all believers. In addition, the prophets repeatedly counseled the community in times of national crisis to fast, to repent, to alter habitual behavior, in order to wake up to the peril in which they stood.[2]

There was a particularly strong ascetic streak in the Christian community from the third to the fifth centuries A.D. The Alexandrians, Clement and Origen, incorporated the idea of ascetic behavior into their theologies. Perhaps the name most frequently associated with asceticism is that of Antony (d. 356), the monk immortalized in Athanasius' famous biography, who retired to the desert to fight the demons, protesting the wedding of church and state after Constantine.

This tradition continued through the age of the martyrs and into the Middle Ages, which witnessed extreme forms of ascetic behavior. Although all the medieval saints put a high priority on self-denial, one thinks especially of the severe practices of Francis of Assisi (d. 1226), who treated his own "Brother Body" with such severity, or of the extremes of self-torture practiced for a while by Henry Suso (d. 1366). In some religious orders ascetic practices such as fasting, chain wearing, and flagellation continued in some form well into this century, especially in Europe.

In its more striking forms, Christian asceticism has been characterized by withdrawal from society into the desert, open struggle with demonic forces, fasting, constant prayer, sleep deprivation, virginity, a strong sense of the end of the world, and self-inflicted mortification, often in imitation of the hero-martyrs.[3]

---

[1] Diarmuid O. Murchu, "Early Christian Asceticism and Its Relevance Today" in *Irish Theological Quarterly* 50 (1983–84), p. 86.

[2] Margaret Miles, "The Recovery of Asceticism" in *Commonweal* 110 (January 28, 1983), p. 40.

[3] *Ibid.*, p. 83.

Greek dualism has greatly influenced our understanding of asceticism within the Christian tradition. This dualism opposes body and soul, matter and spirit. Many Christians viewed the body as a major obstacle to holiness and therefore in constant need of containment, suppression, and control. Because our ideas of asceticism are still influenced by this dualism, we moderns have a hard time understanding why or how asceticism could be good for us. We no longer view the body in opposition to the soul. Asceticism seems unhealthy at best and harmful to full human development at worst.

RECENT INTEREST IN ASCETICISM

IN SPITE OF THESE DIFFICULTIES, there seems to be significant interest in asceticism and in the ways in which it can be meaningful in contemporary life. These approaches point to the impoverishment of Christian life that would result in eliminating asceticism altogether, but they are also wary of extreme, harmful forms of asceticism. Asceticism is viewed as a way to the fullness of life. It is a way to ward off the death-dealing power of idolatry, of obsessive compulsions, of illusions and egoism. Ascetic practices can foster conversion, gather and focus energy, and, when reconnected with love, avoid the dangers of self-preoccupation and self-congratulation while enhancing service to neighbor.[4]

However, much of the discussion takes as a starting point the traditional ascetical categories such as fasting and abstinence. And while there is value to this approach, it is limiting if it is the *only* or the *primary* approach. The recent changes in theology and spirituality such as the turn to the human subject, the importance of human experience and of the socio-cultural context in which we live, make it imperative to look at asceticism (and many other aspects of the Christian life) from a fresh viewpoint.

THE ASCETICISM OF EVERYDAY LIFE

WE MUST START by recognizing the difference between ascetic practices in which one chooses to engage and the opportunities for asceticism that are built into daily existence. Most discussion about ascetic practices addresses the former

---

[4] See Margaret Miles, *Fullness of Life: Historical Foundations for a New Asceticism* (Philadelphia: Westminster Press, 1981), and Karl Rahner, "New Asceticism" in *The Practices of Faith* (New York: Crossroads, 1983).

type, such as the choice to renounce food or sexual activity, social contact, or goods and pleasures of some kind. We are aware that such practices can be very life-giving and productive of a deeper love of God and neighbor. Yet any form of conscious ascetic practice has its dangers. We are all familiar with the Reformation discussion of works righteousness and the danger inherent in attempting to win salvation by our own activity. This effort involves performing ascetic practices in order to store up a large bank balance of grace toward an eternal reward. A second danger attached to choosing asceticism is egoism. One can become focused on the behavior, lose touch with its roots in love, and begin to assume a "holier-than-thou" attitude toward others. Stories of extreme asceticism cause us to question the authenticity of such practices and the image of God behind them.

But there is another way to think about asceticism. I call it the asceticism of everyday life, and I suggest that for the majority of Christians it will be primary. A wise friend once said to me, "You never need to go to Lent. Lent always comes to you." In other words, if we live in even a minimally conscious way, we cannot help but see that life brings most of us all kinds of opportunities for self-denial. In this approach, we begin not with a category from the past such as fasting but with reverent attention to the stuff of our daily lives. When we focus too exclusively on the old categories, it rarely occurs to us that the primary locus of asceticism is our ordinary experience.

What follows presumes a basic orientation toward love of God and neighbor. It also presumes a desire, at some level of consciousness, to live in imitation of Jesus, including participation in his loving and life-giving suffering for us. This perspective also presumes an incarnational theology in which we take seriously the gospel message that what we do for the least of persons (ourselves included) we do for God.

At issue here is one's perception and understanding, in faith, of the *meaning* of everyday existence. Ultimately, such a vision of life is a gift of God, but the ways in which this gift is accepted and nurtured will vary from person to person. The one universal prerequisite is some kind of regular reflection on how God is present in one's life. For some, the primary catalyst is learning that such a contemplative stance is possible and then choosing to look at life in this manner. For others, regular communal worship will feed the desire to see God in all things. For yet others, the loving witness of other people will call them to a reverent outlook on life. And finally, some will be assisted by more traditional spiritual disciplines such as set periods of prayer, solitude, fasting, and spiritual direction. The danger is to view the matter in too narrow a fashion, failing to realize that the paths to falling more deeply in love with God are infinite. Let me mention three. They are confronting illusion, aging and death, and parenting.

CONFRONTING ILLUSION

L IFE BRINGS NUMEROUS OPPORTUNITIES to move from illusion to reality. Some illusions are inherited from culture, nation, or family. We see ourselves as better, more generous, or more intelligent than others. It is also possible to cling to the illusion that we are not worth anything or that we are incapable of good actions. Other illusions are created as defense mechanisms. We have illusions about ourselves, about our children, about our situation in life, about friends, about God. In some situations the illusion is more positive than the truth. In others, less so. In either case, they are false and therefore incapable of serving as a foundation for building a loving and authentic life.

In general, we like our illusions. They are familiar and comfortable, and we cling to them even though they lead to a dead end. We close our eyes when the truth intrudes on our picture, and we rarely seek outside perspectives from persons who might see more clearly than we do. Responses from other people that make us especially upset or angry can point to some part of the truth about ourselves that we are not willing to face.

An asceticism of everyday life points to an alternative in which we grow in the desire for the truth of our situation. We undergo the necessary stripping as the layers of illusion are peeled away. We engage in the discipline of seeking the truth, of being on the watch for clues to the false dimensions of our lives. We become willing to die to the old, self-centered self so that a new creation may emerge. Such an asceticism may involve the time and energy required to get at the truth of some political situation, local or global, and the action one must take as a result of knowing the truth. For others, it may mean facing up to the growing chasm between true inner feelings and dispositions and the self that is presented to others. It may mean watching attentively for the signals that others send us about the blocks to truth we have set up in our work and relationships. Such a process entails pain and suffering but can lead to new life.

AGING AND DEATH

SECOND EXAMPLE of everyday asceticism is the universal experience of aging and death. We might add here the experience of illness, great and small, suffered by many people. Often this opportunity first knocks in middle age. One's energy level and body functions begin to decline. The options are to cling ferociously to youth or to see our physical diminishment and the mental strain that can accompany it as part of a larger picture in which suffering and limitation become channels for participation in Christ's sufferings—gestures of acceptance that nurture love and life in ourselves and others.

The letting go intensifies when death approaches. For the elderly and seriously ill, the stripping can be extreme—physical movement, eyesight, hearing, memory, even speech may slip from one's control. How vulnerable we become—an opportunity to open ourselves ever more fully to the loving presence and care of God. In some ways the practice of fasting, for example, pales in the light of this invitation to lay down one's life with courage and love.

The loved ones of the sick and elderly are invited to their own brand of asceticism. How do we deal with the fatigue and burnout of daily hospital visits? How do we manage to keep up the daily round of responsibilities that do not abate when someone in the family is ill or dying? How do we allow God to share the burden of grief and the letting go of a friend or child or spouse? The weight of such experiences can crush us or be seen as a call to lay down our lives in love, to open ourselves to the consoling grace of God's love, and to emerge as persons fully alive in the Spirit.

In the past we have looked too exclusively to unusual ascetic models and have failed to see the heroism all around us. Even a visionary such as Thomas Merton, the Cistercian monk of Gethsemane (d. 1968), can, on occasion, seem to miss the more ordinary examples of everyday asceticism. In a recent story in the *New Yorker*, Marvin Barrett offers a vivid description of the trauma of heart attack and cancer, and of life in the intensive care unit. He concludes, "Merton writes about the marginal man, the monk, the displaced person, the prisoner, those who live in the presence of death and go beyond it to become 'witnesses to life.' Why does he leave the other experts off his list—the old, the desperately ill?"[5]

---

[5] Marvin Barrett, "A Kind of Dying," *The New Yorker* (October 12, 1987), pp. 40–43.

PARENTING

A FINAL EXAMPLE is one experienced by a great number of people: raising children. In our society the challenge of raising children is perhaps the ascetic opportunity *par excellence*. This is not to deny the profound joys and rewards of parenting—receiving unexpected gestures of love and gratitude such as a simple flower or a homemade birthday card; participating in the process of children's maturation; watching them and helping them to become loving persons; seeing them accomplish their goals and grow in learning and self-reflection. But whether one has children or is simply helping or observing others raise them, one cannot but be struck by the minefield facing most parents today. How do we love children well? How do we allow them to become who they are meant to be, free from our excessive attempts to mold them into something else? How do we trust them? How do we expose them to values? How do we cope with alcohol, drugs, misuse of sexuality, indifference, selfishness, boredom, consumerism? How do we gracefully and lovingly let them go when the time comes?

Parents get a lot of bad press. For the most part, parents have deep desires to love their children well, and they suffer untold agonies—both in discerning how to raise their children and in experiencing some of the failure that is an inevitable part of the process. Child rearing is almost always an invitation to asceticism.

Some examples point to the loving self-denial that is at the heart of the asceticism of everyday life. Who is not familiar with the rigors of carpooling to school, soccer games, piano lessons, and science fairs? Young parents who both need to be employed face hard decisions about child care. A full night's sleep, time to oneself, the freedom to come and go as one pleases—all this must be given up, and given up in a way that is quite different from the monk who chooses to rise once or twice during the night to recite his prayers. Huge chunks of life are laid down at the behest of infants. And then, later, parents must let go, allowing children to create their own futures in freedom.

Who has not agonized over children who become victims of drugs, who lose all interest in learning, or who enter into other patterns of self-destructive behavior? What parent has not felt helpless after exhausting every possible mode of action without success? Suffering with children often extends into the second and even third generations, with grandparents and great-grandparents continuing to be deeply involved in the lives of their families.

Of course, one must be aware of the spiritual potential of everyday asceticism in order for it to be meaningful. There is nothing automatic about it. It is part of one's total spirituality that includes a desire for God, an openness to the gifts God offers us, a willingness to learn about and confront the patterns of sinfulness in our lives. True asceticism is nurtured by a loving, attentive, contemplative stance toward the persons in our lives, by a willingness to cross over and walk in another's shoes, a desire to be patient and to commit to the long haul. Asceticism also demands freedom. Most often we have little control over the sufferings that life brings, but we do have something to say about how we will respond to these opportunities. How we respond can lead us to the fullness of life or to a life of anger, resentment, cynicism, and despair.

But what a shame if we miss these daily invitations to self-denial, to the free and loving surrender of life for another, and think that choosing to fast one day a month is the only avenue of asceticism available to us. "As you did to the least of my brothers and sisters, you did to me" (Matt. 25:40, AT). The spiritual life is a journey into the fullness of life and love in God and in one another. Ascetic practice is one means that can be used to this end. The asceticism of everyday life is the primary means available to Christians on their journey toward union with God in love.

It is time for the Christian community to make a paradigmatic shift of images. The model of asceticism for the Christian community can no longer be the emaciated, celibate monk with the tortured face. The struggle of the loving, selfless parent can be a model for all of us, whether we are physical parents or not. As church, we are called to become more aware of the loving asceticism of everyday life. Only then will we be able to appreciate the heroic death to self that surrounds us, celebrate the presence of God in these forms of self-sacrifice, affirm, encourage, and console one another, and look to the best of them as models in our own search for a life-filled existence.

Community

Community

Memory *in* Congregational Life

by Bruce C. Birch

A FEW YEARS AGO a member of our congregation objected to part of a litany being written for the reception of new members. It was a segment giving thanks to all of those who had labored in the communities of faith which went before us. It remembered with gratitude our ancestors in the biblical communities and those who carried the work of the church through subsequent history. This man said he objected because he felt little or no tie to those people. For him the church was important because of the support and witness of this congregation in the immediate present.

Later the same evening, older members were telling new members about aspects of life in that congregation which meant the most to them. The man who had objected earlier said the oneness of community he felt when we gathered around the table for the passing of bread and wine in Holy Communion was the most meaningful to him. Someone immediately challenged him, "Dave, did you think the sacraments were originated by our worship committee?" As members of Christian congregations we owe a great debt to our past, but most of us are not very conscious of that debt.

How are congregations influenced by the past? Why is awareness of that past important? How do we bring that past to greater consciousness in the life of the congregation? How do we draw on the resources of our past to enable our mission as the church in the present? These are questions I hope to focus on by looking at the role of memory in the life of the congregation.

THE FORMATION OF CONGREGATIONAL LIFE

S EVERAL FEATURES which are clear in the biblical formation of congregational life deserve renewed attention in our assessment of how the past addresses modern congregational life.

First, congregation is formed in response to God's initiative of grace. In the Old Testament, Israel is brought into being as the people of God by God's deliverance of the Hebrews from bondage in Egypt

(Exod. 14–15; Deut. 32:6). In the Exodus event, God freely entered human history in an act of grace toward slaves with no worldly standing. This graceful act was motivated by love alone (Deut. 7:7-8). This Exodus experience became for Israel a model throughout succeeding generations for the way God's saving grace is experienced. As with Israel at the sea, those who trust in God's grace can experience hope out of despair and life out of death. God opens up the future in unexpected ways.

At Mount Sinai the congregation comes into being as a covenant community in response to God's salvation. Exodus creates a delivered people, but it is in the covenant at Sinai that Israel becomes an organized congregation in response to God's saving action. In the covenant texts we see Israel struggling to give concrete expression to its life as a delivered people. Faith cannot exist in the abstract. It must issue forth in the way we live as community in the world. In the New Testament the dynamic is virtually the same. God's grace in Jesus Christ initiates and calls us to response as the church. In crucifixion and resurrection we see once again the drama of God's salvation. Death becomes life. Despair turns to hope. This resurrection faith is experienced as God's grace generation after generation in the church. When Pentecost comes and the church is born, it is in response to God's grace and made possible by God's Spirit (Acts 2). The earliest Christian congregation in Jerusalem immediately sets to work organizing its life in patterns of worship, common life, and missional activity in the world consistent with the grace they have come to know in Jesus Christ (Acts 2:43-47; 4:32-37).

It is important in our own congregational life to see faithful community as a response to the grace which comes from God and not as the source of God's grace itself. Thus, the agenda for congregational life is always set by God's will, prayerfully and reflectively considered, rather than the congregation's own self interest.

Congregation is also formed around memory and vision. Memory is oriented to recalling what God has done and how faithful response has been made to God's action. Vision is oriented to anticipating what God is yet doing in the world and to aligning congregational life to serve that action of God's grace. The cultivation of memory and vision issues forth in the congregation's identity and mission. The community of faith stands with one foot rooted in a historic tradition from which it draws its identity as God's covenant people. Its other foot is firmly planted in a future, God's future, toward which it lives in anticipation of the fulfillment of God's desire for love, justice, and wholeness.[1]

As in the biblical communities, memory and vision, identity and mission, are necessary and interrelated in the life of modern congregations. Though these aspects of congregational life are frequently treated as an either-or, overemphasis on either distorts the life of the church. Those who stress memory and identity exclusively (e.g., Bible reading as a devotional end in itself apart from mission) run the risk of becoming the fossil church. A fossil is an extraordinarily faithful witness to the past, but it is incapable of responding to the present or the future. Those who stress vision and mission without rootedness in faith memory run the risk of becoming the chameleon church. Having no identity of its own, it is likely to take on the coloration of whatever ideology, cultural context, or fad happens to surround it.[2]

It is clear biblically that the congregation is the chief agent of memory in the life of faith. Primarily in its local congregational form, the church is the bearer of biblical and historical tradition. The canon of scripture itself grew out of materials that became authoritative in the life of local congregations and only later were recognized by wider "official" forums of church life. Thus, local congregations must become self-conscious about the continuation of this important task of passing on the church's memory.

The biblical congregations formed around memory and vision have a distinctive character. In both Old and New Testament, congregations are called to model life as alternative communities in the midst of their prevailing cultural settings.[3] Those who had received and acknowledged the gift of God's grace could not simply reflect the patterns of life in the surrounding cultures. To know God's grace made a difference in relationship to God, to other persons of faith, and to one's neighbor in the world.

In the Old Testament, *covenant* was the term applied by the congregation to its model of alternate life. The covenant model set forth a vision of community which intimately tied relationship with God to relationship with the neighbor. From the very beginning one's

---

[1] This same dual quality is discussed as being and doing aspects of Christian life in Bruce C. Birch and Larry L. Rasmussen, *Bible and Ethics in the Christian Life* (Minneapolis: Augsburg, 1976, revised edition, 1989).

[2] The images are suggested by Jürgen Moltmann, "Christian Theology Today," *New World Outlook*, LXII (1972), p. 483.

[3] Recent thinking about biblical community as alternative community may be found in Walter Brueggemann, *The Prophetic Imagination* (Fortress, 1978), ch. 1, and Bruce C. Birch, *What Does the Lord Require? The Old Testament Call to Social Witness* (Philadelphia: Westminster Press, 1985), ch. 3.

neighbor included not just other believers but sojourners, strangers in the gate, and aliens in your midst.

In the New Testament the pattern of calling to alternative community and temptation to worldly accommodation is remarkably similar to what we see in Israel's story. The early church organized its life in ways that were radically different from those of the Hellenistic world. They forsook ownership of goods and shared economic resources on the basis of need. They ignored the political divisions of their world and converted women and slaves and persons of all economic and social classes or nationalities. The politics of the early church were based on servanthood and not power, community and not status.

In our congregations remembering in the biblical sense will involve a constant calling to a life lived in tension with the world—but lived for the sake of the world. Memory in the life of the congregation is never limited to the comfort of discovering one's historic identity. The very content of that biblical identity is discomforting, since it calls us to the difficult task of alternative life amid the constant cultural pressures on the church to conform. But precisely this tension is the creative one from which the church's mission arises and is empowered. That mission is to mediate the grace of God we have already experienced to a broken world in need of healing grace. The congregation's own life as an alternative community in the covenant model is one of the significant ways that mission is carried forward.

THE ROLE OF MEMORY IN CONGREGATIONAL LIFE

THE MOST IMPORTANT function of memory in the congregation is in the formation of identity and character. We are shaped as community by what we call to memory from our biblical and historic traditions. The importance of congregational activities of remembering is often underestimated. Many of those most committed to the renewal and effectiveness of the church have focused almost entirely on the question "What is the church to do?" But since scripture and tradition (the sources of the church's memory) seldom tell us precisely what the church is to do, many in active local congregations treat scripture and tradition as little more than distant historical background.

Alongside the concern for congregational doing must be concern for the congregation's being, "Who are we to be?" Memory plays a primary role in forming our identity, values, perceptions, dispositions, and intentions. The character of Christians and Christian congregations becomes as important as their conduct.[4] When we come to know and internalize the Hebrew affirmation that creation is good or the Pauline insight into the universality of the gospel, "all are one in Christ Jesus," then we are shaped in our basic identity and character in ways that affect our "doing" as congregations.

Enhancing the role of memory in the formation of congregational identity and character is a long-term and ongoing task. Without long-term cultivation in the life of the congregation, references to the Bible or to a particular historic tradition will only be sprinkled into the church's activities to lend justification to priorities already determined on other grounds. On the other hand, nurtured over the course of a congregation's ongoing life, the images and insights of biblical and historical memory will be available as part of the identity the church carries with it into every decision on priorities or action of missional calling. Congregations which do not know something of their biblical and historic roots can seldom do more than reflect their own cultural context in the world.

THE SOURCES AND ARENAS OF MEMORY IN CONGREGATIONAL LIFE

THE SOURCES of congregational remembering are the Bible and tradition. A congregation must reach back to find its roots in the biblical communities of faith or it will lose touch with those traditions that make the church Christian. All that we know of God rests on scriptural foundations, for even our discernment of divine activity in our own time is dependent on knowing who God revealed the divine self to be in biblical tradition. Sharpening our understanding of the God who called Israel and the church into life can give us new eyes to see the grace of God in our midst.

We relate to biblical memory not simply by leaping back from our moment to biblical times and experiences. We have access to biblical memory through some historic faith tradition. That tradition is also a part of congregational remembering.

---

[4] Recent Protestant work in theology and ethics has given new emphasis to the formation of character in the life of the church. See Stanley Hauerwas, *Vision and Virtue* (Notre Dame: Fides, 1974), and *Character and the Christian Church* (San Antonio: Trinity University Press, 1975).

The influence of tradition may find its most powerful expression for many congregations in the ongoing influence of its own local history. Examples of powerful local memory which can shape congregations in important ways are the continuing effect of a previous pastor, the local conflicts and issues that have affected the community, a special mission focus that led to the founding of a local congregation. These must be acknowledged and understood as a part of our remembering which needs critical reflection as surely as does scripture or denominational tradition.

The arenas of congregational remembering are worship, religious education, and the life of the congregation as a community. We can look briefly at the dynamics of memory in each of these arenas.

In many ways Christian worship can be considered a ritual act of congregational remembering. Although its central purpose is celebration, it is based on the remembrance of what God has done in Jesus Christ and on the remembrance of who we are called to be as God's people, Christ's church.

In Christian worship we are surrounded by signs and symbols which evoke congregational memory. Architectural designs and objects of art and furnishings speak of particular biblical or historic traditions. These may run the gamut from austere to ornate, but every worship setting with its symbols speaks to the congregation of a particular pattern of faith memory.

Our liturgies are filled with word images rooted in and meaningful only in reference to our faith memory. Participation in Christian worship is itself an exercise in Christian remembering. Broadening our understanding of the images and traditions used in our liturgies can pay great dividends. By the same token, efforts to enrich the liturgies we use can broaden the range of remembering to which congregations are exposed in worship.

Several elements within the liturgy are of special importance in nurturing congregational memory. The reading of scripture in worship is for many church members the only regular, direct exposure to the Bible. The use of the historic creeds ties the gathered congregation to earlier central affirmations of the church. The sermon proclaims God's word anew to the congregation, but not as an act of the moment only. In proclamation we lay claim anew to the memory of our faith in the confidence that it has a word to speak to us in our own moment. The preacher proclaims not out of his or her authority alone, but on the basis of God's word mediated in scripture and tradition. Finally, the sacraments are unique vehicles of congregational remembering, since they not only speak God's word but reenact it in the community. Sacraments have a unique capacity to make memory present in our midst in ways that renew and empower the congregation for its mission in the world.

In the educational life of the church the nurture of congregational memory is a central task. Reflection on and study of the Bible and of our diverse historic traditions is an obvious part of the church's educational task. But it has not always been given the central attention it deserves, because the nurture of congregational memory itself has been so often devalued. In many congregations Bible study is still primarily a matter of children's church school and not a high priority for active adult church members. Changing patterns of family and vocational life leave less time for the study and reflection that enrich our faith memory. Even where active educational programs are in place, well-intentioned curricula actually screen people off from direct contact with the sources of congregational remembering. We study what someone else says about the Bible rather than learning to study the Bible itself. Many church members have become consumers of other persons' biblical reflection rather than producers of biblical reflection themselves.

Memory is also nurtured in the shape and quality of congregational life. To be serious about Christian community as a calling and not simply as a part of institutional structures will require drawing upon faith memory for the images and understandings which will inform the life of the congregation. The life of any given congregation will model the memory images it has chosen to hold before its people. In mission has it chosen to consider "the least of these," as Jesus urged? In evangelism does it have genuine good news of the gospel to proclaim, or is it simply seeking statistical growth? Does it encourage and enable the life of prayer and spiritual devotion with its personal dimensions of congregational remembering, or is it more interested in populating its committees? In pastoral care, does it offer images of hope drawn from the wellsprings of faith, or does it leave people with the hollow platitudes of secular life? The modeling of these choices from faith memory for congregational life will be affected by worship and study, for all of these arenas interrelate.

A final word must be said about the social location of congregational memory. The process of nurturing and appropriating faith memory in the life of a congregation does not go on in a vacuum. It is a dynamic process affected by what we bring with us to the process of remembering. In particular, the process is affected by our social location in the appropriation of the church's memory.

New awareness of the importance of this insight has come from the emergence of insistent and perceptive voices in feminist, ethnic, and third-world theologies. They have shown us how frequently a white, middle-class, male social location is assumed as normative and how often the process of congregational remembering has failed to see or hear texts and traditions that address the concerns of women, people of color, the poor, the dispossessed. Congregations must be aware that within their own membership social location will cause different persons looking at the same biblical text to hear a different word addressed to them, and they must be prepared to honor those perspectives as authentic encounter with God's word. The task then becomes to hear and understand the different shape that our remembering takes because of social location, and to work toward finding ways of joining in the common work of the body of Christ.

Even where such differences are not apparent in a local congregation, awareness of those perspectives from social location in denominations and in the global church must be fostered. Use of resources that show us the view of scripture or tradition through other eyes can be helpful. For example, *The Gospel in Solentiname* simply records the discussions of gospel passages by village folk in Nicaragua, but what they find in those texts is powerfully and movingly different because of the social location from which they hear the scripture.[5] The same experience of new eyes and new ears for congregational remembering can be found in resources that reflect on women's experience or the African American experience or the experience of any segment of the church which occupies a social location different than our own.

THE ENHANCEMENT OF MEMORY IN CONGREGATIONAL LIFE

SINCE MEMORY is crucial in the life of the local congregation, how can congregational memory be fostered and enhanced?

1. Empower the laity for nurturing congregational memory. Clergy are not the principle guardians of faith memory.

---

[5] Ernesto Cardenal, *The Gospel in Solentiname* (Maryknoll, NY: Orbis Books, 1976). See also Robert McAfee Brown, *Unexpected News: Reading the Bible with Third World Eyes* (Philadelphia: Westminster Press, 1984).

Laypersons with opportunity and training for leadership in all arenas of the church's life can be the needed leaven in the loaf for generating seriousness about the role of memory in congregational life.

2. Improve opportunities for Christian education. There are still many congregations where sustained educational programming is available only to children. Adult education (where it exists) is often episodic and lacking in any long-term strategy for the nurture of memory.

In children's education, programs and curricula for teaching the Bible to children are still dominated by the idea that the Bible is an adult book and can only be taught to children in diluted forms that do violence to the biblical stories and their natural power. We need a recovery of appreciation for the simple power of biblical storytelling done with integrity and skill. Steeping children in the stories of the Bible builds up a fund of faith memory. But that fund does not need to be immediately tapped for the drawing of morals or the direct application to life experience.

Both children and adults should be given more opportunities for learning basic skills and tools that make direct study and interpretation of the Bible possible. Too much of our educational efforts in building biblical memory involve teaching about the Bible and little contact with the Bible itself.

Teacher training for congregational education programs should include opportunities for deepening knowledge and understanding of the Bible and our historic traditions for their own sake. Training events usually focus on help for the preparation and teaching of lessons in the classrooms. But those charged with deepening the faith memory of the congregation in study and reflection must have opportunities to deepen their own encounter with biblical and historical memory without immediately having to think in terms of application or use of that material in educational programs.

3. Renew and reform membership preparation. If membership in a congregation is to be meaningful, it must be accompanied by some serious opportunity for renewing or building faith memory. Some of the most successful membership preparation processes involve study, reflection, and prayer by potential members with their sponsors from the membership

of the congregation. Over a period of years this can have a broad and profound effect on the church's memory and on openness to new memory-enhancing aspects of the church's life.

4. Emphasize visual image and symbol. We should not think that enhancement of congregational memory is solely accomplished by words. Historically the church has a rich tradition of expression in the visual arts, but the close relationship between artistic expression and the life of the church in many earlier periods is not characteristic of our own time. Lack of such visual expressions of faith is often defended as making money available for urgent arenas of the congregation's missional program. The danger, however, is an impoverishment of the spirit that ultimately affects the energy and vision by which we pursue the mission of the church.

There are surely many other areas and methods for the enhancement of memory in congregational life. As long as these efforts are seen in conjunction with the church's vision for mission and not as an end in themselves, this nurture of congregational memory can prove richly empowering to the local congregation. "God heard their groaning, and God remembered [the] covenant . . ." (Exod. 2:24). In the hour of our need God has always remembered us. In the midst of the broken world to which the church is sent let us remember God. Let us give thanks for the remembering of those who went before us, enabling us to know of the God who called us into being as a people and to recognize that same God present in our midst yet today.

Adapted from an article by the same title appearing in *The Congregation: Its Power to Form and Transform*, ed. by C. Ellis Nelson (Atlanta: John Knox Press, 1988).

Meditative Bible Study

by John S. Mogabgab

IETRICH BONHOEFFER once compared reading the Bible to meditating upon a letter from a loved one. We do not approach such a letter objectively, analytically, or hurriedly, as we might a newspaper or newsletter from our congressional representative. Rather, we linger over the words, savor them, and allow them to soak into the very center of our being, because we know that in this letter we are being addressed by someone who loves us.

The purpose of a Bible study group with a meditative orientation is to follow Bonhoeffer's suggestion. Thus do we enter what Karl Barth called "the strange new world within the Bible," a place where we are instructed in the meaning of being in the world but not of it.[1] In the following pages I will describe one way of structuring such a group, and conclude with a few things about the content and method of the study.

STRUCTURE

N THIS SECTION I want simply to enumerate the essential procedural matters associated with meditative Bible study groups. First, how much time is involved? As a general guideline, two hours is an appropriate amount of time to set aside for the group. This will allow for gathering, settling down, listening to God's word, reflecting upon it, sharing the harvest of these reflections, closing, and departure. The person who initiates the idea of such a group should decide on a time period that will fit the schedules and responsibilities of prospective participants. Minor adjustments (such as starting or closing time) may be made after the group has met for several sessions. Frequency of meeting must also be settled. Ideally, the group would gather weekly during an evening relatively free of other church programs or meetings.

The place of meeting must also be determined. Although much could be said in favor of coming together in a private home, there are advantages to meeting in a comfortable room at the church. The

---

[1] Karl Barth, *The Word of God and the Word of Man*, trans. Douglas Horton (New York: Harper & Row, 1957), pp. 28–50.

church will probably be less prone to distracting interruptions. At the same time, that it is the church rather than a home accentuates the fact that this is not primarily a social gathering. And finally, using the church in this way can help people recognize that the church is not merely a Sunday morning congregation but a community of faith active throughout the week as well.

There are two forms of leadership in meditative Bible study groups. The first is usually assumed by a person knowledgeable enough about scripture and theology to provide gentle, unobtrusive guidance to the group. This role might be assumed by a pastor, deacon, or director of Christian education. But it could also be taken on by someone who is involved in extension courses in theology, or who has been for some time interested in and committed to the discipline of Bible study (as this is encouraged, for example, in Cursillo, The Walk to Emmaus, and Tres Dias). It would be appropriate to view this person as one whose leadership consists of facilitating spiritually informative and empowering conversation among the group members.

The second form of leadership involves responsibility for the group on a particular evening, and thus should rotate among the members. This person will do basic exegetical work on the text to be studied prior to the meeting and will therefore be prepared to answer historical, critical, or other "factual" questions related to the text. This person will also convene the gathering, read the scripture for the day, and close the gathering at the end of the session.

Many formats might be used to organize the two hours of group time. The one suggested here is offered simply as a pattern to stimulate your own thought. The session's leader calls the group together and invites them to become still before the Lord. This quieting and centering may be found through certain relaxation techniques or simply through silence. After the group has become quiet, the leader reads the scripture for the first time. At the conclusion of the reading, the leader invites participants to a silence of three to five minutes. The leader may give some guidelines for the use of these quiet moments, such as to note which words or images from the text especially stand out in each participant's mind. The leader concludes this period of silence by reading the text a second time, perhaps varying the pace and emphasis to suggest another interpretation of the words. Again, this reading is followed by a similar period of silence.

This silent time might be used by group members to enter imaginatively into the text if it is a narrative portion of the Bible.

They might be encouraged to use all their senses to locate themselves in the scene portrayed in the words of the text. What does it look, smell, sound, and feel like to be there? Where are they in relation to the main characters or the central action? Do they identify with any of these characters, and if so, in what ways? Or the leader might suggest that participants take note of any resonances or resistances the text stimulates in them. Such feelings are often clues to how and where God's word is actively addressing us. Once more, the leader concludes this silent time with another reading of the text. Before doing so, he or she should announce that this third reading will be followed by an open-ended silence which will be broken when someone in the group is ready to offer a response to God's word. Approximately fifteen minutes before closing time, the leader for that day should note the time and suggest that conversation be brought to a conclusion. The last ten minutes of the session might then be devoted to intercessory prayers (perhaps shaped by the text for that day and the sharing it has encouraged). Let the group conclude with the Lord's Prayer.

Should the group remain open to newcomers, or should membership be closed after a certain number of members have joined or a certain number of sessions have passed? There are some who feel that such groups should remain open so that individuals feel free to attend as they are able. Others believe that the intimacy which can grow in these groups would be inhibited by an open membership policy. Certainly decisions on these matters ought to be informed by discussion with prospective group members. But since the outcome of such discussion will also be influenced by the content and method of meditative Bible study groups, it is time to turn our attention to these aspects of this environment for listening.

CONTENT AND METHOD

WHERE DOES A GROUP BEGIN its study of the Bible? The choice of how to enter into the great drama of God's works recounted in scripture deserves special consideration. It will depend upon the expressed interests of prospective participants, the style of preaching in the local congregation, and that church's understanding of its unique calling in the community, as well as the theological and educational convictions of those who start the group. But given these and other factors unique to each congregation, there are three basic approaches to scripture that will determine the actual content of the group meetings. These are straightforward and require little commentary.

The first approach involves a continuous reading of scripture. This will mean selecting a book, letter, or series of these, and simply working through them consecutively. The fact that such an approach has an organic continuity that builds over time might lead some leaders to decide that if this option is selected, the group should not be open to new members after a certain point. If this decision is made, then others who express interest in participating would become the nucleus of a new group.

The second approach to scripture is thematic. In this style of Bible study, selected themes such as healing, political ethics, or biblical economics determine the selection of texts for each session. Here, a good concordance, various commentaries, and dictionaries of the Bible are especially useful. This approach lends itself to either open or closed group formats, depending in part on how frequently attention moves to a new theme.

Finally, the third approach to the Bible is through a lectionary. Lectionaries include some of the strengths of the two other approaches: since they are based on the liturgical year, they touch on themes appropriate to each holy season, and within each season the lectionary selections tend to build upon one another as in the continuous reading of scripture. In churches where the clergy preach from a lectionary, this approach to Bible study has special merit. To have meditated upon the Sunday readings some time during the previous week often helps group members find new riches in the Sunday liturgy and homily. Because this approach to scripture is linked to weekly worship, it is especially appropriate to use with a group that wants to remain open to new members, or to more casual participation on the part of original members. Like Sunday worship, each week's group meeting will build on the previous week and yet be a meaningful event in and of itself.

What does it mean to speak of a method of meditative Bible study groups? Perhaps more than anything this refers to the spirit and focus of such gatherings. Their purpose is not to collect interesting facts about scripture but to discern how God is speaking to us in and through God's word. Their aim is not merely to talk about this word, keeping it safely objective and at arm's length, but to allow even our talking to be a form of listening to the word we have heard.

There are some simple disciplines that will foster the deeper listening that nourishes spiritual growth. For example, God's word to us is not an abstract theorem or principle. It comes to us in and through the eminently concrete experiences of people located in history. So, too, our listening must be rooted in and informed by our own location in all its dimensions (psychological, interpersonal, sociological, political, economic, geographic). We should strive for honesty in what we share with the group, and we should speak only for ourselves and refrain from interpreting or rephrasing what others have said. We should, therefore, resist the temptation to judge others either openly or in the secret places of our heart. We might pray for openness to receive as gifts the words our Christian brothers and sisters choose to entrust to our care. And we need to be aware of the importance of attending with all our energy to what scripture actually says, instead of speculating about what it does *not* say.

If we can practice these disciplines of listening, trusting that when we gather in Christ's name he is present with us, then we will experience the mutual penetration of scripture and personal life so well described by Maria Boulding: "The story to which you listen in scripture and your own life as you live it are mutually illuminating: you can hear the word in scripture because you know the hidden word in your life, but it is the scriptural word which is a lamp for your steps and a light for your path as you go back again to the task of living."[2] May your steps take you along the paths that lead to spiritual wholeness.

---

[2] *The Coming of God* (Collegeville, MN: The Liturgical Press, 1982), p. 79.

Liturgy *as* Holy Play

by Don E. Saliers

O NE SUNDAY, in a church I was attending, a woman who received communion in her motorized wheelchair was coming through the line to greet the clergy at the conclusion of worship. It had been a particularly festive eucharistic celebration, with vibrant young voices leading us in the psalm, including a lively procession of small children with cans and boxes of food for a special offering, following the bread and wine brought to the altar. Looking up at the pastor with wide eyes under the brim of a wondrous straw hat she exclaimed, "Didn't we dance today!"

I was suddenly awakened from my routine, if pleasant, after-liturgy greeting next in line. Her remark from the wheelchair startled me into re-perceiving the service just ended. Yes, I realized, yes we had indeed danced—young and old, well-dressed and blue-jeaned, able-bodied and the seemingly not so—all had been in a place of movement toward and around the presence of God incarnate. We gathered, sang, watched, listened, spoke, stood, some kneeling, and processed (on foot and otherwise) to and from a table, some joining hands. Suddenly I saw what we all should know: Christ is in our midst, inviting us to this moving circle of grace.

Her exclamation brought to mind the saying attributed to Jesus in the Acts of St. John, which depicts the hymn shared with the circling disciples after the meal in the upper room: "Whoever does not dance, does not know what is coming to pass. Amen."

How easy it is to miss the essentials. How much we fail to see and hear, even in the most ordinary gatherings for the worship of the Holy One. Could it be that every such faithful gathering—whether in great festivity or on those "dull" Sundays—is a time and a place for sacred play, the dance and song around the holiness of God-with-us? What is it that brought the psalmist to sing, "Let everything that breathes praise the LORD!" What are we missing which echoes in the lines of the twentieth-century church musician-poet Erik Routley:

In praise of God meet duty and delight,
angels and creatures, men and spirits bless'd;

in praise is earth transfigured by the sound
and sight of heaven's everlasting feast.[1]

Who among us, once having heard and sung (perhaps even danced) the disarming simplicity of what the Shakers taught us, can forget:

'Tis the gift to be simple, 'tis the gift to be free,
'tis the gift to come down where we ought to be,
and when we find ourselves in the place just right,
'twill be in the valley of love and delight.

These are hints and guesses, clues of a revelatory truth. The worship of God in the gathered community is, at its heart, what Romano Guardini called "holy play."[2] For him to liken our worship to play is a bold thing. Yet this is a venerable truth, and is at the origin of true Christian worship and life. Holy play is not the same as restless frivolity or frantic leisure. Rather, it is characteristic of what happens to human beings in community, large or small, who come into relation with the holy love of God for us and for the whole world. To be child-like in wonder and delight, as well as to be confronted together with what it is to be human in the presence of God—these are the qualities and effects of such play.

A little known Easter carol sings: "the whole bright world rejoices now, *hilariter, hilariter.*" Here is a lost language which lies at the heart of the mystery of authentic Christian worship and life. There is a "hilarity"—a high-spirited freedom and joy released by the glory of Christ. Perhaps the oldest hymn, apart from New Testament canticles, still used widely in Christian liturgy is the evening hymn known by its ancient Greek name, the *phos hilaron.* Some of us know this as "O Gladsome Light." Underneath our smoothed-out versions is a deep meaning: the gracious delight and challenging *hilaron,* the light of Christ, illuminating each day's waning, which is the light of the whole world's salvation. In that light we see the very brightness of God's glory.

We do well to consider the biblical and recurring notion that liturgical praise and prayer is to the Christian life as playful and faithful

---

[1] Lyrics from the hymn "For Musicians" by Erik Routley, copyright © 1977 by Hope Publishing Co., Carol Stream, IL. All rights reserved. Used by permission.

[2] Romano Guardini, *The Spirit of the Liturgy,* trans. Ada Lane (New York: Benziger Brothers, 1931), pp. 85–106.

love-making is to a healthy marriage: marked by deep respect and joy, not always ecstatic nor fully expressed, but capable of such deep communion as nowhere else is to be found. Yet, unlike human nuptial bliss, God extends to every soul and to every communal gathering in God's name the invitation to dance and sing in lamentation, in solemn thanksgiving, and in playful ecstatic praise.

Certainly there are strong differences among traditions and churches concerning how much and what kind of hilarity is admissible in the presence of God. And we must recall that David dancing before the ark and Herodias' dance before Herod are both, ambiguously, in scripture. The Puritans, like some of the early Christians influenced by Plato, and surrounded by demeaning pagan rites and the pleasures of gladiatorial games, placed strong strictures on holy play. There was to be no laughter or whistling on the Sabbath; or, earlier, no flute-playing or literal dancing in the liturgy. We can understand these responses to the loss of seriousness about human weakness and the sin of the world. Play as such can be self-destructive and even cruel. Yet it is just the deeper sense of liturgy as holy play which is required in order to understand our humanity and the created order appropriately. Otherwise, we can easily be consumed with our own religious self-seriousness.

How can authentic and faithful Christian liturgy free us to become who we are in God's grace? Two insights are worth pursuing. First, we human beings are created in the image of God, prefigured in the divine becoming human. So we are the object of God's joy as a creating and redeeming God. The Source of our life intends that we should ourselves play in some manner as God does. We are meant to regard the beautiful, and to learn a kind of improvised delight in the simple as well as the deepest matters. We learn to praise God, that everything may be received as gift; we learn to eat and drink together in Christ, that all our meals may be holy, and that we learn to be bread for others. Such a lightness of being knows how to take things seriously, but not so seriously as though we ourselves were finally in charge of the world, much less the whole creation. So Christian liturgy takes sin seriously, but God's grace even more so. This is surely a mark of the "glorious liberty of the children of God" of which the New Testament speaks!

The second insight concerns the divine promises which are at the heart of every liturgical gathering. In Christ the whole world is drawn to God and redeemed, and moved in the direction from which the vision of God's future beckons. The play of liturgy and its power to shape Christian life is thus both future-oriented in hope, and future-present in foretaste. Consider how many of our hymns sing this, whether in Advent through Epiphany, or in Easter-Pentecost. Our central prayers cry this out:"Your kingdom come. . . ." and *maranatha!* (Come, Lord Jesus). At the heart of our baptism and the eucharistic meal is this empowering promise: "Nothing can separate us from the love of God in Christ Jesus." No wonder we speak and enact together the reality of serving the world "until Christ comes in final victory, and we feast at his heavenly banquet."[3] No wonder some traditions say, "Therefore let us keep the feast."

In a neglected little book, Hugo Rahner speaks of the "sober seriousness" and the "eager lightness" of the Christian life. This is what we yearn for in our liturgical gatherings over time as well. To live prayerfully and gracefully is to live as we worship. "This eager lightness of touch," Rahner remarks, "is never mere frivolity, for frivolity is always the sign of a secret despair; whereas [persons] who play this game of God [are] secure in the knowledge that [they] proceed from God's own creating and protecting hand."[4]

But even more powerful than the virtue of "sober seriousness" coupled with "eager lightness" at the heart of liturgy as holy play is the radical claim of Easter freedom. As Jürgen Moltmann claims, "Easter freedom does not permit us to escape from the world or to forget about it . . . both the laughter of Easter and the sorrow of the cross are alive in liberated [human beings]."[5] The radical graced ability to laugh with those who laugh and weep with those who weep, and to gather up both suffering and joy into the song, prayer, and movement about the table in worship—this is the miracle of holy play. This is what authentic liturgy empowers and illuminates: our human being restored and made child-like before God.

In the world of the cynical, the hateful, and captivity to death, such a time and place for re-creation and transformation is indeed a divine miracle in human flesh. This is exactly what is promised to the faith community if we have ears to hear, eyes to see, and hearts open to God's way with us in Jesus.

Our existence here is always the arena of contrasts. The world is

---

[3] *United Methodist Hymnal* (Nashville: The United Methodist Publishing House, 1989), p. 10.

[4] Hugo Rahner, *Man at Play*, trans. Brian Battershaw and Edward Quinn (New York: Herder and Herder, 1967), p. 26.

[5] Jürgen Moltmann, *Theology of Play*, trans. Reinhard Ulrich (New York: Harper & Row, 1972), p. 32.

joyful and beautiful; it is tragic and filled with terrors. The gift of freedom in authentic worship of a faithful community involves vulnerability, fragility, and, above all, openness to the surprising grace of God. So liturgy as holy play has deeply serious meaning, whether in the children's "innocent" dancing in a procession of gifts, or in the deeply worn paths of confession and forgiveness and hymns of joy in the midst of suffering. Only when our worship knows the range of gratitude and awe, of suffering with others alongside fiesta with God and the gathering with the "saints by the river" will we come to play well. Only when we learn to improvise with the prayer and work of Jesus Christ throughout all the seasons of life will we come to understand liturgy as holy play.

When we bring a sense of gratitude, joy, and delight to the liturgy, the living celebration of the Gospel in word and song reveals, over time, its own intrinsic delight. Yet without a community of persons, with ample biblical texts, a good range of hymns and psalms, knit together with adequate prayer forms, ritual actions, and a balance of Word and sacrament, such holy play does not come to light. We are to be living reminders for one another as well so that over time a community develops a common set of affections for the things of God and a sense of improvising because we know the forms and rhythms of worship well enough. Thus we can never quite predict which dimension of the liturgy—texts, sound, sight, gestures, movement, ritual act—will occasion the sense of free encounter and play before God. On some occasions, all the parts work together. Even when that does not happen, we can be attentive to receiving back, as the psalmist says, "a greater joy," "a new song."

Why do we settle for so little? Why do we not perceive and practice the essentials? She was so right, "Didn't we dance today!" And just then I caught sight of the *hilaritas* of which Christians have spoken and sung since the beginning, and of perhaps why Dante called the final story of God and the world the *Divine Comedy*.

Living *the* Eucharistic Prayer

by Gail Ramshaw

IT IS DIFFICULT to describe how liturgy forms the faithful in the spiritual life. Yet throughout the world's liturgical movement, liturgists devoutly desire for participation in the liturgy to form the faithful into the community of God. But we who are eager for the formation of persons as Christians must beware that we do not merely gun our engines on the theory that more and better liturgy, like more gasoline, will get this church moving. For we know that there are countless people who regularly participate in Christian liturgical celebrations whose lives appear to be untouched by the experience.

We speak autobiographically, or we probe Christian history, or we interpret studies, but we do not know how and when the liturgy is experienced as the vehicle for God's Spirit. We speak to one another only our hopes that the liturgy which has brought grace into our lives will do the same for others, children and adults alike. Many of the techniques for formation which are popular among newly-converted adults are inappropriate for my daughters, still young children who were baptized as tiny infants. Yet I can hope that their weekly participation in the Eucharist will form in them an attitude of praise, prayer, and service which will join them to other Christians in an increasingly secular culture.

Simply said, here is the liturgical logic: that the weekly ritual of assembling around Christ in prayer for the world will form in Christian people the mind of praise and the habit of service. Prayer is to shape us by giving us hope for compassion. Unfortunately, much of the prayer written by white, middle class, North American Christians has been so dwarfed by psychological rhetoric that intercession has more in common with personal therapy than with baptismal formation. The nineteenth-century faith in Jesus as personal Savior has met the twentieth-century human potential movement, and this results too often in prayers about how I can be more fulfilled this week. To find a prayer for Christian formation, let us look to the classic western eucharistic prayer with its elements of praise, remembrance, and petition, and let us ask together how to live the prayer.

A GOOD AND JOYFUL THING

It is right, and a good and joyful thing
always and everywhere
to give thanks to you,
Sovereign of the Ages. . . .
You created all things
and called them good.[1]

ARISTOTLE SAID that a story needs a beginning, a middle, and an ending. But the literature of this century indicates a world in which such naive order has been destroyed. Stories begin in the middle, proceed with a logic all their own, and stop without concluding. In many novels, the calendar day is the only shape given the protagonist's tale. The death of the omniscient narrator suggests a world in which we can speak only a private vision of personal values. The incoherent violence of recent movies seems to cement in American consciousness, rather than purge away, the terrible pattern of Vietnam, where our highest ideals began questionably, proceeded dishonestly, and ended "not with a bang but a whimper."[2] Adopted children, in a mythic search for origins, locate their birth parents, discovering only one or two slight, middle-aged aliens. Like digital clocks, we live minute by minute, the sweep of life obscured by the orange flashing figures, numbers as isolated as we ourselves.

How would it be were we formed by the beginning of the eucharistic prayer?

In the first place, we would have assembled on the Sabbath. Endless, orderless time would be benevolently laid before us in units we could grasp, and we would give priority to the first day of the week by assembling with others who shared this calendar of grace. Like the disciples in John's Gospel, we would gather on the first day of the week with sure knowledge that at such a weekly meeting God would be present to bless us. This is no small thing, this communal affirmation of a human order to the universe, this peaceful acknowledgment that our time begins together in God, this shared value that

---

[1] Here and throughout I am using the form of the eucharistic prayer found in *Holy Communion* (Nashville: Abingdon, 1987), Supplemental Resource #16, Service 20, pp. 46–47. Copyright © by The United Methodist Publishing House. Used by permission.

[2] T.S. Eliot, *The Complete Poems and Plays* (New York: Harcourt, Brace & World, 1958), p. 59.

from such an assembly flows life in abundance. Assembling on Sunday is like acting out Genesis 1 in which the universe, rather than mindlessly expanding into more vacuum, is benevolently ordered for the good of humankind by a God who teaches us praise. Thus merely to assemble with the baptized on Sunday is to recreate the modern universe, giving it a beginning in God and a middle in grace, with hope for an end in fulfillment and peace.

The eucharistic prayer, like the Sabbath, situates the community in a graceful world. We begin by praising God. We acknowledge God as an Abba God, the loving parent who arranges the nursery to the child's best advantage, who protects the infant from final evil, who nurses, instructs, and chides better than all the human parents and all the mythic gods and goddesses who fill our lives and storybooks. God creates the world, we say. We form our community around this assertion, that the world has its meaning in and from God and that as we are in God, we participate in its meaning. God saves the world, we say. We form our assembly around this belief, that contrary to appearances evil has been overcome by and in God, and that as we are in God we together are saved. Were the assembled community to enter fully into this opening paragraph of praise, our formation as Christians would have made a substantive beginning.

IN REMEMBRANCE OF THESE
YOUR MIGHTY ACTS

Holy are you,
and blessed is your eternal Word,
who became flesh
and came to dwell among us
in Jesus Christ. . . .

"HUMANKIND CANNOT BEAR very much reality," wrote T.S. Eliot, and one way that we protect ourselves is to forget.[3] The old saw is true: women do not quite remember the pains of childbirth. That I was in pain I remember. What the pain was like to have made me scream so wildly, I cannot recall. We forget the sufferings of the race, and assassinations in our country, and the quarrels in the family; and we try to relax in an easy chair with earphones gently playing only New Age music. Yet another way that we

---

[3] *The Complete Poems and Plays*, p. 209.

protect ourselves is to overlook. There is a man lying on the train platform, crying out in pain, but I am in a hurry; I must not miss my appointment; it might even be a setup. It is as if each person has a certain capacity for pain, and it is usually quite filled to the brim. Whether our pains be personal, familial, social, or political, there is no room for the suffering of others.

To pray the eucharistic prayer is to be the community which focuses on the Suffering Servant. In the center of the prayer we remember Christ, the one who heeded the cry of the man on the platform even to his own death. We call to our remembrance, making the memory alive and well, that God is among us as one who serves the suffering ones. God sees human suffering and remembers it. And God's response to the cries in the emergency ward and around the world was to bind up our wounds, pouring on oil and wine. To pray this prayer together is to take on the mind of Christ, to don with the name "Christian" the lifestyle of the Servant. Let the church be the donkey on which Jesus lays the wounded man; we are to carry those who are newly anointed and communed. To pray this prayer is to recall against our self-protective amnesia the death of Christ and to hear, in spite of our headset, the cries of all in need. John's Gospel teaches us that the meaning of the Last Supper is seen in Jesus' washing his disciples' feet. So we come to the table ready to serve.

ONE IN MINISTRY TO ALL THE WORLD

By your Spirit make us one with Christ,
one with each other,
and one in ministry to all the world,
until Christ comes in final victory
and we feast at Christ's heavenly banquet.

OUR CULTURE IS EXHAUSTED by its frantic search for community. No wonder our children are enchanted by reruns of "Little House on the Prairie" with its evocation of a mythic time when small neighborhoods lived with shared values in communities marked by friendliness and concern. The reformed drug addicts visiting our schools eagerly petition everyone to join their enthusiastic campaign for a drug-free society, and I see in their fervor the old delight in group identity: "We are reformed addicts; we call you to our mission." Such a sense of group identity, such shared goals, such communal responsibility and support are increasingly rare in a society which seems overwhelmed by trying to embrace too much too fast. Now we do not look any longer to the pages of the *National Geographic* for pictures of foreign patterns of life. We see them across the hall of our apartment building.

To pray the eucharistic prayer is to invoke God the Paraclete. In this prayer we pray for the Paraclete to come among us, to make us one, to bring all the needy into our heavenly city. We pray that the Paraclete will continuously voice our concerns before God's throne, that there might finally be some action toward mercy and renewal. Together we pray for communion and even in the prayer begin to enjoy the communion which we seek. But the communion of God's imaginings is so far beyond our own that always in the eucharistic prayer we are drawn to a deeper sense of what human communion is: not wearing similar clothes or seeking the same entertainment but discovering a bond of love which God alone can create.

We are formed by our culture to live in chaos without praise, in the moment without sympathy, and in lonely search for communion. To pray the eucharistic prayer is to praise God for a world mercifully saved, to remember the suffering ones as a faithful servant would, and to petition together so heartily for communion in this world that our lives naturally follow our prayers. Thus we learn not to molder away our lives watching television, with its sound blocking out the needy world, its emptiness a symbol of our own barren lives. We join with a community that sings hymns on Sunday morning, that remembers Christ and hears the needy, and that in praying for communion becomes a community of servants.

ALL GLORY AND HONOR

Through your eternal Word Jesus Christ,
with the Holy Spirit in your holy Church,
all honor and glory is yours,
Almighty God, now and for ever.

THE EUCHARISTIC PRAYER forms us by bringing us to God. God is the Abba, ordering the world in mercy; God is the Servant, identifying with all the needy; God is the Paraclete, forming us into community. The doctrine of the Trinity need not be an archaic and sexist way to draw silly pictures of God. For Christians, the doctrine of the Trinity hints at the mystery of God and calls us into a human existence made in the image of this mysterious and merciful

God. The institutional church is always buying some new method for catechesis and some new theory of education, and the prophets on the edge of the church are always calling out their prescriptions for conversion and reform. Yet no sooner have we sold our decade's soul to a method or a cause when we see our convictions as limitations. The doctrine of the Trinity, which classically provided the church with its outline for eucharistic praying, also offers to the church a program for catechesis and its inspiration for amendment of life.

How would it be were our catechesis and conversion formed by the doctrine of the Trinity? Here are some suggestions for our congregational education and service committees: The families of the newly-baptized infants would recommit themselves to regular eucharistic praise and service. Our children would learn the Bible stories of God's benevolent love and would hear the lives of the saints, who are co-servants with us, part of the community for which we strive. Mystagogical catechesis would be revived among us, with adults growing more deeply each paschal season into the mystery of life with God. Rather than mirror the aimless race of contemporary culture, congregational life would be marked by the beauty of hospitality and peace. The "least of these" would be the most honored in our midst, as we remember with St. Lawrence that the treasures of the church ought not be the new copes in our sacristy but the homeless in our cities. We would see every need, every sorrow, every stranger, with the eyes of a servant. We would stand together to support one another in the pain of seeing. We would break through the solipsism that sets in after the evening news by choosing one or two people who need our care, one or two cooperative efforts, and by working for the communion for which we pray.

These are only several suggestions, merely starters, for the church's formation by the liturgy. We are to be formed by the church's prayer to become such prayers in the world, such instances of praise, service, and community, such personifications of joy, sympathy, and hope. We are so formed, not by successful church programs or popular media techniques, but by the Spirit of God, who draws us by God into God. May God, Abba, Servant, and Paraclete, teach us so to pray.

The Work of the People

INVOLVING THE CONGREGATION
IN LITURGY

by K. C. Ptomey, Jr.

LITURGY—literally "the work of the people." In his now well-known analogy, Søren Kierkegaard pointed us toward a true understanding of liturgy by asking us to think of worship as a theater. Who are the actors, prompters, and audience? The typical answer might be: "Well, the worship leaders, clergy, and choir, are the actors. The audience is the gathered congregation." In this understanding the worship leaders perform for the congregation. But Kierkegaard suggested that in fact worship leaders are really prompters who stay behind the scenes. The worshipers are the actors, and the role of worship leaders is to enable them to do their work. In this analogy, God is the audience!

This insight turns the traditional understanding of liturgy inside out simply by reminding us that liturgy is indeed the work of the people. We do not truly worship God when we go to a church building and act as spectators to a performance by clergy and musicians. We worship when we are actively engaged in doxology, in praise of Almighty God.

Unfortunately, few congregations have found practical ways to implement this concept. In most congregations it is a great challenge to engage the people actively and meaningfully in worship. Too many of us are still members of the audience, passively observing what the actors are doing on the stage. It is no wonder that one priest writes that ". . . celebrations of the liturgy suffer the common syndrome of modern living—a lack of people power."[1]

However, in some churches, worship is slowly once again becoming the work of the people. Where this is happening there is an excitement and a vitality in worship that is true doxology. One way leaders in local congregations can engage communicants more actively in the liturgy is through the use of liturgy teams. Because there is a difference between the way in which the more "liturgical"

---

[1] Al Hanzal, "Liturgy and People Power," in *Modern Liturgy Handbook*, ed. John P. Mossi, S.J. (Ramsey, NJ: Paulist Press, 1976), pp. 84–87.

denominations and the Protestant and free church denominations approach the matter of worship, I will treat them separately.

For the past five years in the church which I serve, a Presbyterian congregation of approximately 1,800 members, we have used liturgy teams to develop the services for each Sunday. We currently have a different team for each month of the year. In the past we have used other approaches such as a team for the same Sunday of the month for a six-month period (e.g., first Sunday team, second Sunday team) or a team for a liturgical season (e.g., Advent team, Christmas team, Epiphany team). Having a team for each month has worked best. This approach requires only a limited commitment from the team members and provides the continuity of developing four or five Sunday services in succession.

The teams are recruited and trained in the fall and begin their service in January of each year. Teams consist of three to five members, depending upon how many volunteers are available. Each team has a captain who is responsible for coordinating the work of the group. It is helpful for each team to include at least one person who has a proven facility for using the English language.

We conduct a three-hour training session in which we orient the volunteers to the shape of the Sunday liturgy. Brief explanations are given of the various elements of the service, the rationale for the order in which these elements are arranged, and the movement of the liturgy from the call to worship to the climax in the Eucharist and then through to the dismissal. Time is also spent introducing various resources, all of which are kept on a shelf in the church library and reserved for the use of the liturgy teams.

The second half of the training event is a workshop in which teams are given an opportunity to use various psalms and other texts from the lectionary as resources in actually writing various parts of the service. We find that contemporary translations of the psalms provide rich material for use as calls to worship, confessions, words of assurance, and other elements of the liturgy.[2] The rationale for using actual biblical texts in the various parts of the service is that the center of the liturgy is the word of God written in the scriptures, proclaimed in the homily, and enacted in the sacraments. Using the words of scripture throughout the service reinforces the centrality of the word of God in Christian worship.

---

[2] See especially Nancy Schreck, O.S.F., and Maureen Leach, O.S.F., *Psalms Anew* (Winona, MN: St. Mary's Press, 1986).

W E ENCOURAGE TEAMS to borrow from resource material as well as actually to create the various pieces of the service. We have found that expecting teams to create every service out of nothing may lead to some poor writing! But we have also discovered that as teams study together and build services, they grow in their appreciation for the language of liturgy and become quite poetic in their writing.

One confession. It is true that liturgy teams may not create prayers, responses, and so forth which are as well written or as lyrical as some of the great gems of our liturgical heritage. Most people simply do not possess the facility for language which is of the same quality as that found in the *Book of Common Prayer* or *The Book of Common Order*, for instance. There is a trade-off. In exchange for language that soars, the worshiper gains a sense of continuity and comfort.

The raw material which the teams have at their disposal includes a list of the lections for each Sunday, the hymns and anthems which have been chosen by the musicians, and sermon briefs from the preacher. These briefs indicate the particular text or texts upon which the sermon will focus and a two- or three-sentence summary of the direction in which the preacher intends to move with the text.

Sermon briefs are a key to the success of this program. The preacher must give the liturgy team a clue as to which lection or combination of lections will be treated by the sermon, as well as what aspects of the text will be developed.

The teams are not asked to be indentured to the sermon briefs. They are asked to study the lessons and discuss them using the sermon notes as a guide. But the teams are then free to develop the liturgy as they feel led. Teams which try to be slavishly thematic may create liturgy that is forced and stilted. Thus, guidance is provided in the sermon briefs, but freedom of expression is encouraged.

The discipline of preparing sermon briefs six to eight weeks ahead of time can be a helpful one for the preacher. He or she is forced to consider Sunday lections in relation to one another rather than treating each Sunday in isolation. Sometimes a series of sermons will take shape, or the preacher will discover an entirely new interpretation as the scriptures from various Sundays speak to one another.

Once a liturgy team has written a service, it is reviewed by the pastor. Respect for the work which teams have done is essential in maintaining incentive and ownership. We have chosen to edit only for grammatical correctness and inclusiveness. We may clean up a sentence here and there, but we never rewrite an entire piece.

This brief description of the liturgy planning process in one church is a model which can be adapted for use in almost any church. In traditions which use a formally adopted order of worship and a prayer book, the challenge of involving laypersons in the liturgy is a bit different, but liturgy teams can still play a vital role in shaping the weekly worship of the congregation. Most denominations have developed new or revised prayer and/or worship books during the past ten years which provide options for almost every aspect of the liturgy. There may be two or three suggested calls to worship or prayers of confession or responsorial psalms. The responsibility of a liturgy team then is to choose from among the options that are offered based upon a pre-determined theme for the service. The liturgy team, in consultation with the clergy, would choose a theme. Typically the theme would emerge from one or more of the lections for the day. The priest or preacher would be asked to suggest directions the sermon or homily would be taking on that Sunday.

T HE LITURGY TEAM might also work with the musicians to choose hymns and other service music that support and undergird the theme of the day. Additionally, the team might want to work with the visual aspects of the liturgy, suggesting or creating banners, vestments, mime, lectern decorations, and so forth, all of which fit with the theme for the day. Members of the team might choose to bake the communion bread or even make the wine! One congregation with which I am familiar has a member who for several decades has provided homemade blackberry wine for communion.

Modern Liturgy Handbook, edited by John P. Mossi, S.J., is an excellent resource for those seeking to engage laypersons in the development of the weekly services in the more liturgical churches. In this collection of essays, Mossi covers the spectrum of liturgical planning such as the theological and theoretical basis for using lay liturgy teams, practical tips for organizing and using teams, the environment of worship, music, and drama in the sanctuary, and children's liturgies. Mossi also comments on practical ways for liturgy teams and clergy to work together. This is an important area of concern, especially in churches in which responsibility for planning the weekly liturgy has been exclusively in the hands of the clergy.

In any tradition, recruiting, training, and involving laypersons in developing weekly services of worship is effort well spent. Over the past five years in the church which I serve, approximately two hundred persons have been involved as members of liturgy teams. Through their work on the teams they have learned a great deal about worship and liturgy. They have gotten to know one another and have struggled together with the meaning of worship and with how to enhance the worship experience in the local church. They have become better worshipers in every way. Since they now know the liturgy inside out, they approach worship as informed participants who understand the dynamics of the liturgy as well as the work that stands behind a well-developed service. They are more attentive because their critical and analytical faculties are attuned to the fine points of liturgy. Certainly they are better participants, more enthusiastic and responsive. The worship of the church, in other words, belongs to them. But not only to them. The whole congregation becomes more involved. This is reflected in an increased level of feedback, enthusiastic participation in the weekly liturgy, recognition of the thematic character of the liturgy, and heightened appreciation for the whole service of worship as opposed to interest in only one or two aspects of the service. All of these reactions are indicative of a real sense of ownership.

When there is congregational ownership of worship there is true encounter with the living Christ in worship. Worship is no longer a performance the people come to see but an experience of communion with God. One must be careful not to propose that there is a "sure-fire" formula to use to create an experience of communion with God. God is not at our disposal. But there is a predictable progression from formation of liturgy teams, to better understanding of all aspects of the liturgy, to a sense of ownership on the part of the congregation, to a heightened level of congregational participation, to a deeper and more profound encounter with God in worship. A congregation grows in faith as well as in mission and service when worship is truly an encounter with God. I believe the use of lay liturgy teams as outlined in this article is one way to move a congregation toward a fuller life of worship and mission.

Not incidentally, there are ramifications for ministers who become involved in this process. I have suggested that the use of liturgy teams forces us to be better organized and to become better at planning our preaching. But I have found in addition that God has spoken to me through the prayers, responses, and other aspects of the liturgy which have been shaped by our liturgy teams. I have discovered connections between lections, hidden themes, and entirely fresh insights into the scripture through the work of the lay people of the liturgy teams. Also, I can truly worship in a way I was unable to when I took full responsibility for shaping the liturgy. Anxiety about the various parts of the service is relieved and I can enter into worship as a participant along with the congregation. There is now a depth to my worship life which is the direct result of sharing responsibility for worship with lay persons.

Having worked now for about ten years in situations in which liturgy teams have played a major role in shaping worship, I would never return to my previous approach of taking full responsibility for the worship life of the congregation. I know that congregations benefit and that I benefit from sharing the load and the joy of creating and leading the liturgy. I am certain that the Spirit can work with us in wonderful ways when we are willing to work together, people and leaders, laypersons and clergy, in offering our praise and thanksgiving to God. Then liturgy truly becomes the work of the people.

Speaking *the* Truth *in* Love

by Thomas Ward

If your brother sins against you, go and tell him his fault, between you and him alone. If he listens to you, you have gained your brother. But if he does not listen, take one or two others along with you, that every word may be confirmed by the evidence of two or three witnesses. If he refuses to listen to them, tell it to the church; and if he refuses to listen even to the church, let him be to you as a Gentile and a tax collector.

—Matthew 18:15-17 (RSV)

SOME YEARS AGO an Oklahoma church made national news in a court case that has stayed in my mind. In March 1984 Marian Guinn sued the Collinsville Church of Christ for $1.3 million. She alleged that the elders of that church had invaded her privacy by following the disciplinary steps outlined in Matthew 18:15-17.

Marian Guinn had been a member of the Collinsville Church of Christ; she was also a divorcée with four teen-aged children. Ms. Guinn admitted to having a relationship with Pat Sharp, a former mayor of Collinsville. Sharp was divorced as well. The elders of the church had talked with Ms. Guinn privately. When she refused to listen to them and renounce her relationship with Sharp, they denounced her publicly for the sin of fornication. They also exhorted other members of the congregation to avoid her company.

In bringing suit against the church, Marian Guinn's attorney compared the elders' action to that of the church leaders in Nathaniel Hawthorne's *Scarlet Letter*. He said that their invasion of her privacy had caused her serious emotional distress. In their defense, the elders said that everything they had done was done out of love and concern for Marian—that they saw her acting against the norms of scripture, against the standards of the church she was in covenant with, and against her own well-being. A twelve-person jury, only four of whom were members of any religious body, awarded Marian Guinn $390,000 in the case. The church is in the process of appealing the decision.

My first response on reading about this case was sympathy for Marian Guinn. I thought to myself, *Surely the elders of that church could have found a more compassionate way of confronting a wayward member.*

I know that groups in power can be oppressive. The will of the majority can tyrannize a minority, especially a minority of one. I recalled Calvin's Geneva, where church and state worked together to burn Michael Servetus at the stake in 1553, and Salem, Massachusetts, where church and state again combined to hang John Proctore and Rebecca Nurse in 1692 for allegedly consorting with the devil. These examples, in turn, reminded me of the Sanhedrin working with the Roman government to crucify Jesus of Nazareth.

Closer to home, the minister of our church in Mississippi publicly denounced my father from the pulpit for attending a high school fraternity dance. My father stayed away from organized religion until my mother was pregnant with me. Beyond this, I remembered the public pressure of some churches in that same town as I grew up. Sin seemed limited to smoking, drinking, and any activity remotely associated with human sexuality. Such pressure seemed narrow and judgmental rather than compassionate.

The longer I thought about this court case, however, the more another perspective emerged. What about the character of the church, the Collinsville Church of Christ or any other congregation? What does the church stand for? What are its standards, its norms, its boundaries? What is its discipline? How should these be made known and upheld?

Mainline North American Christians are ambivalent. On the one hand, we want the church to take stands on all areas of our life, from the private to the public, from sexual conduct to the nuclear arms race. On the other hand, we reserve the right to set our own personal values above the standards of the church when we disagree, or when those standards apply to us in a pointed way. We want a church with integrity. But we also want our privacy and the validation of our personal opinions and moralities.

As the rector of a local mainline congregation, I see this ambivalence both threatening the integrity of our individual and corporate lives and offering us the opportunity to strengthen our life together in Christ. The threat lies in our taking our energy away from the community when we disagree with its norms. The opportunity lies in our learning to speak the truth in love within the boundaries of the local congregation.

The local congregation needs norms, standards, and limits. Without these there is no integrity to its common life. But the congregation also needs the creative dissent of individuals and groups which sense that the Spirit of Christ is violated by a particular rule or its application. When a minority, even a minority of one, withdraws its energy from the congregation, both the minority and the congregation lose the opportunity to hear the truth that God may be speaking to them in their disagreement. The minority might learn that its dissent is not the righteous insight it first believed it to be. The majority might learn that God still speaks through particular persons and circumstances and that God's truth is not limited to set rules or structures.

This view of congregational life places great demands on all of the individuals in the congregation as a whole. It entails a higher degree of commitment to the local congregation and to the discipline of speaking the truth in love than is usually the case in current mainline Christianity.

ILLUSTRATIVE OF THE PROBLEMS and opportunities of our ambivalence are baptism and marriage as we administer them in the congregation I serve. Persons who have been away from or on the periphery of the church for some time often come to one of its priests wanting their newborn child baptized. The problem here is that these persons have not indicated by their previous behavior that they intend to fulfill the vows and promises they are about to make, i.e., seeing that the child they present is brought up in the Christian faith and life and helping this child to grow in the full stature of Christ by their prayers and witness. The opportunity is that the parents of a newborn child, having witnessed the miracle of birth, are often more open to the miracle of rebirth than they are at any other time. What is called for is the pastoral art of telling the truth in love: confronting the lapsed with the vows of their own baptisms while assuring them of the empowering gospel of grace. One without the other will not do. Nor will such telling be faithful without the congregational representatives listening to the truth these new parents have to tell. It may be that the congregation has not been as supportive to this couple as it might have been.

Analogous problems and opportunities arise in relation to marriage. Couples often come to the church seeking a ceremony in an attractive setting with beautiful music. The church sees this ceremony as the focal point of a faithful relationship within a faithful community. If either or both of the partners has not been faithful to his or her baptismal covenant, there is some reason to question whether he or she is prepared for the covenant of life-long monogamous union in Christ. On the other hand, the gift of falling in love with another human being may be the epiphany that enables the commitment of this couple, individually and together, to the One who has loved them to this special moment. Marriage offers the community and its members an opportunity to discern the work of the Spirit and to tell the truth in love.

That we turn to the church at such significant points in our lives, whether we have been faithful to the church or not, points to our hunger for genuine community and for the Lord who calls such community into being. At the same time, other ways of life call to us as well. Christianity has never occurred in a vacuum; it has always shaped and been shaped by its cultural context. Our current cultural context affects our way of being Christian in this time and place.

In the best-selling analysis of American culture entitled *Habits of the Heart*, sociologist Robert Bellah and his associates hold a mirror before us. They trace four central strands in American thought: republican, biblical, utilitarian individualism, and expressive individualism. Bellah sees utilitarian individualism in terms of career success; its prototype is the manager. He sees expressive individualism in terms of self-fulfillment; its prototype is the therapist. "Between them, the manager and the therapist largely define the outlines of twentieth-century American culture."[1]

Bellah's thesis is that these two forms of individualism are undermining the republican and biblical strands of our culture, that we are losing the healthy balance that makes public life possible, and that we need to restore this balance by recovering our republican and biblical heritage.

An extreme form of the expressive individualism that Bellah refers to can be seen in what its author, Fritz Perls, calls "A Gestalt Prayer":

> *I do my thing, and you do your thing,*
> *I am not in this world to live up to your expectations,*
> *And you are not in this world to live up to mine.*
> *You are you and I am I.*
> *And if by chance we find each other, it's beautiful.*
> *If not, it cannot be helped.*

Taken alone, such expressive individualism makes no place for genuine community.

---

[1] Robert N. Bellah, Richard Madsen, William M. Sullivan, Ann Swidler, and Steven M. Tipton, *Habits of the Heart: Individualism and Commitment in American Life* (Berkeley and Los Angeles, CA: University of California Press, 1985), p. 47.

In explaining why she voted to award Marian Guinn the $390,000 in damages for the Collinsville Church of Christ's invasion of her privacy, one juror said, "He was single, she was single, and this is America."

This quotation implies that, at least from the perspective of this juror, sexual relations between single consenting adults is an ethical norm in the United States. This perspective exemplifies the expressive individualism that Bellah describes and Fritz Perls exalts. However, it does not describe the sexual ethical norms of most congregations that call themselves "Christian." Again, we must have such norms if we are going to tell the truth in love; many, if not most, of these norms are going to differ from the norms of twentieth-century North American culture.

While the one Church of Jesus Christ is not visibly united, congregations which bear the name "Christian" also share a central basic assumption from which we derive all our other values. We believe in Jesus Christ, crucified and risen, and in the church, called into being by God's action in the Christ, conveyed to us by the Holy Spirit.

Both our individual and private values on the one hand and our public and cultural values on the other are to be tested by the risen Christ in the midst of his holy people. While no one local congregation has exclusive claims to God's truth and while that truth finally resides in the risen Head of that Body of which we are all members, the local congregation is the place where we are formed in Christ and where we must learn to tell the truth in love.

We twentieth-century Americans, in the church and outside the church, yearn for such a community in which we may know others and be known by them. But we also fear such knowledge and the commitment that makes such knowledge possible. Where do we experience such community? Who takes the risk to tell us when we are drinking too much or working too much or neglecting our family or allowing a friendship to become more than a friendship? What would our response be if another took the risk of confronting us with his or her perception of God's truth about us? Would we listen? Would we become defensive? Would we end the relationship? Would we take the risk of giving words to our perception of that person's life in relation to the risen Christ? Could we do this in a spirit of concern for the other's well-being rather than in a spirit of superiority, competition, or control? We long for a community in which we might ask and answer such questions in love, and yet we fear such questions and the community that might foster them.

The churches that gave birth to the New Testament were just such communities. Paul writes to the church in Rome and says, "Do not be conformed to this world but be transformed by the renewal of your mind. . . . Let love be genuine; hate what is evil, hold fast to what is good. . . . Live in harmony with one another . . ." (Rom. 12:2, 9, 16, RSV). To the church in Ephesus he writes, ". . . speaking the truth in love, we are to grow up in every way into him who is the head, into Christ, from whom the whole body, joined and knit together by every joint with which it is supplied, when each part is working properly, makes bodily growth and upbuilds itself in love" (Eph. 4:15-16, RSV). That Paul wrote such passages exhorting the communities to love and live in harmony with one another is evidence that these early congregations had their conflicts, just as twentieth-century congregations have theirs. That we still read, study, and respond to such passages bears witness to the word that God still speaks to us through them.

Speaking the truth in love is the means our Lord has given us for the building up of his Body, the church. The passage in Matthew which the Collinsville Church of Christ applied in confronting Marian Guinn is a variation on this theme, derived from the experience of another early Christian congregation. It presupposes that the risen Lord is present when two or three are gathered in his name. It also presupposes that the congregation wills to share the character of its Lord. In fact, the entire eighteenth chapter of Matthew forms a discourse on the relation between the congregation and the individual, calling on members to "become like children" (18:3), not to "despise one of these little ones" (18:10), and to forgive one another without limit (18:21-34). The chapter forms a treatise on reconciliation and forgiveness, with the passage on speaking the truth in love (18:15-20) as the centerpiece.

Here the local congregation has character, the character of the risen Lord. The community matters, and so does each individual in it. Forgiving and being forgiven are the manifestation of the Spirit: ". . . as the LORD has forgiven you, so you also must forgive" (Col. 3:13, RSV). The norms, limits, and boundaries of the congregation are intended to foster growth in Christ.

None of us wants to be denounced in church as Marian Guinn was or as my father was. Nor do we want to do the denouncing. Few of us would want the theocracy of Calvin's Geneva or Salem, Massachusetts, in the late seventeenth century. On the other hand, many of us in this pluralistic culture yearn for a Christian community of genuine love in which we are known for the wounded pilgrims that we are.

I believe that it is God's will for us twentieth-century North American Christians that our local congregations be such communities of spiritual formation. For many congregations, this is going to entail forming smaller groups or cells, accountable to larger structures but small enough to allow trust to grow, so that we might know one another in the depths and the heights and take the risk of telling the truth in love. It is also going to entail an increased commitment to the local congregation for many mainline Christians.

The church must become our primary community, the place of our being conformed to the image and likeness of Jesus Christ, in whose image and likeness we are made. Speaking the truth in love is not only the means to this end; it is the end we seek. For Jesus Christ is God's Word and God's Truth. He is the love we are called to embody.

Anger: *An* Instrument *of* Peace

by C. Gordon Peerman, III

A S CHILDREN are wont to do with their parents, our three-year-old son has once again been instructing me, this time in the uses of anger. Recently we had a house guest staying with us for several days. Our son Alex upon first meeting our guest engaged this man with his usual open-heartedness and led him by the hand into the full range of his little boy enthusiasms. Our guest, a big, sturdy, sixty-year-old man initially was charmed by the attentions of this small whirlwind round his feet, but after about a day his response changed.

My wife and I first noticed that our guest would correct Alex in what felt to us a heavy-handed fashion. He would engage Alex in physical "play" which was too rough even for this child who delights in rough-housing. Our guest seemed to enjoy pushing Alex beyond the limits of fun into distress, then minimizing Alex's protest or upset by saying, "That's not hurting you." At this point my wife or I would intervene, breaking up the battle between the three year old and the sixty year old.

As the visit wore on, I was getting increasingly angry at the way our guest was attempting to control, correct, and intrude upon our son. Yet I was feeling stuck in the tension between wanting to protect our son and wishing to avoid conflict with our guest. When our guest told us he had straightened out his own children with the back of his hand, we got the hint, and I responded with a cold silence.

Finally things came to a head. Our guest was "teasing" Alex again, calling him a "rascal." There wasn't any humor in this name-calling, only an attempt to needle. I was about to intervene, ostensibly on Alex's behalf but more out of my own mounting resentment, when Alex took care of the matter himself. Drawing himself up to his full forty inches, Alex got into his antagonist's face and angrily said, "My name isn't rascal! My name is Alex!" There followed one of those moments of silence in which all present know that the balance of power has shifted. My wife and I exchanged a glance of a certain satisfaction. The teasing and the bullying stopped for the moment.

For Alex, anger is simply a part of life. Each night as he goes to bed we engage in a three-question ritual of asking him, "What made you happy today? What made you sad? What made you angry?" He loves to ask both of us the same questions, and it is sometimes arresting to consider the questions and reply in a way that is truthful and comprehensible to him. He especially enjoys asking us that last question, growling like a lion as he says the word "angry." He could hardly know how much he is helping me by asking his question in such a playful way. For knowing how to be with my own anger, how to be with myself when angry, how to be with others at whom I am angry, how to be with others who are angry with me—this has been the great growing edge for me for several years now.

ATTENTIVENESS

THE WELL-KNOWN PRAYER commonly attributed to St. Francis of Assisi begins, "Lord, make us instruments of your peace. Where there is hatred, let us sow love. . . ." The prayer continues with a series of antitheses: where there is injury/let us sow pardon, discord/union, doubt/faith, despair/hope, darkness/light, sadness/joy. One can read these antitheses in an either/or fashion. On this reading my task as an instrument of peace is not to feel or express hatred, doubt, despair, or sadness, but to suppress them and enact their opposites. On the other hand, one could read these antitheses in a both/and fashion. On this reading the path to authentic love goes directly through hatred, the path to authentic union through discord. The Christian life then is less an uprooting of hatred and discord than an attentiveness to them so that the kingdom of peace might be cultivated.

Practically speaking the suppression of anger has an unfortunate way of leaking out sideways in sarcasm, of indirect expression through bodily illness, or directly exploding in aggression. The attempt to uproot negativity doesn't work. There is, however, a way of feeling and expressing anger that goes beyond denial, masochism, or retaliation. This way employs not suppression but attentiveness to anger, a willingness to wait and watch with it, then the discerning of what if any action to take. Anger is first felt, then detoxified and metabolized in a non-destructive way.

This capacity for simple attentiveness to one's anger is foundational, for without it one cannot begin to discern what to do with that anger. Before we do anything with anger, we must learn how to be with it. From the desert fathers we hear the story of "a brother [who] asked one of the elders: 'What is humility?' The elder answered him: 'To do good to those who do evil to you.' The brother asked: 'Supposing a man cannot go that far, what should he do?' The elder replied: 'Let him get away from them and keep his mouth shut.' "[1]

If we can learn when angry first to keep our mouths shut, we may develop the capacity to attend to our anger before we visit it on someone. If we can keep our mouths shut, we might then learn to discern when and how we should open our mouths in anger. What the desert fathers and mothers called "the custody of the tongue" is a capacity which grows out of a genuine *ascesis*, or practice. Within the enclosure of silence we can practice watching anger being transformed into peace. The first step in this transformation is simple, gentle attentiveness to our anger.

The Vietnamese Buddhist monk Thich Nhat Hanh offers retreats to Vietnam veterans in our country, teaching them about this sort of attentiveness. Nhat Hanh tells of one American commander who lost four hundred seventeen of his men in a single battle on a single day and had been unable for twenty years to get past his anger at the useless loss of these lives. Another man had out of anger and revenge taken the lives of children in a Vietnamese village, and had after that time lost all his peace. Ever since that time, he had not been able to sit alone with children in a room. Nhat Hanh taught these men and other veterans what he calls the practice of mindfulness, which is simply sitting and watching one's breath come and go, and looking after one's anger, seeking neither to suppress it nor drive it out, but simply to watch it in an affectionate and caring way.

"When we are angry," Nhat Hanh writes, "we are not usually inclined to return to ourselves. We want to think about the person who is making us angry, to think about his hateful aspects: his rudeness, dishonesty, cruelty . . . and so on. The more we think about him, listen to him, or look at him, the more our anger flares. His dishonesty and hatefulness may be real, imaginary, or exaggerated, but in fact the root of the problem is the anger itself, and we have to come back and look first of all inside ourselves. . . . Like a fireman, we have to pour water on the blaze first and not waste time looking for the one who set the house on fire. 'Breathing in, I know that I am angry. Breathing out, I know that I must put all my energy into caring for

---

[1] Thomas Merton, *The Wisdom of the Desert* (New York: New Directions, 1960), pp. 53–54.

my anger.' " Caring for our anger: that is very different from visiting it upon someone or hoarding it in bitterness. Still, we might wonder how to practice such caring.

Nhat Hanh suggests that in our homes we set aside a room where we can be alone and breathe in gentle mindfulness. He calls this breathing room "an Embassy of the Kingdom of Peace," a refuge which should not be violated by shouting. A child about to be shouted at would be safe within the grounds of the Embassy. A parent, too, might take refuge in this room, to sit down and restore him- or herself. This is a room not for talk, but for silence. In this Embassy is not the stony silence of angry withdrawal, but the gentle, transforming silence of attentiveness. The urge to attack comes and sits in the room of attention. If we can listen first to ourselves without doing anything, we may in time open up a space to listen receptively to another, even to another's anger, hurt, or disappointment.[2]

A TTENTIVENESS TO ONE'S ANGER is not a quick fix. It is the antithesis of the "get it out of your system" school for dealing with anger. It is the recognition that my anger is first my own, not made by another's actions, but more often arising out of a threat to my need for security, affection, or control.[3] Life will offer me regular challenges to these needs; and, unless I can develop a certain detachment in the face of these threats, I will find myself inevitably controlled by anger when threatened. There is a different, less attached ground on which to stand in response to these threats: It is discovering in prayer my life hid with Christ in God. On this ground, as in Nhat Hanh's breathing room, I may find a different way to be with my anger.

One of the most maddening aspects of life together in the local church is the difficulty of actually getting conflict and our anxiety about conflict into a room where both can be addressed. Private griping, the nursing of grievances, and playing "nice" split congregations into factions of disenchantment and mutual demonizing. Given the inevitability of conflict in our common life, a congregation might, rather than ignore or avoid conflict, offer to incorporate it by setting aside a regular time and place to be attentive to conflict within the community, in essence, to *invite* the negative in a structured way.

---

[2] Thich Nhat Hanh, "Peace Is Every Step," *Parabola* Vol. XVI, No. 4, pp. 73–78.
[3] See Thomas Keating, *Invitation to Love* (Rockport, MA: Element, 1992), pp. 5–13.

A forum for first teaching attentiveness to one's anger in prayer and then discerning how to respond, if at all, would do more for genuine community formation than all the appeals to charity and loving-kindness will ever do. Lest this forum degenerate into a shoot-out, training for pastoral leaders in ways of prayerful attentiveness to anger and a framework for the discernment of appropriate responses should be carefully elaborated. No persons should avail themselves of such a forum unless there is clarity about its purposes and limits. If I am not hopelessly romantic, the local church, in offering such a forum, would at the same time be offering Christian formation in a very different way of being with anger than avoidance of conflict. This different way is entering directly into the anxiety of experiencing anger and discerning what action to take.

DISCERNING ACTION: BEYOND RETREAT OR RETALIATION

THIS DIFFERENT WAY of being with anger we can see over and over in the life of Jesus. When the Pharisees put to Jesus the question over the lawfulness of paying taxes to Caesar (Matt. 22:15-18), we get to watch how Jesus handles malice. The Pharisees attempt first to set Jesus up with some smooth words, pretending to appreciate his honesty. Then they seek to entrap him with their question: Is it lawful to pay taxes to Caesar? If Jesus says no, he appears to be subversive of the Roman state; if he says yes, he seems to collaborate with a foreign occupying force.

Jesus will grasp neither of the alternatives. Instead he confronts the Pharisees with their malice and their true motive of trying to trap him. "You hypocrites! Why are you trying to catch me out?" We should note that in the face of this concealed hostility Jesus neither retreats from his assailants nor retaliates in kind. Nor does he discuss the question on the terms in which the Pharisees present it. He first simply names the question for what it is: a malicious attack.

At times in my work in pastoral counseling I find it helpful to say to a client something like, "You are so angry with me you want to leave," or "You're mad at the way I am with you," or "You feel contemptuous of me." Simply having anger named in a neutral fashion— neither acquiescing, nor forbidding, nor fleeing from it—may open up a space in the client for receptive attentiveness to anger.

In our common life as Christians there is a reluctance, if not an absolute inability, to name hatred by its proper name. Either we respond to malice with masochism, mistakenly believing that passively enduring it is somehow Christlike, or we eventually retaliate with some act of hatred of our own. Of course, our own hatred may come in a form as cleverly disguised as that of the Pharisees: withdrawing, pretending to submit, placating, yet all the time steaming inside.

Someone once described masochism as a safe way to hate. Rather than expressing my own anger openly, I allow someone to do me in out of my own self-disregard. Jesus will not allow the Pharisees to skewer him with their question. He assertively points attention to their malicious intent and risks further inflaming their hatred by unmasking them. In so doing he serves them notice that he will not be intimidated by their hatred.

There is a story from the life of D. W. Winnicott, a British pediatrician and psychoanalyst, which has much to say about the creative uses of anger. Winnicott once described an orphan boy who briefly lived with him and his wife, a boy who had a pronounced capacity to induce intense feelings of hatred in those around him. The boy was prone to destructive fits of temper, and Winnicott felt that it would be a mistake to try to show the boy some false sort of love when he was behaving hatefully.

Winnicott dealt with his own hatred of this very trying child by taking him, when in the middle of a fit, "by bodily strength" and putting him outside the front door. There was a bell that the boy could ring and he was told that, if he rang it, he would be readmitted and nothing would be said about his fit. Each time Winnicott put him outside, he told the boy he hated him for what he had just done. It was easy for Winnicott to say this, he explained, because it was true. Moreover, saying this was important not only for the boy's therapeutic progress, but just as importantly because it enabled Winnicott to continue working with him, as he said, "without losing my temper and without every now and again murdering him."[4]

By putting the boy outside the way he did, Winnicott made a strong statement. Reduced to its essence, the statement is: "I will not allow you to do that here." It is a statement about boundaries, about what is acceptable or tolerable and what is not. The statement uses the force of anger in a non-destructive way, without attacking, to draw a boundary.

Many of us do not have a clue how to express anger non-destructively. We either attack others directly and malignantly or

---

[4] Gerald Schoenewolf, *The Art of Hating* (Northvale, NJ: Jason Aronson, Inc., 1991), p. 6.

indirectly and secretly. Or we attack ourselves for having what seem to be such ugly impulses. Jesus is the model of one who is non-violent toward himself and nonviolent toward others, and he has much to teach us about the handling of anger in this regard. Calling aggression by its name and setting limits are capacities Jesus demonstrates again and again. While he will not retaliate evil for evil, he often draws boundaries as in the cleansing of the temple, in his refusal to answer by what authority he acts, in forbidding his disciples the use of force at the time of his arrest. His very refusal to retaliate is one of the most forceful expressions of his own boundaries: he is willing to go to the cross rather than retaliate.

Parker Palmer makes a fine distinction between false crosses and true crosses. "[S]ome crosses are false, not given by God, but placed on us by a heedless world and received by an unhealthy part of ourselves. Christian tradition has too many examples of masochism masquerading as the way of the cross. So we have the problem of distinguishing valid crosses from invalid ones, crosses which lead toward the centerpoint from crosses which lead to desolation."[5] Long before Jesus is nailed to the wood of the true cross, he takes up the cross of confrontation with those who would lay false crosses of desolation on the backs of his contemporaries. Not once does he bid his followers take up the false cross of masochism. Nor does he pretend to be nice when belittled or devalued. It is a false cross of desolation to pretend to be nice when hate is what is in your heart. It is a false cross of desolation to become the target of hateful behavior only to respond with perpetual placating in the hope that the aggressor will be appeased. It is a false cross of desolation to respond to destructive hate with more destructive hate and so escalate and perpetuate conflict. The true cross of Jesus is a middle way between getting even and getting away. It is attentiveness to one's own anger so that one may become an instrument of peace.

BECOMING AN INSTRUMENT OF PEACE

AFTER EASTER last year I made a ten-day retreat to engage in a deepening of the practice of centering prayer. This took place at St. Benedict's Monastery in Snowmass, Colorado with Father Thomas Keating, his staff, and fifteen other retreatants. Centering prayer is a preparation for contemplative prayer, resting in

---

[5] Parker J. Palmer, *The Promise of Paradox* (Notre Dame: Ave Maria Press, 1980), p. 50.

God. It is not so much the absence of thoughts as detachment from them and "ever so gently" returning to one's desire to be with God.[6] We had been forewarned that our accommodations might offer a certain lack of privacy, but I had not anticipated a roommate who suffered from sleep apnea, that unforgettable pattern of snoring which alternates the snore with a long silence of no breathing at all. The walls would shake with the inrush of air past my roommate's tonsils, then all would be quiet for an unpredictable time, until the cycle began again with a blast of sound. After two nights of no sleep I began to hope that in the long silence between snores my roommate might have died. Alas, he snored on, so I told him of the problem, and we agreed I should wake him up if he continued the assault. There then ensued the nightly ritual of my waking him, and truth bids me acknowledge I did enjoy the look of startled terror in his eyes when I did so.

Once I finally began to get some sleep, then my problems with the retreat could begin in earnest. Extended periods of centering prayer were followed with conferences by Thomas Keating which I found both stimulating and unsettling—stimulating in that I found his presentations compelling and attractive, unsettling in that a practice of centering prayer looked dangerously like it might change my life in ways for which I was unprepared. In the silence of centering prayer I was getting lots of opportunity to be attentive to the anger bubbling up in me. Some of the fellow retreatants were honoring the rule of silence more in the breach than the observance, and privacy, a core value of mine, was in short supply. The tension in me was mounting, as was my resistance to the retreat.

By day seven I must have been getting some sleep because I had this dream. I was back home and was doing some work on my car, having taken one of the wheels off. I went inside my house, only to find when I returned to the car that all four wheels were now off and the car was resting disabled on its axles. Furious and wondering who might have done this, I watched a man get off a bus and walk toward me and the car. This man bore a strong resemblance to Thomas Keating. He acknowledged that he had removed the wheels and furthermore, he had done a bit of rearranging under the hood. I started yelling at him, attempting to throttle him, and demanded to know if he was competent to overhaul my car. Before he could

---

[6] Thomas Keating, *Open Mind, Open Heart: The Contemplative Dimension of the Gospel* (Amity, NY: Amity House, 1986).

respond I awoke, the tension in me now dissipated by the dream. With the explosion of the dream a deep sense of peace settled in, my resistance to the retreat resolved itself, and I was laughing at the uncanny wisdom of the unconscious.

Both the context and content of the retreat were conspiring to disable my usual manner of getting through the day, and I was mad about it. Thomas Keating and the practice of centering prayer were beginning to rearrange my habitual patterns of responding to threats to my security, sources of esteem, and ability to control others and events. In centering prayer I could be attentive to my reflexive, habitual emotional responses to these threats, watch them over and over arise and recede, and ever so gently return to rest in God. This was a different, more detached ground from which to view my anger. The anger was there, but it became less urgent, and my need to get rid of it or do something about it quickly could diminish if I sat with it attentively. Gentle attention to the anger, letting it go rather than forcing it away, and returning to rest in God: Something in me was getting overhauled.

Later the next day after one of the periods of prayer, I asked the group to notice that we were not keeping the rule of silence, and that unless we negotiated a change with one another my preference was to maintain the silence at the times prescribed. Others agreed; some dissented; in the end we resolved to be more attentive to the rule.

Here was a situation I did not control, both the context and content of a retreat. In response to my lack of control of the context and in response to the tensions surfaced by the content of the retreat, I found myself with mounting anger. Here on retreat, however, there was lots of time to be attentive to this anger, watch it come and go, ebb and flow. I had the luxury of waiting to see how it might resolve itself and of deciding how I wished to respond, without withdrawing from the retreat or retaliating out of my discomfort. When at the right time I could state my own preference about the rule of silence from a more detached ground, I felt as though I really joined the group and somehow had finally shown up for the retreat.

I believe that many of us fundamentally fear that if we feel and express our anger we will be attacked or condemned to isolation, and this fear is not without some merit. If we express our anger in destructive ways, we will surely invite repudiation. Moreover, there is within Christian communities so much rhetorical emphasis on union that having real differences and discord may quickly be labeled as un-Christian and pressure mounted to sweep anger under the rug.

With hatred left unresolved, the path to authentic unity is blocked; we are left to settle for enduring or avoiding one another, if not covertly or openly attacking or undermining. We will only experience unity as we discover that we can survive feeling hatred, disappointment, and disillusionment both in ourselves and from others, and work to find non-destructive means of metabolizing such negativity.

Jesus' resurrection appearances showed his disciples that he had taken to himself human hatred, without fleeing from it or attacking. He returned to them bearing peace, and with the gift of the Holy Spirit made them instruments of his peace. He will make us instruments of his peace as we suffer the anguish of our own anger and that of others and learn slowly, attentively, ever so gently to let God transform it into compassion and peace. In working through discord to unity, through hatred to love, through injury to pardon, we join with the disciples in the experience of reconciliation on the other side of the cross. Anger is the cross of love; and we do not finally come into the kingdom of peace except by way of this cross.

The Pastor as
Spiritual Guide

by Tilden Edwards

RECENTLY I PARTICIPATED in a Sunday morning liturgy at a Russian Orthodox church. At the end the priest remained in front of the altar with a metal cross in his hand. The people came to the priest and kissed the cross as he silently smiled in recognition of each person.

That gesture expresses the nature of the pastor as spiritual guide: one through whom others are drawn to kiss the Lord of Life, and know the severely loving smile subtly present for us through all things.

All members of Christ's body share this pastoral privilege in some form by right of their baptism. This cannot be emphasized enough. My purpose here, however, is to look at the ordained pastor as one who has special responsibility to guide the people's understanding and sharing of the ministry and the good news it carries.

This view reflects the pastor primarily as a practitioner rather than a functionary. As practitioner, the pastor is centrally involved with caring for souls—for their being and becoming in God, individually and corporately. This care grows out of the pastor's own desire for the fulfillment of St. Paul's prayer: "May [God] give you the power through [God's] Spirit for your hidden self to grow strong . . ." (Eph. 3:16-19).

An enormous weight of functionary expectations focused on tasks of institutional and social maintenance is placed on pastors. These tasks can eclipse the heart of the pastor's calling to be a practitioner who models the values of soul-care. Often this sad situation is reinforced by the dominant values of the congregation. A mutual, unconscious complicity arises between pastor and people to avoid the truth of God, in the name of God. The people are not willing or yet graced to face into the price of the gospel. That price involves relinquishing one's ego attempt to overcontrol, possess, and secure life. Only then can we live truly open to the liberating abundance and shared life promised us in Christ.

The pastor as a practitioner of spiritual guidance needs to approach ministry as a calling to attend to both this context of resistance and the liberating reverberations of God's Spirit among us. Such personal sensitivity will help the pastor tune in to what is most significant in the church's life and the pastor's own ministry: in preaching, teaching, prophecy, counseling, meetings, prayer and faith sharing groups, sacramental rites, programs, and community outreach. Indeed, the pastor is at least indirect spiritual guide through everything he or she does and is.

Historically a very specific form of individual spiritual guidance grew up that came to be called "spiritual direction" in the Western Church.[1] Spiritual friendship, companionship, discipling—whatever it is called, spiritual direction is disciplined focus on one's whole life from the vantage point of the Holy Spirit's hidden movements in it.

Spiritual direction is not problem solving focused on oneself. Rather, it is an opportunity to drop into the subtle, mysterious energy of the Spirit. With their guide, people seek to appreciate that living presence shaping their unique Christ-nature, and to discern its particular calling to share their gifts for ministry. It is also a time when they can look at their unique ways of noticing and inviting the Spirit's presence in and among them day by day, i.e., through personal spiritual disciplines. This ministry perhaps is the most intimate form of guidance: going through "the pain of giving birth to you . . . until Christ is formed in you" (Gal. 4:19).

Some pastors are specially called to this unique form of guidance relationship. How can they best carry on such personal guidance? It needs to begin with the pastor's own guidance. As John of the Cross reminds us, "The person that is alone without a spiritual guide, and has virtue, is like a glowing ember that is alone. It will become more frigid rather than hotter."[2]

SUCH HELP comes from many sources. God sometimes sends a particular person to be a soul friend for the long haul—a priceless treasure, a human sacrament with whom God's hidden Yes in one's life surfaces. Just knowing that there is someone who particularly cares and prays for their deepest liberation and calling in God, even if they see the person infrequently, empowers clergy to remember what is most important day by day. Perhaps knowing the

---

[1] Cf. my book *Spiritual Friend: Reclaiming the Gift of Spiritual Direction* (Mahwah, NJ: Paulist Press, 1986) for a historical, theoretical, and practical review of this subject.

[2] J.M. Neufelder and Mary Coelho, *Writings on Spiritual Direction by Great Christian Masters* (New York: Seabury Press, 1986), p. 5.

spiritual friend's intimacy with them in prayer is one reason why the tradition of relatively infrequent meetings has grown up, once a month being about average. The Eastern Orthodox tradition especially considers the spiritual companion's gift of ongoing intercessory prayer the most important dimension of the relationship.

When guide and guided do meet, they probably will have prayer and hopefully silence together for a few minutes, and then the guided will let rise as transparently as possible his or her sense of grace threading through life (which may be in very rough as well as smooth circumstances). The one receiving guidance will share responses to perceived grace: joy, compassion, fear of surrender, resistance, and perhaps testing of particular callings to discipline, lifestyle, relationships, and ministries. The guide listens and, when so moved, gently questions, affirms, and perhaps suggests a particular focus for attention between sessions. Through this process both guide and guided need to remember that the Holy Spirit is the real director. Such awareness can lighten the sense of personal inadequacy and threat in undertaking such guidance. Guidance is best when both partners are least self-conscious and least *trying* to do anything but be openly present. The awareness beneath the ego-conscious surface is where people are most permeable to the Spirit, and where they glimpse the unique image of God in Christ that they are becoming.

If pastors are drawn to such a relationship with someone they know, they need to risk asking for it. If there seems to be no one at hand, pray for such a person to appear and stay alert. It is usually best for the person to be outside the pastor's congregation and family, since clergy often have complicated relationships in these contexts that can become barriers to simple mutual presence to the Spirit. If pastors are drawn to a relationship with someone who also wants them as guide, it is important to give one another an unambiguous hour of special focus rather than mixing talk about one another in the same hour. This promotes disciplined, sustained focus on one person.

If pastors have no one with whom they are willing to open themselves spiritually in this way, they become less trustworthy guides of others. Bernard of Clairvaux said, "He becomes the disciple of a fool who sets up to be his own teacher,"[3] and that foolishness can spill over to others. Of course, their own responsible discernment of the Spirit must have the last word. But pastors need someone with whom to expose and test it.

---

[3] *The Letters of St. Bernard of Clairvaux*, trans. Bruno Scott James (Chicago: Henry Regnery Co., 1953), p. 133.

Since pastors usually have so many responsibilities, it is not possible for them to guide many individuals regularly. Such one-to-one guidance is a gift, demonstrated by people spontaneously coming to them. Their guidance gifts may lie elsewhere, for example, in preaching, teaching, or small groups. Therefore, it is wise to identify several laity in the church who are so gifted—people to whom others naturally seem to gravitate spiritually. The pastor can support these people and offer them further educational help if needed.[4] Gifted laity, like pastors, are likely to feel inadequate at the thought of being recognized as spiritual guides and need reminding that their central confidence for this ministry must rest in the Lord, not in themselves.

All pastors inevitably are involved in occasional guidance: in crises, informal conversations, and many other circumstances. The strong formation in pastoral counseling received by most clergy today tends to make them too problem and management oriented in their approaches to these people's situations. The pastor's unique gift (in contrast to that of the psychological counselor) is a well-conditioned and sensitive eye that can sense the Spirit at work (or being blocked) in a person's life, and the ability to talk about this as the person seems able to receive it.[5]

As people have become increasingly conditioned by society to be ego problem oriented, attempts to reveal a deeper dimension of reality at work in their situations can be difficult. The church needs a more comprehensive approach to spiritual formation. The great potential advantage of the pastor is that the pastor can approach spiritual guidance in the context of other mutually reinforcing and long-term forms of guidance in the faith community.

I N SPIRITUAL GUIDANCE pastors need to remember that the Spirit resonates differently in people's lives. Some find themselves called primarily to strong direct social action, others to solitude. Some are called to intensive study, others to simply personal service. Others are guided to creating beauty, to contemplative or ecstatic presence before God, or to energetic hospitality. Still others need to be affirmed

---

[4] Various programs nationally provide training for such laity, including the Shalem Institute in Bethesda, MD.

[5] For a practical and profound view of human nature and development that helpfully bridges the best of psychological and spiritual awareness today, I refer you to Gerald May's *Will and Spirit: A Contemplative Psychology* (New York: Harper & Row, 1982), and to his *Care of Mind, Care of Spirit: Psychiatric Dimensions of Spiritual Direction* (New York: Harper & Row, 1982).

in the Spirit's hidden presence through times of patient waiting, dryness, resistance, and pain. The spiritual disciplines involved in these paths and phases may vary significantly, depending upon our personalities and situations.[6]

Spiritual formation needs to help sensitize people to these different authentic possibilities for themselves and others. Small groups that meet weekly for a period of months can expose people to a range of spiritual disciplines. With the group's support they can test and choose which ones seem most right for them to practice regularly. Such groups also provide: 1. collective stimuli for their members, freeing them to take on a serious spiritual attentiveness that they otherwise might not sustain; 2. an intimate and sustained way of learning to respect differences in practice; 3. an opportunity for the pastor to get in touch with the souls of people in a way that otherwise might not happen, and in-touchness that can feed into sermons and other forms of pastoral guidance; 4. a context for spiritual teaching, wherein the pastor can help connect the fragments of discipline and intent into a coherent way of life; 5. an atmosphere of honesty and support wherein people feel free to raise their deepest spiritual questions and be gently nudged, as they seem ready, to release their fear of God and anxious securing of life, hopefully realizing a deeper life of trust in Christ that overflows into compassion.[7] In an average church there is usually a small group of such people ready for deeper formation each year. Such small group guidance could be a staple annual offering of the pastor and gifted lay leaders.

Because fullness of life is impossible for me until it is fulfilled for you and all creation, spiritual formation as well as individual guidance needs to take place within an awareness of our shared journey. Life in the Spirit can never be private, because that Spirit is uncontainable. It is an opening energy that circulates freely through creation, bringing one hand into another, the flower from the seed, the living from the dead. It is the divine energy that shapes life into one coinherent, cosmic Body of Christ, moving fitfully toward its fullness in God.

Personal guidance exists in this context. So also does that corporate guidance which is called for when Christians need to attend the Spirit's collective calling at various levels of community. The pastor

---

[6] Cf. my *Spiritual Friend*, pp. 112, 160.

[7] Cf. Gerald May, *Pilgrimage Home* (Mahwah, NJ: Paulist Press, 1979) for a practical understanding of group spiritual formation, especially in the context of Christian contemplative tradition.

moves between the corporate and individual dimensions of spiritual guidance, turning one time this way and another time the other, symbolizing and actualizing their connectedness with one another and with the larger Body of Christ.

The process of deepening the church's life in Christ today requires that spiritual guidance be taken with great seriousness. Both clergy and laity are forever in danger of sinking too deeply into functionary modes that cheat pastor, people, and community of authentic spiritual practice. The best place for pastors to begin in this struggle is with themselves. Guidance for parish practice will emerge organically out of the pastor's deepening sensitivity to the Spirit's caring life moving in and through himself or herself and the faith community. The forms of pastoral guidance will be manifold, but all authentic forms will be united by a single-hearted desire for fullness of life in the risen Christ.

Desert Listening

by Wendy M. Wright

The abbot Anthony said, "Fish, if they tarry on dry land, die: even so monks that tarry outside their cell or abide with men in the world fall away from their vow of quiet. As a fish must return to the sea, so must we to our cell: lest it befall that by tarrying without, we forget the watch within." [1]

THEIR WORDS AND NAMES echo through the centuries and fall on our ears with the haunting, foreign ring of oriental temple bells: Abba Anthony, Amma Syncletica, Abba Marcarius, Abba Poemen. Yet these fathers and mothers of the deserts of Egypt, Palestine, and Syria are our own Christian spiritual forebears.

If we listen carefully to their words, words uttered over fifteen centuries ago, we learn that these desert dwelling ascetics were engaged in a life of intense listening. They were zealous disciples of Christ who had left the "world" which formed people in its own image of power, self-aggrandizement, greed, lust, and luxury and had fled to the desert to be formed in the image of Christ, to die to themselves and thus become persons of charity, humility, compassion, and continual prayer. Their practice was fiercely ascetic, their disciplines many. But at the core of their life was the practice of silent listening. Only in the stillness of a single focused attention, they felt, could they sift through the myriad, conflicting voices that crowd the human heart. Only in the solitude and silence of the wilderness, they believed, could they discern the voice of God.

The harsh ascetic impulse of these early Christians may be far from the spiritual needs of twentieth century North America, but their quest for intentional listening is not. We, too, have an urgent need to ferret out the small, still whisper of divine prompting that so easily gets submerged in the rowdy chorus of voices that clamor for our attention in the busyness of each day. To listen deeply; to listen with a tender, yielding heart; to listen adventurously enough to be utterly surprised at what we hear—this we all need to be able to do. We all need, in one way or another, at one time or another, to enter

---

[1] *The Desert Fathers*, trans. Helen Waddell (Ann Arbor: University of Michigan Press, 1985), p. 63.

the desert and listen there mutely, intently for God. The ammas and abbas can be our guides.

LISTENING WITHIN

A certain brother went to Abbot Moses in Scete, and asked him for a good word. And the elder said to him: "Go, sit in your cell and your cell will teach you everything." [2]

ENTERING THE PHYSICAL DESERT was never an easy prospect for the early spiritual fathers and mothers. Theirs was a harsh life, fraught with danger and marked by hardship. So, too, with the inner desert of the heart. Journeying through the treacherous maze of "worldly" temptations was not over when they left the world. In the desert they discovered that the image of the world was engraved deep in their own spirit. Thus the greater and more difficult journey was not from the cities of the Roman Empire to the solitudes of Egypt, Syria, or Palestine; it was through the crooked pathways of the heart. To make those paths straight for the advent of the Lord was the spiritual struggle in the wilderness.

Each of us, like the ammas and abbas of old, must engage to one degree or another in the inner wrestling that is the perennial lot of the reflective human person. There are so many competing voices, so many conflicted selves, so deafening a din when we turn our ears inward, that sorting out the messages we hear can be daunting. The Christian tradition, from the era of the desert onward, has referred to the task of this layered inner listening as the discernment of spirits.

The myriad interior voices were characterized by the desert dwellers as having their origins in a variety of spirits—the spirit of the "world," of the demonic realm, of God, of nature. The task (whatever one thought of the other voices) was somehow to distinguish the intonation of the divine voice from the rest. This was and is no simple task. At rare graced moments in our lives we may stand, as it were, on a mountaintop, looking down with clarity and perspective, able to discern in that rarefied atmosphere the sharp retort of God's clarion call. But most of our lives are spent wandering in forested plains or hidden valleys where it is difficult to distinguish which leaf-strewn clearing is in fact the path that will eventually get us to the next

---

[2] Thomas Merton, *The Wisdom of the Desert* (New York: New Directions, 1960), p. 30.

mountaintop. In the midst of those shadowy forests the clarion call is more like a faint echo one strains to hear in the distance, unsure of its origin or nature. The desert ascetics were engaged in the process of picking out the divine Spirit from among spirits, the voice of God from multiple voices. To do that they had to be keen listeners. So do we.

LISTENING TO THE SPIRITS

Amma Syncletica said, "We must arm ourselves in every way against the demons. For they attack us from outside, and they also stir us up from within; and the soul is then like a ship when great waves break over it, and at the same time it sinks because the hold is too full. We are just like that: we lose as much by the exterior faults we commit as by the thoughts inside us. So we must watch for the attacks of men that come from outside us, and also repel the interior onslaughts of our thoughts." [3]

THE LANGUAGE OF THE SPIRITS in the desert is baroque and perhaps alienating to our present-day sensibilities. We are more likely to give psychological interpretation to our inner voices than to attribute them to demonic sources. Nor do we tend to be as mistrustful of fantasy or thoughts as the ancient ascetics seem to have been. Be this as it may, it remains true that we, like they, must wrestle with the conflicting claims, desires, and values that confront us from both the outside and the inside. And this involves intense listening.

There are various models of discernment given to us by the Christian tradition. Most famous perhaps are two from the sixteenth century. Ignatius of Loyola, the Spanish founder of the Jesuits, focused his attention on the interior movements that he termed consolation and desolation. Ignatius believed that to people immersed in a "worldly attitude," the spirit of light (God's Spirit) presented itself as hard and forbidding (as desolation) while the spirit of darkness was attractive and compelling (consolation). For persons well embarked on a life of spiritual progress, the presentation of the spirits was in reverse. God's Spirit was in desires and movements that ultimately led to consolation and peace, while the evil spirits' intentions could

---

[3] *The Sayings of the Desert Fathers*, trans. Benedicta Ward (Kalamazoo, MI: Cistercian Publications, 1975), pp. 196–197.

be detected in desires and prompting that ended in confusion and anxiety (desolation).

A second model of interior discernment is found in the writings of the Spanish Carmelite John of the Cross. John presented a schema of human spiritual growth in which interior and exterior purification was the operative principle. Thus, for the most part, painful inner experiences ("dark nights" as he termed them) of desolation, abandonment, doubt, and so forth were part of God's purgative process of drawing the person closer in pure love by withdrawing him or her from attachments of any kind, inner and outer. God's path was thus often through the path of stripping and self-emptying.

A THIRD MODEL of discernment, quite different from either of the sixteenth-century models that focus on affectivity (inner yearning), is one originating in the seventeenth-century Quaker practice of silent listening. Perhaps (although separated by centuries and the abyss of culture) this model captures something of the desert discernment that might be of special value to us today. The early Quakers taught (and Quakers still do) that one must wait in silence for the Spirit to speak, that one's listening is primarily receptive. The tendency in the early Quaker Movement for people to "hear" excessive and bizarre promptings was soon tempered by the practice of communal listening, in which an individual prompting by the Spirit was attended to by the entire community and the authenticity of its message tested in the silence they shared. The Quakers perceived that there was a "weight" to the silent meeting, that silence itself was layered, having depth and texture, and that to learn to be attentive to the varied qualities of the layers was to begin to discern the presence of the Spirit of God.

Personal discernment is not a practice that can be easily systematized into any formula, especially not a simple one. But perhaps what we might take away from these earlier models are two ideas. First, attention to the quality and direction of one's inner affectivity is part of the art. Second, whatever one thinks, feels, or experiences is best weighed in the medium of profound silence. Spiritual listening is not listening to words, to arguments, to pros and cons, to positions and opinions. It involves listening to the delicate intersection of the human heart, with its desires and dreams, and the vast and silent mystery that is God.

LISTENING TO ONE ANOTHER

Some old men came to Abba Poemen and said to him, "When we see brothers who are dozing at the synaxis, shall we rouse them so that they will be watchful?" He said to them, "For my part when I see a brother who is dozing, I put his head on my knees and let him rest." [4]

INNER LISTENING is essentially a solitary task. Ultimately, you or I alone can enter the inner deserts of our own experience. Only you or I can decipher the complex codes that make up our own dreams, inner images, and self-understanding. Yet this solitary listening, as Quaker practice and desert tradition both confirm, is really best done in concert with others—with a spiritual guide, with the support of a few fellow travelers, and most especially within the context of a supportive faith community. The desert wisdom figures knew this. They knew it was too easy to be self-deluding, that we are often too identified with the habitual way we perceive things to hear the music of what might be a radically new song that God is inviting us to sing.

Thus, to embark on this taxing journey long ago, one needed a sure guide. The abbas and the ammas were such leaders, recognized by the quality of their lives. Their compassion, humility, charity, and purity of heart shown luminously in all that they did and said. They were perhaps the first spiritual guides in the Christian tradition, men and women who listened not only to the whispered voice of God in their own inner longings and wrestlings but persons who listened to God in the wrestlings and longings of others as well. These deep listeners, practiced in peeling back the layers of silence, pierced to the core the hearts of fellow seekers and laid bare for them the voice of the living God.

If a disciple wanted the wisdom of the desert, she would seek out a wise one who could teach her not by imparting information, but by simply being. If a disciple desired to learn, he would ask a wise one for a word. This word was a dynamic and unique gift from master to disciple. Meant for the seeker alone, the word served as a sort of desert koan on which to reflect or to chew. It was not to be analyzed but taken into the heart, digested, and lived. The wise ones knew from experience the tricky labyrinth of the human heart and knew the word for a given disciple that could illumine the path to greater understanding and fuller faith.

---

[4] Ward, *The Sayings of the Desert Fathers*, p. 151.

Although the specific ministry of spiritual direction (undertaking to act as guide for others in a formal way) requires training and accountability, and the gift of spiritual discernment is charismatic in nature and not simply a learned skill, we are all occasionally called to listen to one another in the manner of the desert: to help one another listen for the faint echo of God's distinct voice in the cacophony of voices filling our lives. It is that sort of informal listening to another, done in what perhaps is best termed a contemplative mode, that complements the intense listening of our own inward journey.

CONTEMPLATIVE LISTENING

It was said of Abbot Agatho that for three years he carried a stone in his mouth until he learned to be silent.[5]

ONE OF THE MOST ESSENTIAL aspects of Christian community, and often one of the most overlooked, is the aspect of listening. Like the desert ammas and abbas, we can become listeners to each other's hearts, fellow travelers who hear each other into fullness and into God.

Listening is a helping skill that is familiar to many of us these days. It is practiced by counselors, pastors, social workers, psychiatrists, and psychologists, among others. However, I would say that for the most part listening of this kind is somewhat different than desert listening.

Persons in helping professions learn to listen empathetically as well as analytically. They learn to encourage warmly a person's self-disclosure, to enable a person to articulate his or her own perspective, and to identify areas of confusion, pathology, or need that might be addressed. Through helpful listening of this sort we (whether we are professional counselors or not) may help one another become more functional as social beings.

The motivation with which we typically undertake this task is a problem-solving one. We want to fix things. Perhaps at the root of our desire to fix things is an aesthetic impulse. There is deep in the human heart an insatiable longing for beauty and harmony, a painful aching to experience life as we sense it might be: fulsome and delightful in its symmetry and grace. This is a religious impulse of the first order. There is not a religious tradition in existence that does not

---

[5] Merton, *The Wisdom of the Desert*, p. 30.

define how human life must be crafted in order to be beautiful. One way we usher one another into the beauty we perceive as ultimate is by listening for what might be fixed, healed, or changed.

Fixing what is broken or healing what is injured is indeed part of what the spiritual life is about. But there is more. There is also a certain disorder, characteristic of creativity, that belongs in the aesthetic realm as surely as do the patterns of order we perceive as satisfyingly beautiful. Creation is a messy business. It involves hard work, practice, temporary successes, as many or more false starts, the surprise of unexpected discovery, the disappointment of failed vision. The listening we do for one another must also embrace this wild and uncontainable aspect of creativity. For, if what we are doing here on our little human pilgrimages is more than simply surviving, simply living reactively to the multitude of social pressures that bombard us, if we are seeking to shape and form ourselves according to a deeper and more ultimate aesthetic vision, then we must be willing genuinely to risk the pain and chaos that lead to new birth. Our spiritual listening must reflect this process.

Thus, listening as a spiritual discipline is related but not identical to the listening practiced in helping settings today. First and foremost, spiritual listening is a contemplative undertaking and not a problem-solving task. It is essentially prayer. A contemplative attitude pervades the listening done by spiritual seekers. They do not seek to encounter human life as a problem to be solved or fixed but as a mystery to be entered and plumbed. There are certainly innumerable problems that we must solve in order to live well. But simply disposing of the problem in one's life does not necessarily lead one into the immensity and profundity of the living God.

Spiritual listening as a contemplative discipline pushes us beyond the immediate impulse to order and fix to the embrace of the whole of human life with all its ambiguity, failure, and paradox. We are pushed to a level of listening beyond our own powers of analysis to the grace and the gift of divine life itself. We are invited into a realm of apprehension that surpasses our words, plans, schemes, and panaceas. We move into silence and into the creative work of God.

To listen this way is to listen with heart and mind opened wide. It invites us to be changed along with those to whom we listen. It exposes the limitations of our solutions, even of our questions. It sensitizes us to the ultimately mysterious way God moves incarnationally in the unique particularity of each human life. Life is not ultimately problem but mystery. To listen to its depths is finally to find oneself on one's knees.

LENSES OF LISTENING

Abbot Mark once said to Abbot Arsenius: "It is good, is it not, to have nothing in your cell that just gives you pleasure. For example, once I knew a brother who had a little wildflower that came up in his cell, and he pulled it out by the roots." "Well," said Abbot Arsenius, "that is all right. But each man should act according to his own spiritual way. And if one were not able to get along without the flower, he should plant it again." [6]

DESERT LISTENING is contemplative. At its deepest it surrounds the vast and multidimensional range of human experiences in an embrace of radical love. It waits in the mystery of silence to receive the word of God.

Yet even while we listen at that depth, our listening is influenced by interpretive lenses of various kinds. We hear the data we receive in the context of the ideas and values with which we are familiar. Thus, when we listen to one another, we bring our own frame of reference to the encounter. The desert ammas and abbas knew this; and it is important that we be similarly aware for at least two reasons. First, when listening to another, we need to be sensitive to the unique way that God acts in that man or woman's life. His or her perception of God-with-us will have a particular nuance, a special lilt. It will not sound like yours or mine. If God truly works through the incarnational medium of the individual person, then God's presence will be shaped by the life circumstance, culture, language, personality, and history of that particular man or woman.

Second, the way we understand what we hear is strongly shaped by the interpretive schemas we carry with us. If we have given meaning to our lives through the categories of addiction and co-dependency, or feminist theory, or biblical literalism, we are likely to hear another primarily in that mode of understanding. None of these (or other) theories can exhaust the ways we can think about our own and others' experience. All may be helpful in making sense of and improving our conditions; but none is synonymous with the word at the core of silence which undergirds all life. To be aware of the

---

[6] Merton, *The Wisdom of the Desert*, pp. 67–68.

assumptions—theological, psychological, and multicultural—that frame our listening can free us to listen more creatively, more adventurously to the Spirit that is active in a multitude of ways in our brothers and sisters.

LISTENING IN LOVE

> *A brother asked the abbot Pastor, saying, "If I should see my brother's fault, is it good to hide it?" The old man said to him, "In what hour we do cover up our brother's sins, God shall cover ours; in what hour we do betray our brother's shames, in like manner God shall betray our own."* [7]

ONE OF THE MOST arresting and, to my mind, the most touching qualities of desert listening as it is expressed in the pithy sayings of the abbas and ammas was its quality of compassion. As austere as desert advice could be in terms of a seeker's own practice, the same kind of severity was rarely found in the advice given about listening to one another. Rather there was a tender solicitude toward the human condition and an insistent reminder that genuine humility requires one to be conscious of one's own need for God rather than focused on the shortcomings of others.

We might well heed this call to compassionate listening today. Amma Theodora's advice to teachers, given some fifteen centuries ago, is apt for listeners as well.

> *[She] said that a teacher ought to be a stranger to the desire for domination, vain-glory, and pride; one should not be able to fool him by flattery, nor blind him by gifts, nor conquer him by the stomach, nor dominate him by anger; but he should be patient, gentle and humble as far as possible; he must be tested and without partisanship, full of concern, and a lover of souls.* [8]

To listen tenderly and lovingly to the petty foibles, the painful longings, the relentless thirst for God that crowd into the consciousness of each of us is to listen, in fact, to God's own longing to live among and transform us. To listen to one another in this way is indeed to be a lover of souls.

---

[7] Waddell, *The Desert Fathers*, p. 97.
[8] Ward, *The Sayings of the Desert Fathers*, p. 72.

The Clearness Committee

A COMMUNAL APPROACH TO DISCERNMENT

by Parker J. Palmer

MANY OF US face a series of difficult dilemmas when we are trying to deal with a personal problem, question, or decision. On the one hand, we know that the issue is ours alone to resolve and we believe that we have the inner resources to resolve it—but those resources are often hidden from us by layers of inner "stuff." On the other hand, we know that other people might help us discover our resources and find our way—but by exposing our problem to others we run the risk of being invaded by their judgments and assumptions and advice, a common and painful experience. As a result, we too often privatize these vital questions in our lives. At the very moment when we need all the help we can get, we find ourselves cut off from our own inner resources *and* from the resources of community.

For people who have experienced these dilemmas, I want to describe a method invented by the Quakers, a method that protects individual identity and integrity while drawing upon the wisdom of other people. It is called a "Clearness Committee." If that name sounds like it is from the sixties, it is—the 1660s! From their beginnings over three hundred years ago, Quakers needed a way to draw on both inner and communal resources to deal with personal problems because they had no clerical leaders to "solve" their problems for them. The Clearness Committee is testimony to the fact that there are no external authorities on life's deepest issues, not clergy or therapists or scholars; there is only the authority that lies within each of us waiting to be heard.

Behind the Clearness Committee is a simple but crucial conviction: *each of us has an inner teacher, a voice of truth, that offers the guidance and power we need to deal with our problems.* But that inner voice is often garbled by various kinds of inward and outward interference. The function of the Clearness Committee is not to give advice or "fix" people from the outside in, but to help people remove the interference so that they can discover their own wisdom from the inside out. If we do not believe in the reality of inner wisdom, the Clearness Committee can become an opportunity for manipulation. But if we respect the power of the inner teacher, the Clearness Committee can be a remarkable way to help someone name and claim his or her deepest truth.

The Clearness Committee's work is guided by some simple but crucial rules and understandings. Among them, of course, is the rule that the process is confidential. When it is over, committee members will not speak with others about what was said—and they will not speak with the focus person about the problem unless he or she requests a conversation.

1. Normally, the person who seeks clearness (the "focus person") chooses his or her committee—a minimum of five and a maximum of six trusted people with as much diversity among them as possible in age, background, gender, etc.

2. The focus person writes up his or her issue in four to six pages and sends this document to members of the committee in advance of the meeting. There are three sections to this write-up: a concise *statement of the problem*, a recounting of *relevant background factors* that may bear on the problem, and an exploration of any hunches the focus person may have about *what's on the horizon* regarding the problem. Most people find that by writing a statement of this sort, they are taking their first step toward inner clearness.

3. The committee meets for three hours—with the understanding that there may be a need for a second or third meeting at a later date. A clerk (facilitator) and a recording clerk (secretary) should be named, though taping the meeting is a good alternative to the latter. The clerk opens the meeting with a reminder of the rules, closes the meeting on time, and serves as a monitor all along the way, making sure that the rules are followed with care. The recording clerk gives his or her notes to the focus person when the meeting is over.

4. The meeting begins with the clerk calling for a time of centering silence and inviting the focus person to break the silence, when ready, with a brief oral summary of the issue at hand. Then the committee members may speak—but everything they say is governed by one rule, a simple rule and yet one that most people find difficult and demanding: members are forbidden to speak to the focus person in any way except to ask honest, open questions. This means absolutely no

advice and no amateur psychoanalysis. It means no, "Why don't you . . . ?" It means no, "That happened to me one time, and here's what I did . . . ." It means no, "There's a book/therapist/exercise/diet that would help you a lot." Nothing is allowed except *real* questions, honest and open questions, questions that will help the focus person remove the blocks to his or her inner truth without becoming burdened by the personal agendas of committee members. I may think I know the answer to your problem, and on rare occasions I may be right. But *my* answer is of absolutely no value to you. The only answer that counts is one that arises from your own inner truth. The discipline of the Clearness Committee is to give you greater access to that truth—and to keep the rest of us from defiling or trying to define it.

5. What is an honest, open question? It is important to reflect on this, since we are so skilled at asking questions that are advice or analysis in disguise: "Have you ever thought that it might be your mother's fault?" The best single mark of an honest, open question is that the questioner could not possibly know the answer to it: "Did you ever feel like this before?" There are other guidelines for good questioning. Ask questions aimed at serving the focus person's needs rather than at satisfying your curiosity. Ask questions that are brief and to the point rather than larding them with background considerations and rationale—which make the question into a speech. Ask questions that go to the person as well as the problem—e.g., questions about feelings as well as about facts. Trust your intuition in asking questions, even if your instinct seems off the wall: "What color is your present job, and what color is the one you have been offered?"

6. Normally, the focus person responds to the questions as they are asked, in the presence of the group, and those responses generate more, and deeper, questions. Though the responses should be full, they should not be terribly long—resist the temptation to tell your life story in response to every question! It is important that there be time for more and more questions and responses, thus deepening the process for everyone. The more often a focus person is willing to answer aloud, the more material he or she, and the committee, will have to work with. But this should never happen at the

expense of the focus person's need to protect vulnerable feelings or to maintain privacy. It is vital that the focus person assume total power to set the limits of the process. So the second major rule of the Clearness Committee is this: *it is always the focus person's right not to answer a question.* The unanswered question is not necessarily lost—indeed, it may be the question that is so important that it keeps working on the focus person long after the Clearness Committee has ended.

7. The Clearness Committee must not become a grilling, a cross-examination. The pace of the questioning is critical— it should be relaxed, gentle, humane. A machine-gun fire of questions makes reflection impossible and leaves the focus person feeling invaded rather than evoked. Do not be afraid of silence in the group—trust it and treasure it. When silence falls it does not mean that nothing is happening or that the process has broken down. It may well mean that the most important thing of all is happening—new insights are emerging from within people, from their deepest sources of guidance.

8. From beginning to end of the Clearness Committee, it is important that everyone work hard to remain totally attentive to the focus person and his or her needs. This means suspending the normal rules of social gathering—no chit-chat, no responding to other people's questions or to the focus person's answers, no joking to break the tension, no noisy and nervous laughter to indicate that we "get it." We are simply to surround the focus person with quiet, loving space, resisting even the temptation to comfort or reassure or encourage this person, but simply being present to him or her with our attention and our questions and our care. If a committee member damages this ambiance with advice, leading questions, or rapid-fire inquisition, other members— including the focus person—should remind that person of the rules, and he or she should not argue the point. The Clearness Committee is for the focus person; the rest of us need to learn to recede.

9. The Clearness Committee should run for the full time allotted. Don't end early for fear that the group has "run out

of questions"—patient waiting will be rewarded with deeper questions than have yet been asked. About thirty minutes before the end of the meeting, the clerk should ask the focus person if he or she wants to suspend the "questions only" rule and invite committee members to mirror back what they have heard the focus person saying. If the focus person says no, the questions continue, but if he or she says yes, mirroring can begin, along with more questions. "Mirroring" does not provide an excuse to give advice or "fix" the person—that sort of invasiveness is still prohibited. Mirroring simply means reflecting back the focus person's own words and behavior to see if he or she recognizes the image—and with each mirroring the focus person should have a chance to say, "Yes, that's me. . . .", or, "No, that's not. . . ." In the final ten minutes of the meeting, the clerk should invite members to celebrate and affirm the focus person and his or her strengths. This is an important time, since the focus person has just spent a couple of hours feeling vulnerable. And there is always much to celebrate, for in the course of a Clearness Committee people reveal the gifts and graces that characterize human beings at their deepest and best.

10. Remember, the Clearness Committee is not intended to "fix" the focus person, so there should be no sense of let-down if the focus person does not have his or her problems "solved" when the process ends. A good clearness process does not end—it keeps working within the focus person long after the meeting is over. The rest of us need simply to keep holding that person in the light, trusting the wisdom of his or her inner teacher.

T HE CLEARNESS COMMITTEE is not a cure-all. It is not for extremely fragile people or for extremely delicate problems. But for the right person, with the right issue, it is a powerful way to rally the strength of community around a struggling soul, to draw deeply from the wisdom within all of us. It teaches us to abandon the pretense that we know what is best for another person and instead to ask those honest and open questions that can help that person find his or her own answers. It teaches us to give up the arrogant assumption that we are obliged to "save" each other and learn, through simple listening, to create the conditions that allow a person to find his or her wholeness within. If the spiritual discipline behind the Clearness Committee is understood and practiced, the process can become a way to renew community in our individualistic times, a way to free people from their isolation without threatening their integrity, a way to counteract the excesses of technique in caring, a way to open new channels for the Spirit to move among us with healing and power.

MODIFICATIONS FOR RETREATS

WHEN WE PRACTICE the Clearness Committee process at a retreat, several of the preceding guidelines are modified given the brevity of the time available and the need to give all participants an experience as members of a committee:

1. At a retreat, I will assign members to committees, but before doing so, I will ask each focus person for a confidential list of any persons he or she especially wants to work with—or feels unable to work with.

2. At a retreat, focus persons are not required to write a lengthy statement, but are asked to reflect on the three areas (see #2, above) so they can present them orally to the committee at the start of the session in a concise (10 minutes or so) but helpful way.

3. At a retreat, meetings normally last only two to two and a half hours, and the "clerking" is done by everyone involved rather than a specifically appointed member. Committee members who do not find it distracting to take notes during the proceedings can make a gift to the focus person by giving him or her those notes when the meeting is over.

This article, revised in September 1994, differs substantially from the version originally published in *Weavings*.

Commonweal

Commonweal

Sharing *in the* Pain *of* God

DIETRICH BONHOEFFER'S REFLECTIONS ON CHRISTIAN VULNERABILITY

by Geffrey B. Kelly

I N A LETTER FROM PRISON that his best friend, Eberhard Bethge, would treasure for its words of faith and courage, Dietrich Bonhoeffer wrote that to learn what God has promised and to experience fulfillment in God, one had to "persevere in quiet meditation of the life, sayings, deeds, sufferings, and death of Jesus." He went on to declare that living close to God and in the light of God's presence was an entirely "new life" because in God all things had become possible.

Bonhoeffer was not speaking here of the unleashing of human potential for grandiose deeds. Rather, he was coming to grips with the fearful reality of his own death. The July 20, 1944 plot against the life of Hitler had failed. The noose of the Gestapo was being drawn ever more tightly around those of his band of conspirators who, though already in prison, were implicated in the assassination attempt. Soon Bonhoeffer, cut off from any contact with his family, would be transferred to the dreaded Gestapo prison and then, just a few short weeks before Hitler committed suicide, placed in a van for that long journey to the death camp at Flossenbürg.

But Bonhoeffer's words, smuggled out of prison by a friendly guard, were not those of a man in despair over his fate. Rather, they were as death-defying as those Paul spoke in declaring that nothing in this world or in the beyond could ever separate him from the love of God that he had experienced in Christ Jesus his Lord (Rom. 8:28-39). To Bethge Bonhoeffer confided his conviction that "no earthly power can touch us without his will and that danger and distress can only drive us closer to him. It is certain that . . . our joy is hidden in suffering, and our life in death." That certainty, he said, came from their fellowship in Jesus, whose death on the cross was seen by Bonhoeffer as God's "Yes and Amen" and "the firm ground on which we stand."[1]

---

[1] Dietrich Bonhoeffer, *Letters and Papers from Prison* (New York: Macmillan, 1971), p. 391.

A WOUNDED GOD

IN PRISON Bonhoeffer had come to experience more deeply the pathos of God's "weakness" and "foolishness" while the warring world was refining its malevolence and Christ was being tortured and crucified anew on Nazi Golgothas. The extent of God's love for God's people he now saw not in the power of God to eradicate evil and to assuage grief but in the way God had made divinity itself vulnerable in the stark, unfathomable reality of Jesus' humanity. Bonhoeffer took comfort from the word of Mark 15:34 in which Jesus cries out in despair from the cross, "My God, my God, why have you forsaken me?" (NRSV). This passage had become a word from God telling Bonhoeffer that not even Christ could avoid the human consequences of sacrificing oneself for the sake of others, sharing both the earthly blessings and sufferings of his people. "Like Christ," Bonhoeffer wrote, "Christians must drink the earthly cup to the dregs, and only in doing so is the crucified and risen Lord with them, and they crucified and risen with Christ."[2] Bonhoeffer sensed that Christ was not like a God who came to earth from on high, to remain supremely aloof except to intervene at certain moments with opportune miracles, and then depart virtually untouched by the world's harshness. Christ experienced the absence of God at the very moment when he ached for deliverance. In Christ, God does not offer any glib answers to the agonizing problem of human grief. God chooses to suffer with those who suffer. This realization of God's eloquent silence in the midst of suffering became at once Bonhoeffer's greatest consolation and most demanding challenge.

This sense of God's solidarity in their distress with the weakest of God's children, in fact, inspired Bonhoeffer to write one of his most moving poems from prison, "Christians and Pagans." In the opening lines of this poem Bonhoeffer describes how people, both Christians and unbelievers, go to God when they are troubled, begging from God the liberation and peace for which they long. But the second verse abruptly tells Christians that they are those who paradoxically must stand with God to help a needy God who shares the pain of those who cry out for deliverance from their suffering.

> People turn to God when God is sore bestead;
> they find God poor, disgraced, without roof or bread,

---

[2] Bonhoeffer, *Letters and Papers from Prison*, p. 337.

attacked by sin, thus weakened, and deprived of life.
A Christian stands by God to share God's pain and strife.[3]

In the concluding verse Bonhoeffer writes of how God goes to every person, pagan and Christian, with the bread that feeds the spirit. For both, God hangs in death and for both God offers pardon and solace. God has, in short, become in Christ a wounded God vulnerable to all the pain that people endure in life's journey back to God. The thought that God too bears the hurts and rejections of the innocent, that God suffers with all God's children, and is a hidden presence even in their lonely, degraded deaths at the hands of a criminal ideology, inspired in Bonhoeffer that extraordinary peace of mind admired by both his fellow prisoners and warders.

THE HUMILIATED ONE

I N MANY WAYS, too, the understanding of how God in Christ accepts the pain that can come only when one loves another with the intensity of divine love became the motivating force in Bonhoeffer's own decisions to make common cause with the most defenseless and vulnerable of his brothers and sisters, the Jewish people and the outcasts perishing in Nazi death camps. Even before his involvement in the church struggle and the conspiracy, Bonhoeffer saw in the God to whom he had dedicated his ministry the same God who had proclaimed an irresistible oneness with the grubby poor, a God who fully shared in the sorrows and joys of people. In a memorable conference to his Barcelona parishioners in 1928, he told his people that the way of Christ to God was the divine light shining "down on those who are ever neglected, insignificant, weak, ignoble, unknown, interior, oppressed, despised; here it radiates over the houses of prostitutes and tax collectors. . . . Here the light of eternity has been cast on the toiling, struggling, and sinning masses." Bonhoeffer concluded that conference with the observation that Christianity inverts the values systems of society by preaching the "unending worth of the apparently worthless and the unending worthlessness of what is apparently so valuable. The weak shall be made strong through God and the dying shall live."[4]

---

[3] Bonhoeffer, *Letters and Papers from Prison*, pp. 348–349. Author translation.

[4] Bonhoeffer, "Jesus Christ and the Essence of Christianity," in *A Testament to Freedom: The Essential Writings of Dietrich Bonhoeffer*, ed. Geffrey B. Kelly and F. Burton Nelson (San Francisco: HarperSanFrancisco, 1990), p. 54.

The paradoxes of that statement of God's having identified with those whom society would brand as worthless were intensified in an Advent sermon from the same period in which Bonhoeffer preached to his people that they were "faced with the shocking reality: Jesus stands at the door and knocks, in complete reality. He asks you for help in the form of a beggar, in the form of a ruined human being in torn clothing. He confronts you in every person that you meet. Christ walks on the earth as your neighbor as long as there are people."[5] The coming of Christ for Bonhoeffer was not merely a Christmas day event but the everyday opportunity to welcome into their midst Christ in the person of the poor and the ruined outcast. Bonhoeffer had counseled his parishioners to find their Christ in the most vulnerable of people, the homeless beggar and the ragged human being with little to offer in return.

Bonhoeffer urged the same faith on his students. In one of the most powerful segments of his Christology lectures, he raised the question that would stand out in his later prison letters. "Who is this Jesus whom we seek?" The question became his invitation to his students to search out the contemporary presence of Jesus in the "incognito" of the least of their brothers and sisters. Bonhoeffer linked this aspect to the way Jesus is fully God and fully man as the "humiliated one" who has entered fully into the pathos of human existence. In effect, Jesus chooses to confront people in his contemporaneous presence where they least expect him. As Bonhoeffer insisted with his students, Jesus enters the world "in such a way as to hide himself in it in weakness and not to be recognized as God-man. He does not enter in the kingly robes of a *morphe theou* (Greek, 'form of God'). His claim which he as God-man raises in this form must provoke contradiction and hostility. He goes incognito, as a beggar among beggars, as an outcast among outcasts, as despairing among the despairing, as dying among the dying."[6] This "incognito" was for Bonhoeffer not only the point of God's vulnerability in becoming human but also the central problem of Christology: Jesus challenging his followers to look for him not primarily in the privileged of this earth but in the lowly who were the object of his Father's special predilection. In his sensitivity to Christ's incarnate nearness in the

[5] Bonhoeffer, "Predigten in Barcelona: 1. Advent, 2. Dezember 1928." English trans. Geffrey B. Kelly in *A Testament to Freedom*, p. 196.

[6] Bonhoeffer, *Christ the Center* (San Francisco: Harper/Collins, 1978), p. 107.

beggar, outcast, despairing, and dying, Bonhoeffer could see both the woundedness of God and the riskiness of being a Christian. A Christian had to obey Christ even when it cost the most in terms of status and respectability.

For Bonhoeffer, it was not sufficient merely to label oneself a church-going Christian and to bask in one's religiosity as attestation of one's faith in Jesus Christ. Bonhoeffer argued that the Christian Church's boast of being herald of God's love for people was only a vain trumpet blare if its credibility was not grounded in a Christlike solidarity with the oppressed and in its willingness even to endure the bloody cross of persecution for the sake of those it would, in God's name, deliver from evil. It is in keeping with his conviction about the task of Christians in the midst of the pain inflicted on the innocent that Bonhoeffer was to make this remarkable claim in his *The Cost of Discipleship*, namely, that Christians may have to renounce even their own dignity in order to reach out in compassion to those in distress. "They [Christians] have an irresistible love for the downtrodden, the sick, the wretched, the wronged, the outcast and all who are tortured with anxiety. They go out and seek all who are enmeshed in the toils of sin and guilt. . . . They will be found consorting with publicans and sinners, careless of the shame they incur thereby. In order that they may be merciful they cast away the most priceless treasure of human life, their personal dignity and honor. For the only honor and dignity they know is their Lord's own mercy, to which alone they owe their very lives."[7] Bonhoeffer's words here are particularly apropos for church goers who fear to forsake their own privileges if that is the cost of truly following Christ in the path of peace and justice. In Bonhoeffer's spiritual reflections, fidelity to one's Christian vocation entails the closest possible communion with the suffering Christ. Such is the "cost of discipleship" in which the shame of being called disloyal citizens is often the price Christians must pay to be truly those who would obey the difficult word of the Sermon on the Mount and take the example of their crucified Lord seriously. For Bonhoeffer, Christian faith demands that we accept God's own vulnerability in embracing those to whom society deals the living death of rejection and neglect. This is the only way Christians can bring God's healing into the lives of those in whom Jesus is bruised and rejected anew.

---

[7] Bonhoeffer, *The Cost of Discipleship* (New York: Macmillan, 1963), pp. 124–125.

THE CROSS OF CHRIST

IT IS NOT SURPRISING to discover that at the center of Bonhoeffer's Christian decision to make himself vulnerable within the hate-filled world of Nazism lies the primary inspiration of Martin Luther. Luther's own life underwent a dramatic change when, moved by God's word, he took as the *leitmotif* of his reform the experience of God's encountering him in Christ, not in a theology of glory, but in lowliness and suffering, becoming one with people in their weakness, guilt, and pain. The Christian believer, Bonhoeffer noted in words that echoed Luther's own forceful acknowledgment of the liberating power of Christ's cross, lives "by the grace of God which comes to people and comes to every person who opens his or her heart to it and learns to understand it in the cross of Christ."[8] Luther's orientation in his life and writings to God's paradoxical "strength in weakness and wisdom in foolishness" was itself drawn from the powerful hold on him exerted by the cross of Christ. This is the same cross that Bonhoeffer described, in a memorable passage from his *Life Together*, as blocking the path of Christians, interrupting their lives and disrupting their well-set plans for a day and for a lifetime. He reminds his seminarians, whose experience at Finkenwalde is the background of the book, that they cannot enjoy the luxury of the priest who can piously walk by the poor man left for dead by thieves. Followers of Christ must be like the Samaritan, willing to have God "constantly crossing our paths and canceling our plans by sending us people with claims and petitions. We may pass them by, preoccupied with our more important tasks, as the priest passed by the man who had fallen among thieves, perhaps—reading the Bible. When we do that we pass by the visible sign of the Cross raised athwart our path to show us that, not our way, but God's way must be done."[9] That "way," for Bonhoeffer, entailed a willingness to open one's heart and resources to those, regardless of their race, religion, and status, who are struck down by the evil forces within every society. The suffering of people is the way the cross of Jesus Christ encounters Christians who might religiously kiss a replica of the dying Christ but shrink from personal encounters with the real Jesus—not a polished icon but a victim making demands on one's compassion and faith. For Bonhoeffer, the cross is the only way for Christians to discern what Christ is

---

[8] Kelly and Nelson, *A Testament to Freedom,* p. 56.

[9] Bonhoeffer, *Life Together* (New York: Harper & Row, 1954), p. 99; also in *A Testament to Freedom,* p. 356.

demanding of his contemporary followers and to discover, in the alleyways of destitution and the shadowy recesses of poverty and despair, Christ's contemporaneous presence.

Speaking on the theology of Karl Barth while a student at Union Theological Seminary in New York, Bonhoeffer turned to the same theme: where the cross of Christ is to be seen, that is where God must be recognized in an unheard of way by Christians attuned to human misery. This is a God "revealed in the poor life of a suffering man; God revealed on the cross; God revealed in . . . sin and death. . . . Faith sees God coming most closely . . . where a man hanging on the cross dies in despair. . . . This is the real world of biblical faith, which sees God's work not on the top, but in the depth of mankind."[10] If God's way of being with people is epitomized in the brutal anguish and death of Jesus, then the Christian path to God means "sharing the suffering of Christ to the last and to the fullest."[11] It is the cross of Jesus Christ that interrupts the best planned career in order to invest the Christian vocation with its most genuine meaning. God's love is shown paradoxically in the ever escalating demands God makes on the Christian. What should result is neither correct doctrine nor mindless attention to liturgical rubrics, the trademarks of the organized religion in which even Nazis were comfortable. The cross of Christ was a call to solidarity with and action for every person downtrodden by a nation's heartlessness. Hence Bonhoeffer's sobering phrase that the gift of Christ to people "is not the Christian religion, but the grace and love of God which culminate in the cross."[12] The cross of Christ is not an idealistic blueprint for a better world. Jesus' cross offers, rather, liberating solace to the wounded victims of this world who sigh for a God who cares and for Christians who can share their anguish and alleviate their pain.

RESPONSIBLE AND FREE ACTION

GOD'S VULNERABILITY in the crucifixion of Jesus and in solidarity with the least of Jesus' brothers and sisters, enjoined on all those who call themselves Christians, fills the pages of Bonhoeffer's collected writings. His convictions about God's

---

[10] Bonhoeffer, "The Theology of Crisis," in *No Rusty Swords: Letters, Lectures, and Notes, 1928–36*, ed. Edwin H. Robertson (New York: Harper & Row, 1965), pp. 363–364.

[11] Bonhoeffer, *The Cost of Discipleship*, p. 98.

[12] Kelly and Nelson, *A Testament to Freedom*, p. 56.

woundedness in the most vulnerable of God's people help explain why he could state so matter-of-factly from prison that the way of God's weakness and powerlessness in the world "is precisely the way, the only way, in which God is with us and helps us. Matthew 8:17 makes it quite clear that Christ helps us, not by virtue of his omnipotence, but by virtue of his weakness and suffering." [This passage from Matthew cites Isaiah 53:4: "This was to fulfill what was spoken by the prophet Isaiah: 'He took up our infirmities and bore our sorrows.' "][13] Bonhoeffer's emphasis on God's paradoxical power in human weakness sends an unmistakable message to the cruel leaders of any society that would use their might to crush the lowly. Bonhoeffer exposes the hypocrisy behind the pious pretense of military dictators that they are merely agents of God's power unleashed against the so-called evil forces of a disruptive peasantry or of a subversive underclass of poverty-ridden citizens.

Bonhoeffer's willingness to make common cause with those branded by such modern ideologies as less-than-fully-human *Untermenschen* was inspirited by the example of Jesus, who dared his followers to search for him not in the clouds of heavens, or on the thrones of earthly majesty, or at the banquets of the affluent, but in the places where people can only cry out to God in their distress. To enter into solidarity with the oppressed of Nazi Germany, as Bonhoeffer did, made one a sharer in God's own vulnerability. The mystery of personal suffering is not that God permits it but that God suffers in the loneliness, anguish, and tragic deaths that scream out their denial of a God who cares. In their pain those who suffer call out to the Spirit of Christ in those who hear not the lament of strangers but the heart-rending cry of brothers and sisters. God's communion with people is never so intense as when human suffering seems to belie the existence of goodness, justice, and hope.

It is at this troubled point of human pathos that Bonhoeffer recognized his own calling to be an instrument "in the hand of the Lord of history." Knowing that "we can share in other people's sufferings only to a very limited degree," nonetheless, Bonhoeffer insisted it was the vocation of all who would be like Christ to "have some share in Christ's large-heartedness by acting with responsibility and in freedom when the hour of danger comes, and by showing a real compassion that springs, not from fear, but from the liberating and redeeming love of Christ for all who suffer. Mere waiting and

---

[13] Bonhoeffer, *Letters and Papers from Prison*, pp. 360–361.

looking on is not Christian behavior. The Christian is called to compassion and action, not in the first place by his own sufferings, but by the sufferings of his brothers and sisters, for whose sake Christ suffered."[14] These words, sent to his family and fellow conspirators just before his imprisonment, are a clear statement of how Bonhoeffer embraced the Christian life as a call to suffer with and to respond with courage to those in whom Christ experienced a twentieth-century crucifixion. The cost of their solidarity with Christ in the countless victims of Nazi brutality would be their liberty and their lives. The liberating and redeeming love of Christ reaches people through preaching the word of God and celebrations of the Lord's Supper, to be sure. But that word is also spoken in the Christ who has entered into communion with the most downtrodden and vulnerable of his brothers and sisters for whom, in the compassionate outreach of their fellow Christians, the cross of Christ is still the light shining in darkness.

---

[14] Bonhoeffer, *Letters and Papers from Prison*, p. 14.

Birthing Compassion

by Sue Monk Kidd

IN HIS BOOK, *The Power of the Powerless*, Christopher de Vinck tells a simple story:

> *One spring afternoon my five-year-old son, David, and I were plant-*
> *ing raspberry bushes along the side of the garage. . . . A neighbor*
> *joined us for a few moments. . . . David pointed to the ground. . . .*
> *"Look Daddy! What's that?" I stopped talking with my neighbor*
> *and looked down.*
>
> > *"A beetle," I said.*
>
> *David was impressed and pleased with the discovery of this*
> *fancy, colorful creature. My neighbor lifted his foot and stepped on the*
> *insect giving his shoe an extra twist in the dirt. "That ought to do*
> *it," he laughed.*
>
> *David looked up at me, waiting for an explanation, a*
> *reason. . . . That night, just before I turned off the light in his*
> *bedroom, David whispered, "I liked that beetle, Daddy."*
>
> > *"I did too," I whispered back.*[1]

De Vinck concludes this story by saying, "We have the power to choose." So we do. We have the power to choose how we will respond to every living thing that crosses our path, to all the fancy, colorful creatures which God has set in motion upon our fragile planet, from beetles to human beings. Sometimes our feet are quicker than our hearts.

Compassion often eludes me. I remember the time I wept before a television image of a homeless man lying in an American gutter. Three weeks later I stepped over a homeless man on a sidewalk in New York without looking back. Perhaps I gave my shoe an extra twist on the cement, I don't recall. But as I strode away, I had the odd feeling that somewhere Someone was looking at me, waiting for an explanation, a reason.

"Be compassionate as your Father is compassionate" (Luke 6:36, JB). Sometimes I wonder how seriously we have taken these words of

---

[1] Christopher de Vinck, *The Power of the Powerless* (Garden City, NY: Doubleday and Co., 1988), pp. 3–5.

Jesus. I only know there is too much suffering in the world. Too many homeless, hungry, abused, rejected, poor, lonely, sick, grieving, fragmented, defeated, lost, and oppressed. There are too many bombs, too many wars, too many squashed beetles. The world is hip-deep in tears. Compassion is not an option. It is a matter of survival.

Remember the line in *The Little Prince*—"It is only with the heart that one can see clearly"? What renders the heart, even the "good, Christian heart," so full of blind spots? Why is compassion so elusive? Why are our feet sometimes quicker than our hearts?

YOU CAN'T FORCE THE HEART

THE BEGINNING OF AN ANSWER came to me the summer I was twelve, though I scarcely knew it at the time. I had gone to a nursing home with a youth group from my church. Frankly, I was there under duress. My mother had not heard my pleas that I be spared the unjust sentence of visiting a nursing home when my friends were enjoying the last day of summer vacation at the city swimming pool. Smarting from the inequity, I stood before this ancient-looking woman, holding a bouquet of crepe paper flowers. Everything about her saddened me—the worn-down face, the lopsided grin, the tendrils of gray hair protruding from a crocheted lavender cap. I thrust the bouquet at her. She looked at me, a look that pierced me to the marrow of my twelve-year-old bones. Then she spoke the words I haven't forgotten for nearly thirty years. "You didn't want to come, did you, child?"

The words stunned me. They were too painful, too powerful, too naked in their honesty. "Oh yes, I wanted to come," I protested.

A smile lifted one side of her mouth. "It's okay," she said. "You can't force the heart."

I tried to forget her. For a while I hated her for the rebuke. Then I passed it off as the harmless twittering of an old woman. Years later though, as I began to follow the labyrinth of my spiritual journey, I discovered the truth in her words.

You can't force the heart. Genuine compassion cannot be imposed from without. It doesn't happen simply by hearing a sermon on love, or being sent on a loving mission. How often have we set out to love the world—or even more difficult, to love some tiresome, undeserving, mule-headed person on our street—and given up, feeling exasperated, unappreciated, used, tired, burned out or just plain cynical? The point is, you don't arbitrarily make up your mind to be compassionate so much as you choose to follow a journey that transforms your heart into a compassionate space.

Compassion, which is the very life of God within us, comes through slow and often difficult metamorphosis deep within the human soul. It happens through a *process*. If we look closely at the workings of creation, we find that God nearly always works through process and passages. Think of it. First there is a seed, then a sprout, then a blossom, and finally fruit. God does not begin with a butterfly but with a larva that becomes a chrysalis and finally a creature with wings. Neither does God speak a star into existence but sends dust floating in space, then interstellar gas, the slow heating of temperatures, and eons later, a star. Perhaps most mysterious of all is the unfolding process of ovum, fetus, baby, child, adolescent, adult. The universe is designed to move stage by stage, from incompletion to completion. Now why should we suppose that God designed the heart any differently than the rest of creation? It, too, has its stages.

Meister Eckhart, the fourteenth-century theologian and mystic, used imagery which highlighted the truth that divine life, like human life, is implanted internally and comes about through a process of gestation and birth. "We are each meant to be mothers of God," he wrote.[2]

For Eckhart, birthing God essentially meant birthing compassion. He believed compassion to be the ultimate fruit of our birthing, a slow breaking out of divinity from within us. God *is* compassion, he insisted; therefore, as God is born more deeply in the soul, so too is the compassionate life.

The stages and movements in this birthing process entail a gradual shifting of spiritual consciousness. We move from a false and separated way of relating to the world, which I call being in the *Collective They*, to a union with our True Self, which means realizing the *Authentic I*, and finally to a sense of interconnectedness with all that is, which brings us to the birth of the *Compassionate We*.

The movement is portrayed somewhat in a story contained in the charming little book, *Tales of a Magic Monastery*:

> I sat there in awe as the old monk answered our questions. Though I am usually shy, I felt so comfortable in his presence that I found myself raising my hand. "Father, could you tell us something about yourself?"
> He leaned back. "Myself?" he mused. There was a long pause. "My name used to be Me. But now it's You."[3]

[2] Matthew Fox, *Meditations with Meister Eckhart* (Santa Fe, NM: Bear and Co., 1983), p. 74.

[3] Theophane the Monk, *Tales of a Magic Monastery* (New York: Crossroad, 1981), p. 18.

We might ask ourselves what name we wear deep inside. "Our spiritual journey is undertaken in order that we may discover our real name, that is, our true identity," wrote Alan Jones.[4] This identity is found not in the name They, or the name I, but in the name We. As we birth God more fully, we draw on new sets of values and orientations which reshuffle our identity and rename us within. We take on a we-consciousness, which is the deep and sure ground of compassion.

THE COLLECTIVE THEY

THE FIRST NAME we wear, however, is They. It can be startling to realize that much of the time we are not living out of our own unique truth and God-given purpose but from scripts written by culture, friends, family, church, job, and traditions. We spend much of our lives taking on a story for ourselves to live in. Rather than questing for our own individual truth, we may live out the expectations thrust upon us from without. The power of the collective to give us our sole identity and to "author" our lives and our beliefs is enormous. Let me give you a small example of what I mean.

When I was six years old someone asked me, "What do you want to be when you grow up?" At that age, living in a small Georgia town in the 1950s, I could only think of four careers for women—they were the only stories I knew: teacher, nurse, secretary, and housewife. By some process of elimination, I picked nurse. From that moment on, I began to get little nurse kits for my birthdays. The librarian at school set aside the biography of Florence Nightingale for me, and if someone cut their finger, I was called in as the designated bandager. At sixteen, my parents arranged for me to be a volunteer at the local hospital. Everyone expected me to be a nurse, and I was like wet cement taking on the expectations. Indeed I got my BS degree in nursing and worked nine years, even teaching nursing in a college before I stopped and said to myself, "This is not who I am. I am not really a nurse inside. I'm a writer." By that time, the cement had hardened and I had some jack-hammer work to do, breaking up the old name imbedded within and releasing a new identity.

Frequently we take on the scripting of the world in order to protect and serve the ego. We create patterns designed to keep us

---

[4] Alan Jones, *Journey into Christ* (San Francisco: Harper & Row, 1977), p. 110.

invulnerable from the slings and arrows that come whenever we diverge from "they-ness," to borrow philosopher Martin Heidegger's term. I continued with nursing, not because it is a noble profession that stirred my deep gladness but because I did not want to risk upsetting others, not to mention my own, ingrained notion of who I was. I wanted to please. I wanted to protect myself from the uncertainty of starting over. In such ways our consciousness becomes centered in the outer roles and masks we wear, rather than in the True Self within.

I have had to struggle to pull myself from the suction of the Collective They on all sorts of fronts. At various times I have lived out of narrowly prescribed identities which I accepted and internalized from the collective: dutiful and submissive wife, ever-sacrificing mother, armored career woman, perfectionist, pleaser, performer, good little girl who never colored outside the lines drawn for her. Sometimes I was so busy being tuned into outside ideas, expectations, and demands, I failed to hear the unique music in my own soul. I forfeited my ability to listen creatively to my deepest self, to my own God-within. I was wearing the name They.

When I wear this name I am limited in my ability to relate to others in a genuinely compassionate way. I am separated from them by the masks that keep me from being real with them. Stuck in the Collective They, I am more apt to have mixed motives, hidden agendas, a what's-in-it-for-me bottom line. I am apt to relate out of my ego needs, from the subtleties of my false selves and from mandates and demands placed on me from others rather than love born in my own heart.

We are called to unravel the illusions we live with in order to find our true and essential being. Thomas Merton wrote often of the spiritual life as a movement from false selves to the True Self, from fabrications to real identity. He wrote:

> For me to be a saint means to be myself. Therefore the problem of sanctity and salvation is in fact the problem of finding out who I am and discovering my true self. [5]
>
> One's actual self may be far from "real," since it may be profoundly alienated from one's own deep spiritual identity. To reach one's real self, one must in fact be delivered from that illusory and

---

[5] Thomas Merton, *Seeds of Contemplation* (New York: New Directions, 1949), p. 26.

false self whom we have created. . . . To use common figures of speech, we must "return to ourselves." [6]

AN AUTHENTIC I

ONE DAY driving down the street, I asked myself, "Sue Monk Kidd, who are you?" And right away the obvious answers came. "You are Bob and Ann's mother, Sandy's wife, Leah and Ridley's daughter, a writer, a member of Grace Episcopal Church. . . ." All nice things. Then I asked myself, "So, if all those roles were stripped away, *then* who would you be?" The question jolted me. It brought me to stand before the bare mystery of my own being. Was there something deeper at the very core of me that was purely and truly my "I"?

I came to believe, along with many of the mystics of the church, that our true identity goes beyond the outer roles we play. It transcends the ego. I came to understand that there is an Authentic "I" within—an "I-Am" or divine spark within the soul which mystics have called *scintilla animae*. Eckhart wrote:

> *There is something in the soul which is only God. . . . The seed of God is in us. If the seed had a good, wise and industrious cultivator, it would thrive and grow up into God. Now the seed of a pear tree grows into a pear tree . . . the seed of God into God.* [7]

Here is where our real selfhood is rooted, in the divine spark or seed, in the image of God imprinted on the human soul. The real self is not our creation, but God's. It is the self we are in our depths. It is our capacity for divinity and transcendence.

Unraveling external selves and coming home to our real identity is the real meaning of soul work. I remember a time in my life when I actually thought the term "soul work" referred to the evangelistic effort of "winning souls." That hints at how little attention I had paid to the soul as the seedbed of the divine life. I eventually found that the soul is more than an immortal commodity to win and save. It is the seat and repository of the inner Divine, the truest part of us. In fact, when Paul writes, "It is no longer I who live, but Christ who lives in

---

[6] Thomas Merton, *The New Man* (New York: Farrar, Straus and Giroux, 1961), pp. 63–64.

[7] Meister Eckhart, *Breakthrough: Meister Eckhart's Creation Centered Spirituality in New Translation*, introduction and commentary by Matthew Fox (Garden City, NY: Doubleday and Co., 1980), pp. 103, 118.

me" (Gal. 2:20, RSV), I believe he is referring to the crucial soul work of coming home to this Authentic I.

A few years ago, struggling with false selves, wearing masks as if life were a masquerade party, I began to feel the suffocation that happens when we cut ourselves off from the True Self. I went away to Springbank, a Dominican retreat center nestled among live oaks in the low country of South Carolina. I went to try and remember who I really was. I walked in the front door, and there tacked on the wall was a picture of the pregnant Madonna and these words:

> *This image represents each person who is trying to birth the Real Self, the Imago Dei that is taking shape within. For that conception to move to its fullness, we all need time to be quiet, to be reflective, to be centered in our deep places.*

In the Christian mystical tradition, to move from the Collective They to an Authentic I involves setting up an honest dialogue with the soul. It means becoming partakers of solitude, silence, and prayer, particularly contemplative prayer. In these ways, as well as through other spiritual disciplines, we recover the I-Am in the ground of our soul. "Prayer unites the soul to God," wrote Julian of Norwich.[8]

During that retreat, I walked beneath the trees alone with God, alone with my real name, praying wordless prayers, touching the space of mystery, going to my center. That time produced the energy needed to shift my awareness back toward an Authentic I, which is the necessary prelude for real compassion.

A COMPASSIONATE WE

THE EMERGENCE of one's Authentic I awakens a fresh awareness that God is the life of us all and we are one in God together. Without this movement our journey would be in danger of privatism and selfishness. Teresa of Avila taught adamantly that true prayer and uniting with the True Self flows outward in compassion. "It is in the effects and deeds following afterward that one discerns the value of prayer. . . . If we fail to love our neighbor, we are lost," she wrote.[9]

It is inevitable. The journey of birthing God leads to our neighbor. It refocuses our heart-vision. We move from what Paul

---

[8] Julian of Norwich, *Showings*, trans. Edmund Colledge and James Walsh (New York: Paulist Press, 1978), p. 253.

[9] St. Teresa of Avila, *Interior Castle*, trans. Kieran Kavanaugh and Otilio Rodriguez (New York: Paulist Press, 1979), pp. 76, 102.

Tillich referred to as "our essential solitude" into a deeper and more expanded relationship with others and creation. We discover that God so loved the world he gave us one another.

I took part in a retreat once in which the leader gathered the group into a circle and handed out three balls of colored yarn. She asked us to toss the balls back and forth to one another across the circle, each holding onto a piece of it. The result was a beautiful, multi-colored web stretched across the center of the circle. "Each of you take turns and wiggle your thread," the leader instructed. What we found was that every movement vibrated the entire web. And it dawned on me—this immeasurable truth we were portraying. We are each a thread woven into the vast web of the universe, linked and connected so that our lives are irrevocably bound up with one another. I looked at those faces around the circle in a new way. The old adage, "I am my brother's keeper"—or in this case, my sister's keeper—melted into something new: I am my sister. And suddenly I wanted to gather them to me and do what I could to heal them and bless them and affirm to them how beautiful they were.

Such interconnection is what Jesus was getting at when he said, "As you did it to one of the least of these . . . you did it to me" (Matt. 25:40, RSV). This deep knowledge, born from the heart, draws us into a compassionate posture toward the entire cosmos. As Madeleine L'Engle once said to me during an interview, "We need to realize that what we do affects the stars." We are also linked through God's web to humpback whales and hummingbirds and the trees in a rain forest. In the book *The Color Purple* the character Celie said she knew if she cut a tree, her arm would bleed. That is the oneness of wearing the name We.

Living out of the Compassionate We also means blending our tears with the world's in a way that heals and creates community. The word *compassion* literally means *com* (with) *passion* (suffering). Compassion is not, therefore, having a sentimental feeling of pity; it is sharing the pain. It means a "suffering with" that flows from the life of God in the soul, not from ego-motivations.

When compassion wakes up in us, we find ourselves more willing to become vulnerable, to take the risk of entering the pain of others. We open our lives to them in a genuine willingness to be known. We tell them our own story of suffering as a way of offering healing and hope. We feel their heart bleeding into ours; we catch their tears. We relieve their pain as much as we are able, and by relieving theirs, we relieve God's.

Once when I was going through a difficult time, my husband touched his finger to the tears winding down my face, then touched his wet finger to his own cheek. His gesture spoke volumes to me. It said: "Your tears run down *my* face, too. Your suffering aches inside *my* heart as well. I share your wounded place." It is with such compassion that we lift our finger to the world's teary face.

While reading Elie Weisel's book *Night*, which is the chronicle of his suffering in a Nazi concentration camp, I came upon a story that spread before me a metaphoric picture of what it means to live in the Compassionate We as a community.

Nazi soldiers herded the Jews out of their barracks before dawn into a thickly falling snow in order to wait for a train that would transport them to another camp. Without food and drink for three days, the Jews stood in the snow till evening, forbidden to sit or even bend over. The snow formed a layer on their shoulders. One thirsty man took out his spoon and began to eat the snow that had accumulated on the shoulders of the person in front of him. The act spread through the line until that collection of separate individuals, each of whom had been struggling alone with their pain, became a community sharing their suffering together.[10]

I could feel the image burn in my mind, and I knew that in some way this is how we would survive as a human family, by becoming a place of nourishment for our brothers and sisters, by quietly shouldering their pain and their healing. We would survive as we became a We-community, sharing our sufferings in a great and holy act of compassion.

A WOMB FOR COMPASSION

WHEN WE SEEK compassion, we must remember that ultimately the heart cannot be forced. But it *can* become a womb where compassion is gestated and birthed. In fact the Hebrew word for womb and compassion come from the same root word, portraying the connection between them. According to Meister Eckhart we are called to the "divine maternity bed" in the core and ground of the soul. There we birth God. There we birth the name We. And with this holy name we will look with the eyes of the heart at all creatures, great and small, and walk gently upon God's bruised planet.

---

[10] Elie Wiesel, *Night* (New York: Avon Books, 1958), p. 109.

The Kingdom

GOD'S DOMINATION-FREE ORDER

by Walter Wink

D URING MY SOPHOMORE YEAR of college I took my first class in philosophy taught by a devout atheist and materialist. In the face of his seasoned polemic against God and all things religion, the intellectual house of cards that was my adolescent faith collapsed. I was no longer able to believe in God (though I was certain that the God who no longer existed was still calling me into the ministry!).

Toward the close of the spring semester, I was in church, surveying the wreckage of my faith, when I heard—really *heard*—the scripture reading about seeking first God's kingdom and righteousness, and everything else being provided (Matt. 6:25-34). Suddenly it occurred to me: This promise is falsifiable. It can be put to scientific test. During the coming summer I will stake my life on this passage being true, and, if God is real, by the end of the summer I will know. I will act *as if* this statement were true. I will prove or disprove it empirically.

That test proved stunningly successful. I now knew there was a God, freed from the debris of childish expectation. But what, really, was the kingdom of God that I was seeking? For my pietistic bent, it seemed to be a completely personal relationship with God—not so much a kingdom as a private audience.

Seminary and graduate studies enlarged the compass of the kingdom by giving it historical perspective. Israel's long agony with kingship, its yearning for a righteous nation, its visions of a coming benevolent divine rule, were met by Jesus' proclamation that the kingdom of God was indeed dawning in his own ministry. My teachers helped me to understand *where* the kingdom was and *when* the kingdom was, but not *what* the kingdom was.

Where is the kingdom? Already in our midst, wherever anyone is liberated or healed or exorcised or forgiven or transformed. Where is the kingdom? Already inside of you, in your soul, your depths, the

---

moment you receive into yourself the reality that Jesus proclaimed.

Thus the hotly disputed reading of Luke 17:21, "the kingdom of God is *entos* you" (which can be translated either as "the kingdom of God is *within* you" or "the kingdom of God is *among* you" or "in the midst of you") is wrongly regarded as an either/or. It can only be both/and. That, at least, is how the earliest commentary on the verse puts it: "The kingdom of God is inside of you, and it is outside of you."[1] The reign of God cannot just be inner or outer; it must be both or it is neither.

When is the kingdom? It is, my teachers demonstrated, past, present, and future. God has reigned, reigns, and will reign. In the formula of the Book of Revelation, God is the one who is and who was and who is to come (Rev. 1:4). The kingdom was manifested in the life of Israel and the ministry of Jesus. It has been seen, fitfully, in the history of the church. It happens today, whenever people in the thrall of addiction or the power of delusion or the gall of hatred are liberated to their true lives. And it will come in all its fullness and power at the consummation of history. In an even tighter formula, the kingdom is already/not yet. And, we learned, "kingdom" is not as helpful a translation as "reign," which stresses the exercise of God's sovereign power more than the area or domain over which it presides.

All that was helpful, and right, as far as it went. But when I asked, *what* is this "reign," the answers became thin. Re-reading the books of that era, I am struck by how similar to my privatized pietism was the German theology that dominated the post-war epoch. Here was a generation that had been through the worst carnage in the history of the world, and they could write page after page with never so much as an allusion to that searing bloodbath through which they all had come.

I found this astonishing. It was clear that the "reign of God" of these German theologians had very little to do with the real lives of people suffering oppression, deprivation, or death. Instead, they spoke interminably about a fairly minor theme in scripture, justification by grace, as if by constant reiteration they could persuade themselves that their complicity in or compliance with Nazism could be forgiven. Of course it could! But why not just come right out and *confess* it, rather than forever going on about justification by grace, as if the theological principle could take the place of public acknowledgment of guilt?

This highly individualistic notion of God's reign was at last mercifully shattered by black, liberation, and feminist theologies. Born

---

[1] Gospel of Thomas 3.

in situations of extremity and injustice, these new approaches enabled us, for the first time, to grasp the political dimension of God's reign. God was not simply attempting to rescue individuals from their sufferings at the hands of an unjust system, but to transform the system so as to make and keep human life more human.

Despite all of these advances in understanding, however, I still was puzzled. I had a better handle on the reign of God, but still lacked any kind of precision. Was this reign simply the acknowledgment of God's supremacy in one's heart? But how was that different from my pietistic origins? Was it the establishment of a just order "on earth, as it is in heaven," as the Lord's Prayer puts it? But every such utopian effort has ended miserably, even catastrophically. Very few people still believe that the corporations and institutions and political systems that grow rich at the expense of the multitude (the "principalities and powers") will voluntarily relinquish their advantage. So many of those who have hurled themselves against the ramparts of evil have been cut down like flowers.

PERHAPS WE NEED TO START all over again from the beginning. "Kingdom" in scripture refers to the regnant political order: an authoritarian system in which the king ruled supreme. The Hebrew root behind king and kingdom means "to possess, to own exclusively." Kingship seems to have arisen with the great conquest states, around 3000 B.C.E. As these massive empires spread from Mesopotamia, they brought with them hierarchical power relations, unjust economic relations, oppressive political relations, ranking, aristocracy, taxation, standing armies, and war. Violence became the preferred means for adjudicating disputes.

Kingship was not, then, a primordial arrangement, but a rather late arrival. And it was especially late arriving in Israel. Having had their fill of the oppression of kingship when they were slaves in Egypt, the Hebrews attempted to develop egalitarian politics and economics. By means of the sabbath year and jubilee legislation, they sought to institutionalize their slave revolt. Debts were to be canceled every seven years in order to prevent foreclosure of land, slaves were to be freed, and the land was to lie fallow. Every forty-nine (or fifty) years, rural property sold to satisfy debts was to be restored to its ancestral owners. Much of this legislation was ignored in various periods of Israel's life. But the intention was clear: to prevent the large disparity between rich and poor from taking hold in Israel.

More important for this discussion, there was to be no king in

Israel. Yahweh alone would be their leader. Interestingly, Yahweh was never called "king" prior to the rise of the monarchy in Israel. Likewise, most pre-monarchical houses were of roughly the same modest size, whereas after the monarchy began there were palaces and hovels. When the people requested a king at last, Samuel warned them of the consequences: an aristocracy, military conscription, a standing army, a military-industrial complex to make weapons, taxation to support it all, the enslavement or forced enrollment of sons and daughters to serve the king, the seizure of lands and goods under royal pretext (1 Sam. 8). But the people persisted, and the rest of Israel's history, down to the Babylonian exile, is the sad tale of power politics played out with all the intrigue and injustice of the pagans. Israel, called to be different than the nations, had become a nation like all the rest. It had entered fully into the worldwide network of principalities and powers that I call the Domination System.

ISRAEL'S PROPHETS began to look to the future for the end of human kingship and the restoration of God's direct rule. Or they dreamed of a new line of David that would avoid all the evils that David's actual line had caused. Not surprisingly, the hope for a future king or anointed one is infrequent in the Hebrew scriptures, and missing altogether in the Psalms. Having been burned repeatedly, many were ambivalent or downright negative about bringing back an institution that had been the source of so much misery.

The immediate context of the New Testament was not the Jewish kingship, which was defunct during most of that period, but rather the Roman imperium. The expression "kingdom of God" is actually fairly rare in the Hebrew Bible and the later Jewish writings. With Jesus, however, that phrase suddenly became central. Against the kingdom of Rome the early Christians proclaimed the kingdom of God. Against Caesar's imperial rule they placed God's imperial rule. "Kingdom of God" thus needs to be seen in its political context. It is a counter-assertion, against the hegemony of the Roman empire, that Rome and its pretenders are not ultimate, that God's rule will prevail in the affairs of the world, and that Jesus' followers owe allegiance to none other than God. Like many other counter-assertions, however, "kingdom of God" was in time twisted into a legitimation of divine kingship, both of God's totalitarian rule and the rule of God's regents on earth.

But there is an even more decisive context for the gospel. Rome, after all, was only the latest in a long line of empires that had straddled the world. It was not Rome alone, but the Domination System itself that was the problem. Jesus' message has traditionally been treated as a timeless, eternal, contextless teaching proclaimed in a sociopolitical vacuum. But his teaching and deeds are directed at a specific context: the Domination System. Jesus' message is a context-specific remedy for the evils of the Domination System.

"Kingdom of God" had always seemed to me to be an empty expression. It denoted God's rule, but gave no indication as to what that rule entailed. It was Riane Eisler, a Jew whose family barely escaped Austria after the Nazi takeover, who enabled me to see for the first time the world-historic significance of Jesus' proclamation of the kingdom. Since the rise of the conquest states five thousand years ago, she observes in *The Chalice and the Blade*, no one has articulated such a consistent critique of domination as the Jew Jesus. The Hebrew prophets had, to be sure, already envisioned elements of his program, and Socrates had anticipated certain aspects of his critique, but no one came close to matching Jesus' perception of the nature of the Domination System and what was needed to replace it. That new alternative he called the "kingdom of God." In order to specify its actual content I paraphrase that expression as "God's domination-free order."

What were the elements of that critique? Virtually every statement in the Gospels! No summary can capture the vast sweep of Jesus' vision. Do yourself a favor: Read straight through the four Gospels noting every reference to domination and its cure. When I first did that, I was staggered. I could scarcely sleep at night. I had never seen it before, and it was right there, waiting to be recovered.

Here are only a few items in his critique.

JESUS AGAINST DOMINATION

Jesus repeatedly attacked domination in all its forms:

A dispute also arose among them [the disciples] as to which of them was to be regarded as the greatest. [Jesus] said to them, "The kings of the Gentiles lord it over them; and those in authority over them are called benefactors. But not so with you; rather the greatest among you must become like the youngest, and the leader like one who serves. For who is greater, the one who is at the table or the one who serves? Is it not the one at the table? But I am among you as one who serves."

(Luke 22:24-27, NRSV)

JESUS DOES NOT CONDEMN ambition or aspiration; he merely changes the values to which they are attached: "Whoever wants to be first must be last of all and servant of all." He does not reject power, but only its use to dominate others. He does not reject greatness, but finds it in identification and solidarity with the needy at the bottom of society (Matt. 5:3-12; Luke 6:20-23). He does not renounce heroism, but expresses it by repudiating the powers of death and confronting the entrenched might of the authorities unarmed.

His rejection of domination hierarchies could scarcely be more complete than when he taught, astonishingly, "Happy are those servants whom the master finds awake when he comes. Truly I tell you: He will hitch up his robe, seat them at table [literally, 'have them recline,' as at a formal banquet or feast], and come and wait on them" himself (Luke 12:37)!

These are the words and deeds not of a minor reformer, but of an egalitarian prophet who repudiates the very premises on which domination is based: the right of some to lord it over others by means of power, wealth, shaming, or titles. In his beatitudes, his healings, his table fellowship with outcasts and sinners, Jesus declares God's special concern for the oppressed.

His followers are not to take titles: "But you are not to be called rabbi, for you have one teacher, and you are all students. And call no one your father on earth, for you have one Father—the one in heaven. Nor are you to be called instructors, for you have one instructor" (Matt. 23:8-10, NRSV). His followers are to maintain domination-free relationships in a discipleship of equals that includes women. The hierarchical relationship of master and slave, teacher and student is not to persist. "I do not call you servants any longer, because the servant does not know what the master is doing; but I have called you friends" (John 15:15, NRSV).

Jesus' actions embody his words. According to the Fourth Gospel, Jesus washes the disciples' feet, a task considered so degrading that a master could not order a Jewish slave to perform it (John 13:1-20).

ECONOMIC EQUALITY

THE GOSPEL OF JESUS is founded on economic equality because economic inequities are the basis of domination. Ranking, domination hierarchies, and classism are all built on accumulated power provided by excess wealth.

Breaking with domination means ending the economic exploitation of the many by the few. Since the powerful are not likely to abdicate their wealth, the poor must find ways to transcend the Domination Epoch while still in it. So Jesus adapts the sabbath year legislation by challenging creditors not only to forego interest, but to ask no repayment whatever. To those who wish to follow him, he counsels selling everything, and warns the rich that they have no access whatever to the new society coming (Mark 10:17-27). To the religionist's dream of being able to be "spiritual" and still amass wealth within an unjust system, Jesus pronounces an unconditional No: "You cannot serve God and wealth" (Matt. 6:24; Luke 16:13, NRSV).

His followers were to begin living now "as if" the new order had already come, seeking first God's reign and God's justice. Jesus and his disciples lived from a common purse. The early church "had all things in common, and they sold their possessions and goods and distributed them to all, as any had need" (Acts 2:44-45).

It is the poor whom God elects and blesses, the meek and brokenhearted and despised who will inherit God's coming reign on earth. It is the merciful not the mighty, the peacemakers not the warriors, the persecuted not the aristocrats, who will enter into the joy of God (Matt. 5:3-12; Luke 6:20-26).

In parable after parable, Jesus speaks of the reign of God using images drawn from farming and women's work. It is not described as coming from on high down to earth; it rises quietly and imperceptibly out of the land. It is established not by aristocrats and military might, but by an ineluctable process of growth from below, among the common people.

In sum, Jesus is not looking for a kingdom for himself or anyone else where power can be wielded in order to *impose* God's will on the world. He is inaugurating a domination-free society.

NONVIOLENCE

AN EGALITARIAN SOCIETY presupposes nonviolence. For violence is the way some are able to deprive others of what is justly theirs. Inequality can only be maintained by violence.

Jesus repudiates violence. Luke depicts the disciples requesting permission to call down fire from heaven on inhospitable Samaritans; Jesus rebukes them (9:51-56). When a disciple cuts off the ear of the high priest's slave in an attempt to save Jesus from arrest, Jesus is shown commanding, "No more of this!" (Luke 22:51, NRSV)—an injunction the church took literally for the next three centuries. Matthew has

Jesus say, "Put your sword back into its place; for all who take the sword will perish by the sword" (Matt. 26:52, NRSV). Turning the cheek, stripping naked, carrying a soldier's pack the second mile (Matt. 5:39-41) do not at all mean acquiescing passively in evil, but are a studied and deliberate way of seizing the initiative and overthrowing evil by the force of its own momentum.

The last supper and the crucifixion display Jesus' nonviolent breaking of the spiral of violence by absorbing its momentum with his own body. What Jesus distilled from the long experience of his people in violent and nonviolent resistance was a way of opposing evil without becoming evil in the process. He advocated means consistent with the desired end: a society of justice, peace, and equality free of authoritarianism, oppression, and ranking. His method and his goal incarnated God's domination-free order.

These are but a sample of Jesus' critique of domination. Jesus also directed that critique against the law, which was intended to mitigate violence and injustice, but which had been subverted by the Domination System and made to serve the powerful, the wealthy, and the shrewd. He prophesied the end of the temple, with its reliance on sacral violence and its depiction of God as requiring blood in order to be appeased for human sin. He broke with the laws of *ritual purity* by means of which Israel kept itself separated from the Gentiles; as a consequence, the church opened its doors to Gentiles without requiring that they first become Jews. He criticized the *family* for its role in perpetuating the patriarchal system. And most remarkable of all, he related to *women* in total disregard for the mores of his society, declaring them full members of the household of God and equal with men.[2]

This, then, is something of Jesus' answer to the Domination System. As I mentioned earlier, the "good news" is Jesus' context-specific remedy for the evils of the Domination System. Only as we see the Domination System as the context to which the gospel was addressed do we begin to grasp something of the content of what Jesus meant by "the kingdom of God." Where is God's reign? Wherever domination is overcome, people freed, the soul fed, God's reality known. When is God's reign? Whenever people turn from the idols of power and wealth and fame to the governance of God in a society of equals. What is God's reign? It is the transformation of the Domination System into a nonviolent, humane, ecologically sustainable, livable

---

[2] All this is treated in considerably more detail in my book *Engaging the Powers* (Philadelphia: Augsburg Fortress Press, 1992).

environment fashioned to grow people and grow them well.

The meaning of God's "kingdom" is thus incredibly simple: It is the coming of God's domination-free order. That is a message so elementary that even a small child can understand it. It means, for children, no more beatings; for women, no more battering and rape; for men, no more violence and war.

This message has never been more relevant. The world has never been more needy.

Power, Powerlessness, *and* Power

by Henri J. M. Nouwen

S ITTING IN A PLANE and looking down on broad landscapes filled with rivers, lakes, and mountains, with winding roads and little villages, it is easy to wonder why it is so hard for people to live peacefully together on our earth. The astronauts, seeing our blue planet from their space shuttle, were so overwhelmed by its beauty that it seemed impossible to believe that its inhabitants were busy destroying one another's homes and killing one another through war and exploitation.

Distance sometimes helps us gain a sharper vision of our human condition and raise some critical questions. I would like to take a look at our world from a distance—not from the physical distance of a plane or a space vehicle, but from the spiritual distance of our faith. I want to look at us human beings from above, with the eyes of God. Jesus always looked at the human condition from above and tried to teach us to look as he did. "I come from above," he said, "and I want you to be reborn from above so that you will be able to see with new eyes" (see John 3:1-3, NJB). This is what theology is all about. It is to look at the rich variety of all that is with the eyes of God and so discern the way to live.

I want to offer you a theology of weakness. I want to look with God's eyes at our experience of brokenness, limitedness, woundedness, and frailty in the hope that such a vision will offer us a safe way to travel on earth. I will focus on three words: power, powerlessness, and power. I first want to explore the power that oppresses and destroys. Then I want to show how that power is disarmed through powerlessness. Finally, I want to proclaim the true power that liberates, reconciles, and heals.

THE ILLUSION OF POWER

W HEN GOD looks at our world, God weeps because the lust for power has entrapped and corrupted the human spirit. Instead of gratitude there is resentment; instead of praise there is criticism; instead of forgiveness there is revenge; instead of healing there is wounding; instead of compassion there is competition;

instead of cooperation there is violence; instead of love there is fear.

God weeps at the sight of our beautiful planet with thousands of maimed bodies lying on battlefields, lonely children roaming the streets of big cities, prisoners locked behind bars and thick walls, mentally ill men and women wasting their time in the wards of large institutions, and millions of people dying from starvation and neglect. God weeps because God knows the anguish we have brought upon ourselves by wanting to take our destiny in our own hands and by lording it over others.

When we look around us and within ourselves with the eyes of God, it is not hard to see the all-pervading lust for power. Why are Serbs killing Moslems? Why are Protestants and Catholics throwing bombs at each other? Why was the president of Sri Lanka murdered, the prime minister of Belgium kidnapped, and why did the political leader of France commit suicide?

Let's look into our own hearts! Aren't we constantly concerned with whether we are noticed or not, appreciated or not, rewarded or not? Aren't we always asking ourselves whether we are better or worse, stronger or weaker, faster or slower than the one who stands beside us? From elementary school onward haven't we experienced most of our fellow human beings as rivals in the race for success, influence, and popularity? As soon as our own safety is threatened, we tend to grab the first stick or gun available, telling ourselves that our survival is what really counts even if thousands of others are not going to make it. Aren't we so insecure that we will snatch at any form of power that gives us a little bit of control over who we are, what we do, and where we go? I know my sticks and guns. Sometimes my stick is a friend with more influence than I; sometimes my gun is money or a degree; sometimes it is a little talent that others don't have; and sometimes it is special knowledge, or a hidden memory, or even a cold stare. I will grab it quickly and without much hesitation when I need it to stay in control. And before I realize it, I have pushed my friends away.

God looks at us and weeps because, wherever we use power to gain a sense of self, we separate ourselves from God and each other. Our lives then become "diabolic" in the literal meaning of that word: "divisive."

But there is something worse than economic and political power. It is religious power. When God looks at our world, God not only weeps but is also angry—angry because many of those who pray, offer praise, and call God "Lord" are also corrupted by power. In anger God says: "These people honor me only with lip service, while their hearts are far from me. Their reverence of me is worthless; the lessons they teach are nothing but human commandments" (Isa. 29:13, NJB).

The most insidious, divisive, and destructive power is the power exercised in the "service" of God. I am overwhelmed by the number of people who have been wounded by religion. An unfriendly word by a minister or priest, a critical remark in church about a certain lifestyle, a refusal to welcome people at the Lord's table, an absence during an illness or death, and countless other religious hurts often remain longer in people's memories than other more secular rejections. Thousands of separated and divorced men and women, numerous gay and lesbian people, and all of the homeless people who have felt unwelcome in the houses of worship of their brothers and sisters in the human family— all these and more have turned away from God because they experienced the abuse of power when they expected an expression of love.

The devastating influence of power in the hands of God's people becomes clear when we think of the crusades, the pogroms, the policies of apartheid, and the long history of religious wars. Less obvious is that many contemporary religious movements create the fertile soil for these immense human tragedies to happen. In these days of economic and political uncertainty, one of the greatest temptations is to use our faith as a way to exercise power over others and thereby supplant God's commandments with human commandments.

It is easy to understand why so many people have turned away in disgust from anything vaguely connected with religion. When power is used to proclaim good news, good news soon becomes bad news. And that makes God angry. But God looks at our world not with sad and angry eyes only; God is merciful, and God's mercy is far greater than God's sadness and anger. As the psalmist says: "God's anger lasts but a moment" (Psalm 30:5, NJB). In an all-embracing mercy God chooses to disarm the power of evil through powerlessness— God's own powerlessness.

POWERLESSNESS

WHAT WAS AND IS God's response to the diabolic power that rules the world and destroys the people and their land? God chose powerlessness. God chose to enter into human history in complete weakness. That divine choice forms the center of the Christian faith. In Jesus of Nazareth, the powerless God appeared among us to unmask the illusion of power, to disarm the prince of darkness who rules the world, and to bring the divided human race to a new unity. It is through unmitigated powerlessness that God shows us divine mercy. The radical, divine choice is the choice to reveal glory, beauty, truth, peace, joy, and, most of all, love in and through the complete divestment of power. It is hard, if not impossible, for us to grasp this divine mystery. We keep praying to the "Almighty God." But all might is absent from the one who reveals God to us saying: "Whoever has seen me has seen the Father" (John 14:9, NRSV). If we truly want to come to love God, we have to look at the man from Nazareth whose life was wrapped in weakness. His weakness opens for us the way to the heart of God.

People with power do not evoke intimacy. We fear people with power. They can control us, and force us to do what we don't want to do. We look up to people with power. They have what we do not have, and can give or refuse to give according to their will. We envy people with power. They can afford to go where we cannot go, and do what we cannot do. But God does not want us to be afraid, distant, or envious. God wants to come close, so that we can rest in the intimacy of God like children in their mothers' arms.

Therefore God became a baby. Who can be afraid of a baby? A baby is completely dependent on its parents, nurses, and caregivers. How can you fear a baby you rock in your arms? How can you look up to a baby that is so small and vulnerable? How can you be envious of a baby that only smiles at you in response to your tenderness? Yes, God wanted to become so powerless that eating or drinking, walking or talking, playing or working would be impossible without people's help. Yes, God became dependent on human beings for growing up and proclaiming the Good News. Yes, indeed, God chose to become so powerless that the fulfillment of God's own mission among us became completely dependent on us. That's the mystery of the incarnation. God became human, in no way different from other human beings, to break through the walls of power in total weakness. That's the story of Jesus.

And how did that story end? On a cross, where the same human person hung naked with nails through his hands and feet. The power-lessness of the manger became the powerlessness of the cross. People jeered at him, laughed at him, spit in his face, and shouted: "He saved others; he cannot save himself. He is the king of Israel; let him come down from the cross now, and we will believe in him" (Matt. 27:42, NJB). He hung there, his flesh torn apart by lead-filled whips, his heart broken by rejection by his friends and abuse from his enemies, his mind tortured by anguish, his spirit shrouded in the darkness of abandonment—a ravaged portrait of total weakness, total powerlessness. That's how God chose to reveal to us the divine love, bring us back into an embrace of compassion, and convince us that anger has been melted away in endless mercy.

But there is more to be said about the powerlessness of God revealed in Jesus of Nazareth. There is not only a powerless birth and a powerless death, but, strange as it may seem, a powerless life.

Jesus, the powerless child of God, was blessed in powerlessness. When, after a hidden life in Nazareth, Jesus began his ministry, he first offered us a self-portrait (Matt. 5:3-10). "Blessed are the gentle," he said. Jesus did not break the bruised reed. He always cared for the little ones. "Blessed are those who mourn," he said. Jesus did not hide his grief, but let his tears flow when his friend died and when he foresaw the destruction of his beloved Jerusalem. "Blessed are those who hunger and thirst for justice," he said. Jesus didn't hesitate to criticize injustice and to defend the hungry, the dying, and the lepers. "Blessed are the merciful," he said. Jesus didn't call for revenge but always and everywhere healed. "Blessed are the pure in heart," he said. Jesus remained focused only on what was necessary and did not allow his attention to be divided by many distractions. "Blessed are the peace-makers," he said. Jesus did not stress difference, but reconciled people as brothers and sisters in one family. "Blessed are those who are persecuted," he said. Jesus did not expect success and popularity, but knew that rejection and abandonment would make him suffer.

The Beatitudes are Jesus' self-portrait. They represent a portrait of the powerless God. It is this portrait that we glimpse wherever we see the sick, the prisoners, the refugees, the lonely, the victims of sexual abuse, the people with AIDS, and the dying. It is through their powerlessness that we are called to become brothers and sisters. It is through their powerlessness that we are called to deepen our bonds of friendship and love. It is through their powerlessness that we are challenged to lay down our weapons, offer each other forgiveness, and make peace. And it is through their powerlessness that we are constantly reminded of Jesus' words: "You foolish people, is it not necessary to suffer and so enter into glory?" (see Luke 24:25-26, NJB). Indeed, God's powerlessness and the powerlessness of the human race, of which God became part, have become the door to the house of love.

THE POWER OF LOVE

OUR WORLD IS RULED by diabolic powers that divide and de-stroy. In and through the powerless Jesus, God disarmed these powers. However, this mystery confronts us with a new and difficult question: How do we live in this world as witnesses to a powerless God and build the kingdom of love and peace?

Does powerlessness mean that we are doomed to be doormats for our power-hungry society? Does it mean that it is good to be "soft," passive, subservient—always allowing the powers of darkness to dominate our lives? Does it mean that economic weakness, organizational weakness, physical and emotional weakness have now, suddenly, become virtues? Does it mean that people who are poorly educated, poorly organized, and poorly prepared for their tasks can now brag about their poverty as a blessing that calls for gratitude? When we read Paul's words: "My strength is made perfect in weakness" (2 Cor. 12:9, KJV), do we imagine that we are dealing with a weakling who uses his low self-esteem as an argument to proclaim the Gospel?

We touch here on one of the most dangerous traps of a theology of weakness. If we can become free from the enslaving powers of the world only by being enslaved by weakness, what kind of freedom is that? If a theology of weakness becomes a theology for weaklings, then such a theology is a comfortable excuse for incompetence, submissiveness, self-denigration, and defeat in all fields!

This is far from a theoretical possibility. Financial, intellectual, and spiritual weakness is sometimes interpreted as a divine privilege; competent medical or psychological help may be delayed or avoided in the conviction that it is better to suffer for God than not to suffer; careful planning, aggressive fund raising, and intelligent strategizing for the future are frowned on as lack of faithfulness to the ideal of powerlessness; the sick, the poor, the handicapped, and all who suffer too often have been romanticized as God's privileged children without much support to free them from their fate. Friedrich Nietzsche, the nineteenth-century German philosopher, rightly criticized a theology of weakness. For him it was a theology that kept the poor in their poverty and gave the rulers of the religious establishment a chance to keep their "faithful" in a state of subservient obedience. Indeed, there is a spirituality of powerlessness, of weakness, of littleness that can be extremely dangerous, especially in the hands of those who feel they are called to speak and to act in God's name. Of them, Jesus says: "They tie up heavy burdens and lay them on people's shoulders, but will they lift a finger to move them?" (Matt. 23:4, NJB).

A theology of weakness challenges us to look at weakness not as a worldly weakness that allows us to be manipulated by the powerful in society and church, but as a total and unconditional dependence on God. This evangelical weakness opens us to be true channels of the divine power that heals the wounds of humanity and renews the face of the earth. A theology of weakness claims power—God's power, the all-transforming power of love. A theology of weakness shows God weeping for the human race entangled in its power games and angry that these same power games are so greedily used by so-called religious people. A theology of weakness shows how God unmasks the power games of the world and the church by entering into history in complete powerlessness. But a theology of weakness wants, ultimately, to show that God with immense mercy offers us the divine power to walk on the earth confidently, with heads erect.

God is powerful. Jesus didn't hesitate to speak about God's power. He said: "In truth I tell you, there are some standing here who will not taste death before they see the kingdom of God come with power" (Mark 9:1, NJB). Wherever Jesus went there was the experience of divine power. Luke writes: "Everyone in the crowd was trying to touch him because power came out of him that cured them all" (Luke 6:19, NJB). When a woman who had suffered from a hemorrhage for twelve years touched the fringe of Jesus' cloak, trusting that Jesus would cure her, Jesus said: "Somebody touched me. I felt that power had gone out from me" (Luke 8:46, NJB). Jesus was filled with God's power. Jesus claimed for himself the power to forgive sins, the power to heal, the power to call to life—yes, all power. The final words he directed to his friends are full of this conviction. He said: "All power in heaven and on earth has been given to me. Go, therefore, make disciples of all nations" (Matt. 28:18, NJB).

Power is claimed, and power is given. In and through the powerless Jesus, God wants to give us the power that Jesus had and send us into the world to cast out demons, to heal the sick, to call the dead to life, to reconcile the estranged, to create community, and to build the kingdom of God. A theology of weakness is not a theology for weaklings but a theology for men and women who claim for themselves the power of love. It is this power that frees them from fear and enables them to put their light on the lampstands and do the work of the kingdom. Yes, we are poor, gentle, mourning, hungry and thirsty for justice, merciful, pure of heart, peacemakers, and persecuted by a hostile world. But we are not weaklings, not doormats. The kingdom of heaven is ours, the earth our inheritance. We are comforted, have our fill, experience mercy, are recognized as God's children, and see God. That's power, real power—power that comes from above.

You and I are called to move from power to power through powerlessness. As fearful, anxious, insecure, and wounded people we are tempted constantly to grab the little bit of power the world offers us. These threads of power make us puppets jerked up and down until we are dead. But insofar as we dare to be baptized in powerlessness, always moving towards the poor who have no worldly power, we will be plunged right into the heart of God's endless mercy. We will be free to reenter our world with the same divine power with which Jesus came. We will be able to walk in the valley of darkness and tears, unceasingly in communion with God, with our heads erect, confidently standing under the cross of our life.

It is this power that engenders leaders for our communities, women and men who dare to take risks and new initiatives. It is this power that enables us to be not only gentle as doves but also as clever as serpents in our dealings with governments and church agencies. It is this power that allows us to talk straight and without hesitation about money with people who have financial resources, to call men and women to radical service, to challenge people to make a long-term commitment, and to keep announcing the Good News everywhere and at all times. It is this divine power that enables us to become saints who can make all things new.

BECOMING SAINTS

ARE THERE ANY DISCIPLINES to keep us moving from dividing power to uniting power, from destructive power to healing power, from paralyzing power to enabling power? Let me suggest three disciplines that can help us look from above with the eyes of God.

The first discipline is to focus continually on the poor in this world. We must keep asking ourselves: Where are the men, women, and children who are waiting for us to reach out to them? Poverty in all its forms—physical, intellectual, and emotional—is not decreasing. On the contrary, the poor are everywhere around us. As the powers of darkness show their hideous intentions with increasing crudeness, the weeping of the poor becomes louder and their misery more visible. We have to keep listening. We have to keep looking.

The second discipline is to trust that God will truly care for the poor that are given to us. We will have the financial, emotional, and physical support we need, when we need it, and to the degree that we need it. I am convinced that there is a large body of people ready to help with money, time, and talent. But that body will remain invisible unless we dare to take new risks. If we want to have all our bases covered before we act, nothing exciting will happen. But if we dare to take a few crazy risks because God asks us to do so, many doors, which we didn't even know existed, will be opened for us.

The third discipline is the hardest one. It is the discipline of being surprised not by suffering but by joy. What was true for Peter will be true for us: As we grow older, we will have to stretch out our arms and allow ourselves to be led to places we would rather not go (see John 21:18). There is suffering ahead of us, immense suffering, a suffering that will continue to tempt us to think that we have chosen the wrong road and that others were more shrewd than we. But don't be surprised by pain. Be surprised by joy. Be surprised by the little flower that shows its beauty in the midst of a barren desert. And be surprised by the immense healing power that keeps bursting forth like a spring of fresh water from the depth of our pain. With an eye focused on the poor, a heart trusting that we will get what we need, and a spirit always surprised by joy, we will be truly powerful. We will walk through this valley of darkness performing miracles because it is God's power that will go out from us wherever we go and whomever we meet.

Let me conclude with a little story about John and Sandy. John and Sandy are two very simple people. We all have Johns and Sandys among us. One day John said to Sandy, "We've never had an argument. Let's have an argument like other people have." Sandy asked, "But how can we start an argument?" John answered, "It's very simple. I take a brick, and say, 'It's mine,' and then you say, 'No, it's mine,' and then we have an argument." So they sat down and John took a brick and said, "This brick is mine." Sandy looked gently at him and said, "Well, if it's yours, take it." And so, they could not have an argument.[1]

As long as we keep bricks in our hands and speak about mine and thine, our little power games gradually will escalate into big power games and our big power games will lead to hatred, violence, and war. When we look at life from below, our fears and insecurities lead us to grab bricks wherever we can. But when we dare to let go of our bricks, empty our hands, and raise them up to the One who is our true refuge and our true stronghold, our poverty opens us to receive power from above, power that heals, power that will be a true blessing for ourselves and for our world.

---

[1] A contemporary rendering of a story from the tradition of desert spirituality. See *The Wisdom of the Desert Fathers*, trans. and intro. by Sister Benedicta Ward, S.L.G. (Oxford: SLG Press, 1975), p. 60.

This article is published as a separate booklet by Crossroad.

An All-Embracing Love

by Esther de Waal

WHAT DOES IT MEAN to say in western society today that we are members one of another? For many that must have a hollow ring. The concluding sentence of a recent article describing life in New York today catches the atmosphere not only of life in a big city but widespread elsewhere: "I am all the time looking over my shoulder." If we are no longer at ease with each other, neither are we at home with the earth itself, the mother whom we have exploited, abused, dishonored. Nor, finally, are we at home with ourselves; and the journey on which we pursue that lost self seems to go deeper and deeper into an apparently bottomless pit. On my most recent transatlantic flight I had an experience that I find repeated time and again. A young man sitting next to me handed me the book which he said had the answer to all life's problems. One glance was enough to show that it said little that had not been said before, and probably said better, on the subject of self-help and self-fulfillment. We search to find a sense of interconnectedness at all levels, but the thirst that drives us on remains unquenched.

Reading the scriptures and above all saying the psalms remind us of what our highly individualistic and cerebral society has forgotten. For Israel the cosmos was a whole, a community in which everything had its place, a community in which God delighted as all the creatures of God's creating, human and nonhuman, were woven into one web, a web in which all the strands held together, interrelated and interconnected, their fine tuning resting in the hand of God. Here men and women, orphans and strangers, animals and plants all had their territories within the soil community. Humans and everything else fitted into place like the pieces of a jigsaw puzzle, each one touching a neighbor and through that neighbor the whole.[1]

The price we have paid for the neglect of this vision is only too apparent as we watch not only the ecological and environmental crises that now surround us but also the social exploitation (whether open or hidden) which denies many millions of people the chance to live lives of full human dignity. There is an uncanny resemblance between

---

[1] See Edward P. Echlin, "Christian Wholeism Within Creation Under God," *The Month* (November, 1990), pp. 450–457.

the way we handle the earth and the way we handle people—neglect or failure of respect in the handling of one seems to parallel neglect and lack of reverence for the other. "It seems as though it is only in recent times that we have come to realize fully how extensive and how essential the intercommunion between earth and person really is." This opening sentence of a newsletter from a center of Christian spirituality in Australia shows that this awareness is worldwide. And yet it has always been there. The rational mind of the west, with its scholastic and cerebral approach, has overlaid something that was early, primal, fundamental in our consciousness. This awareness has also been present in our Christian tradition, and it is time to reappropriate this part of our heritage.

BOUND INTO THE WHOLE

THE CELTIC PEOPLES, coming as they did from the earliest roots of Christianity, knew a closeness to the earth as they knew also a closeness to one another in their rural and tribal society. When asked by the heathen to tell them something of his God, St. Patrick, the great figurehead of the Celtic church, does not reply with some credal statement of belief. He answers them with this great creation affirmation, a song of praise which celebrates the whole of the universe as being a whole, the work of a loving creator God.

> *Oh God, God of all men,*
> *God of heaven and earth, seas and rivers,*
> *God of sun and moon, of all the stars. . . .*
> *He has a dwelling in heaven and earth and sea*
>   *and in all things that are in them.*
> *He inspires all things, he quickens all things,*
> *He is over all things, he supports all things.* [2]

Patrick himself, as he tells us in his *Confession*, had first learned to pray when he lived for ten years in Ireland as a slave looking after herds in all seasons and all weathers, wrestling with the elements day and night, and turning this into prayer. This is the kind of praying that unites a person with the earth itself. It finds magnificent expression in St. Patrick's Breastplate, yet another affirmation of the unity of the

---

[2] *Prayers and Praises in the Celtic Tradition*, ed. A. M. Allchin and Esther de Waal, (Springfield, IL: Templegate Publishers, 1987), p. 20.

whole created order that binds men and women into the whole. Here we see all the powers, angels and archangels, patriarchs, prophets and apostles, and so on to the sun and moon, fire, wind, sea, earth, and rock, until at last there is each one of us created, enfolded in Christ.

Handed on in oral tradition from generation to generation in Ireland and in Scotland, this sense of our total humanity was kept alive in the Celtic lands even if elsewhere it became neglected, forgotten, overlaid. At the end of the last century, Gaelic scholar Alexander Carmichael toured the highlands and western isles of Scotland and talked with the local men and women who lived there. He found that at the start of each day a mother would teach her children to stand outside the house and listen to the birds as they celebrated the end of darkness and the dawning of a new day. The mother would ask the children if we humans could be dumb when the creatures themselves greeted the light in this way? Also she would teach them to celebrate the new day, the totality of creation—first the universe itself and then each one of us within that universe—using the homely imagery of making cloth, which would be a familiar part of the family livelihood.

I believe O Lord and God of the peoples,
That thou art the creator of the high heavens,
That thou art the creator of the skies above,
That thou art the creator of the oceans below.

I believe O Lord and God of the peoples
That thou art He who created my soul and set its warp,
Who gave to my body breath, and to my soul its possession.[3]

Delight in this all-embracing love can only lead to a response of gratitude, an outpouring of praise in the face of such generosity. Another morning prayer from the Outer Hebrides ends with these words:

Each day may I remember the source of the mercies
Thou hast bestowed on me gently and generously.

Each thing I have received from Thee it came,
Each thing for which I hope, from Thy love it will come,

---

[3] *The Celtic Vision*, ed. Esther de Waal (Petersham, MA: St. Bede's Publications, 1990), p. 20. This is a selection of poems, prayers, and blessings from Carmichael's six volume work, *Carmina Gaelica*.

Each thing I enjoy it is of Thy bounty,
Each thing I ask comes of Thy disposing.[4]

In the round of daily work which followed, in farming and fishing, in the household chores, in milking, spinning, weaving, or whatever it might be, the Celtic peoples would do what had to be done and yet at the same time see beyond the action to God. Each activity was undertaken with care, with integrity, and with the awareness that it was an occasion for finding the presence of God and for actually doing the task in partnership with God. In this way the Celtic peoples became co-creators with God. Noel Dermot O'Donoghue, telling us of his experience of growing up near Killarney in Ireland, describes a very simple example of how this consciousness would transform one of the most ordinary of actions in everyday life. If you visited a house where the people were in the middle of churning, you would enter with the greeting "God's blessing on the work." Then you would take the churn staff in your hand and strike the cream with it a number of times, helping the cream to break into good butter. And this ritual, although so completely ordinary and mundane, carried depth of meaning. It was a sharing in the work and in the community created by that work, but it was also an involvement of men and women in the process of creation itself.[5]

Just as there was a daily pattern of prayer and blessing, so there was a yearly rhythm in which each succeeding activity on the land carried its own ritual. When the farmer went out to sow his seed, his work was equally labor and liturgy; he was his own priest. Sowing always took place on a Friday because Friday was the day of death and burial and Christ, who is king of Friday, is the seed of the new world of the resurrection of men and women and of nature. The Celtic peoples never forgot that creation comes with pain. The gift of creation and the pain of the gift were received with equal thanksgiving. The skies, the winds, the weather may bring abundance but they may also bring blight or famine. If we are to rediscover a sense of our place within the whole created order, it is vital not to forget this perspective. Otherwise we allow ourselves to escape into something that can easily become facile and romantic. If our lives are intertwined one with another and with the whole, then we must also expect to share in the pain, confusion, and suffering of the whole.

---

[4] *The Celtic Vision*, p. 34.

[5] Noel D. O'Donoghue, "Celtic Creation Spirituality," *The Month* (November, 1990), p. 421.

Perhaps we can see this particularly clearly in the poetry of the early Celtic hermits. The destiny of their eremitical vocation led them to live the life of the desert not in the sandy wastes of Egypt but in remote and isolated parts of Wales, Ireland, Scotland (which still to this day are called *disserth* or *dysart*). Here deep in woods, on a lonely island, or perched high on a cliff face, they found themselves in places of quite outstanding and extraordinary beauty. They, before anyone in Europe, had a vision of the natural world in an almost unnatural purity. It was a vision that came from lives of prayer, prayer which united them with the world. Their lives became intertwined with the times, colors, and rhythms of the life around them, with the changing light of day and night and with the birds and the beasts who became their friends, perhaps even their co-hermits. This life of renunciation was also a life totally fulfilled. It is caught for us in this imagined dialogue between King Guaire of Connacht (d. 663) and his half brother, the hermit Marban. When the king asks Marban why he no longer sleeps upon a feather quilt, he gives an answer that becomes an apologia for the hermit life.

> *I have a bothy in the wood—*
> *none knows it save the Lord my God;*
> *one wall an ash, the other hazel,*
> *and a great fern makes the door.*
>
> *The door posts are made of heather,*
> *the lintel of honeysuckle;*
> *and wild forest all around*
> *yields mast for well-fed swine.*
>
> *This little secret humble place*
> *holds tenure of the teeming woods;*
> *maybe you will come to see?—*
> *but alone I live quite happy.*[6]

Marban lives alone and yet has not made himself separate from the world. The life of solitude is far removed from lonely individualism. Only because hermits have learned to be at home in themselves can they also be totally at home in the world. Hermits carry within

---

[6] Another translation is to be found in *Prayers and Praises in the Celtic Tradition*, p. 30.

both the joy, the pain, and fractures of that world. The cell becomes a microcosm of the world where, as in the world, there is constant struggle. So the hermit also writes of wailing to heaven, of frequent showers of tears, of a cold, anxious bed. To be part of common creation is to be part of the anguish of the world. "The heart is but a small vessel," writes St. Macarius, "and yet dragons and lions are there, and there are poisonous creatures and all the treasures of wickedness; rough, uneven paths are there, and gaping chasms. There likewise is God, there are the angels, there life and the Kingdom, there light and the apostles . . . all things are there."[7] Here is a real opening up to the whole universe—to the birds, the plants, and the animals no less than the sun, the moon, the stars, and not least, to men and women. All become brothers and sisters, part of common creation. In some mysterious way, relating to the great diversity of creatures was also relating to the whole of oneself, a fraternizing with the obscure parts of one's own self, the inner darkness and the inner depths. Thus the inner world becomes as open as the outer, a world without walls and without frontiers.

---

[7] Quoted in Igumen Chariton of Valamo, *The Art of Prayer: An Orthodox Anthology*, trans. E. Kadloubovsky and E. M. Palmer, ed. and intro. by Timothy Ware (London: Faber & Faber, 1966), p. 19.

Horizonal Persons

by E. Glenn Hinson

*Do not be conformed to this world, but be transformed by the renew-
ing of your minds, so that you may discern what is the will of God—
what is good and acceptable and perfect.*

—Romans 12:2 (NRSV)

THIS MEDITATION concerns "horizonal persons." By "horizonal"
I mean persons who can look beyond the horizon of their
age and culture and see what God is trying to bring into
being. I mean what Paul means in Romans 12:2, persons not simply
shaped in the mold of their own age but transformed by a recycling of
their understanding so that they have a sense of what is God's will—
what is good and acceptable to God and contributes to God's ultimate
purpose.

Our age needs horizonal persons. Arnold Toynbee, the dis-
tinguished metahistorian, observed in a volume published on his
eightieth birthday that this civilization we are creating poses the
greatest threat to our survival as persons of any civilization which has
existed since our ancestors became human. Using a biblical parody, he
went on to say that, whereas nature chastised us with whips, this
civilization is chastising us with scorpions. "A change of heart is the
heart of the matter."

NOT SHAPED IN THE MOLD OF THIS AGE

HORIZONAL PERSONS are, in the first place, persons not shaped
solely in the mold of the age and culture in which they live.
To some extent, of course, we are all shaped in the mold of
our age and culture; otherwise, we could not contribute to and benefit
from that culture. Our parents induct us into our culture's ways.
Teachers carry that process farther.

Sometimes our culture does too good a job on us. It beats,
hammers, molds, engraves until we become its captives. This molding
process begins in our earliest years and continues throughout the rest
of our lives. Twenty years ago, for instance, my daughter joined the
Barbie set. We bought a Barbie doll. That was a very innocent thing

to do, for Barbie cost only $3.85. But Barbie came without any clothes. You can't let Barbie go around naked; we bought a Barbie dress. If Barbie was going to be a real American lady, she couldn't get by on one dress; we bought a Barbie wardrobe. If Barbie had a Barbie wardrobe, she had to have Barbie furniture; we bought Barbie furniture. If she had Barbie furniture, she had to have a Barbie house; we bought a Barbie house. If she had a Barbie house, she might get stuck at home too much; we bought a Barbie car. Sometimes Barbie needed to get away on longer weekends; we bought a Barbie camper. When Americans grew sensitive to ecological concerns, Barbie joined them; in this case a friend gave my daughter a Barbie bicycle.

Art Buchwald, the noted political humorist, estimated that in eleven years with Barbie, his daughter spent hundreds of dollars. I have recently learned that one can buy the whole set for $261, but the price is not the main point. The point is how culture shackles us, how it shapes us in its mold. How do we attain liberation from our chains?

TRANSFORMED BY A RECYCLING OF UNDERSTANDING

THIS IS WHERE the second characteristic of "horizonal persons" enters the picture. "Horizonal persons" are persons transformed by a recycling of their understanding.

Paul uses here the Greek way of looking at our problem. In the Greek view the human mind (*nous*) is the source of thought, attitudes, and behavior. If we are not to be *con*formed to the age and culture in which we live, we must be *trans*formed by a recycling or renewal of understanding. The key to liberation lies in *recycling of the understanding*. How is that effected? Experience suggests two ways. One is by education and the other by conversion.

To shape the mind in certain ways is the primary purpose of education. The higher persons climb up the educational ladder, the more they should gain critical perspective and from thence freedom to choose. Education forces persons to compare and contrast their culture's ways with the customs of other cultures and to evaluate them under that searchlight. In time it should snip away some of culture's cords that hold people in thrall.

Many critics, however, point out that in the United States higher education doesn't always do what it is supposed to do. Often it reinforces cultural stereotypes and models. Indeed, Theodore Roszak has indicted American higher education for creating and perpetuating "the single vision"—the way of empirical observation and rational reflection and neglecting and negating what he calls "the powers of transcendence." Recently, Yale professor of law Stephen Carter has charged that the judicial and legislative branches of American government, contrary to the intentions of the founding fathers of the country, stack the deck *against* religion in virtually every realm of American public life, but especially the schools, and thus assure the triumph of secularity.

We do not have to look far to discover how "the single vision" has come to dominate American higher education and then to pervade the rest of the public educational system. American educational institutions were founded originally by the churches and served mainly religious purposes. When Americans created the "land-grant colleges," now the state universities, they directed them to supply "knowledge for use"—knowledge which would increase production and offer direction in elevating the standard of living for all Americans.

Public institutions of higher learning have effectively met the demands of the American public. Unfortunately, as they have supplanted church-supported educational institutions in determining the course of instruction at all levels, they have not tried to balance the empirical/rational powers with the "powers of transcendence," and most church-related schools have felt compelled to follow in their train. The net result is serious neglect of the humanities in which the powers of the artist and the poet and the contemplative would receive a fair amount of attention. Allocation of federal moneys to higher education points up the priorities. During the sizzling sixties, forty percent went to military, thirty-seven percent to medical, twenty percent to other sciences, and three percent to social sciences.[1] Nothing went to humanities, unless you count the training of CIA agents in foreign languages as humanities. Those who pay the piper called the tune, and they did not ask for studies which would enhance "the powers of transcendence."

Such benign neglect is why another approach is required. Some may cringe a bit at the sound of the word conversion, for it has often taken on trite and superficial meanings in the American context— walking down a sawdust trail, taking a preacher's hand, and filling out a membership card. Consequently, we would do well to be sure we understand the concept behind the word.

---

[1] Clark Kerr, *The Uses of the University* (New York: Harper & Row, 1963), p. 54.

Paul associated conversion with radical change, not just once but for the rest of one's life. In his own case the persecutor stopped trying to halt the Christian movement and became its ardent advocate and fearless friend, filling up, he told the Colossians, "what is lacking of the sufferings of Christ in his own flesh on behalf of Christ's Body, the Church" (Col. 1:24, AT).

Conversion focuses particularly on recycling of understanding. "In Christ there is a new creation. The old [humanity] has passed away, the new has come" (2 Cor. 5:17, AT). Believers seek "that mind which was also in Christ Jesus" (Phil. 2:5). No longer does the human personality and inclination prevail. Rather, the living, ascendant Christ in us determines and directs thought and attitudes and behavior, for we have in ourselves "the mind of Christ."

HAVING A SENSE OF GOD'S WILL

THE NET RESULT of this transformation through recycling of understanding is to "have a sense of what is God's will, what is good, acceptable to God, and contributes to God's ultimate purpose." No goal, surely, has inspired human hearts more, yet also generated greater frustration, than the desire to know and to do the will of God. Much of the latter may stem from misunderstanding of the concept.

Many conceive of the will of God as a track laid out before them which, if they will get on it and stay on it, will assure that their lives run smoothly, but, if they jump off of the track, will bring only sadness and despair and lead to wreck and ruin. Others think of the will of God as a blueprint which, if properly read and followed, will help them build a sturdy house in which they may live safely and happily.

The Apostle to the Gentiles gave a different twist to this concept. In his letters the will of God, what pleases God, or what is acceptable to God has to do with what kind of persons we are, with attitude and outlook. God wants us to be persons who live our lives from the vantage point of a covenant with God through and in Jesus Christ, conscientized and sensitized and tenderized by love, making the very best decisions we can make in the circumstances in which we find ourselves.

In 1 Thessalonians 4:3 Paul tells husbands that God's will is their "sanctification," that they treat their wives as persons rather than as objects for their sexual gratification. In the next chapter he says that the will of God is to "rejoice always, pray incessantly, [and] give thanks in every circumstance" (5:16, AT). In both instances the will of God has to do with attitude and outlook conditioned by the indwelling Christ.

In the "household code" of Ephesians, obviously sensitive to strongly felt betrayal of the gospel's promise of liberation, slaves are directed to serve human masters "as Christ" without hesitancy and not to act like the proverbial slaves who did only what they had to and sought to retaliate as often as they could. Christian slaves should serve Christian masters as if they served Christ and not human beings, thus "doing the will of God soulfully (*ex psyches*)" (Eph. 6:6). Once again, the will of God is a matter of attitude, outlook, sensitivity. God is interested in what kind of persons we are and will be quite content with any number of choices we, like children, may make. Indeed, Paul perceived here one of the central paradoxes of the Christian life.

In Philippians 2:12-13 he fingered that paradox pointedly: "Work out your own salvation with fear and trembling, for it is God who is effecting in you both the motive and the ability to do what pleases God." Notice what Paul does *not* say, that is, that God will *choose* for you. God has created us "in God's own image and likeness" (Gen. 1:27, AT), capable of making our own choices. God has given us a share in God's own creative and redemptive work and asked us to exercise our freedom responsibly. God is pleased when we seek God's counsel, like earthly parents are pleased when their children do the same, but God will not decide for us.

Yet, paradoxically, God does supply two boosts—motive and ability to do what pleases God. Grace, according to Augustine, *adds* something to nature; it does not replace it. If we open like a flower opening to the morning sunshine, God will pour love energies into our vital centers so that we may do far more than we could ever expect to do. "Horizonal persons," then, are not simply persons who have not been completely shaped in the mold of the age in which they live. They are also transformed by a recycling of understanding so that they may open to the beams of God's love. To sharpen the picture, I will single out one such person, the Quaker saint John Woolman.

John Woolman was born in 1720 in West Jersey. A sensitive child reared in a devout Quaker home, at age twelve or thirteen he did something which further sandpapered his sensitivities to the world around him. Walking one day, he spied a mother robin feeding her young on the nest. Impulsively, he picked up a rock and hurled it at the mother robin. The rock struck the mother robin and killed her. John Woolman learned that one act of cruelty often exacts another.

To keep the babies from starving, he had to climb up and kill them too.

At age twenty John Woolman began working for a Quaker merchant as a clerk. In that capacity he had to write a bill of sale for a female African American slave. He did so with pangs of conscience, explaining to the owner and purchaser that he was "not easy" to do that. But he overrode a tender conscience.

At age twenty-six John Woolman started traveling around the colonies as a "minister" in the Society of Friends. On this first journey he witnessed the plight of persons held in bondage against their wills. From that time until his death of smallpox in England in 1772, he spent about one month out of every year traversing the colonies to plead with Quakers to free their slaves. He became what I would call a "quiet revolutionary."

Lest he become so "encumbered by the affairs of this life" that he could not follow God's leading, he gave up a prosperous merchandising business of his own and earned his living as a tailor. He stopped wearing dyed suits because the dye for coloring men's suits came from indigo, a product of slave labor. He no longer used sugar, rum, or molasses made in the West Indies, for they too were produced by slavery. Yet, loving and sensitive soul that he was, he worried lest too many follow his example and bring greater hurt to those he wanted to help. In 1763 he gave up riding on horseback or in carriages because slaves could not ride. When he stayed in a Quaker home where there were slaves, as he prepared to leave in the morning, he would press some money into his hosts' hands and ask them to give it to a slave so that the latter could buy his or her freedom.

Little by little, John Woolman gained new and profound insight into the chief source of injustice. He saw it in the way whites broke treaties they made with Indians. He saw it on his trip to England in 1770 in the way shippers took advantage of sailors—virtually shanghaiing them into service, working them long hours in awful conditions, and paying pitiful wages. He saw it too in England in the stagecoach traffic. To make time, drivers whipped the horses mercilessly. Often, on a long run, horses went blind or dropped dead in the harness. And young post boys, hired to post the mail, froze to death riding outside the coach in winter or were maimed or killed falling under the wheels as the stage lurched forward before they could get a secure grip after posting the mail. John Woolman refused to ride stage coaches or even to post mail by them.

In all of these matters John Woolman discerned that injustice resulted not so much from deliberate intention to harm as from *insensitivity*, from *unthinking*. Slave owners, at least Quaker owners, usually did not deliberately try to hurt slaves; they simply let their desire for comforts and conveniences, what Woolman labeled "superfluities," override their sensitivities to other human beings. If we lived by *agape*-love, if we lived by the Golden Rule, he insisted, we could not act without thinking about how what we did impacted the lives of others.

John Woolman did not live to see the end of slavery even among Quakers. Nonetheless, he did not allow the magnitude of the slavery problem to deter him from throwing his straws into the wind. He lived with Romans 8:28 steadying his course, the conviction that "in everything God is working together for good with those who love God, with those who are called according to God's purpose" (AT). For him this meant that small efforts matter. And thanks largely to the persistent "horizontal" efforts of John Woolman, by 1787 (note the date!) no American Quaker owned a slave.

Not many, perhaps none, of you who read these words will walk the high plateau John Woolman traveled. The world has not seen many equals. Yet can you and I, too, not act on "horizonal perceptions," living with sensitivities sharpened to the way our desires and our actions impact the lives of others not merely in the United States but around the world? Can we, for instance, go on driving gas guzzlers knowing that we who make up six percent of the world's population consume more than forty percent of all energy produced annually? Can we, for another instance, continue long honored habits of consuming high protein foods such as beef knowing that it takes eight times as much cereal grain fed through beef cattle to produce a certain amount of protein than if we ate the grain directly?

Obviously in both cases we can, but not if we are acting on "horizonal perceptions," sensitized and tenderized to the way what we are doing impacts the whole creation. And our age needs persons who act on horizonal perceptions. It needs churches, government agencies, political parties, and groups of many kinds who will do so. The call is God's; the challenge is ours.

Contributors

BRUCE C. BIRCH is professor of Old Testament at Wesley Theological Seminary. He is an ordained member of the Baltimore Annual Conference of The United Methodist Church and teaches frequently in various church settings. His most recent book is *To Love As We Are Loved.*

ROBERTA C. BONDI is professor of Church History at Candler School of Theology at Emory University in Atlanta. A graduate of Oxford University, she has a particular interest in the spirituality of early monasticism and is currently working on a book entitled *Houses,* a collection of family stories. She is also the author of *Memories of God: Theological Reflections on a Life, To Love as God Loves,* and *To Pray and To Love: Conversations on Prayer with the Early Church.*

ELIZABETH J. CANHAM, an Episcopal priest, is director of Stillpoint Ministries, a retreat center in Black Mountain, NC. She is a graduate of London University and also holds the D.Min. in creative ministry from Graduate Theological Foundation of Indiana. She leads workshops and retreats, teaches in two seminaries, and acts as a local church consultant. She is the author of *Pilgrimage to Priesthood, Praying the Bible,* and *Journaling with Jeremiah,* and co-author of *Where Love and People Are.*

ESTHER DE WAAL is an Anglican lay woman living on the borders of Wales. Her main interests lie in the fields of Benedictine and Celtic spirituality, and she gives retreats and writes widely in both these areas. Her most recent book on the Celtic tradition is *Every Earthly Blessing.*

DEBORAH SMITH DOUGLAS holds degrees in literature and law, and has served the Presbyterian Church (USA) as deacon, elder, and teacher. She has deep affinity for the sacramental and mystical theologies of the Anglican and Roman Catholic traditions and writes and speaks on spiritual issues for a variety of Christian periodicals and organizations. She lives in Santa Fe, NM with her husband and their daughters.

ELIZABETH A. DREYER is associate professor in the Department of Ecclesiastical History at the Washington Theological Union in Silver Springs, MD. She is the author of *Passionate Woman: Two Medieval Mystics, Manifestations of Grace,* and *Earth Crammed With Heaven: A Spirituality of Everyday Life.*

TILDEN EDWARDS, an Episcopal priest, is executive director of the Shalem Institute for Spiritual Formation in Bethesda, MD. He is the author of six books on the spiritual life including *Living in the Presence* and *Sabbath Time.*

E. GLENN HINSON is John F. Loftis professor of Church History and professor of Spirituality at Baptist Theological Seminary in Richmond, VA. He taught more than thirty years at The Southern Baptist Theological Seminary in Louisville, KY. He has written extensively in both Church history and spirituality. Recent writings include a new edition of *A Serious Call to a Contemplative Lifestyle* and *Spirituality in Ecumenical Perspective*. Hinson also serves on the advisory board of *Weavings*.

GEFFREY B. KELLY, STD, is professor of systematic theology at La Salle University in Philadelphia. Since 1974 he has been secretary of the International Bonhoeffer Society, English Language Section. He is the author of *Karl Rahner: Theologian of the Graced Search for Meaning* and *Liberating Faith: Bonhoeffer's Message for Today*. Also, he is co-author of *A Testament to Freedom: The Essential Writings of Dietrich Bonhoeffer*.

SUE MONK KIDD, a popular speaker and retreat leader, is the author of five books on spirituality. Her most recent publication is *When the Heart Waits: Spiritual Direction for Life's Sacred Questions* (Harper & Row, 1990).

HENRI J. M. NOUWEN is a Roman Catholic priest of the Diocese of Utrecht, Holland. He is a spiritual director of Daybreak, the L'Arche community near Toronto, Canada. Widely known as a speaker and retreat leader, he has a special interest in Latin America and has made several trips to that region. He is the author of numerous books, including *Our Greatest Gift* and *Here and Now*.

PARKER J. PALMER is an independent writer, teacher, and activist. He travels widely in the U.S. and abroad giving workshops and retreats on spirituality, community, education, leadership, and social change. His books include *To Know As We Are Known* and *The Active Life*. He holds a Ph.D. in sociology from the University of California at Berkeley.

WILLIAM O. PAULSELL is presently senior minister at North Christian Church in Columbus, IN. His publications include *Taste and See: A Personal Guide to the Spiritual Life, Letters from a Hermit, Tough Minds, Tender Hearts,* and numerous articles.

C. GORDON PEERMAN, III, is an Episcopal priest and pastoral counselor living in Nashville, TN. He holds degrees from the University of Virginia, Yale University, and Vanderbilt University.

K. C. PTOMEY, JR., has served as the pastor of Westminister Presbyterian Church, Nashville, TN, since 1981. He has published articles on liturgy and preaching in *Weavings, The Presbyterian Survey,* and *Reformed Liturgy and Music*.

GAIL RAMSHAW, a scholar of liturgical language, is a graduate of Valparaiso University (B.A.), Sarah Lawrence College (MA), the University of Wisconsin (Ph.D.), and Union Theological Seminary, New York (M.Div.). Her publications include *God Beyond Gender, Christ in Sacred Speech*, and *Worship: Searching for Language*, and numerous articles and liturgical helps.

DON E. SALIERS teaches theology and worship and is director of the Masters of Sacred Music Program at Emory University. Among his recent publications are *Worship As Theology: Foretaste of Glory Divine, The Soul in Paraphrase: Prayer and the Religious Affections,* second edition, and as co-author, *The New Handbook for the Christian Year.*

MARJORIE J. THOMPSON is an ordained minister of the Presbyterian Church (USA). Currently she serves as adjunct faculty for Vanderbilt Divinity School and teaches regularly in the United Methodist Academy for Spiritual Formation. She is the author of *Family: The Forming Center* and *Soul Feast: An Invitation to the Christian Spiritual Life*, and regularly contributes to *Weavings*, an ecumenical journal of the Christian spiritual life. Other of her writings have appeared in *Worship, The Upper Room Disciplines,* and *The Abingdon Preacher's Annual.*

EVELYN UNDERHILL (1875-1941) was an Anglican, a mystic, and a pioneer among twentieth century women in the church and the spiritual life. She was a worker in the war effort of World War I and a pacifist in World War II. She was the author of approximately forty books.

THOMAS WARD is presently Chaplain of the University of the South, Sewanee, TN. He has served Episcopal parishes in Mississippi and Tennessee, most recently Christ Church, Nashville.

WALTER WINK is professor of Biblical Interpretation at Auburn Theological Seminary in New York City. Previously, he was a parish minister and taught at Union Theological Seminary in New York City. In 1989—1990 he was a Peace Fellow at the United States Institute of Peace in Washington, DC. He is the author of numerous books including *Engaging the Powers: Discernment and Resistance in a World of Domination.*

WENDY M. WRIGHT holds a Ph.D. from the University of California at Santa Barbara and currently teaches on the Theology faculty at Creighton University. She also teaches regularly in several graduate ministerial programs including Seattle University's SUMORE program, Creighton's Christian Spirituality Master's program, and the United Methodist Academy for Spiritual Formation. Her expertise falls in the areas of history of spirituality, family spirituality, spiritual direction, and women and spirituality. Her academic work has focused on the Salesian spiritual tradition founded by Francis de Sales and Jane de Chantal. She is the author of numerous publications including two by Upper Room Books: *The Vigil: Keeping Watch in the Season of Christ's Coming* and *The Rising: Living the Mysteries of Lent, Easter, and Pentecost.*

Index

The following is a guide to the articles in this collection which indicates where they originally appeared in Weavings.

THE WORK OF THE PEOPLE: INVOLVING
THE CONGREGATION IN LITURGY
K. C. Ptomey, Jr., Vol. IV/4 (July/August 1989)

SPEAKING THE TRUTH IN LOVE
Thomas Ward, Vol. III/4 (July/August 1988)

ANGER: AN INSTRUMENT OF PEACE
C. Gordon Peerman, III, Vol. IX/2 (March/April 1993)

THE PASTOR AS SPIRITUAL GUIDE
Tilden Edwards, Vol. II/4 (July/August 1987)

DESERT LISTENING
Wendy M. Wright, Vol. IX/3 (May/June 1994)

THE CLEARNESS COMMITTEE: A WAY OF DISCERNMENT
Parker J. Palmer, Vol. III/4 (July/August 1988)

Commonweal

SHARING IN THE PAIN OF GOD: DIETRICH BONHOEFFER'S
REFLECTIONS ON CHRISTIAN VULNERABILITY
Geffrey B. Kelly, Vol. VIII/4 (July/August 1993)

BIRTHING COMPASSION
Sue Monk Kidd, Vol. V/6 (November/December 1990)

THE KINGDOM: GOD'S DOMINATION-FREE ORDER
Walter Wink, Vol. X/1 (January/February 1995)

POWER, POWERLESSNESS, AND POWER
Henri J. M. Nouwen, Vol. X/1 (January/February 1995)

AN ALL-EMBRACING LOVE
Esther de Waal, Vol. VIII/3 (May/June 1993)

HORIZONAL PERSONS
E. Glenn Hinson, Vol. X/2 (March/April 1995)

Playboy and the Making
of the Good Life in Modern America

PLAYBOY

and the MAKING of the GOOD LIFE in MODERN AMERICA

Elizabeth Fraterrigo

OXFORD

UNIVERSITY PRESS

2009

131218

OXFORD
UNIVERSITY PRESS

Oxford University Press, Inc., publishes works that further
Oxford University's objective of excellence
in research, scholarship, and education.

Oxford New York
Auckland Cape Town Dar es Salaam Hong Kong Karachi
Kuala Lumpur Madrid Melbourne Mexico City Nairobi
New Delhi Shanghai Taipei Toronto

With offices in
Argentina Austria Brazil Chile Czech Republic France Greece
Guatemala Hungary Italy Japan Poland Portugal Singapore
South Korea Switzerland Thailand Turkey Ukraine Vietnam

Copyright © 2009 by Oxford University Press, Inc.

Published by Oxford University Press, Inc.
198 Madison Avenue, New York, New York 10016

www.oup.com

Oxford is a registered trademark of Oxford University Press.

Library of Congress Cataloging-in-Publication Data
Fraterrigo, Elizabeth.
    Playboy and the making of the good life in modern America / Elizabeth Fraterrigo.
        p.   cm.
    Includes bibliographical references and index.
    ISBN: 978-0-19-538610-3
    1. Playboy Enterprises.   2. Playboy (Chicago, Ill.)   3. United States—Social
conditions—1945—   4. United States—Moral conditions—20th century.   5. Social change—
United States—History—20th century.   6. Arts and society—United States—History—20th
century.   7. Liberalism—Social aspects—United States—History—20th century.   I. Title.
    PN4900.P5F73 2009
    051—dc22   2009011643

9 8 7 6 5 4 3 2 1

Printed in the United States of America
on acid-free paper

ACKNOWLEDGMENTS

Many individuals and institutions have provided generous assistance for this book and I am pleased to have the opportunity to express my gratitude to them in these pages. I would like to thank the librarians and archivists of the Charles Deering McCormick Library of Special Collections at Northwestern University; the Chicago History Museum; the Kinsey Institute for Research in Sex, Gender, and Reproduction, Inc.; Lied Library at the University of Nevada, Las Vegas; the E.M. Cudahy Memorial Library of Loyola University Chicago, and the Schlesinger Library at Harvard University. I am also grateful for the help of several people at Playboy Enterprises, especially Lee Froelich, who facilitated access to company archives in Chicago, and Steve Martinez, who helped me navigate collections at the Playboy Mansion in Los Angeles. Marcia Terrones oversaw requests for permission to reproduce material from the magazine. Jill Boysen deserves many thanks for her patience and diligence in tracking down images for the book. Special thanks go to Leroy Neiman, whose work "At Ease" graces the dust jacket. Lastly, I thank Hugh Hefner for allowing me to peruse his personal scrapbooks and for graciously agreeing to be interviewed for this book.

At several stages of research and writing, I was fortunate to have received financial support from the following sources, for which I am grateful: the Arthur J. Schmitt Dissertation Fellowship and the DePersis-Urbanek Fellowship in Women's History from Loyola University Chicago; the Carter Manny Dissertation Award from the Graham Foundation; a Summer Fellowship from the College of Liberal Arts at the University of Nevada, Las Vegas; and funding from the history department at UNLV for travel to collections. I also wish to thank Ed Shoben, former dean of the College of Liberal Arts at UNLV, and Eugene Moehring, former history department chair, for granting a course reduction during the 2006–07 academic year that provided much-needed time to work on the book.

During its earlier life as a dissertation, this project benefited from the wisdom and support of many people. Susan Hirsch's graduate course on women's and gender history inspired my initial thinking about the history of masculinity and bachelorhood. Patricia Mooney-Melvin never let me forget that careful thinking and clear prose go hand in hand. Where I approach clarity in these pages, she deserves much credit. By chance, Lew Erenberg had a box of old *Playboy*s in his office at a crucial moment when I was casting about for a topic in his graduate seminar, and I learned from him the value of thinking critically about popular culture as a meaningful site of expression. I am grateful not only for his guidance of the dissertation that grew out of that seminar, but also for his encouragement and advice as I transformed the dissertation into this book. I also wish to thank my fellow history graduate students as well as the members of the Women's Studies Graduate Scholars Program at Loyola University Chicago, who provided intellectual companionship as this project first took shape and helped make graduate school a fulfilling experience. The Newberry Library Urban History Dissertation Group provided helpful feedback as well as a forum for intellectual engagement while I was writing.

Las Vegas has served as a fascinating setting in which to ponder capitalism, consumption, sexuality, and self-indulgence—themes that suffuse this book—and for many years, the history department at the University of Nevada, Las Vegas, provided a welcome and rewarding environment in which to do so. Faculty, staff, and students in the history department supported this project in various ways. I am thankful to many for reading and commenting on material or for offering helpful advice, especially Gene Moehring, David Wrobel, Mary Palevsky, David Holland, Yuma Totani, and Marcia Gallo. My late colleague, Willard Rollings, and his wife, the late Barbara Williams-Rollings, saved me many trips to special collections by providing me with a cache of *Playboy*s after I remarked that it would be helpful to have the magazine on-hand as I worked on the book. Joanne Goodwin, Andy Kirk, Greg Brown, Kevin Dawson, Kathy Adkins, and Lynette Webber offered encouragement and shared my enthusiasm for this project over the years. Stimulating discussions with students in my fall 2007 colloquium on gender history and in my fall 2008 course on American popular culture energized me as I reworked parts of the manuscript. Leisl Carr Childers cheerfully carved time from a busy schedule to read page proofs. Michelle Lettieri coaxed me away from the computer for much-needed and rejuvenating breaks. Special thanks go to my friends and colleagues Michelle Tusan and Elizabeth White Nelson. Michelle Tusan gave helpful feedback on portions of the manuscript, along with constant encouragement and sage advice that kept me on track. Elizabeth White Nelson read multiple drafts, asked probing questions, and offered thoughtful comments that vastly improved this work.

I owe her a special debt for her unflagging interest in this project, even when my own energy was waning, and for making her constructive criticism all the more palatable by dispensing it along with delicious and memorable meals.

I am also enormously grateful for the insightful comments and suggestions from the readers for Oxford University Press, which enriched and helped shape this book. At OUP, Susan Ferber has been a patient guide through every stage of the publishing process and her skillful editing has much improved the manuscript. Jessica Ryan deserves thanks for shepherding the book through the production process and Stacey Hamilton for her careful copyediting.

Many friends and family members now know a great deal about *Playboy*, and I am grateful to all of them for their kind patience over many years as the conversation turned yet again to this book. I am especially thankful for the enduring friendship of Maureen McMahon and Brian Skaggs, who have provided, in addition to a place to stay in Los Angeles, much laughter and many fond memories over the years. My parents, Fred and Louise Fraterrigo, have been a constant source of support and encouragement, and my mother deserves special thanks for patiently allowing me to vacillate between my incessant talk about this book and my requests that she not ask how it was coming along.

Finally, I owe my greatest debt of gratitude to my husband, Ray Clifford, who has lived with my distractions and endless rumination about *Playboy* and postwar America for quite some time. This book simply would not exist were it not for his patient support, encouragement, endless humor, and love, which have sustained me throughout this project. This hardly makes up for any of it, but Happy Birthday!

CONTENTS

Playboy and the Making
of the Good Life in Modern America

INTRODUCTION

IN THE EARLY 1960s, a journalist reported on the growing number of "girly" magazines "entrapping young American men in a Never-Never Land, where bachelorhood is a desired state and bikini-clad girls are overdressed, where life is a series of dubious sex thrills, where there's a foreign sports car in every garage, a hi-fi set in every living room, and 'Home Sweet Home' is a penthouse pad."[1] *Playboy* stood as her quintessential example. Launched by Hugh M. Hefner in 1953, *Playboy* promoted an image of the young, affluent, urban bachelor—a man in pursuit of temporary female companionship and a good time, without the customary obligations of marriage or fatherhood. And by the end of the decade, the urbane world of glamorous living and sexual excitement presented in its pages was glimpsed by some one million readers each month. *Playboy* and the values it represented garnered significant attention. Competitors tried to duplicate the magazine's winning formula. Advertisers targeted acquisitive, aspiring young playboys, showcasing the profusion of fine things money could buy. Stylish, sexually magnetic bachelors loomed larger than life in motion pictures. Supporters praised the magazine's celebration of the libertine spirit, while detractors condemned it for the nudity and freewheeling lack of commitment promoted in its pages. Fans and critics alike recognized the challenge to traditional morality and family life posed by *Playboy*'s brand of good living.

At the outset, Hefner assumed a modest role for his magazine, promising to stress entertainment over serious social or political matters. "We don't expect to solve any world problems or prove any great moral truths," he wrote in his opening editorial. "If we are able to give the American male a few extra laughs and a little diversion from the anxieties of the Atomic Age, we'll feel we've justified our existence."[2] Despite this proposal for lighthearted fun in a publication he subtitled "entertainment for men," Hefner's magazine took on far greater importance as it set about redefining the good life for Americans in the decades after the Second World War. Its sexual content and glamorous depictions of bachelorhood made it roguish for the 1950s, but in its heyday, *Playboy* was more

than a magazine filled with pictures of nude women and advice on how to mix the perfect martini. Hefner's interest in the good life, his vision of sexual liberation and high living, propelled his magazine into mainstream debates about society, economics, and culture in postwar America.

Exploring the world created in the pages of *Playboy,* this book looks at transformations in postwar middle-class society. It begins by examining changing modes in gender roles and family life. In the years after World War II, the men and women who raced to the altar and generated the baby boom endorsed the roles of male breadwinner and female homemaker. They also grappled with their identities, however, and expressed frustrations as they negotiated these roles. As breadwinners, men bore a twofold burden. Societal expectations about adult responsibility harnessed male energy to a job in support of the family, while the group-orientation of the corporate workplace, where more and more men earned their pay, undermined a sense of masculine individualism and achievement. Within the home, social prescriptions calling for marriage as a partnership conflicted with existing views about female subordination in marriage, and despite potent cultural images of domestic bliss, many women failed to find fulfillment in the household realm. Women's paid employment, especially among married women, increased in the postwar era, the number of women in the workforce growing by approximately two thirds from 1940 to 1960.[3] In these years, sexual mores were also in transition. Moralists attempted to beat back the liberalizing trend begun before the war, which wartime upheavals and the expansion of the national marketplace had only accelerated. Anxious members of Congress solicited testimony on the spate of "immoral" and "offensive" material flooding drugstores and newsstands. Religious and civic leaders warned of the social dangers of moral laxity. A conservative public morality was often sharply at odds with private sexual practice, while women endured the burden of a double standard that called for them to guard their virtue against male advances. Broader cultural values were also in flux. A Victorian code of self-restraint and decorum had been largely broken down a half-century earlier, replaced by a cultural creed attuned to the expanding consumer society. While depression and war had stymied Americans' ability to attain personal pleasure and material well-being, the nation's return to peace and prosperity breathed new life into these aspirations. The entrenchment of a consumer ethic prizing self-gratification played a vital part in fueling the engines of postwar consumer capitalism.

Policy makers, public intellectuals, advertisers, and other cultural observers often invoked the notion of "the good life," an abstract concept encompassing the apparent comfort, security, and abundance made possible by postwar prosperity. Middle-class families enjoying an expanded realm of leisure and consumption formed the focal point of one pervasive vision. Emerging from

World War II and the uneasy period of readjustment that followed, Americans experienced growth and mobility in various guises: rising levels of productivity fueled by consumer spending, the nationwide construction of suburban housing developments, the population upsurge of the baby boom, the movement of people from cities to suburbs, and the upward mobility of an expanding middle class. Hailed as evidence of national achievement, these physical and cultural features of the postwar landscape were also buttressed by government and business policies as well as cultural support. Privileging new single family dwellings, federal mortgage guarantees spurred home ownership and suburban growth. Federal income tax policies favored married couples in which wives did not work outside the home. Advertisers targeted families in their efforts to sell, with consumer spending on household goods fueling the postwar economic boom. Popular culture kept pace, as television shows such as *Ozzie and Harriet* (1952–1966), *Father Knows Best* (1954–1960), and *Leave It to Beaver* (1957–1963) celebrated the white, suburban, middle-class family. The mass weeklies also highlighted the nuclear family, as did women's magazines such as *Ladies' Home Journal* and *McCall's,* which coined the term "togetherness" in 1954. As America squared off against the Soviet Union, the traditional family enjoying consumer plenitude served as an important symbol in the ideological battles of the Cold War.[4] This vision upheld the primacy of the family and supported conventional gender arrangements and sex norms, while also affirming the socioeconomic order.

Playboy magazine played a significant role in defining an alternative, often controversial, and highly resonant version of the good life. For all the popularity of the Playmates, the nude or seminude women who graced the center pages of each issue, there would have been little to make *Playboy* stand out from the numerous men's magazines that traded in female flesh had it not been for the larger editorial context that surrounded them. Hefner aimed to reach a male audience "a little more interested in urban living—in the nice things about an apartment, hi-fi—wine, women and song." He positioned his magazine as a challenge to the wholesale acceptance of postwar domestic ideology. Like the early version of *Esquire* magazine, which served as inspiration, *Playboy* had lifestyle features that allowed readers to envision an upscale, masculine identity based on tasteful consumption and sexual pleasure.[5] Each month, "modern living" features showcased a world of fashionable attire, gourmet food, sports cars, and exotic vacations. Luxurious bachelor pads housed well-stocked liquor cabinets and the latest hi-fi equipment, providing a modish backdrop for collections of abstract art and jazz records. All of these consumptive delights were meant to be enjoyed with a lovely, single, sexually available girl who had no intention of charting a course to the altar. Hefner meant for his publication to

be experienced as a total package, a "veritable handbook for the young man-about-town" that showed readers how to acquire the finer things while enjoying life every step of the way. For Hefner, the good life meant the freedom to fashion a lifestyle of one's own choosing. The one he promoted was "the playboy life," where expensive goods and sexually available women were plentiful, obligations were few, and "the name of the game was fun."[6]

Playboy, author Barbara Ehrenreich has observed, was an important player in a male "rebellion" against 1950s dictates for responsible manhood, which called on men to serve as the providers for economically dependent housewives.[7] According to this view, men took umbrage at the constraints of breadwinning and challenged the family ideal well before feminists encouraged women to opt out of the role of "happy housewife."[8] While disdain for the yoke of familial responsibility undoubtedly found expression in *Playboy,* in fact, the magazine joined a broader chorus of anxiety and dissatisfaction voiced by both men and women over so-called traditional gender arrangements and idealized suburban family life. As historians have shown, images of domestic fulfillment and discontent appeared together in widely read magazines. Popular works of social criticism addressed pressures for conformity in the offices and tract-developments of modern America. Novelists, filmmakers, and other commentators exposed the hidden pitfalls of affluence and pointed to the problems of marital tension and gender discord.[9]

As it joined in these wide-ranging discussions of postwar society, *Playboy* extolled the virtues of singlehood. "Never before have so many men-about-town had the wherewithal necessary for enjoying the good life, never before have men had more leisure time and been more in the mood to enjoy it," *Playboy* announced. "Of course, some women have altar-egos, [*sic*] but all the pitfalls of a playboy's existence can be successfully avoided by paying strict attention to the words of wisdom to be found on these pages each month."[10] *Playboy* advised readers where to meet women and how to win them, showcasing an alternate world where young men did not have to settle down. In Playmate pictorials and lifestyle features, the playboy's many companions took the form of young coeds, secretaries, aspiring actresses, and the like. Whether she was a shopgirl or a flight attendant, her identity centered not on home and family, but on her job, or perhaps her choice of automobile, or the way she liked to spend the weekend. Most of all, she appeared physically attractive and sexually willing, and a wedding ring was no prerequisite for sex—only a jazz recording on the turntable and a properly mixed cocktail to set the mood.

As *Playboy* crafted these alluring images of singlehood, the success of the magazine stemmed from its simultaneous existence at the margins and at the center of postwar society. *Playboy* attacked pressures for early marriage,

traditional gender arrangements, and sanctions against premarital sex. But Hefner's vision of the good life, though rebellious, was also carefully fitted to the mainstream of society. *Playboy* promoted prolonged, commitment-free bachelorhood with the implication that delaying adult responsibility would ultimately strengthen marital bonds. The playboy and his bevy of female companions challenged the conservative, family-centered society without upsetting the gender order; the women in *Playboy* were not wives and mothers, but they remained supportive and solicitous to men. In seeking to free heterosexual relations from marriage and in scrupulously crafting a squeaky-clean image for his Playmates, Hefner sought initially to expand, rather than explode, the boundaries governing sexual behavior and expression. Finally, highlighting the link between work and leisure, he affirmed the centrality of consumption to postwar society, but in the guise of the well-heeled bachelor, he made the individual, rather than the family, its centerpiece.

Playboy's celebration of singlehood and sexual freedom, its glamorous images of affluent young bachelors and liberated but compliant single girls, resonated in the popular culture and consumer society of postwar America. Drawing inspiration from the playboy, by the early 1960s, the "Single Girl," an unmarried, working girl, had taken her place alongside him, both figures providing models of unfettered individualism and self-fulfillment. In the wider culture as the decade wore on, the barriers to sexual expression continued to erode as purveyors of popular culture defeated proponents of traditional morality in the nation's courtrooms and marketplaces. A relaxation of mores governing sexual behavior paralleled the easing of restraints for sexual expression. Increasingly, sexual pleasure was released from the bonds of marriage, affirmed as a vital and fulfilling part of adult life. Changes in sexual morality were also linked to developments in the consumer society. Policy makers and captains of industry after World War II upheld economic growth as the fount of national well-being. In order to partake in the ongoing consumption upon which growth depended, historians have argued, Americans had to come to believe that indulging in all the unnecessary items made possible by mass production was, in fact, a positive endeavor, even a moral one. The widespread adoption of an ethical framework that sanctioned pleasure-seeking brought to fruition earlier trends and helped sustain the nation's consumer society. *Playboy* tied the pursuit of pleasure to national purpose, a connection that affirmed and helped further the drift of postwar society. Helped along by advertisers and other spokespersons for the consumer economy, pleasure and self-fulfillment, achieved through the acquisition of material goods or in the form of sexual experience, became goals cemented to middle-class life.

Playboy marks continuity from the early years of the Cold War era through the more pronounced upheavals and movements for social change of the 1960s and 1970s. *Playboy* is popularly depicted as one of the shock troops of the sexual revolution. The hedonistic aspects of the counterculture and sexual revolution were not merely the products of a generation in revolt against the conservative 1950s but were also rooted in postwar cultural formulations of singlehood and personal consumption, which prized individualism and fostered an ethos of pleasure-seeking and self-gratification.[11] Similarly, *Playboy*'s representations of women shaped later discussions of gender equality and consumer society. Not everyone was comfortable with rising American materialism; concern over the nation's moral complacency voiced by critics aligned in the 1960s New Left also inspired a reassessment of the commodification of sexuality evident in *Playboy* and elsewhere. As they took stock of the institutions they viewed as supporting a sexist society, feminists denounced *Playboy*. The women's liberation movement of the 1960s and 1970s was not just a reaction to the idealization of women as domestic goddesses; it was also a response to the modified version of female domesticity crafted in *Playboy* and supported by popular depictions of the Single Girl, which detached women from the home and family but gave them far less social or economic freedom than men enjoyed. Indeed, in the eyes of many critics, the magazine merely replaced the image of woman-as-housewife with that of woman-as-sex object. While the materialism that underpinned "the playboy life" and the wider society proved remarkably resilient, *Playboy*'s representations of gender nonetheless had unintended consequences. If in presenting a limited role for women outside the family it sowed seeds of discontent, *Playboy* also demonstrated how roles could be refashioned or even abandoned in the consumer society.

Broadly speaking, these developments signaled a transformation in the decades after World War II from a society that endorsed traditional gender roles and placed a high premium on the family as its primary unit to one that held the individual in the highest regard and afforded men and women a far wider range of options in their social roles. At the same time, the outward espousal of conservative moral values gave way to greater acceptance of sexual freedom, while lingering, traditional values of hard work and self-restraint receded, displaced by an emphasis on self-indulgence and consumption. All of these complex changes were bound up in *Playboy*'s mandate for the good life.

Although Ehrenreich termed the playboy "a new style of male rebel," this figure was not created out of whole cloth in the 1950s. The playboy—a youthful, unmarried, urban male known for his seductive prowess and upscale consumption—represented a maturation of cultural trends that accompanied the rise of commercial capitalism and fueled the growth of a consumer society in

the decades bracketing the turn of the twentieth century. The nation's industrial expansion and transition from proprietary to corporate capitalism prompted the creation of new cultural forms along with a significant reorientation in values. Because its viability depended on ever-expanding markets for its products, fostering desire and encouraging consumption became central features of the new economic system. Notions of "abundance," rather than "scarcity," became defining elements of American culture as values associated with nineteenth-century modes of production, including thrift, hard work, and self-restraint, gave way to an ascendant ethos of consumption. The new ethos encouraged the pursuit of pleasure, personal expression, and self-fulfillment. Burgeoning cities, meanwhile, nurtured a popular culture instrumental in shaping the sensibilities associated with modern life. Department stores, motion pictures, and modern advertising elevated the value of outward appearance and personal magnetism and encouraged the pursuit of leisure and consumption.

As men and women found new avenues for self-expression in the realm of public amusements and nightlife, earlier codes of morality calling for social decorum and sexual restraint began to break down. Family and community no longer watched over courtship; instead, couples "went out" on "dates" in the new commercial venues—dance halls, movie theaters, cabarets, amusement parks. In the developing peer-directed social world, courtship took place within a cash nexus where a man spent money taking a woman out, expecting and frequently receiving some degree of sexual favor in return. College campuses, in the early decades of the twentieth century, further nurtured a leisure-oriented youth culture that embraced new styles of sociability and sexual practice. These developments had important implications for men and women, as gender, racial, and class identities became bound up in patterns of consumption and shaped by the values being disseminated through the new forms of media and popular culture.[12]

The commercial diversions and institutions of American cities also supported a flourishing bachelor subculture in the late nineteenth and early twentieth centuries. Emphasizing male autonomy and homosocial intimacy, bachelor culture centered on saloons and barbershops, pool halls and rooming houses, spaces that met the material and social needs of single men and provided an alternative to traditional modes of domesticity. At the same time, popular literature highlighted bachelorhood and gave expression to the values and characteristics associated with modern configurations of masculinity. Filled with sensational crime stories and sports features, the *National Police Gazette* included salacious illustrations of women as well, serving as "the unofficial scripture" of bachelor culture. In the early decades of the twentieth century, Bernarr Macfadden's periodicals, *Physical Culture* and *True Story,* showcased youthful vitality and sex

appeal as important components for male success. While some magazines still promoted visions of masculine achievement in the business world through hard work and self-restraint, others began to emphasize successful interpersonal relationships managed through careful consumption and a pleasing personality. By 1933, as Tom Pendergast has shown, *Esquire* magazine brought together many of these elements into a vision of masculinity attuned to modern life with an editorial package touting sexual virility, style, taste, and personality.[13]

Urban life and popular culture, then, supported a thriving bachelor subculture and brought forth new visions of middle-class masculinity.[14] The developments of this period, however, also ignited concerns about moral economy, the relationship of gender to consumption, and the potential disaffection of modern work. For men in the growing ranks of the professional-managerial middle class, the increasingly regimented workplaces of corporate capitalism had the potential to alienate and emasculate the white-collar employees who toiled there. Consumer culture, with its plethora of manufactured goods, offered security and material well-being, but its inducements to consume and its commodification of appearance and personality also provoked unease. Additionally, the nascent consumer ethic did not obliterate older, traditional middle-class values of economy and self-discipline; longtime ideals linking manhood to the productive sphere lingered, complicating men's efforts to embrace the values of modern society. Important questions remained, therefore, about men's relationship to the economic system and the consumer society it fueled. Although a number of cultural forms accommodated and promoted the new values, tensions persisted between these and earlier standards. Images of bachelorhood and ideas about masculinity that emerged from the formation of modern, urban culture helped form the basis for the articulation in the postwar period of a masculine figure—the playboy—who served as a vehicle for exploring and resolving these lingering tensions and many others.

Advertisers and marketers had attempted to cultivate masculine consumption in the first half of the twentieth century, but in the 1950s, commodity consumption remained a problematic activity for middle-class men. It carried a feminine taint, cast as a sphere of activity for women and redolent of frivolity, in contrast to the more serious arena of male production. Moreover, the sea of commodities for sale could be overwhelming, especially for those newly acclimating to middle-class status. In tones that presumed a readership of savvy consumers, modern living features in *Playboy* thus showcased the latest gadgets and trends while also carefully explaining them. Readers received advice from "The Playboy Advisor" on everything from cufflinks to caviar. Whether in the form of a color-coded chart spelling out the necessities of the basic wardrobe or in a floor plan for a lavishly appointed penthouse apartment, *Playboy* helped

men become accustomed to the sphere of domestic consumption. The idealized playboy offered a model for living that demystified the male consumer, showing him how to display style and taste to assert status in the social hierarchy while sanctioning a pleasure-seeking approach to life. The magazine promised that young males from most walks of life could achieve playboy status and express themselves through consumer practices and leisure pursuits.[15]

Although some critics denounced the magazine, excoriating its nude photographs as immoral, others viewed *Playboy* as much more than a "girly" magazine. Assessing the widening consumer society, contemporary observers discussed and debated status anxiety, purchasing habits, the erosion of class differences, and the merits of advanced capitalism. Given its claim of serving as a consumer handbook, *Playboy* fit naturally into such discussions, and thus commentators in mainstream publications as well as erudite journals pondered the implications of the popular magazine. They believed *Playboy*'s potency lay not in its risqué photographs, but in its capacity to capitalize on consumer uncertainty in an increasingly image-conscious society. Moreover, they worried about the magazine's seeming promotion of self-interest above concern for the community and its celebration of pleasure-seeking in all aspects of life. Critics charged that the lifestyle showcased in *Playboy* produced anxious consumers or, alternately, lazy spendthrifts.

While hedonism undoubtedly underpinned the playboy lifestyle, Hefner's pronouncements for pleasurable consumption presupposed hard work. Hefner's own public persona suggested an amalgam of industriousness leavened with pleasure. The successful editor and publisher extolled work as an important arena in which the playboy made his mark among men. His revised work ethic provided the rhetoric with which to disarm critics of *Playboy*'s sexual content by arguing that his magazine inspired young men to work hard to achieve the good life. In highlighting the link between the spheres of production and consumption, work and play, he posited private consumption as the key to economic growth and thus national well-being.

As Hefner offered a resolution of the tensions between hedonism and national purpose, his magazine also put forth identities for men and women that promised to ease the strains of gender confusion in the years after World War II. Americans at mid-century expressed concern that the line dividing male from female, masculine from feminine, was becoming increasingly blurred. Some contemporary observers believed postwar society had become particularly inhospitable to men. Surveying a multitude of changes in the workplace and family life, in popular culture and national character, they generated a discourse on gender upheaval that understood American masculinity as under siege and in crisis.

The sense of gender confusion, as well as the various explanations offered for it, was nothing new. During the late nineteenth and early twentieth centuries, a confluence of social, cultural, and economic changes focused attention on manhood and inspired concerted efforts to renegotiate gender configurations. Work in the burgeoning offices of urban America offered little outlet for rugged individualism, and policy makers, civic leaders, and medical experts fretted over the enervation of "overcivilized" white, middle-class men. Critics also voiced concern about women's role in shaping society. They cited the undue influence women wielded as they reared male children at home and in schools, infused Protestantism with sentimentality, and exerted an unwelcome feminizing effect on American culture. At the same time, women aggravated the gender status quo and challenged male power by attending college, seeking work outside the home, and attempting inroads into male political culture with their demands for voting rights. Perceptions of this assault on American manhood and the sense that masculinity needed reasserting informed many developments, including arguments for a vigorous foreign policy, a growing obsession with competitive sports, and the misogynistic campaigns of anti-suffragists, as well as the rise of masculine domesticity—men's increased involvement in household matters as an effort to revitalize the overly feminized domestic sphere.[16]

Those who voiced concern about the decline of masculinity after World War II pointed to similar issues and culprits. Once again, modern work was blamed for undermining individualism, and the consumer society came under scrutiny for its feminizing effects. In the home, the male breadwinner–female homemaker arrangement drew criticism for burdening men with dependent wives and for fostering a decline of patriarchal authority while men were out winning bread for their families. Given that the "second wave" of feminism has often been viewed as the pivotal moment in the disruption of traditional gender arrangements, it may seem incongruous that so much concern was voiced earlier over women's increasing power and the erosion of difference between the sexes.[17] Yet, as a variety of social changes, including women's heightened workforce participation, greater visibility in public life, increased discretionary spending, and expectations for marital partnership, called into question rigid formulations of appropriate gender roles, many experts and observers attempted to uphold "traditional" male and female roles. Debating what constituted proper masculine or feminine roles and spheres of activity, these commentators often expressed a firm commitment to clear gender differences in the face of unsettling change.[18]

Playboy's utterances on this subject were well-tuned to this debate. While Hugh Hefner never spoke in terms of "crisis," he did address the confusion of the

"sex roles" responsible for sowing discontent in marriages and breaking down the social order. In Hefner's view, men and women found happiness when they adhered to separate, complementary roles. To erode the distinctions between the sexes was to invite trouble. The magazine and its founder fell back on essentialist assumptions that men and women were naturally endowed with different characteristics that gave them a corresponding place in the social order. While they provided cultural space for the fashioning of identities outside narrow prescriptions for the male breadwinner–female homemaker, Hefner and other *Playboy* contributors denounced changes that caused too much slippage in the "sex roles." The substance that filled the categories "masculine" and "feminine" could, to some extent, be reconstituted so long as those changes did not allow women to assume the power or prerogatives reserved for the masculine role. *Playboy* imagined roles for women other than wife and mother, for example, but did not initially provide space for them alongside the playboy when it came to social and sexual freedom. Similarly, cultural formulations of the working girl, who placed herself in service to men, reconciled women's increased role in the economic sphere with concerns about women's power. Within this context, *Playboy* did not just print pictures of nude women. The magazine actively engaged in a project of formulating gender, often overtly, sometimes implicitly, for which nude pictures served as just one important element.[19]

Depending on one's viewpoint, *Playboy*, by the late 1960s, symbolized either the fruition of the consumer society's imperatives or its most egregious flaws. Advertising, motion pictures, and popular entertainers celebrated self-indulgent singlehood and a relaxation of sexual mores, key tenets of the kind of "playboy life" Hefner promoted. The path to self-fulfillment implicit in this material-oriented, pleasure-seeking lifestyle, however, rested on a fragile foundation of gender inequality. It further posed a white, middle-class model of masculine success that remained out of reach for most African Americans. And for those who did achieve it, critics blamed the successful for buying into a system that was morally bankrupt. Among those attacking the ethos of playboy-style achievement were "second-wave" feminists. Yet the relationship between *Playboy* and the women's movement was not merely an oppositional one. During the 1960s and 1970s, *Playboy*'s support of liberal feminist causes such as reproductive freedom, which made sense in the framework of "the playboy life," made Hefner a frequent but uncomfortable ally of the women's movement. Meanwhile, *Playboy* opposed more radical feminist demands for gender equality. In consciousness-raising groups and at protest rallies, in position papers and feminist newsletters, women attempted to theorize the significance of *Playboy* magazine in a sexist society and debated the implications of *Playboy*'s support for feminist goals. Under

fire from these critics, *Playboy* struggled to reconcile its pronouncements for personal liberation with an editorial program that did not appear to extend to women the same liberation it had promised men. Investigating this complex relationship, this book illuminates the ways in which *Playboy* was shaped by feminism and vice versa.

Playboy's idealization of a sexually liberated, consumer-oriented, hard-working bachelor-individualist offered valuable commentary on a society in transition and placed the magazine at the center of discussions about sex and freedom, politics and pleasure in postwar America. Exploring these discourses, the chapters that follow are arranged both thematically and chronologically. Chapter 1 situates Hefner's early adulthood and his founding of *Playboy* magazine within the context of rising affluence, a boom in family life, and perceptions of gender upheaval. Hefner drew on an editorial strategy devised by *Esquire* magazine in the 1930s to craft a magazine that critiqued familial obligation, sexual conservatism, and women's impingement on male power, offering the playboy as a model for male liberation. Chapter 2 turns to economic life, exploring questions of production and consumption in postwar America. It examines the construction of Hefner's public persona as the Self-Made Man for the consumer society, his articulation of moral economy in support of "the playboy life," and the role of his magazine in mapping consumption as the terrain on which status claims were increasingly staked. Chapter 3 looks closely at the spatial context for "the playboy life." *Playboy*'s representations of the bachelor pad and the city mobilized concepts of space and gender to critique the "feminization" of society evident in the growth of suburbia, while claiming space for men in a revised domestic sphere. Chapter 4 explores the configuration of gender, work, and consumption in the persona of the working girl who served as the idealized companion for the playboy. Popular representations of working-girl femininity such as those put forth by Helen Gurley Brown attempted to reconcile ideas about the primacy of women's domestic role with the fact of women's increasing workforce participation. Though the Single Girl was liberated from traditional domesticity, she remained situated within the traditional gender hierarchy, her marginal social and economic status making her a suitable companion for the playboy.

The last two chapters trace the ascent and decline of Hefner's "Playboy empire," analyzing celebratory appraisals and condemnations of *Playboy* emanating from several fronts. Chapter 5 considers the "Playboy empire" in its heyday during the 1960s. It traces the popularity of *Playboy* and positive depictions of bachelorhood in an increasingly sexualized climate and examines an emergent singles culture and hedonistic counterculture as elements of the

"permissive society." By examining the racial dimensions of *Playboy* and the origins of a groundswell of criticism aimed at the consumer society, this chapter also explores the implications of this pleasure- and status-seeking lifestyle in a social order marred by commercialism and inequality. An important champion of the "permissive society," in the next decade *Playboy* became a casualty of the "lifestyle revolution" it helped spearhead, undermined by the social changes it so heartily welcomed. Chapter 6 recounts *Playboy*'s attempts to remain relevant in a highly sexualized marketplace as well as its significance as a symbol of feminist grievances. In important ways, *Playboy*'s evocation of self-indulgence was more fitted to the mainstream than ever before, a position that ironically made it appear outmoded. The magazine also faltered under feminist attacks on its version of socially and sexually emancipated womanhood. Examining the relationship between *Playboy* and feminism sheds light on the strategies employed by *Playboy* to reconcile demands for gender equality with its commitment to personal liberation and its earlier configuration of gender roles. It also exposes the origins of key fissures in the women's movement. Toward the end of the 1970s, a conservative moral backlash attempted to beat back the "popular hedonism" that seemed to grip society during that decade. Yet, even as *Playboy* came under attack from conservatives and antipornography activists, the personal freedom, self-fulfillment, and materialism that infused its vision of the good life remained firmly affixed to American culture. An epilogue thus considers the cultural legacies of *Playboy* and the broader transformations and debates of which it has been a part. Understanding the forces that contributed to *Playboy*'s diminished import in American society after the early 1970s as well as its continued place in the mainstream—a trajectory of decline and diffusion—helps make sense of the tensions in today's sexualized popular culture and consumer society.

"*Playboy* isn't very serious," Hefner remarked in 1955. In fact, it offered a send-up of "the kind of life part of the reader would like to live. It offers him an imaginary escape into the world of wine, women and song. Then the other part of him says he has to go back to his family responsibilities and his work." If the magazine offered escapism—and in the opulent setting of the playboy's penthouse apartment and in the nubile young women that graced its centerfolds, it supplied plenty of this—then the form of its particular vision of escape and the relief it promised from a society in transition reveals much about postwar America. Even as he claimed his magazine merely provided entertainment, Hefner made another insightful assertion as well. "If we have an editorial policy it's only by implication: 'Live and let live. It's a wonderful world and let's enjoy it,'" he explained. "It's a kind of argument for a liberal democratic society with emphasis on the freedom of the individual."[20] This was, in fact, the philosophy

that underlay the specific vision of upscale liberation outlined in his magazine. As millions turned to its pages, that philosophy and vision helped to make *Playboy* the focus of appreciative and critical discussions about modern American society. Examining how ideas about the substance and meaning of the good life took shape and were contested in the decades following World War II enables us to see how and why, in important ways, American culture has come to resemble the playboy life.

1 "WE AREN'T A 'FAMILY MAGAZINE'"

Sex, Gender, and the Family Ideal in Postwar America

IN MARCH 1953, amid reports on U.S.-Soviet tensions, the latest accusations made by a Red-baiting Senator Joseph McCarthy, and the opening of a "Modern Living Exposition" to showcase the newest ranch house designs, the *Chicago Daily News* ran a two-page story, "How a Cartoonist Lives" (see figure 1.1). The story featured the young Hefner family at home in a newly refurbished apartment.[1] Hugh Hefner, wife Millie, and baby daughter Christie appeared in photographs that highlighted Hefner's taste in modern decor and his clever use of cartoons to decorate the nursery. Images of the smiling family in their living room revealed nothing of the dissatisfaction in Hefner's ailing marriage. The story made no mention of the frustrated cartoonist working his way through one dull office job after another, attempting repeatedly but so far unsuccessfully to strike out on his own. Nor did the sunny pictorial offer any hint that by year's end Hefner's latest venture, *Playboy* magazine, would hit newsstands and catapult him to millionaire status and revitalized singlehood. In little time, a young married father became a spokesperson for sexually liberated bachelorhood, an unusual achievement in an era typically cast as one marked by conformity, renewed commitment to domesticity, and sexual conservatism. Hefner tapped into powerful undercurrents of discontent running through postwar society.

COMPROMISES IN THE ADULT WORLD

In spring 1946, Hefner received his military discharge, having spent two years as a camp clerk stationed in various locations in the United States while the war raged to conclusion in Europe and the Pacific. Eager to get on with life after the

1.1 *Hugh Hefner posed with his wife and baby daughter for a feature story,*
"How a Cartoonist Lives," in 1953. Hefner took pride in the new furniture and
modern decor of his apartment. Despite appearances of domestic tranquility, he
was disenchanted with family life. The launch of Playboy *within the year allowed*
him to fashion an opulent new lifestyle as the footloose, millionaire editor and
publisher of the popular men's magazine. (Chicago Daily News)

interruption of military service, the twenty-year-old Chicago native was also
anxious about what the future might bring. Hefner had thrived in high school,
enjoying immense popularity and voted one of the students most likely to succeed by his fellow classmates. Now he worried about making the grade in college
after a two-year break from schooling and wondered if he would ever achieve
success and find fulfillment in a career. He was further troubled over doubts
about his girlfriend, questioning his feelings for her and the prospects for their
continued relationship.[2] Such hesitations at the personal level resonated at the

national level, as Americans, after a decade and a half of depression and war, looked to an uncertain future.

Across the country, Americans were adjusting to peacetime and to the social and cultural transformations unleashed by the war. Fueled by its immense productive capabilities, the nation congratulated itself for its defeat of fascism and assumed a preeminent place in global affairs, yet faced an uneasy peace. Now Americans confronted the anxieties of the Atomic Age, a prospect made all the more urgent as the convenient wartime alliance between the United States and the Soviet Union gave way to the protracted tension of the Cold War. On the home front, the war generated massive mobility, which disrupted traditional social controls and enabled a loosening of morals. Social dislocations of wartime threatened to undermine the family—separating husbands from wives, parents from children—and to destabilize traditional gender roles. The movement of women into traditionally male occupations aided the war effort but caused strains as many wondered how women would retain their femininity and uphold responsibilities to home and family. In the immediate aftermath of the war, perceptions of increased juvenile delinquency and a sharp spike in the divorce rate generated concern about the resilience of the social fabric. Meanwhile, although the war pulled the nation out of the depths of the Great Depression, Americans faced the bumpy road of economic reconversion. The end of the war brought inflation, widespread labor unrest, housing and food shortages, and uncertainty as to whether or not economic crisis would return.[3]

In the fall of 1946, as the nation recovered from a wave of industrial strikes and struggled through the economic shock brought by the lifting of price controls, Hefner enrolled with the aid of the GI Bill at the University of Illinois, where his girlfriend was a student. He immersed himself in college life, majoring in psychology and taking extra summer courses to make up for lost time. Despite a heavy course load, he also managed to become involved in campus activities. He edited the campus humor magazine, *Shaft*, where he introduced a new feature, the "Coed of the Month," and drew cartoons for the *Daily Illini*. Hefner became engrossed in another publication as well: the first Kinsey Report on male sexuality, issued in 1948. Fascinated with the study's revelation of the chasm between publicly espoused norms and private sexual behavior, Hefner began to read a wide range of material dealing with sex, from medical journals to books on sex law. He continued to date Mildred Williams, the fellow high school classmate whom he met just before leaving for the army. They were engaged in December 1948. Upon graduating a few months later, he returned to Chicago to search for work in advertising or publishing but had to settle instead for a desk job at a manufacturing company. In June 1949, he and Millie

were married and, after a brief Wisconsin honeymoon, moved in with Hefner's parents.[4] Like many other young men in the early postwar period, in just a few short years, Hefner went from high school, to the army, to college, to marriage and a steady job. As the nation embarked on an unprecedented period of economic growth, Hefner settled down to the routine of married life. But he could not shake the gnawing sense that somehow he had missed out on something along the way.

The initial path Hefner followed as a young man fit the pattern set in the early postwar period by "young marrieds" who collapsed the attainment of adult milestones—education, job, marriage, and parenthood—into a very short timeframe. In comparison to other American men who married after World War II, Hefner was not particularly young, at age twenty-three, to have tied the knot.[5] Americans rushed to the altar, driven in part by desire for security after the prolonged crises of depression and war. Furthermore, the economic recovery brought by wartime, and the prosperity that followed, put marriage within reach of young couples. At the same time, men and women encountered incentives and pressures that spurred the trend to early wedlock. Providing adult status and privileges, marriage also sanctioned sexual activity, while popular advice literature suggested that those who failed to assume the adult responsibilities of family life suffered from maladjustment. As the Cold War intensified, rhetoric calling for containing communism abroad found a complement in what Elaine Tyler May has termed "domestic containment." Strong, stable nuclear families promised refuge and fulfillment for husbands and wives while fortifying the nation against the threat of internal subversion and social disorder.

Both at home and on the job Hefner's early adulthood reflected postwar trends. Settling back into his boyhood home on Chicago's Far West Side, he and his new wife joined the ranks of more than two million couples living with relatives. This was typical of "young marrieds," whose parents often subsidized their first years of marriage with money for household expenses or a place to live. The severe postwar housing shortage also prompted young couples to double up with extended family, a need that would be eased by the explosive growth of suburbia.[6] His first job in a personnel department was characteristic of the transforming workplace, too. "Personnel," with its aim of managing human resources in order to keep the organization running smoothly, served as a key component of the increasingly rationalized world of work. As a paid employee, Hefner earned his income in the manner of growing numbers in the American labor force. Between 1947 and 1957, the number of salaried middle-class workers in the United States increased by 61 percent, a trend that reflected the displacement of the individual entrepreneur by the hired employee who

increasingly worked in the area of "management." While some Americans desired the security of a steady job in a big company, the nature of the regimented workplace and its demands for conformity inspired widespread criticism in the postwar period.[7] For his part, Hefner found his first job and the many that followed wholly unsatisfying.

Hefner's efforts to shed the bonds of a corporate job drew on his fascination with sex, his fantasies about urban life, and his lifelong interest in writing and cartooning. He quit his first job and began a brief stint in graduate school studying sociology at Northwestern University, where, analyzing the legal proscription of many acts that Kinsey identified as commonplace, he produced a term paper on the need to reform the nation's sex laws. He left after one semester, taking employment as an advertising copywriter for a department store, while devoting his real energies to creating *That Toddlin' Town: A Rowdy Burlesque of Chicago Manners and Morals.* Hefner billed his book of original, racy cartoons as "a humorous poke" at the city's "institutions, its culture, its sex life," and the publication enjoyed a measure of local success. He next picked up work as a promotional copywriter for *Esquire.* This magazine's "urbane sophistication" had appealed to him as an adolescent, but Hefner found his work there dull. When *Esquire* relocated its offices to New York in 1951, he remained in Chicago with plans to start a magazine devoted to that city. Unable to raise enough money to launch *Pulse: The Picture Magazine of Chicago,* he abandoned the project. In the meantime, news of Millie's pregnancy sent the young couple searching for a place of their own. Hefner and his wife finally moved out of his parents' house and transformed an aging apartment into the modern design showroom featured in the *Chicago Daily News.*[8]

Hefner landed another job at Publisher's Development Corporation (PDC), which put out such titles as *Art Photography, Modern Sunbathing, Sunbathing Review,* and *Modern Man.* During the war years, popular pinups of Rita Hayworth and Betty Grable had glorified female curves, while images of buxom, long-legged women festooned military aircraft. Fueled by the demand of U.S. servicemen, publications featuring "cheesecake" in the form of illustrated pinups and nude photography had increased in number and in circulation in the forties. *Modern Man* was typical of the kind of "girlie" magazine available by the early 1950s. The U.S. Post Office Department exercised de facto censorship powers by denying discounted mailing rates to publications viewed as unfit for public consumption, so *Modern Man* accepted no subscriptions, relying solely on newsstand sales. Within each issue was an eight- to ten-page "Modern Man Gallery"—photos of nude women cloaked in the language of "art photography." *Modern Man* captured Hefner's attention as he contemplated a different approach, thinking the sexual content

could pervade the editorial package of a magazine, rather than be relegated to a thinly disguised "sexual ghetto."[9]

By early 1953, Hefner had changed jobs once more, taking a position as circulation manager for a magazine called *Children's Activities*. Having garnered through his various jobs and personal ventures a range of publishing and editing experience, he again thought about starting a magazine. "I'd like to produce an entertainment magazine for the city-bred guy—breezy, sophisticated," Hefner noted in the "cartoon autobiography" that served as a personal diary. "The girlie features would guarantee the initial sale, but the magazine would have quality too." Inspired by a 1930s book of risqué cartoons, *Stag at Eve*, Hefner planned to call his publication *Stag Party*. Searching for something to call attention to it, he discovered that for $500 he could obtain the celebrated, but seldom seen, nude calendar photographs of Marilyn Monroe.[10] Hefner secured a modest bank loan using his new furniture for collateral and offered stock in the magazine to friends and family. Short on cash, he also offered payment in stock to those who contributed material for publication and located items in the public domain that he could reprint for free. In letters of introduction, he touted both the nude pinup of Monroe and his *Esquire* connection and received an encouraging number of advance orders for the first issue. Shortly before *Stag Party* went to press, Hefner received a warning letter from the attorneys of *Stag* magazine compelling him to find another name. *Top Hat, Bachelor, Gent, Gentlemen, Satyr,* and *Pan* received brief consideration, until a friend remembered an automobile called a "Playboy," a name Hefner found reminiscent of the "Roaring Twenties." In fact, it was also the name of a short-lived publication from that decade.[11] With its F. Scott Fitzgerald connotations, Hefner decided it had the sound he wanted, and *Playboy* hit newsstands in November 1953.[12]

For Hefner, *Playboy* served as a medium through which to espouse his own musings on society, and the ideal "playboy" crafted in the magazine was in many ways a creation based on his own personal longings. "Both at home and at work," he recalled, "I was dying on the vine." In his youth, he had "envisioned marriage as the apex of romance for a couple in love, a haven for erotic and romantic bliss until death do us part." Instead, he explained, "that naivete on my part had died a cruel death, and I was finding it increasingly difficult to honor the conventions of society rather than follow my own convictions." His abbreviated path to responsible manhood had left him longing for some excitement in his life. "I knew it was less than what I really wanted, but I thought that was one of those things you had to settle for," he reasoned. "My marriage was like the jobs I had before I started *Playboy*—the kind of compromises most of us make in the adult world."[13] At first, he crafted a world of urbane excitement and sexual adventure that existed only in the pages of his magazine. Soon, he

was living life anew, jettisoning his role as family man and conjuring his fantasies into existence through hard work and good fortune.

After several lackluster attempts to break into publishing and achieve financial independence, Hefner found success in *Playboy*. But he was true to his ambitions of creating a men's magazine that appealed to more than just the physical interests of its readers. In its opening editorial, *Playboy* announced an intention to fill "a publishing need only slightly less important than the one just taken care of by the Kinsey Report."

> If you're a man between the ages of 18 and 80, *Playboy* is meant for you. If you like your entertainment served up with humor, sophistication and spice, *Playboy* will become a very special favorite. We want to make clear from the very start, we aren't a 'family magazine.' If you're somebody's sister, wife or mother-in-law and picked us up by mistake, please pass us along to the man in your life and get back to your *Ladies' Home Companion*.[14]

Proclaiming its departure from family-oriented fare, Hefner promised entertainment for adult men. With so much of popular culture geared to the presumed interests and moral sensitivities of women and children, this was an important assertion. While the many women's and family-oriented general magazines of the 1950s color popular memory of the era, *Playboy* also joined the growing field of specialized magazines directed toward the male reader after World War II.[15] Hefner promised a departure from those as well. "Most of today's 'magazines for men' spend all their time out-of-doors—thrashing through thorny thickets or splashing about in fast-flowing streams," Hefner explained. He hoped his magazine "would be welcomed by that select group of urbane fellows who were less concerned with hunting, fishing, and climbing mountains than good food, drink, proper dress, and the pleasure of female company."[16] Hefner thus crafted a vision of the urban, heterosexually-virile, consuming male. It was not an entirely new concept but a skillful rendition of an existing prototype, which gained coherence in the pages of *Playboy* magazine and struck a responsive chord with readers in the 1950s.

FROM *ESQUIRE* TO *PLAYBOY*

The relationship between *Esquire* and *Playboy* was apparent. Letters in the "Dear Playboy" section called attention to the link, one asserting, "I remember *Cap'n Billy's Whiz Bang* and the *Esky* of the early thirties. Yours is the

most refreshing mag to hit the stands since they passed away." The popular media also picked up on the connection, *Time* calling *Playboy* "an oversexed young version of the 23-year-old *Esquire*."[17] From an editorial perspective, there was little revolutionary about *Playboy* when it entered the marketplace. The magazine borrowed heavily from the pathbreaking formula of *Esquire* in the 1930s, which promoted a vision of upscale, masculine consumption and heterosexual vitality as a welcome break from a female-oriented consumer society.

Founded in 1933, *Esquire* was the creation of David Smart and William Weintraub, two men whose backgrounds lay in promoting menswear. Recognizing that a magazine essentially brought together audiences and advertisers, Smart and Weintraub crafted a periodical for the well-heeled clientele of men's clothing stores in order to provide a venue for the advertisers of men's apparel. The editorial concept for the new magazine was devised by editor Arnold Gingrich who, according to *Esquire* historian Kenon Breazeale, identified both "a readership and a cause" in the guise of the "neglected male."[18] In its first issue, for instance, *Esquire* announced a reprieve for beleaguered males living in a consumer society geared toward feminine interests:

> It is our belief, in offering *Esquire* to the American male, that we are only getting around at last to a job that should have been done a long time ago—that of giving the masculine reader a break. The general magazines, in the mad scramble to increase the woman readership that seems to be so highly prized by national advertisers, have bent over backward in catering to the special interests and tastes of the feminine audience. This has reached a point...where the male reader, in looking through what purports to be a general magazine, is made to feel like an intruder about gynaecic mysteries.

To be sure, a man reading the general magazines occasionally found a few items aimed at him. But these features were included "somewhat after the manner in which scraps are tossed to the patient dog beneath the table." "What we can't figure for the life of us," *Esquire* continued, "is why woman readership should be valued so highly as to make a step-child out of the interests of male readers." *Esquire*'s editors promised to give the new magazine "an easy natural masculine character—to endow it...with a baritone voice." The magazine made no apologies to those concerned about its resultant "moral tone." "The endorsement of the Boy Scouts or the Campfire Girls, or even of the Federation of Women's Clubs, has never been *Esquire*'s objective," its editor explained. Before anyone took them to task for including items "that are (or should be) over the head of little Johnny aged nine," *Esquire* instructed critics to "take another look at the

qualifying caption" that appeared beneath the magazine's title. "The Magazine for Men" was not for women and children.[19]

These and other editorial pronouncements did not mean *Esquire* shared nothing in common with the women's magazines, however. Although Gingrich cited the *New Yorker* and *Vanity Fair* as inspiration, in fact, *Esquire* borrowed a formula established by women's magazines in the 1920s, which, in addition to visuals and fiction, included an assortment of "lifestyle" features that functioned in concert with advertising to inspire consumption. As *Esquire* put it, its "departments," which included art, books, theater, movies, music, potables, sports, and men's attire, comprised "a contemporary guide to gracious living."[20] Showcasing an array of goods and leisure pursuits, the magazine pointed the way to an upper middle-class masculine identity formulated around consumption.

The economic crisis of the 1930s, which left many male breadwinners unable to support their families, undermined male authority and status in the home. Priced at fifty cents amid the Great Depression, *Esquire* cultivated an audience among an upper middle-class segment left relatively unharmed by the decade's economic woes. Identifying itself as a magazine with "class" rather than mass appeal, it stressed to advertisers the disposable income of its acquisitive, upwardly mobile audience:

> Remember that laying down a half dollar for a single copy of a magazine that doesn't teach you anything and that you don't particularly need, is in direct ratio to laying out $115 for a suit of clothes or $3500 for an automobile—it isn't necessary but it's fun if you can afford it. In society, a man may do that and still be a rank parvenu. But in business, where the only aristocracy is the dollar, and the dislodgable [*sic*] dollar at that, he's class.

Neither the magazine nor its advertisers, *Esquire* claimed, had interest in attracting an audience of "dime dispensing tycoons" and "diamond tiara'd dowagers"—both "rotten prospects for people with things to sell," for their "needs are few and their wants are fewer still." When it came to advertising, "class" did not mean "heavy moneyed circulation, but ready moneyed."[21] Hefner similarly pitched his magazine to acquisitive young men with cash in their pockets and set about showing them how best to spend it.

Esquire's audience may have possessed the requisite disposable income, but gendered assumptions about practices such as grooming, interior decorating, cooking, and shopping required the magazine to recast tasteful consumption as an appropriate activity for male readers.[22] In the first issue *Esquire* asserted its aim to be, "among other things, a fashion guide for men. But it never intends to

become, by any possible stretch of the imagination, a primer for fops." *Esquire*'s readers had "too much inherent horse sense" to become overly concerned or fastidious about fashion, a preoccupation that might cast doubt on one's masculinity.[23] *Esquire* also disparaged women's cooking and decorating abilities in order to make room for male interest in such activities. Lest there be any lingering taint of effeminacy, *Esquire* simultaneously constructed women as objects of the male gaze in a variety of images that served to confirm the heterosexual masculinity and affirm the superiority of the male reader.[24] Most memorable of these were the stylized, airbrushed illustrations of scantily clad women by George Petty and Alberto Vargas.

Fiction and articles from top-name authors gave *Esquire* highbrow literary appeal, while risqué cartoons and jokes provided lowbrow humor, a mixture one critic called an "unholy combination of erudition and sex."[25] The resulting editorial package constituted *Esquire*'s ideal reader as a modern, sexually virile, masculine consumer who paid no heed to traditional virtues like civic duty or manly self-restraint:

> He is a very shaky bet to endow any universities, or to leave monuments behind him in the shape of any such good and lasting works when he goes. He drinks too much. He drives too fast. And he swears, upon no provocation at all. As his pal, we will stoutly maintain that his interest in sex is healthy, but we cannot deny that it is lively. And he hasn't been to church since the last time he ushered at a wedding...try as we may, we have yet to find a subject that he considers sacred.

The audience to which it appealed, *Esquire* admitted, was irreverent and unconventional. But if the average reader was a rake, he was also an important mark for advertisers: "He's a sailor with his money—he sails for every new thing that comes into his ken and more often than not, for no good reason. He's rather inclined to be vain and self-indulgent—apt to be a trifle over eager to be first with new things, from cocktail recipes to clothes and cars." *Esquire*'s promotional literature soothed concerns about the lowbrow aspects of its content and the readership to which the magazine appealed, arguing for the viability in the commercial mainstream of a risqué publication appealing to adult, male self-indulgence. "Quite possibly," *Esquire* conceded, "you would hesitate to take him into the bosom of your family, or even to propose him for membership in your club. But you couldn't possibly hesitate to accept his business, because the Grade A spender is the prime prospect." After all, *Esquire* reasoned, "if you're in business to sell...do you insist on having your every prospect up to meet the wife and kids before you will accept his money?"[26] According to *Esquire*, one did not have to like the fact that it flouted

conventions or printed material unsuitable for children in order to seize a profitable opportunity. Such arguments, which detached capitalist enterprise from traditional morality, continued to gain credence as the twentieth century progressed.[27]

The creation of *Esquire* marked an important development in the construction of a modern, masculine persona, which resonated with the early twentieth century's increasing emphasis on personality, self-expression, and display while countering the perceived feminine orientation of the consumer society. During World War II, David Smart added even more "cheesecake," boosting the magazine's appeal to American GIs. Special editions were provided free to servicemen, its popularity prompting comedian Bob Hope to quip that American soldiers were ready to fight "at the drop of an *Esquire*." The bawdy publication, however, was also a target of Post Office censors. Even though each issue contained much non–sex related content, Postmaster General Frank C. Walker revoked *Esquire*'s second-class mailing permit in December 1943, alleging that the magazine was not of an acceptably edifying nature to receive such privileges. Following a two-year legal battle, the Supreme Court ruled in *Esquire*'s favor, declaring that the U.S. Post Office Department could not act as moral arbiter, a decision that portended the court's expansion of the realm of material deemed fit for public consumption. While its airbrushed pinups reached the height of popularity during the war, the magazine's literary merit and its smart, sophisticated lifestyle package dissipated along the way. Gingrich, whose vision had shaped the magazine in its 1930s heyday, departed in July 1945.[28] *Esquire* entered the postwar period lacking editorial focus and beset by competition from numerous "girlie" magazines. By mapping out a masculine consumer lifestyle and an editorial strategy for securing it, however, *Esquire* had provided a ready template for a newcomer. In Hefner's judgment, the marketplace had a need for such a magazine in the 1950s.

Playboy fast became a publishing sensation. With more than 300,000 paying readers by the end of 1955, it surpassed *Esquire*'s circulation by 1958 and boasted a paying readership of more than one million by 1960.[29] *Playboy*'s fashioning of a lifestyle marked by tasteful consumption and heterosexual virility broke little new ground. Instead, Hefner's genius lay in recognizing the void created by *Esquire*'s decline and in capitalizing on postwar circumstances that made possible a successful reinvigoration of that magazine's early editorial strategy. Whereas the economic conditions of the 1930s had limited the audience to which *Esquire*'s consumer lifestyle appealed, a newfound level of affluence that made possible the translation of consumer fantasies into reality enabled *Playboy* to promote earlier images of the hedonistic bachelor to their fullest

potential. At the same time, the sense that men needed a reprieve from a society overly concerned with propriety and catering to women's tastes and interests resonated with even greater intensity in the postwar period, exacerbated by the widespread changes taking place across America.

MARITAL TENSION AND GENDER ANXIETY IN POSTWAR AMERICA

Hefner's personal misgivings about marriage took shape as the hallmarks of the good life centered on hearth and home were still forming. Amid rising prosperity, rampant suburbanization, and a cultural celebration of the nuclear family, *Playboy* emerged as a contestant in an ongoing dialogue about a society in transition. The publication of Betty Friedan's *The Feminine Mystique* in 1963 has received credit for first exposing the cleavage between the myth of the "happy housewife" and the lack of fulfillment women found in this role. Friedan's assessments were not new, however, nor were women's roles the only ones under scrutiny as observers critiqued postwar gender and family ideals. As historian Eva Moskowitz has demonstrated, women's magazines articulated "a discourse of discontent," training the spotlight on women's dissatisfaction with the prescribed role of housewife even as it encouraged them to adjust to that role. *Life* magazine's Special Issue on the American Woman (1956) devoted attention to restless housewives and the husbands who bore the brunt of their frustrations.[30] Social guidance films warned of marital strife, depicting husbands and wives as they quarreled over decision making and went unappreciated in their respective roles. By the mid-1950s, fictional works and sociological studies addressed the anomie and discord of suburban life, where wives lacked meaningful contact and social interaction during the day and husbands faced the stress of work and the endless worry about paying the bills for this particular version of the American dream.

Among such works, John Keats's *The Crack in the Picture Window* and August Comte Spectorsky's *The Exurbanites* painted bleak pictures of housewives who threw themselves into housekeeping and child-rearing while envying the interesting lives of their husbands; in turn, husbands found their spouses frustrated and embittered. Keats, for example, chronicled the fate of archetypal tract-dwellers John and Mary Drone, who faced a life of drudgery and financial hardship after purchasing a "box on a slab" in a suburban development. In this cautionary tale, as John Drone commutes to and from his job in the city, he fails to see how the monotonous routine of housework and childcare is breaking Mary's spirit. He allows her to talk him into buying a bigger house,

thinking a more spacious home will solve her problems. He ends up working two jobs, along with a third during the Christmas season, to pay for it. Having been seduced by the promises of domestic consumption, they have only exacerbated their problems and remain miserable. The subjects of Spectorsky's 1955 bestseller enjoyed a higher standard of living in the far-flung locales outside New York City than the Drones of Rolling Knolls, but they faced the same pressures of boredom, financial worry, and marital conflict.[31]

Contemporary studies supported the images sketched in these popular depictions. William H. Whyte described the new suburbia as the dormitory of the Organization Man—"packaged villages" marked by unsettling mobility, where the desire to fit in was the chief concern of residents and the "tyranny of the group" precluded efforts for individual expression. *The Split-Level Trap*, a study of suburban Bergen County, New Jersey, addressed similar concerns, endeavoring to learn where and how "this archetype of the mobile world, this Disturbia— has gone wrong." According to its authors, the pressures of suburban life—the isolation of young wives from kinship networks, the lack of defined mores in a development full of strangers, the demanding and confining roles of homemaker and breadwinner—caused stress and nervous breakdown, findings *Cosmopolitan* magazine cited in an article it called "Crack-ups in the Suburbs."[32]

In the postwar period, concerns about the pressures and frustrations of family life circulated alongside exhortations to enjoy "togetherness." In *Playboy*, themes of suburban discontent informed the magazine's positioning of its ideal reader in a swinging, urban bachelor pad, while the unfulfilled housewife served as a foil for the sexually vital single girls who appeared in the magazine. *Playboy* also took up another strand of criticism pervasive in postwar culture, as popular writers and public intellectuals voiced concern over a series of troubles thought to be plaguing the American male. Discomfort with changes in the workplace and family life found expression in discussions of gender upheaval and pronouncements that masculinity was in a state of crisis.

Assertions of masculine crisis exaggerated the impingements on male power at mid-century. As historian Gail Bederman has argued about the so-called crisis over manhood in the late nineteenth and early twentieth centuries, white, middle-class men never doubted their right to wield power; they merely looked for new ways to reassert their claims to power.[33] Similarly, in the postwar period, men continued to hold the upper hand when it came to accessing credit, education, jobs, income, political power, and public space, and women's abilities and social contributions were still rather narrowly envisioned. Those who did express consternation about women's infringements on male authority had little doubt that men were naturally supposed to have that authority. Yet they worried about a constellation of developments that produced stress and

anxiety in daily life, seemed to undermine male power, and called into question the coherence of masculine identity.

Although middle-class men more than a half-century earlier had grappled with the changing nature of capitalism and its ramifications for their identities as producers, the relationship between the structure and values of the corporate economy and the individual received widespread attention after World War II with the appearance of several publications. Together, they pointed to profound shifts in American culture that, in turn, posed important implications for men and masculinity. "The twentieth-century white-collar man," asserted C. Wright Mills, "is always somebody's man, the corporation's, the government's, the army's; and he is seen as the man who does not rise." Mills's *White Collar* (1951) described the transition from a middle class composed of independent shop owners, entrepreneurs, and professionals to a new middle class of wage earners toiling in large companies. According to David Riesman, where once individuals had been "inner-directed," guided from within by a "psychological gyroscope," now they were "other-directed," equipped with a "social radar" attuned to the signals emanating from those around them as well as from mass culture. The resultant "other-directed" society limned in *The Lonely Crowd* (1950) valued consensus and emphasized getting along with others. Whyte's *The Organization Man* (1956) similarly noted a transformation from a Puritan ethic prizing individualism to a social ethic, which favored the group and emphasized the individual's need to belong.[34]

These critics pointed to a social order that subdued individualism and encouraged conformity. Moreover, emphasizing passivity over assertiveness and sensitivity to others over personal initiative, the social order they sketched valued characteristics typically cast as feminine. Thus, although they spoke broadly about national character or the new middle class, they addressed circumstances of consequence to white, middle-class men. Together with those who popularized their insights, they described a society that in effect had become "feminized."[35] A female character in the novel *No Down Payment* provided an apt summary of the trend:

> About the only real difference between how a man and his wife live now is that she has children. They do pretty much the same kind of work— she pushes buttons and runs machinery at home, he does it at work or he's being pleasant to somebody as a sales man. Mostly they drink about the same, go out about the same, have the same kind of fun in bed. The girls are even getting bigger...

In this estimation, both the ease of postwar living and the nature of postwar production eroded the differences between the sexes. Neither work nor leisure seemed to afford opportunities for fixing masculine identity.

As some commentators pointed to a society grown more feminized due to economic forces and shifts in social organization, others found a more imme-diate culprit in the American woman. Summing up critics' complaints during the early years of the Cold War, a time when dissent was equated with dis-loyalty, Betty Friedan offered one explanation for the ease with which women were blamed for men's troubles. "No one has ever been blacklisted or fired for an attack on the 'American woman.'... Safer to take it out on his wife and his mother than to recognize a failure in himself or in the sacred American way of life." As Friedan acknowledged, women formed a convenient target, their alleged attempts to dominate men and their undue feminizing influence pro-viding a suitable explanation for unsettling changes in American society. In blaming women for the distress of the American male, many commentators engaged in a sort of historical amnesia, envisioning a unique moment of crisis and overlooking the fact that objections to women's influence at home and in society were not new. Others drew connections to the past but viewed the postwar moment as the apex of women's long-standing attempts to seize male power. That women "dominated" men was a common charge, but accounts of how exactly women came to do so contained many inconsistencies and expressed many of the era's tensions.

No one was more vitriolic in blaming women for society's ills than Philip Wylie, who began his attack on the American woman with *Generation of Vipers* in 1942 and went on to continue his tirade in *Playboy. Vipers* reached its twentieth printing by 1955. In it, the acerbic Wylie denounced "momism," doting mothers who produced a nation of ineffectual men, easily dominated by women.[36] Although critics identified women as parasitic housewives and smothering mothers during the 1950s, women's presence outside the home, in fact, expanded after World War II. Women's postwar workforce participation increased steadily, with married women's income often providing the cushion that allowed families to enjoy a middle-class existence. Whether they focused their energies exclusively on the home or ventured outside of it, women were charged with trying to usurp power from men. As women enjoyed signifi-cant control over the home and increasingly entered a public sphere typically regarded as a male preserve, some warned that they began also to assume the masculine role.[37]

"She's winning the battle of the sexes," proclaimed the cover of *Look* mag-azine's special issue on the American woman. Elsewhere critics charged that men were embattled in daily life, while women had it easy. After all, men were required to prove themselves even before they entered into matrimony. As one social scientist put it, a man had to "demonstrate some vocational proficiency and achieve at least a modicum of economic security" before he married.

"Relatively speaking, the prerequisites for the female," on the other hand, were "only that she should appear at the ceremony with clean face and proper costume." Popular accounts suggested that despite the dissatisfactions of work in the "organization," men found it difficult to break free, bound as they were by their familial obligations. A cartoon illustration for a *New York Times Magazine* article on the "American Man in a Woman's World" showed a man looking up at a signpost, where "marriage" and "parenthood" pointed one way, "career" another; "home" and "risk" lay in entirely opposite directions (see figure 1.2). Sloan Wilson's novel, *The Man in the Gray Flannel Suit,* addressed this same perception. When his wife berates him for becoming a cynical corporate "yes man," Tom Rath pointedly underlines the ties between family-centered consumption and conformity. "You're talking like a typical American woman," he tells her. "You want it both ways. 'Don't play it safe,' you say, 'and can we get a new car tomorrow?'" The angst-laden questions posed by each installment of *Look* magazine's series on "The American Male" (1958) were telling as well: "Why Is He Afraid to Be Different?" "Why Do Women Dominate Him?" "Why Does He Work So Hard?"[38]

If the man who failed to provide for a wife and family shirked the duties of responsible manhood, men who married also faced the feminizing influences of their wives. "You can have hair on your chest and bulges in your biceps and still be more feminine than Ava Gardner," explained one article in the *Nation's Business,* which informed readers that masculinity waned the longer a man stayed married. "In plain English," the author summed up, "that means your missus is making you feminine!" Wives subdued the behaviors associated with free-spirited bachelorhood. According to one study, they even restricted their husbands' alcohol consumption, a particularly egregious situation when a husband needed a drink to take the edge off the demands of breadwinning. In the literature on masculine decline, married men were either emasculated by their domestic responsibilities or else had no role at all in a home where a wife had seized male power. Opined a psychiatrist, the American woman was "thoroughly spoiled. She has plenty of pushbuttons, but not enough to satisfy her—so she also pushes her husband." "Does the American father have any role at all, beyond procreation and money-making?" asked one *Look* author, while another proclaimed that fathers had too many roles to fill. "Today's breadwinner" served as "part-time nursemaid, kitchen helper, handyman and mechanic," all amounting to "more hard work at the end of a hard day." According to *Look,* desertion, bachelorhood, and homosexuality—the "flight from masculinity"— were among the ways the American male warded off female domination.[39]

Playboy's unflattering portrait of marriage represented a seamless addition to this rhetoric about the beleaguered male, beginning, as Barbara Ehrenreich

1.2 *This cartoon, which appeared in the* New York Times Magazine *in 1957, captured sentiments about the links between familial responsibility and conformity. For the breadwinner charged with supporting a wife and children, security was the hallmark of a good job. Home and risk were in opposite directions. (Abner Dean)*

has observed, with an article on alimony titled "Miss Gold-Digger of 1953."
Subsequent issues added the harrowing details. Conniving, selfish, and indo-
lent, too many women were only after money. If she wasn't soaking the poor
sap who married her ("when a modern day marriage ends…it's always the
guy who pays and pays…"), she was using the court system to stick him with
child support payments ("when the charge is bastardy, the wily woman wins").
Some women never involved the courts at all, living contentedly on their
husband's income. Cautioned one *Playboy* contributor, "When the little doll
says she'll live on your income, she means it all right. But just be sure to get
another one for yourself." "Unlike many-sided man," warned "Open Season on
Bachelors," "woman has only *one* goal in life—marriage." Women were "perfectly willing to crush man's adventurous, freedom-loving spirit" to get the
financial security they craved. Some withheld sex, coercing men to marry; others granted sexual favors, guilting men into wedlock. Before readers fell prey to
such ploys, *Playboy* urged them to "take a good look at the sorry, regimented
husbands" who trudged down the street in a "woman dominated land" and
consider their fate.[40]

Playboy's depiction of marriage critiqued social conventions that required
men to bear the financial burdens of family life. Bachelorhood offered a pleasant alternative. "You can have only one wife at a time, but the bachelor can be
surrounded by girls of all kinds," explained one author. Men, after all, craved
variety. "Monogamy is a flop," declared another. Marriage amounted to "under
the counter sex varietism masquerading as easy divorce."[41] More than simply denoting an anti-marriage posture, however, such hyperbolic portrayals
of scheming, freeloading, and controlling wives represented one facet of the
magazine's participation in prevailing debates about gender upheaval. In addition to publishing stories on the perils of marriage and the freedom of bachelorhood, *Playboy* engaged in further rumination on masculinity, feminization,
and the proper place of men and women in postwar America, issues taken up in
discussions on the problems of a "womanized society."

Seeking to upgrade the editorial content of his magazine, Hefner recruited
A. C. Spectorsky, author of *The Exurbanites*, to join him in Chicago as *Playboy*'s
associate publisher in 1956. Spectorsky was instrumental in securing contributions from Philip Wylie, who continued in *Playboy* the diatribe against women
first articulated in *Generation of Vipers*. Though that book is perhaps best
remembered for its attack on "momism," Wylie had also criticized America's
"Cinderella myth." The tale was a rags-to-riches story, except that unlike the
Horatio Alger hero who pulled himself up by his bootstraps, Cinderella's good
fortune came from marrying rich—the prince she met at the ball saved her
from a lifetime of drudgery. In Wylie's estimation, this tale had particular

resonance in the United States, where technology produced an idle class of married women whose husbands worked to support them. Moreover, mass media inspired women to seek Cinderella status. "There is, the American legend tells her, a good-looking man with dough, who will put an end to the onerous tedium of making a living." Supported by a man, the woman controlled the purse strings, her spending transforming American cities into: "(a) markets for home-consumed goods; (b) markets for the sale of goods to make home-keeping a minimal-cinch; (c) markets offering female vanity-goods; and (d) minimal-cinch homes." In the modern-day version of the Cinderella myth, the corporation turned the pumpkin into a Chevrolet.[42] Wylie's discussion of Cinderella anticipated his later contributions to *Playboy*, which deplored the inexorable power of the marketplace and the exacting nature of modern life, attributing both to female domination. In articles titled "The Abdicating Male and How the Gray Flannel Mind Exploits Him" (1956), "The Womanization of America" (1958), and "The Career Woman" (1963), Wylie sketched a popular and consumer culture that catered to female tastes and interests, where "dominated" men financed women's endless consumption and found themselves under siege at home, in the leisure realm, and in the workplace from women who competed with men and intruded on male spaces.

In Wylie's estimation, society was not just becoming "feminized," it was becoming "womanized," which in the language used to debate a gender system in flux meant a society dominated by "masculinized" women. George Frazier, writing in *Esquire*, offered a similar assessment. In the past, "notwithstanding their homespun clothes and unrouged cheeks, their hard days work and their harassment by nature," American women recognized that they were born "to love and to look up to their men—and, naturally, to bear their children too." Now women were confused, making incessant demands on male pocketbooks, "craving" equality, and wanting careers of their own while still insisting on the courtesies typically afforded to women as the "weaker" sex. "Crisis of masculinity be damned, the problem is the crisis of femininity," declared *Esquire*. "Whatever happened to the girl who was loving rather than just loved, serene rather than strident, comforting rather than competitive?"[43]

In Hefner's words, "womanization" meant the development of a "female-oriented society...A matriarchy instead of a patriarchy," which stemmed from long-term social changes and caused neuroses in contemporary society. In his view, the current state of anxiety began when "the woman, continually in a subordinate role, was pushed into a more dominant position. Women's suffrage gave them the vote, etc. All very positive things," he admitted. But after 1950, the pendulum of progress had swung too far. "We've gotten ourselves into a situation where...the [roles] of the sexes...are becoming less and less

defined.... You'll find more and more that women are competing with men whether they are married or not. It exists in jobs, but it exists in a good deal more than that." Hefner offered an account of the clearly defined roles that had recently given way to confusion. America had risen to greatness as a patriarchal society, Hefner explained. "We may have always thought that mom was pretty swell, but none the less, in the simpler society that existed in frontier days, dad was boss." He continued:

> You know it goes back to the very beginning of time. The man goes out and kills a saber-toothed tiger while the woman stays at home and washes out the pots. Fair, unfair, good, bad, or indifferent, the roles were clearly defined. Sadly, as they become less defined and more confused, we get into a situation such as we have today with a tremendous amount of national neuroses and real confusion in terms of the woman in a state of emotional flux. She wants to dominate the male, and the man gets into a position in which he feels dominated, and thus the woman loses identity. Without it things begin to be very unhappy. Marriages collapse, etc.

Hefner echoed concerns expressed in *Life* magazine, which attributed America's "disturbing divorce rate," in part to "wives who are not feminine enough and husbands not truly male."[44] In Hefner's formulation, neither men nor women could find contentment without the clear sense of identity that came from these complementary, separate roles. To be sure, he conceded, the postwar world was changing, but men and women had to adjust to its new circumstances without losing site of their natural relationship to one another.

The problem of "womanization" inspired a lengthy roundtable discussion in *Playboy* in June 1962, which began with an editorial statement on the "growing national awareness" of women's increased power in society, advances that merited praise. "We are not male chauvinists," declared *Playboy*. But in many ways, women's "meteoric ascendancy" had given "grave cause for alarm to women as well as men." Outlining the varied dimensions of a female-oriented, woman-dominated society, *Playboy* rehearsed the rhetoric on masculine crisis. One had only to consider the proliferation of advertising and mass media directed at women, the "massive upsurge in feminine purchasing power, the kitchen-oriented redesigning of homes, the wall-to-wall décor of American automotive appointments," or the "blurred distinctions between the sexes" in business as well as in "household chores, leisure activities, smoking and drinking habits, clothing styles, upswinging homosexuality and the sex obliterating aspects of togetherness." Given these developments, *Playboy* wondered "whether women are being masculinized even faster than the country is becoming womanized. Or is it, perhaps, that men are being effeminized?"[45] Participants in the "Playboy

Panel" included renowned psychoanalyst Dr. Theodor Reik; noted literary figures Alexander King and Norman Mailer; Edward Bernays and Ernest Dichter, experts in the fields of public relations and marketing; and Herbert Mayes, the top executive at *McCall's,* one of the leading magazines for women. Addressing a range of topics from the male's loss of authority at home to women's conflicting demands for rights *and* deferential treatment, to women's consumer power and expectations for male sexual performance, panelists failed to reach consensus on the extent to which society was becoming "womanized," but agreed that changes in men's and women's roles threatened a sense of male superiority.

Playboy concluded with a forecast for renewed harmony between the sexes as men and women adjusted to their transforming gender roles:

> There is a new spirit on the land, evident in our readership, which would suggest that the younger urban people of this country are coming to a new awareness of both masculinity and femininity. That is, the men are increasingly aware that one can be masculine without being hairy-chested and muscular; the women, that one can be intelligent and sensitive—and witty and wise—and at the same time be completely feminine.

Pointing to this "new awareness" of gender implied the acceptance of some fluidity in the range of attributes, behaviors, and activities comprising masculinity and femininity, yet also presumed the continued expression of essential qualities that marked the natural boundaries between men and women. *Playboy* embraced the notion that the substance constituting masculinity could change, while never doubting that men were meant to have certain prerogatives that women did not enjoy. *Playboy* executive Victor Lownes explained in the *Saturday Evening Post,* "I guess we do express an antifeminist point of view, and we might be somewhat in error in not giving the exceptional woman full credit. But we firmly believe that women are *not* equal to men."[46] Hefner saw the program of gender difference to which he was so firmly committed as a harmonious system of complementary roles for men and women, but it was also hierarchical, with men maintaining the dominant position in terms of status and power. Rather than reverting to stereotypes of rugged masculinity or hearkening back to the patriarchal days of what Hefner called "a simpler society," *Playboy* envisioned a masculine persona in tune with a modern, sexually liberated, consumer society, freed of the burdens of breadwinning and untainted by the feminine associations of consumption. Furthermore, as the closing remarks of the "Playboy Panel" suggested, the playboy's exuberant singlehood provided a model that promised to ease tensions between embattled men and women. "As our nation becomes emancipated from the notion of associating sex with sin, rather than with romance, and as young people are increasingly freed of

feeling guilty about a play period in their lives before settling down to marital maturity, so the attitudes of the sexes may well become more healthy toward each other," *Playboy* concluded. In this estimation, the womanization problem was tied to society's veneration of the family and its insistence on confining sex to marriage, which had the unhealthy effect of constricting men's and women's roles and pitting them against one another. It followed, then, that rethinking the place of sex in society could actually combat the problem of marital discord and gender upheaval.

SEX AND SOCIETY IN POSTWAR AMERICA

Hefner knew the "girlie" pictures in his magazine would help sell it, but the sexual content took on even greater import as he began to imagine *Playboy* as a vehicle through which to advocate for a prolonged period of "play" in life and to crusade against what he called the evils of sexual Puritanism. Hefner had experienced firsthand the disparity between social conventions and sexual behavior, and his disappointing marriage seemed to offer proof that the pressures on young men and women to find a mate and settle down early in life only created discontent. Back in college, he and Millie had traveled to a nearby town, checked into a motel room, and consummated their relationship. It was the first time either had experienced sexual intercourse, and they became engaged only a few months later. Millie graduated ahead of Hefner and left to take a teaching job in another part of the state. The couple reunited for weekend visits, but in time, Millie grew inexplicably distant. During one visit, she broke down in tears and finally confessed to having an affair—"the most traumatic experience of my life," Hefner later recalled. Though devastated, he decided not to break off the engagement. Because society placed such a premium on female virginity, he reasoned, once that status had been lost, it was not very difficult for a woman "to fall into an affair." Almost immediately after beginning wedded life, though, he resented the confines of a monogamous relationship and regretted marrying right out of college.[47] As his magazine gained a following, he gradually asserted his belief that revising the place of sex in society would produce a healthier, less guilt-ridden, and better adjusted one.

In the words of one commentator, in the 1950s, Americans followed a moral standard that defined a gentleman "as a man who would rather commit adultery than mention it in the presence of a lady."[48] The codes governing sexual morality at mid-century affirmed heterosexual desire but confined it within a framework of marriage. The existing double standard upheld expectations for

premarital chastity for women, while tolerating a male's (hetero)sexual exploits before marriage; within this system, women who provided sexual outlets were differentiated from "nice girls."[49] Hollywood's Production Code Administration, U.S. Post Office Department censors, local blue laws, and numerous citizen watchdog groups provided formal and informal mechanisms of control, keeping a ready eye on public displays that threatened to transgress the bounds of morality or offend good taste. This meant not only that purveyors of popular culture risked censorship or prosecution by deviating from accepted norms, but that obscenity statutes as well as guidelines for television and motion pictures permitted sexual expression only to the extent that it did not threaten to corrupt society's most susceptible members. In this regard, sexually explicit material remained at the margins, associated with guilt and secrecy, yet also further eroticized by its transgressive nature. Though conflict between moral traditionalists and purveyors of commercialized leisure was not new, the upheaval of the war years and the expansion of the national marketplace accelerated the pace of change and exacerbated these strains in the 1950s. Americans experienced a disconnect between publicly espoused norms and private behavior, as well as tension between, on the one hand, a popular culture that made sex more visible and threatened sexual mores and, on the other, the forces of conservatism trying to keep change at bay. Compared to the pronounced sexual liberalism of the late 1960s and 1970s, the era appears as a time of sexual conservatism, but sex was not absent from postwar culture. Sexual innuendo permeated mainstream cultural forms. Furthermore, efforts to censor and prohibit sexual expression constituted an important growth of public discussion that opened up cultural space for the development of further discourse.[50]

Alfred C. Kinsey's investigations into human sexual behavior, for example, prompted a public outcry at the same time they made sex a viable topic in the mainstream media. Based on thousands of detailed interviews, Kinsey's first cataloguing of sexual experience, *Sexual Behavior in the Human Male*, appeared in 1948. The book provoked shock and outrage among some members of society but also sparked enormous interest. One newspaper reported that a practical joker had wired a copy of the book left on a shop counter so that curious customers sneaking a peek received an electrical jolt. Hundreds of requests, many on "bar-stained stationery" accompanied by labels soaked off of Kinsey liquor bottles, arrived at the Kinsey Distilling Corporation in response to rumors that labels could be exchanged for a free copy of the book.[51] Other Americans were just as eager to purchase the Kinsey Report, which, despite its technical language and dense statistics, sold more than a quarter of a million volumes.

The long-awaited companion, *Sexual Behavior in the Human Female* (1953), stirred frenzy in the media. Advance press copies prompted editorials alternately

praising the groundbreaking study or denouncing its prurience. Some newspapers printed statements explaining that they would not review the publication because the language needed to discuss Kinsey's findings offended good taste. More important, such information threatened to "corrupt the morals" of young people, particularly those eager "for 'authority' to overturn the bounds of respectable and restrained conduct." Other journalists chose to review the book but carefully excised the "graphic language," which readers "seldom encountered outside medical books." Religious leaders called the study and the widespread publicity it enjoyed "a shocking indictment of the morality of our age." But the very fact that the Kinsey Report sparked such acrimony brought the topic of sex into a public forum. Mainstream publications such as *Newsweek* summarized the Kinsey Report in articles that discussed "onanism," petting, and extramarital relations.[52]

And there was still the matter of Kinsey's findings. Although subsequent researchers questioned Kinsey's methodology and conclusions, the report on male sexuality stunned readers with its announcement that masturbation was normal, that premarital and extramarital sex was widespread, and that homosexual activity was far more common than most believed.[53] Like the report on male sexuality, the study of women indicated a wide discrepancy between sexual practice and social decorum, but seemed to offer even greater cause for alarm because, as one newspaper put it, women were "bound by a stricter moral code." One irate woman called Kinsey's statistics "a figment of a monstrous imagination" meant "to undermine and degrade the virtues of the American woman." Meanwhile, a man surmised that one could not trust Kinsey's data on women because one could not trust women to tell the truth. Notwithstanding such disbelief, Kinsey's statistics exposed the fiction of publicly espoused sex norms.[54]

Along with the controversy stirred by Kinsey, postwar fashions and youth culture provided further evidence of tensions and concerns over sexual expression. Embodied in the vocal style and swiveling hips of Elvis Presley, sexuality took center stage in a new form of music that appealed to youth. With its urgent rhythms, suggestive lyrics, and origins in African-American and working-class communities stereotypically associated with a lack of restraint, rock and roll, with its sexual overtones, excited young people but worried middle-class parents and community leaders who led the charge against it. A sexually expressive youth culture also gave cause for concern. While adults expected young couples who "went steady" to engage in physical displays of affection, fear of sexual transgression—that young people would go too far—was linked to wider fears of social disorder and the rupturing of family life. Sexual activity, if properly "contained" within marriage, promised to bolster the family and thereby strengthen the fabric of society, a belief that helped spur early marriage for

young men and women. At the same time, the proliferation of maternity homes and a booming adoption market, not to mention demand for the services of illegal abortionists, all of which provided ways to cope with consequences of sexual indiscretion, pointed up the inadequacy of early marriage to fully contain youthful sexuality. Clothing styles emphasizing female curves also drew attention to sexuality. In the 1950s, the availability of undergarment structuring materials such as elastic and metal, off limits to bra manufacturers during the war, transformed breasts into sculpted shapes.[55] Fashion epitomized the strains in a cultural system that prized feminine beauty and encouraged a degree of sexual expression within courtship, while placing on young women the burden of halting male sexual advances.

The years after World War II also brought an increase in the production of sexually explicit material as well as sustained debates over its suitability for public consumption. Although *Esquire* had won its hard-fought battle against post office censors, the proliferation of "girlie" magazines, pulp paperbacks, and comic books prompted a congressional investigation in 1952. Chaired by Ezekiel Gathings (D-AR), the Select Committee on Current Pornographic Materials sought to define obscenity, assess the scope of offending publications, and propose remedies for curtailing their distribution. Alarmed by the perceived increase in "undesirable" material, the committee nevertheless was unable to reach a unanimous decision about how to define obscenity, much less what to do about it. Dissenters on the committee opposed advocating what in their view amounted to censorship.[56] This is not to suggest that *Playboy* entered a wide-open marketplace in the 1950s, for Hefner, too, faced the efforts of post-office censors and drew the ire of church officials in the heavily Catholic city of Chicago. It took a federal district court to compel the post office to grant discounted mailing privileges to *Playboy* in 1955. In a case dismissed for lack of evidence, Hefner was charged with contributing to the delinquency of a minor for the appearance in the magazine of Miss January (1958), a college student whom officials claimed had been underage when the photos were taken. A gritty sexual scene in a fictional story that appeared in the July 1962 issue necessitated a long memo of justification from Hefner to calm the nerves of skittish advertisers. And Hefner stood trial on obscenity charges for publishing nude photographs of Jayne Mansfield in June 1963. A conviction would have brought $400 in fines, but the case ended in a hung jury.[57]

Postwar efforts to combat public expressions of sexuality represented a rearguard action against change. Conflicts that pitted "pariah capitalists" against proponents of traditional morality provided evidence of the growing power of the marketplace to challenge and redraw social boundaries. Along these lines, beginning in the 1950s, independent films and foreign movies, which fell outside the purview of the Production Code Administration, gradually began

to undermine Hollywood's self-censorship guidelines. Although religious and civic groups threatened boycotts, such films attracted audiences and proved profitable. Meanwhile, as numerous cases wound their way through the court system, the Supreme Court gradually began to narrow the realm of material judged obscene. In doing so, the court revised a longtime test of obscenity. In the fifties, the court ruled that only a work evaluated in its entirety and determined to be "utterly without redeeming social importance," could be found obscene. No longer was the consideration whether a work might corrupt a vulnerable individual—the young innocent—but "whether to the average person, applying contemporary community standards," its "dominant theme" appealed to "prurient interest." Such decisions did not center on whether or not one had the right to consume whatever material one wished, but on where to draw the line that separated legitimate from illegitimate matter. The revised measures of obscenity, in shifting concern away from the protection of the impressionable innocent, had the effect of legitimizing cultural production aimed at an adult market rather than at a family-oriented mass market, opening the door for increased production and distribution of sexually oriented material.[58] In this changing climate Hefner took on the role of progressive crusader as he sought to expand the bounds of the permissible.

Hefner possessed a long-standing interest in the legal and ethical considerations circumscribing sex. The fact that cultural purveyors, in their pursuit of mass markets, appealed to conservative sensibilities so as not to risk offense merely contributed to the sense that society had grown more "feminized," and seemed to substantiate Hefner's appeal to the "neglected males" of the 1950s. As he explained, there was no way to produce a publication for an adult male audience that would also be suited "to Mom and the kiddies."[59] In his view, the family-oriented society and its strictures on sexual expression denied a healthy, adult interest in sex. The form and content of his magazine seized on the era's furtive interest in sex while also avowing that men's attention to *Playboy*'s nude pictorials and frank revelry in sexual matters was perfectly normal and appropriate. In attempting to legitimate first, men's interest in nude pictures of women, and second, a period of premarital sexual activity, *Playboy* sought to widen, but not to obliterate, the boundaries of acceptable behavior by redefining the terms of sexual permission and restraint.

The bachelor's heterosexual activities technically defied social prescriptions confining sex to marriage. The single man who did not violate these sanctions, however, risked being branded a homosexual. Kinsey's finding that 37 percent of males had reached orgasm through at least one homosexual act fueled anxieties about masculinity by raising the possibility that virtually anyone might be a homosexual, a status linked to male weakness in popular discussions. In

the chilling climate of the Cold War, sexual "perversion" and subversion were readily linked. The Lavender Scare that racked the nation's capital in the 1950s took shape amid concern over American moral degeneracy and fear of weakness against the threat of Soviet expansion. Suspected homosexuals faced FBI surveillance and police harassment; men and women who failed to conform to gender prescriptions were purged from military and government service as security risks.[60] Hefner strategically positioned his magazine in this homophobic climate. "A picture of a beautiful woman is something that a fellow of any age ought to be able to enjoy," he commented. "If he doesn't, then that's the kid to watch out for." Hefner related that "there were two kinds of boys—those who liked to pull the wings off flies and those who liked girls. We confess to a preference in the latter. The deviates, the perverts, the serious juvenile delinquents—they're not interested in healthy boy-girl relationships." He asserted in another interview, "There's something wrong, either psychologically or glandularly, with some guy who isn't interested in pictures of pretty girls." Constructions of homosexuality as male weakness and a potential threat to national security meant that *Playboy*'s nudes, rather than harming society, affirmed heterosexual virility. "We're admittedly very much a heterosexual magazine in the full Freudian sense of the word," he told another journalist. "The so-called family magazines treat sex sensationally, making it seem ugly and dirty. Sex to them is the doctor's bag, the unhappy marriage. Sex to us is beautiful girls. If dressing up and taking a girl out for a night on the town is delinquency, then maybe we need more delinquents." From this perspective, *Playboy*'s success offered evidence of national well-being.[61]

Moreover, there was nothing threatening about *Playboy*'s brand of "pretty girls." Hefner made important modifications to the nudes found in other magazines for men, the Playmate appearing in glossy full color when others were printed on pulp paper in black and white. Following the inaugural issue with Marilyn Monroe, *Playboy* published stock photographs of anonymous females. Soon exhausting this supply, *Playboy* began to showcase models photographed specifically for its pinup, and Hefner's instructions for these features reveal the middle ground he sought for these sexually alluring images. Hefner admonished photographers not to submit "beach pin-ups, study poses and arty salon shots." Instead, he explained, "We want to see fresh, young things in bedroom and bath...in filmy negligees, silky nightgowns, and similarly dressed as girls really are. We want the surroundings to be logical and the girl real to the reader." Finding just the right level of "exposure" was critical. He informed one photographer, "To keep it sexy but acceptable, we'll want the breasts exposed, and yet covered.... This distinction is a very important one for us—as we don't want to run anything as innocuous as a straight pin-up, and at the same time we don't

want to run out and out nudes." Hefner also thought it important to provide a context for each Playmate. He issued copious instructions on the kinds of settings and props to be used—a college dorm room, a man's pajama top, two mixed drinks on a table—in order to suggest a particular scenario for each monthly feature (see figure 1.3). The result, as he put it, was "nudity with validity." In these images, he explained to one photographer, "the camera becomes our guy who is present but unseen."[62]

To Hefner, "a nude that has no name" held "relatively little appeal." He further honed the feature by creating an identity for the Playmate, publishing a story that provided biographical information about each model, along with a series of photos of the fully-clothed Playmate partaking in her everyday activities. The resulting images suggested that "nice" but somehow sexually self-aware "girls" disrobed for *Playboy*'s cameras, while the accompanying text affirmed that the Playmate existed not in a world apart from the reader, but all around him.[63] Like the Gibson Girl a half-century earlier or the World War II–era pinup, the Playmate, Hefner suggested, exuded an all-American type of beauty. "She is never sophisticated, a girl you cannot really have. She is a healthy, simple girl—the girl next door," he explained. "Please remember that the October Playmate is supposed to be a college coed," he reminded one photographer, "so try to get her to strike a fresh, provocative but rather innocent expression. In other words, don't have her looking too sultry or ultra-sophisticated." In crafting the squeaky-clean girl next door, Hefner sought to remove the tawdriness that surrounded nudity and sex, pressing for the mainstream acceptance of greater sexual expression while claiming legitimacy for his magazine. *Playboy* did not promote wanton sexual activity, nor sex with just anyone, after all. It carefully pointed to a healthy, male sexual appetite, channeled toward wholesome girls who appeared in an upmarket format. Attesting to Kinsey's finding that engaging in sexual fantasy was a regular activity for males, "Dear Playboy" letters occasionally alluded to the centerfold's function as a masturbatory aid, such as one that recounted, "I got as far as Sharon Rogers and couldn't go on. The rest of the magazine had to be an anti-climax." Others simply expressed enthusiasm for the latest Playmate in the manner of one that exclaimed "Wow! 'Miss October'...was really the most."[64]

The sexually alluring "girl" who posed for the magazine's centerfold contrasted with "women" who pressured men for marriage, only to become burdensome, resentful housewives. Her title changed after the first issue, from a Sweetheart, which connoted a level of romantic commitment, to the Playmate of the Month, suggestive of fun and only temporary companionship. There was also no mistaking the femininity of the Playmate and her place in the gender order. An average age of twenty-one, the Playmate embodied youthful sexuality

1.3 *Miss October dons her clothing in a young man's college dorm room. Moving away from the art-photography approach typical of nude pinups, Hefner strived to create a context for each Playmate, showcasing young women in a variety of suggestive settings. He also sought to achieve just the right amount of exposed skin so that his pinups would appear provocative but not lewd. (Reproduced by special permission of* Playboy *magazine © October 1955 by Playboy.)*

in keeping with popular images of voluptuous women acting as feminine play-things.[65] Hefner's espoused preference in women mirrored the cinematic shift away from strong, independent female characters. Certain actresses "never had any sexual effect on me, the *femmes fatales*, the old ones, or the intelligent ones," he claimed, explaining that he did not know "what to do" with an intelligent woman. He found "nothing sexy in Greta Garbo or Marlene Dietrich," women who portrayed assertive characters in Hollywood films, but he "got the mes-sage" from young starlets like Brigitte Bardot and Marilyn Monroe. Boyhood infatuations with Dale Arden of the Flash Gordon serials and actresses Jean Harlow and Alice Faye sparked his enthusiasm for blonde bombshells. Hefner described his own preferences about women, reproduced in the pages of his magazine: "I tend to be attracted to the sort of woman who isn't competitive and doesn't feel frustrated or resentful because she isn't in charge." "In my rela-tionships," he explained, "I do not look for equality between men and women. I like innocent, affectionate, faithful girls."[66]

In addition to crafting representations of "girls" that both confirmed the healthy, heterosexual appetite of the male reader and countered the image of the competitive, overbearing woman, *Playboy* challenged conventional notions that cast as a failure the man who remained single for too long. The ideal bach-elor crafted in its pages was not some maladjusted narcissist, but an exuber-ant man enjoying an extended period of youthful freedom before assuming the responsibilities of adult life. In Hefner's view, social and religious strictures against sex outside of marriage channeled men and women prematurely into commitment and failed to account for the human desires and needs of the unmarried adult. Sexual pleasure was a vital facet of the good life, he argued, but the confinement of sex to marriage had wrongly turned matrimony "into a church-state license for sexual intercourse." Throughout the 1950s, Hefner's magazine portrayed an active sex life as an important feature of the playboy's lifestyle, and in the early 1960s, Hefner spoke at college campuses, debated reli-gious leaders, and preached "The Playboy Philosophy" on the need to reform sex laws and revise attitudes that condemned consenting adults for engaging in sexual activity. Although *Playboy* was avowedly heterosexual, Hefner's com-mitment to sexual liberation eventually prompted an attitude of forbearance toward homosexuality; this view was expressed in the magazine only after the excesses of the Lavender Scare had passed, however. "Our belief in a free, ratio-nal and humane society demands a tolerance of those whose sexual inclinations are different from our own," he explained, "so long as their activity is limited to consenting adults in private and does not involve either minors or the use of any kind of coercion." That said, Hefner wrote, "We confess to a strong personal prejudice in favor of the boy-girl variety of sex."[67]

Yet, for as much as he advocated a healthy, guilt-free, "liberated" approach to sex outside of marriage, seduction figured problematically in standard depictions of "boy-girl" sexual encounters in the magazine. Articles and features suggested that opportunities for unmarried sexual pleasure abounded if one had the playboy's skill. But assumptions underpinning images of seduction still positioned men in conflict with women, for whom sex brought the risk of pregnancy and greater social condemnation. As feminist critics would later point out, these constructions held out the bachelor's pleasure as the overriding concern. "When a fellow first meets a girl," explained one *Playboy* article, "a lot of questions run through his mind, among them, can she be had?" And if so, how much effort would it take? "Being an efficient sort of guy, you don't want to waste a lot of promotion on a push-over." Readers had to learn how to ascertain "if a girl is a prospective playmate or a professional virgin." Another article, stating that "there are two distinct kinds of men: those who get it often and easily, and those who don't," informed readers how to become members of the first category. *Playboy* advised that persistence would pay off. "Don't be afraid of a negative answer. A girl has a right to at least one 'no' before she yields, and the sooner you get that over with, the further you'll get." More important, readers were reminded, "Many girls who will do your bidding will never verbally agree to it." Winning her over was all part of a well-played game, as another item called "Playboy's Progress" illustrated. Here, the playboy employed a number of tactics, including selecting romantic music for the hi-fi and reading aloud passages from the Kinsey Report. That the power to seduce women was a chief attribute of the playboy is not surprising, given the entrenched "sexual brinkmanship" of the 1950s, where virtuous women were expected to halt men's advances and men were expected to press for as much sexual contact as they could get.[68] The savvy bachelor had to convince prospective playmates to overcome the social conventions inhibiting carefree sex, and as a connoisseur of many things, including women, the playboy knew just how to coax a woman into bed. Rather than breaking down the double standard, such images worked within its framework, the important difference being that, in theory, the playboy thought no less of the playmate once he bedded her. Though the playboy's companion might be sexually willing, however, she was not sexually aggressive, for to initiate sexual advances was to take on the masculine role. The distinct, complementary roles for men and women, which promised to ease postwar gender discord, required a male seducer and a female object of seduction.

A decade after Hefner typed out the first issue, *Playboy* had developed into a slick monthly with a well-defined editorial package containing articles and fiction, cartoons and jokes, nude pictorials and other visuals, and regular lifestyle

features on everything from overseas travel to proper evening attire. Hefner worked tirelessly to separate his publication from the unsophisticated men's magazines with their grainy, black-and-white nudes and bear-wrestling adventure stories.[69] Upgrading its editorial content represented an important step in securing an elevated position among *Playboy*'s rivals. Spectorsky's role as editorial director ensured a steady stream of fiction and articles from prominent authors. *Playboy*'s increasing circulation also made it possible to offer one of the highest fees in the magazine trade for writers, which in turn, increased the quality and quantity of literature and reportage that filled its pages. Hefner wanted *Playboy*'s advertisements to support its editorial flavor as well, but many advertisers were reluctant to associate themselves with such a racy magazine. Until his publication could secure ads from the big-name, upmarket purveyors of products and services suited to the lifestyle he was promoting, *Playboy* carried little in the way of advertising. The magazine turned a profit on newsstand and subscription sales alone.

Not long after launching *Playboy,* Hefner moved out of the apartment he shared with his wife and young child, working night and day in the apartment serving as the magazine's new office space. He made no serious attempts at reconciling with his estranged wife, though he fathered a second child in 1955, a pregnancy he only later discovered had been planned by Millie. By 1957, *Playboy*'s growing staff occupied a four-story building at 232 E. Ohio, where Hefner slept in a back room behind his office and enjoyed the sexual companionship of various young women throughout the day. Hefner's self-proclaimed interest in "innocent, affectionate, faithful girls" was perhaps unsurprising given the devastation of Millie's infidelity. Reinventing himself as the suave bachelor-publisher of *Playboy,* he embarked on a series of encounters, from casual trysts to more intense, drawn-out affairs, with countless young women, many of whom posed for the magazine or worked in its offices. Hefner expected devotion from his "special girls" and dated much younger women, an unequal dynamic further enhanced by his position as head of the self-contained world of *Playboy*. In the meantime, his days as a family man, if not a breadwinner, were over. The divorce became final in April 1959; Hefner was ordered to pay $1,400 a month in support of his ex-wife and two children, a sum he could easily afford.[70] He moved into an opulent mansion on the city's North Side, the ultimate bachelor pad for a still relatively young man, newly single once more.

Hefner had come of age harboring a "romanticized" view of marriage, with no sense of a "viable alternative" to wedlock for "middle-class, moral young people." Heartbroken over his fiancée's affair, he had attempted nevertheless to find happiness in a marriage he later deemed "over before it began." In the early 1960s, renewed bachelorhood found him pondering the need for a more

sensible approach to acquiring the trappings of adulthood. "I was typical," he informed one interviewer. "I wanted to get through school, get married, get the house in the suburbs—become established in some sort of job or other. Well, in doing that, it is quite possible to marry too early, settle down too quickly, and never really find out who you are." As Hefner further refined and articulated the concept behind *Playboy*, he expressed more clearly that his magazine was neither wholly against marriage nor in favor of lifelong bachelorhood. Instead, a longer sanctioned period of bachelorhood would allow men to assume adult responsibilities after they had formulated a clear sense of identity and had come to know what they wanted in a spouse and out of life. "I think you've got to find yourself before you find your life-long mate," Hefner explained. "And too many people find their mate first and only find themselves in later years if at all." *Playboy* advocated expanding the timeline for the achievement of adult milestones that had been collapsed so unusually by the young men and women who rushed to the altar in the postwar period. "We're concerned with a period of life that is not really long enough. A period of play at the finish of education and before taking the responsibility of having a family." Far from undermining the family, Hefner reasoned, society's acceptance of the play-period celebrated in his magazine could ultimately strengthen the family. "*Playboy* tries to give the American male an identity and the right frame of reference. So if you spend the bachelor years doing what *Playboy* suggests, you wind up with a happier, more stable marriage."[71] In this regard, Hefner offered a justification of *Playboy*'s apparent challenge to marriage, family, and sexual conservatism as serving the best interests of society. And when the playboy did settle down, he did not have to abandon the range of interests sustained by the magazine. He could continue his well-honed pursuit of pleasurable consumption and keep the nation's economy humming along.

2 "WORK HARD AND PLAY HARD, TOO"

Modern Living and the Morality of the Playboy Life

> Playboy was not planned as a publication for the idle rich, so much as in recognition that with the prosperity of post-war America, almost everyone could have a piece of what we described as *the playboy life*—if he were willing to expend the necessary effort.
>
> —Hugh M. Hefner, "The Playboy Philosophy," 1964

IN DECEMBER 1962, with his magazine making headlines across the nation, Hugh Hefner issued the first installment of "The Playboy Philosophy," in which he spelled out "for friends and critics alike—our guiding principles and editorial credo." Over the next three years, Hefner addressed a panoply of topics—antiquated sex laws, First Amendment rights, organized religion, free enterprise, communism, prostitution, witchcraft, and more—all the while arguing for individual freedom in a less repressive society. In the second of what became a twenty-five-part editorial, Hefner discussed the gradual resuscitation of "optimism, individuality, and spirit of adventure" in the American people, which in his view had been squelched by nearly two decades of depression and war. As he saw it, *Playboy*'s depiction of the good life played a role in promoting initiative over conformity and restoring faith in America. "Our editorial emphasis is on entertainment and leisure-time activity rather than on the ways in which man earns his daily bread," he wrote, "and yet our articles, on the creature comforts and the infinite variety of man's more elegant, leisure-time possessions, clearly stress that these are the prizes available in our society in return for honest endeavor and hard work."[1]

Hefner believed the promise of material reward energized the individual and the nation. Thus, the idealized figure in his magazine possessed a specific outlook toward work, matters of taste, and the pursuit of pleasure, as an early description of the playboy made clear:

Is he simply a wastrel, a ne'er-do-well, a fashionable bum? Far from it: He can be a sharp-minded young business executive, a worker in the arts, a university professor, an architect or engineer. He can be many things, provided he possesses a certain point of view. He must see life not as a vale of tears, but as a happy time, he must take joy in his work, without regarding it as the end of all living; he must be an alert man, an aware man, a man of taste, a man sensitive to pleasure, a man who— without acquiring the stigma of voluptuary or dilettante—can live life to the hilt. This is the sort of man we mean when we use the word playboy.

The playboy was neither a freeloading hedonist nor an ascetic overachiever, but a man who exuberantly pursued a full life of work, pleasure, and play. And the *Playboy* reader, as one advertisement for the magazine asserted, was "the sort of man who insists the best things in life aren't free, but very much worth working for."[2] These views made Hefner an important spokesperson for the liberal consensus that developed during the Cold War, which presumed that economic growth and private consumption would serve as the wellsprings of prosperity and a more democratic society.[3]

American economic life at mid-century brought several interrelated tensions to the forefront. The postwar economic juggernaut was hailed for providing an expanding middle class with its highest-ever standard of living. The nature of modern work, however, seemed to stifle individualism. For Americans unaccustomed to abundance, the profusion of available goods not only upended traditional notions of frugality and restraint, but it also intimidated novice consumers. Through his magazine, Hefner offered a resolution for these strains. *Playboy* promised to instruct readers in the fine art of consumption, cultivating taste and imparting expertise on a variety of matters. In an increasingly status-conscious society, the magazine reconciled competing desires for individualism and belonging: the playboy's connoisseurship made him part of the in-group and set him apart from the crowd.[4] At the same time, Hefner acknowledged the potential alienation in the organized world of advanced capitalism, yet he cast work as a meaningful enterprise. And not only did men earn the rewards of the good life through their efforts, in both their work and play they drove the economy forward and contributed to the strength of the nation. Hefner thus negotiated a compromise between a lingering ethos that prized restraint and hard work and the ascendant consumer ethic of mid-twentieth-century America, reanimating the links between production and consumption, work and play, while preaching that "the playboy life" was indeed a moral one.

CONFORMITY AND THE UNCOMMON MAN

Although Hefner's own life experience and the meteoric rise of *Playboy* was deemed "a sort of libidinous Horatio Alger story" by *Life* magazine, the average reader of his publication was less likely to be a wealthy, self-made millionaire than a white-collar "organization man" or a college student on his way to becoming one. *Playboy* emerged at a moment when this archetypal male and the nature and meaning of the work he performed elicited anxious commentary. For those who found accomplishment in the white-collar managerial realm, Donald Meyer has written, "success turned on suspension of self, and upon the neutral exposure of every faculty to the teeming signals demanding interpretation and integration. One might ask whether the role required any 'self' at all." Vulnerable to the whim of clients and supervisors, ever wary of competitors, the corporate employee, according to many popular accounts, was thus forced to manipulate his personality in order to manipulate others. Frank Wheeler, the central character in Richard Yates's *Revolutionary Road*, provides a fictional example of one man's hyperawareness of his own image. In Yates's discordant tale of postwar suburbia, Wheeler spends each day at his desk shuffling papers from one pile to another, accomplishing little, but perfecting the appearance of keeping busy. Forever glancing in mirrors or catching his reflection in the window, he takes stock of his appearance and uses his social radar to assess each situation so as to affect the appropriate demeanor and response. Wheeler's "self" is contrived for everyone else's reception. Similarly, Sloan Wilson's protagonist Tom Rath in *The Man in the Gray Flannel Suit* senses the need to get along when he considers saying something he thinks his boss will not want to hear. "I should quit if I don't like what he does, but I want to eat, and so, like a half million other guys in gray flannel suits, I'll always pretend to agree, until I get big enough to be honest without being hurt. That's not being crooked, it's just being smart." He contemplates his fate: "How smoothly one becomes, not a cheat, exactly, not really a liar, just a man who'll say anything for pay."[5]

The striving employee at the mercy of the corporation received memorable treatment in Billy Wilder's 1960 film, *The Apartment*. The film told the story of corporate drone C. C. Baxter (Jack Lemmon), an employee of Consolidated Life. Lacking backbone and desperate to move up the corporate ladder, he finds himself turning over his apartment to the insurance company's married executives, who revel in pseudo-bachelorhood with various girlfriends before returning each night to suburban domesticity. Although Baxter tires of roaming the city until his "guests" have gone home, when the personnel director, Sheldrake, pressures him for the key to his apartment, Baxter exchanges it for a cherished promotion to a perfunctory junior executive position. He is on

his way up, moving from a desk in the accounting pool to a small office with a window and his name on the door. The plot turns when Baxter secretly falls in love with Fran, the elevator operator whom Sheldrake has been taking to the apartment. When she lingers one night after Sheldrake rushes for the train home to his family, Baxter returns to find a distraught Fran has swallowed a bottle of sleeping pills. Disregarding his own feelings for her, he nurses her back to health and helps the two reconcile. He is rewarded with a new position as Sheldrake's assistant, which comes with a luxurious office and a key to the executive washroom.

While this film frowned on the corrupt executives who wield control over Baxter's future, it also highlighted the complicity of the individual selling his soul to the company for the sake of advancement. Though a likeable protagonist, Baxter is a spineless character who finds redemption only in giving up his aspirations for the executive office. Finally, he puts his feelings for Fran and his own sense of right and wrong ahead of his career. No longer aiming to please others and instead following his inner-directed moral compass, Baxter refuses to let Sheldrake bring her to the apartment any longer. In a closing scene, he hands over his key to the executive washroom instead of the key to his apartment. The film ends with Baxter reclaiming his dignity and getting the girl. He is, however, out of a job.

A spate of humorous publications, among them *The Executive Coloring Book* (1961), provided an apt summary of the troubles said to plague the nation's corporate employees and signaled the extent to which discussions of conformity had become widespread. Modeled on a child's coloring book, text and drawings lampooned conformity in the corporate world. For example, a drawing of a man, clad in his underwear and holding a briefcase and his suit, was captioned: "This is my suit. Color it Gray or I will lose my job." Lines of identical men boarding a commuter train bore the caption: "You meet lots of interesting people on the train. Color them all gray" and so on (see figure 2.1). At once self-important, dyspeptic, and popping pills to alleviate job-related stress, the executive, according to this tongue-in-cheek book, was nothing more than a pretender who did not know how to make decisions and feigned interest in his customers. Significantly, the boss and the wife of the executive were identical, suggesting that the breadwinner, at home or in the office, found no respite from being bossed.

The "organization man," swathed in gray flannel and doubly burdened by family and work, appeared in popular discussions as a cog in the corporate machinery, disconnected from any real sense of production and forced to subdue his will to the team—a conforming, emasculated, small man. *Playboy* did not share these sentiments but kept abreast of such perceptions, publishing

THIS IS MY TRAIN. It takes me to my office every day.   You meet lots of interesting people on the train. Color them all gray.

2.1 *William H. Whyte's* The Organization Man *and Sloan Wilson's* The Man in the Gray Flannel Suit *contributed essential watchwords to discussions of postwar malaise.* The Executive Coloring Book *lampooned the corporate drone and signaled the pervasiveness of the critique of American conformity. (The Funny Products Company, 1961)*

articles that acknowledged the stresses and demands its upwardly striving readers no doubt faced in the workplace. *Playboy* excerpted satirist Shepherd Mead's lampoon of the workplace, *How to Succeed in Business without Really Trying.* "A Junior Executive is expected to suffer," Mead explained. "If you cannot manage it, you must at least appear to. An ulcer is excellent. Grow one if you can, but if you can not, a bottle of milk placed conspicuously on the desk will do nicely." In another piece, Mead wryly commented on the underdeveloped physique of the average male office worker who used his mind, not his muscles, on the job. Women, Mead complained, refused to recognize a man's narrow shoulders as "a badge of honor," a symbol of his white-collar status. Instead, they were "often caught gazing at fellows with second-rate minds and seemingly broad shoulders." Mead's humor pointed up contemporary concerns that the white-collar treadmill, in addition to subjecting men to the power of the corporation, lacked the overt masculine associations of physical labor and caused stress and anxiety. *Playboy*'s cartoons that depicted an affair between the boss and the employee's wife further poked fun at perceptions that the workplace unmanned the employee. Another article, "Executive Chess" (October 1958), offered "power plays and potent ploys for upward strivers on the business scene." This article promised guidance on successfully navigating office politics in the other-directed world of the organization. Within the office a man waged "the war of personality." He "jockeys for status, strives for upward mobility, may devote more time to the techniques of interoffice guerrilla warfare than to the business which pays his salary." The competent player reaped rewards of "power, prestige and property." Success did not come without sacrifice, however. The businessman had "to be ever vigilant and on guard," denying every impulse to fully trust others. Furthermore, the effort to get ahead meant "friends cannot be freely chosen. Subordinates must remain subordinate, colleagues remain competitors. Intimacy is always potentially dangerous. And to all this we may add the probability of ulcers."

Playboy considered the question of conformity in a November 1962 "Playboy Panel on Business Ethics and Morality." Invoking the language of the mass-society critics, *Playboy* queried: "Are we 'other-directed' sheep lacking any system of individual values? Are we becoming 'organization men' who unquestioningly follow our corporate party lines without thought as to consequence?"[6] The panel brought together politicians, heads of industry, and critics of American business for a discussion on the conscience of the corporation and the place of the individual in the increasingly "organized" world. While the panelists in this feature debated a number of woes afflicting American business, a sustained response to the question of conformity came in the recasting of the self-made man, in the guise of J. Paul Getty and Hugh Hefner.

In his column as *Playboy*'s "Contributing Editor for Business and Finance," billionaire Getty told readers how to succeed in the business world. For over a decade, Getty counseled readers on investing in the stock market and amassing a fortune. He penned articles that advised how to make wise executive decisions, cope with crises, manage underlings, and—most important—retain one's individuality. Getty called for creativity, initiative, and a sense of adventure in the business world. Whereas Mead satirized the "organization man," Getty annihilated him. The "mystique of conformity," Getty wrote in his first article, "has produced the lifeless card-board-cutout figure of the organization man who tries vainly to hide his fears, lack of confidence and incompetence behind the stylized facades of conformity." Conformity, he asserted, stemmed from the links between familial responsibility and fear of risk-taking, a connection that cast both the bachelor and the entrepreneur in a favorable light. Fear of failure might cause men to play it safe, but a self-interested woman was ultimately to blame for keeping a man "in his conformist's strait jacket." Sounding a familiar note, Getty opined, "Wives have a habit of raising harrowing specters to deter a husband who might wish to risk his safe, secure job and seek fulfillment and wealth via imaginative and enterprising action."

Like Hefner, Getty was the picture of entrepreneurial success. His experience as a wealthy oil tycoon provided the basis for the words of wisdom doled out to readers. Frequently citing his own enterprise as a "wildcatting operator in the Oklahoma oil fields," Getty relayed countless other success stories of men who set out to earn their fortunes. Yet wealth alone did not make the man. In an essay titled "The Educated Barbarians," Getty urged readers to cultivate their cultural sensibilities, a view much in line with *Playboy*'s outlook on enlightened consumption as a marker of status and masculine success. "Far from emasculating or effeminizing a man, a cultural interest serves to make him more completely...male....It stimulates and vitalizes him as an individual," Getty wrote. "The cultured man is almost invariably a self-assured, urbane and completely confident male....Be it in the board room or a bedroom, he is much better equipped to play his masculine role."[7]

Getty personified the type of individual Hefner labeled the "Uncommon Man"—a throwback to the optimism of an earlier generation and a harbinger of things to come. Hefner offered an instructive account of the recent past as he explained this figure's resurgence. "The first 30 years of the 20th Century were characterized by our unbounded faith in ourselves, both individually and as a nation," Hefner suggested in a glowing estimation of the past. "We were enjoying the results of the industrial revolution, and if the streets were not literally paved with gold, it was only a technicality." Hefner described a time when young Americans consumed the stories of Horatio Alger and believed that "any boy

could grow up to be President of the U.S., or of U.S. Steel." Fictional characters like Frank Merriwell and real-life heroes such as Charles Lindbergh personified the rhetoric of individual achievement. The sense of unbounded possibility reached a pinnacle during the 1920s. "It was a yeasty time, a time of innovation and adventure, when new notions and ideas were accepted almost as quickly as they were born." Exuberance ended with the stock market crash in 1929.[8]

Hefner's view of the nation's experience of crisis downplayed evidence of vitality and purpose. The 1930s witnessed a vigorous labor movement, a flourishing of leftist artists and intellectuals, and a thriving popular culture, all of which critiqued American institutions but also embraced the promise of American ideals. World War II brought forth an important measure of national unity and commitment toward a common goal, the defeat of fascism.[9] These experiences, however, had little to do with the sort of individual striving and material reward that Hefner saw as the cornerstone of the nation's social, political, and economic well-being. In his view, the 1930s stood out as a time when the popular media ridiculed "initiative, ambition and the accumulation of wealth." Concern for the average man turned into "Deification of the Common Man," which de-emphasized the individual in favor of the group. During World War II, the need to fight a total war against fascism prompted Americans to give up willingly "what individuality they had left." Finally, the anticommunist investigations of the postwar era had left a smothering blanket of conformity over the nation.

A new generation, Hefner explained, had broken "the fetters of conformity." One could find evidence of this break with the past in the Beat movement. Yet, while Hefner conceded that the artists and poets of the late 1950s countercultural Beat movement symbolized a resurgence of individualism in America, his magazine evinced only a limited affinity for these bohemians. *Playboy* addressed the Beat phenomenon in articles that described the unusual features of its rebellious, alternative lifestyle, but the magazine could not endorse its challenge to American materialism. *Playboy* editor Ray Russell assessed the divide between the magazine's version of the good life and the Beat rebellion. "We liked the sort of freedom they espoused, the liberated atmosphere, the artistic expression in poetry and prose," he explained. "We were in favor of any kind of sexual liberation, as long as it was heterosexual lib. All that was positive. But we also felt there was a lot in it counter to what we promoted in *Playboy*." He went on to explain:

> The sandaled, dirty feet, unwashed aspects of the beats ran against the grain of the well-groomed, button-down, Aqua Velva look our reader wanted. The antiestablishment attitude, lack of material ambition, or

desire to get ahead, which typified the beats, was not what *Playboy* was all about. We were telling people how to make out, not just with girls, but in business and in their jobs. We thought readers getting a bigger car or a bigger apartment was great. There was a lot about the beats we liked and a lot that was not part of our orbit or our world.[10]

According to Hefner, *Playboy*'s followers, "sharing the rebellious spirit of the Beats, and equally ready to throw off the shackles of sameness and security," comprised "a much more significant and larger segment" of a "new generation" eager to overturn the old order in America. "Both groups refused to accept the old ideas and ideals passed along by the previous conformity-ridden generation," Hefner explained. "But whereas the Beat part of this new generation rejected the old in a negative way, simply turning their backs on society and ceasing to communicate, the rest searched for new answers and new opportunities in a spirit that was positive in the extreme." The exuberant, young, upwardly mobile men who embraced leisure and affluence stood in contrast to the antimaterialist, antiestablishment Beats. In 1958, *Playboy* termed them the "Upbeat Generation."

The theme of generational change was in sync with contemporary appraisals. In his 1961 inaugural address, John F. Kennedy announced that "the torch" of leadership had been "passed to a new generation of Americans." Kennedy, a picture of youthful verve, offered a marked contrast to the dowdy Eisenhower who had presided over the perceived blandness of the 1950s. *Life* magazine highlighted "a new breed of American" in a special issue on "The Take-Over Generation," profiling the young men and (some) women moving to the forefront of politics, business, and education. Of his Upbeats, Hefner claimed, "They are bringing the country alive again and they are, we're certain, the only hope America has for the future." In contrast to the nihilistic, vagabond Beats, *Playboy*'s band of cultural rebels recalled an earlier generation. The "spirit and attitude of the Upbeats is right out of the first part of this century—it's the same optimistic viewpoint and zest for living that made America great in the first place," Hefner explained in his "philosophy." "In the 1930s and 1940s we lost our faith in ourselves, we hid our individual identities within groups, decisions were made by committees, companies were run by boards; today, a younger and less fearful generation seems willing to look the future straight in the face and spit in its eye."[11] *Playboy* served as "the voice" of "the Upbeat Generation," and Hefner positioned himself as its leader, a forward-looking individualist in step with the needs of modern society. Strikingly, he drew much of his inspiration from his perceptions of the 1920s, particularly the decade's associations of hedonism, loosening sexual mores, and revelry in urban nightlife. Hefner

encouraged men to reclaim the sense of adventure and desire for personal achievement that he believed the intervening decades of depression and war had eradicated.

The pictorial feature entitled "Playboy's House Party," which appeared in May 1959, provided an example of just how well pluck and hard work paid off. The photographs documented a weekend get-together at the Miami bachelor digs of an entrepreneur named Harold Chaskin. The home contained many of the same elements highlighted in designs for bachelor pads that *Playboy* commissioned and showcased in the magazine. More important than the indoor swimming pool, underwater bar, and powered, retractable roof, however, was the trajectory of the accompanying narrative, which sounded the familiar strains of Alger's fictional stories. Chaskin had arrived in Miami "a youthful New Yorker" with a suitcase full of his worldly belongings "and his entire financial holdings—$40 in cash." He started his own business, became a major national tile manufacturer, and attained the material rewards of the good life, *Playboy*-style: a swinging bachelor pad equipped with five beautiful girls, who "for a lark...bathe together in the manner of ancient Rome."[12] Ambition and effort paid dividends in consumer luxuries—and sexual fulfillment—for the Upbeats.

Hefner's rising fame made him the subject of a documentary film in the early 1960s. "I'm a rebel," Hefner claimed in the film, "a man out to work hard and play hard, too. Because you've only got one time around in this old world and if you don't make the most of it, you've got no one to blame but yourself." His magazine celebrated this vigorous approach to life. "We don't believe in the old taboos and the old sacred cows, and neither does most of the rest of the new generation," he wrote to the editors of the Minneapolis *Tribune*. "They want new answers to old questions and are willing to forego the certainties of security for some of the risks incurred by independent endeavor." He cast his own achievements as a modern tale of individual courage and triumph. "The success of Playboy and its Publisher," he wrote, "proves that it is still possible in America to take nothing but an idea, plus a dedication to it, to build a success story equal to any ever told." Of *Playboy*'s critics, he continued, "I'm quite certain that I work a good deal harder for what I believe in...and I must confess that I probably play a good deal harder, too, and that I think, is the way it should be. I must say most sincerely that I am one of the happiest, most fulfilled guys on this good earth: I dreamed a very big dream, and it came true."[13]

Observed one journalist of the work habits that allowed Hefner to realize his dream, "He seems a mass of pure kinetic energy, sprinting between desks carrying a half-swigged Pepsi-Cola in one hand like a track man carrying a baton. With the possible exception of sex and work, Pepsi-Cola is his only major

addiction." *Playboy*'s promotional machinery emphasized Hefner as the quintessential, ultra-achieving, hardworking playboy. Ironically, the energy needed to sustain his breakneck pace came increasingly from the use of the stimulant Dexedrine, which by the late 1950s had become a dependency that made marathon work sessions with Hefner almost unbearable for many of his employees. His reliance on the drug wreaked havoc with his schedule, leading him eventually into a reclusive phase as he ignored the normal rhythms of the day. Yet it did not deter his efforts at self-promotion nor diminish the growing *Playboy* mystique. Hefner instructed staff members to feed a steady stream of publicity items to the press. "Anything we can do to build a personal romantic image, the notion of young executive on the go, etc.," Hefner asserted, "are all very positive and more firmly establishing us on the local and national scene."[14]

He also took care to convey that the production of the magazine—the work that went into it—was as enjoyable and titillating as the finished product. A description in the June 1957 issue of *Playboy* sketched this image of Hefner at work: "In his vigorously masculine office on the top floor of the new Playboy building, he edits copy, approves layouts....There is an electronic wall in his office, very much like the one featured in *Playboy's Penthouse Apartment*, that includes hi-fi, AM-FM radio, tape and television, and will store up to 2000 LPs. Brubeck, Kenton or Sinatra is usually on the turntable when Hefner is working." Here, work was not drudgery, but a pleasurable activity undertaken in a site filled with hi-tech toys. Other features offered a "behind the scenes" look as male staff members created various pictorials, with *Playboy*'s office personnel occasionally serving as models. The 1962 film documenting Hefner and his growing *Playboy* empire also illustrated the connection between toil and pleasure. "The magazine is without question a reflection of my personality, of my own adolescent dreams and aspirations," Hefner stated in a voice-over. Footage showed Hefner "at work" in the office, discussing future assignments with cartoonist Shel Silverstein while "playing" on a bongo board, pipe in hand. The voice-over continued, "I think that it's when you're young that the world is the greatest adventure, and if you can keep this same kind of attitude on things then you're apt to get the very most out of life." As his celebrity grew, Hefner's publicized lifestyle set within his opulent mansion declared that a life surrounded by beautiful women and expensive toys was the clear reward of hard work.[15] But the distinctions between the work realm and the leisure realm blurred. Even the work of promoting his magazine on the late-night television program *Playboy's Penthouse* was also Hefner at play, imbibing alcohol, mingling with entertainers, enjoying the performances of his celebrity musical guests.

For Hefner, *Playboy* represented a labor of love, and in his public image work and play did not form discrete oppositional spheres, but were intertwined.[16]

Here was a self-made man who achieved success not through self-restraint or thrift, but by approaching all of life, work and play, "with gusto and relish." In an era concerned with stifling conformity and the "rat race," Hefner embodied a new ideal, where work was more than the sphere of activity that financed consumption; it was an exhilarating realm in its own right, which also made possible the enjoyment of leisure. And leisure offered more than compensation for a stultifying job; it formed an area of enrichment and identity that was part of a full life. The success he achieved was measured not in terms of power or financial gain, though he accrued both, but in his ability to enjoy a bountiful and pleasurable lifestyle, the symbol of which became the Playboy Mansion. This dynamic was at the heart of his pronouncements for the Upbeat generation. The goal was not to become a captain of industry or president of the United States. Pursuing work and play with enthusiasm, one could grow up to live like Hugh Hefner, or at least a middle-class version of him. *Playboy* readers were reminded of the publisher's mantra. "Hefner...advocates neither a life of hedonistic irresponsibility nor one of joyless drudgery; he believes in a balance of work *and* play," wrote the editor of the Playboy Forum.[17] This was not a message during the magazine's first decade of publication about unbridled self-indulgence, but a statement about toil and pleasure, risk and reward, that gave middle-class men permission to enjoy the good life and helped set the stage for the materialism of later decades.

"MAN AT HIS LEISURE": MODERN LIVING IN *PLAYBOY*

The postwar economic boom fueled expectations for the elimination of class differences and elevated leisure and consumption to unprecedented heights in American life. Policy makers pitted the variety and abundance of consumer goods available to American families against the Soviet economic system, a comparison made most famously in the 1959 "Kitchen Debates" between Richard Nixon and Nikita Khrushchev. Casual clothing styles, a boom in tourism, the growth of hobbies and do-it-yourself activities, and the bustling trade in home entertainment goods all pointed to an expanding leisure realm. "Zestful Americans enjoy their new leisure," proclaimed *Life* magazine in a special double issue on "The Good Life." Articles and advertisements celebrated the pastimes and products enjoyed by American families and extolled the dramatic impact of leisure-related spending on the nation's economy.

Life also expressed ambivalence about whether the "new leisure" constituted a bane or a boon to society. As the symbol and by-product of prosperity, the

"new leisure" gave rise to concerns about the effects of too much easy living and free time. Affluence held out the possibility of hedonism and sparked concerns that the nation might be growing "soft." Others wondered about the pressures of leisure time, as Americans sought meaningful activities to fill the spaces of the day. Such ambivalence revealed a tension between lingering notions of self-restraint and the postwar culture's increasing emphasis on pleasure, self-indulgence, relaxation, and fun.[18] *Playboy,* of course, expressed no concerns about affluence. Unlike husbands and fathers, for whom embrace of the "new leisure" meant family vacations, home handiwork projects, backyard barbecues, and neighborhood cocktail parties, the bachelor's singlehood gave him tremendous liberty in determining how to spend his time and money.

Hefner claimed to edit *Playboy* according to his own preferences, telling one interviewer in 1955, "As I develop, so will the magazine." In June 1957, readers received an introduction to the man with whom they presumably shared so much. "This month we'd like you to meet Editor-Publisher Hugh M. Hefner," began the Hefner-penned copy, "the man responsible for the pulse, the personality, and the very existence of this magazine." Accompanying the text was a photograph of Hefner, his eyes fixed on the camera, leaning casually against a stairway railing inside *Playboy*'s new offices. A young woman gazed admiringly at him from behind. The introduction continued:

> The lean, restless young fellow who presides over *Playboy* is something of a phenomenon in the publishing world.... His dress is conservative and casual, he always wears loafers, and a bottle of Pepsi-Cola (which he consumes at the rate of two dozen a day) is never far away.... He is essentially an indoor man, though he discovered the pleasures of the ski slope last winter. He likes jazz, foreign films, Ivy League clothes, gin and tonic and pretty girls—the same sort of things that *Playboy* readers like.... None of this is too surprising, of course, for *Playboy*'s unprecedented popularity with the young urban male is a direct result of the fact that the editor-publisher and his audience see eye-to-eye.

Hefner positioned himself not as a man possessing a particular political or social viewpoint, but as an individual identified by a coherent set of tastes and consumer preferences, central features of the modern, masculine identity constructed in *Playboy*. In its capacity as a "handbook for the young man-about-town," *Playboy* informed readers how to spend their well-deserved money and leisure time so as to maximize pleasure and accrue status.[19] Articles on topics such as gourmet food, liquor, fashion, travel, furnishings, art, music, automobiles, and other luxury items—from private jets to pleasure boats—instructed the reader in the fine art of "modern living."

Many of *Playboy*'s service features were devoted to grooming and personal appearance. Historian Kathy Peiss has noted that earlier attempts to market products used to bolster male appearance had met resistance, but wartime military service, which subjected men to regimented scrutiny, helped inspire more careful attention to appearance. Postwar manufacturers of male toiletries invoked images of strength and heterosexual vitality, emphasizing the "romantic male" in advertisements that linked product usage to sexual activity.[20] *Playboy* approached the cultivation of male appearance by casting good taste and sex appeal as masculine attributes. As a case in point, consider a feature on "The Man in His Bath." Language describing the bathroom and its accouterments thwarted any feminine connotations of luxuriating in the act of personal grooming. Words were chosen to convey substance and function. Showers and hampers were "available in massive and masculine versions," which gave "the rite of the bath a properly rich setting." "Plump, huge, soft towels" were said to be "sumptuous yet virile in color and design." "On a handy, hefty brass hook," one found a "voluminous terry robe to don when stepping from a long, relaxing soaking in the oversize tub." The smart bachelor knew just when to enjoy a cool shower, which occasion called for a tepid bath, how to achieve the perfect shave, and so on. "The true bathophile is as discerningly selective of his soaps, brushes, shaving gear, grooming aids and other accouterments, as he is in selecting his wines and women." Connoisseurship mattered, even in the bathroom.

Men's attire also received regular attention in *Playboy*. The magazine's fashion editors proceeded with care, cultivating a tone that assumed a well-bred, in-the-know audience, while at the same time working to explain fashion for young male readers. An article on building a basic wardrobe suggested this paradoxical approach: "Three suits will be laughably inadequate to the great majority of *Playboy* readers, but—hell—you've got to start somewhere." For the first decade and a half, *Playboy* steered a conservative course in the fashion mainstream. Jack Kessie served as the magazine's first fashion editor, dispensing advice originally under his own name, and later under the more compelling pen name Blake Rutherford. "Conservative in all departments," wrote Kessie, "we lean heavily toward these distinctive details of styling that point up the man as being *quietly* well dressed." *Playboy*'s reserved, Ivy League tendencies extended to most occasions. Kessie/Rutherford criticized the man whose "sense of Ivy-bred style takes a nose dive" as soon as he found himself "liberated from the suit-and-tie ritual." Men who made the wrong choices for their casual attire ran the risk of unwittingly "competing with women to see who can look prettier."[21] The playboy remained secure in his masculinity with the magazine as his guide.

The well-dressed man projected "an air of distinction, of poise and commanding presence." Careful attention to personal appearance attracted women and won the admiration and approval of one's male associates. Following *Playboy*'s directives for a "sensible, color-coded wardrobe" garnered one the "self-confidence that goes with being well turned-out from head to foot, the approval (even emulation) of your fellows, and the prideful smile of any lass in the company of a tastefully-garbed guy." While acknowledging that designers and advertisers largely dictated style, *Playboy* promised to set readers straight on which trends to follow and which fads to ignore. For example, Jack Kessie's "The Shorts Story" discussed men's walking shorts as a stylish alternative to trousers. "The remarkable thing," wrote Kessie, "is the way that advertising agencies have been able to build acceptance for such an item in so short a time.... We feel this is good, but certainly some further facts, definitions and warnings are in order." "Being well-appointed is not a hit-or-miss proposition," Kessie/Rutherford explained in another article. "It is a carefully-planned stratagem involving a broad view and a close watch on details. But once mastered, it is a process that becomes as effortless (and rewarding) as sampling 20-year-old Armagnac from a snifter." Until readers reached that level of comfort, *Playboy* provided a chart to help them properly coordinate shirts, ties, hats, socks, and shoes with their three basic suits of navy, gray, and brown (see figure 2.2). The well-dressed college male, according to another feature, in order "to avoid classification as an oddball," owned four classic crewneck sweaters in conservative colors and steered clear of the "interesting" sweaters meant for boating or resort-wear. The right wardrobe thus served as an outward display of status. Shopping for it provided a fresh outlet for masculine expression.[22]

Playboy's fashion articles furthered the total vision of the playboy lifestyle (see figure 2.3). "Spring House Party," for example, envisioned an affluent, weekend gathering at a country house where riding, golf, tennis, and a dance at the country club rounded out the weekend's activities. After taking readers through numerous wardrobe changes over the course of the imaginary weekend, the article concluded with two key points of etiquette. The houseguest should bring a proper house gift, perhaps a bottle of fine, imported liquor. Also, referring to the playboy's presumed sexual exploits, the author cautioned one to think carefully before mentioning at breakfast the view of the garden he'd enjoyed the night before: after all, was it his bedroom that overlooked the garden, or that of the female guest with whom he had managed to spend the night? Similarly, "Meet Me at the Club," which began by describing a "nifty sports car...with the carefree smile on the driver's face...purring toward a private club" wrapped fashion in the imagery of free-and-easy affluence.[23]

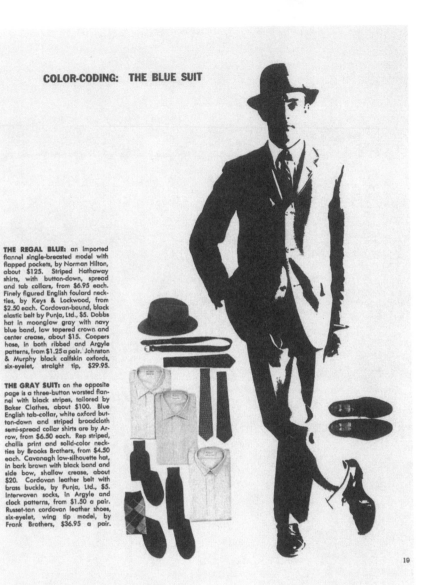

COLOR-CODING: THE BLUE SUIT

THE REGAL BLUE: an imported flannel single-breasted model with flapped pockets, by Norman Hilton, about $125. Striped Hathaway shirts, with button-down, spread and tab collars, from $6.95 each. Finely figured English foulard neckties, by Keys & Lockwood, from $2.50 each. Cordovan-bound, black elastic belt by Punja, Ltd., $5. Dobbs hat in moonglow gray with navy blue band, low tapered crown and center crease, about $15. Coopers hose, in both ribbed and Argyle patterns, from $1.25 a pair. Johnston & Murphy black calfskin oxfords, six-eyelet, straight tip, $29.95.

THE GRAY SUIT: on the opposite page is a three-button worsted flannel with black stripes, tailored by Baker Clothes, about $100. Blue English tab-collar, white oxford button-down and striped broadcloth semi-spread collar shirts are by Arrow, from $6.50 each. Rep striped, challis print and solid-color neckties by Brooks Brothers, from $4.50 each. Cavanagh low-silhouette hat, in bark brown with black band and side bow, shallow crease, about $20. Cordovan leather belt with brass buckle, by Punja, Ltd., $5. Interwoven socks, in Argyle and clock patterns, from $1.50 a pair. Russet-tan cordovan leather shoes, six-eyelet, wing tip model, by Frank Brothers, $36.95 a pair.

19

2.2 In Playboy's role as a "handbook" for the young urban male, fashion features coached readers with clear instructions on how to properly attire themselves. "Color Coding the Basic Wardrobe" spelled out all the pieces one needed to accessorize a brown, blue, or gray suit. (Reproduced by special permission of Playboy magazine © April 1957 by Playboy.)

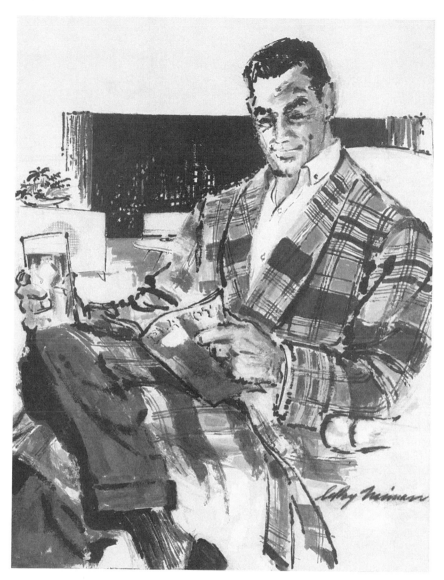

2.3 *Service features highlighted trends and encouraged consumption while also advancing the total vision of the playboy lifestyle. This illustration of a man relaxing with a drink and an issue of* Playboy *accompanied an article on "Lounge Wear for the Man of Leisure," a detailed report on dressing gowns, robes, host coats, smoking jackets, and pajamas. (Leroy Neiman work titled "At Ease" from* Playboy *magazine, February 1956. Reproduced by special permission of* Playboy *magazine © February 1956 by Playboy.)*

"Playboy's Sports Car Jacket" served as the requisite attire for this important symbol of the good life. While Detroit turned out huge, chrome-laden, finned autos for the family, *Playboy* commenced its love affair with the two-seat sports car, the automotive antithesis of "togetherness." Although primarily interested in foreign models, *Playboy's* attention to sports cars served the symbolic purpose attributed by Thomas Hine to the two-seat 1955 Ford Thunderbird, which "went completely against the grain of a family-centered society," by offering "a dream of irresponsibility, detachment, escape." Some managed to make this dream a reality. Victor Lownes, who lived a playboy-like existence in Chicago, New York, and eventually London as president of Playboy Club operations in Britain, walked out on his wife one morning in 1953 after she asked her usual question, "What time will you be home for dinner?" Married since the age of eighteen, to the then-twenty-five-year-old Lownes, the innocent query had "the ring of a prison regulation." Despite a comfortable marriage, he explained, "A wife just didn't fit into my concept of life in the fast lane—no room in the sports car, so to speak."²⁴ Hefner, too, after leaving his wife, tooled around Chicago in his Mercedes-Benz 300 SL Roadster convertible, that is, until he began riding around in a chauffeured limousine.

If the playboy required three basic suits around which to build his wardrobe, he needed, at least according to one article, six motor vehicles to fill out his collection. "The Compleat Sports Car Stable" highlighted the half-dozen cars that belonged in the garage of the automobile connoisseur. *Playboy's* sports car authority, Ken Purdy, wrote, "No single sports car is going to be enough for the city man of means and discernment, who leaves the utility sedans to his duller fellows, the same blokes who take their two-pants suits where they find them and order red wine or white without specifying vineyard or vintage." *Playboy* readers, of course, knew better when it came to buying clothes and ordering wine. Articles on food and drink, most of them penned by Thomas Mario, gave instructions on masculine cookery and told the reader what to eat and which beverages to consume. The playboy indulged his many appetites, no less a masculine act than appreciating feminine beauty. A Mario article about wine, for example, was followed by a Playmate pictorial called "Le Rouge et Le Blanc," which showcased two semi-undressed women, one a redhead, the other a blonde. Comparing their attributes, *Playboy* noted that "the true playboy, a connoisseur of both wine *and* women, will want to savor the unique qualities of both."²⁵

In addition to offering advice on fashion and dining, *Playboy* obsessed over hi-fi equipment and jazz. "A high fidelity system...is commonly accepted as a badge of sophisticated masculinity," *Playboy* noted. "Indeed, one hears it said that high fidelity has supplanted the etching as a sure lure to seduction." Although rock and roll music commanded attention outside the pages of the

magazine, *Playboy* clung steadfastly to jazz throughout the 1950s and well into the 1960s. Jazz critic Leonard Feather devoted one of his columns to the new sound. "While it is undeniably true that rock 'n' roll sinks its roots in the authentic rhythm-and-blues era of jazz history," Feather asserted, "it is, for the most part, a bastardized, commercialized, de-based version of it." Elsewhere, *Playboy* claimed rock and roll put forth "strange sounds masquerading as music" offering "more beat than talent."[26]

Why did *Playboy* exhibit such a strong allegiance to jazz? Certainly, Hefner was a fan, and many of *Playboy*'s young editors had come of age listening to the strains of the big bands of the thirties and forties. But jazz held a deeper significance as it related to the image of urbanity crafted first by *Esquire* and taken up by *Playboy*. For a magazine that claimed spiritual kinship to the jubilant urban culture of the "roaring twenties," jazz conjured images of cabarets and nightclubs, moral laxity, and an irreverence for social conventions. Arising from the musical interactions of performers from diverse racial and ethnic backgrounds, jazz had provided cultural space in which to challenge social and cultural boundaries and continued to be a medium in the 1950s through which musicians opposed conformity and conservatism. The association of rock and roll music with teenage culture provided yet another reason for the magazine's fondness for jazz. According to Leonard Feather, rock and roll appealed primarily to "adolescent rebellion and insecurity." He offered this further assessment:

> Man has evolved from lower forms of animal life and in this, he shares a common origin with the monkey. In the same way, jazz and rock 'n' roll are related. But from its original ragtime beginnings—through dixieland, swing, bop, progressive and cool—jazz, like man, has learned to walk erect and speak with intelligence. Rock 'n' roll shares a common beginning with jazz, but it has evolved no further than the primitive, gibbering ape.

Rock and roll was unsophisticated. Thus, the superior taste of *Playboy* readers set them apart from "a majority of Americans" seemingly enthralled with the "musically mediocre." *Playboy* inaugurated an annual jazz poll in 1958 and went on to host an enormously successful jazz festival in Chicago the following year. The magazine's first jazz poll confirmed that "the *Playboy* reader is a very special guy—hip, aware, sophisticated, discriminating, in the know." Results of the poll "showed readers to be as sharp in matters of jazz as we already knew them to be in sports cars, food and drink, attire, and women."[27]

Travel also played an important part in the world of the idealized bachelor, and several editorial staples highlighted the image of the man-about-town who was also a citizen of the world. "Firm believers in the idea that travel is

broadening and endorsers of the notion that the true sophisticate must, of necessity, be a cosmopolite," *Playboy*'s editors presented an "International Issue" in May 1957. It included a travel essay on Monaco, a detailed account of tiger hunting in India, a fashion feature devoted to selecting and packing a travel wardrobe, and an expanded "International Datebook," a regular column that enumerated the goings-on in various tourist hot spots around the world. In addition, the issue carried humorous sketches of Tokyo drawn by "itinerant cartoonist" Shel Silverstein, the first of many such drawings documenting his far-flung exploits. Along with Silverstein, *Playboy* sent impressionist painter LeRoy Neiman around the globe to observe and depict scenes of foreign locales and their exotic inhabitants. Neiman and Silverstein each served as a contemporary flaneur whose recorded impressions allowed readers to gaze vicariously at the modern world.[28]

Playboy's portrayal of cosmopolitanism and travel fit comfortably within a cultural milieu that celebrated postwar affluence and posited the beneficence of the American socioeconomic system. In the context of the Cold War, tourism symbolized the pleasures of consumption and leisure made possible through free enterprise. Rising incomes and paid vacation time, together with a booming automobile industry, the construction of the interstate highway system, and the development of tourist-class jet travel all fueled an upsurge in the vacation and travel industry. To be a tourist signaled a level of prosperity that gave one the time and money to spend on holiday, devoted to taking in spectacles and experiences marked as out of the ordinary. Thus *Playboy*'s evocations of the globetrotting male found a ready audience in an expanding middle class for whom recreational travel was becoming a normal activity.[29] *Playboy*'s travelogues posited tourism as particularly suited to the romantic, affluent, pleasure-seeking male whose itineraries were far from the stuff of family vacations.

The playboy traveled both for business and pleasure. Status accrued to the business traveler, no downtrodden, Willy Loman–like traveling salesman, but a jet-setting, debonair businessman flitting from city to city in high style. One *Playboy* advertisement presented a well-dressed businessman, briefcase in hand, stepping smartly from a DC-7, a young woman gazing fondly upon him from the steps of the airplane. Overseas travel especially imparted an air of refinement and distinction. Another ad showed a young couple running playfully beneath the Eiffel Tower: "A young man tagged for traveling in high style, the Playboy reader is as apt to 'live it up' in the City of Light as he is to take off for the pleasure playgrounds of the 'in' out-islands. Decidedly in a class by himself, he can easily afford the time and space for world-roaming rewards." Other scenarios indicated that the sporting playboy enjoyed upmarket pastimes like skiing and sailing, as usual with an attractive woman in tow. "A young man...apt

to be mooring his craft in a Caribbean harbor when he's not plying his craft at the executive level," the *Playboy* reader had a penchant for travel. From its initial "International Datebook" column, the magazine went on to publish a series of articles on major cities and vacation destinations. In the early 1960s, *Playboy* also began to promote its own specially chartered tours. In addition to taking the reader on a tour of foreign capitals and major American cities, *Playboy* spotlighted such vacation havens as Acapulco, Spain's Costa Brava, Tahiti, the U.S. Virgin Islands, Jamaica, Hawaii, and Sardinia, along with such exotic experiences as traveling on the Orient Express or attending Carnival in Rio.[30] Photographs showed a man and his date partaking in various urban scenes: strolling through the nighttime city, walking through a market, dining out, watching a scantily clad showgirl performing at one of the in-spots. Taking up the theme of the globe-trotting playboy, another series of pictorials first published in 1960 focused almost exclusively on the unclad "Girls of..." various locales. Relying on stock prose, each feature hit upon recurring themes as it revealed the exotic inhabitants of faraway places. One learned from this series that "girls" from around the world preferred American men, were remarkably easy to meet, and were eager to form liaisons. More important, they were all secure in their femininity—indeed, they reveled in it—and possessed none of the competitive spirit of their American sisters.

A letter pitching the magazine to advertisers promised that *Playboy* reached "the young men who are spending their way up in the world." If a wide disparity existed between the most luxurious elements of the "dream fodder" showcased in *Playboy* and the average reader's ability to attain it, readers nonetheless formed a vast reservoir of purchasing power. "What we seem to have is the *Esquire* man," an enthusiastic Hefner wrote to a prospective marketing consultant, "but we've got him ten years younger." *Playboy*'s average reader in 1955 was twenty-nine. Commenting on the magazine's ability to attract advertisers, he mused, "It seems to me we've a wonderful story in terms of 'best buying age,' for it is at this point in life that basic brand selections are made that will last a lifetime."[31] The magazine reported on the spending potential of its followers in "Meet the Playboy Reader," acknowledging that this data was "meaningful" to advertising directors "faced with the problem of selling their particular audience to the gray flannel gentlemen in the ad agencies along Madison Avenue." Young men between the ages of eighteen and thirty-four made up about 75 percent of the magazine's readership, and 70 percent had some college education. Not all readers fit the most fundamental aspect of the playboy image: marketing studies showed about half were single, "free men," the other half "free in spirit only." Nevertheless, the average reader was a young, educated man with money to spend and a tendency to put it toward the kinds of things

promoted in *Playboy*. The household of the *Playboy* reader boasted a median income of $7,234; the upper half of the magazine's readership pulled in around $10,000 a year. *Playboy* readers smoked and drank more than the average and spent more money on travel, clothing, automobiles, and household goods. Not surprisingly, Diner's Club, the first independent credit card company, was an early advertiser in *Playboy*, drawn by the acquisitive, upwardly mobile audience the magazine promised to deliver. One *Playboy* feature offered a send-up of the consumerism promulgated in each issue: "The playboy lives on credit. He has a credit card for everything. He hasn't paid cash for anything in the last ten years. Next week he is joining a new credit card company.... With this company's credit card, you can sign for monthly bills you receive from other credit card companies."[32] The magazine's service features, by instructing readers in the art of "modern living," took the guess work out of choosing among the dizzying array of goods available in postwar America. At the same time, in cultivating the consumptive habits of its readership, *Playboy* helped mobilize its audience into an increasingly important unit of society—the consumer demographic.

"A CHAMPAGNE ATMOSPHERE": THE PLAYBOY CLUB

Where and how he enjoyed his leisure time was just as important a fixture of the playboy's identity as the various products he purchased. In *That Toddlin' Town*, his book of original cartoons published in 1951, Hefner sketched a drawing of a Clark Street strip bar, where a topless woman paraded down a runway in front of a motley crowd. The caption below read: "What we need is some little gimmick to give the place class."[33] Hefner recognized the possibilities in linking sex to an upmarket atmosphere. He later commented, "When you put sex and status together you can't miss."[34] By the end of the decade, Hefner had come up with just the "little gimmick" needed to create a space where men could gape at female flesh in a tasteful and sophisticated climate, a place with "class." His gimmick? The Playboy Bunny. The classy locale? The Playboy Club (see figure 2.4).

Although the most luxurious elements of the good life depicted in *Playboy* existed in the realm of fantasy, the opening of the first Playboy Club in 1960 solidified notions of affluence, youthful vitality, sexuality, and pursuit of pleasure in an actual space, a place where one could live out the image of the well-heeled man-about-town *and* come face to face with scores of beautiful women. The Chicago venue became the flagship club in a leisure-and-entertainment empire that would come to include dozens of nightclubs, resorts, hotels, and

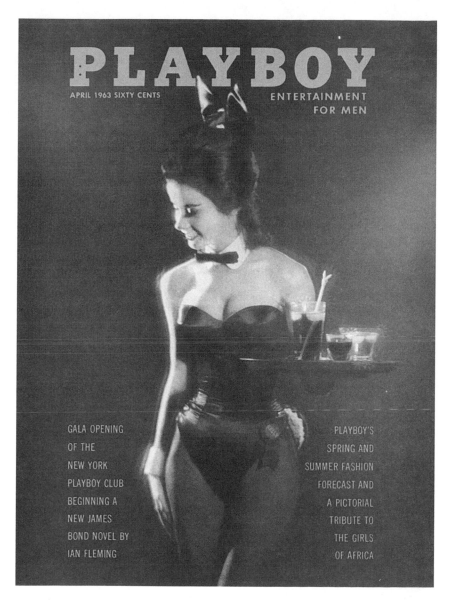

2.4 *The Playboy Bunny was meant to provide upscale titillation in the tasteful surroundings of the Playboy Club. Playboy magazine promoted the clubs, and the popularity of the clubs' iconic Bunnies, in turn, brought more publicity for the magazine. (Reproduced by special permission of* Playboy *magazine © April 1963 by Playboy.)*

casinos worldwide. The Playboy Clubs tapped into the desires of both Hefner and his readers. In the late 1950s, Playboy's office at 232 E. Ohio stood near Rush Street, the primary thoroughfare of Chicago's North Side nightlife district. Here, stylish supper clubs, smoke-filled, late-night jazz clubs, and bistros lined the street alongside seedier bars and strip clubs. Working late into the night, Hefner, with friend and colleague Victor Lownes, regularly headed out to nearby nightspots like the East Inn, Chez Paree, Black Orchid, Trade Winds, or the Cloisters.[35] Occasionally, their late-night talk turned to the possibility of operating a private club. In 1956, Playboy spotlighted the Gaslight Club, a restaurant and cocktail lounge that featured "gay nineties" music hall ambience, complete with waitresses dressed in skimpy costumes and fishnet stockings. Advertising executive Burton Browne had started this members only "key-club" in 1953, and it had since caught on in two other cities. When readers wrote to Playboy asking how they could join the club, Hefner and Lownes realized they had a ready clientele for a place of their own.[36]

Chicago offered plenty of nightspots that served drinks and provided various degrees of sexual titillation. Low-end strip joints along West Madison Street traded openly in female flesh. Anyone willing to pay exorbitant drink prices could find female companionship at the bars populated by B-girls along North Clark Street and around Rush Street. For upscale excitement, one could take in a floor show at numerous supper clubs or enjoy the chorus girls at the Chez Paree. Just as he had attempted to make pictures of nude women more respectable, Hefner set about upgrading the sex found in many of the more sordid venues. Unlike the strip joints and "clip joints" where the B-girls worked, the Playboy Club offered a posh space where one could enjoy the presence of attractive females without fear of being fleeced. In that sense, the clubs combined the sexual aura of the strip clubs with the more refined feel of the Chez Paree, adding the gimmicky exclusiveness of the members only Gaslight Club. If the playboy lived in a swank penthouse apartment, his private club would share the same contemporary decor. At the failed Colony Club at 116 E. Walton, workers gutted and transformed the interior into a hip, modern nightclub. Outside, the doorway to the old brick building was outfitted with a canopied, multicolored entryway emblazoned with a black and silver rabbit-head logo. On opening night, hundreds of charter members waited in the cold to pass through that door and into a realm where the most popular men's magazine had come to life.

Keyholders entered the "Playmate Bar" on the first level of the club. There, in place of the painting of a nude woman that hung over the bar in many a Victorian-era saloon, illuminated reproductions of Playmate centerfolds decorated the walls. It was one thing to gaze at the magazine's centerfolds in the privacy of one's home, or even to pass the magazine around at a party;

the illuminated nude photographs that hung next to tables created a shared space that invited and sanctioned men to enjoy them with their fellow sophisticates. The centerfolds' presence in this environment—a place where bachelors brought dates and husbands brought wives—further suggested that such images, and a male's desire to look at them, were perfectly appropriate. That the Club employed a number of former Playmates added to the titillation. "Look around you [at the centerfolds]," *Playboy*'s promotional literature urged, "many of these same young ladies are on hand to wait on members and their guests." The undressed woman in the photograph on the wall could indeed turn out to be the same Bunny-costumed woman who took one's drink order.[37]

The Playmate Bar also featured state-of-the-art technological accouterments. A custom-crafted stereo installation boasted more than 1,000 carefully selected records and tapes. Copies of Playboy's playlist were available to patrons who wanted a guide for building their own audio collections. Walking up the staircase to the second floor, visitors entered the "Living Room," covered with Playboy's specially designed rabbit-head logo carpeting and outfitted with low, plush chairs and coffee tables. Here, visitors could gather around a piano bar or relax in front of the fireplace. The Living Room hosted live performances and jazz combos and offered casual buffet dining. "Playboy's Cartoon Corner," a small sitting area in the back of the Living Room, featured original cartoon artwork from the pages of the magazine. Keyholders could relax in the "plush, masculine surroundings" of the third-floor Playboy Library, which showcased name entertainers between midnight and closing time in special "After Hours" shows. The Library was intended to suggest a cabaret-like intimacy, as guests sat on cushions arranged on the floor. Later, the "Penthouse" room was added upstairs.[38]

According to one promotional brochure, every room in the Chicago Playboy Club evoked "the warmth, the intimacy and the fun of a private cocktail party, with fine food, drink, entertainment." But the "numberless beautiful women—many of them Playmates from past issues of the magazine"—represented the most notable aspect of the club. Indeed, the bachelor-pad ambience served as the setting for the club's main attraction. Abandoning his original idea of dressing the club's female employees in frilly nightgowns and calling them Playmates, Hefner aimed to come up with a more practical uniform. The resultant Playboy Bunny embodied a feminine version of the magazine's rabbit mascot. Outfitted in what looked like a strapless, one-piece bathing suit finished off with fluffy tail and satin ears, the Bunny resembled something of a modern-day chorus girl, which *Playboy* was quick to point out: "Not since the Ziegfeld Girl of the Twenties has the concept of the all-girl girl so completely captured the public eye and imagination."[39]

Playboy touted the club as "a meeting place for the most important, most aware, most affluent men of the community" with membership "limited to the men of substance and influence in each urban area." Unlike traditional businessmen's clubs that required sponsorship and levied a hefty membership fee, any male with $25 could buy a lifetime membership. The Playboy Clubs were democratic in this regard, especially in comparison to clubs and lodges that excluded individuals on the basis of ethnic or racial identity or newly moneyed status. *Playboy* promised, "Whether you're entertaining a dinner date or an important client, every facet of this Club makes you *feel* like a member, lets you *impress*." *Playboy* trumpeted the frequent attendance at its clubs of various Hollywood film stars and musical entertainers, whose presence inspired "celebrity parties... highlighted by Bunnies twisting enticingly" atop the Living Room's Piano Bar. The clubs promised elbow-rubbing with celebrities, as well as special treatment to make each member feel like a "very important playboy," or VIP, the name Playboy chose for its members' magazine, as well as for the clubs' elaborate dining rooms. The New York club was the first to offer a VIP room for special occasions, where one could enjoy a ten-course haute cuisine meal. Instead of the "man-sized" drinks and dinners found elsewhere in the club, the VIP room boasted elegant crystal, silver, and china as well as service by Bunnies wearing special blue-velvet and silver trimmed costumes that matched its décor. *Playboy* recruited dozens of multilingual, foreign-born women to fill these posts; exotic Bunnies further marked the VIP room experience as something out of the ordinary.[40]

By 1963, Playboy boasted a quarter-million keyholders with six clubs in operation and plans to establish nine more. The desire to attract newcomers to the expanding chain of clubs meant creating an aura of classy sophistication with wide appeal, what one journalist called "mass merchandising a champagne atmosphere at beer prices." Except in the special dining rooms, the clubs sold everything from steak dinners to martinis for $1.50, a policy that simplified operations and ensured high margins on liquor sales. It also rendered the club-going experience less intimidating for the newly affluent young man-about-town. According to one observer, "The chain of Playboy Clubs is a middle-class phenomenon not unlike the supermarket, and it has been successful for many of the same reasons: low prices, good value for the money, a reassuring uniformity of layout and product, and tight control of quality and operations from a central headquarters."[41] The clubs offered a faux-exclusivity in an atmosphere that was racy but not raunchy, providing a setting and experience that privileged the male gaze while trading in the ascendant currency of display, leisure, and fun.

THE MORALITY OF "THE PLAYBOY LIFE"

As more and more men continued to join the ranks of *Playboy* readers and key-club members, critics began to assess seriously the implications of *Playboy*'s success. In an article in the journal *Commentary*, one scholar condemned *Playboy* for a single-minded devotion to sex, arguing that its editors offered "a vision of the whole man reduced to his private parts." A. C. Spectorsky dismissed the complaint in his letter to the editor of *Commentary*:

> We feature girls because they're attractive, stories because they are entertaining, jokes because they are funny. Our vision is not that of man reduced to his private parts, but of man enlarged through his capacity to interpret and enjoy life, one aspect of which—but by no means the only one—is the healthy enjoyment of sex.

Spectorsky took issue with an attack that focused so narrowly on the magazine's sexual content, explaining, "To derogate *Playboy* with a discussion limited to sex is to ignore much of the substance of the magazine." Many critics continued to view the nonsexual content as a veneer for the "smut" at the magazine's core, accusing *Playboy* of catering to "peep show tastes."[42] Others, however, gave careful consideration to the whole package offered by *Playboy*, finding it shrewdly attuned to specific features of postwar America, and thus in a disturbing position to challenge the social and ethical framework of society.

"*Playboy* has a strong, almost irresistible appeal for the young man who is struggling to establish his own identity, to define his own personality, to work out his style of life," suggested a religious commentator in 1960. Writing in *Motive*, Reverend Roy Larson continued:

> Caught up in a reaction against 'blah,' he does not want to be just another person, but wants to show, by his manners, his personal taste in music, food, drink, and apparel, that he is someone who is distinctive....And so he needs impersonal guidance and direction and help. Where does he get it? From *Playboy*, of course.

In his view, *Playboy* became a sort of bible. Its modern living features carried the weight of the Ten Commandments—for example, "Thou shalt not wear double breasted suits....Thou shalt not eat Velveeta Cheese." Its pronouncements formed a substitute religion for young men making their way in the world of consumer possibilities. Theologian Harvey Cox offered a similar assessment in *Christianity and Crisis*. Drawing on David Riesman's delineation of the "other-directed" character type, Cox argued that in a fast-changing

society increasingly oriented toward consumption, young men were confused by "a plethora of mass media signals and peer group values." He explained, "For the insecure young man with newly acquired time and money on his hands who still feels uncertain about his consumer skills, *Playboy* supplies a comprehensive and authoritative guidebook to this foreboding new world to which he now has access." In his view, "highly mobile, increasingly affluent" young readers looked to *Playboy* for "a total image of what it means to be a man."[43]

Larson and Cox were correct in recognizing *Playboy*'s function as expert advisor and in understanding the significant links between taste and status in postwar society. Americans turned increasingly to experts after World War II. The social and cultural changes that transformed postwar America undermined traditional forms of authority, which now seemed inadequate to address the new features of the highly mobile, prosperous, consumer-oriented society. Living in the new postwar suburbs, for example, many young wives and mothers found themselves separated from the traditional assistance of older kin; *Betty Crocker's Picture Cook Book* and *Dr. Spock's Baby and Child Care* both promised modern, expert guidance and sold millions. Ernest Dichter, a pioneering figure in the study of consumer behavior, reported that in the mobile society, new entrants into the middle class increasingly acquired values and attitudes from the mass media, turning especially to newspapers, magazines, advertisements, and radio and television programs for guidance when it came to matters of taste.[44]

To postwar observers, the field of consumption had become important terrain on which one staked a claim to social position. Russell Lynes articulated the significance of taste and its links to status in 1949, detecting a social structure based on taste and intellectual pretension made up of highbrows, middlebrows, and lowbrows. In his estimation, displays of taste were replacing wealth and family as determinants of prestige.[45] Vance Packard, whose works included *The Status Seekers* and *The Hidden Persuaders*, widely read critiques of postwar social configurations and the advertising industry, likewise noted the important role patterns of consumption played in the delineation of social hierarchy, even amid upward mobility. Packard disputed the notion that postwar prosperity was fostering a "classless" society; but as people strived for upward mobility, he argued, and as distinctions in income between many blue-collar and white-collar workers collapsed, the status one derived from consumer practices, rather than income, became the measure of social position.[46] Packard cited the work of Dichter's Institute for Motivational Research, which he claimed had discovered the lucrative potential for advertisers to target those who had recently achieved white-collar status. These people, especially, needed guidance since

the changes required to take up the new role are far from "painless." There is often considerable uncertainty and self-doubt. The Institute suggests this is the "fertile moment" to develop new brand loyalties by helping the newcomer feel comfortable with his new collar. This can be done, it says, by helping him know the ins and outs of the proper trappings. "The typical 'white-collar' products," it says, "such as fashionable clothing, fashionable home interior products of all kinds, golfing equipment, more sophisticated foods must make this type of person feel that he belongs."

Packard warned that such upwardly mobile individuals, anxiously adjusting to their newfound affluence and status, were susceptible to the manipulation of advertisers. To put it bluntly, status anxiety fueled empty consumption. Indeed, economist John Kenneth Galbraith had voiced a similar concern in *The Affluent Society,* a critique of Americans' commitment to economic growth as the measure of national success. In it, he argued that society's faith in consumer spending focused the nation's efforts and resources on expanding an economy based on the production and consumption of unnecessary goods. In these views, the consumer economy was in many ways like a house of cards, the entire structure resting on the fragile supports of planned obsolescence and the ability of savvy advertisers to exploit status anxiety and promote ongoing consumption. Or, as Cox, in his critique of *Playboy,* put it, "Those liberated by technology and increased prosperity to new worlds of leisure" now became "anxious slaves of dictatorial taste-makers."[47]

Playboy's attention to self-centered consumption was also charged with promoting a virulent strain of individualism. According to this view, *Playboy*'s "emphasis upon self-fulfillment" was antisocial and "anti-Christian." A life "lived with 'gusto and relish' is divorced from any concern for the neighbor," opined an editorial in the *Catholic World.* "It is life lived in pure concern for self." In this estimation, *Playboy* taught individuals how to achieve the trappings of a pleasurable, fashionable existence but provided no framework for connecting these status-conscious sophisticates to one another or to any purpose greater than self-indulgence. "The only neighbor Hefner apparently knows is the Playboy sitting at the next table in a luxurious Playboy Club, watching and being watched over by a Playgirl Bunny, who himself knows how to get what he wants either in food, or clothes, or sex, or automobiles, or liquor, or high fidelity."[48] According to this perspective, *Playboy*'s brand of good living seemed to lead inevitably to social atomization.

Growing criticism in the early 1960s inspired Hefner to draft a response, which took the form of the twenty-five-part editorial series "The Playboy Philosophy." In doing so, he crafted a statement of purpose that made him a

significant advocate of what Ernest Dichter called "the morality of the good life." As historian Daniel Horowitz has shown, Dichter, through his countless market research studies and published books, was an active participant in the reshaping of postwar society and staunch supporter of the Cold War consensus.[49] Dichter saw the consumption of goods as a positive, moral endeavor that provided psychological well-being by satisfying desires, while also supporting a democratic society and free-market economy. His outlook, delineated in *Strategy of Desire,* dismissed concerns that advertisers manufactured desires for unnecessary goods or that consumption fostered hedonism and profligacy. "Strictly speaking, a new car, a color TV set, cigarettes, beer, or French wines are not necessities," Dichter conceded. "But they all represent aspects of a full life." Consuming such seemingly unnecessary goods satisfied legitimate psychological needs while also energizing capitalism. "If we were to rely exclusively on the fulfillment of immediate and necessary needs, our economy would literally collapse overnight," Dichter proclaimed. Thus, those whom Packard viewed as hucksters, Dichter perceived as the heroes of the consumer society. That people did not need for survival the things they consumed made the task of the advertiser, marketing executive, or salesperson all the more imperative. As he put it, "The real salesmen of prosperity, and therefore of democracy, are the individuals who defend the right to buy a new car, a new home, a new radio." Before one sold a product, one first had to sell "*a positive philosophy of life*" that conveyed optimism about the future and endorsed the immediate self-gratification that came from consumption. According to Dichter, Americans needed to abandon lingering values of thrift and restraint and embrace a moral outlook in sync with the demands for self-indulgence generated by the postwar consumer economy. He even called upon those in the communications industry to use their media pulpit to spread the news about "the morality of the good life."[50]

Hefner served as one such prophet. With his magazine already a compendium on the pleasures of consumption, Hefner used his "philosophy" to give further definition to "the playboy life," providing the necessary ethical framework to go along with it. To critics who charged that his attention to individual fulfillment promoted a selfish lack of concern for others, Hefner countered with the "difficult truth" that "U.S. religion and free enterprise are, in certain respects, incompatible." "If what many of us profess to believe religiously were actually applied to American social, political and economic life," he argued, "we would have a system more nearly socialist than capitalist." Like Dichter, Hefner made no apologies for the economic system that rewarded with material gain the striving individual. "Americans have traditionally 'worshipped the Almighty Dollar'... and suffered a gilt-edged guilt complex as a result." But the competition and the material reward that inspired people to achieve had resulted in the

nation's high standard of living. Hefner positioned his magazine as a buttress for American consumerism:

> Thus Playboy exists, in part, as a motivation for men to expend greater effort in their work, develop their capabilities further and climb higher on the ladder of success.... The acquisition of property—and in the 1960s property may mean a handsome bachelor pad, elaborate hi-fi rig and the latest sports car—is the cornerstone of our American economic system. And a publication that helps motivate a part of our society to work harder, to accomplish more, to earn more, in order to enjoy more of the material benefits described—to that extent, the publication is contributing to the economic growth and strength of the nation.[51]

In this formulation, property did not mean land or other patrimony passed on from fathers to sons, but material possessions available to anyone with the cash—or credit—to buy them. In that sense, Hefner offered an optimistic vision that defined American citizenship in terms of the freedom to consume; theoretically, American men everywhere could aspire to playboy status and enjoy the fruits of a good life predicated on affluence and leisure.

Some postwar observers expressed concern that affluence would lead Americans to lose their competitive edge. After all, Soviet scientists had bested the U.S. space program with the launch of *Sputnik* in 1957, and Soviet athletes had defeated Americans in recent Olympic competitions. John F. Kennedy also made the so-called missile gap a campaign issue in 1960, claiming that the United States had fallen behind in the arms race. Whereas some worried that prosperity allowed the nation to grow "soft," Hefner argued that *Playboy* helped to keep the nation fit in the contest against the Soviet Union. His magazine's attention to material reward stimulated "young men to educate themselves so they can make enough money to enjoy these benefits. In this way we can help overcome the educational gap between ourselves and the Russians."[52] Furthermore, in a society confronted by the "much-discussed New Leisure," the magazine's attention to "leisure-time living" served the further good of helping individuals to adjust, motivating them to "personally examine and develop aspects of their individuality, interests, talents and activities perhaps previously dormant."[53] According to these assertions, *Playboy* did not exploit status anxieties; it showcased the finer things, a world of high-class, high-status goods and experiences that inspired democratic participation in the nation's free-market economy. In this regard, Hefner also had an answer for those charging that *Playboy*'s representations of "recreational sex" reduced sexuality to a "packageable consumption item." The Playmate, he argued, served as yet another motivating force, symbolizing high-class romance and sexual pleasure. Hefner

summed up this view in a statement that only bolstered critics' complaints while remaining wholly in keeping with his view of moral economy. "Playmates," he explained, "are real people and they are one of the good things in life that you can enjoy when you get up there and work hard and play hard."

Americans deserved to live *Playboy*'s version of the good life, Hefner proclaimed. The lifestyle projected in the magazine had far-reaching resonance due to the historical and cultural moment in which it took shape. Emerging in the midst of widening affluence, a consolidating consumer ethos, and growing emphasis on taste and status in formulations of social hierarchy, *Playboy* helped shepherd along these important transformations. *Playboy*'s "modern living" features, travelogues, and nightclubs created a vibrant tableau of a masculine identity fashioned around material acquisition and pleasure. The magazine's painstaking reconnaissance of the consumer landscape helped to transform readers into an important market for a variety of personal goods. The self-interested nature of the playboy's consumption stood in contrast to the conservative impulses of family-oriented spending, yet Hefner offered a justification for his magazine that shrewdly placed it at the center of national purpose. If postwar commentators fretted about the problem of conformity or the banalities of a society enjoying too much prosperity, Hefner saw only promise in rising affluence—the chance for more people to enjoy "the playboy life." Its pursuit fueled the economy and kept Americans competitive. Unlike the rebellious Beats, adherents to "the playboy life" neither dropped out of society nor posed a serious challenge to the economic order. Instead, their striving to get into "the sophisticated upper crust" drove them to "work hard and play hard, too."[54] Hefner helped propel the diffusion of a consumer ethic in postwar America, not by advocating unbridled hedonism, but by articulating the link between work and play, a connection that in effect granted permission for pleasure. Most readers would never attain the level of material comfort enjoyed by Hefner, nor were they likely to experience the same degree of autonomy and independence when it came to their livelihood. Nonetheless, *Playboy* envisioned its followers as energetic, virile free agents whose "upbeat" outlook and self-possession brought them financial success and whose paychecks financed a world of high-status consumption, on the town or in the penthouse.

3 PADS AND PENTHOUSES

Playboy's *Urban Answer to Suburbanization*

IN SEPTEMBER 1959, the *Chicago Daily News* announced the imminent construction of a "Snazzy Four Story Home" to be built in an area of the city known as the Gold Coast. Illustrated by renderings of a sleek, modern town house fit snugly between two stately brownstones, the story detailed the luxurious amenities of the proposed home, from the three-story atrium surrounding an indoor swimming pool to the twenty-four-foot state-of-the-art electronic entertainment wall in the living room. The opulent residence was meant to serve as bachelor quarters for the recently divorced Hugh Hefner, a far cry from the modest family apartment that appeared in the *Daily News* seven years earlier. *Playboy*'s editor-publisher purchased a narrow lot in the wealthy Near North Side neighborhood on which to build his new home, but the deluxe modern town house never materialized. While the project was still in the planning stages, Hefner spotted a four-story brick and limestone mansion in the same neighborhood and deemed it a palace befitting the "Czar of the Bunny Empire," as the *Saturday Evening Post* dubbed him. He acquired the property at 1340 North State Parkway that soon attained widespread fame as the Playboy Mansion.[1]

No longer destined to occupy an actual space in the cityscape, the "snazzy home" resurfaced as "The Playboy Town House" in the May 1962 issue of *Playboy* magazine (see figure 3.1). An "ultra-urban island of individuality in a sea of look-alike" dwellings, the proposed structure represented "the best of all possible worlds for the unattached, affluent young man happily wedded to the infinite advantages of urbia."[2] *Playboy*'s description of the town house commented on several salient features of postwar American culture. In an era of mushrooming "ticky-tacky" subdivisions and popular discussions of conformity, it emphasized individuality. In the midst of dramatic economic growth, suburbanization, and a marriage and baby boom that elevated the nuclear family to iconic status, it evoked affluence, but conjured

3.1 *Plans for this three-story town house were initially drafted as a proposed residence for Hugh Hefner. When he instead purchased the property that became the Playboy Mansion, the drawings were transformed into a fantastic "modern living" feature, "The Playboy Town House." (Reproduced by special permission of* Playboy *magazine © May 1962 by Playboy.)*

an image of a single man, married only to his urban lifestyle. The Playboy Town House represented just one of several *Playboy*-commissioned designs and photographic essays on bachelor "pads" that appeared in the magazine between 1956 and 1970. Together these features formed part of a critical, imagined urban landscape that gave spatial coherence to *Playboy*'s vision of the good life. *Playboy*'s "man about town" enjoyed a world of urban commercial amusements and resided in a bachelor pad.[3] Anchoring the playboy in the posh spaces of the penthouse and the city, the magazine addressed both the apparent encroachment of women into the public sphere and the "feminized" spaces of suburbia. In doing so, it upheld a positive image of a glittering cityscape that countered expressions of concern over the decline of the American city.

Popular assumptions juxtaposed a private, domestic female realm of the suburb with a public, productive male world of the city.[4] Such categories did not reflect a society bifurcated along these lines—women worked in the city, after all, and men lived in the suburbs—but they did have conceptual power, which invested these spaces with meaning about the value and the appropriate "place" of men and women in society. The symbolic dichotomies of urban/male, suburban/female helped to structure *Playboy*'s response to suburbia and the way in which the magazine couched its depiction of both urban living and domestic space. They were also subject to manipulation. Amid the growing emphasis on family and suburbia, *Playboy* retrieved men from the "feminized" suburbs and relocated them, rhetorically, in the "masculine" space of the city. Drawing on popular depictions of technological ease and affluence, the magazine attempted to "masculinize" the domestic sphere, which it also located in the city. Notably, *Playboy*'s attention to consumption in interior spaces reflected society's drift toward privatization, a development that in time helped to destabilize the gendered urban-suburban dichotomy. *Playboy* had little need to uphold urban living as a marker of masculinity once men were comfortable in the domestic sphere. In this regard, *Playboy*'s representations of gender and space did not merely reify existing categories of difference; its efforts to refashion masculinity exposed the ways in which gender roles and the spaces where men and women enacted them could be transformed.

"A PLAYBOY'S PAD"

In his opening editorial, Hefner proclaimed that *Playboy* would be unlike most other men's magazines with their focus on rugged outdoor activities:

We don't mind telling you in advance—we plan on spending most of our time inside. We like our apartment. We enjoy mixing up cocktails and an *hors d'oeuvre* or two, putting a little mood music on the phonograph, and inviting in a female acquaintance for a quiet discussion on Picasso, Nietzsche, jazz, sex.[5]

From the beginning, *Playboy* located its readership within a specific spatial context while outlining the range of interests around which the playboy lifestyle revolved. Awareness of liquor, music, food, hi-fi equipment, fine art, even philosophy made the playboy a connoisseur, with its attendant meanings of refinement and sophistication. In turn, his connoisseurship was linked to seduction and sexual indulgence, and all were situated within the realm of the bachelor pad.

The special issue of *Architectural Record* on modern designs for the American family home showcased "Architecture for the Good Life," according to the president of the American Institute of Architects (AIA) in 1956.[6] *Playboy* grounded its vision of the good life in a different kind of space, providing a detailed view of ideal bachelor quarters in a two-part feature called "Playboy's Penthouse Apartment," which appeared in September and October of that same year (see figure 3.2).[7] "A man yearns for quarters of his own," began the narrated tour. "More than a place to hang his hat, a man dreams of his own domain, a place that is exclusively his."[8] Text and illustrations escorted readers through a spacious open floor plan composed of six interconnected spaces—living and dining areas, kitchen, bathroom, bedroom, and study. An entry hall opened onto the "active zone," a combination living-dining room with adjoining kitchen that one could partition from the rest of the apartment. Adjacent was the "quiet zone"—the master bedroom with its custom-made oversized bed and connected study. Outfitted with modern furnishings, including built-in Knoll cabinets, Saarinen armchairs, and Japanese Shoji screens, the penthouse featured a neutral palette and striking textural contrasts from its cork tile floor, to the stone fireplace hearth, to an exposed brick wall. Expansive window walls afforded views of the city. Well-concealed closets and built-in cabinets held the playboy's possessions—sports gear, clothing, gourmet food, expensive liquor, pipes, stamp collection. Gadgetry abounded in such forms as a high-tech entertainment wall, an ultrasonic dishwasher, and the bedroom's console of switches and buttons that gave the playboy complete control over the apartment.

In 1956, the Women's Congress on Housing convened to address women's needs and desires as consumers of domestic space, signaling the primacy of the single family home and the paramount position women held within it.[9] That same year, in the interior spaces of the penthouse, *Playboy* outlined an antidote to suburban domesticity:

3.2 "Playboy's Penthouse Apartment" appeared in September and October 1956. The two-part feature took readers on a tour through the open floor plan of a lavishly appointed bachelor pad, providing a marked contrast to the family-centered suburban home. (Reproduced by special permission of Playboy *magazine © September 1956 by Playboy.)*

A man's home is not only his castle, it is or should be, the outward reflection of his inner self—a comfortable, livable, and yet exciting expression of the person he is and the life he leads. But the overwhelming percentage of homes are furnished by women. What of the bachelor and his need for a place to call his own? Here's the answer, Playboy's penthouse apartment, home for a sophisticated man of parts, a fit setting for his full life and a compliment to his guests of both sexes. Here a man, perhaps like you, can live in masculine elegance.

Assertions about the need for masculine space coalesced against the backdrop of new postwar suburban housing forms and the critique of a "feminized" society. Take for example Philip Wylie's account of "The Womanization of America," which appeared in *Playboy* in 1958 and linked emasculation to women's gradual invasion of male space. In his estimation, the onslaught had begun decades earlier when saloons, which once provided a place for male bonding, gave way to speakeasies that catered to female patrons by serving colorful, fruit-flavored "feminine" drinks. In time, Wylie explained, "the American male had lost his authority as symbolized by the places where he drank. Sawdust vanished and

the stand-up bar was rare.... By then, the one remaining masculine redoubt was a man's club." But women laid siege to the men's club, too. In all such "luckless clubs" where the "battle axes moved in," the traditional masculine decor—"the big stone fireplaces, the vast, dim, peaceful libraries and the heavy, wonderful chairs"—soon vanished. The evolution of the single family home illustrated the further demise of male space. "Where once man had had a den, maybe a library, a cellar poolroom, his own dressing room—and good, substantial floors and walls to protect his privacy," Wylie explained, "he now found himself in a split-level pastel creation with 'rooms' often 'created' by screens his wife moved about as often as she changed her flower arrangements." The result was a sense of displacement. "He thereafter hardly ever knew where he was, in his own home. All he knew was that the beloved old place now looked like a candy box."[10] Although writing about a standard of living well out of reach for the average male, Wylie's hyperbolic account suggested an important link between changing gender roles and the material world. The lines in the "battle of the sexes" had been drawn all across the urban landscape.

Wylie was also responding to transformations in the shape, setting, and meaning of the American home, which saw the disappearance of gender-specific spaces in favor of the "family room." By the mid-twentieth century the tendency toward smaller dwellings composed of less formal, multipur-pose spaces had been well established. In the postwar era, vast acres of new single family dwellings, built with innovative mass production techniques and financed with federal mortgage guarantees, promised to solve the nation's hous-ing dilemma. Ascendant visions of family togetherness and a fascination for the relaxed "California lifestyle" combined with cost considerations to make the open-plan ranch house the most prominent postwar housing form.[11] To crit-ics like Wylie, too much family togetherness, as symbolized by and contained within the family home, undermined masculinity. "What of this new brand of compulsive closeness, lauded as a social virtue and sweeping the country like a seven year virus?" asked *Playboy*'s William Iversen as he lamented the lack of privacy in the modern home and lampooned togetherness. "Is it something you catch from sitting around a suburban living room watching the Lawrence Welk show? A mystic sense of oneness that comes from making a burnt offering of prime sirloin on an outdoor grill?" Iversen called for "apartness," intoning, "Togetherness-haters, unite—you have nothing to lose but your Janes." "The American home," Wylie asserted, "is becoming a boudoir-kitchen-nursery, dreamed up by women, for women, and as if males did not exist as males."[12]

Suburban males could lay claim to the domestic sphere through "domestic masculinity," embracing handiwork and home improvement projects, but *Playboy* shunned this type of activity and its association with familial responsibility. In

the 1950s, do-it-yourself projects received widespread attention in the popular press, offering men a masculine foothold within the home in the form of the garage or basement workshop.[13] *Life* magazine, for example, sketched "the new American domesticated male" who focused his interests and expended his energy on home and family. Mowing the lawn behind a noisy machine gave him "a sense of power and a gadget to tinker with." Building the backyard barbecue pit kept him "busy nights and weekends" and encouraged family togetherness. Such efforts constituted "a boon to the household" as well as a "boom for industry." *Life* even speculated, "Probably not since pioneer days, when men built their own log cabins, have they been so personally involved in their homes."[14] *Playboy*'s representations of the city and the bachelor pad suggested distaste for such work. Rather than exert himself in productive labor around the house, the playboy would be a consumer of domestic space in his own right.

In "The Dream House and How to Avoid It," Shepherd Mead presented the urban apartment and suburban home as separate spheres for the exuberant bachelor and the harried husband. Single men chose "carefree apartment living" in the city, while married men were dragged by their spouses to suburbia. According to Mead, a married man soon discovered that "every woman wants a home of her own. From the very moment you move into your apartment, she will make it clear that she thinks of it only as a temporary expedient—until you find your dream house." Not only did the exiled suburbanite face separation from city friends and a longer commute to work, he also missed the "protective wing of the building superintendent and handy man," who freed the apartment-dweller's time for more important matters.[15] The playboy, after all, had no physical need to enlarge his home for a growing family. Nor had he the psychological need to build something with his own hands. During his leisure time, he aimed to have fun. Mead's admonishments to avoid suburbia suggested the attributes of the dwelling most attuned to the playboy lifestyle. While male efforts to maintain the suburban home stemmed from familial responsibilities, the urban bachelor pad, demanding little time or effort, bespoke the free-and-easy existence of the single man.

Thus, throughout the description of "Playboy's Penthouse Apartment" an emphasis on ease and serenity prevailed. Skylights lend "a romantic atmosphere to the entrance-way," where a closet panel "slides easily aside, a light goes on automatically." At the end of the hall, the "apartment beckons warmly" to the playboy. Entering the living space, he turns his attention to the "magnetic glow" cast by the fireplace. Through open windows, he gazes at the "winking towers of the city." From this vantage, he can take in the "enchanted view from the window wall." In the study, he reposes in a contoured Herman Miller armchair with footstool, which offers such perfect support that "you and the chair are like twin spoons nested together." In the bedroom, "soft mood music flows

through the room and the stars shine in the casements as you snuggle down."
One had no need to depart from the city in search of refuge, for the penthouse
represented an urban haven, "a physical expression of [the] dream" to be "an
active part of the city's excitement and sophistication, and yet to know a measure of isolation from its frantic tempo and noises."[16] Indeed, the bachelor pad
itself took over the wifely duties of greeting and soothing the man returning
from the realities of the outside world.

Yet, given the problematic meanings attached to the bachelor's position outside the family, his dwelling constituted a potentially disruptive site. The 1949
Alfred Hitchcock thriller *Rope* brings into focus the image of the bachelor pad
as a site for sexual transgression. Filled with refined artwork and furnishings
and offering a sweeping view of the skyline, the high-rise apartment in *Rope* is a
sinister place. It serves as the setting where two bachelor roommates carry out a
twisted plan to strangle a former classmate, conceal his body in the apartment,
then host an elegant dinner party in the victim's honor with his unwitting family members as guests. *Rope* hints at a homosexual relationship between the
two young men, implying, for instance, that they share one bedroom in the
two-bedroom space. In this manner, it links their murderous capacity to their
sexual "perversity," the apartment serving as the stage on which they act out
both "crimes."[17] In the hetero-normative climate of the 1950s the unmarried
man prompted suspicion about his sexual orientation. *Playboy*'s pad emphasized the bachelor's heterosexuality by gearing its technologies for seduction.
For example, the built-in bar in the living room:

> permits the canny bachelor to remain in the room while mixing a cool
> one for his intended quarry. No chance of missing the proper psychologi-
> cal moment—no chance of leaving her cozily curled up on the couch with
> her shoes off and returning to find her mind changed, purse in hand, and
> the young lady ready to go home, damn it.

Similarly, a self-timing dimmer let the bachelor "gradually and subtly dim the
lights to fit the mood—as opposed to the harsh click of a light switch that
plunges all into sudden darkness and may send the fair game fleeing." A cleverly
placed switch turned off the telephone ringer so that "a chatty call from the date
of the night before won't shatter the spell being woven." Juggling the numerous
women in his life, the playboy also made good use of the answering machine
that helped him manage the many telephone calls he received. Thus, through
the mention of multiple girlfriends and his success at seducing women, the narrative emphasized the penthouse as a site of heterosexual masculine pleasure.
This construction of the pad as "lair" also formed a frequent trope for *Playboy*
cartoons and inspired a setting for several films in the 1950s and 1960s, most
memorably the 1959 comedy *Pillow Talk* (see figure 3.3).[18] In the film, Rock

3.3 *The playboy's heterosexual vitality was grounded in the space of the bachelor pad, which served as the setting and subject of many cartoons in the magazine. (Reproduced by special permission of* Playboy *magazine © November 1966 by* Playboy.*)*

Hudson portrayed smooth-operator Brad Allen, opposite Doris Day. The film glamorized Brad Allen's single status and womanizing ways, highlighting his automated bachelor pad as the playpen for a healthy, robust heterosexual male. Equipped with controls that dimmed lights and locked doors, played mood music and transformed the sofa into a bed at the flip of a switch, his apartment formed the perfect lair for seducing women and provided an important contrast to the pastel frills of Doris Day's abode.

The bachelor pad drew on contemporary housing trends while carefully opposing the feminized and family-centered spaces and culture of postwar suburbia.[19] Popular expectations of material abundance and the ease of a "push-button society" in postwar America resounded in *Playboy*'s representations of the domestic realm and the household technologies that filled it. The family home represented a sphere in which the power of modern technology, in the form of climate-regulating systems, electrical appliances, and new synthetic materials, could be harnessed to facilitate a life of controlled comfort. Postwar images of extravagant or futuristic domiciles reinforced the link between domestic comfort and modern technology. Shortly before the appearance of "Playboy's Penthouse Apartment," for example, *Life* magazine ran a "Modern Living" feature complete with photographs and floor plan, showcasing the "push-button paradise" of a Los Angeles family. The extravagant home stood on a one-acre plot and included pools for swimming and wading, along with a tennis court. *Life* paid greatest attention to technological novelties like the motorized "human Lazy Susan," seven rotating lounge chairs designed to give sunbathers an even tan. This "mechanical dream house" also featured a bar that dispensed whiskey at the touch of a button, beds that raised themselves for making at the flip of a switch, and an elaborate system of controls that played soft music, opened draperies, and filled the bathtub.[20]

The idealized penthouse and subsequent pads shared much in common with the highly mechanized or futuristic family homes touted in the popular press, but in the penthouse technology was meant to facilitate the desires and leisurely pursuits of the bachelor. The description of "Playboy's Patio Terrace," for instance, emphasized its gadgetry for preparing and serving food and beverages; for entertaining, including a television that could be raised, lowered, and rotated 360 degrees all by remote control; and even for controlling the climate of the outdoor patio (see figure 3.4).[21] The penthouse boasted an ultrasonic dishwasher like the one found in Disneyland's "House of the Future." Technology figured most prominently in the bedroom, where a control panel built into the headboard gave the playboy complete mastery of his environment, even allowing him to start breakfast in the morning with the simple throw of a switch.[22] At a time when men were encouraged to demonstrate commitment to family

3.4 *"Playboy's Patio Terrace," one of* Playboy's *commissioned designs, was described as a "refreshingly feasible answer to the city squire's quest for a touch of outdoor living." It featured a cantilevered sun deck, fully equipped outdoor kitchen, revolving television set, and pool. (Reproduced by special permission of* Playboy *magazine © August 1963 by Playboy.)*

and channel their masculinity by acting as home handymen, *Playboy* presented instead a state-of-the art existence where everything could be controlled at the touch of a button, and where one's own desires came first.

In order to "masculinize" further the domestic realm, *Playboy* had not only to draw attention to the bachelor's heterosexual identification, but also to massage assumptions about what constituted "normal" maleness. Men's interest in their physical surroundings required adherence to "masculine" taste and style. *Playboy* appropriated modern design as a masculine idiom, avoiding elements with feminine or familial associations. Devoid of artifice and frivolous decoration, masculine design was, by implication, superior. The playboy's pad was thoroughly modern, outfitted with high-priced furnishings designed by contemporary trendsetters such as George Nelson, Eero Saarinen, and Charles Eames.[23] The penthouse was no place for Early American–style furniture, dinette sets, or affordable embellishments—what Thomas Hine has called Populuxe—found in an average tract-dweller's home.[24] Nor would one find the popular hues like sea-foam green, canary yellow, or flamingo pink that brightened everything from appliances to flooring to cabinets in many postwar houses. A neutral color scheme, with a few bold accents in blue and green, enhanced the sleek, modern feel of the penthouse. If readers remained unconvinced of modern design as an expression of masculinity, the narrator

pointed out the "complete absence" of such feminine mainstays as "bric-a-brac, patterned fabrics, pleats and ruffles." More overt masculine touches existed in such furnishings as the kitchen stool "constructed from [a] rugged, contoured tractor seat." Describing the bachelor's lavatory, *Playboy* juxtaposed the "compartmented drawers," holding "the potions, lotions, notions, sundries and other mysteries"—items potentially associated with feminine acts of primping and beautifying—with the "bold and vigorous primitive paintings reminiscent of the prehistoric drawings in the caves of Lascaux."

Although *Playboy* also implied that its smart, functional floor plan represented a particularly masculine scheme, the open plan of the penthouse differed little from the open-plan ranch house.[25] Built-in wall units, light fixtures, and preinstalled television sets in Levittown's ranch houses, for instance, signaled a modern existence made affordable for an expanding middle class. *Playboy*'s proposed living quarters drew upon such notions but surpassed them, replacing the solitary television set, for example, with the extravagant flush-mounted equipment of its high-tech entertainment wall. Contrary to Wylie's demands for "good substantial walls," within the "active zone" (living and dining area, kitchen) and "quiet zone" (bedroom, study, bath) of the penthouse, furnishings and partitions could be manipulated to rearrange areas. The real difference between the family home and the pad lay in the use of space. In the family home, for instance, partitions could transform multipurpose rooms into play and hobby space for children.[26] The playboy's apartment, on the other hand, could be transformed into *adult* play space for a crowd of friends or more intimate play for two. The dining room was perfect for a "full-production gala dinner" or "all-night poker games, stag or strip." While many suburban tract houses afforded little privacy for their inhabitants—indeed, Levittown houses offered only one bathroom—the playboy's lavatory promised total comfort and privacy, boasting such accouterments as a tanning bed, magazine rack, ashtray, and telephone. Although the playboy lived by himself, the apartment's study, where he might don a smoking jacket, described as "good balm for the inner man," allowed him to "get away from the rest of the house and be really alone."[27] There he could recline in his Herman Miller armchair, a "lord-of-the-domain chair reserved for you alone." The provision of private space within the privacy of the penthouse furthered the fantasy of a domestic realm divorced from the imperatives of a child-centered family home.

Playboy also made the bachelor at home in the kitchen. The magazine's attention to men's culinary prowess came at a time when assumptions about "women's work" limited men's role in the kitchen and involvement in food preparation to barbecuing, carving meat, and drying dishes. In the 1930s, *Esquire*'s depictions had laid the groundwork for a male interest in activities

typically coded as "feminine," but assumptions in the 1950s about what comprised appropriate roles for men and women, along with the strong association of effeminacy with homosexuality, meant that *Playboy* also had to rationalize men's claim to activities seemingly outside a "normal" male purview.[28] *Playboy* circumvented the kitchen's association with women's caregiving and housekeeping roles and instead tied the bachelor's domestic skills to his masculine status.[29] Such a formulation drew upon distinctions between men as chefs and women as cooks, a distinction *Esquire* made in its 1949 *Handbook for Hosts*. *Esquire* shunned routine cookery, equated with femininity, and instead focused on "the little known recipes of internationally famous chefs, the unexpected touches which transform an ordinary food into an extraordinary dinner, the *super* dishes that will establish your reputation as a cook even if you *never* learn to bake a cake or disguise a left-over."[30] Masculine cookery was something quite extraordinary, an opinion *Playboy* shared. In its descriptions of the bachelor's activities in the kitchen, *Playboy* thus minimized the drudgery and emphasized the spectacle of cooking. In the penthouse, for instance, the kitchen could be partitioned from the rest of the apartment, "But since the urban male prides himself on his culinary artistry [the kitchen] may, more often, be open onto the dining room, so the host can perform for an admiring audience while sharing in conversation." The kitchen also boasted, in addition to an impressive storage system for the playboy's wine collection, an induction stove and a radiant broiler roaster. "The manipulation of this broiler, and the sight through the dome of a sizzling steak, will prove for your guests a rival attraction to the best on TV." The playboy, of course, was the real center of attention. The narrative assured, "You'll be the director of this show." Whereas the kitchen in the open-plan family home served as a "command center" for mothers engaged in cooking, cleaning, and supervising young children at play, the penthouse kitchen put the playboy on display.[31] For him, the kitchen served not as a workspace, but as a stage; cooking represented a leisurely pursuit, not part of a day's labor in caring for family.

The playboy's interest in the kitchen did not extend to less glamorous forms of labor. "Unless you're a very oddball bachelor indeed," *Playboy* noted, "you like to cook and whomp up short-order specialties to exactly the same degree that you actively dislike dishwashing, marketing and tidying up." Thus, plans for the penthouse emphasized "an easy-to-keep clean setup," as the *Miami Daily News* observed, "for a man can hardly look masculine shaking the feather duster over the tables when the doorbell rings." Like the technology in the rest of the apartment, the kitchen's devices helped affect a particular persona—in this case, the bachelor as suave, culinary wizard—while also facilitating a life of ease. In the kitchen of "Playboy's Duplex Apartment," nonperishable items paraded by on

a motorized conveyor belt so the playboy need not spend time searching his cabinets. In another feature, electric cookware freed him "from the tyranny of the kitchen" and its connotations of women's domestic labor.[32]

In addition to its inclusion in the bachelor pad features, the playboy's kitchen received regular attention in the magazine. Thomas Mario's monthly "Food and Drink" columns highlighted the performance of the bachelor chef and linked cooking with seduction and sexual pleasure.[33] The columns also separated the gourmet recipes suitable for a playboy's skilled efforts from the basic food women prepared for their families. Throughout, food preparation and consumption were couched in gendered terms. "A woman may make the best patty of chicken in the world," Mario explained, "but it takes a man to place a thick shell steak over a bed of live ashen white charcoal." He scolded the playboy gourmet who invited a "few pals over for a buffet dinner" and asked them "to perch on kitchen stools while he mashes the potatoes. That's woman's work." Cooking red meat was clearly a man's job, but Mario also managed to give salad-making a manly spin. "Actually a good salad maker must have many of the traits and skills that we sometimes think of as feminine—meticulousness, patience, cleanliness and a very alert sense of touch and taste." Mario explained that "these are not exclusively feminine virtues, and for some reason, it takes a man to master the really fine art of the salad bowl." Significantly, despite all these rationalizations, the playboy refrained from baking, for in the 1950s the cake served as "an icon of American womanhood."[34] *Playboy* did not attempt to refashion such a powerful symbol of femininity into a masculine enterprise.

FOR YOUNG CITY GUYS

Playboy's *Penthouse*, a syndicated television program that aired in 1959 and 1960, made clear that the bachelor made his home in the city. Hosted by a tuxedo-clad, pipe-clutching Hefner, weekly episodes welcomed viewers into a cocktail party in progress, attended by entertainers and celebrities and adorned by fashionable women. The opening sequence followed a sports car as it made its way through the bustling traffic up Chicago's Lake Shore Drive toward the heart of the city. To the strains of an original jazz composition by Cy Coleman, the camera panned across downtown to an illuminated tower in the nighttime skyline. The next shot showed the automobile as it stopped in front of a high-rise, then cut to an interior of an elevator as it climbed to the top-floor penthouse. The doors opened and the camera/viewers were invited by Hefner to join in the

festivities. As these opening credits suggested, the playboy spent only part of his time indoors. He was also an active inhabitant of the city.

Playboy's attention to the city took shape against a backdrop of developments that signaled the erosion of a male public culture and stirred concern about the fate of urban centers. "What goes on in those male sanctuaries— the strictly 'men only' restaurants, the 'no women allowed' saloons and poker games?" Richard Gehman queried readers of *Cosmopolitan*. "They're only a symptom—but a growing one—of man's struggle to retain his masculine identity."[35] As businesses identified the family as the primary unit of consumption and vied for its dollars, traditionally masculine spaces and pastimes were becoming sanitized, softened, and feminized. Proprietors dressed up previously all-male spaces such as diners and bowling alleys in order to make them respectable venues for housewives and their children. They took their design cues from the new suburbia, embracing materials popular in middle-class homes such as Formica, vinyl, and terrazzo. Bowling alleys wooed families by brightening interiors, limiting the sale of alcohol, and even experimenting with spaces for childcare and laundry facilities. Major League Baseball targeted families by attempting to upgrade the crowds and the stadiums in which they gathered. Retail, often envisioned as a woman's domain, assumed an even larger place in the postwar landscape. As Lizabeth Cohen has explained, the earliest department stores had created "feminized space" within urban districts otherwise organized around "male-dominated" commercial and leisure activities. Isolated from this heterogeneous street culture, postwar suburban shopping malls marked a departure from early city department stores, as builders created quasi-public spaces oriented toward women and families. Meanwhile, the sprouting of malls across the United States affected development in the urban center, since business leaders intent on reviving downtown viewed the declining city in gendered terms. Believing not men but women cared about cleanliness and safety, developers in the 1950s aimed downtown beautification efforts toward female shoppers. Commenting on a diminishing male-oriented urban public culture, Ernest Havemann painted this picture:

> Thirty or forty years ago 6 pm was the hour when millions of Americans were slicking up to go out for the evening. Now most of them are feeding the kids and getting ready to wash the dishes together. In many cities today you could shoot a cannon through the downtown streets at night without harming anybody but an occasional forlorn stranger, wandering pitiably in search of excitement. The old traditional hangouts of the unmarried male have disappeared from the American scene.

Of course, this description overlooked the continued popularity of night-life districts like the one where Hefner routinely played on Chicago's North Side and which inspired his own foray into the nightclub business. Yet all of these developments pointed to the domestication of space and, as Havemann observed, to the primacy of the family and fed perceptions that, quite literally, men were losing ground to women.[36]

At the same time cultural and commercial interests were organizing the new suburbia around women and families, the postwar city was becoming associated with deterioration and danger. Historians have traced the city's waning fortunes to several factors. In the postwar period, discriminatory lending practices promoted suburban homeownership at the expense of urban revitalization. African-American migration to urban centers spurred racial fears, prompting panic-peddling and "white flight." Disinvestment siphoned taxes and jobs from cities, leaving them cash-strapped. Those who remained generally faced deteriorating housing stock and limited economic opportunities. Together these trends combined to speed the erosion of the center city and the shift instead to the decentralized metropolitan area, and in the process "racialized" the image of the city and the social problems it came to represent.[37] Meanwhile, as the Cold War intensified, civil defense experts added another layer to the growing stigma by pointing out that the urban center would be the bull's-eye in the event of an atomic attack. Proponents of decentralization argued that besides removing people from harm's way, "dispersal" was "Good Business." American cities, in their estimation, suffered from decaying infrastructure, obsolete commercial districts, and blighted areas that drained public coffers. From this perspective, as Paul Boyer points out, that they were also subject to attack was merely "the final nail in the coffin."[38] Grim representations and predictions about the city circulated at mid-century. "Our cities are prime targets for atomic attack," civil defense films and publications warned. Film noir, beginning in the mid-1940s and continuing into the next decade, showcased urban disorder. As Eric Avila has explained, this new cinematic form captured the dark underbelly of urban life associated with the "blackening" of the city in terms of its racial composition and the crumbling of the urban culture that had peaked in the early decades of the twentieth century. Taking the "modern city as both setting and subject," film noir presented an "erotic portrayal of an urban wasteland" that revealed deep ambivalence toward the city.[39]

If some presaged an urban wasteland, *Playboy* offered an urban wonderland. While noir's male antiheroes met their doom in the city, betrayed by treacherous women, the playboy enjoyed his scads of Playmates. He used the city as his playground and seduction aid, embracing life at every turn. While the suburb buffered the white, middle-class family from the urban realm, the city offered a

haven from the stifling domesticity symbolized by the suburban home. In keeping with mainstream discussions that spoke in universalizing terms about "The American Male," *Playboy* presented a white, affluent young man as its ideal type and promoted a positive image of urban life at a time when the city was becoming linked to the specter of racial change, decay, and even atomic disaster.[40]

"Since ancient times, men have associated true sophistication with cities," asserted a *Playboy* promotion in 1957. "Our word 'urbane,' meaning suave, elegant, polished, refined, is a direct descendant on the Latin *urbanus* (belonging to a city)....It's a matter of solid statistics that *Playboy* is *the most urban men's magazine in America*." As Hefner said of himself, the readers of his magazine, and the ideal playboy depicted within its pages, all were "city guys." Hefner, who claimed to edit the magazine to suit his own tastes, provides a starting point for understanding the centrality of the city to the vision of masculinity purveyed in *Playboy*. Hefner described himself as a "city-bred" fellow, his magazine suited to "indoor" interests that grew out of his own youthful longings. For Hefner, the city became the site for the projection of fantasies about an alternative to his mundane responsibilities. He recalled, "I remember, in the days prior to *Playboy*, walking the streets of Chicago late at night, looking at the lights of the high-rise apartment buildings and very much wanting to be a part of 'the good life' I thought the people in those buildings must be leading." His impression of the city also stemmed from a nostalgic view of the urban culture of the "roaring twenties," a decade he had hardly experienced but imagined as a "yeasty time" of joyful exuberance quite different from the seriousness of the early 1950s.[41]

That Hefner's own fantasies about the good life had been nurtured in an urban context helps account for the shape and direction of his magazine. Equally important, while the spatial milieu for the idealized nuclear family was the feminized suburban home, bachelor culture was inexorably entwined with urban culture. The bachelor subculture that flourished around the turn of the twentieth century hinged directly on the commercial diversions and all-male institutions afforded by urban life.[42] It made sense, then, that the magazine's imaginary bachelor figure would inhabit and celebrate the urban realm. After all, Hefner did not invent the playboy out of whole cloth in the 1950s. *Playboy* drew upon the associations of city living with singlehood, freedom, mobility, and sexual license that coalesced during the heyday of the bachelor.

Throughout its first decade of publication, *Playboy*'s advertising, editorial content, and publicity consistently invoked the city. A 1958 article on fashion, "Summer in the City," offers just one example of how the magazine's many service features emphasized the pleasures of urban living. Drawing attention to the "smart young folk" inhabiting a city that "shimmers romantically and excitingly" in the summer heat, the text challenged the supposed comfort and ease of suburbia.

We know some happy commuters who bitch bitterly about their daily stint in the city and talk big about the bucolic joys of their split-level junior estates. But we also know (and tend to identify with) quite a few happy toilers in the city salt mines who get a sadistic clout out of going from office to railroad station... to watch the poor pseudo-hayseeds scurrying to make the 5:05... dutifully homeward bound to the little viragoes who, 40 minutes hence will be waiting for them in the jet-propelled marsh-mallow called a station wagon.

The alternative—the bachelor's brief ride in his sports car to an apartment where a bevy of girlfriends awaited—was not hard to imagine. The urban man and his many dates comprised "part of a club of working city people" who regularly finagled their way out of invitations for exurban weekends, preferring instead "the glamorous city summer scene."[43] Weaving together imagery of city living, work, and leisure, this article's advice on summer fashions became secondary to the task of grounding the playboy in a world of urban pleasure.

"A young man having the time of his life, the Playboy reader really enjoys the quick pace, the fun and excitement of city living," proclaimed one ad for the magazine. In 1958, *Playboy* inaugurated a campaign to sell advertising space, employing the memorable slogan "What Sort of Man Reads Playboy?" Each month, the campaign sketched a suave, alluring masculine persona while touting readers' considerable purchasing power. Various ads showed him consuming beer at a city beach, scrutinizing a vodka brand in a liquor store, buying tickets at the cinema, hosting a party. Others declared him a trendsetter with the income to buy the car of his choice, and followed him around as he shopped for shoes, selected hi-fi equipment, bought a shirt and tie, and used or purchased everything from toiletries to television set. In contrast to the housewife who shopped for her family in a suburban mall, the playboy was a self-indulgent urban consumer at large. Typically picturing a bachelor with an attractive young woman as his date or gazing at him from a distance, these ads neatly tied together youth, sex appeal, and consumption against a backdrop of city living (see figure 3.5).[44]

Other regular features invoked urban leisure. The paintings of *Playboy* contributor LeRoy Neiman gave artistic expression to the good life. An instructor from the Art Institute of Chicago, Neiman specialized in

capturing people engaged in the pursuit of pleasure, with a special emphasis on the glitz and glitter of nightlife.... Wealthy men and fashionable women enjoying their wealth. Boxers at Johnny Coulon's South Side gym. Late-night action at the strip joints along Clark Street. Gamblers, pugs, bars, high life and low life—from the Pump Room to the seediest Rush Street dive.

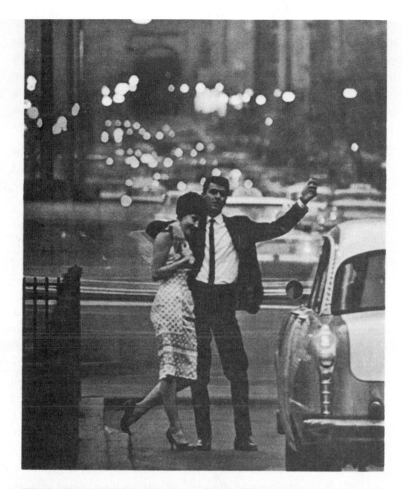

WHAT SORT OF MAN READS PLAYBOY?

A young man who knows his way around—uptown or downtown—the PLAYBOY reader's arrival signals the start of an eventful evening. And with good taste—from wine to women—he's a man who dines and drinks out often. Facts: 89% of PLAYBOY readers enjoy at least one drink, 43% at least three, in a restaurant or bar each week. For 30%, it's just natural to end an evening with a cordial note. Sure lift for your beverage sales: a campaign in PLAYBOY. It will do wonders for your spirit. (Source: *Playboy Male Reader Survey* by Benn Management Corp.)

Advertising Offices: New York • Chicago • Detroit • Los Angeles • San Francisco • Atlanta

3.5 Playboy *touted its audience of acquisitive young men to advertisers. Employing images of the man-about-town and the memorable slogan "What Sort of Man Reads* Playboy?" *each month the magazine highlighted the consumer habits and purchasing power of its readers. (Reproduced by special permission of* Playboy *magazine © April 1964 by Playboy.)*

Rooted in impressionism, with striking, bold use of color, Neiman's most notable work in *Playboy* consisted of "Man at His Leisure," a series that began in 1958
and ran for fourteen years. His style and cosmopolitan subject matter resulted
in a romanticizing of city life. Dubbed the "Painter of the Urban Scene," Neiman
produced canvases "bristling with bottles and babes, croupiers and cash regis-
ters," which portrayed a masculine realm of urban leisure where sex, money,
liquor, and sport came together.[45] The monthly "Playboy after Hours" section
reinforced the magazine's orientation toward nightlife, situating beneath an
illustration of a nighttime skyline its reviews of dining and drinking hotspots
in various cities as well as the latest in theater, movies, and music.

Playboy also showcased major cities in a series of articles aptly called
"Playboy on the Town." Slick photographs of skylines, streetscapes, and nightlife venues took readers on a grand urban tour. *Playboy*'s travelogues helped
focus what scholar John Urry has called the "tourist gaze" in specific ways, linking cosmopolitanism with sexual possibility.[46] Like the "sex takeouts" of other
men's magazines, they titillated with a visual and textual account of where the
action was, charting a detailed course in each city, complete with directions for
comportment. *Playboy*'s travel features suggested that knowing a city meant
knowing where to find (and how to seduce) its female inhabitants. In short,
they linked urban spectacle to sexual pleasure.

Many of the magazine's features showcased specific locales such as New
York, Chicago, or San Francisco. More important than *Playboy*'s attention to
actual cities was its construction of the city writ large, which it marked as a
masculine space. Unlike the Single Girl, whose marginal economic position
either made her dependent on men or called for careful planning and saving if
she wished to enjoy the commercial pleasures of the city, the bachelor was thoroughly independent, his city a place for exercising male prerogative. *Playboy*
certainly depicted the presence of women in the city. They were the girls in
the shops, the secretaries in the playboy's office building, the dates he escorted
around town and invited up to his penthouse. For the playboy, available women
were part of the urban fabric. But the city itself was constitutive of a modern
masculine identity, symbolizing affluence, sophistication, vitality, and heterosexual license.

"DISNEYLAND—FOR ADULTS ONLY!"

Even as *Playboy* extolled the virtues of the city and shunned the familial connotations of suburbia, its focus on entertainment technologies and consumption in the domestic sphere mirrored the postwar trend toward privatization

that eventually rendered the urban celebration unnecessary. Nothing better exemplifies this development than the Playboy Bed and Hefner's personal life, both in and out of it. The Playboy Bed—complete with bar and refrigerator—received its own feature in 1959. Three years later, "The Playboy Town House" introduced readers to its "single most dramatic piece of furniture," an oversized, round, rotating bed. In April 1965, a photographic essay gave readers a look at "The Playboy Bed" as it had been constructed in the Playboy Mansion. There, the motorized unit vibrated at three speeds to gently massage its occupant (and any guests), lull him to sleep, or awaken him with a vigorous shake. The bed made a commute to the office unnecessary, because the headboard housed filing cabinets, a speed-dial telephone, and an intercom system. One could manipulate the bed to face a television, a fireplace, a snack bar, work surface, or a couch, "transforming the space between into a conversation area." Playboy's publicity machine made Hefner's unusual sleeping quarters one of the most visceral symbols of the self-indulgent lifestyle he promoted. More than symbolizing "some kind of potentate's serving of sex," as journalist Tom Wolfe put it, the bed represented "a fantasy of a potentate's control of the environment."[47] Taking the push-button infatuation to an extreme, the bed went beyond practicality and convenience. It represented a customized private space that catered to one's every whim, making the outside world increasingly less relevant.

In January 1966, readers received the grand tour of Hefner's living quarters in a twenty-one-page spread on "The Playboy Mansion," with its game room and bowling alley, twenty-four-hour-a-day restaurant-quality kitchen, underwater bar, and swimming pool complete with "woo grotto." The magazine also drew attention to the top-floor Bunny Dorm, which housed many of the cocktail waitresses who worked at the nearby Playboy Club and added to the mansion's visual interest.[48] One visitor called the mansion a "Disneyland—for adults only!"—a fitting reference, given the mansion's redolence of amusement and abandon. Even more to the point, Hefner's mansion shared with Walt Disney's theme park the achievement of a carefully regulated space, insulated from the outside world through architecture, technology, and the efforts of a compliant staff. Originally intended to be Hefner's ultimate bachelor pad in the city, the Chicago mansion had become instead a "total environment" that rendered the city increasingly insignificant. "In short," the text explained, "the Mansion is Hefner's own self-created, self-contained, self-controlled environment, almost symbiotically sensitive and responsive to his personality and predilections."[49] Lacking for nothing inside its walls, Hefner shunned the outside world, wondering, "What the hell was it I was supposed to go out for?"[50]

In 1968, reprising his role as host of a swinging apartment party for a new television show, *Playboy after Dark,* Hefner began making regular trips to Los Angeles, where the program was produced. While taping one episode, he met Barbara Klein, a UCLA student working as an extra on the set. Hefner was smitten, and, in little time, she became his "special girl." His Los Angeles sojourns grew longer and more frequent so he could spend time with the young woman who pursued her show business ambitions under the stage name Barbi Benton. During one of Hefner's visits, Benton showed him a property she had found—a thirty-room Tudor Gothic-style residence situated on five and a half acres in Holmby Hills, an exclusive neighborhood of Los Angeles. Hefner purchased and undertook a major renovation of the property, which became known as Playboy Mansion West. After splitting time for several more years between Chicago and Los Angeles, he decided to make the sun-drenched estate in southern California his permanent home.

A 1975 feature took readers on a tour of Hefner's private Shangri-La, where he had created an idyllic playground for himself and his companions complete with exotic wildlife, ponds, swimming pools, waterfalls, grotto, gently rolling hills, and forests. The outdoor paradise was encased in a sophisticated matrix of electronic security, keeping the inhabitants inside safe and secluded from the outside world. This was a far cry from earlier images of a penthouse overlooking a vibrant skyline whose occupant was "an active part of the city's excitement and sophistication." In a sense, Hefner had forsaken the city, at least as it had been imagined in the 1950s and 1960s. "Wandering through these woods," *Playboy* noted, "you realize that this is one of the few places where you can still feel such a sense of seclusion and security in a major American city at night." The narrated tour hinted at an "urban crisis," but one that existed far outside the mansion's walls. "There is little chance of being mugged at the Mansion; if anyone jumps out of the bushes while you're taking this stroll, it will probably be a playful Playmate."[51]

Hefner's migration to Los Angeles calls to mind the shift of population and capital from the older urban centers of the Northeast and Midwest to the sprawling metropolises of the southwestern Sunbelt.[52] His relocation also represented the fruition of the postwar suburban impulse for privacy and control. Living in an elaborate version of the privatized suburban family home, Hefner had no reason to leave Playboy Mansion West. Although his particular level of comfort and insulation required a level of affluence that far surpassed the means of most Americans, his self-contained private world was in sync with an expanding middle class focused on acquiring the comfortable and stylish accessories of modern domestic life. Hefner offered a model for living as a master of

a private domain, where consumption, leisure, and one's own pleasure formed the measures of success and where the world outside one's doors seemed to matter less and less.[53]

"A WOO GROTTO IS WHERE YOU FIND IT"

"Congratulations; you've done it again," proclaimed a letter in "Dear Playboy." "I must know the estimated cost of *The Playboy Town House* so that I may keep this goal before me until I attain it." Another letter griped, "Who the hell can afford it except Hefner or Getty?" *Playboy* made a small attempt to reconcile the contradictions between the fantasies it projected and the economic realities of its audience. The editor advised that the town house would cost about a quarter of a million dollars, but with some modification—eliminating the retractable roof and the elevator—the price might be brought below $200,000, still an outrageous sum for the average reader in 1962. More important, concepts found in the Town House plan might be adapted or incorporated into other urban settings, an accommodation *Playboy* employed in subsequent features. "We want the reader to feel about this that it is elegant, original, exciting—and that it is an 'answer' to his fantasies and aspirations," *Playboy*'s A. C. Spectorsky instructed staff members about the patio terrace feature.

> We can take liberties with size and shape, and with potential expense, if the net result is two-fold: one, to make the reader want it; two, to do the job in such a way that the man with a suburban back-yard, or a town house patio, or much less space, or not enough money, can derive excited pleasure from looking at the finished product, and also single out suggestions which will spring to his mind as being adaptable to his own particular situation.

For instance, readers were reminded that "Playboy's Patio Terrace" was "replete with elements and details that can readily be adapted to individual preferences determined by available space and finances." Within the "grand scale" of "Playboy's Entertainment Wall" one found "countless kernels of ideas both for solving spatial problems and for working according to monetary limitations." All of the bachelor pad features showcased "purchasable furniture and gear and gadgetry," as Spectorsky put it. Moreover, even if *Playboy*'s ideal bachelor pads represented an unattainable object of desire, they also suggested that, to an important extent, the playboy lifestyle was predicated on a

state of mind. Even if one's "pad" amounted to a single lounge chair in a paneled suburban rumpus room with a playmate centerfold tacked to the wall, *Playboy*'s commissioned designs worked to legitimate striving for cultural—and physical—space for the desiring male subject, a point illustrated in an editorial response from "Dear Playboy." A letter queried why "Playboy's Town House" had not included a secret "woo grotto" like the one in the Playboy Mansion. *Playboy* replied, "A Woo Grotto is where you find it, Roger; it isn't built—it's made."[54]

In imagining the playboy's pad as well as his larger urban playground, *Playboy* responded to the social and spatial transformations of postwar America. The bachelor pad features garnered tremendous response from the magazine's readers, many of whom were married homeowners.[55] The fantasy spaces promising erotic fulfillment, adult activities, and occasional peace and quiet likely spoke to them. For unmarried readers, too, from college students to young upwardly mobile professionals, *Playboy*'s pads and penthouses focused fantasies of consumption, pleasure, and prosperity in a specific spatial context. That *Playboy* envisioned an alternative to married life in suburbia, one that struck a chord with readers, does not mean most men were unhappy with their homes and families. But scrutinizing the form of *Playboy*'s answer to suburbia helps unravel some of the tensions and concerns surrounding the changing circumstances inhabited by postwar American men. More than a blueprint for bachelorhood, the city writ large and the bachelor pad within it served as idealized sites where postwar cultural tensions could be addressed and thus offered a powerful critique of suburbia and of a gender order in flux.

Examining the magazine's representations of space reveals the rhetorical strategies involved in attempting to reaffirm male privilege and power at a time when gender boundaries were shifting and the physical spaces of the city and of the family home were being transformed. *Playboy*'s evocation of a masculine city to counter a feminized suburbia served to reconstitute and thus lay claim to the "private" domestic sphere. Importantly, *Playboy*'s strategy for reclaiming domestic space departed from activities like partaking in household management and childrearing or embracing handiwork, efforts identified by historians as masculine domesticity or domestic masculinity.[56] Such activities relied on a productive and familial context for men's recovery of the private realm. *Playboy* jettisoned the family and instead forged a combination of domesticity and masculinity in the figure of the consumption- and pleasure-oriented bachelor. Although in time the city became less critical as a foil to a feminized suburbia, the magazine's celebration of urban living, singlehood, and sexual freedom portended the urban singles scene

that took shape in the 1960s and represents an important link to the young urban professionals, or "yuppies," of the 1980s. Indeed, *Playboy*'s urban lifestyle anticipated later gentrifiers, occupants of cities enlivened by a reinjection of capital, who consumed urban space as commodity and spectacle.[57] In the meantime, the spatial dimensions of "the playboy life" served to accommodate the growing privatization of American life and the centrality of consumption within it, providing a vision of masculinity that could be grounded most anywhere, even in the comfortable interior spaces of the sprawling metropolis.

4 THE IDEAL (PLAY)MATE

Gender, the Workplace, and the Single Girl

THE PLAYBOY COULD not live life "to the hilt" without plenty of free-spirited young women to squire around town and invite up to his apartment. The good life Hugh Hefner imagined for young males presumed a certain type of young female, a woman looking for pleasure rather than security. Playmate pictorials and other features idealized the qualities of the young, unattached women who served as the playboy's temporary companions, and in Playboy's clubs, voluptuous Bunnies seemed to bring the image to life. Beyond the pages of Hefner's magazine and outside the doors of his clubs, single women captured the popular imagination as well, and the emergence of a cultural figure to serve as the ideal companion for the fun-loving bachelor marked an important development of the 1960s. She was envisioned variously as the working girl, office girl, bachelor girl, or bachelorette but was best known according to the formulation put forth by Helen Gurley Brown: as the "Single Girl," who moved to the cultural fore as an image of modern, independent, self-supporting, and sexually fulfilled womanhood.

Brown fashioned a vibrant lifestyle for the unmarried woman, urging her to embrace rather than lament her single status. The Single Girl both emulated and modified the playboy's lifestyle, finding fulfillment in getting and spending, but in ways that reflected the social and economic inequalities circumscribing women's lives. Brown's vision for the Single Girl was right in step with *Playboy*'s sensibilities about the proper role of women in society. Her working-girl heroine challenged the sexual double standard and posited alternative roles for women besides caring for a house and family. At the same time, her independence remained limited, contingent on her charm and her relationships with men. And she did not upset the gender order by becoming too ambitious. In this regard, the Single Girl did not oppose traditional notions of femininity and domesticity so much as she deployed these attributes outside the context of home and family by enacting a different sort of "working-girl" femininity.

In Brown's advice manuals and in the guise of the Bunnies who worked in Playboy's clubs, the happily unmarried, feminine, vital young woman appeared to be liberated from cultural conventions, making her own way and comfortable with her place in the world. Yet her apparent freedom, reliant on a tenuous sexual capital, was framed by overarching sexist attitudes and structures.

SEX AND THE SINGLE GIRL IN THE CONSUMER SOCIETY

Helen Gurley Brown's first advice book, *Sex and the Single Girl* (1962), rejected gender roles that posited marriage, motherhood, and homemaking as the fruition of female existence, not unlike another well-known publication of the early 1960s. Betty Friedan, of course, also voiced strong opposition to traditional domesticity in her 1963 book, *The Feminine Mystique*. Friedan criticized the image of happy, housebound femininity peddled by women's magazines. She advocated for middle-class women's entrance into the male-dominated business and professional realms as a solution to the housewife's lack of fulfillment. Like Friedan, Brown made a strong case for female autonomy, but offered a different strategy for achieving it. She articulated a relationship between feminine identity, paid employment, and consumption that accepted women's limited career opportunities and construed marriage to be the eventual goal, while placing sexuality and commodity consumption at the center of a prolonged stage of pleasure-oriented singlehood. Her work, Brown insisted, was "not a study on how to get married but how to stay single—in superlative style."[1]

Born in Green Forest, Arkansas, in 1922, Brown began a long string of secretarial jobs at the age of eighteen, working to support a widowed mother and a sister crippled by polio. At the age of thirty-seven she married a motion picture producer, a wealthy and well-connected man who encouraged her to write the best-selling *Sex and the Single Girl*.[2] "For seventeen years I worked hard to become the kind of woman who might interest him," Brown explained. "And when he finally walked into my life I was just worldly enough, relaxed enough, financially secure enough . . . and adorned with enough glitter to attract him." In her books and, later, as editor of *Cosmopolitan*, which she transformed into the premier magazine for the urban working girl, Brown celebrated the Single Girl, affirming her autonomy and her right to pleasure as an individual entity—until the right man came along.[3]

Brown's agenda for the Single Girl aimed to transform the unmarried woman into a self-sufficient, vibrant character, one likely to attract and catch a

man; at the same time, these same qualities would enable her to embrace and enjoy singlehood, ultimately giving her greater freedom in choosing when and whom to marry, if at all. "I believe that as many women over thirty marry out of fear of being alone someday—not necessarily now but *some* day—as for love of or compatibility with a particular man," Brown wrote. "The plan seems to be to get someone while the getting's good and by the time you lose your looks he'll be too securely glued to you to get away. Isn't it silly? A man can leave a woman at fifty (though it may cost him some dough) as surely as you can leave dishes in the sink." Like Hefner, Brown advocated for a period of liberated singlehood to be enjoyed in its own right but that, in the long run, might also make for stronger marriage bonds. She opined, "How much saner and sweeter to marry when you have both jelled. And how much safer to marry with part of the play out of his system *and yours*."[4] Although marriage was still the goal, Brown cautioned against equating a husband with security and stressed the importance of self-reliance. Thus the Single Girl worked to earn her own keep, her financial independence giving her access to travel, entertainment, cosmetics, clothing, apartment furnishings, and meals out.[5]

Succeeding as a Single Girl was no easy task, for she existed in a society oriented toward couples and families. Chapters titled "The Availables: The Men in Your Life" and "Where to Meet Them" listed places where one might encounter men. Brown noted, "It really is important to surround yourself with men every day to keep up your morale." She explained, "A married woman already *is* something"—namely, someone's wife. "Whatever hardships she endures in marriage, one of them is *not* that she doesn't have a place in life." But if the single woman did not enjoy the social status conferred upon wives in a family-oriented society, her singlehood gave her vital attributes that wives lacked, attributes that provided more opportunity for enjoyment and made her even more enticing to men. The Single Girl, for instance, had time and energy to devote to her physical appearance as well as the "the freedom to furnish her mind." Brown explained:

> She can read Proust, learn Spanish, study *Time, Newsweek* and *The Wall Street Journal*. Most importantly, a single woman, even if she is a file clerk, moves in the world of men. She knows their language—the language of retailing, advertising, motion pictures, exporting, shipbuilding. Her world is a far more colorful world than the one of P.T.A., Dr. Spock and the jammed clothes dryer.

The Single Girl existed outside the world of housework and child care. Her job provided access to men and made her more attractive than the housewife. "A single woman never has to drudge," Brown explained. "She can get her

housework over within one good hour Saturday morning plus one other hour to iron blouses and white collars. She need never break her fingernails or her spirit waxing a playroom or cleaning out the garage." Furthermore, her income facilitated self-indulgence. "She has more money for clothes and for trips than any but a wealthily married few," Brown claimed.[6]

Achieving "single bliss" did not come easily, however. Brown cautioned, "You have to work like a son of a bitch." Brown served as a taskmaster, taking readers through the various dimensions requiring cultivation and upkeep if one wished to succeed as a Single Girl. She began by outlining the basic dicta:

> You must develop style.... Brains are an asset but it doesn't take brainy brains.... Whatever it is that keeps you from saying anything unkind and keeps you asking bright questions even when you don't quite understand the answers will do nicely.... Fashion is your powerful ally.... Roommates are for sorority girls.... Your figure can't harbor an ounce of baby fat.... You must cook well. It will serve you faithfully.... You must have a job that interests you, at which you work hard.

As these pronouncements suggest, enjoying "the good single life" required maximum effort on several fronts. The Single Girl had to work hard at her job in order to live independently and finance the necessary Single Girl accouterments. "What you do from nine to five has everything to do with men," Brown advised. "A job is one way of getting *to* them. It also provides the money with which to dress for them and dress up your apartment for them." She also had to become an accomplished consumer, skilled in the use of appearance-enhancing commodities. Brown gave instruction on fashion, shopping, and applying makeup and perfume, all with a view to enhancing one's desirability to men. The Single Girl expended great effort on her body, maintaining an attractive figure through diet and exercise, taming unruly hair, manicuring nails, retraining a high-pitched voice to achieve a pleasant tone. Even her projection of sex appeal and femininity called for carefully honed interpersonal skills. "You can't afford to leave any facet of you unpolished," Brown maintained.[7] The price of liberated singlehood was measured in the time and money spent on this ongoing body project, the aim of which was to attract men.

While marriage remained a long-term goal, the Single Girl no longer led the life of the spinster while she awaited a proposal. Brown promised a welcome reprieve for those who complained of the "radically restricted" social life deemed appropriate for unmarried women. As one woman opined in a letter to the *New York Times,* single women chose marriage and family "not entirely [for] a love of hearth and home," but because they faced few socially acceptable alternatives. In this climate, she contended, the unmarried woman

"tends to become fanatically devoted to her work because she is not permitted anything else." Sloan Wilson described the city in 1956 as "a pitiless place for most unmarried girls once they get outside the family and social structure in which they have been brought up." The "career girl," he observed, "may have looked glamorous on the street but most of the unmarried ones lived in lonely little walk-up apartments, and their social lives consisted largely of going to the movies with girls like themselves."[8] *Sex and the Unmarried Woman,* a popular anthology of professional and scientific literature, focused on the "sexual problems" of the single female arising from social norms that confined sex to marriage. Likewise, Estelle Ries's *The Lonely Sex* offered single girls much sympathy along with plenty of advice for finding a husband. Until she found a mate, the unmarried woman was encouraged to channel her energies into vicarious domesticity by becoming a favorite aunt. Obsessing over the possibilities of pregnancy, disease, and emotional disturbance that might come from sexual dalliance, *The Lonely Sex* went so far as to prescribe a special diet and even colonic irrigation to ward off sexual desires for which the unmarried woman had no appropriate outlet.[9] In contrast to these views, Brown meant for the Single Girl to enjoy her independence *and* her sex life. "Theoretically, a 'nice' single girl has no sex life. What nonsense!" she asserted. Brown challenged the double standard that demanded women remain chaste until marriage, encouraging single women to search actively for pleasure, just like the playboy. Brown, in fact, wanted to title her book "Sex *for* the Single Girl," but her publisher thought it sounded too risqué.[10]

In her many romantic comedies of the 1960s, Doris Day's working-girl characters clung steadfastly to virginity until marriage. In *That Touch of Mink* (1962), for example, Day's character Cathy Timberlake is so anxious about sleeping with rich playboy Philip Shayne that she imagines the other hotel guests can picture the duo on the large canopy bed that awaits in their hotel room. "They know!" she frets, certain that everyone can tell she is planning to have unmarried sex with Mr. Shayne. Unnerved by the prospect, she breaks out in hives. Brown's version of the Single Girl had no such hang-ups. Her disregard for the double standard was commensurate with the advice dispensed by the Playboy Advisor, who encouraged men and women alike to abandon their old-fashioned sense of propriety. Launched in 1960, the Playboy Advisor furthered the editorial viewpoint of the magazine by concocting letters from inquiring "readers," to whom it furnished helpful replies. To "three girls with a problem," who wanted to know how to turn down men's sexual advances, the Advisor responded, "The best way to say no to 'that certain question' is simply to say 'no'—and if pressed for a reason, to give the most honest explanation you can." But, he continued, they should realize virginity was overvalued—"It

is a perfectly natural and healthy thing for women to have some sex life prior to marriage and the tradition that places such stress on female 'virginity' is more conducive to frustration and suffering than anything else." Another "reader" explained that although he came close to having intercourse with a woman, he stopped himself. The woman had become upset and told friends that he was "a latent homosexual." "I want to know what I did wrong," the letter continued. "I mean, doesn't the gentleman's code count for anything anymore?" Responded the Advisor, "You're getting exactly what you deserve. Rather than upholding any 'gentleman's code,' you've violated it by your refusal of the girl's ultimate gift.... People like you give chivalry a bad name." Another "reader" offered a similar problem. Having abstained from sex with his girlfriend because he wished her to be a virgin when they married, he learned that she had been sleeping with an acquaintance. He was advised by *Playboy* to "have a heart-to-heart talk with her and promise to provide at home what she's been forced to seek on the road."[11] The Playboy Advisor dismissed the traditional prizing of female chastity before marriage. To be sure, upholding the double standard would have conflicted with the magazine's pronouncements about the "girl next door," namely that she was a sexually willing creature and thus a suitable companion for the playboy. But in asserting that the "girl next door" could enjoy premarital sex without losing value as a potential spouse—or as a person, for that matter—*Playboy* was also affirming women's right to step out of narrowly prescribed roles. Brown, too, saw no reason for a woman to remain on the sidelines of sexual experience just because she lacked a ring on her finger. There would be no anxiety-induced hives for *her* Single Girl.

Brown's views on sex supported those put forth in *Playboy*. Her vision of commodity consumption was similarly aligned with the glamorous lifestyle and consumer ethic advanced in the magazine, but with some significant modifications. The Single Girl's position in the consumer economy was shaped by the gender inequality that limited her access to high-paying jobs and career advancement. *Playboy* ranged from fantasy wish book to helpful primer as it showcased consumer goods and exotic vacations for upwardly mobile men. Brown's advice tome, on the other hand, devoted an entire chapter to the art of pinching pennies. Because the Single Girl's economic security was tenuous, strong elements of restraint and delayed gratification ran through Brown's advice for achieving "the good single life." Hers was not the "buy now, pay later" world of credit available to the playboy, who presumably possessed the funds needed to buy luxuries, but couldn't be bothered with paying cash. Brown warned against borrowing from creditors and stressed frugality. This approach did not keep her from pursuing the trappings of affluence, but it meant she had to proceed carefully. "Under my system," she explained, "you start funds for the

things you want—car, vacation, hi-fi, television, fur coat, furniture. You sneak up on these luxuries."

The Single Girl scrimped on items so long as they did not detract from her outward appearance of glamour. She was not a bargain-basement shopper. She made wise purchases of quality merchandise and saved money by doing her own tailoring and cleaning her garments at home. Her hi-fi was service-able, not top-of-the line. The Single Girl did require her own apartment, for, as Brown explained, "If you are to be a glamorous, sophisticated woman that exciting things happen to, you need an apartment and you need to live in it alone!" But she saved money by avoiding expensive neighborhoods and build-ings with views and fireplaces. "Be prepared to sink money" into some furnish-ings, Brown advised, but she went on to provide further guidance on how to hunt inexpensive decorations to supplement the key pieces.[12] Brown's stress on economizing extended to the Single Girl's diet. "Try to like kidneys, hearts, liver, brains," Brown encouraged readers. "Every nutritionist says they give you more health returns than filet mignon. Oh yes…they cost one-sixth as much." The Single Girl saved her extravagant meals for guests. Brown supplied a few special recipes so the Single Girl might occasionally impress partygoers or charm men. But if gourmet food provided a routine seduction aid for the bachelor, it was an expense the Single Girl avoided. In a chapter called "The Care and Feeding of Everybody," Brown posed the question, "When do you have him over?" Her answer: "Reciprocity is not entirely in order with beaux. I think the correct ratio between times on the town and dinner *intime* in your apartment is about twenty to one!" Unless one saw marriage on the horizon, women had no reason to make a financial investment in the relationship. "If you aren't engaged…you don't really have to pay back dinner ever. Part of the price bachelors pay for staying single is to spend money taking girls out. No use making their bachelorhood easy by feeding them like little mother." Along such lines, besides counting her pennies, the Single Girl had another important strategy for accessing the world of consumer goods. "Expect and encourage gifts from men," Brown wrote. "They are part of the spoils of being single."[13] In this regard, Brown embraced the possibilities for negotiating financial and sexual exchange implicit in dating. In her advice books, what one got out of a date was all part of a well-played game.

The Single Girl thus marked an evolution from the unmarried, working "women adrift" who populated the nation's cities in the early twentieth cen-tury. As historians have shown, these young women often earned paltry wages based on the assumption that women worked only to supplement the income of a real breadwinner, whether a father or husband. They survived by sharing expenses with roommates, skipping meals, and walking to work, while often

relinquishing part of their meager pay to help support family members. Some working women also participated in a system of "treating," bestowing sexual favors on men in exchange for gifts, meals, clothing, or a night out, a practice that alarmed reformers. For struggling unmarried female workers, the "gifts" they received from men provided the incremental difference between success and failure in the city.[14] In contrast to these earlier working women, the Single Girl brought home a paycheck for herself, earning money so as to partake in the luxuries the consumer society had to offer. She shunned roommates. Living alone was "sexy" and signified independence, thus making her more attractive to men and aiding in her pursuit of what Brown termed "the good single life." Brown refused to see the sexually active Single Girl as a "fallen" woman and instead celebrated her sexual autonomy as a critical component of her individual freedom. Like earlier working women, though, the Single Girl's income was still largely determined by her gender. She used her sexuality to engage in a cash nexus, flirting, dating, or sleeping with men whose gifts supplemented her income.[15] Such gifts did not provide the measure of survival but made possible the enjoyment of various consumer goods, the new "necessities" made possible by postwar affluence. In this manner, although Brown's writings were in step with *Playboy*'s agenda for sexual freedom and fun, her advice pointed to the bachelor girl's existence at the margins of the playboy's luxurious lifestyle. The dapper playboy was affluent and charming. Thrift and cunning were needed to make it as a Single Girl.

SEX AND THE OFFICE

The term *Single Girl* had important connotations not only about a woman's marital status, but about her economic status as well. The married woman got from her relationship to her husband an identity and an income stream; the Single Girl had to earn her own keep. Work, then, was central to the Single Girl's identity. Since her status as a woman shaped her limited job prospects and thus her earning power, her economic station was tied to her subordinate position in the gender hierarchy. Brown's vision for the Single Girl fit within an existing framework of gender inequality and assumptions about a woman's place. Discussion of work in *Sex and the Single Girl,* as well as in her second book, *Sex and the Office,* promoted a form of working-girl femininity in keeping with the historically gendered division of office work and supportive of existing stereotypes about the office as an eroticized space. In Brown's formulations, the working girl provided a contrast to the housewife derided in popular

discussions as a parasite and a drudge. Yet the working girl's femininity also paralleled the domesticity of the housewife in important ways, making her an acceptable cultural figure amid concerns about "sex role" upheaval and the "womanized" society.

While women who took wartime jobs were encouraged to relinquish them to returning soldiers at the end of World War II, women's workforce participation actually increased in the postwar period. By the end of the 1950s, almost 40 percent of all women over the age of sixteen held a job or sought paid employment, and the number and proportion of women working outside the home continued to increase throughout the twentieth century. As a result, women's share of the workforce also grew.[16] Popular discussions of working women highlighted several tensions. Those who believed women belonged in the home clashed with critics of the economically dependent housewife. Such a view also conflicted with the growing demand for women's labor brought on by economic expansion. At the same time, women's expanding presence in the workplace added to the sense of gender disorder and female encroachment into a male realm.[17] By 1960, almost one in three working women was employed in a clerical job, with women comprising 96 percent of the nation's secretaries, stenographers, and typists.[18] In the context of concerns about woman's place, clerical jobs were readily able to absorb female workers because the work had become sex-typed in a way that affirmed the gender order.

Examining the gendered development of modern office work, historians have shown that excluding women went hand in hand with the professionalization of many business occupations, a factor that left women with few alternatives to clerical work. At the same time, the feminization of clerical work sparked concern that women entering previously all-male office spaces posed a threat to workplace morality and productivity. Women, according to these concerns, distracted male employees and were vulnerable to temptation and male advances.[19] In the wake of feminization and mechanization, clerical positions, once occupied by men and offering potential advancement within a company, became devalued and ceased to be a stepping-stone to promotion. Furthermore, beliefs that women's paid employment marked but a temporary phase on the way to marriage served to justify pigeonholing women into the most routinized and lowest-paying jobs. The time and money invested in training them for better jobs, the logic went, would be wasted when women left to get married. Generally speaking, the result of all this was the bifurcation of job opportunities for men and women that replicated the gender hierarchy, with men installed as managers and supervisors over female clerical workers who labored in low wage, dead-end jobs.[20]

The creation in the early decades of the twentieth century of such a hierarchical, heterosocial office environment, according to Sharon Hartman Strom:

> virtually guaranteed that young office workers would be in some kind of submissive power relationship with an older man. Bosses could choose private secretaries and stenographers on the basis of appearance. Single women and married men could have illicit love affairs. Women clerks might receive unwelcome sexual advances. The possibility of the man using his power to gain sexual advantage—or, perhaps, of the young woman using sexual attraction to gain a supervisor's attention—was clearly present.

Assumptions about femininity shaped expectations of the private secretary or stenographer, who was supposed to exhibit independence and resourcefulness, while also providing her employer with "the services of her gender: domesticity, passivity, charm, and endless patience."[21]

A promotional booklet, *Memo—How to Be a Super-Secretary,* produced in the early 1950s by typewriter manufacturer Remington Rand, illustrates how these attributes continued to factor into expectations for female clerical workers. According to its author, the ideal secretary remained "pleasant, even under strain.... You never sulk.... In the office, you have just one mood ... fair and sunny ... you wear it no matter how you feel." "You are silent about your own personal troubles ... about office feuds and gossip," the guide continued. "You protect your chief from the interruptions and details which he considers unimportant and you *check first to make certain which these are.*" Not only did the "super-secretary" maintain a pleasant disposition and shield her male boss from the mundane details of work, she remained modest. "You are truly humble," intoned the advice booklet. "Be indispensable ... but don't let on you think that you are! ... If you originate an idea, you give the credit to your boss because you know when he advances you advance with him." This ideal office worker carried her domesticity into the workplace. "You are a good housekeeper. You keep your boss's desk and office neat.... And you do it *always,* not just in streaks when the mood strikes you." She was attentive and faithful: "You listen with undivided attention to your chief's instructions and comments.... You are loyal. You put the interests of your boss first ... even above your own.... When you can prevent him from making mistakes, you do it without his being aware." Finally, the "super-secretary" provided endless cheerleading and support. "You are a one-woman publicity campaign. You carry the torch ... give him encouragement when he is feeling low ... put up with his bad humor when he has to let off steam ... make him feel he's a pretty wonderful person."

Gal Friday, a magazine devoted to the working woman, offered similar sentiments in its characterization of female employees. The magazine took its name from the oft-used term for a female assistant that called forth the subservient helpmate from *Robinson Crusoe.* The opening editorial explained, "Oh, we know you well Gal Friday. You're jack of all trades, morale booster, glamor girl [*sic*] and bustling worker. You're office manager, teletype operator, file clerk, receptionist, executive secretary, administrative assistant." *Gal Friday* limned the quintessential female office worker—a woman who used her charm, appearance, and domestic skills to make the office run more smoothly. "We've seen you…finding your son's pencils, your husband's ties…and somehow finding the time to put yourself together and emerge ready to find your boss' pencils, his clients' files—and on and on. You're chief cook and rubber plant waterer. Low man on the totem pole, young lady on her way up."[22]

Brown sketched a working girl in step with these popular assumptions about women's role in the office, a figure that posed a contrast to the housewife's associations with drudgery and unattractiveness, while bringing her domesticity into the workplace. "Men don't like drones or slugs in offices any more than they like having them around the house," Brown asserted. To be sure, the Single Girl performed her share of menial work in the office, but she did so pleasantly, dressed to the nines, and sufficiently compensated by the available men who surrounded her. "On an attractive girl a great job looks and smells good too," she explained, "even though certain mundane choring goes into the making of that job." Since appearance was one of her chief resources—"it's a fact bosses love to have chic, sleek cats around to show off to company"— Brown coached readers on proper wardrobe and makeup.[23] The working girl she envisioned was more stylish and attractive than the housewife, but like a good wife, she behaved in a solicitous and feminine manner toward her male coworkers. Brown contended that secretarial work, "being a Miss Girl Monday through Friday," provided the best "in" to the business world. Whether one aimed to remain in this position or move up, Brown instructed secretaries to treat bosses with "love and devotion." "Other people give the man trouble. You must be there to help him gird on his armor for battle and then bind up his wounds when he returns," she intoned. The Single Girl was even more loyal and supportive than the boss's wife. "I don't feel there's any justifiable cause to criticize a boss ever," Brown maintained. "You are *for* all his schemes, up to and including his taking over the company. It's easier for you than for his wife, who may see his power play costing her the cabanas, the flagstone *and* the swimming pool." She bolstered his ego by "delivering discreet personal compliments" and was urged "to collect the best gossip the office has to offer—rumors of mergers and firings too. Pass them on each day as a little love offering." Nor was the

boss to be the only recipient of the Single's Girl's domesticity and feminine charms, for Brown encouraged her to win over the mailroom boy with chocolate fudge for his birthday. "Of *course* you are a little mother to *all* the growing boys around the place. You dispense Band-Aids and smiles to anyone who is wounded on the job, aspirin and Bromo to those who got the wounds the night before." Brown also provided luncheon recipes so the Single Girl could woo her man with an office picnic, as well as menus and ideas for the various office parties the Single Girl was sure to be hosting. Above all, she advised, "You should feel empathy in your bosom."[24]

Such domestic, feminine behavior confirmed that the working girl posed no threat to the gender order. Femininity, Brown asserted, "is a matter of accepting yourself as a woman." In language that recalled the criticism of the "dominating" woman, she explained: "Some girls 'hate' men because they secretly envy their 'superior advantages,' their jobs, their ability to exploit.... Man-haters secretly envy men's penises." The Single Girl modified prescriptions about femininity, domesticity, and woman's role, deploying these attributes in the workplace in order to bring personal pleasure and to advance her work-related social life. As Brown advised in *Sex and the Single Girl,* "If you really like men but would just like to seem a little softer and less self-sufficient, go on a 'helpless' campaign. Let a man push open every door.... Have difficulty with packages. He'll help carry. *Expect* to have your cigarette lighted." And, most important, she counseled, "Get it straight in your head that anyone who wants to kiss you or sleep with you isn't handing you a mortal insult but paying you a compliment."[25]

An attractive personal secretary outside one's door, along with the size and location of one's office, the dimensions of one's desk, and the thickness of the wall-to-wall carpeting on the floor, represented an important symbol of status and power in the workplace, according to the author of *Survival in the Executive Jungle.* Businessmen found it more difficult to select a secretary than to hire someone for a "top position." "The reason," he explained, "is that the applicant is a woman and you are a man.... You'll quickly notice whether she's comely or homely. No detail of her figure, from neckline to ankle will escape you.... While outwardly you may appear to be interviewing her with cold objectivity and businesslike manner, she knows this isn't so, and so do you." Given these dynamics, the young executive hiring a secretary for the first time sometimes mistook "a girl's job-seeking charm as an invitation for an affair." The skewed power relationship between a male boss and his female underling in the potentially sex-charged atmosphere of the office served as a cultural trope that informed representations of workplace relationships while also setting the parameters within which the Single Girl earned a living. Although this author warned against it, office hanky-panky, especially the boss's hijinks with

his private secretary, provided the fodder for many a punch line or storyline. For instance, Hefner's college magazine, *Shaft*, ran a feature charting the prospects for various professions. The heading "Private Secretary" offered the following information:

> You Need: A well rounded set of qualifications. Willingness to display qualifications under restricted circumstances (tight sweaters).
> You Take:...shorthand if your employer is female or over 85.
> You Get: Pinched, patted, played up to, for, and with. Insults from your boss's wife. Insulting suggestions from the boss...
> You Should: Get some indoor track training.

A later generation of feminists would identity this scenario as sexual harassment, but at mid-century popular stereotypes often defined such activities as horseplay and a staple of the workday. In this vein, a novelty coin engraved with the words "Do It" on one side and "the Hell with It" on the other promised to help harried executives make quick decisions. "One flip helps you decide in a trice whether to chase her around the desk; another flip helps *her* decide whether to accept your gracious invitation to the romp."[26]

Elsewhere the office was portrayed as a sexual meeting ground, the available office girl compensation for the daily grind. In Richard Yates's novel *Revolutionary Road*, Frank Wheeler's wife and children, and his own sense of ineffectuality, keep him tied to his job. Yates described Wheeler's Monday morning commute following a weekend quarrel with his wife: "Riding to work, one of the youngest and healthiest passengers on the train, he sat with the look of a man condemned to a very slow, painless death. He felt middle-aged." After a sexual tryst with a woman from his office, however, Wheeler leaves her apartment exultant, feeling "like a man." His masculinity restored, the evening commute to the suburbs becomes an experience befitting a man.

> Could a man sit meekly massaging his headache and allowing himself to be surrounded by the chatter of beaten, amiable husks of men who sat and swayed and played bridge in a stagnant smell of newsprint and tobacco and bad breath and overheated radiators?
>
> Hell, no. The way for a man to ride was erect and out in the open, out in the loud iron passageway where the wind whipped his necktie, standing with his feet set wide apart on the shuddering, clangoring floorplates, taking deep pulls from a pinched cigarette....And when he came to his own station, the way for a man to alight was to swing down the iron steps and leap before the train had stopped, to land running and slow down to an easy, athletic stride as he made for his parked automobile.[27]

Wheeler's ability to take charge with the office girl makes up for the emasculation he experiences at home and in his work. Demonstrating his potency in this aspect of his life enables him to recast his evening routine into a masculine endeavor.

Brown likewise cast the Single Girl as a figure who provided solace and excitement for men facing tedium at home or on the job. She also wholeheartedly embraced the notion of the sex-charged office, a view best expressed in her recounting of a customary practice in one of the many offices where she worked.

> When I came in from school every afternoon, some of the men would be playing a dandy game called "Scuttle." The Scuttle rules were simple to get the hang of. All announcers and engineers who weren't busy at one particular time would select a secretary or file girl, chase her up and down the halls...catch her and take her panties off. Once the panties were off, the girl could put them back on again if she wished. Nothing wicked ever happened. De-pantying was the sole object of the game. While all this was going on, the girl herself usually shrieked, screamed, flailed, blushed, threatened and pretended to faint, but to my knowledge no scuttler was ever reported to the front office.

While this behavior would later be deemed sexual harassment, Brown presented this as harmless fun, recalling, "As a matter of fact, the girls wore their prettiest panties to work." For Brown, the office was a sexual meeting ground, where sexual dalliances provided fun and possibly even an avenue for advancement. "Now...it seems obvious to me that if you aren't meeting any men through your job, you are in the wrong job," she wrote in *Sex and the Single Girl*. The better the job, the better the men to which the Single Girl had access. "And though it may seem to the untrained eye that you are selflessly working on office projects together," Brown wrote, "what you are really doing is sinking into them like a cobalt treatment so that you may make off with them after work—if that's your pleasure."[28]

Sex and the Office upheld stereotypical views about a woman's supportive role in the workplace as well as her reliance on personal appearance and sex appeal to get ahead. In a section headed, "What to Wear to Be Especially Sexy," she suggested that women "go choir-girl occasionally with a chalk-white collar and cuff set....Nothing pleases some men more than thoughts of deflowering innocence." "No, presumably you wouldn't flirt with office menfolk *all* the time," Brown explained in *Sex and the Office*, "but a lot of this attitude of love and listening can prevail when you take dictation, chat with men in conferences, ride with them to meet the client, walk from office to office. Again,

I would say, make every man you work with, from the mailroom boy up, just a little bit in love with you. You'll have a rich, full office life." Sex appeal and success went hand in hand. After two chapters devoted to projecting the right image, Brown concluded, "All right, there you are—your face, your figure and your office all gussied up to absolute perfection so that lovely things can happen to you. Let's go on now to what you can make of your job—by working *very* hard and looking *very* delectable."[29] Brown instructed women to work hard so as to make themselves indispensable to employers and to demand to be compensated accordingly. But the recurring theme in her books of astute men who "discovered" a woman's abilities, nurtured her talents, and facilitated her success supported a notion of the world of work as male-dominated and male-privileged. Her suggestions for career advancement in *Sex and the Single Girl*, for example, depended on one's physical appearance, drew upon stereotyped "feminine" talent or skills, or hinged upon a single girl's relationship to the right person, most often a man. Brown's passive language was telling. As she put it, she aimed to help one become "the kind of person a career can happen to."[30] This roundabout approach to advancement was perhaps unsurprising, given Brown's road to success. Her first step out of the secretarial ranks and into a job as a copywriter came when she repeatedly entered and finally won a writing contest sponsored by *Glamour* magazine. Her husband, film executive David Brown, encouraged her to write *Sex and the Single Girl*. He edited the manuscript and shopped it around to publishers. It was David Brown, too, who developed the magazine prospectus that eventually launched Brown's career as the editor of *Cosmopolitan*. Like Brown, then, the ideal Single Girl set herself up for success by looking good and working hard, then waited and hoped for opportunity to knock. If she managed to climb to a job above the level of secretary, she offended no one by maintaining her working-girl femininity.

Just as Brown's notions about the Single Girl's sex life were in accord with the views of the Playboy Advisor, her heroine's activities in the workplace kept well within the bounds of conventional views on appropriate feminine behavior and thus resembled *Playboy*'s representations of the working girl. One *Playboy* fashion feature painted this picture of the city-dwelling male office worker: "Once dressed, he phones down to the doorman to get him a cab, takes the lift to the street and rides to his office. En route he may pleasure himself by gazing on one of the city's finest sights: young, chic, svelte office girls in summer dresses heel-tapping their way to work." In one photograph, the man in his private office studies papers on his desk while a female coworker gazes at him. "On his mind, designs," read the caption. "On hers, designs on him."[31] Although its overt subject matter was men's attire, this feature also offered telling information about gender and work. The playboy occupied a position of

socioeconomic privilege, riding in a taxi while the office girls walked to work. Although the women on the street constituted a "sight" for the male spectator, within the office the woman in the photograph turned her gaze on the studious male. Like Brown's Single Girl, she maintained more than a professional interest in her male coworker, a situation with great appeal for the playboy.

While the playboy asserted his prowess in the masculine world of business, images in the magazine upheld gender stereotypes that placed men in charge of the marketplace while working women occupied service-oriented, secondary positions. In these images, women were sexy and sexually available, but not competitive. Inspired by *The Executive Coloring Book,* a drawing in "The Playboy Coloring Book" showed a curvaceous young woman standing inside a posh office:

> This is the Playboy's office.... The girl in the picture is the playboy's private secretary.... He has just told a story to his secretary. Color her face red. The playboy's secretary cannot type, or spell, or take shorthand. Color her hair yellow, and her eyes green, and her lips red, but leave her mind blank. The playboy's secretary has a funny birthmark, but it is covered by her blouse. If you wait for a few minutes, perhaps you can color the birthmark.[32]

This was self-parody, of course, but envisioning the office as a setting for sexual dalliance was in keeping with *Playboy*'s eroticization of everyday life. It also reflected attitudes and beliefs about women's roles in the white-collar office, which had helped determine appropriate female tasks and shaped office culture. *Playboy* pictorials featuring office girls such as "Playboy's Girl Friday," "Legal Tender," and "Honey in the Bank" showed women performing various tasks in their respective workplaces alongside seminude photographs. While an insurance company evoked "images of monolithic statistical tables," suggested one, the office's nineteen-year-old secretary-turned-Playmate was sure to enliven the place.[33]

As early as December 1954, with the feature "Photographing a Playmate," *Playboy* had glamorized the real-life work that went into creating a Playmate pictorial. Art Director Art Paul appeared in the photographs, busily overseeing the project with the unclothed model, Terry Ryan. "Photographing Your Own Playmate" (June 1958) continued the theme (see figure 4.1). "The first thing you *don't* need is a professional model.... We, for instance, find our Playmates in lingerie shops, airplanes, country clubs—and in our own offices." The eighteen-year-old Playboy receptionist, when asked to disrobe for this pictorial, "did the proper amount of hemming and hawing for a couple of days" before agreeing. Captions accompanying the photographs explained that fully clothed test shots

PHOTOGRAPHING YOUR OWN PLAYMATE

EVER SINCE NICÉPHORE NIEPCE took the first photo back in the 1820s, photographing pretty girls has been a popular pastime; and in recent years, about the most popular photographs of pretty girls have appeared in PLAYBOY as Playmates. With the idea of giving you a few pointed pointers on shooting a Playmate of your own, here's the way PLAYBOY goes about it:

The first thing you *don't* need is a professional model. There's an extra added attraction to the fact that your fair subject is a secretary or a clerk in the book store where you picked up that copy of Burton's *British Mammals* yesterweek. We, for instance, find our Playmates in lingerie shops, airplanes, country clubs — and in our own offices.

Judy Lee Tomerlin, 18, is a receptionist on the fourth floor of the PLAYBOY Building: she is attractive, personable, and fresh from Tennessee, having been with us just under half-a-dozen months at the time we began thinking about her as a Playmate. Modeling experience, professional or amateur: none. Perfect for our purpose. We broached the subject. Judy Lee was aware of our previous

one of our office girls
helps us show you how to take
a prize pin-up photo

PLAYBOY receptionist and potential Playmate.

4.1 Playboy *often constructed for readers a glimpse of what went on "behind the scenes" to produce a magazine devoted to pleasure and entertainment. Pictorials like this one, which showcased the making of a Playmate of the Month photograph with a Playboy receptionist in the starring role, suggested the business of* Playboy *was every bit as exciting and glamorous as the world depicted in its pages, and that prospective Playmates could be found all around in daily life. (Reproduced by special permission of* Playboy *magazine © June 1958 by Playboy.)*

helped her to overcome her initial shyness. Features like this one reinforced the squeaky-clean vision of the Playmate—she was not a professional model, only a nice young girl, who after careful consideration decided to take off her clothes for *Playboy*. At the same time, they added to the image of *Playboy* as a sexually liberated environment and the workplace in general as a source of erotic possibilities.[34]

Cartoons provided another source of visual imagery of men and women in the workplace. Along with those depicting models, nurses, nudists, or other women identifiable only as potential sex partners, cartoons in which humor turned on an employer-employee "office" relationship appeared regularly in *Playboy*. In *Playboy*'s office-themed cartoons, viewers were meant to recognize the sexual/power dynamics that underpinned the relationship between the male boss and his female employee. Secretaries filed into the executive's office to "compensate" for their typing errors. Lascivious office parties formed the backdrop for sexual trysts between managers and female underlings. White-collar men took pleasure fondling or gazing at the buxom office girls in their midst. Earlier images of the working girl as office vamp or innocent victim resonated in these cartoons.[35] The typical dictation scenario illustrates these points. Whether she willingly participated in the dictation-as-sexual-encounter gambit or naively insisted on doing her job, the working relationship between the boss and his secretary, especially as it existed within his private office, was routinely depicted as one filled with sexual possibilities. In one cartoon, a woman with exaggerated breasts sits in her boss's lap, oblivious to his sexual advances. He admonishes in the punch line, "Will you please stop taking down what I'm saying?!" In another version, the secretary perched on the lap of her boss warns, "Better not give me another raise too soon—I don't want my mother to start worrying." Other cartoons depicted the boss chasing his secretary around the desk, staring at her cleavage, making suggestive remarks, or touching her body.[36] Such exaggerated shows of aggression poked fun at male lechery while presenting the attractive office girl as fair game for male advances.

Many cartoons also suggested that in the workplace, women traded on their sexuality, using sex to make up for poor job skills or to secure a pay raise. In one instance, a man climbs in bed with a woman who asks, "Will I get time-and-a-half?" In another, a voluptuous woman tells a prospective boss, "I can type, take shorthand, file, and I'm a pushover." Other scenarios involved women applying for positions for which they needed no actual job skills. In one, a prospective candidate enters the personnel department to find her interviewer waiting for her in bed. In another, an employer desperately calls after a departing female applicant, "Wait, how about longhand, then? Can you take longhand?" Similarly, a boss asks his secretary, "I wonder, Miss Potter, if you'd be interested in how

you might be able to get away with atrocious typing such as this?" In another cartoon, as two secretaries sit idly at their desks, one of them tells a man about to enter the manager's private office, "Well, I can tell you what *we* had to do to get *our* raise, but I doubt if the information will do you much good."[37]

These cartoons were not meant to be taken as direct representations of reality, of course. Full-page, single-frame cartoons used the technique of exaggeration in order to make the punch line instantly legible to the reader. The meaning of even the most hyperbolic depiction would have been lost, however, without a prior understanding of hierarchical gender roles and their replication in the workplace. Sex might be understood to be the primary theme of these cartoons, but the humor drew on cultural tensions and turned on several underlying assumptions. In these images, women occupied a subordinate position that went beyond their place at the low end of the office totem pole. Their value derived not from their job skills but from physical attractiveness and sexual availability. While many cartoons depicted female office workers as subject to male advances, those that showed foolish men succumbing to women's sexual power gave expression to concerns that women actively used their sexuality to advantage. Yet female sexual capital, however powerful, was not a lasting commodity; men in these images ultimately held the positions of enduring authority.

"There weren't any Petty Girls working at *Esquire*," Hefner once complained about his stint in 1951 as a copywriter for that magazine's promotions department. He was referring to artist George Petty's airbrushed female figures, which graced the pages of *Esquire* throughout the 1930s. Enthralled by *Esquire* in his youth, Hefner had gone into the job with high expectations. "I kind of had the feeling that it would be an extremely stimulating and exciting atmosphere in which to work, that it would be markedly different from just another office job," he told an interviewer. He soon discovered, however, that "working there was just a nine-to-five routine. It lacked the glitter and glamour from inside that I had anticipated when I was younger."[38] While *Esquire*'s offices were devoid of real, live Petty Girls, Hefner made sure that the photographic equivalent, the Playmate, enlivened his own place of business.

More important, he made sure to advertise that fact. Janet Pilgrim, who appeared in the July 1955 issue of the magazine, held the distinction as the first Playmate of the Month to be constructed as the "girl next door." She also worked in *Playboy*'s offices, and the way Hefner presented that information is instructive. Pilgrim, whose real name was Charlaine Karalus, worked for *Playboy* and was dating the married Hefner at the time. Hefner chose her pseudonym as a jesting poke at sexual Puritanism.[39] The story about Janet Pilgrim that accompanied her pictorial "revealed" that she worked in

the magazine's subscriptions department. Hefner later explained that when she asked him for an addressograph machine, he promised to get her one if she posed for the magazine. Soft-focused photographs of the unclad young woman told the outcome of that exchange. This narrative thus presented Janet Pilgrim as the ultimate incarnation of the sexually alluring, devoted office girl: a young woman who decided to shed her clothes for her boss and his company, not only providing him with a pinup for his magazine but doing so in order to obtain the equipment she needed to perform her regular job more efficiently. The popular Janet Pilgrim went on to reprise her role as Playboy's "Office Playmate" in two more issues. Although she received offers of modeling and other jobs after her initial appearance in the publication, the loyal Miss Pilgrim was happily continuing to manage its subscriptions, readers of the December 1955 issue learned. In fact, *Playboy* informed them, she dutifully agreed to pose for the holiday issue "when we suggested that it would probably increase the number of Christmas orders."

Images of Hefner as the embodiment of the urbane, fun-loving bachelor, and his company as a realm of erotic possibilities became important promotional tools that shaped the public image of the magazine and its founder. Hefner played this angle to advantage. Discussing the evolution of the Playmate from a nameless nude to the girl next door, Hefner in the early 1960s told the story about Janet Pilgrim, the "little gal working for us" with whom he struck his bargain. "We had an attractive staff even then," he mused. The presence of attractive and sexually inviting young women at his company became part of Hefner's well-told story about his own success. While working at *Esquire,* Hefner claimed, he had promised himself that if he ever got his big break he "was going to make my office all the things that I'd always imagined an office ought to be and that's what *Playboy* is.... It's funny, a good-looking girl can be just as efficient as an ugly one."[40] Publicizing the affair between the young woman and the still-married Hefner would have been unseemly in 1955; it was enough to show Janet Pilgrim doing her job, with a shadowy, unidentifiable male figure (Hefner) in the background of her Playmate of the Month photograph, to establish the mystique of the Playboy office, and to suggest the erotic possibilities of the workplace in general.

The solicitous, sexually available "office girl" provided a contrast, then, to the wife whose demands for financial security tied her husband to his job, as well as to the overly-ambitious woman who competed with men in the workplace. Increasingly, according to a 1962 article in *Business Week,* men in the workplace heard "the tap of high heels moving up from behind on the ladder to business success." Although their sheer numbers made women's presence in the workforce more visible, in reality, females who held positions of authority over men

were still few and far between. The specter of the woman finagling her way into the male domain of executive privilege, however, prompted exaggerated warnings in *Playboy*.

"Everybody here is completely flipped by your idea of doing the ultimate take-out on career women, compared to whom Mom is an absolute delight," Editorial Director A. C. Spectorsky informed Philip Wylie in August 1962. "We would really like a no-hold-barred [*sic*] tearing apart of this miserable humanoid who calls herself woman." Spectorsky claimed an intimate knowledge of this nefarious strain of working woman. "Having worked for Street & Smith Publications, I speak with considerable feeling about these chromium-plated, castrating, driven, vicious, unhappy, destructive, asexual or anti-sexual devouring, insatiable... [women]." "You are the man to do it," Spectorsky assured Wylie about the proposed article, "and we are the guys to print it." As Wylie's subsequent attack on career women worked its way through *Playboy*'s editorial pipeline, Spectorsky encouraged editors to make clear that although "so far, men have not deigned to rise in anger and smite down these bitches... increasingly the real hipsters among men are recognizing them for what they are and have either managed to keep them at arms length or anticipate their ploys."[41]

Wylie's final piece lambasted women for intruding into the male realms of the professions and management and for using positions within the fashion, advertising, and television industries to exert a feminizing influence on American culture. The career woman, he wrote, has an "obscene compulsion: She must compete with, and if necessary, cripple manhood and masculinity." How did she compete with men? Through her "characteristic methods: espionage, blackmail and, if she is up to it, whoring."[42] Indeed, *Look* magazine's investigation into the plight of the American male had noted that women in the workplace posed the threat of "unfair competition" if they chose to use their "attractiveness in a business battle." The "habitat" of the career woman "is man's," Wylie proclaimed, "and she has infiltrated every cubic foot of it with the single exception of the toilet." In his view, women who sought positions of power stepped outside the bounds of appropriate female behavior. They infiltrated both symbolic and actual male space, stopping only at the men's lavatory. That the "executive washroom" was simultaneously understood to be the men's room suggests a spatial metaphor for the ideological barriers to women's ascent up the corporate ladder. That women might dare to infiltrate the executive (male) washroom implied a transgressive desire to occupy male space and assume a male role.

"A woman's place is in her place, and that is true both at home... and in the office," advised Shepherd Mead. The problem with the career woman was that she did not know her place. "She gives orders and competes with men on

their own ground.... She even gives orders *to men,* something that has to be experienced to be appreciated." Moreover, the woman executive jeopardized the status of the workplace as a sex-charged haven from home. She threatened, for instance, to remove attractive secretaries from the office. "Before you know it," Mead cautioned, "the office may become a drab and unfriendly place, one where you will find no solace and little comfort." How to combat this peril? Mead advised men to create the impression that the woman executive was "always breaking into the middle of a dirty story" and, by implication, invading male space. Once she was out of the way, the office could resume its comfortable functioning with those "women trained to be the hand-maidens of the modern business man."[43]

Exaggerations about the power of the "career woman" upheld a vision of the business world as a male realm, where women were meant to occupy a supportive role that reflected their place in the gender order. Wylie called upon men to combat women who stepped out of line:

> Let us, then who are still masculine, or who wish to become masculine, and those who would undertake to restore a birthright now stolen by the career sisterhood...let us unite to celebrate womanhood as feminine, as gorgeous, as titillating and sexy—and let us hoot down with hearty bass guffaws any and all vulgar...dames who try to stride in and put a stop to our fun.[44]

Women, as presented in pictorials and cartoons in *Playboy,* were on hand to massage male egos, serve as "eye candy," and provide respite from the doldrums or frustrations of a hard day's work. Those who competed with men for personal advancement and success in the business world, however, drew harsh criticism. These were, after all, "masculine" pursuits.

Taking such assumptions into consideration, Brown's program for the working girl's advancement required an extravagant outward showing of femininity. Addressing what she termed "sneaking up on the boys career-wise," she cautioned, "don't worry, we'll be so gentle and ladylike they won't mind a bit. In an ideal world we might move onward and upward by using only our brains and talent but, since this is an imperfect world, a certain amount of listening, giggling, wriggling, smiling, winking, flirting and fainting is required in our rise from the mailroom." If perchance the Single Girl did advance to a job above the level of secretary, she retained her working-girl femininity, posing no threat to male egos. She continued to look lovely. "You're the new girl success who bears no resemblance whatever to that tweedy, walrus-shaped thing of the past," Brown explained. She surrounded herself with feminine decor. "It's okay to let your office achieve a

well-cluttered look of 'art objects,'" Brown further counseled. "An austere, businessy office wearing a girl inside suggests she's pretending not to be one or else has no imagination." She still proved more interesting than the mousy housewife. "A girl with appointments to keep and places to go and who doesn't seem *needy* is *exciting*." She continued to display her feminine charms and enact her workplace domesticity, "listening, babying, flirting" with men in the office. She even stashed away a bottle of liquor for emergencies. "Naturally a lady doesn't hoist her bottle and guzzle away like one of the boys, but if one of the boys has run out of his own J&B, you produce *yours*. (Doesn't a mother run for the snake-bite remedy or mustard poultices when her boy is bitten or ailing?)," Brown queried. Furthermore, the working girl who achieved a better job had no interest in power. Once the Single Girl had climbed to the next rung on the ladder of success, Brown advised humility. "Never mind whether you've got a secretary and several phones to lord it over—the big thing is whether it provides you a more exciting day and a closer relationship with men on *their* level."[45]

Although the hardworking and lucky Single Girl might eventually become a career girl, Brown accepted a rather low glass ceiling for women in a chapter titled "The Key to the Men's Room." The business world, she conceded in a section headed "The Fellows Won't Let You in Their Club," was still a man's world. "Who wants to play dominoes at their 'for men only' luncheons anyway...or choke to death in their smoke-filled, segregated dining room?" she asked. Brown recognized such spaces and activities as realms of power and offered women's relative gains and a glamorous lifestyle as a panacea for women's exclusion from them. "It's quite a new thing for men and women to be companions anyhow....A little more time is needed to integrate completely," Brown explained, "and naturally there will always be some things men and women won't do together, and women wouldn't want them to. Meantime, I'm sure you have a million projects for your lunch hours, the most important of which might be to grab a nap against a very big evening or big meeting."[46]

While assuming a social space for the independent, self-fulfilled single woman, Brown accepted that it was, in fact, still a man's world, where men had greater access to money and power and often mediated between the Single Girl and public life. The Single Girl's marginal position in fact made her a fitting companion for the playboy—her challenge to the established social order went far enough to make her an available partner for an evening on the town or a night in the playboy's round, rotating bed, but she did not stray too far from a traditional feminine role. Instead, she accepted the gender status quo, cultivating feminine charm and sex appeal as coping strategies amid the social and economic inequality faced by women. As compensation for her efforts, she

gained access, albeit on a more limited basis, to the world of consumer goods and pleasurable experiences that comprised the "the good single life."

"A BUNNY'S TALE"

The Playboy Club provided a male-oriented leisure space designed to bring to life the pages of a magazine that promised "entertainment for men." For the young, mostly single women who donned the Bunny costume, the club was a workplace. Fashioned as exemplars of the sexually alluring, available companion to the playboy, many of these women experienced a newfound measure of independence in the Playboy Club, while existing within a framework that upheld notions of working-girl femininity and ideas about woman's role. Like the Playmate or the office girl, the Bunny represented an undemanding, sexually appealing female, working to pay her own way and solicitous toward the men whom she served. In this regard, the Bunny shared much in common with the Single Girl.

Ensconced in a costume that emphasized her curves and prohibited by regulations from meeting boyfriends or husbands outside the club, the Bunny appeared unattached and sexually available.[47] That many Playmates became Bunnies, and vice versa, added to their appeal. In August 1962, *Playboy* noted that twenty-four young women had already made the leap from Playmate to Bunny. Miss August, Jan Roberts, represented the first "Playmate to be discovered among the hutch honeys already decorating club premises."[48] The following summer, *Playboy* ran its first of numerous Bunny pictorials, which presented the club employees in classic girl-next-door fashion.[49] "The Bunnies of Dixie," for example, introduced readers to Sara Patricia Atkinson, in language that highlighted her femininity and her delight in free-spirited consumption:

> She's blonde and blue eyed, with a gentle voice, a delicate mouth and a smile that could melt Sherman's statue. When you talk to Sara, she speaks shyly of her devotion to her family, her childhood on her father's farm in rural Georgia, and her feeling of cozy security at the Atlanta Club. What does she do in her spare time?... "I have a little burgundy Mustang— my prize possession," she says. "A real fast one, with four on the floor. It flies.... I love the wind and I love speed—planes, cars, anything, just so long as they're fast."[50]

One photograph showed Atkinson at work in her Bunny costume, while another presented her standing outdoors on a farm wearing considerably less.

While *Playboy* strived to craft a desirable identity for the Playmates who appeared only as two-dimensional images on a page, in the clubs, customers encountered the Bunny as a living, breathing person. Yet a measure of fantasy and abstraction surrounded her as well. Bunnies were not allowed to date customers, nor reveal their last names, telephone numbers, or home addresses—rules intended to protect them and, more important, to safeguard the clubs' liquor licenses.[51] While, theoretically, this meant a keyholder had no hope of seducing a Bunny, it also meant she existed just out of reach, making no demands, offering only service and visual pleasure. Consider, for instance, *Playboy*'s description of Bunny Camille, "one of the few pig-tailed Bunnies in captivity." *Playboy* noted how skillfully she poured drinks for her customers. She also possessed "a very fine frame, which the keyholder is free to visually enjoy while the beer is slowly, ever so slowly, filling his glass."[52] The Bunny pictorials, which revealed personal information and very often what little flesh the costumes usually covered, made the prospect of interacting with the clubs' hostesses even more enticing. Club members often wrote to *Playboy*, requesting pictorials and information about their favorite cocktail waitresses. These photo essays became a prominent feature in *Playboy*, carrying out the dual purpose of promoting the clubs and helping to sell magazines.[53]

"To the keyholder," extolled *Playboy*, "the Bunny is a personal Girl Friday—warm and friendly, unobtrusively efficient, and a delight to behold."[54] Nothing epitomized the sense of the club as a masculine space privileging the male gaze more than the Bunny Watchers' Society, a fraternity of keyholders who gathered in the Playmate Bar each afternoon to enjoy a free drink while they observed their favorite cocktail waitresses. Bunny Watchers sported special black blazers with the Playboy rabbit insignia, drank from monogrammed Bunny Watchers mugs, and enjoyed a game that involved guessing the measurements of their cottontailed hostesses. Yet, while the clubs represented a quasi-private realm for the men who comprised their fee-paying membership, many of the women whose costumed bodies and pleasant demeanor served as the main attraction envisioned the clubs as *their* space. The clubs served as a stage for feminine performance that provided a mixed bag of empowerment and objectification within a context of male privilege and corporate control.[55]

Behind the scenes in the club's dressing room, young women went through a process of transformation that would have met with approval from Helen Gurley Brown. They applied makeup, donned false eyelashes and hairpieces, and stuffed their costumes with everything from gym socks to plastic bags to fill out the bust-line. Finally, pinning on a tag with their special "Bunny name," they became the objects of male fantasy.[56] Training for the job, which required no experience, encouraged young women to think of their work as a

stage performance. Advertisements to fill the new hutches around the country announced "casting sessions—staged like a call for a Broadway play." Others proclaimed, "This is show business!... [T]he perfect opportunity for beautiful young ladies interested in a glamorous and rewarding career."[57] Many women found the "performance" aspect of the job freeing, as it enabled them to take risks in fashioning and refashioning an identity. Said one Bunny, "I relished playing the role of 'good girl' wearing a provocative costume: 'Come hither, but don't touch.'" Recalled another, "I bought a red wig, then a short curly one, and had a ball role playing. I could be anyone I wanted to be." "When we walked onto the floor of the Club, we were on stage," explained a third. Knowing that she was the center of attention and capable of handling her job gave this woman a sense of confidence. As she put it, "This was your space. You owned it."[58]

In such a performance, the better one played the part, the more money she earned. Despite women's increasing presence in the workforce, paid labor was often still viewed as a temporary activity before settling down to family life, and women faced limited prospects for employment. As one former Bunny remarked, "There weren't many choices if you hadn't found a husband by the time you graduated high school." Working at the Playboy Club offered a decent living and flexible work hours, although there was a hierarchy within the hutch. A novice server might start out in the Playmate Bar, but the real money went to experienced Bunnies working in the showrooms. The bulk of one's earnings came from cash tips. "In answer to questions regarding income," Playboy's "Bunny Manual" advised, "Bunnies should not give out definite facts and figures to customers but should imply that the girls make extremely good wages.... This not only has a tendency to make members tip generously, but also increases the prestige of our Bunnies generally." Although they were instructed not to "push drinks," for Playboy did not want its clubs to resemble the unseemly B-girl joints, young women recognized that the more drinks they sold, the more money they earned. Moreover, "Bunny of the Week" contests rewarded the waitress who served the most drinks.[59] As added incentive, girls with the highest drink averages got the best schedules. Thus, Bunnies worked to maximize their earnings by cashing in on charm and sex appeal. Bunnies strived to establish a rapport with keyholders. Some kept detailed lists of customers' tipping habits and made sure they could address each one by name. Said another, "You'd have people eating out of your hand just by remembering their names and making them look good to their friends."[60] Where clubs wooed customers with the promise of attentive treatment from beautiful women, Bunnies obliged, playing the game to their advantage.

"Inside the Club," one former New York Bunny recalled, "we paraded like starlets in our showgirl costumes." The theatricality and associated "fame"

spilled over to life outside the club. *Playboy* publicized the clubs and sold magazines by spotlighting the clubs' young female employees. Public fascination led to radio and television guest spots for many Bunnies, as well as participation in Bunny of the Year contests, which later became televised pageants. In that sense, while *Playboy* purveyed an image of status for men, for some women, the money they earned at the clubs and their association with *Playboy* put them in touch with a measure of glamour and celebrity.[61] Yet, when all was said and done, a Bunny was still a glorified cocktail waitress working long hours in an uncomfortable costume. Designed to invite male stares, the costume occasionally resulted in further unwanted attention. One Bunny remembered that tails had to be made from fire-retardant material because customers tried to light them on fire. Others faced unwelcome advances from keyholders.[62] The job necessitated, as one writer put it, becoming "well versed in ways of taming a wolf without losing a customer." Tactics ranged from enlisting a fellow Bunny to spill drinks in the lap of an overly fresh patron, to quoting Shakespeare in the hopes of revealing one's intellect along with one's flesh.[63] Strict rules against cavorting between Bunnies and customers, in place to protect the clubs' liquor licenses, did help keep patrons in line. Bunnies were instructed to inform customers that they were not allowed to socialize with keyholders. "The management always backed you up, and as a result we all developed 'attitudes,'" said one former club employee. Another put it more bluntly: "We were major cock teasers, and that was our image as Playboy Bunnies."[64]

Protected by management and by their own coping skills against unruly customers and established as the cause célèbre of the clubs, many women felt their sense of femininity affirmed. For one, achieving status as a Playboy Bunny banished any self doubt about whether she was "attractive, feminine, [and] sexually alluring." Others commented on the sense of empowerment. "You soon start to realize how great the power of a woman's sexuality is—and how you're using it."[65] For some, however, recognizing the potency of their sexuality caused misgivings. "Getting by on your looks is a double-edged sword. I knew I could get what I wanted with my body, but I never respected that and I didn't feel good about it." "When you get dressed up in an outfit like that, it makes you question what the role is that you're really playing." Spending time in the image-obsessed environment of the clubs could also be unnerving: women faced weight regulations and the possibility of being fired for lack of "Bunny image," often a euphemism for being too old.[66]

While *Playboy* touted the glamour of its Bunnies, these cottontail-clad women also elicited scathing criticism. One reviewer observed rather harshly, "On the whole, I found most bunnies to be vacuous maidens cut out of the same mold, with billowy hairdos, heavy eye make-up, large busts and derrieres,

a consuming passion for the large sums of money they are earning and a bovine acceptance of their off-duty roles as companions for Hefner and his executives." Further condemnation came when future feminist activist Gloria Steinem published her exposé on the clubs after infiltrating them as "Bunny Marie" in February 1963. Steinem painted an unflattering portrait of unintelligent, over-worked, underpaid girls whose biggest assets were the plastic dry-cleaning bags propping up their breasts for club members to ogle. Hefner's habit of discussing the Bunnies in the aggregate—"We total over 24.5 tons of bunnies. Their collective chest measurement is 15,156 in., which is about one-quarter of a mile"—did little to dispel such views.[67] To dismiss these women merely as passive dupes in a sexist enterprise, however, overlooks a more complex reality.

For many women, working at Hefner's chain of key-clubs opened a door to greater opportunity. Flexible hours, decent wages, a chance to transfer to clubs in various cities, and a tuition-reimbursement program enabled women to go to school, travel, support a family, or live independently as they planned their futures. Even as it afforded a greater measure of autonomy, however, working as a Playboy Bunny involved a performance of working-girl femininity that prized physical appearance and deferential service to men. As *Playboy* put it, Bunnies combined "the wholesomeness of airline stewardesses, the glamour of showgirls, and the warm efficiency of hostesses at a swinging house party." "Bunny-ing," then, combined physical labor with glamour and celebrity, feminine caregiving roles with a newfound measure of economic independence, sexual performance and display mixed with personal empowerment. In this sense, these women experienced something akin to the turn-of-the-century working women for whom sexuality was both liberating and constraining.[68] Brown and many of the women employed as Playboy Bunnies were unapologetic about cultivating femininity through consumption and display and using physical appearance to get ahead. As she followed the path to independence blazed by the Single Girl, the Bunny embodied the tensions in this particular form of liberation.

Brown's Single Girl fit easily into the harmonious system of gender roles supported by Hefner. She made few demands on the male pocketbook, aside from accepting the occasional gift or evening on the town, and instead made her own way as a working girl. Like the playboy, she strove to work hard and play hard, too; yet she had no pretensions about achieving much power or earning vast sums of money through her role in the workplace. Instead, she accepted her marginal economic position and limited job prospects with a smile on her well-made-up face. Though she may not have enjoyed the same degree of autonomy and plenitude as the playboy, the Single Girl shared his sensibilities. Like the

playboy, the Single Girl asserted a right to participate in the consumer culture and to enjoy sexual pleasure as a free agent. She did not shun marriage, but enjoyed a prolonged period of singlehood before settling down; more important, the experience and financial independence she gained as a Single Girl gave her the option to choose or decline marriage. In this regard, this important cultural figure was both a handmaiden to the liberalization of sexual attitudes in the 1960s and the ascent of a consumer-oriented singles culture.

Brown's vision accepted the sexist underpinnings of society and the limitations they placed on women's ambition and independence. Many of the tensions and accommodations present in her work would be challenged by the end of the decade. The consumer nexus that buttressed the relationship between the Single Girl and the playboy, where women embraced commodities and used sex appeal to access men, and men utilized the trappings of status to attract and seduce women, came under attack in the late 1960s as part of a larger groundswell of protest against the consumer society. The attitudes and social structures that made it both expedient and limiting for women to embrace sex appeal as their primary asset came under fire from the women's liberation movement. Indeed, so-called second-wave feminists—in their demands for equal pay and equal opportunity, their protests against sexual harassment and workplace discrimination, and their denouncement of menial, gender-stereotyped tasks that formed the domain of female office workers—strongly opposed the formulation of working-girl femininity found in Brown's works. The "good single life" outlined by Brown was a dilution of *Playboy*'s more robust promises of abundance and pleasure for men, but self-fulfillment lay at the heart of both enterprises. Although the Single Girl's unequal status would be challenged by feminists, the pleasure-seeking, commodity-focused approach to fulfillment at the center of her ideal would continue to resonate.

5 "FOR US IT IS THE GOOD LIFE"

The Ascendant Playboy Life

WRITING IN HARPER'S *Magazine* in 1967, journalist David Halberstam reflected on the years he spent as a foreign correspondent in Poland, until his unflattering reports about the government caused him to be expelled from the country. Before leaving Poland, Halberstam recounted, he wanted to show his appreciation to a Polish intellectual who had remained a loyal friend during the skirmishes with state officials that resulted in his expulsion. To his surprise, Halberstam's Polish friend requested a subscription to *Playboy*, "the most important magazine there is." When the American journalist suggested that there were other magazines more suitable for the caliber of this man's intellect, his friend reportedly told him:

> But you don't understand how important Playboy is.... It is for us the greatest American export in the world. For us it is the good life. The boy, the girl, the pad, with fancy lighting and sports car. The wine bottle, half-empty, then the lights out. The pinup girls. But are they pinup girls? No, not at all, they are secretaries, girls next door, and miracle, they are taking off their clothes, all of them. Your secretary is taking off all her clothes.

When Halberstam protested that the magazine did not depict reality, his friend stopped him, explaining, "It doesn't matter that all American young men don't live like *Playboy* heroes; what matters is that we think they do. For us *Playboy* is the symbol of your good life."[1]

As this perhaps apocryphal account suggests, *Playboy*, and the lifestyle rendered in its pages, captivated audiences in the 1960s. A robust one million by 1960, circulation climbed steadily to more than five million by the end of the decade. In the meantime, Hefner's initial publishing venture spawned an entertainment empire that included nightclubs, resorts, casinos, hotels, and countless other licensed products and services, while also creating two iconic figures, the Playmate and the Playboy Bunny. Both Hefner and his growing "Playboy

empire" received widespread media attention. To fans and critics alike, "playboy" had become synonymous with the affluent, stylish, sexually liberated hedonism purveyed in the magazine.

Not only did *Playboy* reach ascendancy in the 1960s, but the values, gender formulations, and cultural style it promoted increasingly reverberated through American culture. From its inception, the magazine had carefully rebelled against the traditional restraints and adult responsibilities of the family-oriented society. In the late 1950s and 1960s, the magazine's celebration of singlehood and sexual liberation, its images of suave, stylish men and free-spirited yet submissive young women, echoed in the popular culture and consumer society of postwar America. Imitators attempted to copy *Playboy*'s winning formula. Popular entertainers embodied the playboy's self-indulgent style. Numerous motion pictures projected the image of the fashionable, sexually magnetic bachelor onto the big screen. In the wider culture as the decade wore on, the barriers to sexual expression continued to erode, then crumbled. Young people in the burgeoning urban singles culture as well as in the 1960s counterculture embraced the "new morality" and its affirmation of personal desires. More and more, cultural trends and changing social mores emphasized personal freedom, consumption, and pleasure, touchstones of the good life found in the pages of *Playboy*. As lighthearted depictions of liberated sexual encounters and lavish consumption increasingly permeated American culture, deeper issues were at stake. African Americans faced formidable barriers as they sought entrée into the playboy life, raising questions about the racial identities of the "American consumer" and the "all-American girl" that underscored the failings of a purportedly democratic society. And as the 1960s progressed, critics attacked the materialism of the consumer society but could not shake loose from its moorings the pleasure-seeking ethos on which it rested.

THE COLLEGE MARKET AND *PLAYBOY* IMITATORS

With the postwar expansion of college enrollment, young campus men facing a world of consumer and leisure possibilities had *Playboy* to show them the way (see figure 5.1). *Playboy* was a hit on college campuses, where fraternity brothers shared each issue, Playmate centerfolds decorated dormitory walls, and a quarter of all copies of the magazine were sold.[2] In 1961 the Cornell University marching band even entertained the halftime crowd at the Cornell-Harvard football game by falling into formation in the outline of a familiar bow tie–wearing rabbit. Students at Dartmouth carved an ice Bunny for their winter

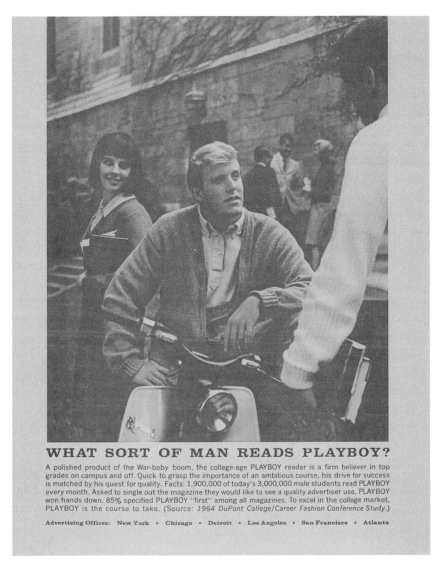

WHAT SORT OF MAN READS PLAYBOY?

A polished product of the War-baby boom, the college-age PLAYBOY reader is a firm believer in top grades on campus and off. Quick to grasp the importance of an ambitious course, his drive for success is matched by his quest for quality. Facts: 1,900,000 of today's 3,000,000 male students read PLAYBOY every month. Asked to single out the magazine they would like to see a quality advertiser use, PLAYBOY won hands down. 85% specified PLAYBOY "first" among all magazines. To excel in the college market, PLAYBOY is the course to take. (Source: *1964 DuPont College/Career Fashion Conference Study.*)

Advertising Offices: New York   •   Chicago   •   Detroit   •   Los Angeles   •   San Francisco   •   Atlanta

5.1 *College students embraced* Playboy, *a fact it eagerly pointed out to advertisers.* Playboy *catered to students with special collegiate issues each September. (Reproduced by special permission of* Playboy *magazine © September 1964 by Playboy.)*

carnival. *Playboy* specifically addressed the young male college student audience with September "back to school" features that included a college football preview and a report on campus fashion trends. It also established a College Bureau, which organized student representatives on each campus to promote the magazine and help sell *Playboy* products. Fraternities held "Playboy Parties," decorating with Playmate centerfolds, cartoons, magazine covers, and banners provided by *Playboy* for the occasion, and organized their own "Playmate contests."[3] One amateur Playmate became the real thing when fraternity members at Carnegie Tech sent *Playboy* a snapshot of the coed they selected at a house party and suggested that she grace the centerfold.

Becoming a strong presence on college campuses, in turn, helped attract advertisers looking to tap the market of upwardly mobile young men who favored the magazine. Advertisers adopted the language of "the playboy life" in trying to reach them. One menswear maker introduced the "Playboy" tuxedo into its line of formal attire. "Too Pooped to Play, Boy?" asked a No Doz ad, suggesting the product enabled one to enjoy a night on the town after a hard day's work. A men's slacks manufacturer, invoking the magazine's "What Sort of Man Reads Playboy?" ad campaign, posed the question, "What sort of man wears Raeburns?" Botany 500 produced a "Young Bachelor" line of apparel for young men, while Bacardi Rum advertised the Bacardi party "for fun-loving playboys." These products and advertisements underscored the popularity of the magazine and the awareness that the single males to whom it appealed made up an important segment of the consumer society. More than half of the male college students in one marketing study said they read *Playboy* regularly. When asked in what magazine they were most likely to look at the advertisements, more readers identified *Playboy* than any other.[4]

Imitation was the best form of flattery, and the proliferation of copycat men's magazines that filled newsstands confirmed *Playboy*'s success. *Caper* appeared in 1956, dubbing the woman who appeared in its two-page color center spread the "Caperette." *Fling* commenced in 1957. It promised to take readers on a "round-the-world pleasure trip" and offered a "Fling Folio" with "colorful pages of sophistication and spice" in the middle of each issue. Whereas *Playboy* offered "entertainment for men," *Fling* took the slogan "Passport to Pleasure" and in place of *Playboy*'s frisky rabbit mascot adopted the "King of Fling," a rotund little sultan aboard a magic carpet. Each month, the magazine provided a photographic look at the newest member of "The King's Harem." Others jumping on the bandwagon of *Playboy*'s success included *Rogue, Dude, Gent, Swank, Candid,* and *Cavalier.* Each carried a "cheesecake" centerpiece with such titles as Mademoiselle of the Month, Date of the Month, Rogue Girl, and Miss Weekend, the latter bringing together notions of leisure time and

sexual possibility.[5] Though modeled on *Playboy*'s formula, the imitators never matched it in quality or readership. The best-selling among them reached a circulation of a few hundred thousand compared to *Playboy*'s millions. Taken as a whole, the popularity of such men's magazines formed part of a growing trend as the pleasure-seeking bachelor came to occupy an increasingly visible place in American culture.

THE RACIAL LIMITS OF "THE PLAYBOY LIFE"

Unlike Halberstam's friend in Poland, who wished for a taste of the good life that seemed to abound in the United States, African Americans did not glimpse the nation's affluence from distant shores. They were citizens of the United States, cast as outsiders by the persistent racial discrimination and segregation that kept them from partaking fully in American freedom and prosperity. The vision of success put forth in *Playboy* posited a definition of American citizenship based on equal access to the marketplace. Theoretically, all American men could aspire to the playboy's status and enjoy his material comforts. Like the mass publications of the 1950s, however, *Playboy* assumed a white middle-class audience and represented a world of white affluence. *Playboy* and its mandate for the good life factored into African Americans' struggle for equality in several ways. African-American publishers created a magazine that attempted to extend "the playboy life" to black audiences overlooked by *Playboy*. African-American newsmen challenged *Playboy*'s exclusion of black women from its famous centerfolds. Their public exchanges with Hefner, while prompting editorial changes, also pointed to *Playboy*'s authority as the premier arbiter of American beauty, and thus spoke to the tremendous cultural power of the magazine. Members of the press also railed against the discrimination practiced in Playboy's franchised nightclubs in the Jim Crow South, highlighting the hypocrisy of a society that preached democracy but failed to practice it. Finally, as *Playboy* increasingly expanded its scope beyond "entertainment for men" to address vital social and political matters, African-American writers and civil rights activists reached an audience of millions.

Founded in 1957, *Duke*, like legions of other imitators, copied *Playboy*'s successful formula, but addressed explicitly an audience of African-American males hard-pressed to find themselves in the pages of *Playboy*. The short-lived *Duke* faced a particular set of challenges in wooing African-American readers with a publication oriented toward sexuality and consumption. When John H. Johnson founded *Ebony* magazine in 1945, for instance, he faced the task of breaking into the mass market with a publication directed to a black audience

that neither offended readers by ignoring racial issues nor put off potential white advertisers by focusing too directly on racial problems. Modeled on the large-circulation mass magazines such as *Life* and *Look, Ebony* tried to focus on the "happier side of Negro life," embracing consumption even as it addressed issues of special concern to its audience. African Americans' postwar struggles for advancement involved efforts to gain equal access to American political and economic life but stemmed also from rising frustrations over the discrimination that continued to cut them out of the widening consumer society.[6] Johnson had addressed this very point in an editorial explaining *Ebony*'s attention to African-American consumption:

> To berate colored Cadillac owners for not spending their money instead on good race causes is to deny Negroes the right to reach for equality on every level of U.S. life. As long as there are rich and poor people in this country, there will be rich and poor Negroes. And that means there will be Negroes with Cadillacs. It cannot but do every Negro's heart good to see one of their number driving the finest car, wearing the finest clothes, living in the finest home. It is a worthy symbol of his aspiration to be a genuinely first class American.[7]

As Johnson understood, American notions of citizenship were bound up in the consumer society. To be an American was to be a consumer, and vice versa.

In keeping with this sentiment, *Duke* attempted to justify its departure from the day's pressing racial issues by cultivating an upmarket, African-American male consumer. The first installment of *Duke* appeared in June 1957, launched by former employees of the Johnson Publishing Company, publisher of *Ebony*. Among them were jazz critic and musician Dan Burley and Sylvestre C. Watkins, editor of the *Anthology of American Negro Literature*. *Duke*'s initial pitch was like a page straight out of *Playboy*:

> *Duke* will strive to cater to the sophisticated, urbane tastes of our Ivy-minded males who have advanced fully enough so that virility is more than a word and adult truly connotes manhood in all its glories. We have no causes and no axes to grind except to bring moments of pleasure to he-men and their female friends of like mind with an amusing, delightful package of assorted goodies.

Only two years earlier, *Jet* magazine had trained the spotlight on racial violence and inspired civil rights activists by publishing photographs of the mutilated corpse of Emmett Till, the fourteen-year-old African-American boy murdered in Mississippi for speaking to a white woman. *Duke*, however, promised to showcase only the pleasant aspects of life, a point underscored by letters

printed in the "Dear Duke" section of the magazine, which commended the publication's attention to less serious matters. One letter cautioned, "Don't run a lot of those lynchings and white folks hating Negro stories. I read enough of that kind of stuff in the colored weeklies. I want to read the kind of stories they run in the other big magazines. If you do that, you've got my money every month." "So you fellows are putting out a new colored magazine," another letter began. "Well, that sounds good but if you are going to fill it up with a lot of civil rights stories and things about white people keeping colored people down, you'd just as well stop right now.... In fact, I've quit buying colored magazines just because they always give you the bad side of things and we've had too much of that already."[8] *Duke*'s publishers promised to dedicate the magazine "to the simple things in life like pleasure and gaiety."

Like the earliest issues of *Playboy, Duke* made use of reprinted material, including fiction by Erskine Caldwell and a Langston Hughes story, "Sugar Brown," from the April 1934 issue of *Esquire*. In scope, content, design, and layout, *Duke* followed the *Playboy* template, right down to its fifty-cent newsstand price. Even the illustrations that graced the jokes page, Male Tales, were reminiscent of the whimsical female gremlins, or "femlins," created by LeRoy Neiman to decorate the pages of *Playboy*'s Party Jokes. The centerpiece of the magazine was its "Duchess of the Month" pictorial. Like the Playmate pictorial, the feature included photographs of female models in various daily activities. Given racist stereotypes of black males as "oversexed," the images of the Duchesses remained relatively modest, with no bared breasts or full nudity. Editorial content specifically addressed an African-American male audience, with articles on "The Myth of Our Virility" and the "Evolution of the Conk," but *Duke* did not mention civil rights. Instead, like *Playboy*, the editorial package highlighted the masculine consumer, linking sex and status. An early editorial identified the magazine's market as a "select group of quite worldly gentlemen and some of their more sophisticated lady friends.... They are what the French call bon vivants.... They enjoy good clothes, good food, good drink but do not mind departing that descriptive formula when it comes to female companionship."

Though *Duke* did not overtly address the civil rights movement, the magazine did not ignore the struggle for racial equality so much as it took as its starting point the presumption of egalitarian consumption. Where *Playboy* tapped into desires for material comfort and pleasure with its extravagant images of the bachelor's lifestyle, *Duke* expanded the fantasy, offering a vision for an upscale African-American masculine identity that extended the notion of "consumer citizenship" across racial lines. Throughout its short existence, *Duke* offered readers an image of African Americans, not as a group struggling for access to the good life, but as successful participants in the consumer society. When it

failed to find support, the *Chicago Daily Defender,* one of the nation's leading African-American newspapers, lamented its passing, noting "we still feel the gap left by the magazine."[9]

Although *Playboy*'s idealized bachelor was an affluent white man, Hefner, in fact, espoused a personal commitment to racial equality. His first job in a personnel department had involved rejecting "Jews, Negroes, and guys with long, foreign names," a task he found repugnant. While African-American men and women were largely absent from the magazine's early issues, Hefner's late-night television program, *Playboy's Penthouse,* presented a racially integrated, cocktail-party atmosphere. Often this amounted to black entertainers such as Ella Fitzgerald, Nat King Cole, Sammy Davis, Jr., Sara Vaughn, and Ray Charles performing and socializing with predominantly white guests. Occasionally, African-American couples joined the white men and women mingling in the background to create the impression of a party in progress, and in at least one episode, Hefner discussed racial integration. The interracial mixing kept the show from being syndicated in the still-segregated South, but it received praise on another front. The *Daily Defender* commended the "many interracial formats" of *Playboy's Penthouse,* calling it "one of the most democratic programs on the air."[10] Hefner's Playboy Clubs provided another venue in which racial integration was endorsed. The club circuit provided a setting for black entertainers to cross the color line, helping to get their start performers such as comedian Dick Gregory, first hired for a three-week stint at the Chicago club in 1960 for $250 a week.[11] And, in theory, Playboy Clubs admitted any male who could afford to purchase a "key," a colorblind approach to membership that affirmed Hefner's notions of democratic consumption.

This approach proved no match for Jim Crow, however. As part of the grand opening of the Playboy Club in New Orleans, Mayor Victor H. Schiro presented Hugh Hefner with an honorary key to the Crescent City. Hefner, in return, bestowed upon the mayor a key to Playboy's newest "hutch." "Like all other keyholders," *Playboy* noted, "His Honor will find that his key opens Playboy Club doors, present and future, everywhere." An article chronicling the opening festivities went on to describe the club, explaining that the building's facade had been left intact due to local laws prohibiting exterior architectural changes in the city's French Quarter. This was not the only law that affected operations at the Louisiana club. State statutes and municipal ordinances that barred racial integration meant that as far as African-American club-goers were concerned, *Playboy* could not make good on its promise that a key to one club would open doors to all others.[12]

"Can a Negro Be a Playboy?" queried John Wilcock in his column for the *Village Voice* in October 1961. "Playboy—that self-styled swingingest of magazines

with its liberal principles and broad-minded policies—invites people to join its club through the pages of its magazines...and then refuses them admittance if they happen to be Negroes. Even if they're members." Wilcock condemned the recently opened New Orleans Playboy Club, where local laws excluded African-American keyholders from the premises, and contemplated a lawsuit against Playboy Clubs International. Meanwhile, *Jet* magazine drew attention to "two tan citizens" asked to leave the club on opening night. The *Daily Defender* reported that its own sports editor, Tommy Picou, a keyholder at the Chicago Playboy Club, had been denied admission to the French Quarter locale.

The negative publicity drew an impassioned response from Hefner. "We feel that it is very unfair that a liberal organization that is *forced* to comply with a local situation is picked out as a primary target for criticism," Hefner complained in the *Village Voice*, "when so many major national companies, not necessarily private social clubs and not necessarily in Louisiana (nor even in the South, for that matter) *voluntarily* practice discrimination without it ever occurring to Mr. Wilcock to devote an entire column to embarrassing them." "I think it is an ironic thing that because of our excellent track record we are singled out for criticism when a situation arises where we find ourselves, like the Negro, forced to compromise in order to exist in a southern state," he wrote to *Jet* magazine. The *Defender* reprinted the letter Hefner sent to Picou after learning of the incident:

> We believe in the acceptance of all persons in all aspects of life on the basis of individual merit and without any regard to race, color or religion. Do I mean that we are "tolerant" and that we believe in economic integration but not social integration? No, Mr. Picou, I mean we believe in being "colorblind" straight down the line!

Hefner pointed to Playboy's previous efforts in support of racial equality, from donating the opening night's proceeds from the 1959 Playboy Jazz Festival to the Chicago Urban League to maintaining the "integrated party format" of *Playboy's Penthouse*, despite the fact that its racial mixing limited the show's access to southern markets. At issue, Hefner explained, was not Playboy's policy on race, but the legal ability of the franchisee to discriminate. When the franchise owner of the Miami club barred African-American keyholders, Playboy Clubs International bought back the club. In New Orleans, however, Hefner's hands were still tied by local custom and the current arrangement with the franchisee. Not only was he personally opposed to racial discrimination, Hefner pointed out, but its persistence in a nation trying to spread its ideals abroad made the United States look positively hypocritical. "This is even more important when we, as a nation, are trying to talk others into doing business our way...to buy, as it were, franchises in our national way of doing things." The aggrieved sports

editor might return his key to Playboy for a full refund, Hefner conceded, but asked that he not do so, vowing "your key will be...a continual reminder to me that the policies at the New Orleans Playboy Club constitute a problem that must be solved in accordance with the principle of good will to all men." True to his word, the Miami club was desegregated, and within months Playboy Clubs International repurchased the New Orleans Playboy Club.[13]

Soon after, *Playboy* called attention to the clubs' integrated membership, affirming its support for racial equality while casting variety and difference as part of the recipe for urban sophistication. *Playboy* heralded the sixty-seven foreign-born Bunnies tending tables in the VIP rooms and noted that the clubs' "11 Oriental Bunnies are particularly in the limelight this year, which according to the Chinese calendar is 'The Year of the Rabbit.'" Additionally, the magazine announced, "We presently have more than 25 'Chocolate Bunnies.'" In response, one concerned reader queried, "How many chocolate keys do you hand out? I am white." *Playboy* answered, "We couldn't tell you.... The Playboy Club's membership application asks nothing about race." While supporting Hefner's personal convictions on racial equality, the club's endorsement of diversity also flowed naturally from the playboy's modern sensibilities. For the playboy, status stemmed not from racial superiority, but from tasteful consumption. "Anyone who can afford to join our club is welcome to do so," Hefner asserted. Moreover, racial understanding was a mark of sophistication. "I am the symbol of the swingingest, the heppest cat around," Hefner claimed. "Yet I have very strong beliefs in the equality of men. Just as the pipe I smoke becomes a part of the image, so will my deep convictions about human rights." As one journalist summed up, "In short, because the high priest of playboys is that way, then it's upbeat to be liberal; it's square to be prejudiced."[14]

For the hundreds of thousands of African-American readers in the 1960s who purchased *Playboy* each month, the magazine provided vicarious access to a world of pleasurable consumption, status, and sex, in which they were only gradually becoming visible.[15] For much of its first decade of publication, *Playboy* mirrored the cultural forms of the dominant society in its near exclusion of African-American men and women. Just a few months after Hefner defended his clubs against charges of racism, his magazine drew criticism for upholding whiteness as a fundamental ingredient of American beauty. In January 1962 the *Los Angeles Sentinel* reported that photographs of an African-American woman submitted for consideration as a Playmate had garnered a rejection letter from *Playboy* with the explanation: "Current policy still prohibits our featuring as Playmates any girl who is not the generally accepted idea of the all-American beauty. This makes it necessary that we eliminate foreign, Oriental, and Negro girls from consideration."

The *Sentinel*'s Stanley G. Robertson pondered the meaning of such exclusionary practices in a nation marked by racial and ethnic diversity.

> What is the generally accepted idea of the American beauty? Is she tall, short, blonde, brunette, red-headed? Green-eyed, blue-eyed, fair complexioned, dark, or is she a perfect size nine? America is a land of mixtures.... Were we living in such a country as Sweden, where their [*sic*] has not been the great inter-mingling of blood strains as here, one might determine what was the generally accepted beauty of the country. But here, where a recent survey disclosed that, for instance, only eight per cent of the total population of the U.S. are true blonds, how could one say that the generally accepted idea of the American beauty was, for instance, a blonde?

Robertson summed up, "A pretty girl is a pretty girl is a pretty girl...regardless." The *Sentinel* published Hefner's rejoinder, which, like his defense of the Playboy Clubs, expressed dismay that one facet of his enterprise was being made to stand for the whole.

> To take the words from a letter written by a secretary...and suggest that they represent...the attitude of a major publication strikes me as being most unfair. And further than that, to suggest that editorial boundaries or restrictions for a particular feature in a magazine provide evidence of some kind of racial discrimination simply does not make sense. Our Playmate feature was restricted to American beauties...does that mean we discriminate against the rest of the world? Are Negroes excluded from this definition and thus ineligible to become Playboy Playmates? Not at all.

In fact, Hefner asserted, *Playboy* had published "a Negro Playmate in the past." Linda Vargas, the light-skinned woman to whom he referred, had appeared in December 1957, described as "restless" and "lithe...as a satiny, black...cat." "What our secretary was trying to express, and did not express well," Hefner continued, "is the simple fact that the ideal Playmate type we are looking for is a girl of no clearly definable racial background—a beauty, whether dark or light; blonde, brunette or redhead: who has no strong, singular racial characteristic. And this does not refer specifically to Negro characteristics, but to Spanish, Italian, Indian, Asiatic, etc." Each Playmate, he explained, "is selected in the hope that she will represent to the widest number" of readers "the epitome of what they are thinking of as a beautiful woman."

> Now we can't do this by picking one girl one month, and a completely different kind the next month—each and every selection is an attempt to

roll all of the most beautiful, exciting, and interesting qualities in a beautiful girl into one—and each Playmate, hopefully, represents all nationalities, racial characteristics, and physical types, that exist in America.

Yet, Hefner claimed, his interest in finding "girls who represent, not one, single part of our population, but all of it" did not preclude him from considering women drawn from a diverse pool of prospective Playmates. "If I receive test photographs of a really handsome female beauty, exquisite in both face and figure," he promised, "I will want that girl as a Playboy Playmate, whether she is Negro, Chinese, Russian, or Eskimo."[16]

Not only were outside observers questioning *Playboy*'s parochial visions of beauty, staff members were taking stock of the competition. "I have it on good authority that *Cavalier* already has in the works and is planning soon to publish a Negro Playmate," A. C. Spectorsky informed Hefner in January 1963. These exchanges seem to have inspired some reconsideration of *Playboy*'s approach, for not long after, bit by bit, ethnically and racially diverse images of women began to appear in the magazine. In April 1963, *Playboy* published "a salute to the multicolored maidens of a continent of contrasts," a pictorial on "The Girls of Africa." This was a safe foray into new territory, for few of the models showcased had dark skin. The Alberto Vargas drawing in the March 1964 issue, however, was unmistakably "black," and the illustration received attention in the "Dear Playboy" section. According to one letter, "I have noticed, without approval or disapproval, the introduction and gradual increase in appearances of the American Negro in movies, television and magazines. I do not know if this is due to the efforts of integration groups or just due to the American people finally growing up. In any event, from now on, I approve." Another letter offered a more pessimistic viewpoint: "I am willing to accept equal accommodations and equal liberties, but am not willing to accept invasion of privacy in my own home. Had I desired Negro pinups, my subscription would have been mailed to *Ebony* instead of *Playboy*." The letter, signed E. A. Kucharski, warned that "any further attempts at this type of subtle indoctrination will result in immediate subscription cancellation." "So long, Mr. Kucharski," *Playboy* replied.[17]

The following March, the magazine published an African-American Playmate, Jennifer Jackson. The letters that appeared in "Dear Playboy" served to highlight the magazine's more racially inclusive approach to its pictorial features. One letter expressed dissatisfaction with the March Playmate:

We are returning the centerfold from our copy of the March issue of Playboy. Your selection of this Playmate has stirred a great deal of comment on this campus. Your right to publish anything you see fit is recognized

and not to be denied, but it must be admitted that this particular Play-mate has been met with something less than the enthusiasm for those in previous issues. At the risk of being labeled bigots, racists, reactionaries and sundry other things currently in vogue, we entreat you to return to your time-tested format of Playmate selection, which is more in line with the thinking of the vast majority of your readers.

Another praised *Playboy* for allowing the occasion to go by without remark:

Hurrahs and huzzahs are in order for the Negro Playmate of the Month and the manner in which you included her within your publication. Not once was there mention of her race or the color of her flesh; she was merely treated as simply another American young lady with the physical endowments necessary to qualify her for the pull-out page. It was a bless-ing to see her treated as just another citizen and human being—with an abundance of bodily beauty that God chose to give her.[18]

Did the appearance of African-American women in *Playboy* amount to fur-ther racial denigration by exposing black female bodies for a predominantly white male audience, or did the magazine's treatment of this Playmate "as just another citizen," as the letter noted, mark a small gesture toward racial equal-ity? As Joanne Meyerowitz has asserted, racism framed the postwar debate among African-American women over the "cheesecake" published by *Ebony* and *Negro Digest*. For some, assertions about the moral purity of African-American women served to combat racist stereotypes that had long served as a basis for white men's sexual exploitation of black women. Yet, historically, African-American women had also faced racist advertising campaigns for hair-straightening and skin-lightening products that idealized whiteness and promised to "correct" black attributes. From motion pictures to Miss America pageants, American culture continued to offer a narrow vision of female beauty as white. For those wishing to see that vision widened, rather than objectify-ing or exploiting African-American women, "cheesecake" offered "democratic social lessons" about American beauty standards. That was the sentiment of Rosemarie Tyler Brooks, a correspondent for the *Daily Defender*. "Playboy [is] to be commended for their Negro playgirl in the center of their March issue," she wrote. "Let's see more Negro beauties, Mr. Hefner."[19] *Playboy* did place more black women on the magazine's cover and showcased African-American Playmates and Bunnies. It is important to note, however, that the magazine's increasing attention to diversity also stemmed from its construc-tion of the exotic as erotic. The hedonistic bachelor enjoyed variety—lack of variety, after all, was one reason that marriage was to be forestalled. In this

regard, African-American Playmates were akin to the various foreign women who appeared in the features on "Girls of" far-flung locales, serving up a fantasy that allowed the roving playboy to add another notch on his belt. Ironically, the gradual inclusion of African-American and other non-Caucasian women in *Playboy* meant that the magazine promoted a more ethnically and racially diverse range of beauty even as it continued to promote a singular body shape as the ideal. Playmates might hail from a multitude of backgrounds, so long as they had slender frames and ample busts.

The appearance of Jennifer Jackson in *Playboy* garnered praise from the African-American press, which had challenged Hefner's exclusion of African-American women from the centerfold features. *Playboy* also received favorable attention from *Ebony,* which highlighted a young African-American man who had risen through the ranks to become manager of the Hollywood Playboy Club after Hefner observed him as a hardworking busboy at another Chicago nightspot. Columnists for the *New York Amsterdam News* and *Pittsburgh Courier* commended the Playboy Clubs' fair-minded hiring practices. Wrote a columnist about the New York Playboy Club, "Its working staff is most integrated and could serve as an example for others in town with lily-white dealings all around."[20]

In the meantime, in addition to modifying its lily-white representations of ideal beauty, the magazine had slowly offered more editorial content on African Americans' struggle for equality. *Playboy*'s attention to race began with the publication of Nat Hentoff's article, "Through the Racial Looking Glass," in July 1962. The article provided a lengthy analysis of the civil rights movement, assessing the increased militancy of many African Americans and suggesting that many white liberals were out of touch with black frustrations over gradualism. Hentoff explained the appeal of Black Muslims as well as the anguish of joblessness and inadequate education. The article became the first of many thoughtful pieces on civil rights and racial conflict. Moreover, Hentoff's article hinted at a social critique that would gain strength on college campuses and in impoverished urban centers in the coming years. Referring to the Student Non-Violent Coordinating Committee (SNCC), Hentoff wrote, its members "are not at all certain they will be content when full integration is finally achieved. They join with young Negro intellectuals in the North in questioning the essential value structures of American society." As SNCC chairman Charles McDew put it, "Too many of the 'freedom riders' don't think beyond integration. But men ought not to live and die for just washing machines and big television sets." Stated African-American novelist James Baldwin, "People always tell me how many Negroes bought Cadillacs last year. This *terrifies* me. I always wonder: Do you think this is what the country is for? Do you really think this is why I came

here, this is why I suffered, this is what I would die for? A lousy Cadillac?"[21] As Hentoff's article suggested, the consumer ethic underpinning postwar prosperity and endorsed by *Playboy* was coming under scrutiny. It would face even stronger criticism by decade's end.

In September 1962, the magazine published an interview with jazz impresario Miles Davis, which brought forth the musician's experience with the sting of racial prejudice and segregation. It also set a precedent for what became a recurring feature in the magazine—the Playboy Interview, which over the years became a forum for many notable figures to discuss racial issues. African-American author Alex Haley conducted interviews with Malcolm X (May 1963) and Martin Luther King, Jr. (January 1965). The interview with King gave the civil rights leader a forum to discuss his philosophy of nonviolence, while explaining the reality of African-American despair that had become manifest in the riots of the previous summer, sober content for a magazine that had once promised no interest in the world's problems. *Playboy* also published writings by Baldwin and James Farmer, a founder of the Congress of Racial Equality (CORE). The inclusion of these interviews and writers, timely features that also reflected the editors' liberal viewpoints, marked the magazine's growing maturity and presence in the publishing world as a venue for top-notch reportage.[22] *Playboy*'s attention to racial equality extended beyond the pages of the magazine. Hefner supported numerous civil rights organizations and provided $25,000 in reward money for information to aid in the search for James Chaney, Andrew Goodman, and Michael Schwerner, the three civil rights workers slain in Philadelphia, Mississippi, in June 1964. "Every American has a stake in this situation," Hefner asserted as he explained his support for the cause. "It goes beyond any question of race, creed, or color—to the very heart of our democratic system—to the right of every individual to full protection of his life and liberty under the law. It is apparent that without these protections, democracy—and society itself—would fail."[23]

For the publication that emerged six months before the *Brown v. Board of Education* ruling ordered desegregation in the nation's schools, the status line, not the color line, was what mattered. As an exemplar of the good life, an authoritative voice on American beauty, and a proponent of liberal values and individual freedom, *Playboy* was drawn into the public discourse on racial equality. Black publishers tried to extend *Playboy*'s editorial package to an audience of African-American males. Others challenged racial discrimination in *Playboy*'s clubs and in its pictorial features. These episodes highlight not only an important cultural dimension of the civil rights movement, but also *Playboy*'s ascendancy. Even as its limited vision of female attractiveness was questioned, for example, *Playboy*'s powerful role as arbiter of American beauty

was affirmed by such attention. And Hefner's complaints that the New Orleans club was being singled out by critics were not totally unwarranted; indeed, it was *Playboy*'s meteoric ascent and its promise that anyone could achieve its version of the good life that made it a highly visible target of protest. As the struggle for racial equality surged forward, *Playboy*'s attention to the civil rights movement provided readers, both black and white, with thoughtful and impassioned commentary. In line with Hefner's personal convictions, the magazine's liberal viewpoint also fit well *Playboy*'s image of forward-thinking urbanity. After all, much of Hefner's philosophy was given over to lengthy discussions of the rights of the individual in a free society. But if *Playboy* cared more about the status line than the color line, the latter directly impeded African Americans' ability to achieve upward mobility. The stylish way of life that inspired *Duke* was compelling, but often frustratingly beyond reach.

SINGLEHOOD IN POPULAR CULTURE

As *Duke* and other *Playboy* imitators embraced imagery of fun-loving bachelorhood, the suave, sophisticated, single man also became increasingly visible on television and in motion pictures in the late 1950s and 1960s. *Love That Bob,* which aired from 1955 to 1959 and starred Bob Cummings, featured a single guy who encountered numerous young female models through his job as a photographer. Though Cummings dated many women, his bachelorhood was disarmed through his domesticity. He lived with his widowed sister and her teenage son, acting as a surrogate father for his nephew. Similarly, the carefree Beverly Hills attorney in *Bachelor Father* (1957–1962) lived in a penthouse apartment and watched over an orphaned thirteen-year-old niece. The bachelor in *A Family Affair* (1966–1971) inherited a brood of young charges. CBS's *Bringing up Buddy* (1960–1961) followed the comedic trials of a young investment broker who boarded with spinster aunts who were constantly trying to find him a wife. As the decade progressed, such characters began to lose their family-oriented domestic roles. The reincarnation of *Love That Bob* as *The Bob Cummings Show* in 1961–1962 offered a harbinger of things to come. In the new show, Cummings played wealthy Bob Carson, an un-chaperoned, woman-chasing adventurer.[24]

The carefree bachelor made many appearances on the big screen. Perhaps none was more memorable than Rock Hudson's portrayal of Brad Allen opposite Doris Day in the 1959 comedy *Pillow Talk*. The film presented a "boy meets girl" scenario in which the end (seducing the girl) justified the means (pretending to be another man). In the film, Brad, who shares a party line with Jan, is

forever tying up the telephone as he woos his many female conquests. When the two finally meet, Brad recognizes that Jan is not the type of woman to fall for his usual flattery, so he adopts another persona, that of the conscientious, sensitive Rex Stetson. A cad who knows women, he speculates that it will take five dates to work this deception and get Jan into bed. Although Brad and Jan marry at the end of the film, *Pillow Talk* sanctioned Brad's wild-oat-sowing phase of prolonged bachelorhood.

The playboy appeared in various other personages as well. Dean Martin's 1959 hit recording of the duet "Baby, It's Cold Outside" conveyed the verbal dance between a smooth-talking playboy and his hesitant mate. Ignoring his companion's claims that she "really must go," the male figure in these lyrics plies her with drinks and compliments, while dismissing her fears of a damaged reputation should she spend the night. The pop standard might have been the anthem for a generation of young swingers intent on overcoming the reluctance of "nice girls." In 1961, actor Tony Curtis was slated to portray Hugh Hefner in a film about *Playboy*.[25] Although this project never materialized due to disagreements over the script, Curtis portrayed another carefree bachelor in the comedy *Boeing, Boeing* (1965). Curtis played a foreign correspondent whose Paris bachelor pad served as the staging ground for trysts with three airline stewardesses, whom he maneuvers in and out of his apartment with clockwork precision. The playboy's pursuit of sexual pleasure without commitment was also well encapsulated in a statement uttered by Frank Sinatra's character Danny Ocean in the film *Ocean's Eleven* (1960). Confronted by an irate woman demanding to know where he has been since their sexual encounter, Ocean coolly replies:

> I picked you up at the Biltmore bar because I thought you were attractive and I had nothing better to do, and I made a pass at you for the very same reasons. Now I don't know what your reasons were but nobody twisted your arm, made you any promises. So what is this act? Not outraged virtue!

In a few short lines, Sinatra's character denounced the moral pretenses surrounding sexual activity and declared a male right to sex with no strings attached.

Ocean's Eleven presented a group of middle-aged army buddies who lounge and drink, play cards and shoot pool as they plan the perfect caper—the simultaneous heist of five Las Vegas casinos. The film's spectacle of relaxation evoked the playboy's easygoing style, but it was the antics that surrounded the filmmaking that made it especially noteworthy. *Ocean's Eleven* brought together a cast of real-life characters—Frank Sinatra, Dean Martin, Peter Lawford, Sammy

Davis, Jr., and Joey Bishop—for a month of film production by day and well-publicized appearances at the Las Vegas Sands Hotel by night. The extended after-hours party, dubbed the "Meeting at the Summit," typified the ascendance of the playboy's cultural style.[26]

Heralded as the ringleader of the "Rat Pack," Sinatra rose to stardom in the 1940s by capturing the hearts of young bobby-soxers. His public affair in 1949 with Hollywood starlet Ava Gardner, however, tarnished his reputation as a wholesome family man and damaged his career. Sinatra suffered a decline, in part owing to the scandal surrounding his private life. A career-saving role in *From Here to Eternity* (1953) fueled a comeback, and by the late 1950s, he had established a new persona as cool playboy, on-screen in such films as *Pal Joey* (1957) and *Ocean's Eleven* and offscreen as well. Hefner was a longtime fan of Sinatra, but the performer's evolution from teen idol to swinging hipster brought many more men into the ranks of his followers, fans who appreciated his style as well as his music. Sinatra's womanizing, detrimental to his earlier wholesome image, now formed one facet of a total package that made him the object of both adulation and envy. With his recordings for Capitol Records, including such albums as *Songs for Swingin' Lovers, Nice 'n' Easy, Swing Easy,* and *A Swingin' Affair,* Sinatra and his sound, as James Smith writes, "seemed to define the 'cool' of the adult postwar world as dry martinis became the drink of choice in the cities and suburbs of modern America."[27]

Sinatra used his stature in the show-business world to orchestrate everything from movie parts to nightclub bookings so he and his pals could have fun together. As members of the Rat Pack, these entertainers achieved iconic status with their hip, cool style and reputation as all-around playboys. Like Hefner's, their work often seemed like play, and they played with abandon. Together they made movies, performed at the nation's biggest clubs, cut records on Sinatra's record label, cavorted and chased women, and drank, smoked, and gambled into the wee hours of the morning. Although all were at one time or another married with children, they achieved their greatest acclaim at a time when they publicly reveled in a hedonistic bachelor lifestyle. In their notorious late-night carousing, they rejected the domesticated duties of marriage and fatherhood. That so much of their revelry centered on Las Vegas signaled its importance as a place that epitomized the ascendance of a pleasure-seeking ethos in postwar America. Home to opulent casinos and hotels and saturated in sex, drinking, and gambling, this leisure destination upended values of sobriety, self-restraint, and sexual conservatism. Las Vegas made the perfect home for the Rat Pack, who made a spectacle of living by their own rules and thumbed their noses at middle-class propriety and its demands for responsible manhood. Like the models and Playmates

who decorated the set of television's *Playboy's Penthouse,* actresses, showgirls, and other young women—easily discarded and replaced—served as window dressing for their fun. As with the playboy, the rebellious nature of Sinatra and his Rat Pack was a matter of lifestyle. They were not antiestablishment; on the contrary, they participated in a thriving industry that helped fuel the engines of consumer capitalism. Through their personal style and sexual behavior, however, they asserted their independence, challenged conservative mores, and espoused self-indulgence.

While the members of the Rat Pack enacted a hedonistic leisure style, spy novelist Ian Fleming's character, "Bond...James Bond," embodied the playboy's consumer skills and seductive prowess. Agent 007 of the British Secret Service dressed impeccably in hand-tailored suits, relished gourmet food and expensive liquor, and obsessed over exclusive brand-name goods. The ultimate connoisseur, Bond demonstrated his polished taste in all manners of consumption, from his "shaken, not stirred" dry martinis, to his specially crafted brand of cigarettes, to his high performance automobiles. As agent 007, Bond traveled the globe in a series of adventures, defeating villains with high-tech gadgetry and bedding a string of beautiful women along the way.

The hero of Fleming's spy thrillers first appeared in the novel *Casino Royale* in 1953, the same year *Playboy* debuted, and appealed to British audiences for much the same reason Hefner's magazine found success in postwar America. Bond's attention to top of the line products and elaborate meals struck a chord with readers just beginning to enjoy plenitude after years of hardship. More than just a spy thriller, a Bond novel, like *Playboy,* offered a fantasy world that indulged one's sensual appetites on every level, with generous descriptions of fast cars, luxury goods, and liberated sexual encounters. "I write for warm-blooded heterosexuals in railway trains, aeroplanes and beds," noted Fleming of his James Bond series. As he admitted, the target of the books "lay somewhere between the solar plexus, and well, the upper thigh." Readers on both sides of the Atlantic vicariously experienced Bond's unbridled sex life and affluent lifestyle. Moreover, the novels presented exotic locales as the object of Bond's (and the reader's) gaze and constructed "the girl" as the object of a voyeuristic look. In this manner, as Tony Bennett and Janet Woollacott put it, Bond, as bearer of the "license to look" also possessed a "license to consume" foreign spectacles, women, and commodities. As such, like the playboy, he provided a model for masculinity well attuned to modern consumer capitalism.[28] Fleming wrote fourteen Bond stories prior to his death in 1964. Film adaptations of *Dr. No* in 1962 and *From Russia with Love* in 1963 brought Bond to the big screen, greatly increasing his exposure and popularity; the release of *Goldfinger* in 1964 triggered what *Time* magazine called "Bondomania."[29]

Played by actor Sean Connery, the screen-Bond was in many ways the quint-essential playboy. A refined yet virile action hero, Bond derived pleasure from the finer things. He also liked to exhibit his impressive knowledge for others, and even used his connoisseurship to thwart his foes. In *Dr. No,* Bond picks up a bottle of champagne to use as a weapon. "That's a Dom Perignon '55, it would be a pity to break it," Dr. No tells him. Bond replies, "I prefer the '53 myself," an assertion of both his superior taste and his sense of humor. In *Diamonds Are Forever* (1971), his knowledge of clarets enables him to identify a foe imperson-ating a steward on a cruise ship. Bond's gourmet tastes represented just one commonality with the playboy. Just as *Playboy*'s bachelor pads and modern-living features fetishized masculine gadgetry, Bond films highlighted far-out technology. In each film, Bond thwarted enemies with the clever devices pro-vided by his inventive colleague, Q. Similarly, like the globetrotting playboy presented in the magazine, Bond's exploits took place against a backdrop of far-flung locales. And, like the playboy, Bond frequently indulged his appetite for women.

Just as each new issue of *Playboy* showcased a different Playmate of the Month, each new Bond novel or film featured a new "girl," notable for her exotic persona and suggestive identity—Pussy Galore, Kissy Suzuki, and Honeychile Rider, to name but a few. Like a solicitous Bunny or Single Girl, many of the girls whom Bond encountered eagerly put themselves in his service. When that was not the case, Bond's sexual prowess gave him the ability to win women over to his cause, whether they started out on the side of the villain or whether they initially claimed to have no sexual interest in him. Referring to a scene in *Goldfinger,* one *Playboy* writer remarked on this phenomenon, "When [Bond] desperately needs to convert Pussy Galore into an ally, his most potent weapon is himself," a fact that led this writer to ponder just what was "mightier than the sword."

Before Bond ever appeared on the big screen, *Playboy* reported Ian Fleming's gratifying observation that if Bond were a real person, he would no doubt be a reader of the magazine. The obvious connections between the fictional Bond and the playboy were strengthened when *Playboy* serialized *On Her Majesty's Secret Service, You Only Live Twice,* and *The Man with the Golden Gun* between 1963 and 1965 and began running "Bond-girl" pictorials to coincide with the release of each new film (see figure 5.2). Interviews with Fleming and Connery further enhanced the ties. In addition to translating to the screen much of the magazine's iconography of the cosmopolitan ladies' man, the films made overt reference to the kinship between *Playboy* and Bond. In a scene from *On Her Majesty's Secret Service,* 007 perused a copy of *Playboy; Diamonds Are Forever* allowed audiences to see the contents of Bond's wallet, revealing his Playboy Club Key Card.[30]

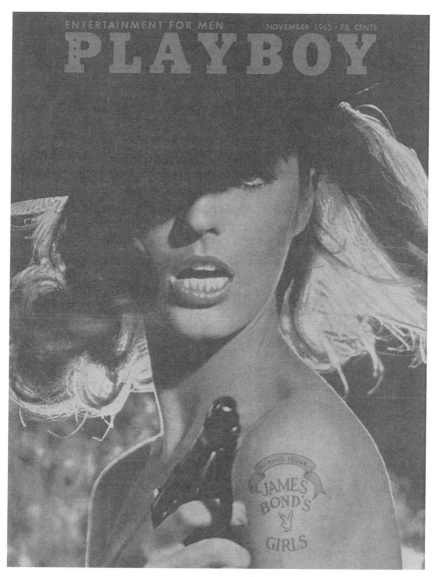

5.2 *The women who starred in Bond films also appeared in* Playboy. *Along with a pictorial on "James Bond's Girls," this issue featured an interview with actor Sean Connery, who portrayed agent 007 on the screen. In the 1960s, Playboy serialized several of Ian Fleming's James Bond novels and promoted the Bond films, fueling the popularity of the suave action hero. (Reproduced by special permission of* Playboy *magazine © November 1965 by Playboy.)*

Bond reached the status of "popular hero" in the mid-1960s, bringing an explosion of press coverage and Bond-themed merchandise and advertising. Colgate-Palmolive launched the 007 line of men's toiletries, with a misogynistic slogan that called forth the linkage of seduction and masculine power in the Bond narratives: "007 gives any man the license to kill...women." During this period, sales of Fleming's Bond novels peaked, and several other Bond-inspired playboy-spy-adventure films appeared. James Coburn played swinging bachelor Derek Flint in *Our Man Flint* (1966) and *In Like Flint* (1967), entertaining four women in his flower-shaped bed. Dean Martin starred in the Matt Helm series beginning in the mid-1960s. In the first film, *The Silencers* (1966), retired spy Helm worked as a men's magazine centerfold photographer until he was called back into service. In the series, Helm lived in a plush bachelor pad complete with fabulous technological accouterments, including a mechanized bed that transported him to a swimming-pool-sized bubble bath. Like Bond, Matt Helm and Derek Flint encountered plenty of available young females.[31]

The "Bond girl" became a cultural phenomenon, helped along by pictorials in *Playboy* and other men's magazines such as *Mayfair*. Significantly, the pictorials became a contractual obligation for the actresses who played Bond's companions. *Playboy* even teamed with United Artists to sponsor a James Bond Girl contest that awarded the winner a role in a subsequent 007 film. Like the Playmate, the Bond girl made no demands for security and marriage. Providing voyeuristic pleasure, she also embodied unencumbered sexuality. Each new Bond girl was "totally lacking in deference, independent, self-reliant, yet also caring, loving, solicitous for Bond's well-being and willing to cater to his every need without making any demands in return"—qualities reminiscent of the Single Girl envisioned by Helen Gurley Brown.[32] Thus, like the Playmate and Single Girl, the Bond girl enjoyed sex outside of the marriage bed, but put herself and her sexuality in service to the male figure in her life.

Beyond the Bond girl, other variants of the Single Girl permeated the nation's entertainment forms in the 1960s and into the next decade. Already a bestseller, *Sex and the Single Girl* received wider notice with the release of a movie version under the same title. On television, the Single Girl appeared in new programs that spotlighted the unmarried working girl while also fitting her safely within acceptable limits of independence and gender advancement. *That Girl* (1966–1971), although ostensibly devoted to the self-sufficient life of a young working girl, contained the independence of the lead character, Ann Marie, through the presence of the men in her life, an overprotective father and a fiancée. Her independence was prelude to marriage. Indeed, *That Girl* went off the air with Ann Marie bound for the altar. Mary Richards, the central character of *The Mary Tyler Moore Show* (1970–1977), took the concept of the

independent career girl further, as Mary remained single throughout the show and succeeded at her job. However, she too remained bound by her relationship to her paternalistic boss and played a "mothering" role to her friends and coworkers. Much as Bob Cummings's domestic life served to contain his bachelorhood, Mary Richards brought her domesticity into the workplace, enacting socially prescribed femininity in a new setting, a formula one scholar described as "Donna Reed repackaged as a working woman."[33]

SEXUAL REVOLUTION AND THE "SWINGLES"

Hefner's vision of the good life was premised on the notion that sex was not a sin. Moreover, he asserted, strictures on sexual expression amounted to censorship and denied an adult interest in sex. More and more in the 1960s, American culture seemed to support this view. The boundaries that governed sexual expression expanded rapidly and dramatically in the second half of the decade, and in a climate of lowered inhibitions, popular culture became saturated with sex. *Time* magazine commented on the proliferation of "Spectator Sex—what may be seen and read" in a feature on "the Second Sexual Revolution" in January 1964. Sex was in the spotlight, from the availability of previously banned literary works such as D. H. Lawrence's *Lady Chatterley's Lover* and Henry Miller's *Tropic of Cancer* and *Tropic of Capricorn* to the cheap, sex-themed novels on display in drugstores and the increasingly risqué nudes found in "girlie" magazines. Fashions for American women featured lowered necklines, as well as dramatically raised hemlines with the advent of the miniskirt. Hollywood films also focused greater attention on sex.

Through the magazine, his "philosophy," and many public speaking engagements, Hefner in the 1960s acted the part of crusader attempting to free society from puritanical constraints. Commencing in 1963, the Playboy Forum, "an interchange of ideas between reader and editor on subjects raised by 'the playboy philosophy,'" became a vehicle for addressing a wide range of issues pertaining to social and sexual repression. Initially seeded with letters crafted by Playboy Forum editor Anson Mount, the monthly feature attacked society's moral and legal strictures concerning sex. Repealing antiquated sex laws, protesting obscenity rulings, supporting advances in birth control and the legalization of abortion, and extricating sex from the marital bed all served as rallying points in *Playboy*'s fight for sexual and personal freedom.

As *Time* astutely recognized, the "sexual bombardment" observed in 1964 was closely tied to a widespread transformation in values. "It is part and symptom

of an era in which morals are widely held to be both private and relative, in which pleasure is increasingly considered an almost constitutional right rather than a privilege, in which self-denial is increasingly seen as foolishness rather than virtue." At the same time, while personal pleasure was elevated to the status of individual right, traditional checks on sexual behavior were eroding. As *Time* pointed out, advances in science and technology had eased fears of such "earthly dangers" as venereal disease and pregnancy. Health care practitioners had begun successfully treating gonorrhea and syphilis with penicillin in the 1950s, and the Food and Drug Administration approved the birth control pill in 1960. The view that "nice girls don't" was also weakening. Attitudes toward premarital sex were relaxing, at least among young people, creating the perception of a more "permissive society." "In short," *Time* concluded, "the Puritan ethic, so long the dominant moral force in the U.S., is widely considered to be dying, if not dead, and there are few mourners."

The trends *Time* identified only intensified as the decade continued. Key Supreme Court decisions in 1966 and 1967 further constricted the parameters of obscenity, enabling purveyors of sex-themed books and magazines to expand their operations and to make their subject matter more explicit. Independent films and foreign movies, which fell outside the purview of the Production Code Administration, had, beginning in the 1950s, gradually undermined Hollywood's self-censorship guidelines. In 1968, the Production Code was abandoned, replaced by a ratings system that did away with censorship in favor of regulations that segmented audiences by age. The new system opened the floodgates for films that dealt with a variety of adult-themed material, including the graphic portrayal of sex. By decade's end, Broadway theaters showcased productions of *Hair* and *Oh! Calcutta!* whose cast members performed in the nude. The liberalization of obscenity laws and the proliferation of sexually explicit material rested on a growing conviction that lines between morality and immorality, good taste and bad, could not be drawn by a few individuals purportedly acting in the public interest. More than ever, determinations about the value of such material were being left to consumers to decide in the marketplace.

The advent of oral contraceptives did not immediately lead to their extensive use by single women, nor did the widespread "promiscuity" associated with the "sexual revolution" occur until the 1970s. Critical developments received notice in the 1960s, however. As with the liberalization of obscenity laws, shifts in sexual attitudes and behaviors were grounded in long-term developments as well as unintended consequences. Mass media and the market economy had steadily eroded traditional forms of moral authority, for instance. And advocates of the birth control pill sought to remedy a "population explosion," not to pave the way for sexual emancipation. While some media accounts, *Playboy*'s

among them, emphasized the most radical activities of the sexual revolution, more important is the extent to which mainstream Americans gradually came to view premarital sex as an acceptable activity and abandoned the notion that a woman's virtue was the measure of her worth.[34] The singles culture of the 1960s was an important barometer of this change.

In his 1958 book, *Sex without Guilt,* Albert Ellis advocated for premarital sex as a healthy form of enjoyment, querying, "Why *must* everyone marry to be a good citizen?" Beginning in the 1960s, the proportion of unmarried men and women living singly or with nonfamily members increased dramatically. In their attitudes and behaviors, many of these young singles seemed to echo the sentiments expressed by spokespersons such as Ellis, Hefner, and Helen Gurley Brown, as they embraced the possibility of sex "without benefit of marriage." College campuses served as important arenas where the new sexual liberalism took hold. The nation's cities, which nurtured an urban singles culture, formed another front. The singles culture was fueled by a high standard of living that made it possible for men and women to forego marriage and live apart from family members. It was also shepherded along by changing attitudes and cultural forms that took a more relaxed view toward delayed marriage. In this regard, the Single Girl and the playboy served as prototypes for the emerging culture of the "swinging singles." Fitting well within the consumer economy, young middle-class singles were glamorized in marketing and advertising that invoked images of sex, youth, and pleasure.[35]

Numerous commercial ventures, from singles bars to apartment complexes, catered to unmarried men and women, sanctioning the shift away from early marriage and moving the cultural focus from the family to the youthful individual. During the 1960s, the explosion in single-family home developments of the previous decade gave way to a resurgence of apartment-building construction. Whereas earlier views estimated apartments as places "for the newlywed and nearly dead," by the mid-1960s, large luxury apartment projects were under way in urban centers. Marina Towers in Chicago and United Nations Plaza in Manhattan were harbingers of the new trend in multiunit housing. At Marina Towers, "a city within a city" that promised plush surroundings, vibrant urban living, and ample opportunities for recreation and fun, singles made up two-thirds of inhabitants; most married residents were couples without children. The building manager admitted that apartments were distributed with a view to mixing residents by gender, remarking, "I didn't want a fraternity on one floor and a sorority on the next." Marina Towers appeared in *Playboy* in the late 1960s in advertisements for liquor and binoculars, the latter implying that the venue was good for girl watching. The site earned a reputation as something of a swinging locale. One apocryphal tale even told of residents climbing up and down the balconies of the sixty-story corncob-like structures to swap mates.[36]

Along with building high-rise rental units, developers kept pace with the growing number of single men and women by creating multiunit complexes in the suburbs. New publications such as *Apartment Ideas* appealed to the singles crowd and emphasized sex and high living in their advertising. The "swinging singles" market even inspired the name taken by a major furniture rental company—Swingles, which encouraged customers in its brochures to "rent a fantasy." The attractive "apartment lifestyle" centered on the swimming pools, party rooms, and other amenities built into the resort-style complexes around the country. In Hefner's hometown of Chicago, the boom in high-rise apartment buildings transformed the streetscape north of downtown. By the early 1970s, developers there unabashedly targeted "swinging singles" with an amenity-laden, no-children-allowed complex named The Satyr. According to its rental agent, the development was meant to be "something akin to the Playboy image." Brochures advertised it as a residence "for lovers and livers...for HEdonists and SHEdonists...Anything goes...!"[37]

For young men and women in the middle-class singles scene, moving after college into a high-rise apartment boasting a rooftop pool and a party almost every night provided an exciting alternative to getting tied down immediately in the role of spouse or parent. In the context of a popular culture that glamorized singlehood as well as the relaxed mores of the "permissive society," staying single for both men and women carried fewer negative connotations and evoked less criticism than it had during the rush to marriage in the 1950s. With less social pressure to marry, greater acceptance of premarital sex, the widespread availability of the birth control pill by the late 1960s, and a growing network of cultural institutions and entertainments geared especially for them, many young men and women began to view an extended period of singlehood as a normal and attractive part of the lifecycle. Indulging a desire to have fun and try new experiences, singles worked, traveled, dated, enjoyed sex—some in exclusive, monogamous relationships, others on a more casual basis—and partook in the city's growing singles scene, socializing with the other young men and women who lived in their buildings and spending time in nearby singles bars. This extended youth culture represented a significant manifestation of "the playboy life."

HIPPIE HEDONISM AND THE PLAYBOY LIFE

As the singles culture reveled in material abundance and navigated the increasingly permissive sexual frontier, others registered concern that American affluence had created a morally and spiritually impoverished society. The optimism

of John F. Kennedy's New Frontier, with which the 1960s began, gave way to growing frustrations and skepticism as the decade progressed. The gradual integrationist approach of the civil rights movement and the egalitarian impulses of Lyndon Johnson's Great Society programs brought no end to racial inequality, urban decline, and stubborn poverty. Faith in economic growth, liberal social change, and Cold War foreign policy was shaken as American cities erupted in racial violence and the nation became embroiled in a war in Southeast Asia.

Writing at a time when unrest on college campuses and criticism of American prosperity was becoming widespread, David Halberstam pondered the aspirations for the good life held by the people he had come to know during his stay in Poland.

> It is something basic as a goal to East Europe, where it does not exist, and difficult to explain in America, where it does and where, indeed, much of the turmoil on campus seems to be in part a revolt against affluence. It includes a decent apartment without uncles and grandmothers, a car, a record player, a pretty girl who can make love without producing children. There is Scotch whiskey there, and the people wear sweaters and blue jeans.[38]

Halberstam presented a glimpse of one perspective from which the growing sexual permissiveness and material well being found in the United States might be envied. If it provided dream fodder for those living outside its reach, however, for young Americans in the student movement and counterculture of the 1960s, the affluent society was a source of growing disdain.

As they issued the Port Huron Statement in 1962, the young people of Students for a Democratic Society (SDS)—"bred in at least modest comfort, housed now in universities, looking uncomfortably to the world we inherit"— were products of the same postwar prosperity that made possible the realization of "the playboy life." In this statement and elsewhere as the decade progressed, young people of the New Left launched a scathing appraisal of a society marred by social regimentation, inequality, complacency, and rampant consumerism. In rhetoric that was often ambitious and idealistic, they spoke in vague but impassioned terms about creating a society based on participatory democracy, where the poverty and racism that persisted under the status quo would be obliterated. The New Left formed one facet of an inchoate mass of students, organizations, activists, and ordinary young men and women that together constituted a wider youth movement of the 1960s.[39] Young people on the left coalesced around multiple issues. Students fought for free speech on college campuses and agitated for civil rights. They protested American policies and military action in Vietnam. More broadly, they attacked the social, economic,

and political institutions that upheld the facade of democracy while breeding conformity and materialism.

Young people's opposition to mainstream values was expressed through the style of the counterculture, whose adherents adopted a bohemian way of life in urban enclaves and college towns throughout America. "Hippies" distanced themselves from the norms and institutions of American society through a variety of ways. Their long, unkempt hair and colorful, free-flowing clothing styles mocked the staid look of the button-down set. They sought out promiscuous sexual relationships in the name of "free love" and lived communally, challenging both monogamy and marriage. They experimented with psychedelic drugs as they tuned into a rock-music sound geared to youth, and they were enthralled with Eastern religion and mysticism. Forging an identity through personal style and cultural practice, the counterculture embraced values of self-expression, personal freedom, community, and pleasure.[40]

The decade's upheavals informed *Playboy*'s editorial viewpoint. In addition to its attention to the civil rights movement, the magazine assessed America's involvement in Vietnam as that conflict polarized the nation. From an initial feature documenting one Playmate's morale-boosting visit with U.S. troops in Southeast Asia, *Playboy* went on to adopt a critical stance against the war, providing space for incisive condemnation of U.S. foreign policy (see figure 5.3). At the same time, *Playboy* highlighted young people's experimentation with alternative lifestyles, while affirming American consumerism. Editorial fare sympathized with the disaffection expressed by young people in the student movement. "Youth—the Oppressed Majority," for example, examined curfews, police harassment of minors, and campus parietal hours. Author Nat Hentoff gave voice to contempt for a higher education system that processed young people into parts for a social order they had no hand in creating but were expected to accept. *Playboy* tuned in to the sensibilities of the counterculture as well. The 1967 hippie-orchestrated "Human Be-In" in San Francisco prompted a lengthy article on the multifaceted youth movement taking shape across America. Herbert Gold's essay, "The Wave Makers," offered a comprehensive assessment, tracing the youth movement's relationship to the earlier Beats, examining the politics of the New Left, and outlining the cultural and sexual practices embraced by the counterculture. Harvard theologian Harvey Cox published a sympathetic piece on "God and the Hippies" that appraised the shortcomings of American society and Western religion and gave credence to young people's search for authentic experience. And a September "back to school" issue tapped into the tumultuous college scene with a Playboy Panel on the student revolt as well as a detailed report on campus sex.

5.3 *Playmate Jo Collins visited U.S. troops in Vietnam after GIs wrote to* Playboy *requesting a lifetime subscription. An earlier* Playboy *promotion had promised that lifetime subscribers would receive their first issue hand-delivered by a Playmate.* Playboy's *coverage of the morale-boosting visit gave way to somber reassessments of U.S. foreign policy as the war intensified and polarized the nation. (Reproduced by special permission of* Playboy *magazine © May 1966 by Playboy.)*

Playboy's coverage of drugs and sex and its embrace of a psychedelic aesthetic also helped position the magazine within the emergent youth counterculture. LSD guru Timothy Leary was the subject of a Playboy Interview, and articles such as "Sex, Ecstasy, and the Psychedelic Drugs" focused on drug use and heightened sexual pleasure. *Playboy*'s "Duplex Penthouse," a commissioned bachelor pad design that boasted a "kinetic bedchamber," also took sex and the drug culture into account. Unlike previous bachelor pads, this one's accessories were geared less to seduction and more toward adapting the environment to enhance sexual experience. "Being turned on electronically by whatever feeds you and your date's audio-visual fantasies is really the name of the bed-game," *Playboy* explained. In this room, "a battery of projectors" transformed the bedroom into "an electric circus of swirling colors that contrast with blinking strobes fired in time to your choice of freaky far-out sounds." Or, alternatively, "the room can glow like an ember, the walls and ceiling pleasantly pulsating,

while you're serenaded by sounds more soothingly conducive to matters at hand." Here was a bachelor pad inspired by the trippy, acid rock light shows of a Grateful Dead concert.[41] Along these lines, *Playboy*'s December 1967 issue featured a cover girl with pink and green psychedelic Bunny ears.

If the bachelor pad decked out with high-end furnishings and stocked with gourmet foods bore only passing resemblance to a hippie "crash pad," the playboy and the hippie still shared important similarities. The counterculture separated sex from marriage, its most utopian members imagining sex as a vehicle for communication, authentic experience, and pleasure. Hefner had long promoted sex for its own sake—because sexuality was a central facet of the human condition, and because it was pleasurable—and in this regard, the hippie's embrace of "free love," unfettered by social conventions and marriage vows, was the apotheosis of this stance. The use of psychedelic drugs, whether to augment the sexual experience or to expand one's consciousness, was similarly in keeping with a philosophy that placed so much emphasis on the individual's pleasure and self-fulfillment.

Among dissenters and their supporters, however, *Playboy*'s purported role as a force of personal liberation prompted skepticism. If *Playboy* could figure prominently in aspirations for the good life, it also served as a telling example of all that was wrong with the prosperous, technocratic society of America, according to one observer. Addressing the discontent expressed by student activists, Vietnam War protestors, and young bohemians, Theodore Roszak, in his 1969 work, *The Making of a Counter Culture*, described the soul-crushing effects of the "technocracy," the social form of an industrial society that had achieved total "organizational integration." Managed by vast reaches of experts and resting on an abiding faith in science and technological progress, this bureaucratized, automated society had sucked the life out of human relationships and created a world without mystery, community, or authenticity. Nothing was beyond its reach:

> Politics, education, leisure, entertainment, culture as a whole, the unconscious drives, and even...protest against the technocracy itself: all of these become the subjects of purely technical scrutiny and of purely technical manipulation. The effort is to create a new social organism whose health depends upon its capacity to keep the technological heart beating regularly.

According to Roszak, the technocratic Leviathan ruled neither by the bullet nor the bayonet. Rather, the system maintained assent through its capacity to provide satisfactions that bred submission and undermined protest. Roszak drew on *Playboy* as his prime example to illustrate this insidious process. Within

the consumer society, he asserted, sexual liberation was a facade, merely "the *Playboy* version of total permissiveness which now imposes its image upon us in every slick movie and posh magazine that comes along." Roszak explained:

> In the affluent society, we have sex and sex galore—or so we are to believe. But when we look more closely we see that this sybaritic promiscuity wears a special social coloring. It has been assimilated to an income level and social status available only to our well-heeled junior executives and the jet set. After all, what does it cost to rent these yachts full of nymphomaniacal young things in which our playboys sail off for orgiastic swimming parties in the Bahamas? *Real* sex, we are led to believe, is something that goes with the best scotch, twenty-seven dollar sunglasses, and platinum-tipped shoelaces. Anything less is a shabby substitute. Yes, there is permissiveness in the technocratic society; but it is only for the swingers and the big spenders.

Hefner had trumpeted a slick, sexualized version of the good life as the payoff for hard work in the consumer society. For Roszak, the commodified version of sexuality put forth by *Playboy* was an exercise in hegemonic power. Hefner's version of the good life was in essence "the reward that goes to reliable, politically safe henchmen of the status quo."[42]

Indeed, for as much as Hefner positioned his magazine as a mouthpiece for rebellion, *Playboy* now represented an important element of the status quo. The opposition to social constraints registered in its pages called for a stylish, sexually alluring posture fashioned around a carefully selected array of commodities. For the same reason Hefner had rejected the Beats, then, *Playboy* was at odds with the counterculture's antimaterialism. One achieved fulfillment through the material rewards that came from participating in economic life, not by "dropping out." In this regard, *Playboy*'s embrace of hippie style in the late 1960s was akin to many other attempts to cash in on the lucrative appeal, rather than the transformative goals, of a photogenic counterculture. Hippie style garnered attention from the "establishment" in the form of the national media and corporate America, whose efforts helped congeal a discernable counterculture while also blunting the oppositional power of its early adherents. Advertisers used "flower-power" imagery to market their products, tying consumption to youthful rebellion. As scholars have demonstrated, those with no interest in dropping out of society and relinquishing material aspirations could still partake in the rebellious atmosphere by sporting long hair and embracing the colorful fashions of the "Peacock Revolution."[43]

If the mass media played a role in giving form to the counterculture, cultural radicals, from their perspective, sensed the power of the marketplace

and expressed concern about its ability to co-opt what they viewed as their culture.[44] When, for example, the major media attention paid to the "Human Be-In" inspired swarms of young people to descend upon Haight-Ashbury, one of the counterculture's earliest groups, The Diggers, held a ceremony marking the "death of the hippie." The radical press expressed similar suspicion about *Playboy*'s attention to the drug scene. Articles appearing in several underground newspapers asserted that *Playboy*, "read by far more pot smokers than any other non-news magazine," was quietly "jockeying for a position to capitalize on legalized marijuana." Citing Hefner's support in the founding of NORML, the National Organization for the Reform of Marijuana Laws, one critic warned, "If *Playboy* could become the popular figure-head of the legalized marijuana movement...Hugh Hefner would be hailed a hero, a far-sighted crusader of social change, and everybody would buy *Playboy*'s brand of marijuana cigarettes." Given its swinging image and marketing expertise, *Playboy* seemed well suited to the task. "Hefner is an expert at commercializing pleasure," this author cautioned. As with so much of the ground staked out by the counterculture, the threat of yet another realm falling prey to these co-opting forces loomed large in this writer's mind. "Many marijuana smokers are having second thoughts about legalization of grass," he concluded, "fearing established corporations will monopolize the market to fatten their own pockets." The underground newspaper *Kaleidoscope* complained, "Rock, sex, communes, superstars, drugs, commix, and a far-out playmate foldout. That's the youth culture right? It sure ain't revolutionary culture but it is the name of the latest sexist shit to slither out of the Playboy Press." This author warned, "Yep, they're trying to co-opt us once again kids. This time it's a bunch of male pigs who want to expand their scope of operations to include US. Instead of nude straight women with set hair, we're now being told to objectify 'hippy chickies' wearing love beads. Far-out man." A letter in the Playboy Forum put it best, "*Playboy* tries to present itself as a hip kapitalist magazine, but...you serve Amerika just as much as the *Wall Street Journal* does."[45] Such criticisms underscored the paradoxical position *Playboy* occupied in the cultural ferment of the late 1960s. These sentiments affirmed the magazine's position as a pillar of American consumer society. At the same time, they portended the challenge the magazine would face as it tried to maintain a self-proclaimed role as a force of rebellion.

Playboy's version of the good life gained substantial ground in the 1960s, the decade witnessing an expansion of "The World of Playboy," along with the further manifestation in American culture of the hedonistic bachelor and the style and values he exuded. Although African-American entrepreneurs experimented with this cultural model, the playboy and the lifestyle package that

surrounded him were of limited utility for African Americans facing segregation and discrimination that kept them from breaking into the ranks of the middle class. Meanwhile, *Playboy* continued to far surpass its rival publications. Promoted as the vanguard of a movement against social and sexual repression, the magazine and the values it supported infused popular culture and helped shepherd along a thriving singles culture. On the surface, the hipsters of the Rat Pack had little in common with the bedraggled hippie youth of Haight-Ashbury, Greenwich Village, and Old Town. The "kings of cool" appealed to the adults of the postwar world; their children had less use for middle-aged men in formal attire whose drug of choice was a dry martini, not LSD. Like the playboy, however, each of these figures drew upon cultural style as a way to articulate disdain for the conservative values of the "establishment." In important respects, the counterculture of the 1960s represented the realization of *Playboy*'s libertine message. The question remained as to what role the magazine of the self-proclaimed rebel, Hugh Hefner, could play now that the barricades of conformity and sexual repression, against which he had self-consciously fashioned his opposition, had been breached.

6 "CASUALTIES OF THE LIFESTYLE REVOLUTION"

Playboy, *the Permissive Society, and Women's Liberation*

IN 1972, PLAYBOY's monthly circulation reached over seven million and the company forecast a thriving future:

> A man gets up in his Playboy town house at Lake Geneva, calls a Playboy limousine to take him to the airport where he gets in a Playboy chartered plane, flies to New York, takes a Playboy limousine to a Playboy hotel in midtown Manhattan, changes into his Playboy suit, takes a Playboy ferry to a Playboy convention center on Randall's island for his business meeting, that night goes to a Playboy restaurant and then to a Playboy theater where he sees a Playboy movie. That's the Playboy environment. And while we don't have all those things yet, we have many of them and we're exploring the rest.[1]

The world of Playboy had its own currency, "Bunny Money," for use at the clubs, and its own landmarks such as "Bunny Bay," site of the Playboy Club-Hotel in Jamaica. Approaching Playboy's Lake Geneva resort, keyholders drove along Cottontail Trail, lined with flagstaffs from which fluttered the Playboy Rabbit banner, along with flags of Canada, Jamaica, and the United Kingdom, all of which boasted a Playboy Club. From a shoestring operation run out of Hefner's apartment, Playboy had grown to become a publicly traded company on the New York Stock Exchange, an IPO in 1971 having provided the capital to finance the explosive growth of Playboy Enterprises, Inc. (PEI). Academics, clergymen, and members of the media continued to ponder *Playboy's* significance in American life. Sedate scientific journals such as *Medical Aspects of Human Sexuality* asked a roundtable of professionals, "What Do You Think of *Playboy?*" while Beyond Illustration—The Art of Playboy, a traveling exhibition of original artwork and sculpture that had appeared in the pages of the magazine, made its way around the country. Televised "Bunny of the Year" pageants

filled the airwaves. Already enjoying a nearly ubiquitous place on the American scene, Playboy Enterprises aimed to expand its operations even further. Only a few years later, the company's future seemed far less certain. In 1975, the corporation began posting losses, its stock price slumped, and little by little Playboy's empire began to crumble.[2]

How did the heady optimism voiced in 1972 give way to such a dramatic reversal of fortune? To an important extent, *Playboy* fell victim to its own success. A casualty of the "lifestyle revolution" it helped spearhead, the magazine foundered in the 1970s as the social and cultural changes it so heartily welcomed threatened to leave it behind. As graphic competitors flooded the marketplace, *Playboy*'s once-daring Playmates and Bunnies and its affuent bachelor lifestyle appeared timeworn. The playboy's lavish accommodations and upscale accessories stretched the bounds of credibility as the postwar economic boom turned to bust in the 1970s and "stagflation" and a crippling energy crisis beset the nation. Hefner's earlier exhortations to work hard and play hard were outmoded for these uncertain economic times, but the permission for self-indulgence implied in this axiom was also no longer necessary when, wherever one looked, it seemed, popular media abounded with endorsements of hedonistic consumption and unrestrained sexual pleasure. In this context, young males no longer needed the magazine to point the way to the good life. Many Americans were pursuing it headlong in a "permissive society" that validated the pursuit of pleasure at every turn.

While the diffusion of an ethos of self-fulfillment meant the magazine, ironically, began to recede in importance, *Playboy* also faltered under charges from a feminist movement in revolt against the supporting part in which women were cast in Hefner's male-centered vision for personal liberation. The freedom from social convention and puritanical restrictions celebrated in the magazine, many feminists averred, was merely a male-defined agenda for access to women's bodies.[3] Feminists targeted *Playboy* both as a symbol of gender inequality and as part of a system of oppression that exploited and objectified women. Inspired by the social movements and cultural radicalism of the 1960s, women as well as men voiced opposition to *Playboy,* in the process articulating a larger concern about their place in a consumer society. Consumption provided a language of protest for these critics: women demanded that they no longer be treated as commodities; men voiced resistance to a masculine mystique caught up in *Playboy*'s inducements to consume women as well as material goods. For many feminists, the images of women peddled in *Playboy* formed an obvious source of indignation, but *Playboy*'s support of reproductive freedom and other feminist causes complicated matters. The debates that ensued over whether or not feminists could find common ground with Hefner or Playboy Enterprises revealed

important tensions in the women's movement. As some feminists began to link the sexually explicit, and increasingly violent, images that proliferated in this era to violence against women, Hefner's magazine was further indicted for making possible the sex-saturated culture in which such images flourished. In the meantime, as *Playboy*'s editors navigated these troubled waters, the magazine attempted to square critics' demands for gender equality with a commitment to notions of gender difference that had long supported male privilege.

"WE'RE GOING RABBIT HUNTING": UNDER SIEGE IN THE SEXUALIZED SOCIETY

For much of the 1960s, *Playboy* informed readers that it stood at the vanguard of a revolution to liberate sex from the bonds of shame and repression. Late in the decade, *Playboy* could no longer claim an identity as an underdog publication in a repressive society. Instead, the magazine found itself immersed in the "Swinging Sixties." "Suddenly the Sexual Revolution made Playboy's winking view of sex look respectable to many readers—and advertisers, too," commented *Business Week* in the summer of 1969 on *Playboy*'s success. "Perhaps it's too respectable, say a minority of skeptics who think the Revolution may be outpacing Playboy—and may leave it behind in the 1970s." From its inception, *Playboy* had managed to dominate the men's magazine field, far surpassing the numerous imitators that cropped up over the years. "A new challenger, an English magazine called *Penthouse*, goes on sale in August in this country," noted *Business Week*, "but Playboy isn't worried."[4]

As it turned out, there was cause for concern. Within the changing social and cultural climate of the late 1960s, *Playboy* was at risk of becoming stale. "It is my feeling that the Playmate picture stories have become so similar in appearance—one issue after the other—that they are in danger of becoming repetitiously dull," Hefner informed A. C. Spectorsky in January 1967. "Something really must be done about them," he complained again the following year. From his position in charge of Playboy operations in Britain, Victor Lownes warned in 1968 that magazine sales there were "suffering because of 'local' competition from *Playboy* type imitators in English and other languages, and because of the relaxation of restrictions on the general mass media. Not only do we suffer because of sales of such magazines as *Playmen, Lui, Penthouse* and *Mayfair,* but we are also suffering because magazines, and even the daily Press, are beginning to relax their restrictions so that they print more and more nudes."[5] As *Penthouse* made its debut in the United States in 1969, founder Bob Guccione

launched a head-on attack against *Playboy*. *Penthouse* announced its entry into the American marketplace in full-page newspaper advertisements depicting the *Playboy* rabbit logo in the crosshairs of a rifle. "We're going rabbit hunting," the ads proclaimed. *Penthouse* mocked Hefner's pretentious crusading, promising "the pictures without the lectures. The pinups without the hang-ups. Writers yes, philosophizers no." According to Guccione, "They were still fighting the sexual revolution. Our starting point was that the revolution had already been won." For all the notoriety of its centerfolds, *Playboy* had not crossed the line that seemed to separate erotic photography from pornography, the display of pubic hair. *Penthouse* challenged *Playboy* in the realm of sexual explicitness, publishing ever more revealing photographs and forcing its predecessor to follow suit. "Remember," Hefner advised photographer Vince Tajiri in 1970, "pubic hair is no longer a taboo in PLAYBOY as long as it is handled in good taste." In the ensuing circulation battle, which became known in the magazine trade as the Pubic Wars, *Playboy* ran its first full-frontal nude centerfold in January 1972 and overall became increasingly raunchy as it tried to thwart its opponent.[6]

PEI also responded to the onslaught from *Penthouse* by launching a more sexually explicit magazine, *Oui,* in September 1972. "What do European men know that you don't know?" queried an advertisement for the new publication. "Say '*Oui*,' and find out." *Oui* promised to open doors to an even more "sophisticated" world than one found in *Playboy*.

> *Oui* is a whole new outlook on life for the young American man. An international point of view. A Continental sense of humor. Fiction, fact and photography by trend-setting contributors from around the world. And the women. Truly unique. Truly beautiful. And quite unlike the girl next door. Become a man of the world... Say yes—to Oui.

In hindsight, the positioning of this new magazine suggests what circulation figures soon made clear: instead of taking on *Playboy*'s competitors, *Oui* was challenging *Playboy*. The "man-about-town" image, *Oui*'s ad copy implied, no longer sufficed in the permissive society. Now, readers aspired to be "men of the world," and the girl next door had been trumped by the "sophisticated" (read: explicit) photographs of the women of *Oui,* such as the one featured in this ad, with hands poised suggestively near her pubic area.[7]

Besides the threat posed by *Penthouse*, *Playboy* soon faced additional competition from coarse imitators *Gallery, Genesis, Coq,* and *Hustler,* which made no attempt to package themselves as "respectable." Even with these new contenders, *Penthouse*'s circulation increased, while *Playboy*'s began to fall in 1973. Advertisers were displeased with *Playboy*'s new levels of explicitness, and by the mid-1970s, Hefner decided he no longer wished to do battle in the Pubic Wars.

Playboy conceded its rivals' domination of the raunchier segment of the market and began to tone down its nude pictorials, though the relative modesty of the 1950s and early 1960s would not return to its pages. Sex-themed content continued to overwhelm the magazine. The marketplace was flooded in the 1970s with graphic discussions and representations of sex, from thriving adult bookstores and X-rated films to popular sex manuals like Alex Comfort's *The Joy of Sex.* Others works, such as Nancy Friday's *My Secret Garden,* Shere Hite's *The Hite Report,* and Erica Jong's novel *Fear of Flying,* emphasized women's pursuit of sexual pleasure.[8] *Playboy* kept pace in the sexualized society by commissioning a Kinsey-esque survey of contemporary sexual behavior and by providing ample reportage on all manner of "liberated" activity. One article, subtitled "the last barrier is down—they're doing it everywhere but in the road," summed up its approach. With sex now highly visible in the public realm and young people more openly engaging in premarital sex, lifestyle features were no longer prescriptive, but focused on the most visible and extreme developments. Articles reported on such practices as marital swinging, group sex, and exhibitionism. Nudity pervaded modern living features. College-oriented issues focused on the best places to go for spring break sex and polled campuses to find those with the most permissive attitudes. *Playboy* also began publishing annual reviews of the year's cinematic "Sex Stars" and "The Year in Sex" along with two new series, "The History of Sex" and "Sex in America," which highlighted a different city in each installment.[9] Meanwhile, other articles and features turned attention to the quest for self-fulfillment nurtured by the therapeutic culture of the 1970s. A new advertising slogan suggested the pleasure-seeking audience courted by the magazine. *Playboy* readers, according to this campaign, had a "lust for life," a catchphrase that seemed to capture the self-gratifying impulses of what journalist Tom Wolfe dubbed the "Me Decade."[10]

As *Playboy* faced the challenge to its supremacy in the men's magazine field, the same forces that had helped open the floodgates for its competitors also threatened the survival of Playboy Clubs International. The Bunny costume and its threat to morals had once been the subject of court hearings; it hardly seemed noteworthy when topless bars lined streets and singles bars offered a place for men and women to mingle without the look-but-don't-touch policy of Playboy's clubs. As one former Bunny put it, "If the guy was on the make, he would go where the action was. What kind of man would want to sit and look at cleavages?"[11] Advertising inserts in *Playboy* still touted the clubs, promising, "The Good Life Is Yours When You Have a Playboy Club Key"; meanwhile, *VIP,* the clubs' membership magazine, tirelessly reported the redecoration or relocation of various venues, all attempts to revive the ailing chain. Updating the venues, however, alienated older keyholders and failed to attract younger

prospects. Additionally, by the 1970s, many clubs once imagined as the epitome of hip urbanity now stood in declining urban areas. Playboy managed to extend the life of the clubs by moving them to suburban locales, following the exodus of business from the city. In the meantime, only Playboy's facilities in Britain thrived, the casinos there shoring up declining revenues from the magazine and masking losses from the rest of the club division. Playboy's profits fell from a peak of $11.3 million in 1973 to $1.1 million in 1975, and its stock dropped to as low as $2.25 a share.[12]

Analyzing the company's woes, one observer opined that Playboy's saturation of the marketplace had caused the image to lose its luster. "Whatever exclusivity once attached to membership in a Playboy Club or a rabbit-embossed Playboy product may now have vanished. All you need to get in a Playboy Club is $25, and you can find Playboy consumer products at Sears." Although payment of a $25 membership fee had always been the only requirement for entry into the clubs, the aura of distinctiveness purchased for this price was indeed gone. The logo that once signified brash individualism and high living lost its cachet once it was emblazoned on ice buckets, Frisbees, key chains, T-shirts, and other tacky merchandise available at Playboy gift shops. The Playboy Bar Tool Set, for example, still promised to add "Playboy status to home entertaining." But just what did "Playboy status" mean anymore? Readers of *Oui* who submitted photographs of fruits and vegetables that resembled parts of the male anatomy hardly seemed like status-conscious sophisticates. Attempting to fill vacant hotel rooms, the company tried to sell itself as a family-friendly venture. The clubs had always welcomed spouses as guests of their keyholder husbands, but the active solicitation of wives and families now signaled a shift from earlier celebrations of footloose bachelorhood. An article on the Lake Geneva Club described the amenities that spouses might enjoy while accompanying their husbands to a convention and promised, "Whatever the choice, a warm welcome awaits the wives." The Playboy name was even removed from its U.S. hotels, signaling that the brand had become a liability. One by one, Playboy shuttered clubs in major cities; those in places such as Omaha, Nebraska, and Lansing, Michigan, remained open, where their position as "the only game in town" helped keep doors open.[13]

Though *Playboy* had much in common with readers seeking self-fulfillment in a decade characterized by intense personal preoccupation, the magazine charted an uncertain course in the permissive society. The lifestyle package and the ethical framework that supported it persisted in the magazine, but became less relevant in a society steeped in the values of the playboy. *Playboy*'s waning fortunes in the 1970s stemmed from a combination of factors, including its overextension into several unsuccessful business ventures and competition

from more explicit magazines in a less-restricted publishing climate. Ultimately, however, the magazine's declining relevance was a function of its success. An expansive leisure realm, an entrenched consumer ethos, and sexual permissiveness all signaled broad acceptance of the values long championed by *Playboy;* it was no longer tenable to position it as an iconoclastic publication. "Hugh Hefner is beginning to seem more and more like everyone's kindly and slightly bewildered uncle," asserted columnist Bob Greene. "Who wants to talk with him about philosophy in a society where stag films are shown from noon on at the old theatre next to the hardware store, and where local businessmen can be masturbated at comfortable massage parlors on their way back from lunch?"[14] In this sexualized climate, the magazine experienced a loss of editorial focus, while American males faced a wide spectrum of diversions in the consumer society that made *Playboy* appear passé.

"WE WILL NO LONGER SELL OURSELVES"

As it struggled to adapt to the more permissive atmosphere and reacted to direct threats from upstarts like *Penthouse, Playboy* faced a challenge on another front as well. By the end of the 1960s, a critical movement for social change confronted *Playboy*'s vision of the good life, calling into question the magazine's pronouncements about personal liberation and its simultaneous support of gender distinctions that endorsed male privilege. In a January 1968 article, author John Clellon Holmes praised "The New Girl," whom he described as interested neither in becoming a "masculinized" woman nor in accepting traditional feminine domesticity. In his view, such developments as the birth control pill, the relaxation of strictures against premarital sex, a breakdown of the double standard, and declining social pressures for early marriage and motherhood had all led to the emergence of the "New Girl." Her acceptance of sexual liberation, making her an ideal companion to the playboy, gained her the adulation of Holmes. Taking stock of the Single Girl, the counterculture, and the urban singles culture, he wrote:

> It is the young single woman in the city, probably no longer a virgin and just as probably regarding this fact not as a troubling loss of innocence but as a valuable gain of experience, who best epitomizes the New Girl. Her life may be either a female facsimile of the hip bachelorhood of her male counterpart...or she may have taken to the lofts with her young man, living in the careless, tribal, improvised poverty of those who have dropped out. But whether her trip is to a dating bar for the purpose of

meeting likely male swingers...or into inner space via LSD...the New Girl's venturesomeness implies, above everything else, an almost complete absence of all those tensions about "being single" that were etched in stress lines around the mouths of girls in their mid-20s heretofore.

Whether a countercultural "hippie chick" or a glamorous Single Girl, the young single woman put forth in this idealized description was anything but strident, taking no interest in competing with men, worrying about marriage, or fighting for women's rights. Indeed, evidence of the "final and complete demise" of feminism, Holmes claimed, could be found in "the fact that the New Left (in whose ranks there are almost as many girls as boys) may be the first radical movement in modern history that does not concern itself with women's rights at all."[15] As developments soon made clear, Holmes's assessment was incorrect. In fact, it was precisely because men in the New Left refused to address the issue of female oppression that many women abandoned it in search of their own movement. Their experiences in both the civil rights movement and the New Left provided female activists with a clear vision of the capacity for social change; fed up with being marginalized in the movement by men, they galvanized to act. Not long after the appearance of the "New Girl" article, a group of women gathered on the Atlantic City boardwalk to toss copies of *Playboy* and *Ladies' Home Journal*, steno pads, bras, false eyelashes, and other artifacts of oppression into a "freedom trashcan." Later, they disrupted the Miss America Pageant by unfurling a banner proclaiming "Women's Liberation." The event marked the opening salvo of a more militant and visible movement for gender equality and made clear that Holmes's glorification of the postfeminist girl had been premature.[16]

Questions about women's role had occupied commentators throughout the 1950s; they received further attention from the Kennedy administration with the creation in 1963 of the Presidential Commission on the Status of Women, chaired by former first lady Eleanor Roosevelt. That year also marked the appearance of Betty Friedan's *The Feminine Mystique*. Although Friedan was not the first to identify women's discontent with their domestic duties, her description of the frustration and despair faced by countless educated women forced to write "occupation: housewife" on the census form resonated widely among wives and mothers who failed to find fulfillment in that role. It also mobilized many of them, inspiring the formation in 1966 of the National Organization for Women (NOW). NOW sought to advance women's status by working within the existing political framework and called for women's equal protection before the law and equal opportunity in the areas of education, employment, and economic life. Stemming from this strategy, the liberal feminist organization championed the Equal Rights Amendment (ERA), first introduced into Congress in 1923.

Meanwhile, women activists in the civil rights organization SNCC and the New Left organization SDS began to formulate a view that women's subordinate position stemmed from more than barriers to male-dominated occupations. Splintering from these groups, they gradually formed a separate movement, calling themselves women's liberationists. Together, the liberal strands embodied by NOW and the more militant efforts of women's liberation formed what historians have termed the "second wave" of feminism.

Young women drawn to the women's liberation movement theorized gender inequality as the result of deep and widespread systems of oppression, namely capitalism and patriarchy. In the numerous small, radical organizations and "consciousness-raising" discussion groups that sprang up, these feminists acknowledged their experiences with sexism, discrimination, and harassment and embraced the notion that the "personal is political"—that an unsatisfying sex life, the burden of housework, incessant pressure to measure up to beauty standards, or the inability to earn a promotion or obtain a safe abortion were not isolated, individual problems but part of a larger structure of gender inequality. Drawing on the "movement culture" of the era, they drafted position papers, launched alternative newspapers, and employed tactics from sit-ins to speak-outs in order to publicize a range of issues.[17]

The Atlantic City demonstration was not the first time *Playboy* was criticized for chauvinistic treatment of women. In 1963, Gloria Steinem had grimly assessed a Bunny's daily routine at the Playboy Club. In 1965, journalist Diana Lurie offered one of the first feminist critiques of "the playboy life," lambasting its implications for women. "Hefner's *Playboy* in a polished, literate package urges Americans to enjoy what they have always frowned upon: hedonism, which *Playboy* calls the 'swinging life'; unmarried sex, which *Playboy* considers a sign of mental health; a suave pseudo-intellectualism, which *Playboy* presents as sophistication." Hefner, she argued, paid lip service to equality for men and women when it came to sexual relationships, but "the way it works out, in both his private life and his magazine, men are a lot more equal than women."[18] While Hefner, in his "philosophy" and elsewhere, espoused his respect for women and his belief that they were equal to men in their value as human beings, such pronouncements often seemed sharply at odds with the magazine, which drew upon and perpetuated stereotypes of woman's subordinate role in society.[19]

Beginning with Friedan's analysis in *The Feminine Mystique* of advertising and magazine fiction, media representations of women provided an important rallying point for the women's movement. If *Playboy*'s linkage of masculine identity to consumption provided a strategy for men to liberate themselves from narrowly defined roles of responsible manhood, feminists perceived the opposite to be true for women. Media constructions of women, they argued,

most often identified them as frivolous consumers or, indeed, as commodities to be consumed. As one woman summed up, echoing Friedan, magazine advertising depicted women as "happy housewives, idiots and sex objects." Following the Miss America protest, feminists launched an all-out assault on sexist images of women in television commercials, in magazines, and on billboards that they felt helped perpetuate the status quo. In December 1969, for example, women picketed outside Macy's department store in response to a Mattel advertisement in *Life* magazine, carrying signs that protested, "Mattel Limits Little Girls Dreams." The offending advertisement promoted different toys for children based on the precept that "girls dream about being a ballerina" while "boys were born to build and learn." The following spring, women held a sit-in at the offices of the *Ladies' Home Journal,* protesting its narrow portrayal of women and demanding promotions for female employees and the creation of a day-care center. NOW initiated a campaign against sexist advertising called the "Barefoot and Pregnant Award of the Week." The organization distributed thousands of stickers proclaiming that "This Ad Insults Women" for supporters to paste on offending ads. Feminists also marshaled their purchasing power, launching "girlcotts" against companies that used offensive advertising. In this context, *Playboy* served as a ready target for feminists concerned about cultural images that perpetuated myths of women's ineptitude, damaged their self-esteem, or portrayed them as commodified "sex objects." Not long after the Miss America protest, men and women at Grinnell College disrupted a *Playboy* casting session on campus. Stripping off their clothing, these students proclaimed, "Playboy is the money-changer in the temple of the body."[20]

Both Hefner and his magazine were caught off guard by the nature and tone of feminist critics. In challenging the family wage ideology that insisted on responsible husbands/fathers caring for financially dependent homemakers, *Playboy* stood on common ground with the liberal elements of the women's movement embodied by NOW. Moreover, as a champion of "sexual liberation," *Playboy* supported legalizing abortion, sex education, and the liberalization of birth control, measures vital to women's reproductive freedom.[21] Many feminist critics, however, viewed this support as merely serving the best interests of the playboy, promoting more sex for men while reducing male responsibilities for unwanted pregnancy. Furthermore, despite the common interest in women's reproductive freedom, women's demands for gender equality and their harsh criticism of the sexist underpinnings of American society threatened the "complementary" gender roles long envisioned in the magazine. Throughout the 1960s, *Playboy* commented on the broad spectrum of social issues that embroiled the nation. To ignore feminism would have meant overlooking a significant social movement, not to mention a major media story of the day. Thus, continuing in its role as a

handbook for young, male readers and as a forum for debate on contemporary issues, *Playboy* confronted the rising tide of second-wave feminism.

The younger, more militant feminists who proclaimed themselves "women's liberationists" soon provoked a sharp response from Hefner. In September 1969, *Playboy* hired a freelance writer, Susan Braudy, who attended dozens of women's liberation meetings in order to prepare an article on the subject. The question of what kind of article *Playboy* ought to publish as its first piece on feminism, however, generated concern and disagreement among the magazine's editors. Months earlier, Hefner had asked for a "nice satirical piece" on what he termed the "super-feminist movement." Spectorsky expressed reluctance to pursue such a course, calling it "a grave error" to "attack the irrational extremists" without also addressing "the real problems" of concern to "intelligent, rational, thinking women." As Spectorsky explained in a memo to Hefner's executive assistant, Dick Rosenzweig, *Playboy,* more than any other magazine, had to proceed carefully when it came to feminism:

> I can imagine no publication that is in a more sensitive position in this matter. We get criticism enough, from young men as well as women, for what they claim is our anti-feminist, women-as-objects stance, and for our Playmates and Bunnies. If we just put down the whole feminist thing in a contemptuous, superior, amused, or one-sided way, it will make us look square and dated.[22]

In light of this precarious position, *Playboy*'s senior editors circulated Braudy's submission and solicited opinions from both male and female staff members as they contemplated whether or not to publish it. While some, mostly men, found the piece an acceptable report on the "radical fringe," others, mostly women, objected to the broad brushstrokes used to paint the entire women's movement. Amid this uncertainty, and apparently without actually reading the article, Hefner stepped in and provided direction.

Hefner issued a staff memo calling for a "devastating piece that takes militants apart." The memo explained:

> What I'm interested in is the highly irrational, emotional, kookie trend that feminism has taken in the last couple of years. These chicks are our natural enemy—and there is, incidentally, nothing we can say in the pages of *Playboy* that will convince them that we are not. It is time to do battle with them and I think we can do it in a devastating way.

While declaring that women should not be confined to narrow domestic roles, Hefner echoed concerns of sex-role convergence that had preoccupied many commentators in the early postwar period:

The society they want is an asexual one....We certainly agree that a woman's place is not in the home, that a woman should enjoy a career, that she should not be limited...to a double standard in sex, etc., etc. But the militant feminist wants much more than this...she wants to play a role exactly comparable to the male's—to compete with him, not simply in a business world, but emotionally—and in every other way. It is an extremely anti-sexual, unnatural thing they are reaching for.

Although he staunchly supported the civil rights movement, Hefner rejected the feminist assertion that gender inequality was comparable to racial inequality, arguing that "the differences between the sexes are and should be more than just physical." Moreover, he pointed out, "the very inclusion of sex in the [1964] Civil Rights Act was intended originally as a joke.... Now that joke has become the law of the land, with many of the obvious ridiculous aspects that have evolved there from." Hefner's rhetoric recalled earlier concerns about "womanization" and the social discord he believed resulted when women tried to "dominate" men and collapse gender boundaries. "Clearly, if you analyze all of the most basic premises of the extreme form of new feminism, you will find them unalterably opposed to the romantic boy-girl society that *Playboy* promotes," he concluded. "It is now up to us to do a really expert, personal demolition job on the subject."[23]

In the wake of this directive, negotiations between Braudy and *Playboy* editors over rewriting the piece failed. Veteran *Playboy* contributor Morton Hunt stepped in to finish the job. The result was "Up against the Wall, Male Chauvinist Pig!" The article explicated and even sympathized with the major points of liberal feminism, then identified a segment of the women's movement as doing its "level worst to distort the distinctions between male and female and to discredit the legitimate grievances of American women." Hunt criticized radical feminist critiques of the beauty and fashion industries as well as feminists' denunciation of the "myth of vaginal orgasm," the Freudian view that defined a "mature" climax as one a woman achieved during vaginal penetration and which thus affirmed the primacy of male-centered sexual activity. According to Hunt, the "rejection of distinctly feminine clothing and of the pursuit of beauty is supposed to free women from squandering their time and energy pleasing (and, thus, being subservient to) men. But as one listens to the extremists, it becomes clear that they are after bigger game—the withering away of heterosexual desire and heterosexual intercourse." In his discussion of "militant man-haters," a term that revealed only slightly veiled concern about lesbian-feminists, Hunt also ironically expressed worry that some radicals, in calling for the eradication of oppressive gender conventions, threatened the

bedrock institutions of marriage and family. Furthermore, while conceding a place for women in the workplace, Hunt envisioned this as secondary to a primary focus on hearth and home.[24]

This was a conclusion with which Hefner disagreed, as he made clear in a subsequent staff memo. "We would never suggest that a man who preferred bachelorhood to marriage was abnormal," he pointed out. "Why treat a woman any differently in this regard?" Hefner claimed to be concerned about the eradication of "all sex-role differences...but that doesn't mean that women shouldn't be allowed the same opportunity to explore their individuality and establish their own personal life styles as men."[25] If Hefner was not pleased with parts of *Playboy*'s initial foray into feminism, his dissatisfaction was emblematic of what had been a confusing series of editorial miscues for all involved. For many critics, Hefner's antifeminist memo—soon leaked to the press—and Hunt's subsequent article only bolstered the view that *Playboy* was an adversary in the fight for women's liberation.

Modeling its efforts on the civil rights and antiwar movements, the women's movement, Patricia Bradley has shown, viewed media attention as the key to publicizing and winning support for its goals. In a perpetual search for fresh angles and bigger headlines, however, journalists tended to seek out the most extreme actions and personalities and to highlight controversy and disagreement among feminists.[26] As an instrument of mass media, *Playboy*'s efforts to spotlight the "irrational" and "kookie" aspects of the women's movement fit within this journalistic paradigm, while they also sought to discredit feminists' criticism of the magazine and its Bunny-empire. Feminist attacks on *Playboy* were inspired by reflective critiques of gender, power, and capitalism, but they were also bold gestures orchestrated to garner media attention. Both sides could play at this game, and *Playboy* and "women's libbers," as they were disparagingly called, became convenient foils in a complicated struggle for social change.

Hefner had already squared off against feminists in March 1970 on the Dick Cavett Show, where Susan Brownmiller challenged, "When Hugh Hefner comes here with a cotton tail attached to his rear end, that's the day we'll have equality."[27] The editorial debacle surrounding *Playboy*'s first article on women's liberation brought more remonstrations against Hefner, his magazine, and its clubs. On April 15, 1970, the Chicago Women's Liberation Union (CWLU) organized a demonstration outside the Playboy Mansion, site of a benefit for the Vietnam War Moratorium Committee. Crowds of protestors, mostly women, blocked the sidewalk, urging couples, politicians, and media figures trying to enter the party to "sign your checks, but don't go in!" Police had to make way for guests to enter the mansion. The CWLU distributed leaflets proclaiming the hypocrisy of protesting the war from the opulent confines of Hefner's mansion:

"Playboy exploits women by using them as sexual objects and by encouraging the consumerism which supports the white man's imperialistic war." Another protestor explained:

> We couldn't forget that Hefner's money and bunnies and TV shows and airplanes and magazines and mansions are the profits of women's bodies and the psychology to which their bodies and the hideous line of Playboy accessories appeal. We couldn't forget the Moratorium's contribution to the further elevation of Hefner's swinger image.

The charge leveled by these demonstrators linked the commodification of female sexuality to capitalism, and capitalism to the war in Southeast Asia. They further understood the legitimizing power among liberals of the Moratorium's association with Playboy. As one protestor put it, "We, and the people who decided not to cross our picket lines, saw the war in Vietnam and the Playboy empire's exploitation and degradation of women as part of the same system, tied inevitably together—and therefore saw total contradiction in being against the war and going into the mansion." "We can't explain the logic behind the demonstration," *Playboy* noted dismissively in a subsequent editorial statement. Two Bunnies carrying "We Love Hugh Hefner" signs were dispatched to the sidewalk to counter the protestors, but television cameras also filmed a Playboy Bunny in an upstairs window, flashing a clenched-fist salute to the picketing women on the street.[28]

The week after the Moratorium protest, a Playboy secretary, Shelly Schlicker, was fired for disclosing Hefner's antifeminist "demolition job" memo to the media. Following her dismissal, as supporters rallied outside Playboy's offices, she read the following statement:

> They think they can stop the growing hostility against *Playboy* by purging their women employees who dare to speak up for their rights. Hefner has made millions selling this air-brushed image of women to insecure men who are taught to want a playful pet rather than a person. But it won't work. We will no longer sell ourselves in return for a pair of ears, a tail and a condescending pat on the behind.[29]

In denouncing Playboy, this ex-secretary's reference to the Bunny's costume and the sexualized gesture of the "pat on the behind" also served to repudiate the vision of "working-girl" femininity that structured expectations for many working women. Playboy became a focal point of demonstrations throughout the country as well as the subject of pointed critiques in a variety of venues, particularly in the feminist underground press. In May 1970, protestors picketed outside the New York Playboy Club in the first of several demonstrations there.

During a taping of the Dick Cavett Show, where Hefner again debated representatives of the women's movement, two women charged the stage, shouting "fascist" and "off the pig!" The next month in Chicago, where a Playboy Action Committee was formed to coordinate efforts, men and women carried signs and distributed leaflets at the Playboy Club. In Boston, men interrupted an MIT fraternity conference held at the Playboy Club, chanting "free our sisters, free ourselves!" In Houston, Playboy representatives looking to recruit Bunnies for various clubs were met by demonstrators. An account of the protest enumerated Playboy's "crimes": first, against women, for presenting the "pitifully shaved, doe-eyed, and air-brushed female as the mere object for male entertainment"; next, against men, for crafting an image of success that "few men can even approach," but that provided "fertile ground for advertisers, who use the magazine to sell would-be Playboys everything from aftershave to automobiles"; and, finally, against "the growing ranks of Amerika's poor and unemployed." To this critic, "The obscene opulence of Hefner's world—the Playboy jets, the clubs and the mansions—are a continual insult to those who literally don't know where their next meal is coming from. And no amount of beautiful naked women or well-dressed men or even interviews with Eldridge Cleaver can cover up that crime." In the face of such condemnation, Playboy continued to maintain that its views on men and women were positive and liberating, but this stance did not dissuade radical critics. When a spokesperson expressed dismay over the homemade incendiary bomb that exploded on the doorstep of the San Francisco Playboy Club, the countercultural Liberation News Service wondered, "Would you expect a butcher to appreciate the horror a vegetarian feels at viewing a beef aging room?"[30]

"WHAT KIND OF MAN IS A PLAYBOY?" CULTURAL RADICALISM AND THE MASCULINE MYSTIQUE

With roots in the civil rights movement and the New Left, the women's liberation movement also had important ties to the counterculture. The stylistic markings of the "hippies" offered a strategy for adopting an antiestablishment posture while remaining within society's materialistic framework, as *Playboy*'s relationship to the counterculture demonstrates. Looking beyond the style of the "hippies" and its ties to the marketplace, however, historians have also highlighted "countercultural aspirations" to affect social change by first transforming individual consciousness. Such transformative impulses also informed

the movement for women's liberation taking shape in the late 1960s and 1970s. Many of the movement's early actions, including the Miss America protest, drew inspiration from countercultural modes of confrontation, such as the yippies' attempts to "levitate" the Pentagon during an antiwar protest or its street-theater "nomination" of a pig for president during the 1968 Democratic National Convention. Moreover, feminists' use of "consciousness-raising" (CR) as a stepping-stone to social activism represented an outgrowth of the counterculture's emphasis on altering consciousness as a precursor to transforming culture. CR meetings enabled individuals to situate their personal lives in a political context, bringing new awareness of one's enmeshment in a larger cultural fabric and inspiring actions to remake it.[31] The activities and rhetoric of the women and men who protested against *Playboy* were rooted in this approach. In feminists' CR discussions and in men's "rap" groups, they came to perceive their personal experiences in a broader context, and then went on to confront "establishment" society with a message about personal liberation and cultural change.

Hefner had expended much time and ink expressing concern for individuals' self-fulfillment and freedom from repression and, when challenged by earlier critics, always promoted the magazine's images of women and their relationship to men as "healthy." Analyzing *Playboy*, some men and women argued otherwise. One matter that received scrutiny was the magazine's potentially damaging effects on women's body image and self-esteem. "As sex objects in *Playboy*, even the women who make it aren't good enough," criticized a woman in a position paper written for a CR group. "Miss April is pretty, tan and possibly naturally blond. But that's not enough for the beat off pictures. For those, she has makeup and false eyelashes, bald legs and armpits, and she hides her hands in all color shots except where they put false fingernails for the foldout." Even film star Brigitte Bardot, she argued, needed a makeover to make the grade in *Playboy*. "The shots are all blurry to hide her defects and in every nude picture she is holding her breasts up with her arm. One picture has a sheer nightie, and her breasts are supported by a flesh colored half bra. Even SHE is not allowed to show it like it is." Said another feminist, "I had pretty much the formative experience of comparing myself to the models in my uncle's *Playboy* magazines in the bathroom. Who can calculate the effect that has on you?"[32]

As women penned their frustrations in radical newspapers and protested outside the clubs, they were joined by sympathetic men who began to articulate the myriad ways in which popular images of masculinity and femininity, particularly those found in *Playboy*, damaged men and women. On June 27, 1970, about eighty individuals picketed and leafleted the Chicago Playboy Club. Men against Cool, a "rap" group that provided a forum for men to discuss how

"both men and women are getting fucked over by the sexual roles in Amerika," planned the action outside the club to confront "the sexist ideology of Playboy." Together with supporters from the gay liberation movement, who earlier that day had marked the one-year anniversary of gay resistance to police harassment at New York's Stonewall Inn, these demonstrators carried signs proclaiming, "Men Should Be Warm Not Cool," "Men Are Brothers, Not Playboys," and "I Have a Small Penis." A recounting of the event in the countercultural *Chicago Seed* pronounced:

> Men need to get together—not as men are together now in offices and governments and armies and football teams, but together in awareness of how we are also oppressed, trapped by the same roles that are supposed to give us an advantageous position. In renouncing the myth of male superiority, we liberate ourselves, allow ourselves to express feelings and needs and fears we have had to suppress before.[33]

As this protestor saw it, men as well as women stood to gain from the elimination of sexism and the reconsideration of gender stereotypes called for by women's liberationists.

Such a view informed the creation of NOW's Task Force on the Masculine Mystique, headed by Warren Farrell, author of *The Liberated Man*. In a letter to NOW members, Farrell counted "war, the Pentagon, West Point, Hugh Hefner, football and the like," among the "most apparent manifestations" of the "problem of masculinity." Beyond identifying these powerful symbols, he outlined numerous ways that education, the workplace, media, and family life might be reshaped to eliminate the gender stereotypes that worked against "women being independent and...men being human" and called for "men's consciousness raising groups" to serve as forums where men could "reexamine their insecurities with sex roles" and recognize their "interest in breaking down the stereotypes."[34] Several hundred men and women gathered in New York in June 1974 for the National Men's Liberation Conference, which was intended to train facilitators for men's as well as mixed-gender CR groups and to launch a national movement. As an outgrowth of this meeting, scores of protestors marched on the city's Playboy Club. "Sex Objects make men Success Objects," they proclaimed. Men carried signs announcing, "The Masculine Mystique Is the Masculine Mistake" and "What Kind of Man Is a Playboy?"[35] At a similar action in Detroit, men protested the Playboy Club—"another cog in Hugh Hefner's empire founded on a degrading image of women and men." Said one demonstrator, "There are a growing number of men who don't see their purpose in life as being to fuck over women and treat them as commodities like expensive cars or clothes."[36]

In the words of one disillusioned former *Playboy* centerfold model: "A Playmate doesn't have a mind or a soul. I don't know what to call her but a *thing*, a thing to be ogled, lusted over, and let's face it, jacked off over." In her estimation, the playboy embraced the motto, "I saw, I conquered, I came."[37] Echoing her assessment, one man contemplated the formative role *Playboy* played in his sex life, acknowledging the ways the fantasies projected in the magazine supported a heterosexist society and shaped his encounters with women. Ashamed of the early sexual encounters he had enjoyed with a male friend, he turned his attention to the "sex objects" found in "pornographic magazines," chiefly *Playboy*. "I began masturbating every day to these images, seeking out the 'perfect body,'" he recounted. When the time came for intercourse for the first time, he related:

> I was scared shitless...What if I can't get an erection? What if she gets pregnant? What if I can only come if I masturbate? What if her body doesn't meet the standards according to Playboy?...For the first time, here was a real woman, a sensitive, thinking person, whom I had somehow to communicate with when we made love. Before it was just me[,] my body and Playboy.

According to this man, connecting to a real woman was an uncomfortable experience. After having sex with his girlfriend, he explained, "I would almost expect her to vanish, like the porno images had when I closed the book." His involvement in the nascent men's movement enabled him to put his experience "into a real perspective, a social and political context, not just an individualistic one." "I am learning," he wrote, "that my sexual hang-ups aren't isolated, but reflect a whole society's sexual oppression, from graffiti on bathroom walls to the myth of the vaginal orgasm." He urged other men to renounce popular images of masculine toughness and sexual conquest. "We must...recognize ourselves as warm, sensitive, vulnerable human beings, not shadows of the images that John Wayne, Hugh Heffner [*sic*] and Charles Atlas have created for us."[38]

Another man who took part in a demonstration outside the San Francisco Playboy Club offered similar insights about the false expectations he and other men in his rap group had gleaned from *Playboy*:

> We as males had all in some way desired the role of playboy. It was a male image that in college I had strongly identified with in my close circle of male friends—to have a nice flashy car to ride around in to pick up women and take them to my cool apartment, turn on some groovy music on my expensive stereo equipment, etc. We were convinced that so much show of wealth, success, etc. would easily seduce any sophomore, junior, or even senior co-ed.

They were disappointed by the divergence between image and reality, discovering that *Playboy* promoted unrealistic expectations for themselves and the women they aimed to seduce. "We were all frustrated. None of us could really afford the car, the apartment, etc and none of the women around could meet up to our fantasies." Recognizing that the image was unattainable, however, did not break its hold.

> We were all aware of the realities but in a subtle way we were still hooked—every month Playboy would be there on our kitchen table. We've all masturbated to those fold out fantasies of the homespun big busted good looking all American girl. We know now what the women think—but we never would really examine the male image part because it was too close to home.[39]

Another man reflected on the way society enforced gender norms by criticizing men who failed to meet certain standards of athleticism, sexual performance, and power.

> Who was it that presumed to choose Joe Namath, the astronauts and Hugh Hefner for my heroes, when I had long ago chosen Beethoven and Walt Whitman? Who was it that decided that my ideal of a woman should be a set of overdeveloped mammary glands in living color on the center spread of Playboy when, in junior high school, I had chosen a tall thin gangly girl who dug literature and writing as I did? (And I rejected her because I couldn't [take] the kidding about my poor choice.)

Shedding the influence of such powerful expectations and cultural representations proved difficult. "You don't need to sample the whole bunch to know that the man's grapes are sour. The problem is wanting them, anyway." Although he recognized the limitations of the playboy ideal, this man wondered if he could exorcise its spell:

> The damage done to my head won't be totally undone in a lifetime. And if, suddenly, the Playboy Bunny should appear and touch me with the magic wand, and...ZAP!...there it was, the giant circular bed, the penthouse apartment, the solid gold convertible, women by the thousands, the power and the glory, what would I choose?...I don't know for sure. And there's the real problem.[40]

Men like this one tied their disapproval of the playboy ideal to a broader critique of the consumer society. They recognized and found limiting that *Playboy*'s vision of masculinity was bound up in the commodification of sexuality. Not only were women treated as consumer items, but sexual desire itself

had been co-opted. "What is wrong with Playboy," commented one man, echoing Theodore Roszak, "is that it takes our legitimate human aspirations, our very human interest in the aesthetics of the body and distorts it, cripples it, and rips it off from us by saying that we can satisfy our interests in the human form by buying the right kind of cuff-links to go with the right kind of shirt."[41]

The men who demonstrated outside Playboy Clubs and reflected on *Playboy* in the radical press lamented the commercialization of sexuality. As their comments make clear, they also recognized and were deeply concerned about the ways in which *Playboy* permeated consciousness and established standards for sexual experience that actually constituted desire. Those who participated in the small pro-feminist movement for "male liberation" were vastly outnumbered by the millions who expressed no misgivings about enjoying *Playboy* or frequenting its clubs. Nevertheless, their views provide a glimpse into the disquiet some men experienced over the inculcation of a playboy mystique in American culture, and their rejection of this model points to another legacy of the counterculture besides the widespread adoption of "hippie" style, though the long hair and colorful clothing of countercultural men also symbolically upended traditional gender distinctions. Hefner had established *Playboy* as a force of rebellion against the limitations imposed on men by pressures for early marriage and breadwinning, but its success had in fact stemmed from the very comfortable place it occupied within the consumer capitalist order. To men who supported women's liberation, questioned the "masculine mystique," or sought freedom from a heterosexist society through the movement for gay liberation, the playboy ethos was just as powerful a force of stagnation and repression as those against which Hefner railed in the 1950s.

In many respects, those who protested the commodification of sexuality were shouting in the wind, not because other men failed to recognize links between capitalism, the consumer ethos, and sexuality, but because few men saw a need to question a deeply entrenched system that seemed to provide material well-being and continued to privilege them relative to women. One man, for example, remarked on the protestors outside the New York Playboy Club: "The almighty dollar is a tough deal to chase but you gotta chase it." He dismissed the protestors' critique of the consumption-oriented treadmill engendered by the "masculine mystique," explaining in language that echoed Hefner's exhortations to work hard and play hard: "To live comfortably you gotta compete, settle down, get in the groove and start working." The connection between capitalism and sexuality, while not lost on him, was of no concern. "Why am I here?" he asked. "You want me to say because this is a symbol of capitalism? Because it's a place for men to relax and look at the pretty girls."[42]

THE AGGRESSIVE CHICK

As women's liberation blasted away outside its doors, within the magazine and in the media, Playboy responded to radical women's critique of the social order in a variety of ways. Cartoons, for instance, examined the "aggressive chick," poking fun at the mystifying ways in which women were challenging the gender hierarchy (see figure 6.1). In one, a young male hippie dictates into a microphone, "Dear diary, Today, Wendy returned my tie-dyed shirt and my Che poster and told me to find someone else to repress and exploit." In another, a man angrily snaps at the woman who has jumped on top of him, "Hey! I'm not through seducing you yet." Yet another showed three women eyeing a magazine centerfold above the caption, "And his measurements are 42–34–36–9½!" On the editorial front, *Playboy* carried Germaine Greer's "Seduction Is a Four Letter Word," which asserted that "seduction" in the form of lies, trickery, and coercion constituted "petty rape." Her argument challenged the long-standing, winking view that condoned the ploys used by the savvy bachelor to bed his mate. For both parties, the publication of this article was strategic, suggesting to *Playboy*'s critics that it was progressive enough to print a feminist's viewpoint, while Greer reached a male audience of millions. A 1974 issue offered, "You've Come a Long Way, Buster," a compendium on masculinity, which pondered men as gendered beings. Features included a quiz, "Just What Kind of Man *Are* You?" along with "Memoirs of a Househusband" and "We Have Met the Enemy and He Is Us." The latter echoed the male liberation rhetoric, asserting that while men frequently envisioned women as a threat to masculinity, they had themselves to blame for creating foolish yardsticks for measuring manhood. At the same time, it gave voice to male anxieties in this changing climate about women's demands for satisfaction in bed and the perplexing state of flux in gender roles. As this writer put it, "Those of us who have sought manhood from birth squirm in the squeeze between manhood as we learned it and the modern abnegations we are instructed to accept."[43]

The battle for hearts and minds continued in the media, with *Playboy* serving as a visible target of feminists' outrage while "women's lib," in turn, provided the company with much public relations ammunition. The magazine defused the potency of feminist demands for gender equality by portraying nude women in traditionally male pursuits, suggesting the inescapability of anatomical difference. For example, as women seized on Title VII of the 1964 Civil Rights Act and the 1972 Equal Employment Opportunity Act in an effort to combat sex-based discrimination in the workplace, a June 1973 nude pictorial on "woman's work" told readers that "it's no big flash that many 'men's' jobs have become fair game—we just want to reassure you that anatomically

"As president of the committee on women's liberation. . . ."

6.1 *Cartoons addressed the challenge to traditional gender roles and the critique of male power posed by women's liberation. This one commented on feminists' affront to the gender order by inverting the familiar imagery of the male boss enjoying the service of his female secretary. (Reproduced by special permission of Playboy magazine © January 1971 by Playboy.)*

everything is status quo." Likewise, the pictorial "Caution: Women at Work!" attempted to eroticize women in "masculine" jobs. "Unfortunately, the jack-hammer seems to be more in control of the situation than its operator," the caption said of a woman astride the power tool wearing only a hardhat, unbuttoned shirt, and work boots. "But it's not hard to see how a person could get carried away, what with the vibrations and all." A second photograph showed the nude woman covered in oil and soot, while the accompanying text teased, "If this pretty... young wildcatter can't bring in a gusher, nobody can." Similar pictorials showcased "Women of the Armed Forces" and "The Women of the U.S. Government."[44]

In the 1970s and into the next decade, as women made advancements in the workplace, nude pictorials of women employed in traditionally male occupations served both as visual celebrations of "titillating and sexy" womanhood and "hearty guffaws" directed at women who encroached upon a male domain. If the sexual scenarios depicted in *Playboy*'s workplace cartoons and the working-girl femininity celebrated by Helen Gurley Brown were becoming grounds for organized protest or sexual-harassment suits, *Playboy*'s images of female workers promised that such upheavals were not cause for alarm. These images suggested that women's gains in both the blue-collar and white-collar "male" job market represented superficial change. Beneath the surface—and the clothing—the female anatomy still signaled a difference between the sexes, one that seemed to provide evidence that the gender order was not in jeopardy. Along such lines, Playboy staged a "Bunny-Lib" protest in Chicago and publicized Hefner's concessions to women's demands. Newspapers carried reports that Hefner was relaxing restrictions on fraternization with keyholders, acknowledging that he had been "a wee bit overprotective" of his Bunnies. The magazine highlighted the "protest" in a photo feature that resembled the working-woman pictorials from the same period, noting, "Today's cottontail may be more outspoken and independent than ever before, but she hasn't lost any of her charm."[45]

Playboy also seized upon publicity created by students protesting its presence on college campuses to shoot its college co-ed features. Photographer David Chan's appearance on Ivy League campuses stirred controversy in early 1979. The Harvard *Crimson* refused to print *Playboy*'s advertisement for models. Others, such as the Yale *Daily News,* did so only after much debate. Throughout his three-month tour of Ivy League campuses, Chan was greeted by angry demonstrators, who chanted "Don't Sell Your Ass to the Ruling Class!" and other slogans. Others wrote angry editorials in campus newspapers or organized speak-outs. Protestors, in turn, were taunted by hecklers. Newspapers, magazines, and television broadcasts covered the fracas.[46] The

resultant feature appeared in the September college issue, the title "Girls of the Ivy League" printed in capital letters. The word "Girls" had a line drawn through it, and "Women" was written above it, apparently a tongue-in-cheek concession to the anti-*Playboy* protestors (see figure 6.2). At Dartmouth, the issue was in such demand that librarians lent it out for only two hours at a time, carefully checking for missing pages each time it was returned. At Yale, first-day newsstand sales of the issue were reportedly seven times the average, and it sold out at Princeton. "Defying demonstrations, censorship and feminist flak," proclaimed the introduction to the pictorial, "coeds from America's most prestigious schools help *Playboy* prove that beauty and brains are not mutually exclusive." One journalist was dubious about this motive, submitting that the magazine trained its cameras on unclothed women from these elite institutions "not because the *Playboy* reader is suddenly seeking a woman to look up to," but because "he is seeking a woman to bring down."[47]

Why did the planned "Girls of the Ivy League" feature draw so much attention? "Do you think there would be this much media coverage or commotion if *Playboy* went to, say, Trenton State?" queried Dan Sheridan, *Playboy*'s news consultant. The author of an article in *Mother Jones* countered, "Of course, *Playboy* would never go to Trenton State College, because *Playboy*, in its attempt to capture and keep the most select portion of the porn market, is playing on the very gentlemanly respectability that Sheridan denounces."[48] Perhaps, but more to the point, many of the Ivy League schools had only recently admitted women into their hallowed halls, and in that sense this pictorial was not unlike the one depicting a bare-breasted woman with a jackhammer and work boots.

Playboy addressed women's advancement in the white-collar workplace in the same vein. "Executive Privilege," an article on office equipment, presented two photographs. Social changes "have created a number of office situations in which females are on top," the text explained. The first photograph depicted the "traditional" arrangement: a man sits at a desk, upon which his female assistant is poised, cat-like, on hands and knees, waiting expectantly to act on his every whim. The second photograph depicted a woman executive with a male secretary. "This man Friday has the boss's routine down pat.... It's not a bad job—once he accepts the idea that there'll be a little hanky-panky now and then." This scenario resolved the tension of the inverted workplace hierarchy: in the photo, the female executive sits with her legs extended on the desk, while she seductively reaches back to grasp the shoulder of her male assistant. Both graphics implied that the male would be satisfied—either with a woman poised to please him or as the object of affection of his attractive female boss. An article called "Sexual Office Politics: A Guide for the Eighties" explored the same theme, noting "two things will happen as more women join the executive ranks—the politics will get tougher and the sex will get terrific."[49] In this interpretation, equal

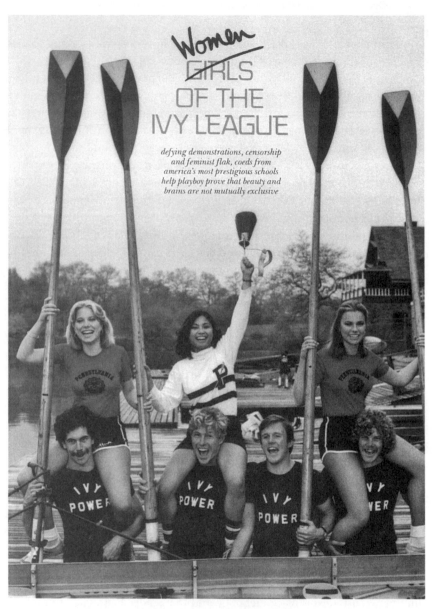

Women ~~GIRLS~~
OF THE
IVY LEAGUE

*defying demonstrations, censorship
and feminist flak, coeds from
america's most prestigious schools
help playboy prove that beauty and
brains are not mutually exclusive*

6.2 *As feminists denounced* Playboy *for objectifying women, the appearance of
the magazine's photographers on college campuses stirred controversy.* Playboy's
*tour of the Ivy League inspired both feminist protests and counterdemonstrations
by antifeminist hecklers as well as free-speech supporters. In the wake of these
debates,* Playboy *struck the word "girl" from the pictorial as a jesting concession
to critics' charges about the magazine's outmoded chauvinism. (Reproduced by
special permission of* Playboy *magazine © September 1979 by Playboy.)*

opportunity in the workplace was noteworthy not so much as a step toward egalitarianism, but as a chance for men to enjoy better sex.

Christie Hefner's ascent to the upper echelons of power at Playboy Enterprises provided another occasion to trumpet the compatibility of feminine sex appeal with women's aspirations for success. Editing and publishing his magazine had once riveted Hugh Hefner's attention, but the company's transformation into a public corporation, its widespread diversification, and its tumultuous fortunes in the 1970s held much less appeal for him; focusing instead on the self-contained pleasures of life at Playboy Mansion West, he began to play a diminished role in business operations. Hefner's daughter was reared by her mother and step-father after her parents divorced in 1959. She kept in contact with her father, however, and though she saw him infrequently during her childhood, the two grew closer after her graduation from college. Christie Hefner joined Playboy as a special assistant to her father in 1975, assuming increasing levels of respon-sibility over the next several years. In 1982, the daughter of *Playboy* magazine's founding editor and publisher assumed the presidency of Playboy Enterprises, Inc. That same year, the December issue of the magazine celebrated her pro-motion with one of its trademark pictorials, this one titled "The Women of Playboy," which featured the female employees of Playboy Enterprises, from secretaries to middle managers and beyond, in various states of undress. "I have an executive position that I earned with energy, talent and dedication, and I'm proud of it," asserted one woman who posed before the camera.[50] The female-authored text that accompanied the images in "The Women of Playboy" touted the skills and workplace accomplishments of these career women, a marked departure from the magazine's rhetoric of earlier decades that rebuked women for competing with men in the "male" business world. The photographs, how-ever, in presenting the female workers in typical *Playboy* form—clad in skimpy lingerie, breasts bared, pubic areas revealed—celebrated women's career gains while assuring readers that with respect to women's allure and sexual availabil-ity, all was more or less business as usual.

Playboy's depiction of women's workplace advancement attempted to uphold sex-based distinctions between men and women at a time when the link between the workplace hierarchy and the gender hierarchy appeared to be weakening. Take, for instance, "The Women of Playboy." The title marked a conscious choice of the word *woman* over *girl*, the latter used in most other pictorials, except, significantly, "The Girls/Women of the Ivy League" and subsequent features such as "The Women of Mensa," which informed read-ers, "They're beautiful, they're sexy *and* they have the bright stuff."[51] If the working-girl femininity that had sustained earlier images was under attack, these "Women of..." images presented a new category of women who were

intelligent, ambitious, and successful in traditionally masculine pursuits, but fit them within a familiar paradigm. Ultimately, they were still nice girls who took their clothes off for *Playboy*.

SLEEPING WITH THE ENEMY? FEMINISM AND THE ANTIPORNOGRAPHY MOVEMENT

An August 1974 NOW press release announced the organization's fifth annual media awards for positive and negative portrayals of women. *Playboy*, along with *Penthouse, Oui,* and others, received a "Meat Market" award "for dehumanizing both women and men." "Eroticism itself is not being objected to," this announcement clarified, "but instead the denial of human dignity." As part of this effort, set to coincide with the August 26th anniversary of women's suffrage, NOW sent letters to *Playboy*'s major contributors, urging them to stop publishing their work in the magazine. Their contributions, NOW claimed, "lent status and prestige" to *Playboy* while endorsing "its exploitation of women's bodies and male insecurities." "We are…aware of the liberal position that *Playboy* has taken on such issues as abortion reform," the letter explained, "but we point out that such reforms also contribute to the greater convenience of the playboy, who does not wish to assume responsibilities." *Playboy*'s progressive stance on certain issues did not excuse its continued disparagement of women.

> The central message of the women's movement, that women are and should be treated as human beings, is completely ignored, distorted or ridiculed in *Playboy* articles, letters, centerfolds, jokes and cartoons.…Whatever function *Playboy* might have played in the past, as a backlash against American sexual Puritanism, has been served and its only function today is to serve as a backlash against the women's movement and women's attempt to achieve a more positive self-image.

Author Joyce Carol Oates had published three short stories in *Playboy*. As one of the recipients of this entreaty, her reply to NOW also appeared in the magazine. Oates sympathized with the impulses behind the letter but called *Playboy* "astonishingly liberal" and disapproved of attempts to squelch expression in the magazine. "In a democratic society," she wrote, "there must be avenues of communication in publications that appeal to a wide variety of people, otherwise writers with certain beliefs will be read only by people with those same beliefs and change or growth would come to an end." Furthermore, she went on to explain,

> My personal belief is that worship of youth, flesh and beauty of a limited nature is typically American and is fairly innocuous set beside the pathological products of hard-core pornography, which glorify not the flesh but its mutilation. Should you compare *Playboy* with sadistic pornography, in which women's bodies are *not* worshipped but destroyed, you would see that your anger over *Playboy* and its hedonistic philosophy is possibly misdirected.

Oates lauded *Playboy* for "exceptionally fine interviews," "important articles," and "some very interesting fiction."[52] In articulating the value of the free exchange of ideas while also contrasting *Playboy* with images of sexualized violence, her reply touched on themes that would lead to growing debate in the second half of the decade and ignite the "sex wars" of the 1980s.

By the 1970s, the array of issues advanced by the women's movement included, along with equity in education and in the workplace, abortion rights and activism against rape, domestic violence, and sexual harassment. Women's antipornography activities of the 1970s evolved out of two endeavors, the critique and reform of sexist media as well as efforts to combat violence against women. In comparison to the inherently hierarchical "complementary" roles Hefner advocated for men and women two decades earlier, *Playboy,* by the mid-1970s, had come to accept the basic tenets of liberal feminism, positioning itself as a staunch supporter. Indeed, NOW and Playboy cosponsored a fundraiser at the Los Angeles Playboy Mansion in 1978 to raise money for NOW's ERA strike force. *Playboy* published a photograph of NOW's Gloria Allred and Christie Hefner looking on as Hefner signed a petition seeking an extension of the deadline for ratification.[53] The initial antipathy between NOW and Playboy and their subsequent alliance in the fight to ratify the Equal Rights Amendment point to the complexity of the issues at stake and the diversity of opinions about what counted as good feminist politics.

In San Francisco in 1976 and in New York in 1979, respectively, Women against Violence in Pornography and Media (WAVPM) and Women against Pornography (WAP) launched protests and organized tours in the urban districts where X-rated theaters and adult bookstores flourished. To these activists, pornography was "anti-woman propaganda," the "ideology of a culture" that promoted and condoned violence against women. Their efforts raised awareness of a burgeoning industry and fueled further initiatives to stamp it out. Much of this energy was directed toward combating "hard-core" pornography, sexually explicit images that often eroticized violence toward women, but magazines like *Playboy* also came under scrutiny, critiqued as part of a larger system of objectification. If pornography was increasingly invoked as a fundamental feminist issue, it also proved a difficult one around which to organize. Although

NOW had, in some ways, broken ground by critiquing and mobilizing against a sexist media, efforts to articulate a viable definition of pornography and to formulate a position on the matter proved acrimonious. Across the women's movement, feminists were far from united on the question of what actually constituted pornography, much less what to do about it. Some believed pornography was devoid of any social value, thus meriting no free-speech protection. Others noted with great concern that efforts to ban pornography led to censorship, long used to oppress women by limiting their access to information about birth control and abortion. Moreover, arguing that the lines between pornography and erotica were notoriously subjective, many questioned what right someone else had to define for them what was or was not an acceptable expression of sexuality.[54] As feminists grappled with the critique of pornography, they were further troubled by *Playboy*'s support of feminist causes. Were women who took their clothes off for *Playboy* sexually liberated or oppressed by capitalism and patriarchy? Had *Playboy*, for all its support of individual freedoms, advanced the cause of women, or was it the enemy? Could women's groups justify taking money from the enemy if it helped advance feminist goals?

As feminists tried to answer these questions, *Playboy* once again trumpeted the cause of individual freedom against its latest foes. Just as Joyce Carol Oates saw value in reaching the audience to whom *Playboy*'s "pictorial aspect" appealed, Christie Hefner likewise argued that *Playboy* played a role in advancing the goals of feminism. Playboy's charitable arm, the Playboy Foundation, as she put it, served as "the conscience of the company," which she believed was "in tune with my liberal feminist viewpoints." Hefner emphasized feminism as meaning options for women, stating, "I believe in and demand the right to choose my own lifestyle and to participate as an equal in the work force and in my personal relationships." In this regard, she argued that *Playboy* was not antithetical to feminism; in its coverage and support for liberal feminist issues like the ERA, it was helping bring men around to the idea of gender equality. "The magazine is reaching men who are in a state of transition, who need help in coming to grips with women. It reinforces their liberal instincts."[55]

Others were less convinced that *Playboy* could proselytize for the women's movement and doubted the company's motives for supporting women's causes. For those who saw links between pornography and violence in a culture where both flourished, Christie Hefner's rhetoric about choices and healthy fantasies was untenable. Like young people in the counterculture, these women registered concern about being co-opted. "Can Playboy Buy Women's Lib?" queried a headline in the radical publication *Majority Report*.

If feminist ethics were scored on a scale of ten, starting say, with renting out one's womb for cloning as zero and ending at the moral pinnacle

of holding off the national guard while squatting in a lesbian separatist halfway house for abused woman, taking money from the Playboy Foundation would rank somewhere just above taking a Revlon ad in a feminist newspaper.

According to this critic, while it was desirable to obtain funding from less vexing sources, the point was to make substantive progress toward achieving feminist goals. As she saw it, *Playboy*'s representations of women *were* damaging to women. She cautioned, however, that "laws against pornography will backfire against all of us who challenge the dominant dicta." In the meantime, it was more important to take Playboy's money and put it to good use. Shared by many organizations, this view condoned accepting money from groups like the Playboy Foundation as a means of "liberating their funds as reparations." Others rejected this mercenary position. "*Playboy* uses its contributions to our work," asserted antipornography activist Catharine Mackinnon, "to transform its position as active oppressors of women into the appearance of being standard bearers of women's equality." Among NOW's national leadership, Christie Hefner's membership on the corporate advisory board of the NOW Legal Defense and Education Fund (LDEF) and the LDEF's acceptance of Playboy Foundation donations produced serious misgivings that Hefner sought "political mileage" from these connections, using them to bolster her own and Playboy's feminist credentials. As another women's liberationist put it, accepting funds from the Playboy Foundation meant taking dirty money. "We are laundering it just as surely as the Nixon administration laundered their money," she argued, and in doing so, "We help the boys look good while all the time we are the losers."[56]

The relaxation of mores and legal restrictions that helped fuel the explosion of pornography had not gone unchecked. The Lyndon Johnson administration formed a presidential commission to investigate the trade in sexually explicit material shortly after the U.S. Supreme Court handed down rulings that allowed for its proliferation. Indeed, Richard Nixon's appeal to the "silent majority" with promises of "law and order" in 1968 and his stunning reelection in 1972 tapped the impulses of many Americans fed up with perceived liberal excess. To Nixon's great dismay, the President's Commission on Obscenity and Pornography, which issued its final report in 1970, detected no significant link between pornography and crime or delinquency. Calling its conclusions "morally bankrupt," Nixon rejected the commission's report.[57] By 1980, an upsurge of conservatism, led by the Christian Right and poised to repudiate the "permissive society" that had gained ground in the 1960s, again confronted the sexualized culture (see figure 6.3). One conservative group charged *Playboy* with the "unbridled promotion

6.3 *With its emphasis on sex outside of marriage, material acquisition, and individual fulfillment,* Playboy *drew substantial criticism as a leading force in the "permissive society" blamed for the breakdown of traditional morality and the decline of the family.* (National Catholic Register, *January 1975*)

of low-commitment sex, recreational drugs, selfish materialism, and adolescent irresponsibility." "Playboy, perhaps more than anyone else in the past 20 years has called America to self-indulge as never before and it appears that we are now reaping the results," proclaimed the anti-Playboy Chicago Statement Foundation. "It's becoming evident that popular hedonism will eventually wreck a society."[58] Such sentiments drove conservative efforts to combat the changes wrought by social and political liberalism since the 1960s. In confronting pornography, the right wing was primarily interested in an anti-smut campaign. As the sex wars got under way, many antiporn feminists actually found themselves on the same side of the issue as Reagan-era conservatives, despite the latter's opposition to abortion rights and the ERA. These strange bedfellows were opposed by an

alliance of anti-"antiporn" feminists and entrepreneurs who championed free speech while profiting from pictures of nude women's bodies.[59]

In editorial statements and articles, *Playboy* cast its opposition to antipornography activists as another battle for liberation against the forces of conservatism, while resisting any attempts to label the magazine "pornography." "For one wing of the feminist movement, the hot issue these days is not equal pay, job opportunities, day-care centers, the Equal Rights Amendment or abortion rights but pornography," wrote Robert Shea, invoking all the planks in a liberal feminist platform in order to suggest that attacking pornography was an ill-conceived effort in light of these worthwhile goals. Antiporn feminists, in his view, had not "advanced an inch in their thinking beyond earlier crusading prudes such as [Citizens for Decent Literature founder] Charles H. Keating Jr., and J. Edgar Hoover."[60] The publication of *Take Back the Night,* an anthology of feminist antipornography writings, prompted a rebuke in *Playboy.* "In the past few months, we've been calling attention to a new kind of Puritanism that is being foisted on us in the guise of liberated feminist thinking. . . . Now comes a book—*Take Back the Night*—that will serve as the *Mein Kampf* of this new totalitarianism," announced an editorial. "In the minds of these women, pornography is no longer an artifact of the sexual revolution—a curiosity or an indulgence. It has become a crime, a conspiracy to commit violence against women."[61]

Even as *Playboy* refuted the charges of antiporn critics, it also refused "to be defined by its detractors," a tactic Hefner had employed with great success in the early 1960s, when, rather than allowing attackers to have the final say about his magazine, he used the "Playboy Philosophy" series to declare its mission. "Nobody can agree on what pornography is, though nearly all definitions have a negative connotation," a *Playboy* article quoted Associate Publisher Nat Lehrman. "*Playboy*'s popularity is not based on pornography, hard- or soft-core. All the sexual images we originate are positive. They have no implication of aggressiveness, hostility or exploitation." "For 27 years, *Playboy* has tried to portray a healthful, robust sexuality based on equality of partners," explained *Playboy* in its denunciation of "The New Puritans." "We are a companion to pleasure. We have tried to destroy the notion that sex was something only bad girls did." Another editorial declared, "While Playboy and the Playboy Foundation have always advocated the right to freedom of speech, Playboy Enterprises has never distributed, nor published, sexual material that we (or the vast majority of the public) consider pornographic."[62]

These articles and editorials emphasized the right to voice dissent as well as to make choices in a free society. Shea, for instance, applauded the picketing and protesting efforts of antiporn feminists as a proper use of their First

Amendment rights, but cautioned that boycotts of vendors carrying popular magazines such as *Playboy* trampled on the rights of consumers. In the so-called secondary boycott, "One group of customers is depriving another group of customers the freedom to choose what it reads or sees.... It is what might be called vigilante censorship."[63] In her review of *Take Back the Night*, Christie Hefner made a plea for freedom of expression and the free market. "I agree with the contributors to this book that the presentation of violence meant to be sexually stimulating is offensive and deplorable," she wrote. "In fact, I refused to see *Dressed to Kill* because the idea of a woman being sliced up was so disturbing and offensive to me. But it never occurred to me that Brian DePalma didn't have the right to make that film." She concluded that "pornographers who make use of violence in their business should be condemned, but not outlawed." Editorial Director Arthur Kretchmer distributed copies of the article to the media, appealing to a shared concern for free speech. With the press "under attack from political zealots," he encouraged editors to quote from Hefner's "reasoned and stimulating" argument.[64]

Hugh Hefner marked his long-standing support of free speech with the creation of the Hugh M. Hefner First Amendment Awards. Feminists seized the occasion of the inaugural event in 1980 to bestow an honor of their own. Standing in front of the Los Angeles Playboy Club, members of Women against Violence against Women (WAVAW) presented *Playboy* with the "Hefner Award" for "encouraging the sexual harassment of working women, for trivializing the sexual abuse of girls, for ridiculing older women, for encouraging racism, and for promoting sexual violence." Meanwhile, the official Hefner First Amendment Awards were presented at a ceremony at Playboy Mansion West. One recipient, Sonia Johnson, had been excommunicated from the Mormon Church for her activities in support of the ERA. Inspired by the action of WAVAW, she refused to accept her award, telling the two hundred guests at the mansion, "I am a feminist first and I can't have my cake and eat it, too." Two years later WAVAW, joined by Women against Pornography (WAP), convinced three individuals, Gene Reynolds, Donna Shalala, and Charles Nesson, to resign their posts as judges for the Hefner First Amendment Awards. The awards, they claimed, were a "*Playboy* publicity scam—a smokescreen aimed at concealing *Playboy*'s business of degrading women." According to one WAP member, "The idea that women's bodies are commodities for men's pleasure and entertainment—like fancy cars and expensive wine—is central to *Playboy*'s 'philosophy,'" a notion that "lowers the status of women in society and legitimizes sexual violence."[65]

Not only were adversaries at odds when it came to defining pornography, but they disagreed on its meaning as well, a difference in viewpoint that helps

explain the contentious nature of this battle. *Playboy* advanced a view that the deluge of sexually explicit material, violent or otherwise, was simply part and parcel of the sexual revolution, which it identified as a movement from repression to freedom that helped make the women's movement possible in the first place. Antiporn feminists viewed the flood of pornography as a backlash against feminism, an attempt to put "uppity women" in their place by "stripping them of their dignity." In articles and editorials, *Playboy* emphasized the healthy sexuality embodied in its images, accusing antiporn feminists who objected to its airbrushed centerfolds as being "anti-sex." Women who condemned *Playboy*, however, voiced concern over the presence of demeaning jokes and cartoons, sexualized images of youth, and its presentation of women as one in a series of commodities. They did not attack the Playmate as a simple representation of a nude female body, but as a constructed package of meaning, couched in this specific context. Perhaps most important, *Playboy*, deemed "coffee-table pornography," came under attack for its powerful role in normalizing photographs of nude women for a male gaze, which critics viewed as having set the stage for the proliferation of "hard-core" porn. "Hefner and his *Playboy* empire seem comparatively mild," the authors of one *Take Back the Night* essay conceded. "But we must remember that it was exploitive images of women such as those promoted by Hefner that laid the groundwork for today's atrocities in pornography and media."[66]

If defining pornography proved difficult, curtailing it proved more so, for efforts seemed always to lead down the illiberal path to censorship. The antipornography ordinances proposed by Catharine Mackinnon and Andrea Dworkin in the 1980s energized supporters, in part because they seemed to offer a different path. The two proposed legislation to allow individuals to bring suit against pornographers for civil rights violations. First initiated in Minneapolis, this attempted intervention into the marketplace met with impassioned resistance. The passage of an antipornography ordinance in Indianapolis in 1984 was challenged in court by a variety of concerned interests—including the American Booksellers Association, *Playboy*, and a group of women who organized the Feminist Anti-Censorship Task (FACT) Force—all of whom questioned its abridgement of First Amendment protection. Over the next two years, FACT chapters sprang up wherever similar ordinances were proposed, including Suffolk County, New York; Madison, Wisconsin; San Francisco and Los Angeles, California; and Cambridge, Massachusetts. FACT registered concern not just over the proposed legislation but with antiporn theory and tactics more generally, which members saw as reminiscent of earlier efforts to safeguard women's purity. The antiporn position was premised on a problematic notion of an "inherently aggressive and destructive" male-identified sexuality.

Antiporn feminists, they argued, conflated sex with violence and condemned as categorically demeaning to women a whole range of images and practices that represented sexual diversity, not degradation. FACT also questioned the wisdom of aligning with right-wing supporters. The Indianapolis ordinance, they pointed out, had been embraced in that city not because it would advance the cause of feminism, but because it could aid in the war on smut. Furthermore, they saw the ordinances as offering "false promises," for at the end of the day, the central problem of subjective definition would remain when it came time to implement the laws.[67] Opponents of the Indianapolis ordinance filed suit and won a court order declaring it unconstitutional, a decision upheld by the U.S. Supreme Court in February 1986.[68]

Amid the flurry of antipornography legislation, the Attorney General's Commission on Obscenity and Pornography, later known as the Meese Commission, commenced its study of the pornography industry with a view to uncovering its connection, causal or otherwise, to criminal behavior. The commission was revisiting a question considered by the earlier President's Commission on Obscenity and Pornography, which had found no important link between pornography and crime or delinquency, a conclusion many critics found unsatisfying, particularly because it had concluded its work shortly before the upsurge in graphic and violent imagery.[69] One unusual indication of how far the line governing sexual expression had moved came in the form of the commission's final report. In the 1950s, when the Gathings Committee investigated the circulation of obscene materials, it deliberately chose to exclude from its published report any excerpts from the works it scrutinized. To include quotations from this material, the committee reasoned, "would be to disseminate obscenity," making the report itself "pornographic." The Meese Commission, however, compiled page after page of quotation and description from the films, books, and magazines under review. The resulting two-volume report reproduced much material commission members deemed pornographic, its explicit content even prompting one critic to boast that she had masturbated while reading the government's report.[70] Though the commission sought to curtail the circulation of graphic sexual material, the very report it produced highlighted the depth of social change since the 1950s.

Playboy received mention many times in the final report, which included troubling testimony such as that of one woman who "alleged that her father had used *Playboy* in connection with his molestation of her when she was a small child." The report also made clear, though, that *Playboy* constituted a different medium from that which primarily interested the commission. The report exonerated publications such as *Playboy*, explaining:

The true pornography industry is quite simply different from and separate from the industry that publishes "men's" magazines, the industry that offers some degree of sexually oriented material on broadcast and cable television, and the mainstream motion picture industry. In some rare instances there may be some linkages between the two, but in general little more than confusion is served by concentrating on these linkages rather than on the major differences.

The commission's content analysis of the April 1986 issue of *Playboy* found that 67 percent of the magazine dealt with topics not related to sex and only 10 percent of its advertising was sexually oriented, making it the magazine with the greatest general interest content and least sexually oriented advertising of all those examined.[71]

Playboy was essentially dismissed as a "men's magazine," a distinction that signaled the entrenchment of its version of sex in the mainstream of society. This did not keep opponents from grouping *Playboy* together with a variety of other much more explicit magazines. Reverend Donald Wildmon, head of the National Federation for Decency, and Christian evangelist Jerry Falwell organized pickets and boycotts of 7-Eleven and other retail stores selling *Playboy* and other magazines. Shortly before the Meese Commission published its findings, executive director Alan Sears issued a letter to several companies explaining that they were among the distributors of pornography about to be listed in the final report. In response, Southland Corporation, parent company of 7-Eleven, along with Rite-Aid and other retailers, announced that they would no longer sell *Playboy, Penthouse,* and *Forum.* Ten thousand stores removed the magazines from their shelves. Hefner saw it as a shakedown—"the first successful use of a national blacklist since the McCarthy era." Playboy Enterprises, Inc., filed a lawsuit asking the court to enjoin the attorney general's office to withdraw its threat. With the court ruling in *Playboy's* favor, the magazine struck back on another front as well, publishing a pictorial, naturally, on "The Women of 7-Eleven." "You know why we are running this pictorial; they know why we are," *Playboy* informed readers. "*Playboy* has always admired the girl next door. And sometimes the girl next door works at the store down the street." In case the point needed further clarification, one woman in the photos sipped from a 7-Eleven "Big Gulp," her cup emblazoned with the logo "Freedom of Choice."[72]

With the court's striking down of the antiporn ordinances, the antipornography campaign faded: "The last gasp of radical feminism," according to activist Susan Brownmiller. Yet tensions remained, even as the liberal viewpoint won out. As *Playboy* celebrated its victory over the Meese Commission in the form

of "The Women of 7-Eleven," the women who posed for this pictorial provided a stark contrast to the actions of other 7-Eleven store employees, who refused even to touch *Playboy* when customers brought it to the check-out counter. Magazines like *Playboy*, said one, told "lies about women." "They define sexuality solely in relation to men. Women in these magazines always do whatever turns men on." This young woman refused to be complicit in the sale of the magazine, explaining, "Most of the men who buy pornography buy something else, too, because they want a brown paper bag. We ring the sale and put everything except the magazine in the bag. We leave it on the counter so they have to deal with it." As the "pornography wars" subsided, the contrast between the "Women of 7-Eleven" who posed for the magazine and those who refused to abet purchasers of *Playboy* in even the smallest way was emblematic of philosophical divisions over the meaning of sexual liberation and women's power. As one journalist summed up, men and women were undecided as to "whether the truly liberated woman is one who can take her clothes off in front of a photographer or one who will kick the photographer in the shins for suggesting it." Those who based their arguments on individual choice in a free market conflicted with opponents who viewed its existence as symptomatic and sustaining of an exploitive system of representation. The antipornography movement revealed a multiplicity of viewpoints concerning the nature of sexual identity and the unclear line between one person's erotica and another's pornography. Efforts to combat the porn industry encountered a slippery slope toward censorship, problematic territory that made unified action almost impossible. Whether or not they included *Playboy* in their definition, for those who viewed porn as harmful to women, the campaign against it was difficult to sustain in the wake of the sex wars because, as Brownmiller has written, "all of a sudden, it seemed so illiberal."[73]

The articles that filled *Playboy*'s pages in the 1970s and 1980s indicated the extent of the social changes that had swept the country. As it had done from its inception, the magazine still served as a useful gauge of the social climate. Although the content had changed since the 1950s, the form remained the same: the unsettling sense that masculinity was in a state of powerful transition. Now, in place of articles on how to avoid marriage, *Playboy* offered advice about proper etiquette for having a woman spend the night and discussed the hidden pitfalls of living together. Warning of the legal claims one's female live-in companion could make on one's property, an article on cohabitation read like an updated version of the primer on alimony, "Miss Gold Digger of 1953." Other articles about custody rights for divorced fathers seemed a far cry from the image of the carefree bachelor who avoided traditional domesticity. Yet, in offering "A

Divorce Manual for Men," *Playboy* continued to act in its long-standing role as handbook for its male readers. In the early 1980s, Asa Baber's "Men" column began offering an introspective evaluation of gender roles and relationships. The inclusion of Cynthia Heimel's "Women" column provided a counterpoint and gave women a small but sustained voice in the magazine. Other articles, like one titled "Frigid Men," broke with the image of the Don Juan and moved on to the continued evolution of sexual attitudes and behaviors. In the wake of more permissive attitudes and a growing popular discourse on women's sexual desire, the hedonistic bachelor and his approach to women seemed anachronistic. The clever playboy no longer needed his bachelor pad and its many accouterments, or even his sexual magnetism, to get the girl into bed. Now he had another problem to worry about: how to perform. Readers also now found articles that addressed negotiating relationships in a changed society: how to deal with a failed marriage, cope with women as the initiators of sex, reconcile past notions of manhood with current demands for sensitivity, and accept women in the workplace on equal footing.[74]

In November 1985, as the Meese Commission sifted its way through magazines, videos, and peep shows, Playboy's Empire Club opened in New York, an updated version of the hip predecessor that first opened a quarter century earlier. The features of the new club pointed to the changes that occurred in the interim. Whereas the Playboy Clubs had limited their membership to men, the Empire Club welcomed men and women. Like the old Playboy Clubs, the new venue featured specially costumed staff. Dressed in updated renditions of the Bunny costume, however, women now served drinks and food alongside male counterparts who showed off biceps and torsos in their sleeveless or shirtless tuxedoes.[75] The gesture toward the transforming relations between men and women and the effort to keep up with the times went without reward. In the early 1960s, people had lined the street outside the daring new club. Now too few came to make operating the Empire Club a worthwhile venture. It closed in less than a year. The young urban professional men and women who frequented the club for a short while had other places to go and spend their money. But these yuppies who forestalled marriage and family, tenaciously pursued work, and spent lavishly represented the latest incarnation of the acquisitive singles culture that embraced "the playboy life," providing a testament to the lasting legacy of the Playboy empire. Later that year, the last of the Playboy-owned clubs quietly closed its doors.

EPILOGUE

America's Playboy Culture

IN 1986, THE year the Meese Commission issued its report on pornography and *Playboy* came under attack from the National Federation for Decency, *Newsweek* featured Hugh Hefner on its cover with the headline: "Playboy: The Party's Over."[1] *Newsweek*'s declaration summed up a number of troubles. Already facing opposition from feminists and conservative critics, *Playboy* further suffered in the 1980s from intense negative publicity over the murder of Playmate Dorothy Stratten. Hefner, *Playboy*, and life at the Playboy Mansion came under severe scrutiny in the public relations battle between Hefner and motion picture director Peter Bogdanovich, with whom Stratten was living at the time of her murder. Bogdanovich blamed Hefner for Stratten's death, charging the young woman had been driven to marry the man who ultimately killed her by the pressures she faced from a sexually aggressive Hefner and an exploitive Playboy machine. Hefner became consumed with the task of defending himself against specious accusations. As Playboy Enterprises, Inc. (PEI) continued to experience financial woes caused by declining circulation, lost advertising, and falling revenues, his health fared no better than the ailing company's. He suffered a stroke in March 1985. For many critics, Stratten's murder turned the centerfold model into a poster child, her death a tragic symbol of the licentious world of Playboy, an exploitive pornography industry, and the depravity of the wider permissive society.[2]

The sexual revolution for which Hefner claimed much credit appeared to be tempered in the 1980s as Americans became aware of the deadly threat of AIDS. Calls for "free love" gave way to warnings about "safe sex." Proponents of a resurgent political and cultural conservatism, citing climbing rates of divorce and teen pregnancy, seized upon the rhetoric of "family values" and attempted to beat back changes wrought by transforming sexual mores and the women's movement. At the same time, even as Reagan-era conservatives repudiated a society they viewed as diminished by liberal excess and sexual wantonness, the

acquisitive individualism of the decade represented a significant extension of the impulses for material reward and self-fulfillment central to *Playboy*'s ethos. The tumultuous cultural climate provided a fitting moment for Hefner, after a full recovery from his stroke, to ease the burdens of his role in his troubled company and to shed his bachelor lifestyle. In 1988, not long after announcing his engagement to Kimberley Conrad, Hefner relinquished to his daughter his position as chairman and CEO of Playboy Enterprises, Inc. Forty years—and innumerable sexual trysts and romantic involvements—after his first attempt to find domestic bliss, he opted once more for married life, wedding the twenty-six year old former Playmate in 1989. For nearly a decade, Hefner lived largely out of the glare of the media spotlight while fathering two sons. Children's toys and activities replaced the notorious adult-oriented revelry of his Los Angeles mansion.[3]

Meanwhile, the magazine Hefner had founded continued to offer its time-honored formula of regular departments, glossy pictorials, and timely articles and features as it moved into the 1990s. The Playboy Advisor doled out advice on style and sex, while regular columns kept readers apprised of "health and fitness" and "money matters," and an "after hours" section reviewed movies, videos, music, and books. Mainstays such as the Playboy Interview and Playboy Forum appeared monthly, as did features on food, fashion, and travel. Fiction and humor, along with topical articles, such as those surveying the sexual land-scape in the age of AIDS, rounded out the familiar editorial program. While the lifestyle package remained intact, the left-leaning politics that informed the magazine's editorial viewpoint in the 1960s and 1970s moved to the center, as *Playboy* registered distain for conservatism on the right and political correct-ness on the left.[4] Meanwhile, having divested PEI. of unprofitable ventures in failing nightclubs, filmmaking, and book publishing, and later, overseeing a corporate downsizing that trimming staff and moving the company out of the Playboy Building it had occupied since 1967, Christie Hefner managed a return to profitability in the latter 1990s.

For much of the decade, Hefner observed his daughter's stewardship of the company from afar, his attention focused largely on his second turn at family life. Preoccupied in his twenties with a desire to make something of himself, Hefner had little use for family life and fatherhood in the 1950s. As a parent again in his sixties, the publishing magnate doted on sons Marston and Cooper. His marriage grew strained, however, in part due to Hefner's strict adherence to a longtime weekly ritual of movie nights, card games, and other gatherings with friends in the self-contained world of the mansion, which frustrated his young wife's desires to make a more traditional home for her family and to escape from the routine of mansion life. In 1998, the couple parted. Hefner emerged

from the split ready to resume a familiar role as America's most renowned playboy.[5]

In April 1998, only months after the Hefners announced their separation, the American Society of Magazine Editors inducted Hugh Hefner and Gloria Steinem, founder and editor of *Ms. Magazine,* a standard bearer for the women's movement launched in 1971, into its hall of fame. It was an incongruous pairing that prompted Steinem to comment, "It's like a conservationist being given an award with a head of a timber company."[6] It was not the first time Hefner and Steinem had crossed paths. Back in 1963, Steinem had worked undercover as a Playboy Bunny and penned a scathing criticism of the Playboy Club for *Show* magazine. By the end of that decade, she was the media darling of the women's liberation movement, the feminist faction Hefner called *Playboy's* "natural enemies." The feeling was mutual. When Steinem interviewed Hefner in 1970, she told him, "There are times when a woman reading *Playboy* feels a little like a Jew reading a Nazi manual."[7] If antipathy remained between the two, a good deal had also changed since then, as the significance of Hefner's enterprise was reassessed and a younger generation of men and women began to embrace *Playboy*.

The honoring of Hefner at the 1998 awards ceremony marked just the beginning of the editor's resurgence in the public eye, as well as the renewed cachet of the Playboy brand. Playboy enjoyed a rebirth in the new millennium. Following his marital breakup, Hefner became a fixture in the entertainment news, cavorting at Los Angeles nightclubs with more than a half dozen platinum-haired girlfriends and hosting lavish mansion parties attended by Hollywood glitteratti. In Chicago, where city officials had once thwarted efforts to hold the Playboy Jazz Festival at Soldier Field, the city's native son was honored in a public ceremony dedicating the site of the first Playboy Club the "Honorary Hugh M. Hefner Way." *Playboy's* fiftieth anniversary drew national media coverage in 2004, and in 2006, Hefner marked his eightieth birthday with much publicized celebrations. Amid this renewed interest in Playboy, women once again donned rabbit ears and cotton tails at a new Playboy Club operated by the Palms Casino in Las Vegas. Meanwhile, on television the hit "reality show," *The Girls Next Door,* followed Hefner's girlfriends through daily life in residence at his swank LA mansion.[8]

The show, which first aired in 2005, was initially imagined as a program geared for an audience of young males. Instead it has garnered an unexpected following among young women. In contrast to sordid tales of seduction that characterized depictions of mansion life in the 1980s, *The Girls Next Door* amounts to a glimpse of well-funded sorority hi-jinks, where three young women pass their time in an endless whirlwind of party planning, field trips, and shopping,

while taking steps toward career goals, all in the pampered and protected environment of the well-staffed mansion. Hefner, who receives letters from young women around the world expressing interest in being his girlfriends, describes the program as a "guilty pleasure" akin to romance novels for the women who follow it.[9] The show offers a fantasy life of good times, with neither the drudgery and responsibility that ordinarily accompanied women's domestic role nor the pressures of the workplace, as the girls dabble in their respective career interests while Hefner appears primarily as a kindly benefactor.

For all of this resurgent attention to the Playboy image, however, *Playboy* magazine has never regained the widespread circulation, immense popularity, and cultural import it once enjoyed. Assessing the flagship magazine of his once far flung empire, Hefner acknowledges that the "uniqueness of *Playboy* and its appeal" were "greatest in its own particular time frame," an era when the publication appeared hip, racy, and unconventional and was able to dominate the field of men's magazines. More than half a century later, *Playboy* occupies a problematic position, simultaneously a publication in the mainstream and one that continues to be linked in the public eye with the sexually explicit material that has proliferated since the 1970s. "Until the success of *Penthouse* and *Hustler, Playboy* was judged by itself as the sexiest version of quality men's magazines. All that changed forever," Hefner opines, with the onslaught of those and other raunchy upstarts. Although *Playboy* gave chase to its competitors in the circulation battles of the 1970s, Hefner ultimately cautioned editors that he did not want to "wind up imitating the imitators." "I was very conscious of and concerned about the fact that the success of *Penthouse* and *Hustler, Penthouse* in particular, were confusing what we were doing…that we were going to be judged in a different way." Subsequent developments only confirmed those worries. Of *Playboy*'s decision to halt pursuit of its coarse competitors, Hefner explains, "We pulled out because we were suffering from and continue to suffer from that association." *Playboy* "wound up being ghettoized on the newsstands."[10]

Reflecting on the magazine's peak circulation in the early 1970s, Hefner notes, "*Playboy* had the marketplace pretty much to itself. Following that period, hardcore pornography arrived. VCRs arrived. Then, later on, the Internet." While the availability of graphic content in these new media forms siphoned away some of *Playboy*'s circulation, Hefner views the Meese Commission, and the impulses behind it, as having left an imprint as well on the magazine's fortunes. "We never got back the convenience stores. We're not distributed or openly displayed in much of America today," he explains. Too, feminist criticism of the magazine as demeaning to women has affected *Playboy*'s ability to garner advertising from companies fearful of recrimination. "When people…say that *Playboy* had a circulation of seven million and…suggest that somehow the magazine has fallen

out of favor," Hefner asserts, "they fail to recognize that we have not played on a level playing field since the 1980s. We suffer…in terms of distribution and advertising." "The only thing that sustains us today, while *Penthouse* is practically out of business, is the fact that the magazine is a good magazine. We had something else to offer. It wasn't all just tits and ass," he quips, invoking the perennial (and correct) adage that "people do read the articles." *Playboy*'s mix of nude pictorials, service features, and high quality writing place the magazine in the difficult middle ground between hard-core pornography, on one hand, and the so-called laddie magazines such as *FHM, Maxim,* and *Stuff,* on the other. Crass in tone, but without the full nudity and negative baggage of *Playboy,* these magazines since the 1990s have found success among a younger male audience, further complicating matters for the publication Hefner created.[11]

Playboy Enterprises has struggled to find solid footing on the shifting entertainment media landscape. Today, *Playboy* boasts a total paid circulation in the United States of 2.6 million, with locally produced editions published in twenty-five additional countries. The magazine remains iconic, though profits are elusive due to declining advertising and circulation revenues. Publishing is just one of PEI's three business groups. An entertainment division operates Playboy TV, which provides adult programming, as well as several Internet sites offering Playboy-themed adult content. For nearly two decades, Playboy's pay-television offerings stopped short of explicit sex. In 2001, PEI purchased Spice Hot, which shows, as one journalist has put it, "porn performers copulating in gynecologist-meets-urologist detail." The acquisition moved the company into the realm of hard-core programming in an attempt to capture some of this lucrative market, although the Playboy name, long intended to connote tasteful representations of sex, remains conspicuously dissociated from the network. Even with this foray into the realm of the explicit, the entertainment division faces a challenge from adult television competitors and freely available web-based content. The third business group, the company's licensing division, puts the Playboy logo on clothing and merchandise as well as the Palms Casino's Playboy Club. Signaling the power and symbolic value of the Playboy brand, it has served as a bright spot of profitability in recent years. In December 2008, as the nation endured a global economic downturn and Playboy's performance flagged, Christie Hefner announced her departure from the company she has guided through mostly troubled financial waters since the 1980s. Although the future remains unclear—the possible sale of the company has recently come under discussion—PEI continues to leverage the Playboy brand and hone its lifestyle package for the contemporary media environment in a search for profits. In April 2009, PEI launched a retooled website, Playboy.com, a digital experience promising "everything men need to enjoy the good life."[12]

Whatever the magazine's prospects, the values espoused in *Playboy* have become the norm for American society and culture. Hefner's magazine began as an instrument of self-liberation, initially serving as an outlet for the expression of fantasies about a life of sexual excitement and high living that seemed a far cry from his own. As the magazine took shape, *Playboy* became a mouthpiece for male liberation, rejecting conventions that saddled men prematurely with familial obligation and confined sex to marriage. "Nice girls" did, Hefner told readers, and, despite the postwar trend toward early matrimony, a young man did not have to wed to be a good citizen. There was a better way to spend young adulthood, one that promised to be much more fun. *Playboy* helped initiate young middle-class males into a society increasingly saturated with goods and oriented toward leisure. The magazine showcased the good life, a world of lavish penthouses, modern furnishings, sports cars, gourmet food, expensive liquor, exotic travel, good music, and of course, beautiful young women. These were the things available to young single men, Hefner told readers, offering a version of "wine, women, and song," remade for the postwar consumer society. If the stylistic markings of this particular vision have undergone change during the course of five and a half decades, *Playboy* nonetheless played a catalytic role in the refashioning of gender roles and sexuality mores since the 1950s, and its underlying messages about pleasure, consumption, and the freedom to find fulfillment in a lifestyle of one's own choosing are now cornerstones of American culture.

Playboy's distaste for traditional domestic roles, affirmation of women's right to enjoy sex outside of marriage, and support for women's reproductive freedom all embolden Hefner to assert, quite seriously, a half-century after starting his magazine, "I was a feminist before there was such a thing as feminism."[13] Reflecting on his contributions, Hefner readily points to a record of support for liberal feminist causes: the Playboy Foundation, founded in 1965, funded sex research and sex education, including the work of Masters and Johnson and SIECUS, the Sex Information and Education Council of the United States; it also supported birth control and abortion rights cases in the lower courts and filed an *amicus curiae* brief in *Roe* v. *Wade*. Beyond these efforts, Hefner rightly notes that one sees, in retrospect, strong similarities between his yearnings for a more vibrant life outside of familial obligation and women's dissatisfactions with postwar domesticity. Betty Friedan's attention in *The Feminine Mystique* to "women's frustration in the household," Hefner explains, "had a direct parallel to my feeling that there was something going on," in terms of the confinement of postwar gender roles, "that just didn't make sense." Such common cause made it difficult for the publisher to fathom the intense ridicule of his Playboy empire from the women's liberation movement. "I only really became conscious of it as feminism when I was attacked," he recalls. "I was

totally blindsided by it, and it was incomprehensible to me. I couldn't understand what they were talking about, where they were coming from, and for a long time, did not have the language to respond. It didn't make any sense to me at all." Hefner believed his magazine's assertion that sex was a part of life to be enjoyed by men *and* women put *Playboy* at the forefront of progressive change. As a result, women's liberation seemed like "a counterculture movement that was attacking us from the rear, because I thought that we were all in it together in terms of sexual revolution. I thought, then and now, that...women...were the real beneficiaries of the sexual revolution."[14]

Hefner's magazine did support the freeing of female sexuality from moralistic constraints, but its representations of gender and sexuality inspired a further critique of society. The liberating potential of *Playboy*'s assertions about "lifestyle" was not lost on feminists. "You're partly responsible for Women's Lib, in a way," Steinem told Hefner during their conversation in 1970. "You supplanted brute strength as a symbol of maleness with sports cars and appliances. If men don't play their Warrior Role, women don't have to play their Mother of Warriors role."[15] The men Hefner took as his constituency already occupied a position of power, however, so the liberation he proposed for them required a modification of the social order, not a dramatic restructuring of it. For many feminists of the "second wave," women were merely accessories of the good life depicted in *Playboy*, not equal partners in pursuing it. *Playboy*'s advocacy of sexual freedom, while challenging conventional wisdom that "nice" girls saved themselves for marriage, sustained existing gender structures. Interest in maintaining clearly defined differences between the sexes meant the magazine sustained stereotypes and assumptions about women's place relative to men, affirming a framework of male privilege. Feminists recognized that the kinds of social and sexual freedom trumpeted in *Playboy* would never fully be available to women without access to traditionally defined male institutions and a reevaluation of male power.

Decades after *Playboy* clashed with feminists, Hefner continues to attribute their criticism of the magazine to a "puritan element" within the women's movement, a view that emphasizes the link during the "sex wars" of antipornography feminists with conservatives, but fails to acknowledge the critique from the left of the commodification of sexuality and the challenge to a male pleasure-oriented heterosexuality levied by feminists in the late 1960s and early 1970s. "Why does a pinup picture turn a woman into something dehumanized?" Hefner wonders about the charge often leveled at his magazine. "Being a sex object is a good thing. It's only negative if that's all you are." For many women in feminism's "second wave," *Playboy* was part and parcel of a sexist media that negatively stereotyped women and emblematized the wider gender inequality that continued to thwart women's aspirations and

made them vulnerable to exploitation. For feminists who saw *Playboy*'s centerfolds and bunny costumes as reducing women to "sex objects," being an object was akin to being packaged and peddled like anything else in the magazine. For Hefner, "sex object" denotes being the focus of desire, a natural element of sexual attraction. "We *should* celebrate our sexuality. We *should* celebrate the difference between the sexes," Hefner says emphatically.[16] Feminists who emphasized the cultural construction, and, thus, mutability of gender roles over the biological differences between men and women posed a challenge to the clear gender distinctions long celebrated in *Playboy*. And the feminist assertion that "a woman needs a man like a fish needs a bicycle," certainly had no place in the "boy-girl society" promoted in his magazine. But Hefner's concerns that "militant feminists" would lead the nation down the path to androgyny did not come to fruition. The Playboy Club in Las Vegas marks the first new club venture since the 1985 opening of Playboy's short-lived Empire Club, which had featured bare-chested men alongside the usual buxom women in an effort to draw a mixed-gender clientele. That failed endeavor, Hefner remarked in 2006, had represented an ill-conceived attempt to pander to women, but there was no need for that at the new club. Women were embracing Playboy "in a way that was unthinkable 20 years ago. What previously was seen as a male chauvinist brand now is seen by women as a source of empowerment," Hefner claimed. "That makes me very happy."[17]

If young women are keen to party at the Playboy club, don tee shirts decorated with the rabbit head logo, or follow the televised exploits of *The Girls Next Door,* they are also members of a generation that has benefited from the fruits of the women's movement. Choice and empowerment characterize women's lives unevenly across the social spectrum, but generally speaking, as author Paula Kamen has shown, American women born since the late 1960s enjoy greater access to information about their own bodies, birth control, abortion, and sexual practices. They also have greater access to education, and therefore, to better jobs, which brings greater economic power and independence. And, coming of age in the wake of the sexual revolution and the women's liberation movement, they are more open to sexual communication. The result of these long-term developments is that young women, who benefit from the previous generation's struggle for change but often lack political consciousness or historical awareness of that fact, have redefined sex, gender roles, and relationships for themselves, in ways that bring self-fulfillment on their own terms.[18] This is a resonance of the kind of social and sexual emancipation Hefner encouraged, but it also required a further feminist critique of the vision of gender and sexuality promoted in *Playboy* during its initial decades of existence.

As women have come to wield greater control over their social and sex lives, cultural preoccupations over definitions of manhood and perceptions of women's power suggest continued anxiety about gender. In the 1980s, the

nascent pro-feminist, anti-sexist men's liberation groups of the 1970s gave way to a different sort of men's movement. The transition was best personified by Warren Farrell, the onetime board member of the National Organization for Women who became a staunch advocate of men's rights. As women continued to advance in society, the men's rights movement evinced perceptions that the gender system was a zero sum game. In the late twentieth century, as author Susan Faludi has argued, economic dislocations, job insecurity, the further erosion of male authority in the public sphere, and the prevalence of America's "ornamental culture," which compelled consumption and elevated appearance over substance, left many men feeling unmoored in an uncertain and superficial world. Where *Playboy*'s bachelor pads and anti-womanization diatribes gave expression to concerns about suburban conformity, feminization, and women's power in the 1950s and 1960s, the ascendant "men's movement" of the 1990s similarly addressed perplexing social changes. Some men went off to the woods on weekend, male-bonding retreats to recapture an essential masculinity lost in the feminized world of modern America. Men also sought relief through membership in the "Promise Keepers," whose adherents hearkened back to a mythologized vision of the nuclear family as they attempted to reassert patriarchal authority in the home. Others pointed to a rising "gender gap" in the nation's schools, where after three decades of female advancement at all levels of education, observers worried that boys were falling irretrievably behind.[19] As with earlier concerns about declining masculinity, these more recent expressions of anxiety overlooked the extent to which men continued to wield authority and power; taken together, they point to an important point of continuity running through the twentieth century, as broad social, economic, and cultural changes repeatedly have been experienced and expressed in gendered terms.

By packaging sex in a tasteful manner, Hefner dissociated "sex" from "smut" for mainstream audiences, ushering in frankness in discussions and representations of sex in popular media and helping to diminish its previous association with guilt and shame. But *Playboy* has generated unintended consequences, too. *Playboy* "certainly made it possible to open up the floodgates," as Hefner puts it, for the deluge of crude, exploitive sexual material that followed. Producers of the *Girls Gone Wild* video series, for instance, have achieved success traveling the country encouraging often intoxicated young women to remove clothing or engage in sexual activity for their video cameras. Asked about this phenomenon, Hefner wonders, "What in the world would motivate a bunch of young, supposedly intelligent women on college campuses" to want "to run out and take their clothes off and maybe have sex in a bus ... just because this bus comes through?" While participating in a *Girls Gone Wild* video is an extreme variant of posing for a centerfold, to be sure, Hefner's sentiments strikingly echo

concerns voiced by earlier critics perplexed by the young women who posed for his magazine's famous collegiate pictorials. The transgression of social boundaries remains titillating and profitable, and those boundaries have expanded considerably since *Playboy*'s heyday. To Hefner, the proliferation of "exploitive crap" is one of the vexing consequences of the erosion of sexual barriers in a free society, the latter one of the by-products of *Playboy*'s success. "We managed actually to introduce democracy to sexuality, a dangerous thing," he asserts. "It gives people choices.... Some people make some very stupid choices. And then sometimes it just has to do with taste."[20]

While choice no doubt characterizes the lives of women and men to a greater extent today than in the past, a sexualized popular culture complicates notions of sexual freedom. *Playboy*'s reach made it an authoritative arbiter of beauty and sex appeal—"hotness" in contemporary parlance—and it has played a tremendous role in driving the culture to embrace narrow standards of physical attractiveness and sexual expression. Author Ariel Levy has written about the standard currently in ascendance: "If you remove the human factor from sex and make it about stuff—big fake boobs, bleached blonde hair, long nails, poles, thongs—then you can sell it. Suddenly, sex requires shopping; you need plastic surgery, peroxide, a manicure, a mall." The commodification of sex is not new, of course. She points to the same marriage today of sexuality and capitalism that helped propel *Playboy*'s meteoric rise in the postwar period and drew vocal condemnation from feminists and other critics in the 1960s. Women's endorsement of mass-mediated images of sexual attractiveness is nothing new, either. What is new, as Levy suggests, is the widespread diffusion of a once-marginal form of sexual representation—a "porn aesthetic"—and its elevation as a standard by which women are measured, along with many young women's sense that by embracing such things as pornography, strip clubs, and *Girls Gone Wild* videos, they can experience the same agency and power as men. Unlike most second-wave feminists, these women do not view such commodified representations of female sexuality as oppressive because their own lives are characterized by the very social and economic independence that the women's movement strived to make possible. Yet efforts to emulate mass-mediated images can seem much less like self-expression than conformity to a stereotyped image of sexuality, a phenomenon that undercuts *Playboy*'s ethos of self-fulfillment.[21]

Hefner did more than advocate for more sex in popular culture and more sex in bed. He also promoted, through his glorification of pleasure-seeking bachelorhood and upscale consumption, a prolonged period of play instead of the hastened attainment of adult responsibility that characterized his generation. Prolonged singlehood is now a common feature of society. By the end of the

twentieth century, the median age at marriage had reached 27 for men and 25 for women. In 2003, the National Opinion Research Center reported that Americans placed the achievement of adulthood at about age 26. In other words, since the mid-twentieth century, the time between childhood dependency and adult responsibility has grown longer. For men and women today, the trappings of adulthood—marriage, family, full-time employment, home-ownership—are milestones achieved later in life than for their counterparts in the 1950s. The trend is due, in part, to economic forces, which have made it more difficult financially for young men and women to reach the benchmarks of adulthood than for those who rushed to the altar in the 1950s. Furthermore, the expansion of higher education and the professionalization of many jobs have prompted young people to stay in school for longer periods and to delay marriage and starting a family.[22]

The forestalling of adulthood speaks to social and cultural transformations as well. Single women in their mid-twenties are no longer viewed as "spinsters." Nor are young men who fail to marry by their mid-twenties deemed irresponsible. Building on the urban singles lifestyle of the 1960s, young urban professionals of the 1980s owed a cultural debt to the imperatives laid out in *Playboy* decades earlier, as well as to feminism. These young, single men and women worked hard and played hard, too, and made individual, rather than family-centered, consumption the focus of their efforts. Instead of the Single Girl's tenuous relationship to the workplace and consumption, female "yuppies" enjoyed the same economic independence and consumer power as the playboy. The ability of white middle-class women to join with their male counterparts in this lifestyle stemmed from their access to higher paying jobs and to the professions, a development made possible by the women's movement. Television's popular *Sex and the City* provided a more recent incarnation of Helen Gurley Brown's "Single Girl" further liberated by feminism, celebrating sex outside of marriage for women. While the family is still an important unit of consumption, the young single with income to spend on the "necessities" of leisure and entertainment helps fuel the consumer economy.

Hefner never meant for the playboy to be taken as a fashionable bum. He was a glamorous consumer, but also a man on the rise in his chosen profession, whose efforts to earn and spend helped drive the economy and kept the nation strong. In the postwar era, America's faith in economic growth required the expansion of the realm of necessities as well as the adoption of an ethical framework oriented toward consumption. Americans were urged to seek self-fulfillment rather than exercise restraint; failure to "live life to the hilt," to borrow a phrase from *Playboy,* meant failing to live up to the standards of the ascendant pleasure-oriented consumer ethos. Although some postwar critics registered concern about its implications, an economy organized around consumption

demanded self-indulgence, and in this regard, self-indulgence became linked to national well-being. The entrenchment of this ethos in today's society helps account for the difficulties policy-makers face in asking Americans to alter habits in favor of sustainable living as well as the nature of the solutions they propose to remedy an ailing economy, like providing tax credits to stimulate consumer spending. The federal call, not to sacrifice, but to consume in the name of national purpose, is the logical extension of earlier expressions of the consumer ethic, none so well formulated perhaps as Hefner's articulation during the Cold War of the moral economy of the playboy life.

From his vantage point in his eighties, Hefner avows, "I can look back over my record and say that I may have misspoken on occasions, but I have been on the side of the angels from the very beginning. My basic views and values...are essentially the same now as they were before."[23] For those who believe Hefner exorcised the devil from the flesh in a magazine that gave expression to desires for material abundance, freedom, and pleasure, his words ring true. For others who view *Playboy* as emblematic of a trend toward rampant consumerism, a sex-saturated culture, and a virulent individualism responsible for family decline and social atomization, the magazine's founder may seem like a much more nefarious force. *Playboy* took the figure of the carefree bachelor as a model for an elongated period of youthful enjoyment, sexual fulfillment, and pleasurable consumption, suggesting that young men who followed the advice of the magazine would ultimately lead more rewarding lives. The views and values of this iconic magazine have come to flow freely in the mainstream of modern America. Along the way, popular discussions of *Playboy* have become, in effect, debates about American life, revealing then and now much about the cultural preoccupations and anxieties of American society.

NOTES

Abbreviations

ACS   Auguste Comte Spectorsky
CHM   Chicago History Museum
CT   Chicago Tribune
CWLU   Chicago Women's Liberation Union Papers, Chicago History Museum
HMH   Hugh M. Hefner
HP   Hugh M. Hefner Papers, 1954–1970. Playboy Archives, Playboy Enterprises, Inc., Chicago, Illinois
HS   Hugh M. Hefner Scrapbook Collection, Playboy Mansion, Los Angeles, California
KIL   The Kinsey Institute Library, Kinsey Institute for Research in Sex, Gender, and Reproduction Inc., Bloomington, Indiana
NOW   National Organization for Women Records, Schlesinger Library, Radcliffe Institute for Advanced Study, Harvard University
NYT   New York Times
PMR   Print Media Response to the Kinsey Report, Kinsey Institute Library
PVF   Playboy Vertical File
SLVFWS   Schlesinger Library Vertical File for Women's Studies Microfilm Collection
SP   Auguste Comte Spectorsky Papers, 1956–1971. Playboy Archives, Playboy Enterprises, Inc., Chicago, Illinois
WEF   Women's Ephemera Files, Charles Deering McCormick Library of Special Collections, Northwestern University

Introduction

1. Marie Torre, "A Woman Looks at the Girly-Girly Magazines," *Cosmopolitan,* May 1963, 42–43.

2. "Volume 1, Number 1," *Playboy,* undated first issue, 3.

3. As *Look* magazine put it, men and women faced new challenges and sometimes longed "for the old, sure ways" as they attempted to "pioneer a new kind of marriage, the partnership." Laura Bergquist, "A New Look at the American Woman," *Look,* 16 October 1956, 35. On the changing context of marriage, see Jessica Weiss, *To Have and to Hold: Marriage, the Baby Boom, and Social Change* (Chicago: University of Chicago Press, 2000); for women's employment, U.S. Department of Commerce, Bureau of the Census, *Historical Statistics of the United States, Colonial Times to 1970* (Washington, DC: U.S. Government Printing Office, 1975), Part I, 131.

4. Frederick Lewis Allen, "My, How You've Changed," *Chicago Daily News,* 9 August 1952. For discussion of the postwar family ideal, see Elaine Tyler May, *Homeward Bound: American Families in the Cold War Era* (New York: Basic, 1988); Stephanie Coontz, *The Way We Never Were: American Families and the Nostalgia Trap* (New York: Basic, 1992); Steven Mintz and Susan Kellogg, *Domestic Revolutions: A Social History of American Family Life* (New York: Free Press, 1988). On suburban growth, see Kenneth T. Jackson, *Crabgrass Frontier: The Suburbanization of the United States* (New York: Oxford University Press, 1985). For popular culture, see Lynn Spigel, *Make Room for TV: Television and the Family Ideal in Postwar America* (Chicago: University of Chicago Press, 1992); Ella Taylor, *Prime Time Families: Television and Culture in Postwar America* (Berkeley: University of California Press, 1989); Karal Ann Marling, *As Seen on TV: The Visual Culture of Everyday Life in the 1950s* (Cambridge: Harvard University Press, 1994). On economic growth, consumption, and national purpose, see Lizabeth Cohen, *A Consumers' Republic: The Politics of Mass Consumption in Postwar America* (New York: Knopf, 2003); Daniel Horowitz, *Anxieties of Affluence: Critiques of American Consumer Culture, 1939–1979* (Amherst: University of Massachusetts Press, 2004); Robert M. Collins, *More: The Politics of Economic Growth in Postwar America* (New York: Oxford University Press, 2000); Charles F. McGovern, *Sold American: Consumption and Citizenship, 1890–1945* (Chapel Hill: University of North Carolina Press, 2006); Robert H. Haddow, *Pavilions of Plenty: Exhibiting American Culture Abroad in the 1950s* (Washington, DC: Smithsonian Institution Press, 1997). On the tensions and paradoxes of postwar change, see Warren Susman with Edward Griffen, "Did Success Spoil the United States?" in Lary May, ed., *Recasting America: Culture and Politics in the Age of Cold War* (Chicago: University of Chicago Press, 1989), 19–37; Roland Marchand, "Visions of Classlessness, Quests for Dominion: American Popular Culture, 1945–1960," in Robert H. Bremner and Gary W. Reichard, eds., *Reshaping America: Society and Institutions 1945–1960* (Columbus: Ohio State University Press, 1982), 163–182. For overviews of the period, see William H. Chafe, *The Unfinished Journey: America since World War II* (New York: Oxford University Press, 1995); James T. Patterson, *Grand Expectations: The United States, 1945–1974* (New York: Oxford University Press, 1996); David Halberstam, *The Fifties* (New York: Villard, 1993); John Patrick Diggins, *The Proud Decades: America in War and in Peace, 1941–1960* (New York: Norton, 1989).

5. Hefner, quoted in "Mike Wallace Interviews Playboy," *Playboy,* December 1957, 61. Kenon Breazeale, in "In Spite of Women: *Esquire* Magazine and the Construction of the Male Consumer," *Signs* 20 (Autumn 1994): 9, wrote that magazines are "calculated packages of meaning," designed to "transform the reader into an imaginary subject." Because

they are "devised and experienced as a whole," magazines are "most meaningfully studied as a system entire," an approach I have similarly employed here.

6. "What Sort of Man Reads Playboy?" advertisement, *Playboy,* November 1966, and "Playbill," *Playboy,* September 1960, 8.

7. Barbara Ehrenreich, *The Hearts of Men: American Dreams and the Flight from Commitment* (New York: Anchor Press, 1983). Ehrenreich was responding to an anti-feminist backlash that blamed the women's movement for a decline in "family values." In pointing out *Playboy*'s role in undermining the male breadwinner–female homemaker compact between men and women, Ehrenreich countered critics' assertions about feminism. She also joined in a wider radical-feminist critique of *Playboy* as the apogee of the consumer society, a view this study seeks to illuminate.

8. The term comes from Betty Friedan's *The Feminine Mystique* (New York: Norton, 1963).

9. Weiss, in *To Have and to Hold,* points out the ways in which the "traditional" family of the 1950s, in fact, represented innovation as well as a single stage in the entire cycle of family life. Joanne Meyerowitz, ed., *Not June Cleaver: Women and Gender in Postwar America* (Philadelphia: Temple University Press); Eva Moskowitz, "'It's Good to Blow Your Top': Women's Magazines and a Discourse of Discontent, 1945–1965," *Journal of Women's History* 8 (Fall 1996): 66–98; Wini Breines, *Young, White, and Miserable: Growing up Female in the Fifties* (Boston: Beacon, 1992); Coontz, *The Way We Never Were;* and William H. Chafe, *The Paradox of Change: American Women in the Twentieth Century* (New York: Oxford University Press, 1991), 175, 182–192, discuss multivalent discourses on woman's role and family life and the process of transformation in the 1950s.

10. "Dear Playboy," *Playboy,* August 1956, 3.

11. Beth Bailey outlines the roots of sexual revolution in widespread changes initiated by World War II in *Sex in the Heartland* (Cambridge: Harvard University Press, 1999). For an overview, see John D'Emilio and Estelle Freedman, *Intimate Matters: A History of Sexuality in America* (New York: Harper & Row, 1988).

12. Ehrenreich, *Hearts of Men,* 41. On the broad social, economic, and cultural changes involved in the formation of American consumer society in this period, see William Leach, *Land of Desire: Merchants, Power, and the Rise of a New American Culture* (New York: Vintage, 1993); Alan Trachtenberg, *The Incorporation of America: Culture and Society in the Gilded Age* (New York: Hill and Wang, 1982); Olivier Zunz, *Making America Corporate, 1870–1920* (Chicago: University of Chicago Press, 1990); James Livingston, *Pragmatism and the Political Economy of Cultural Revolution* (Chapel Hill: University of North Carolina Press, 1994); Roland Marchand, *Advertising the American Dream: Making Way for Modernity, 1920–1940* (Berkeley: University of California Press, 1985); Warren Susman, "Introduction: Toward a History of the Culture of Abundance: Some Hypotheses," in *Culture as History: The Transformation of American Society in the Twentieth Century* (Washington, DC: Smithsonian Institution Press, 2003), xix–xxx; T. J. Jackson Lears, *No Place of Grace: Antimodernism and the Transformation of American Culture, 1880–1920* (New York: Pantheon, 1981). For new amusements and changing mores, see John Kasson, *Amusing the Million: Coney Island at the Turn of the Century*

(New York: Hill and Wang, 1978); Lary May, *Screening out the Past: The Birth of Mass Culture and the Motion Picture Industry* (New York: Oxford University Press, 1980); Lewis Erenberg, *Steppin' Out: New York Nightlife and the Transformation of American Culture, 1890–1930* (Chicago: University of Chicago Press, 1981); Kathy Peiss, *Cheap Amusements: Working Women and Leisure in Turn of the Century New York* (Philadelphia: Temple University Press, 1986); Beth Bailey, *From Front Porch to Back Seat: Courtship in Twentieth Century America* (Baltimore: Johns Hopkins University Press, 1988); Kevin White, *The First Sexual Revolution: The Emergence of Male Heterosexuality in Modern America* (New York: New York University Press, 1993). On college youth, see Paula S. Fass, *The Damned and the Beautiful: American Youth in the 1920s* (New York: Oxford University Press, 1977), and Bill Osgerby, *Playboys in Paradise: Masculinity, Youth and Leisure-style in Modern America* (Oxford: Berg, 2001). For African-American youth culture on college campuses, see Martin Summers, *Manliness and Its Discontents: The Black Middle Class and the Transformation of Masculinity, 1900–1930* (Chapel Hill: University of North Carolina Press, 2004).

13. Howard Chudacoff, *The Age of the Bachelor: Creating an American Subculture* (Princeton: Princeton University Press, 1999), 48, 55–74, 186–210; Mark A. Swiencicki, "Consuming Brotherhood: Men's Culture, Style and Recreation as Consumer Culture, 1880–1930," *Journal of Social History* 31 (Summer 1998): 773–808. On "sporting male" culture, see Timothy J. Gilfoyle, *City of Eros: New York City, Prostitution, and the Commercialization of Sex, 1790–1920* (New York: Norton, 1992), 103–106. For male-oriented periodicals and literature, see White, *First Sexual Revolution*, 27–30, 45–51, 61; Tom Pendergast, *Creating the Modern Man: American Magazines and Consumer Culture, 1900–1950* (Columbia: University of Missouri Press, 2000), 5, 206–223; Guy Reel, *The National Police Gazette and the Making of the Modern American Man, 1879–1906* (New York: Palgrave, 2006); Breazeale, "In Spite of Women"; and Hugh Merrill, *Esky: The Early Years at* Esquire (New Brunswick, NJ: Rutgers University Press, 1995). For advertising and masculinity, see Carole Turbin, "Fashioning the American Man: The Arrow Collar Man, 1907–1931," *Gender and History* 14 (November 2002): 470–491.

14. A key development of twentieth-century American culture, according to Warren Susman, was a shift in values evident in the displacement of "character" by "personality" as the requisite for success. While the transition may not have been as clear-cut as Susman and others have maintained, modern culture did place new demands on and suggested new meanings for the presentation of self, which had important ramifications for men's position within the new visual and consumer culture. Warren Susman, "'Personality' and the Making of Twentieth-Century Culture," in *Culture as History*, 271–285. For a revised reading of Susman's sources, emphasizing the continuity between depictions of character and personality, see Andrew R. Heinze, "*Schizophrenia Americana*: Aliens, Alienists and the 'Personality Shift' of Twentieth-Century Culture," *American Quarterly* 55 (June 2003): 227–256.

15. Pierre Bourdieu, in *Distinction: A Social Critique of the Judgement of Taste*, trans. Richard Nice (Cambridge: Harvard University Press, 1984), identified the process by which a new petite bourgeoisie, anxious about eroding class differences, claimed status

in 1960s French society by constructing taste as a way to differentiate from the lower classes and, in turn, uphold the hegemony of the consumer capitalist system and its privileged place within it. Training this analytical spotlight on the United States, Bill Osgerby, in *Playboys in Paradise,* has deepened our understanding of the ways in which gender and class identities are formed by demonstrating how *Playboy* helped point the way toward a middle-class masculine identity formulated around consumption. For further discussion, see Thomas Weyr, *Reaching for Paradise: The Playboy Vision of America* (New York: Times Books, 1978), and Jesse Isaac Berrett, "The Secret Lives of Consumer Culture: Masculinity and Consumption in Postwar America" (Ph.D. diss., University of California, Berkeley, 1996).

16. Elliott Gorn, *The Manly Art: Bare Knuckle Prize Fighting in America* (Urbana: University of Illinois Press, 1986), 192–93; E. Anthony Rotundo, *American Manhood: Transformations in Masculinity from the Revolution to the Modern Era* (New York: Basic, 1993), 252; Gail Bederman, *Manliness and Civilization: A Cultural History of Gender and Race in the United States, 1880–1917* (Chicago: University of Chicago Press, 1995), 16; Kristin L. Hoganson, *Fighting for American Manhood: How Gender Politics Provoked the Spanish-American and Philippine-American Wars* (New Haven: Yale University Press, 1998); Paula Baker, "The Domestication of Politics: Women and American Political Society, 1780–1920," *American Historical Review* 88 (June 1984): 620–647; Michael Kimmel, "Men's Responses to Feminism at the Turn of the Century," *Gender and Society* 1 (September 1987): 261–283; Margaret Marsh, "Suburban Men and Masculine Domesticity, 1870–1915," *American Quarterly* 40 (June 1988): 165–86; Mark C. Carnes, *Secret Ritual and Manhood in Victorian America* (New Haven: Yale University Press, 1989).

17. Works that view the 1960s as the moment of feminist revolt against an entrenched domestic ideology of the Cold War era include May, *Homeward Bound;* Glenna Matthews, *"Just a Housewife": The Rise and Fall of Domesticity in America* (New York: Oxford University Press, 1987), 197–222; Leila J. Rupp and Verta Taylor, *Survival in the Doldrums: The American Woman's Rights Movement, 1945 to the 1960s* (New York: Oxford University Press, 1987); Maureen Honey, *Creating Rosie the Riveter: Class, Gender and Propaganda during World War II* (Amherst: University of Massachusetts Press, 1984); Sara Evans, *Personal Politics: The Roots of Women's Liberation in the Civil Rights Movement and the New Left* (New York: Vintage, 1979). Works emphasizing the intense transitions already underway in the postwar era include Meyerowitz, *Not June Cleaver*; Weiss, *To Have and to hold;* Joel Foreman, ed., *The Other Fifties: Interrogating Midcentury American Icons* (urbana: University of illinois Press, 1997), and Peter J. Kuznick and James Gilbert, *Rethinking Cold War Culture* (Washington, D.C.: Smithsonian Institution Press), 2001).

18. For examples see Dennis Brissett and Lionel S. Lewis, "Guidelines for Marital Sex: An Analysis of Fifteen Popular Marriage Manuals," *Family Coordinator* (January 1970), 45; Mirra Komarovsky, "Cultural Contradictions and Sex Roles," *American Journal of Sociology* 52 (November 1946): 184–189; A. J. Smith, "How Masculine Are You?" *Real,* January 1954, 46; R. B. Amber, "How Masculine or Feminine Are You?" *Coronet,* July 1955, 73–75; Hannah Lees, "Women Should Not Play Dumb," *Saturday Evening Post,* 28 January 1961, 27; Ralph F. Berdie, "A Femininity Adjective Checklist," *Journal of Applied*

Psychology 43, no. 5 (1959): 327–333. For discussions of masculine crisis, see Beth Bailey, *From Front Porch to Back Seat,* 103–108, and Steven Cohan, *Masked Men: Masculinity and the Movies in the Fifties* (Bloomington: Indiana University Press, 1997); for apprehensions of masculine decline and American political culture and foreign policy during the early years of the Cold War, see K. A. Cuordileone, *Manhood and American Political Culture in the Cold War* (New York: Routledge, 2005); Robert Dean, *Imperial Brotherhood: Gender and the Making of Cold War Foreign Policy* (Amherst: University of Massachusetts Press, 2001); David K. Johnson, *The Lavender Scare: The Cold War Persecution of Gays and Lesbians in the Federal Government* (Chicago: University of Chicago Press, 2004), and Frank Costigliola, "'Unceasing Pressure for Penetration': Gender, Pathology, and Emotion in George Kennan's Formation of the Cold War," *Journal of American History* 83 (March 1997): 1309–1339. James Gilbert's *Men in the Middle: Searching for Masculinity in the 1950s* (Chicago: University of Chicago Press, 2005) reassesses the extent to which American men were concerned about masculine "crisis."

19. This book builds on the insights of scholars who have demonstrated that gender is contingent, constructed in culturally and historically specific contexts, and functions as a critical site for the mapping of difference and thus for the signification of relationships of power. It presumes to be gender "performatively constituted" and articulated within a framework of culturally defined norms for male and female identities. Joan Scott, "Gender: A Useful Category of Historical Analysis," *American Historical Review* 91 (December 1986): 1053–1075, and Judith Butler, *Gender Trouble: Feminism and the Subversion of Identity* (New York: Routledge, 1990), are seminal works. For an assessment of recent trends in the study of masculinity, see Bryce Traister, "Academic Viagra: The Rise of American Masculinity Studies," *American Quarterly* 52 (June 2000): 274–304.

20. Hefner quoted in Alan Whitney, "Playboy: Sex on a Skyrocket," *Chicago Magazine,* October 1955, 32–37. On interrogating what people seek to escape and the form such escapism takes, see Lawrence W. Levine, "The Folklore of Industrial Society: Popular Culture and Its Audiences," *American Historical Review* 97 (December 1992): 1375.

Chapter One

1. William Kiedaisch, "How a Cartoonist Lives," *Chicago Daily News,* 21 March 1953, 8.

2. For Hefner's postwar anxieties, see cartoons in volume 34, HS, esp. "Goo Heffer," 23 May 1946; Bill Davidson, "Czar of the Bunny Empire," *Saturday Evening Post,* April 1962, 35; Thomas Weyr, *Reaching for Paradise: The Playboy Vision of America* (New York: Times Books, 1978), 17–18. For detailed discussion of Hefner's personal life, see the recent biography by Steven Watts, *Mr. Playboy: Hugh Hefner and the American Dream* (New York: Wiley, 2008). Other biographical works include Russell Miller, *Bunny: The Real Story of Playboy* (New York: Holt, Rinehart and Winston, 1984), and Frank Brady, *Hefner* (New York: Macmillan, 1974).

3. For the dislocations caused by the war, see Lewis A. Erenberg and Susan E. Hirsch, *The War in American Culture: Society and Consciousness during World War II* (Chicago: University of Chicago Press, 1996); William M. Tuttle, Jr., *"Daddy's Gone to War": The Second World War in the Lives of America's Children* (New York: Oxford University Press, 1993); George Roeder, *The Censored War: American Visual Experience during World War II* (New Haven: Yale University Press, 1993); Michael C. C. Adams, *The Best War Ever: America and World War II* (Baltimore: Johns Hopkins University Press, 1994); Roger W. Lotchin, ed., *The Way We Really Were: The Golden State in the Second Great War* (Urbana: University of Illinois Press, 2000); Christina S. Jarvis, *The Male Body at War: American Masculinity during World War II* (DeKalb: Northern Illinois University Press, 2004); Karen Anderson, *Wartime Women: Sex Roles, Family Relations, and the Status of Women during World War II* (Westport, CT: Greenwood Press, 1981); Sherna Berger Gluck, *Rosie the Riveter Revisited: Women, the War, and Social Change* (Boston: Twayne, 1987); Maureen Honey, *Creating Rosie the Riveter: Class, Gender and Propaganda during World War II* (Amherst: University of Massachusetts Press, 1984); Elaine Tyler May, *Homeward Bound: American Families in the Cold War Era* (New York: Basic Books, 1988), 58–91. On reconversion, see Jack S. Ballard, *The Shock of Peace: Military and Economic Demobilization after World War II* (Washington: University Press of America, 1983); Lizabeth Cohen, *A Consumer's Republic: The Politics of Mass Consumption in Postwar America* (New York: Knopf, 2003), 100–165; George Lipsitz, *Rainbow at Midnight: Labor and Culture in the 1940s* (Urbana: University of Illinois Press, 1994); Joseph C. Goulden, *The Best Years: 1945–1950* (New York: Atheneum, 1978). For juvenile delinquency, see James Gilbert, *A Cycle of Outrage: America's Reaction to the Juvenile Delinquent in the 1950s* (New York: Oxford University Press, 1986), 24–41.

4. For college, job search, and marriage, see volumes 36–45, HS; "Think Clean," *Time*, 3 March 1967, 77–82.

5. On shortened timeframe for attaining adult milestones, see Jessica Weiss, *To Have and to Hold: Marriage, the Baby Boom, and Social Change* (Chicago: University of Chicago Press, 2000), 17–21. Hasty wartime unions drove up the marriage rate in the first half of the 1940s; they also contributed to the spate of divorces at war's end. By the end of the decade, the divorce rate had nearly returned to prewar levels. The median marriage age among men dipped below 23.0 by 1949 and remained between 22.5 and 23.3 until 1975. For nearly twenty years, until the mid-1960s, the median age for women remained below 20.5. Between 1940 and 1960 the proportion of singles in the adult male population also decreased, from 33.2 percent to 23.2 percent. By 1950, nearly 60 percent of women age 18–24 were married, up from 42 percent in 1940. May, *Homeward Bound*, 8; Susan B. Carter, et al., eds. *Historical Statistics of the United States, Earliest Times to the Present: Millennial Edition* (New York: Cambridge University Press, 2006), Volume I, Part A, 685; Howard Chudacoff, *The Age of the Bachelor: Creating an American Subculture* (New Brunswick, NJ: Princeton University Press, 1999), 254–55; William Chafe, *The Unfinished Journey: America since World War II*, 5th ed. (New York: Oxford University Press, 2003), 117–118.

6. Weiss, *To Have and to Hold*, 25–26; May, *Homeward Bound*, 3–8, 16–36. For a contemporary expression of the view that Americans turned to the family for security and fulfillment, see William Graham Cole, "Early Marriage," *The Nation*, 8 February 1958, 111–113. Examples of prescriptive literature include Hilda Holland, ed., *Why Are You Single?* (New York: Farrar Straus & Co., 1949); Jean van Evera, *How to Be Happy while Single* (Philadelphia: Lippincott, 1949), and Ferdinand Lundberg and Marynia F. Farnham, *Modern Woman: The Lost Sex* (New York: Grosset & Dunlap, 1947). On adjustment, see Barbara Ehrenreich, *The Hearts of Men: American Dreams and the Flight from Commitment* (New York: Anchor Press, 1983), 14–28, and K. A. Cuordileone, *Manhood and American Political Culture in the Cold War* (New York: Routledge, 2005), 118–166. Of thirteen million homes constructed in the United States between 1948 and 1958, 85 percent were created in the suburbs. Eighteen million people moved to suburbia between 1950 and 1960. Kenneth T. Jackson, *Crabgrass Frontier: The Suburbanization of the United States* (New York: Oxford University Press, 1985), 233, 240–241; Steven Mintz and Susan Kellogg, *Domestic Revolutions: A Social History of American Family Life* (New York: Free Press, 1988), 183–186; Chafe, *Unfinished Journey*, 112. On reconversion and housing in Chicago see Laura McEnaney, "Nightmares on Elm Street: Demobilizing in Chicago, 1945–1953," *Journal of American History* 92 (March 2006): 1265–1291.

7. Chafe, *Unfinished Journey*, 111. On college students' expectations for security in the corporation, see William H. Whyte, Jr., *The Organization Man* (New York: Simon & Schuster, 1956), 71–72.

8. Hugh M. Hefner, *That Toddlin' Town: A Rowdy Burlesque of Chicago Manners and Morals* (Chicago: Chi Publishers, 1951); Hugh Hefner, "Sex Behavior and the US Law," paper for Social Pathology course (May 1950) in volume 46, HS; Hugh Hefner, "Christmas 1951" letter in volume 49, HS. For "Millie and Hef's New Apartment," see volume 50, HS.

9. On men's magazines in the 1940s and 1950s, see Theodore Peterson, *Magazines in the Twentieth Century* (Urbana: University of Illinois Press, 1964), 310–316; Audit Bureau of Circulations, *Magazine Trend Report* (Schaumburg, IL, 1965); Michael Kimmel, *Manhood in America: A Cultural History* (New York: Free Press, 1996), 254. For a good example of the "art photography" approach, see "Pin-up Fantasy," *Modern Man*, January 1952, 24. For "sexual ghetto," see Hugh Hefner, "Golden Dreams," *Playboy*, January 1994, 116.

10. Volume 52, HS; Hefner, "Golden Dreams," 121–122. The actress posed for a $50 modeling fee in 1949 before achieving stardom in *Asphalt Jungle* (1950). The photographs received much publicity once "Marilyn" became a household name, with *Life* magazine even printing a small, two-color reproduction of one image. The calendar had not been distributed widely, nor did the images appear in large format or full-color in any magazine. Tom Kelley, "I Photographed Marilyn in the Nude," *Modern Man*, March 1955, 10–14, 43.

11. "Announcing the Birth of Playboy," *Playboy*, v. 1, n. 1 (1919), n.p.

12. Unsure if anyone would buy it, Hefner removed the date at the last minute, thinking the magazine could stay on display until it sold. He sold enough of the 70,000-issue print run to make possible a second issue. Hugh Hefner, [letter to posterity, January 1954], volume 53, HS; "The Illustrated History of Playboy," *Playboy*, January 1979, 264;

Hefner, "Golden Dreams," 121–122, 263–265, 272; Hugh M. Hefner and Bill Zehme, *Hef's Little Black Book* (New York: HarperCollins, 2004), 117–126.

13. Hefner, "Golden Dreams," 114, 266, and "Playboy Interview: Hugh M. Hefner," *Playboy*, January 1974, 72.

14. "Volume 1, Number 1," *Playboy*, undated first issue, 3.

15. *Stag* gave readers "true" adventures and crime exposés, features on sports, hunting, and fishing, and "off-trail articles appealing to the American male." *Male* and *Cavalier* offered similar content, as did *True, Men, Real: The Exciting Magazine for Men*, and *Impact: Bold True Action for Men*. Peterson, *Magazines in the Twentieth Century*, 310–316; Audit Bureau of Circulations, *Magazine Trend Report*; Kimmel, *Manhood in America*, 254; Bill Osgerby, *Playboys in Paradise: Masculinity, Youth and Leisure-style in Modern America* (Oxford: Berg, 2001), 76–78. Tom Pendergast describes postwar efforts to revamp *True* into "*Esquire* for the Beer-and-Poker Set," in *Creating the Modern Man: American Magazines and Consumer Culture, 1900–1950* (Columbia: University of Missouri Press, 2000), 223–238.

16. "Playbill," *Playboy*, December 1954, 2.

17. "Dear Playboy," *Playboy*, July 1954, 3; "Sassy Newcomer," *Time*, 24 September 1956, 71, and "For Young City Guys," *Newsweek*, 7 November 1955, 68. Along with letters published in the monthly "Dear Playboy" section, the magazine went on to include, beginning in September 1960, "The Playboy Advisor," and in July 1963, "The Playboy Forum." At times, particularly in the initial stages of Advisor and Forum, staff members created letters in order to advance editorial goals. Articles and features sometimes were circulated among notable individuals ahead of publication in order to solicit timely or desirable responses. Archival evidence indicates that *Playboy* regularly received unprompted correspondence from readers as well, although PEI does not maintain a collection of letters. While it is not possible to authenticate every letter that appeared in *Playboy*, throughout the text I refer to published letters for the purpose of demonstrating how these sections of the magazine served to address controversy or to further an editorial viewpoint.

18. Kenon Breazeale, "In Spite of Women: *Esquire* Magazine and the Construction of the Male Consumer," *Signs* 20 (August 1994): 5.

19. *Esquire*, Autumn 1933, n.p; "As for Esquire's Moral Tone," *Esquire*, July 1934, 11.

20. Breazeale, "In Spite of Women," 5–6, and *The Sixth New Year: A Resolution* (Chicago: Esquire, 1939), 35.

21. *The Third New Year: An Etude in the Key of Frankness* (Chicago: Esquire, 1935), 29–30.

22. Breazeale, "In Spite of Women," 6–7, and Pendergast, *Creating the Modern Man*, 5, 206–223. On men's grooming practices, see Kathy Peiss, *Hope in a Jar: The Making of America's Beauty Culture* (New York: Metropolitan Books, 1998), 159–166. On fashion, see Carole Turbin, "Fashioning the American Man: The Arrow Collar Man, 1907–1931," *Gender and History* 14 (November 2002): 470–491.

23. *Esquire*, Autumn 1933, n.p.

24. Breazeale, "In Spite of Women," 1, 7, 9.

25. *The Sixth New Year,* 35; Hugh Merrill, *Esky: The Early Years at* Esquire (New Brunswick, NJ: Rutgers University Press, 1995), 4–12, 32; Pendergast, *Creating the Modern Man,* 210.

26. *The Third New Year,* 32–33.

27. Even one of Hefner's self-proclaimed "guiding principles," a quote from Shakespeare, "To thine own self be true, and thou canst not then be false to any man," was also a maxim claimed by *Esquire. Sixth New Year,* 41, and Hugh M. Hefner, "The Playboy Philosophy," *Playboy,* January 1963, 48.

28. "High Court Lifts Esquire Mail Curb," NYT, 5 February 1946, 23; Lois Banner, *American Beauty* (Chicago: University of Chicago Press, 1983), 154–166, 279, and Merrill, *Esky,* 39–41, 81–82, 85–95, 109–120.

29. For circulation figures, see Audit Bureau of Circulations, *Magazine Trend Reports,* for *Playboy* and *Esquire* for 1955, 1958, 1960. Paid circulation did not take into account the magazine's reach among readers who shared issues. See "Dear Playboy," *Playboy,* December 1955, 4; "Sassy Newcomer," 71; "Hefner's Playboy," *Fortune,* May 1957, 216; and "A Dime More a Peep," *Newsweek,* 23 May 1960, 72.

30. Betty Friedan, *The Feminine Mystique* (New York: Norton, 1963); Eva Moskowitz, "'It's Good to Blow Your Top': Women's Magazines and a Discourse of Discontent, 1945–1965," *Journal of Women's History* 8 (Fall 1996): 66–98; "Special Issue on the American Woman," *Life,* 24 December 1956. See the film series produced by McGraw-Hill based on Henry A. Bowman's marriage text, *Marriage for Moderns,* Alexander Hammid, director, "Who's Boss?" (McGraw-Hill Text-Films, 1950); Alexander Hammid, director, "Marriage Today" (McGraw-Hill Text-Films, 1950); Willard Van Dyke, director, "This Charming Couple" (McGraw-Hill Text-Films, 1950); Irving Jacoby, director, "Who's Right?" (McGraw-Hill Text-Films, 1954).

31. John Keats, *The Crack in the Picture Window* (Boston: Houghton Mifflin, 1956); A. C. Spectorsky, *The Exurbanites* (New York: Lippincott, 1955), 218–252. A work of amateur sociology, Spectorsky's book received significant attention and was even synopsized in a half-hour CBS radio broadcast. Excerpts also appeared in *Playboy.* "Radio: Exurbia Revisited," NYT, 31 March 1956, 29. A. C. Spectorsky, "Exurbanites at Play," *Playboy,* April 1957, 21.

32. Whyte, *Organization Man,* 10, 361–363; Richard E. Gordon, M.D., Katherine K. Gordon, and Max Gunther, *The Split-Level Trap* (New York: Bernard Geis Associates, 1961), 27–33; T. F. James, "Crack-ups in the Suburbs," *Cosmopolitan,* October 1960, 60; Mary Merryfield, "It's Brinkmanship vs. Bankruptcy," CT, 12 August 1962, F1.

33. Gail Bederman, *Manliness & Civilization: A Cultural History of Gender and Race in the United States, 1880–1917* (Chicago: University of Chicago Press, 1995), 5–7.

34. C. Wright Mills, *White Collar: The American Middle Classes* (New York: Oxford University Press, 1951), xii, xvii, 188; David Riesman, et al., *The Lonely Crowd: A Study of the Changing American Character* (New Haven: Yale University Press, 1950), 26; Whyte, *Organization Man,* 154, 159.

35. Barbara Ehrenreich, *Hearts of Men,* 33–34, and James Gilbert, *Men in the Middle: Searching for Masculinity in the 1950s* (Chicago: University of Chicago Press, 2005), 50–54.

36. John McPartland, *No Down Payment* (New York: Simon & Schuster, 1957), 87–93; Friedan, *Feminine Mystique*, 203; Philip Wylie, *Generation of Vipers* (New York: Farrar & Rinehart, 1942).

37. Women's share of the workforce grew from 25.8 percent in 1940 to 34.5 percent in 1960. Married women's share of the female workforce increased from 35.9 percent in 1940, to 52.2 percent in 1950, to over 60 percent by 1960. In 1940, only 15 percent of married women worked outside the home; by 1960 that figure had doubled. Mitra Toossi, "A Century of Change: The U.S. Labor Force, 1950–2050," *Monthly Labor Review* (May 2002): 18–24; Leila Rupp, "The Survival of American Feminism: The Women's Movement in the Postwar Period," in Robert H. Bremner and Gary W. Reichard, eds., *Reshaping America: Society and Institutions* (Columbus: Ohio State University Press, 1982), 36; Julie A. Matthaei, *An Economic History of Women in America: Women's Work, the Sexual Division of Labor, and the Development of Capitalism* (New York: Schocken, 1982), 272–273; Weiss, *To Have and to Hold*, 50–53. On concerns about "sex role convergence," see Wini Breines, *Young, White and Miserable: Growing up Female in the Fifties* (Boston: Beacon, 1992), 25–46.

38. Robert F. Winch, "Courtship in College Women," *American Journal of Sociology* 55 (November 1949): 278; Margaret Mead, "American Man in a Woman's World," NYT Magazine, 10 February 1957, 23; Sloan Wilson, *The Man in the Gray Flannel Suit* (New York: Pocket Books, 1955; reprint, New York: Four Walls Eight Windows, 2002), 187; George B. Leonard, "The American Male: Why Is He Afraid to Be Different?" *Look*, 18 February 1958, 95–104; J. Robert Moskin, "The American Male: Why Do Women Dominate Him?" *Look*, 4 February 1958, 80; William Atwood, "The American Male: Why Does He Work So Hard?" *Look*, 4 March 1958, 71–75.

39. Jack Harrison Pollack, "How Masculine Are You?" *Nation's Business*, June 1950, 49–55; Daniel Starch and Staff, *Male vs. Female: Influence on the Purchase of Selected Products as Revealed by an Exploratory Depth Interview Study with Husbands and Wives* (New York: *True—The Man's Magazine*, 1958), 23, 30, 33. "Pushbutton" quote comes from George Frazier, "The Entrenchment of the American Witch," *Esquire*, February 1962, 103. Atwood, "Why Does He Work So Hard?" 73; Moskin, "Why Do Women Dominate Him?" 79–80. See also Martin Tolchin, "Wife Who Wins Battles May Find She Lost War," NYT, 24 May 1960, 28; "Strong Man Called Need of Families," NYT, 5 November 1960, 17.

40. Bob Norman [Burt Zollo], "Miss Gold Digger of 1953," *Playboy*, undated first issue, 6; Martin Abramson, "The Not So Tender Trap," *Playboy*, July 1958, 47; "Comes the Resolution," *Playboy*, January 1957, 77; Burt Zollo, "Open Season on Bachelors," *Playboy*, June 1954; 37–38.

41. Shepherd Mead, "Hasty Marriage," *Playboy*, January 1956, 46–48, 65; Jay Smith, "A Vote for Polygamy," *Playboy*, July 1955, 15–16. See also "The Playboy Coloring Book," *Playboy*, January 1963, 65, and William Iversen, "Love, Death, and the Hubby Image," *Playboy*, September 1963, 92.

42. Wylie, *Generation of Vipers*, 46–48. On Spectorsky's role at *Playboy* and his relationship with Wylie, see Gilbert, *Men in the Middle*, 189–214.

43. Frazier, "Entrenchment of the American Witch," 100–103.

44. Hefner quoted in Simon Nathan, "About the Nudes in *Playboy*," *U.S. Camera*, April 1962, 69–70. Hefner offered this account of gender role confusion without much variation in multiple interviews, including the radio program "Project 62—Playboy of the Modern World," Canadian Broadcasting Company, 4 February 1962, transcript in volume 71, HS; the television program "At Random," CBS, 3 July 1962, transcript in volume 73, HS; and the documentary film directed by Gordon Sheppard, *The Most* (Pyramid Films, 1962). "Changing Roles in Modern Marriage," *Life*, 24 December 1956, 109. See also William Iversen, "I Only Want a Sweetheart, Not a Buddy," *Playboy*, July 1960, 57.

45. "The Playboy Panel: The Womanization of America," *Playboy*, June 1962, 43.

46. Victor Lownes quoted in Davidson, "Czar of the Bunny Empire," 38.

47. Hugh Hefner, interview with author, Los Angeles, California, 14 January 2009. Hefner's dismay over the affair is recounted in Gay Talese, *Thy Neighbor's Wife* (Garden City, NY: Doubleday, 1980), 38–41; Hugh M. Hefner and Bill Zehme, *Hef's Little Black Book* (New York: HarperCollins, 2004), 138, 147–148; and Steven Watts, *Mr. Playboy*, 47–48.

48. Quoted in Frederick Christian, "Sex Cultism in America," *Cosmopolitan*, April 1958, 66–67.

49. This view informed researchers' questions to unmarried male inductees about whether one's first sexual experience had been with a prostitute or a "nice girl." Before a sexual partner was recorded as a "nice girl," respondents had to answer yes to two questions: "Was she a girl you would have married?" and "Was she a girl you would have introduced to your mother and sister?" Leslie B. Hohman and Bertram Schaffner, "The Sex Lives of Unmarried Men," *American Journal of Sociology* 52 (May 1947): 503.

50. For silencing efforts as inciting discourse, see Michel Foucault, *The History of Sexuality*, trans. Robert Hurley (New York: Vintage, 1990), 33–35.

51. Alfred C. Kinsey, Wardell B. Pomeroy, and Clyde E. Martin, *Sexual Behavior in the Human Male* (Philadelphia: Saunders, 1948); Alfred C. Kinsey, *Sexual Behavior in the Human Female* (Philadelphia: Saunders, 1953); *Minneapolis Morning Tribune*, 20 August 1953, PMR; "No Kin," *Time*, 25 October 1948.

52. "Sidelights"; "Public to Get Kinsey Data Tomorrow"; "Kinsey's Book on Women"; "Sex for Sale"; "The Controversy Begins"; "That Book"; "The Editors Look at a Book"; and "City Pastors Call Kinsey Report 'Dangerous' to Morals of Youth," all in volume M–N, newspapers, of PMR, and "All about Eve: Kinsey Reports on American Women," *Newsweek*, 24 August 1953, 68–71.

53. On Kinsey's critics, see Gilbert, *Men in the Middle*, 89–93. For Kinsey's impact on religious views of sex, see R. Marie Griffith, "The Religious Encounters of Alfred C. Kinsey," *Journal of American History* 95 (September 2008): 349–377.

54. "Uproar on Dr. Kinsey"; "Letter to the Editor," Meriden, *Connecticut Record*; "Letter to the Editor," Muncie (IN) *Press*, all in volume M–N, PMR, and John D'Emilio and Estelle Freedman, *Intimate Matters: A History of Sexuality in America* (New York: Harper & Row, 1988), 286.

55. For discussion of rock and roll, see Karal Ann Marling, *As Seen on TV: The Visual Culture of Everyday Life in the 1950s* (Cambridge: Harvard University Press, 1994), 165–182; Michael T. Bertrand, *Race, Rock, and Elvis* (Chicago: University of Illinois Press, 2000);

W. T. Lhamon, Jr., *Deliberate Speed: The Origins of a Culture Style in the American 1950s* (Washington, DC: Smithsonian Institution Press, 1990). For dating and sexual expression, see D'Emilio and Freedman, *Intimate Matters*, 274, 277; Bailey, *Front Porch to Back Seat*, 77–96; Brett Harvey, *The Fifties: A Woman's Oral History* (New York: HarperCollins, 1993), esp. chap 1. For sexual "containment," see May, *Homeward Bound*, 92–102, 118–134. On single pregnancy, abortion, and adoption, see Rickie Solinger, *Wake up Little Susie: Single Pregnancy and Race before* Roe v. Wade (New York: Routledge, 1992); Leslie J. Reagan, *When Abortion Was a Crime: Women, Medicine, and Law in the United States, 1867–1973* (Berkeley: University of California Press, 1997); Elaine Tyler May, *Barren in the Promised Land: Childless Americans and the Pursuit of Happiness* (New York: Basic, 1995), 140–149; Ann Fesler, *The Girls Who Went Away* (New York: Penguin, 2006). For fashion, see Jane Farrell-Beck and Colleen Gau, *Uplift: The Bra in America* (Philadelphia: University of Pennsylvania Press, 2002), 90–94, 126–128; Bailey, *Front Porch to Back Seat*, 73–74; May, *Homeward Bound*, 112. On "sweater girl" contests see Susan Hartmann, *The Homefront and Beyond: American Women in the 1940s* (Boston: Twayne, 1982), 198. "Sweater girl" contests encouraged young women to show off bustlines in tight-fitting sweaters. Reporters first applied the term "sweater girl" to Lana Turner, who appeared in tight-fitting garb in the 1937 film *They Won't Forget*. College fraternities, local merchants, and national knitwear manufacturers organized the contests throughout the 1940s and 1950s. This attention to breasts, along with the codification of a measurement system for bra size, brought into vogue the colloquial usage of bra-cup size or bust, waist, and hip measurements, for example, 36–24–36, to describe a woman's physique.

56. *Report of the Select Committee on Current Pornographic Materials* (Washington, DC: GPO, 1952), 1–2, 34, 12–128. The committee also heard testimony that high school students pooled money to purchase copies of the first Kinsey Report, 101. For the role of women in moral crusades of the 1950s, see Joanne Meyerowitz, "Women, Cheesecake, and Borderline Material: Responses to Girlie Pictures in the Mid-Twentieth-Century U.S.," *Journal of Women's History* 8 (Fall 1996): 23–26.

57. "Sassy Newcomer," 71; Maurice Rosenfield to Paul H. Gebhard, 26 November 1958, PVF, KIL; "Teen-Age Nude Given 15 Days for Contempt," CT, 11 March 1958, 5; HMH to Advertising Staff, 3 July 1962, Folder 3, Box 20, HP (the memo was in response to Calder Willingham's "Bus Story"); "Two Definitions of Obscenity," *Time*, 21 June 1963, 44; "Think Clean," *Time*, 3 March 1967, 80; "Hefner Arrested on Obscenity Charge," CT, 5 June 1963, 20; "Judge Rules Mistrial in Hefner Case," CT, 7 December 1963, 4. For Hefner's take on the obscenity charges, see Hugh M. Hefner, "The Playboy Philosophy," *Playboy*, October 1963, 81, and "The Playboy Philosophy," *Playboy*, November 1963, 49.

58. For "pariah capitalists" see Jay A. Gertzman, *Bookleggers and Smuthounds: The Trade in Erotica, 1920–1940* (Philadelphia: University of Pennsylvania Press, 1999). On Frank Walker, see Merrill, *Esky*, 104–119, and Paul S. Boyer, *Purity in Print: Book Censorship in America from the Gilded Age to the Computer Age*, 2d ed. (Madison: University of Wisconsin Press, 2002), 271–273. On the production code, see David A. Cook, *A History of Narrative Film*, 4th ed. (New York: Norton, 2004), 428–429; Thomas Doherty, *Pre-code Hollywood: Sex, Immorality, and Insurrection in American Cinema, 1930–1934* (New York: Columbia University Press, 1999); Gregory D. Black,

Hollywood Censored: Morality Codes, Catholics, and the Movies (New York: Cambridge University Press, 1994); Frank Walsh, *Sin and Censorship: The Catholic Church and the Motion Picture Industry* (New Haven: Yale University Press, 1996). Concern for the innocent young person in determinations of obscenity followed a standard set forth in the British case *Regina v. Hicklin* (1868). A precedent for evaluating a work in light of its effect on the average adult rather than the vulnerable child was set in *United States v. One Book Called "Ulysses"* 5 F. Supp. 182 (S.D. N.Y., 1933). The new obscenity standard was articulated in *Roth v. United States* 354 U.S. 476 (1957). See Boyer, *Purity in Print*, 275–278; Walter Kendrick, *The Secret Museum: Pornography in Modern Culture* (Berkeley: University of California Press, 1996), 195–203; D'Emilio and Freedman, *Intimate Matters*, 287, and Edward de Grazia, "How Justice Brennan Freed Novels and Movies during the Sixties," *Cardozo Studies in Law and Literature* 8 (Autumn-Winter 1996): 259–265.

59. "Mike Wallace Interviews Playboy," *Playboy*, December 1957, 61.

60. David K. Johnson, *The Lavender Scare: The Cold War Persecutions of Gays and Lesbians in the Federal Government* (Chicago: University of Chicago Press, 2004); John D'Emilio, "The Homosexual Menace: The Politics of Sexuality in Cold War America," in *Making Trouble: Essays on Gay History, Politics, and the University* (New York: Routledge, 1992), 57–73; Alan Berube, *Coming out under Fire: The History of Gay Men and Women in World War Two* (New York: Free Press, 1990), 264–270; Lillian Faderman, "The Love That Dares Not Speak Its Name: McCarthyism and Its Legacy," in *Odd Girls and Twilight Lovers: A History of Lesbian Life in Twentieth Century America* (New York: Columbia University Press, 1991), 139–158, and Stephen J. Whitfield, *The Culture of the Cold War* (Baltimore: Johns Hopkins University Press, 1996), 43–45.

61. Articles and features addressing sexual hypocrisy and the "female point of view" include Ivor Williams [William Iversen], "The Pious Pornographers," *Playboy*, October 1957, 24; "Dear Ann and Abby," *Playboy*, December 1958, 25; Oliver Kinkaid, "The Miss America Joke," *Playboy*, September 1959, 49; William Iversen, "The Pious Pornographers Revisited," *Playboy*, October 1964, 116. Hefner, quoted in "Mike Wallace Interviews Playboy," 83; Nathan, "About the Nudes in *Playboy*," 68, 70–71; Hal Higdon, "Playboying around the Clock with Hugh Hefner," *Climax*, February 1962, 85.

62. HMH to Frances Brenner, 19 November 1954; HMH to Russ Meyer, 29 March 1955; HMH to John Morrin, 18 February 1955; HMH to Hal Adams, 22 June 1955, [no other location] HP.

63. Nathan, "About the Nudes in *Playboy*," 72, and Miller, *Bunny*, 48–50. The first Playmate crafted as the "girl next door" appeared in the July 1955 issue under the pseudonym Janet Pilgrim. That pictorial is discussed in chapter 4. The first triple-page centerfold appeared in March 1956.

64. Hefner, quoted in Oriana Fallaci, *The Egoists: Sixteen Surprising Interviews* (Chicago: Regnery, 1963), 118; HMH to Hal Adams, 22 June 1955. For veiled references, see "Dear Playboy," October 1963, 7 and December 1954, 4 as well as "Dear Playboy," July 1955, 3 and July 1956, 6. *Playboy*'s art director, Art Paul, said of the Playmate concept, "The idea is to think clean." See "Think Clean," *Time*, 3 March 1967, 80. On standard beauty types, see Banner, *American Beauty*, 154–166, 279, and Merrill, *Esky*, 39–41, 85–95.

For more on Playmates, see Maria Buszek, *Pin-Up Grrrls: Feminism, Sexuality, Popular Culture* (Durham: Duke University Press, 2006).

65. Richard Gehman, "Man's Private World," *Cosmopolitan*, May 1961, 42; Anthony F. Bogaert, Deborah A. Turkovich, and Carolyn L. Hafer, "A Content Analysis of *Playboy* Centerfolds from 1953 through 1990: Changes in Explicitness, Objectification, and Model's Age," *Journal of Sex Research* 30 (May 1993): 136–137. On evolving images of women see May, *Homeward Bound*, 42, and Honey, *Creating Rosie the Riveter*, 65–70.

66. Hefner, quoted in Fallaci, *The Egoists*, 120, 123; Hefner and Zehme, *Hef's Little Black Book*, 17; "Playboy Interview: Hugh M. Hefner," 70; Diana Lurie, "An Empire Built on Sex," *Life*, 29 October 1965, 71.

67. Hefner, quoted in "Urbunnity," *Newsweek*, 6 January 1964, 49; Hugh M. Hefner, "The Playboy Philosophy," *Playboy*, April 1964, 177. For a similar argument in favor of premarital sex, see Albert Ellis, *Sex without Guilt* (New York: Lyle, Stuart, 1958).

68. Jules Archer, "Will She or Won't She?" *Playboy*, January 1956; Harlan Draper, "Some Guys Get It," *Playboy*, July 1956, 27, 70; and Harrison Case, "Contour Contact," *Playboy*, June 1957, 23–24, 78; "Playboy's Progress," *Playboy*, May 1954, 22–23. For "brinkmanship," see May, *Homeward Bound*, 127–128.

69. For a self-congratulatory editorial statement on advertising, see "The Size of It," in "Dear Playboy," *Playboy*, December 1962, 28. Spectorsky first appeared on the masthead of the July 1956 issue as "Assistant to the Publisher." He was identified as "Associate Publisher" in January 1957, then "Associate Publisher and Advertising Director" in July 1957. In July 1960, he became "Associate Publisher and Editorial Director."

70. On special girls, see Diana Lurie, "In Hefnerland, Women Are Status Symbols," *Life*, 29 October 1965, 70–73; Sheppard, *The Most*; Hefner and Zehme, *Hef's Little Black Book*, 26–32, 152; for second child, Hugh Hefner, author interview, 14 January 2009. For divorce, *Mildred Hefner v. Hugh Hefner*, No. 59 S 245 (Superior Court, Cook County), Clerk of the Circuit Court of Cook County Archives, Chicago, Illinois.

71. Hugh Hefner, author interview, 14 January 2009; "Project 62—Playboy of the Modern World"; Sheppard, *The Most*; "Urbunnity," 48; and Lurie, "An Empire Built on Sex," 68B. The cartoons in volumes 40–42, HS, convey Hefner's eager anticipation of marriage.

Chapter 2

1. Hugh M. Hefner, "The Playboy Philosophy," *Playboy*, December 1962, 73, and January 1963, 51.

2. "What Is a Playboy?" *Playboy*, April 1956, 73; "What Sort of Man Reads Playboy?" advertisement, *Playboy*, January 1964, 83.

3. On consensus and the politics of growth, see Lizabeth Cohen, *A Consumers' Republic: The Politics of Mass Consumption in Postwar America* (New York: Knopf, 2003); Daniel Horowitz, *Anxieties of Affluence: Critiques of American Consumer Culture, 1939–1979* (Amherst: University of Massachusetts Press, 2004); Robert M. Collins, *More: The*

Politics of Economic Growth in Postwar America (New York: Oxford University Press, 2000); Robert M. Collins, "Growth Liberalism in the Sixties," in *The Sixties: From Memory to History*, ed. David Farber (Chapel Hill: University of North Carolina Press, 1994), 11–44. On the gendered rhetoric of postwar liberalism, see K. A. Cuordileone, *Manhood and American Political Culture in the Cold War* (New Brunswick, NJ: Routledge, 2005).

4. On taste and the mediation of desires to be unique and to belong, see Gregory Votolato, *American Design in the Twentieth Century: Personality and Performance* (Manchester: Manchester University Press, 1998), 28. For more on *Playboy*'s role as taste-maker for young men of the new middle class, see Bill Osgerby's *Playboys in Paradise: Masculinity, Youth and Leisure-style in Modern America* (Oxford: Berg, 2001).

5. "An Empire Built on Sex," *Life*, 29 October 1965, 67; Donald Meyer, *The Positive Thinkers: A Study of the American Quest for Health, Wealth and Personal Power from Mary Baker Eddy to Norman Vincent Peale* (Garden City, NY: Doubleday, 1965), 171–176, 262–268; Richard Yates, *Revolutionary Road* (Boston; Little, Brown, 1961; reprint, Westport, Conn.: Greenwood Press, 1971), and Sloan Wilson, *The Man in the Gray Flannel Suit* (New York: Pocket Books, 1955; reprint, New York: Four Walls Eight Windows, 2002), 183. For more on pressures and alienation of the corporation man, see Arthur Schlesinger, Jr., "The Crisis of American Masculinity," *Esquire*, November 1958, 64–66; C. Wright Mills, *White Collar: The American Middle Classes* (New York: Oxford University Press, 1951), xii, xvii, 182–188, 228–232, 263; William H. Whyte, Jr., *The Organization Man* (New York: Simon & Schuster, 1956), 18, 154, 159; David Riesman, et al., *The Lonely Crowd: A Study of the Changing American Character* (New Haven: Yale University Press, 1950); Greer Williams, "Are You a Good Executive?" *Nation's Business*, July 1951, 41.

6. Marcie Hans, Dennis Altman, and Martin A. Cohen, *The Executive Coloring Book* (Chicago: Funny Products Co., 1961), n.p. Other titles included *The Businessman's Primer* and *The Corporation Coloring Book*. Shepherd Mead, "How to Stop Being a Junior Executive," *Playboy*, July 1954, 43, and "Dressing the Part," *Playboy*, February 1956, 41–42; John Howard Sims, "Executive Chess," *Playboy*, October 1958, 69, 81; "The Playboy Panel: Business Ethics and Morality," *Playboy*, November 1962, 47–72.

7. J. Paul Getty, "Money and Conformity," *Playboy*, February 1961, 52, and "The Educated Barbarians," *Playboy*, August 1961, 118. Getty trumpeted individualism in all his editorials and addressed conformity in the later articles "The Homogenized Man," *Playboy*, August 1964, 61, and "The Myth of the Organization Man," *Playboy*, February 1969, 131.

8. Hefner, "Playboy Philosophy," *Playboy*, January 1963, 42.

9. On the vitality of depression-era culture, see Michael Denning, *The Cultural Front: The Laboring of American Culture in the Twentieth Century* (New York: Verso, 1997); Lewis A. Erenberg, *Swingin' the Dream: Big Band Jazz and the Rebirth of American Culture* (Chicago: University of Chicago Press, 1998); Lary May, *The Big Tomorrow: Hollywood and the Politics of the American Way* (Chicago: University of Chicago Press, 2000).

10. Russell, quoted in Thomas Weyr, *Reaching for Paradise: The Playboy Vision of America* (New York: Times Books, 1978), 49.

11. Hefner, "Playboy Philosophy," January 1963, 49–50; "The Take-Over Generation," *Life*, 14 September 1962. A story by Jack Kerouac, "The Rambling, Rumbling Blues," appeared in the January 1958 issue of *Playboy*. The following month, *Playboy* published a three-part feature called "The Beat Mystique," composed of the following articles: Herbert Gold, "What It Is, Whence It Came"; Sam Boal, "Cool Swinging in New York"; and Noel Clad, "A Frigid Frolic in Frisco," *Playboy*, February 1958, 20–21. For "Upbeat Generation," see "Playbill," December 1958, 3.

12. "*Playboy*'s House Party," *Playboy*, May 1959, 56. In a similar vein, a monthly feature, "On the Scene," spotlighted three rising stars, men who achieved success in their chosen fields.

13. Hefner, quoted in Gordon Sheppard, director, *The Most* (Pyramid Films, 1962), and HMH to *Minneapolis Tribune*, 17 March 1961, Folder 13, Box 17, HP.

14. Hal Higdon, "Playboying around the Clock with Hugh Hefner," *Climax*, February 1962, 13; HMH to Benny Dunn, 16 January 1961 and 12 September 1961, Folder 10, Box 15, HP; Richard Rosenzweig, interview with author, 28 March 2003. For more on Dexedrine use, see Steven Watts, *Mr. Playboy: Hugh Hefner and the American Dream* (New York: Wiley, 2008), 198–200.

15. "Playbill," *Playboy*, June 1957, 2; Hefner quoted in Sheppard, *The Most*. Examples of behind-the-scenes work include "Photographing a Playmate," *Playboy*, December 1954; "Photographing Your Own Playmate," *Playboy*, June 1958; and "Painting a Playmate," *Playboy*, September 1960. For discussion of earlier manifestation of the linkage between work and play, see Lewis A. Erenberg, *Steppin' Out: New York Nightlife and the Transformation of American Culture, 1890–1930* (Chicago: University of Chicago Press, 1981), 201–202.

16. Fascinated observers wondered whether Hefner was a true playboy or a workaholic. See for example Peter Meyerson, "Playboy's No. 1 Playboy," *Pageant* 17 (1961), 32–43; Art Buchwald, "Action's Underwhelming in Boss Bunny's Hutch," 21 October 1967, PVF, KIL; "Urbunnity," *Newsweek*, 6 January 1964, 48, and Don DeBat, "Behind Playboy: Men at Work," *Chicago Daily News*, 26 August 1968, 1. Hefner once summed up the either-or assumptions that circulated about his life in the mansion: "It's either the last thing since Sodom" or "all the girls are there, but there's no fun and games; it's all work." In reality, he claimed, "It is *neither*, it is *both* and that's what it's all about. I get a great deal of pleasure out of both sides of my life, and that is the most difficult thing for people to adjust to." Hefner, quoted in L. Rust Hills, "Esquire Interview: Hugh M. Hefner," *Esquire*, December 1970, 143.

17. "Workboy Philosophy," *Playboy*, October 1965, 171.

18. "Special Double Issue on the Good Life," *Life*, 28 December 1959. For "kitchen debates," see Elaine Tyler May, *Homeward Bound: American Families in the Cold War Era* (New York: Basic, 1988), 16–18; Karal Ann Marling, *As Seen on TV: The Visual Culture of Everyday Life in the Fifties* (Cambridge: Harvard University Press, 1994), 274–281. On leisure, see Marling, *As Seen on TV*, 51–52, 54–59; on development of a "fun morality" emphasizing pleasure and self-fulfillment, see Martha Wolfenstein, "Fun Morality: An Analysis of Recent American Child-training Literature," in *Childhood in Contemporary Cultures*, ed. Margaret Mead and Martha Wolfenstein (Chicago: University of Chicago

Press, 1955), 168–178. For the perils of spoiled or unfit children in affluent America, see Richard E. Gordon, M.D., Katherine K. Gordon, and Max Gunther, *The Split Level Trap* (New York: Bernard Geis Associates, 1961), 141–143, 213; R. M. Marshall, "Toughening Our Soft Generation," *Saturday Evening Post,* 23 June 1962, 13–17; Harry Henderson, "Are We and Our Children Getting Too Soft?" *Cosmopolitan,* August 1954, 16–22. On concerns about the nation's lack of fortitude and the harmful effects of leisure and consumption, see Hanson W. Baldwin, "Our Fighting Men Have Gone Soft," *Saturday Evening Post,* 8 August 1959, 13; Barbara Ehrenreich, *Fear of Falling: The Inner Life of the Middle Class* (New York: Harper, 1990), 15, 29–41; Beth Bailey, "Rebels without a Cause? Teenagers in the 1950s," *History Today* (February 1990): 25–31; Warren Susman, "Did Success Spoil the United States?" in *Recasting America: Culture and Politics in the Age of Cold War,* ed. Lary May (Chicago: University of Chicago Press, 1989), 25–26; Marling, *As Seen on TV,* 51–58; Horowitz, *Anxieties of Affluence,* 101–128. On fears that the American psyche had grown "soft," see Cuordileone, *Manhood and American Political Culture,* 97–105.

19. Hefner, quoted in "For Young City Guys," *Newsweek,* 7 November 1955, 71; "Playbill," *Playboy,* June 1957, 2; "Playbill," *Playboy,* September 1960, 8.

20. Kathy Peiss, *Hope in a Jar: The Making of America's Beauty Culture* (New York: Metropolitan, 1998), 253–255.

21. David Grayson, "The Man in His Bath," *Playboy,* July 1957, 29–30; Blake Rutherford, "Color-Coding the Basic Wardrobe," *Playboy,* August 1957, 17–20; Jack Kessie, "The Well Dressed Playboy," *Playboy,* January 1955, 39; "Verily, the Vest," *Playboy,* March 1958, 28; Blake Rutherford, "Ivy in Action," *Playboy,* July 1957, 20–21.

22. Frederic Birmingham, "Man of Affairs," *Playboy,* October 1958, 39; Jack Kessie, "The Shorts Story," *Playboy,* July 1955, 36; Blake Rutherford, "The Marks of the Well-Dressed Man," *Playboy,* March 1957, 47, 69–70; Rutherford, "Color-Coding the Basic Wardrobe," 17–20; Frederic Birmingham, "The Well-Clad Undergrad," *Playboy,* September 1958, 31–34. On men's shopping, see Richard Gehman, "Man's Private World," *Cosmopolitan,* May 1961, 39–43.

23. Frederic Birmingham, "Spring House Party," *Playboy,* May 1958, 31; Robert L. Green, "Meet Me at the Club," *Playboy,* April 1960, 37.

24. "Playboy's Sports Car Jacket," *Playboy,* May 1960, 45; Thomas Hine, *Populuxe* (New York: Knopf, 1986), 92; Victor Lownes, *The Day the Bunny Died* (Secaucus, NJ: Lyle Stuart, Inc., 1983), 23.

25. Ken Purdy, "The Compleat Sports Car Stable," *Playboy,* April 1957, 23; "The Verities of Vino," *Playboy,* October 1958, 42; "Le Rouge et Le Blanc," *Playboy,* October 1958, 45–53. See also "Status and Speed," *Playboy,* June 1960, 31.

26. "The Compleat Fidelitarian," *Playboy,* October 1957, 31–32; Leonard Feather, "Rock 'n' roll," *Playboy,* June 1957, 77. The article appeared under the usual "jazz" heading in the table of contents.

27. Feather, "Rock 'n' roll," 77. For jazz poll, see "Playbill," *Playboy,* February 1958, 3; for jazz festival, "Festival Finds a Home," *Downbeat,* 25 June 1959, 11; Gene Lees, "Playboy," *Downbeat,* 3 September 1959, 17. On jazz, see Lewis Erenberg, *Swingin' the Dream,* 120–149, 231–234; Ann Douglas, *Terrible Honesty: Mongrel Manhattan in the*

1920s (New York: Farrar, Straus and Giroux, 1995), passim. On postwar jazz, see also John Gennari, *Blowin' Hot and Cool: Jazz and Its Critics* (Chicago: University of Chicago Press, 2006); Jon Panish, *The Color of Jazz: Race and Representation in Postwar American Culture* (Jackson: University Press of Mississippi, 1997).

28. "Playbill," *Playboy*, May 1957, 3. On flanerie, see Keith Tester, ed., *The Flaneur* (London: Routledge, 1994).

29. Shelley Baranowski and Ellen Furlough, introduction to *Being Elsewhere: Tourism, Consumer Culture, and Identity in Modern Europe and North America* (Ann Arbor: University of Michigan Press, 2001), 17; John Urry, *The Tourist Gaze: Leisure and Travel in Contemporary Societies* (London: Sage, 1990), 2–4; Susan G. Davis, "Time Out: Leisure and Tourism," in *A Companion to Post-1945 America*, ed. Jean-Christophe Agnew and Roy Rosenzweig (Malden, MA: Blackwell, 2002), 70; and Karen Dubinsky, "'Everybody Likes Canadians': Canadians, Americans and the Post-World War II Travel Boom," in Baranowski and Furlough, *Being Elsewhere*, 322–325. For more on American tourism during the Cold War, see Christopher Endy, *Cold War Holidays: American Tourism in France* (Chapel Hill: University of North Carolina Press, 2004), and Annabel Jane Wharton, *Building the Cold War: Hilton International Hotels and Modern Architecture* (Chicago: University of Chicago Press, 2001).

30. "What Sort of Man Reads Playboy?" advertisements in *Playboy*, September 1958, July 1963, February 1959, and August 1960; travel features in *Playboy* include Geoffrey Bocca, "Brava Costas!" May 1966, 91; Barnaby Conrad, "Tahiti," March 1961, 80; A. C. Spectorsky, "Those American Virgins," February 1963, 55–59, "Jamaica," January 1960, 56, and "Charter Yachting in the Caribbean," November 1967, 128; Len Deighton, "Hawaii Aye!" June 1968, 140–146, and "Sardinia: Italy's Alabaster Isle," December 1968, 229; William Sansom, "Orient Express," February 1969, 97; "Carnival in Rio," December 1969, 165; "Skiing New England," November 1969, 136; and "Playboy's Weekend House Yacht Party," February 1970, 99.

31. Promotional letter written by Eldon Sellers, Folder 14, Box 3, SP; HMH to Alfred R. Pastel, June 15, 1955 (no other location), HP; *Playboy* reported the results of an independent survey by Gould, Gleiss and Benn, Inc. in the December 1955 "Playbill" section.

32. "Meet the Playboy Reader," *Playboy*, April 1958, 76–77, 63; "The Playboy Coloring Book," *Playboy*, January 1963, n.p.

33. Hugh M. Hefner, *That Toddlin' Town: A Rowdy Burlesque of Chicago Manners and Morals* (Chicago: Chi Publishers, 1951), n.p.

34. Hefner quoted in Simon Nathan, "About the Nudes in *Playboy*," *U.S. Camera*, April 1962, 71.

35. Russell Miller, *Bunny: The Real Story of Playboy* (New York: Holt, Rinehart and Winston, 1984), 72–73; Weyr, *Reaching for Paradise*, 70–71; Frank Brady, *Hefner* (New York: Macmillan, 1974), 159.

36. Jonathan Rhoades, "The Lock on the Barroom," *Playboy*, November 1956, 25; Milton Esterow, "Key Clubs Growing," *NYT*, 17 May 1961, 27.

37. *The Playboy Club*, n.d. [c. 1960], promotional brochure, CHM. On Playmates as Bunnies, see HMH to Victor Lownes III, 2 March 1961, Folder 3, Box 17, HP.

38. "The Playboy Club," *Playboy,* August 1960, 42; "Playboy Club News," *Playboy,* December 1961, 39.

39. *The Playboy Club* and "The Bunnies," *Playboy,* July 1963, 90.

40. The charter price at the flagship club was $50; at other locations it was only $25. "The Playboy Club," 41–42; *The Playboy Club;* "Disneyland for Adults," *Playboy,* October 1963, 160, and "Playboy Club News," *Playboy,* September 1963, [205]. On social clubs' exclusionary practices see Vance Packard, *The Status Seekers: An Exploration of Class Behavior in America and the Hidden Barriers That Affect You, Your Community, Your Future* (New York: David McKay Company, Inc., 1959; 14th printing, 1961), 179–193.

41. "Playboy Holds Key to Nightclub Success," *Businessweek,* 25 June 25, 1966, 88–90. For keyholders and expansion plans, see "Disneyland for Adults," 166; "The New York Playboy Club: Man at His Leisure," *Playboy,* March 1965, 116, and "Pass in Review," *Newsweek,* 10 July 1961, PVF, CHM.

42. Benjamin DeMott, "The Anatomy of 'Playboy,'" *Commentary* 34 (August 1962): 113; "Playboy" and Its Readers," *Commentary* 35 (January 1963): 72; "A Dime More a Peep," *Newsweek,* 23 May 1960, 72.

43. Roy Larson, "The Lowdown on the Upbeats," *Motive,* April 1960, 38, and Harvey Cox, "*Playboy*'s Doctrine of Male," *Christianity and Crisis,* May 1961, 56–60.

44. May, *Homeward Bound,* 26–27; Terence Ball, "The Politics of Social Science in Postwar America," in May, *Recasting America,* 76–92; Marling, "Betty Crocker's Picture Cook Book," in *As Seen On TV,* 202–240; Nancy P. Weiss, "Mother, the Invention of Necessity: Dr. Benjamin Spock's *Baby and Childcare,*" *American Quarterly* 29 (Winter 1977): 519–546; Michael Zuckerman, "Dr. Spock: The Confidence Man," in *The Family in History,* ed. Charles E. Rosenberg (Philadelphia: University of Pennsylvania, 1975), 204–205; Ernest Dichter, *The Strategy of Desire* (Garden City, NY: Doubleday, 1960), 181. The lack of traditional forms of guidance was a theme taken up in John Keats, *The Crack in the Picture Window* (Boston: Houghton Mifflin, 1956); John McPartland, *No Down Payment* (New York: Simon & Schuster, 1957); and Gordon, Gordon, and Gunther, *Split Level Trap.*

45. Russell Lynes, *The Tastemakers* (New York: Grosset & Dunlap, 1949), 310. Lynes categorized most publishers, magazine editors, art dealers, and movie producers—those whom Spectorsky called symbol manipulators and Bourdieu, cultural intermediaries—as upper middle brows. When asked by interviewer Mike Wallace to define himself as "High-brow, middle-brow or low-brow?" Hefner responded, "I consider myself upper-middle." "Mike Wallace Interviews Playboy," *Playboy,* December 1957, 83.

46. Packard, *Status Seekers;* Vance Packard, *The Hidden Persuaders* (New York: David McKay Company, Inc, 1957). Mills made similar observations in *White Collar.*

47. Packard, *Status Seekers,* 310; John Kenneth Galbraith, *The Affluent Society* (Boston: Houghton Mifflien, 1958); Cox, "*Playboy*'s Doctrine of Male," 58. For an excellent discussion of Packard and Galbraith, see Horowitz, *Anxieties of Affluence,* 101–120.

48. J. Claude Evans, "The Playboy Philosophy," *Catholic World,* October 1964, 42–48. For similar views, see Richard N. Johnson, "You'd Be Welcome, Mr. Hefner," *Christian Century,* 18 October 1961, 1238; "An Infinite Number of Monkeys," *Christian Century,* 28

August 1963, 1063; and Gregor Roy, "Plato, the Penthouse, and the Girl Who Hesitates," *Mademoiselle*, March 1965, 199.

49. Horowitz, *Anxieties of Affluence*, 13, 32.

50. Ernest Dichter, *The Strategy of Desire* (Garden City, NY: Doubleday, 1960), 16. Horowitz discusses the significance of Dichter's motivational research along with George Katona's consumer studies in *Anxieties of Affluence*, 48–78.

51. Hefner, "The Playboy Philosophy," December 1963, 78 and January 1963, 50–52; "The Boss of Taste City," *Time*, 24 March 1961, 55.

52. Edwin L. Dale, Jr., "Are We Americans Going Soft?" NYT Magazine, 1 December 1957, 21; Hefner, quoted in Bill Davidson, "Czar of the Bunny Empire," *Saturday Evening Post*, April 1962, 34.

53. Hefner, "The Playboy Philosophy," December 1963, 73.

54. Hefner, quoted in Nathan, "About the Nudes," 74, and Davidson, "Czar of the Bunny Empire," 34. Similar remarks were made in "Project 62—Playboy of the Modern World," Canadian Broadcasting Company, 4 February 1962, transcript in Volume 71, HS, and cited in Marie Torre, "A Woman Looks at the Girly-Girly Magazines," *Cosmopolitan*, May 1963, 45.

Chapter 3

1. "Snazzy Four Story Home for Gold Coast," *Chicago Daily News*, 23 September 1959; Hugh M. Hefner, introduction to Gretchen Edgren, *Inside the Playboy Mansion: If You Don't Swing, Don't Ring* (Santa Monica, CA: General Publishing Group, Inc.), 9, and Bill Davidson, "Czar of the Bunny Empire," *Saturday Evening Post*, April 1962, 34–38.

2. "The Playboy Town House," *Playboy*, May 1962, 84, 105.

3. My investigation of the playboy's domestic realm builds on Barbara Ehrenreich's assertion that *Playboy* attempted to reclaim indoor space for men. See *The Hearts of Men: American Dreams and the Flight from Commitment* (New York: Anchor Press, 1983), 43–44. On the need for scholars to consider how representations of urban spaces inform perception and experience, see Mary Corbin Sies, "North American Suburbs, 1880–1950: Cultural and Social Reconsiderations," *Journal of Urban History* 27 (March 2001): 318–319.

4. Susan Saegert, "Masculine Cities and Feminine Suburbs: Polarized Ideas, Contradictory Realities," *Signs* 5 (Spring 1980): S96–S111; Robert A. Beauregard, *Voices of Decline: The Postwar Fate of U.S. Cities* (Cambridge, MA: Blackwell, 1993), 297–299. For debate on the continued conceptual utility of an urban/suburban dichotomy, see William Sharpe and Leonard Wallock, "Bold New City or Built-up 'Burb? Redefining Contemporary Suburbia," *American Quarterly* 46 (March 1994): 1–30, and Robert Fishman, "Urbanity and Suburbanity: Rethinking the 'Burbs" *American Quarterly* 46 (March 1994): 35–39.

5. "Volume 1, Number 1," *Playboy*, undated first issue, 3.

6. The phrase served as the theme of the AIA's convention in 1956. "Record Houses of 1956," *Architectural Record*, May 1956, 85.

7. The articles proved so popular that *Playboy* published several more plans and initiated "A Playboy's Pad," a regular series of photographic essays on the actual "pads" inhabited by bachelors across America, beginning with "Manhattan Tower" in August 1965. The plans include "The Playboy Bed" (November 1959), "Playboy's Weekend Hideaway" (April 1959), "The Playboy Town House" (May 1962), "Playboy's Patio Terrace" (August 1963), "Playboy's Electronic Entertainment Wall" (October 1964), and "Playboy Plans a Duplex Apartment" (January 1970).

8. "Playboy's Penthouse Apartment," *Playboy*, September 1956, 54–60; "Playboy's Penthouse Apartment Part II," *Playboy*, October 1956, 66–70. Unless otherwise noted, quotations about the penthouse that follow are from these sources.

9. Barbara M. Kelly, *Expanding the American Dream: Building and Rebuilding Levittown* (Albany: State University of New York Press, 1993), 89–90.

10. Philip Wylie, "The Womanization of America," *Playboy*, September 1958, 52, 77. See also Ernest Havemann, "Amid Profound Change Personal Crisis," *Life*, 8 September 1961, 100.

11. On housing designs and family ideals see David Handlin, *The American Home: Architecture and Society, 1815–1915* (Boston: Little, Brown, 1978); Gwendolyn Wright, *Moralism and the Model Home: Domestic Architecture and Cultural Conflict in Chicago, 1873–1913* (Chicago: University of Chicago Press, 1980), and *Building the Dream: A Social History of Housing in America* (New York: Pantheon, 1981); Richard Bushman, *Refinement of America: Persons, Houses, Cities* (New York: Knopf, 1992); Jessica H. Foy and Thomas J. Schlereth, eds., *American Home Life, 1880–1930: A Social History of Spaces and Services* (Knoxville: University of Tennessee Press, 1992); Kelly, *Expanding the American Dream*; Margaret Marsh, *Suburban Lives* (New Brunswick, NJ: Rutgers University Press, 1990). On the ranch house, see Clifford Edward Clark, Jr., *The American Family Home, 1800–1960* (Chapel Hill: University of North Carolina Press, 1986), 193–97, and Kenneth Jackson, *Crabgrass Frontier: The Suburbanization of the United States* (New York: Oxford University Press, 1985), 203–218.

12. Wylie, "Womanization," 77; William Iversen, "Apartness," *Playboy*, May 1958, 35–36, and Margaret Mead, "American Man in a Woman's World," NYT Magazine, 10 February 1957.

13. Steven Gelber, "Do-It-Yourself: Constructing, Repairing, and Maintaining Domestic Masculinity," *American Quarterly* 49 (March 1997): 67–68; Karal Ann Marling, *As Seen on TV: The Visual Culture of Everyday Life in the 1950s* (Cambridge: Harvard University Press, 1994), 58; Kelly, *Expanding the American Dream*, 71–73, discuss the imperative for home improvement projects in Levittown, given the small size of the houses. On earlier manifestations of masculinity within the family home, see Margaret Marsh, "Suburban Men and Masculine Domesticity, 1870–1915," in *Meanings for Manhood: Constructions of Masculinity in Victorian America*, ed. Mark C. Carnes and Clyde Griffin (Chicago: University of Chicago Press, 1990), 111–127.

14. "The New American Domesticated Male," *Life*, 4 January 1954, 42–44. See also "New Do-It-Yourself Market," *Business Week*, 14 June 1952, 70; "Do-It-Yourself Man," *Look*, 22 September 1953, 113–114; and "The Shoulder Trade," *Time*, 2 August 1954, 62.

15. Shepherd Mead, "The Dream House and How to Avoid It," *Playboy*, July 1956, 53–54.

16. "Penthouse Playmate," *Playboy*, August 1959, 55.

17. On the film's implication of the characters' sexuality, see D. A. Miller, "Anal *Rope*," in *Inside/Out: Lesbian Theories, Gay Theories*, ed. Diana Fuss (New York: Routledge, 1991), 119–141.

18. The bachelor pads in the films *All in a Night's Work* (1961), *Boeing Boeing* (1965), and *The Silencers* (1966), for example, served as points of seduction or featured mood-enhancing automated lighting and furnishings. Examples of bachelor-pad themed cartoons appear in the following issues of *Playboy*: January 1959, 27, March 1960, 29, and January 1964, 177.

19. Steven Cohan's "So Functional for Its Purposes: The Bachelor Apartment in *Pillow Talk*," in *Stud: Architectures of Masculinity*, ed. Joel Sanders (New York: Princeton Architectural Press, 1996), 28–41, interprets the penthouse apartment and the similarly appointed pad in *Pillow Talk* as spaces for the hyperperformance of heterosexual masculinity. Cohan argues that Rock Hudson's appearance in the film marked a concerted effort to reconstitute the closeted actor's heterosexual persona after the dissolution of a sham marriage. George Wagner's "The Lair of the Bachelor," in *Architecture and Feminism*, ed. Debra Coleman, Elizabeth Danze, and Carol Henderson (New York: Princeton Architectural Press, 1996), 185, views the idealized pads and the seduction that takes place within them as akin to other architectural programs for spatial control. For additional discussions of *Playboy*'s domestic interiors, see Beatrize Preciado, "Pornotopia" in Beatrize Colomina et al., eds., *Cold War Hot Houses: Inventing Postwar Culture, from Cockpit to Playboy* (New York: Princeton Architectural Press, 2004), 216–253 and Bill Osgerby, "The Bachelor Pad as Cultural Icon: Masculinity, Consumption, and Interior Design in American Men's Magazines, 1930–1965," *Journal of Design History* 18, no. 1 (2005): 99–113. The notion of masculine performance comes from Judith Butler, *Gender Trouble: Feminism and the Subversion of Identity* (New York: Routledge, 1999), 33.

20. "McCulloch's Push-Button Paradise," *Life*, 7 May 1956, 71–78; Kocher, "New House for Family Living," 99; Glenn Fowler, "Builders Depict Home of Future," NYT, 27 January 1957, R1; "House of Future Runs by Buttons," NYT, 11 October 1950, 39; Phyllis Ehrlich, "Push-Button Appliances Will Lighten Housework," NYT, 1 January 1958, 29.

21. "Playboy's Patio Terrace," 96–102.

22. "House of Future Previewed," *Los Angeles Times*, 12 June 1957, 3, and "'House of Future' Built of Plastic," NYT, 16 June 1957, R1. The master bedroom in the "Hotpoint House" model home on display in Long Island in 1950 reportedly featured similar controls, including a button to start the kitchen stove. See "House of Future Runs by Buttons," NYT, 11 October 1950, 39.

23. John Anderson, "Designs for Living," *Playboy*, July 1961, 48.

24. Thomas Hine, *Populuxe* (New York: Knopf, 1986).

25. On the "open plan," see Lesley Jackson, *Contemporary: Architecture and Interiors of the 1950s* (London: Phaidon, 1994), 81–91.

26. Royal Barry Wills, "Space," *Architectural Record*, May 1945, 77; "A Hobby Space for Multiple Use," *Architectural Record*, May 1945, 91; A. Lawrence Kocher, "The New House for Family Living," *Architectural Record*, May 1956, 90, and Jackson, *Contemporary*, 83–88.

27. Blake Rutherford, "Let's Go to My Place," *Playboy*, February 1959, 58.

28. Kenon Breazeale, "In Spite of Women: *Esquire* Magazine and the Construction of the Male Consumer," *Signs* 20 (August 1994): 19–20.

29. Harvey Levenstein, *People of Plenty: A Social History of Eating in Modern America* (New York: Oxford University Press, 1993), 104, 132; Marling, *As Seen on TV*, 213, 218, 243–288. On *Playboy*'s efforts to distinguish the leisurely cooking activities of the bachelor from women's family-oriented labor, see Joanne Hollows, "The Bachelor Dinner: Masculinity, Class and Cooking in Playboy, 1953–1961," *Continuum: Journal of Media & Cultural Studies* 16, no. 2 (2002): 143–155. For more on postwar-era gender and cooking, see Jessamyn Neuhaus, *Manly Meals and Mom's Home Cooking: Cookbooks and Gender in Modern America* (Baltimore: Johns Hopkins University Press, 2003).

30. *Esquire's Handbook for Hosts* (New York: Grosset & Dunlap, 1949), 11.

31. For the kitchen as "hub" of the house, see Kocher, "New House for Family Living," 90; Clark, *American Family Home*, 213–215; Marling, *As Seen on TV*, 250, 262–263; and Jackson, *Contemporary*, 88.

32. Jean Sprain Wilson, "What? No Etchings!" *Miami Daily News*, 6 September 1956, volume 57, HS; "Playboy Plans a Duplex Penthouse," 159, and Thomas Mario, "The Gourmet Bit," *Playboy*, September 1957, 28–29.

33. For examples see Thomas Mario's "Long Live the Lobster," *Playboy*, August 1958, 19; "Santa Claus in a Bottle," *Playboy*, December 1954, 37; "Yo Ho Ho and a Bottle of Rum," *Playboy*, July 1955, 13; "How to Play with Fire," *Playboy*, July 1954, 23; and "The Elegant Omelet," *Playboy*, February 1958, 32.

34. Mario, "The Gourmet Bit," 27; Thomas Mario, "Playboy at the Salad Bowl," *Playboy*, July 1956, 32; Marling, *As Seen on TV*, 224, 226.

35. Richard Gehman, "Man's Private World," *Cosmopolitan*, May 1961, 39–43.

36. Ernest Havemann, "Amid Profound Change, Personal Crisis," *Life*, 8 September 1961, 100. Andrew Hurley, *Diners, Bowling Alleys, and Trailer Parks: Chasing the America Dream in the Postwar Consumer Culture* (New York: Basic, 2001), 68, 57–72; on bowling alleys, see esp. 150–184. For baseball, see Eric Avila, *Popular Culture in the Age of White Flight: Fear and Fantasy in Suburban Los Angeles* (Berkeley: University of California Press, 2004), 146–154, 175. On retail and downtown, see Lizabeth Cohen, *A Consumers' Republic: The Politics of Mass Consumption in Postwar America* (New York: Knopf, 2003), 278, and Alison Isenberg, *Downtown America: A History of the Place and the People Who Made It* (Chicago: University of Chicago Press, 2004), 176, 182.

37. Jackson, *Crabgrass Frontier*, 190–230; Lizabeth Cohen, *Consumers' Republic*, 194–256; Avila, *Popular Culture in the Age of White Flight*, 32–49; Arnold Hirsch, *Making the Second Ghetto: Race and Housing in Chicago, 1940–1960* (New York: Cambridge University Press, 1983); Thomas J. Sugrue, *Origins of the Urban Crisis: Race and Inequality in Postwar Detroit* (Princeton: Princeton University Press, 1996). On investors favoring large-scale suburban development, see Thomas W. Hanchett, "Financing Suburbia:

Prudential Insurance and the Post-World War II Transformation of the American City," *Journal of Urban History* 26 (March 2000): 312–328. Robert M. Fogelson, *Downtown: Its Rise and Fall, 1880–1950* (New Haven: Yale University Press, 2001), 383–388; Michael Johns, *Moment of Grace: The American City in the 1950s* (Berkeley: University of California Press, 2003); and Isenberg, *Downtown*, 183–209, discuss the waning primacy of downtown in the 1950s.

38. Kristina Zarlengo, "Civilian Threat, the Suburban Citadel, and Atomic Age American Women," *Signs* 24 (Summer 1999): 936; Paul Boyer, *By the Bomb's Early Light: American Thought and Culture at the Dawn of the Atomic Age* (Chapel Hill: University of North Carolina Press, 1994), 328.

39. *Survival under Atomic Attack*, produced by Castle Films in cooperation with the Federal Civil Defense Administration, 1951, available at *www.archive.org*; Eric Avila, "Popular Culture in the Age of White Flight: Film Noir, Disneyland, and The Cold War (Sub)Urban Imaginary," *Journal of Urban History* 31 (November 2004): 7. On post–World War II depictions of the effects of catastrophic warfare on urban centers and post-catastrophe urban danger, see Carl Abbott, "The Light on the Horizon: Imagining the Death of American Cities," *Journal of Urban History* 32 (January 2006): 175–196.

40. Romantic comedies, including *Pillow Talk* (1959), *Lover Come Back* (1961), *All in a Night's Work* (1961), and *If a Man Answers* (1962), also provided a positive vision, setting their boy-meets-girl exploits against the backdrop of the city, especially New York.

41. "Most Urban of Them All" advertisement, *Playboy*, May 1957 (emphasis in original); "Playbill," *Playboy*, December 1958, 3; "Playboy Interview: Hugh M. Hefner," *Playboy*, January 1974, 65; Russell Miller, *Bunny: The Real Story of Playboy* (New York: Holt, Rinehart and Winston, 1984), 16; and Hugh M. Hefner, "Playboy Philosophy," *Playboy*, January 1963, 42.

42. Howard Chudacoff, *The Age of the Bachelor: Creating an American Subculture* (Princeton: Princeton University Press, 1999).

43. Frederic C. Birmingham, "Summer in the City," *Playboy*, August 1958, 29–30, 67.

44. See the "What Sort of Man Reads Playboy?" advertisements in the following issues of *Playboy*: January 1959, February 1958, January 1960, April 1964, February 1963, July 1958, August 1958, March 1958, April 1963, June 1963, November 1965, and December 1964.

45. Hugh Hefner, "Golden Dreams," *Playboy*, January 1994, 267; "The World of Leroy Neiman," *Playboy*, July 1978, 134; "Man at His Leisure" features in the following issues of *Playboy*: June 1959, 62; June 1960, 74; September 1963, 150–51; March 1961, 94; and "Painter of the Urban Scene," *Playboy*, April 1958, 49.

46. John Urry, *The Tourist Gaze: Leisure and Travel in Contemporary Societies* (London: Sage, 1990).

47. "The Playboy Bed," *Playboy*, November 1959, 104; "The Playboy Bed," *Playboy*, April 1965, 88–89, 184; Tom Wolfe, *The Pump-House Gang* (New York: Farrar, Straus & Giroux, 1968), 75. Beginning with *The Silencers* (1966), Dean Martin portrayed bachelor Matt Helm, who owned a similarly equipped, round, rotating bed. A retired spy, Helm worked as a centerfold photographer for a men's magazine until he was called back into service.

48. For competing views on the merits of life as a Playboy Bunny, see Gloria Steinem's two-part exposé, "A Bunny's Tale," *Show*, May 1963, 90, and "A Bunny's Tale Part II," *Show*, June 1963, 66; and Kathryn Lee Scott, *The Bunny Years* (Los Angeles: Pomegranate, 1998).

49. "The Playboy Mansion," *Playboy*, January 1966, 207. Readers were first introduced to Hefner's domestic world with "Playmate Holiday House Party" in December 1961, followed by "A Playmate Pillow Fight" in February 1963. On spatial control in Disneyland, see Avila, "Popular Culture in the Age of White Flight," 10–16; and Marling, *As Seen on TV*, 109–118.

50. Hefner quoted in "Playboy Interview: Hugh M. Hefner," *Playboy*, January 1974, 74.

51. "Penthouse Playmate," *Playboy*, August 1959, 55; "The Playboy Mansion West," *Playboy*, January 1975, 215. On Playboy Mansion West, see Roger Ebert, "With Hugh M. Hefner in the American West," *Midwest Magazine*, 20 June 1972, 25–27, and "Up Front," both in PVF, KIL. On the television program, see "Hugh Hefner Faces Middle Age," *Time*, 14 February 1969, 69. For further discussion of Hefner's relationship with Benton, see Miller, *Bunny*, 144–160, and Steven Watts, *Mr. Playboy: Hugh Hefner and the American Dream* (New York: Wiley, 2008), 224–227, 252–258.

52. On western and "sunbelt" cities, see John M. Findlay, *Magic Lands: Western Cityscapes and American Culture after 1940* (Berkeley: University of California Press, 1992); Robert Fishman, *Bourgeois Utopias: The Rise and Fall of Suburbia* (New York: Basic, 1987); Avila, *Popular Culture in the Age of White Flight*; Carl Abbott, *The Metropolitan Frontier: Cities in the Modern American West* (Tucson: University of Arizona Press, 1993); Eugene P. Moehring, *Resort City in the Sunbelt: Las Vegas, 1930–2000* (Reno: University of Nevada Press, 2000); Raymond A. Mohl, ed., *Searching for the Sunbelt: Historical Perspectives on a Region* (Knoxville: University of Tennessee Press, 1990).

53. Wolfe, *Pump House Gang*, 75.

54. "Dear Playboy," *Playboy*, August 1962, 9; ACS to Art Paul, Jack Kessie, and Harvey Stubsjoen, 11 February 1963 (no other location), SP; "Playboy's Patio Terrace," 96, 99; "Playboy's Electronic Entertainment Wall," 122.

55. *Playboy* noted in 1958 that half of its readers were married. According to a 1962 study, among adult males age eighteen or older in households receiving *Playboy*, 70 percent were married, while homeownership in *Playboy* households was 49 percent. These figures, however, do not take into account the magazine's considerable popularity among men living on college campuses, where an estimated one-quarter of all copies of the magazine was sold, nor do they consider the demographics of those who did not purchase an issue but read someone else's copy. "Meet the Playboy Reader," *Playboy*, April 1958, 76–77; Daniel Starch and Staff, *1962 Consumer Magazine Report* (Mamaroneck, NY), 18, 40; "Sassy Newcomer," *Time*, 24 September 1956, 71.

56. Margaret Marsh, "Suburban Men and Masculine Domesticity," 111–127, and Steven Gelber, "Do-It-Yourself," 67–68.

57. Beauregard, *Voices of Decline*, 250–251; Neil Smith, "New City, New Frontier: The Lower East Side as Wild, Wild West," in *Variations on a Theme Park: The New American City and the End of Public Space*, ed. Michael Sorkin (New York: Hill and Wang, 1992), 61–83.

Chapter 4

1. Helen Gurley Brown, *Sex and the Single Girl* (New York: Bernard Geis Associates, 1962), 11.

2. Brown, *Sex and the Single Girl*, 3; Jesse Kornbluth, "Queen of the Mouseburgers," NYT, 27 September 1982, 36–43.

3. Brown, *Sex and the Single Girl*, 4. Laurie Ouellette analyzes Brown's articulation of the upwardly mobile Cosmo Girl as a study in the cultural construction of class in "Inventing the Cosmo Girl: Class Identity and Girl-Style American Dreams," *Media, Culture and Society* 21, no. 3 (1999): 359–383. For further analysis of Brown, see Jennifer Scanlon's recent biography, *Bad Girls Go Everywhere: The Life of Helen Gurley Brown* (New York: Oxford University Press, 2009).

4. Brown, *Sex and the Single Girl*, 4–5.

5. For further discussion of gender and consumption in the guise of the Single Girl, see Hilary Radner, "Introduction: Queering the Girl," in *Swinging Single: Representing Sexuality in the 1960s*, ed. Hilary Radner and Moya Luckett (Minneapolis: University of Minnesota Press, 1999), 9–16 for *Sex and the office*, see Julie Berebitsky, "The Joy of work: Helen Gurley Brown, Gender, and Sexuality in the white-Collar office," *Journal of the History of Sexuality* 15 (January 2006), 89–127.

6. Brown, *Sex and the Single Girl*, 6–7, 34, 89.

7. Brown, *Sex and the Single Girl*, 8–10, 89.

8. Sloan Wilson, "The Woman in the Gray Flannel Suit," NYT Magazine, 15 January 1956, 38, and "Letters," NYT Magazine, 24 February 1957, 4.

9. Estelle H. Ries, *The Lonely Sex* (New York: Belmont, 1962), 66, 79–95; Sexology Corporation, *Sex and the Unmarried Woman* (New York: Award, 1964), 165.

10. Brown, *Sex and the Single Girl*, 7, and "Playboy Interview: Helen Gurley Brown," *Playboy*, April 1963, 53–54. In the interview, Brown discussed her views in favor of legalizing abortion and claimed that her publisher excised this material from her book, fearing it would hurt sales.

11. "The Playboy Advisor," *Playboy*, December 1963, 46; "The Playboy Advisor," *Playboy*, March 1963, 38; "The Playboy Advisor," *Playboy*, September 1965, 67. For introduction of the Advisor, see "Playbill," *Playboy*, September 1960, 5. For origins of Advisor questions, see Mike Laurence to Jack Kessie, 27 August 1964, Folder 12, Box 22, SP.

12. Brown, *Sex and the Single Girl*, 108–111, 119, 197.

13. Brown, *Sex and the Single Girl*, 111, 138–140, 115.

14. On single, working women in the late nineteenth and early twentieth centuries, see Joanne Meyerowitz, *Women Adrift: Independent Wage Earners in Chicago, 1880–1930* (Chicago: University of Chicago Press, 1988); Kathy Peiss, *Cheap Amusements: Working Women and Leisure in Turn-of-the-Century New York* (Philadelphia: Temple University Press, 1986); Elizabeth Ewen, *Immigrant Women in the Land of Dollars: Life and Culture on the Lower East Side, 1890–1925* (New York: Monthly Review Press, 1985); Susan A. Glenn, *Daughters of the Shtetl: Life and Labor in the Immigrant Generation* (Ithaca, NY: Cornell University Press, 1990); Susan Porter Benson, *Counter Cultures: Saleswomen, Managers, and Customers in American Department Stores, 1890–1940* (Urbana: University

of Illinois Press, 1986); Sarah Deutsch, *Women and the City: Gender, Space, and Power in Boston, 1870–1940* (New York: Oxford University Press, 2000).

15. The character Holly Golightly provides another example of the relationship between the Single Girl's sexuality and her marginal economic position. In the demure movie version of Truman Capote's *Breakfast at Tiffany's*, she is a New York party girl who uses her feminine charms to finagle material rewards from men; in Capote's short story she is a prostitute.

16. Susan B. Carter, et al., eds., *Historical Statistics of the United States, Earliest Times to the Present: Millennial Edition* (New York: Cambridge University Press, 2006), Volume II, Part B, 90; Mitra Toossi, "A Century of Change: The U.S. Labor Force, 1950–2050," *Monthly Labor Review* (May 2002): 18–24; Stephanie Coontz, *The Way We Never Were: American Families and the Nostalgia Trap* (New York: Basic, 1992), 158–160. On women's employment during and after World War II, see Susan Hartmann, *The Home Front and Beyond: American Women in the 1940s* (Boston: Twayne, 1982); Karen Anderson, *Wartime Women: Sex Roles, Family Relations, and the Status of Women during World War II* (Westport, CT: Greenwood Press, 1981); Maureen Honey, *Creating Rosie the Riveter: Class, Gender and Propaganda during World War II* (Amherst: University of Massachusetts Press, 1984); Sherna Berger Gluck, *Rosie the Riveter Revisited: Women, the War, and Social Change* (Boston: Twayne, 1987); Ruth Milkman, *Gender at Work: The Dynamics of Job Segregation by Sex during World War II* (Urbana: University of Illinois Press, 1987); Susan E. Hirsch, "No Victory at the Workplace: Women and Minorities at Pullman during World War II," in *The War in American Culture: Society and Consciousness during World War II*, ed. Lewis A. Erenberg and Susan E. Hirsch (Chicago: University of Chicago Press, 1996), 241–262; Amy Kesselman, *Fleeting Opportunities: Women Shipyard Workers in Portland and Vancouver during World War II and Reconversion* (Albany: State University of New York Press, 1990); Elaine Tyler May, *Homeward Bound American Families in the Cold War Era* (New York: Basic, 1988), 58–91; Jessica Weiss, *To Have and to Hold: Marriage, the Baby Boom, and Social Change* (Chicago: University of Chicago Press, 2000), 49–81; Susan M. Hartmann, "Women's Employment and the Domestic Ideal," in *Not June Cleaver: Women and Gender in Postwar America*, ed. Joanne Meyerowitz (Philadelphia: Temple University Press), 84–100.

17. Sloan Wilson, "The Woman in the Gray Flannel Suit," NYT Magazine, 15 January 1956, 28; Bernice Fitz-Gibbon, "Woman in the *Gay* Flannel Suit," NYT Magazine, 29 January 1956, 15, and "That Woman in Gray Flannel: A Debate," NYT Magazine, 12 February 1956, 24–25, 30; Betty Lou Raskin, "Woman's Place Is in the Lab, Too," NYT, 19 April 1959, 17; Hartmann, "Women's Employment and the Domestic Ideal," 84–100.

18. Julie A. Matthaei, *An Economic History of Women in America* (New York: Schocken, 1982), 282.

19. Angel Kwolleck-Folland, *Engendering Business: Men and Women in the Corporate Office, 1870–1930* (Baltimore: Johns Hopkins University Press, 1994).

20. Women did not necessarily view office work in negative terms. That women often saw clerical work as providing decent wages, a clean environment, and a measure of status, however, does not negate the fact that their opportunities for better

pay or advancement were curtailed on account of their gender. Sharon Hartmann Strom, *Beyond the Typewriter: Gender, Class and the Origins of Modern American Office Work, 1900–1930* (Chicago: University of Illinois Press, 1992); Lisa Fine, *The Souls of the Skyscraper: Female Clerical Workers in Chicago, 1870–1930* (Philadelphia: Temple University Press, 1990); Marjorie Davies, *Woman's Place Is at the Typewriter: Office Work and Office Workers, 1870–1930* (Philadelphia: Temple University Press, 1982).

21. Strom, *Beyond the Typewriter*, 348, 372–373.

22. Remington Rand, "How to Be a Super-Secretary" (1951), Subject: Secretaries, SLVFWS; "What Is a Gal Friday?" *Gal Friday*, June/July 1966, 8.

23. Helen Gurley Brown, *Sex and the Office* (New York: Bernard Geis Associates, 1964), 59, 7; Brown, *Sex and the Single Girl*, 98.

24. Brown, *Sex and the Office*, 8–18, 114.

25. Brown, *Sex and the Single Girl*, 86–87.

26. Chester Burger, *Survival in the Executive Jungle* (New York: Collier, 1964), 171, 204–210; *Shaft* (Illini Publishing Company, 1949), University of Illinois Archives, Urbana, IL; "Playboy after Hours," *Playboy*, December 1957, 9.

27. Richard Yates, *Revolutionary Road* (Boston; Little, Brown, 1961; reprint, Westport, CT: Greenwood Press, 1971), 68, 102.

28. Brown, *Sex and the Office*, 285, 6; ibid, 34.

29. Brown, *Sex and the Office*, 227, 33, 49.

30. Brown, *Sex and the Single Girl*, 101.

31. Frederic C. Birmingham, "Summer in the City," *Playboy*, August 1958, 30, 67.

32. Marcie Hans, Dennis Altman, and Martin A. Cohen, *The Executive Coloring Book* (Chicago: Funny Products Co., 1961); "The Playboy Coloring Book," *Playboy*, January 1963, 65. For a similar view of workplace revelry, see Corey Ford, *The Office Party* (Garden City, NY: Doubleday, 1951).

33. "Playboy's Girl Friday," *Playboy*, September 1957, 39–43; "Legal Tender," *Playboy*, December 1959, 73; "Honey in the Bank," *Playboy*, September 1961, 83; "Premium Playmate," *Playboy*, June 1964, 92. See also "The Girls in the Office," *Playboy*, August 1978, 138.

34. "Photographing a Playmate," *Playboy*, December 1954, 20; "Photographing Your Own Playmate," *Playboy*, June 1958, 35. Similar *Playboy* pictorials include "Triple Threat" (January 1964), which highlighted a *Playboy* editorial assistant; "Comely Colleague" (August 1965), which revealed the assistant manager of *Playboy*'s College Bureau; and "Valentine Revisited" (May 1962), featuring a *Playboy* secretary-receptionist. Likewise, "Painting a Playmate" (September 1960) documented the process of producing one Playmate feature in *Playboy*'s offices.

35. Lisa Fine, *Souls of the Skyscraper*, 144. For the type of humor solicited by *Playboy*, see HMH to Hal B. Goldberg, 23 July 1954 (no other location), HP. Other studies of *Playboy* cartoons include Mala L. Matacin and Jerry M. Burger, "A Content Analysis of Sexual Themes in *Playboy* Cartoons," *Sex Roles* 17, nos. 3/4 (1987): 179–187; and Gail Dines-Levy and Gregory W. H. Smith, "Representations of Women and Men in *Playboy* Sex Cartoons," in *Humour and Society*, ed. Chris Powell and George E. C. Paton (New York: St. Martin's, 1988), 234–259.

36. Cartoons in the following issues of *Playboy*: March 1961, 129; October 1960, 116; January 1964, 191; August 1957, 21; July 1960, 69; October 1959, 46.

37. Cartoons in the following issues of *Playboy*: June 1957, 49; August 1963, 54; November 1963, 158; February 1967, 188; April 1965, 132; and December 1965, 261.

38. "Playboy Interview: Hugh M. Hefner," *Playboy*, January 1974, 65; Simon Nathan, "About the Nudes in *Playboy*," *U.S. Camera*, April 1962, 45.

39. She later said of her appearance in the magazine, "Mostly I did it to please Hef." Hugh M. Hefner, "Golden Dreams," *Playboy*, January 1994, 267.

40. "Playboy's Office Playmate," *Playboy*, July 1955, 26; Nathan, "About the Nudes," 72; "A Holiday Evening with Janet Pilgrim," *Playboy*, December 1955, 30; "Janet's Date at Dartmouth," *Playboy*, October 1956, 40. See Gene Shalit to HMH, 8 July 1955; HMH to Gene Shalit, 7 September 1955; and Gene Shalit to HMH, 30 September 1955, all in HP, for a jesting exchange on Hefner's good fortune to have a secretary willing to pose for *Playboy*.

41. ACS to Philip Wylie, 16 August 1962, and ACS to Jack Kessie, 9 October 1962, in Folder 21, Box 19, SP.

42. "Petticoats Rustle on Executive Ladder," *Business Week*, 29 September 1962, 50; Philip Wylie, "The Career Woman," *Playboy*, January 1963, 117–118; J. Robert Moskin, "The American Male: Why Do Women Dominate Him?" *Look*, 4 February 1958, 77–80.

43. Shepherd Mead, "How to Handle Women in Business," *Playboy*, January 1957, 53–54. The article appeared again in the September 1963 issue.

44. Wylie, "Career Woman," 156.

45. Brown, *Sex and the Office*, 3, 49, 62, 146, 135, 58.

46. Brown, *Sex and the Office*, 74.

47. *Playboy Club Bunny Manual* (Chicago: Playboy Clubs International, c. 1965), section 520.2.1–520.2.5.

48. For Bunnies-turned-Playmates, see "Bunny Hug," *Playboy*, August 1962, 61; "Ticket to Success," *Playboy*, February 1967, 96; "Homing Pigeon," *Playboy*, March 1969, 106; "There'll Be Some Changes Made," *Playboy*, December 1970, 166; "Trail-Blazing Bunny," *Playboy*, July 1971, 102; and "Superbunny," *Playboy*, June 1973, 120.

49. "The Bunnies," *Playboy*, July 1963, 90–101, 119–123. Subsequent Bunny pictorials include "The Bunnies of Chicago," *Playboy*, August 1964; "The Bunnies of Miami," *Playboy*, October 1965; "The Bunnies of Dixie," *Playboy*, August 1966; "The Bunnies of Missouri," *Playboy*, March 1967; "The Bunnies of Hollywood," *Playboy*, November 1967; "The Bunnies of Detroit," *Playboy*, August 1969; and "The Bunnies of New York," *Playboy*, May 1971.

50. "Bunnies of Dixie," 103.

51. *Bunny Manual*, section 520.2.1–520.2.5; John Donovan, "Playboy Bunnies Hop to Strict Rules," *Indianapolis Star*, 2 December 1962, PVF, KIL. *Playboy* explained that its no-dating rules were "designed to protect Bunnies from awkward situations that might arise in the Club." See "RSVIP," *VIP*, Fall 1967, 3.

52. "Bunnies of Dixie," 112.

53. On promoting Playmates as Bunnies and vice versa, see HMH to Victor Lownes III, 2 March 1961, Folder 3, Box 17, HP. Playboy also inaugurated a "Bunny of the Year" contest in 1969, publishing an annual pictorial that highlighted contestants.

54. "The Bunnies," 119.

55. A nostalgic account, former Bunny Kathryn Lee Scott's book *The Bunny Years* (Los Angeles: Pomegranate, 1998) nevertheless provides insight into the motivations and experiences of many of the young women who worked at the clubs.

56. In the breast culture of the early 1960s, Bunny costumes, designed to emphasize the bust, came only in generous 34-D and 36-D sizes. Scott, *Bunny Years*, 190; Gloria Steinem, "A Bunny's Tale," *Show*, May 1963, 90, and "A Bunny's Tale Part II," *Show*, June 1963, 66.

57. *Bunny Manual*, 520.1.B; "Playboy Club News" advertisements in these issues of *Playboy*: July 1961, 33; March 1962, 31; and June 1962, 41; "Be a Playboy Bunny," *CT*, 4 June 1961, S12.

58. Quoted in Scott, *Bunny Years*, 153, 155, 228, 193, 135.

59. "General Decorum," *Bunny Manual*, n.p. Accumulating merits cancelled out demerits earned for such infractions as poor appearance or tardiness; enough merits resulted in a monetary prize. *Bunny Manual*, section 520—Appendix "A"; Donovan, "Bunnies Hop to Strict Rules."

60. Quoted in Scott, *Bunny Years*, 188, 135.

61. Quoted in Scott, *Bunny Years*, 133. On fanfare surrounding the "Bunny of the Year" pageant, for instance, see "Ruthy Ross, Singin' in the Reign," *VIP*, Winter 1972, 27, and "A Crown for Coni," *VIP*, Fall 1973, 18–21, 40. On the "discovery" of one Bunny and her subsequent movie role, see "RSVIP," *VIP*, Summer 1973, 4.

62. Scott, *Bunny Years*, 195, 69, 74.

63. "The Bunnies of Missouri," 146, and Scott, *Bunny Years*, 71, 144, 148; George Draper, "Sex and the Single Bunny," *San Francisco Chronicle*, PVF, KIL.

64. Quoted in Scott, *Bunny Years*, 229, 132.

65. Quoted in Scott, *Bunny Years*, 230. See the interviews on 149, 110, and 229 as well.

66. Quoted in Scott, *Bunny Years*, 176, 202. On "weigh-ins" and "Bunny Image," see 196, 225; on regulations for personal appearance, *Bunny Manual*, sections 520.6–520.12. Some Bunnies eventually tried to unionize in order to gain privileges rather than face dismissal for seniority. "Playboy Bunnies Demand Union Rights," *Worker's Power*, 7–20 December 1973; Bowen Northrup, "A Hitch in the Hutch: Playboy Dispute Has Bunnies Hopping Mad," *Wall Street Journal*, 10 February 1967, PVF, KIL.

67. Bill Davidson, "Czar of the Bunny Empire," *Saturday Evening Post*, April 1962, 38; Steinem, "A Bunny's Tale" and "A Bunny's Tale Part II." Hefner, quoted in "Two Definitions of Obscenity," *Time*, 21 June 1963, 44. Steinem's article was subtitled "Show's First Expose for Intelligent People."

68. "Disneyland for Adults," 166; Peiss, *Cheap Amusements*.

Chapter 5

1. David Halberstam, "Love, Life, and Selling out in Poland," *Harper's*, July 1967, 89.

2. Anson Mount, "Playboy's Pigskin Preview," *Playboy*, September 1961, 73; "Sassy Newcomer," *Time*, 24 September 1956, 71.

3. The ad for the college bureau appeared in *Playboy,* September 1957, 77. On college parties, see "Dear Playboy," in the following issues: February 1956, 3; December 1957, 6; and July 1958, 5, as well as "Saucy Sophomore," *Playboy,* September 1958, 41–47.

4. The After Six ad appeared in *Playboy,* December 1957, 11; No Doz, *Playboy,* July 1958, 66, "Too Pooped to Play, Boy?" *Playboy,* December 1957, 79; Raeburns and Bacardi ads, *Playboy,* July 1960, 6; Botany 500 advertisement, *Playboy,* May 1966, 65. On purchasing habits of *Playboy*'s college readers, see Benn Management Corporation, *Male College Student Survey: Conducted for Playboy Magazine* (Chicago, 1963).

5. "Itinerary," *Fling,* vol. 1, no. 1, 1957, 3; "The King's Harem," *Fling* 1, no. 15 (1959), 35. By 1965, *Fling* called itself "the fun-package for men." "Hefner's Playboy," *Fortune,* May 1957, 216; "Playboy Puts a Glint in the Admen's Eyes," *Business Week,* 28 June 1969, 144; Marie Torre, "A Woman Looks at the Girly-Girly Magazines," *Cosmopolitan,* May 1963, 42–43.

6. For civil rights and consumer society, see Lizabeth Cohen, *A Consumers' Republic: The Politics of Mass Consumption in Postwar America* (New York: Knopf, 2003), 44–47, 166–191; Andrew Hurley, *Diners, Bowling Alleys, and Trailer Parks: Chasing the America Dream in the Postwar Consumer Culture* (New York: Basic, 2001), 184–190, 304–310; Alison Isenberg, *Downtown America: A History of the Place and the People Who Made It* (Chicago: University of Chicago Press, 2004), 203–254; Thomas J. Sugrue, *Origins of the Urban Crisis: Race and Inequality in Postwar Detroit* (Princeton: Princeton University Press, 1996), 181–207. On the struggle for racial equality, see Robert Weisbrot, *Freedom Bound: A History of the American Civil Rights Movement* (New York: Norton, 1990); Harvard Sitkoff, *The Struggle for Black Equality,* rev. ed. (New York: Hill and Wang, 1993); William L. Van Deburg, *New Day in Babylon: The Black Power Movement and American Culture, 1965–1975* (Chicago: University of Chicago Press, 1992).

7. Quoted in Thomas David Pendergast, "Consuming Men: Masculinity, Race, and American Magazines, 1900–1950" (Ph.D. diss., Purdue University, 1998), 255. For further discussion on Johnson and *Ebony,* see Tom Pendergast, *Creating the Modern Man: American Magazines and Consumer Culture* (Columbia: University of Missouri Press, 2000), 243–259.

8. Stephen J. Whitfield, *A Death in the Delta: The Story of Emmett Till* (Baltimore: Johns Hopkins University Press, 1991), 145. "New Magazine Aimed for Men," *Chicago Daily Defender,* 13 April 1957, 12; "Duke Debut," *Duke,* June 1957, 2; "Dear Duke," July 1957, 4; and "Dear Duke," June 1957, 4.

9. "Duke's Den," *Duke,* July 1957; Raymond S. McCann, "Off the Record," *Chicago Daily Defender,* 25 June 1958, 10.

10. Hal Higdon, "Playboying around the Clock with Hugh Hefner," *Climax,* February 1962, 86; "Playboy's Penthouse," *Chicago Daily Defender,* 15 November 1960, 22. Off the air, Hefner and *Playboy* supported African-American causes and organizations, and the Chicago Committee of One Hundred bestowed upon him a "Good American Award" for "outstanding contributions in the field of human relations." "Gov. Kerner Joins in Honor to Roy Wilkins," *Chicago Daily Defender,* 3 April 1961, 5; "Chicago Committee of One Hundred to Present Its Good American Awards," *Chicago Daily Defender,* 8 March 1962, 16.

11. "From the Back of the Bus," *Playboy*, October 1962, 132. Hefner later wrote the introduction to a published book of Gregory's humor, *Dick Gregory: From the Back of the Bus*, ed. Bob Orben (New York: Dutton, 1962), 11–18.

12. "The New Orleans Playboy Club," *Playboy*, March 1962, 52.

13. John Wilcock, "Can a Negro Be a Playboy?" *Village Voice*, 19 October 1961, 2; "People Are Talking About," *Jet*, 26 October 1961, Folder 4, Box 18, HP; "New Orleans Club Bars Defender Newsman," *Chicago Daily Defender*, 21 October 1961, 1; John Wilcock, "From Playboy's Hugh Hefner," *Village Voice*, 9 November 1961, 2; HMH to *Jet* magazine, 1 November 1961, Folder 4, Box 18, HP; "Playboy Vows to End Club Bias," *Chicago Daily Defender*, 11 November 1961, 1; HMH to Arthur Greene, 18 June 1962, Folder 4, Box 24, HP; William R. Ming to Roy Wilkins, 30 June 1964, Papers of the NAACP, Administrative File, Board of Directors: Members, William R. Ming, Jr., 1959–1969. On the hypocrisy of American racism in the face of U.S. foreign policy objectives, see Mary L. Dudziak, *Cold War Civil Rights: Race and the Image of American Democracy* (Princeton: Princeton University Press, 2002), and Thomas Borstelmann, *The Cold War and the Color Line: American Race Relations in the Global Arena* (Cambridge: Harvard University Press, 2002).

14. "The Bunnies," 120, and "Dear Playboy," *Playboy*, October 1963, 8; John Wilcock, "From Playboy's Hugh Hefner," *Village Voice*, 9 November 1961, 2; L. F. Palmer, Jr., "Playboy Clubs vs. Jim Crow," *The Courier*, 24 March 1962, in volume 72, HS. For the memo that served as a template for Hefner's various letters to the media, see HMH, "Integration at the Playboy Clubs," Folder 4, Box 18, HP.

15. African Americans constituted about 11 percent of Playboy's paid circulation in 1962, making it the leading men's magazine among black readers. Though this proportion declined to 7.7 percent by 1967, *Playboy*'s circulation increased substantially, producing a net increase of nearly 250 percent in African-American readership. See Daniel Starch and Staff, *Starch Consumer Magazine Report*, and Audit Bureau of Circulations, *Magazine Trend Report*, both for 1962 and 1967.

16. Stanley G. Robertson, "L.A. Confidential," *Los Angeles Sentinel*, 25 January 1962, 4; Stanley G. Robertson, "L.A. Confidential," *Los Angeles Sentinel*, 12 April 1962, 15; "Siren in Search," *Playboy*, December 1957, 47.

17. ACS to HMH, 9 January 1963, Folder 9, Box 22, SP; "Dear Playboy," *Playboy*, June 1964, 21–22.

18. "Portrait of Jenny," *Playboy*, March 1965, 88; "Dear Playboy," *Playboy*, June 1965, 12.

19. Rosemarie Tyler Brooks, "Washington Round-Up," *Chicago Daily Defender*, 27 March 1965, 2; Joanne Meyerowitz, "Women, Cheesecake, and Borderline Material: Responses to Girlie Pictures in the Mid-Twentieth-Century U.S.," *Women's History* 8 (Fall 1996): 19–20. On so-called corrective products for African Americans, see Kathy Peiss, *Hope in a Jar: The Making of America's Beauty Culture* (New York: Metropolitan Books, 1998).

20. "Playboy of the Western Night World," *Ebony*, July 1965, 103–104; Bill Lane, "The Inside Story," *Los Angeles Sentinel*, 25 February 1965, D1; Dave Hepburn, "Playboy Club Opening Postponed; Hefner Empire Includes Many Negroes," *New York Amsterdam*

News, 11 August 1962, 16; "Playboy Clubs Rate Big Negro Personnel," *Los Angeles Sentinel,* 16 August 1962, 16; "Izzy Rowe's Notebook," *Pittsburgh Courier,* 5 January 1963, 17.

21. Nat Hentoff, "Through the Racial Looking Glass," *Playboy,* July 1962, 90.

22. "Playboy Interview: Malcolm X," *Playboy,* May 1963, 53–63; "Playboy Interview: Martin Luther King," *Playboy,* January 1965, 71; James Farmer, "Mood Ebony," *Playboy,* February 1966, 107; James Baldwin and Budd Schulberg, "Dialog in Black and White," *Playboy,* December 1966, 133. Haley's interview formed the basis for *The Autobiography of Malcolm X* (New York: Grove, 1965).

23. Charles J. Livingston, "Gregory's Rights, SOS Draws $$$," *Pittsburgh Courier,* 18 July 1964, 17; "Orchid for the Day," *Chicago Daily Defender,* 29 June 1964, 3; "Gov. Kerner Joins in Honor to Roy Wilkins," *Chicago Daily Defender,* 3 April 1961, 5; "Chicago Committee of One Hundred to Present Its Good American Awards," *Chicago Daily Defender,* 8 March 1962, 16.

24. Lisa Heilbronn, "Breadwinners and Loafers: Images of Masculinity in 1950s Situation Comedy," *masculinities* 2 (Fall 1994): 60–70; Stephanie Coontz, *The Way We Never Were: American Families and the Nostalgia Trap* (New York: Basic, 1992), 171–172; Alex McNeil, *Total Television: The Comprehensive Guide to Programming from 1948 to the Present,* 4th ed. (New York: Penguin, 1996); Dan Einstein et al., "Source Guide to TV Family Comedy, Drama, and Serial Drama, 1946–1970," in *Private Screenings: Television and the Female Consumer,* ed. Lynn Spigel and Denise Mann (Minneapolis: University of Minnesota Press, 1992), 255–259; and Muriel G. Cantor, "Prime-time Fathers: A Study in Continuity and Change," *Critical Studies in Mass Communication* 7 (1990): 280–281.

25. "Playbill," *Playboy,* November 1961, 3. On screenplay disagreements, see Steven Watts, *Mr. Playboy: Hugh Hefner and the American Dream* (New York: Wiley, 2008), 163–164.

26. Robert Legare chronicled the event in "Meeting at the Summit," *Playboy,* June 1960, 34–37. Numerous books have been written on the group known as the "Rat Pack" and on the individuals who comprised it. Richard Gehman's *Sinatra and His Rat Pack* (New York: Belmont, 1961) offers a contemporary account. Others include Lawrence J. Quirk and William Schoell, *The Rat Pack: Neon Nights with the Kings of Cool* (New York: Avon, 1998), and Shawn Levy, *Rat Pack Confidential: Frank, Dean, Sammy, Peter, Joey, and the Last Great Showbiz Party* (New York: Doubleday, 1998).

27. On the affair with Gardner and its impact on Sinatra's popularity, see Levy, *Rat Pack Confidential,* 21–22; Quirk and Schoell, *The Rat Pack,* 39–42; and James F. Smith, "Bobby Sox and Blue Suede Shoes: Frank Sinatra and Elvis Presley as Teen Idols," in *Frank Sinatra and Popular Culture: Essays on an American Icon,* ed. Leonard Mustazza (Westport, CT: Praeger, 1998), 61, 64; Ken Hutchins, "Sinatra's Fans: Discussions in Three Tenses: The Past, the Present, and the Future," in Mustazza, *Frank Sinatra and Popular Culture,* 87.

28. James Chapman, *License to Thrill: A Cultural History of the James Bond Films* (New York: Columbia University Press, 2000), 35; Ian Fleming, "How to Write a Thriller," *Books and Bookmen* (May 1963): 14–15, quoted in Tony Bennett and Janet Woollacott, *Bond and Beyond: The Political Career of a Popular Hero* (New York: Methuen, 1987), 88, 247. For "license to look," see Michael Denning, *Cover Stories: Narrative and Ideology*

in the British Spy Thriller (London: Routledge, 1987), 103–107. For Fleming's "technique of erotic distraction," see A. Bear, "Intellectuals and 007: High Comedy and Total Stimulation," *Dissent* (Winter 1966). I am indebted to Bill Osgerby's fine discussion of the cultural connections between the Rat Pack, James Bond, and *Playboy* in *Playboys in Paradise: Masculinity, Youth and Leisure-style in Modern America* (Oxford: Berg, 2001), 153–162.

29. "Bondomania," *Time*, 11 June 1965, 59. Between 1962 and 1967, five Bond movies were released: *Dr. No* (1962), *From Russia with Love* (1963), *Goldfinger* (1964), *Thunderball* (1965), and *You Only Live Twice* (1967). Based on Fleming's first novel, *Casino Royale*, a sixth "Bond" film, appeared with that title in 1967. This film was not part of the Bond cycle produced by United Artists/Eon Productions. The Columbia Pictures/Charles K. Feldman picture spoofed the Bond films; however, it too points to the overwhelming popularity of the character at this time.

30. Chapman, *License to Thrill*, 81–82, 116–117; Bennett and Woollacott, *Bond and Beyond*, 114–127, 32; Richard Maibaum, "James Bond's Girls," *Playboy*, November 1965, 139; "Playbill," *Playboy*, March 1960, 3; "25 Years of James Bond," *Playboy*, September 1987, 124.

31. For "popular hero," see Bennett and Woollacott, *Bond and Beyond*, 13–20, 29–36. 007 ad in *Playboy*, December 1965, 57. Martin reprised the role in *Murderer's Row* (1966), *The Ambushers* (1968), and *The Wrecking Crew* (1969). Quirk and Schoell, *The Rat Pack*, 245.

32. Bennett and Woollacott, *Bond and Beyond*, 123–124; Victor A. Lownes III to HMH, 1 July 1968, Folder 14, Box 46, SP.

33. Bonnie J. Dow, "Hegemony, Feminist Criticism and *The Mary Tyler Moore Show*," *Critical Studies in Mass Communications* 7 (1990): 263–269.

34. "The Second Sexual Revolution," *Time*, 24 January 1964, 54–59. For changes in obscenity law, see Paul S. Boyer, *Purity in Print: Book Censorship in America from the Gilded Age to the Computer Age*, 2nd ed. (Madison: University of Wisconsin Press, 2002), 282–293. Key court decisions were *Memoirs vs. Massachusetts*, 383 U.S. 413 (1966) and *Redrup* vs. *New York*, 386 U.S. 767 (1967). For Playboy Forum, see Thomas Weyr, *Reaching for Paradise: The Playboy Vision of America* (New York: Times Books, 1978), 107. For changing sexual morality, see Beth Bailey, *Sex in the Heartland* (Cambridge: Harvard University Press, 1999) and "Sexual Revolution(s)," in *The Sixties: From Memory to History*, ed. David Farber (Chapel Hill: University of North Carolina Press, 1994), 235–262, and David Farber, *The Age of Great Dreams: America in the 1960s* (New York: Hill and Wang, 1994), 182–183. The phrase "nice girls don't" is found in Bailey, "Sexual Revolution(s)," 244. Although contemporary observers discussed a sexual "revolution," Bailey points out that it was, in fact, an "evolution."

35. Albert Ellis, *Sex without Guilt* (New York: Lyle, Stuart, 1958), 43; Bailey, "Sexual Revolution(s)," 238; John D'Emilio and Estelle Freedman, *Intimate Matters: A History of Sexuality in America* (New York: Harper & Row, 1988), 305–306. In the late 1960s, median age at first marriage began to rise, reaching 24 for men and 22 for women by the late 1970s and continuing its upward trend for the rest of the century. Between 1960 and 1970, among males aged 20 to 24, the proportion who had never married increased from 53 to 55 percent

and reached 68 percent by 1980, while among women in this age group the proportion who had never married climbed from 28 percent in 1960 to 36 percent in 1970 and by 1980, had reached 51 percent. Derived from Susan B. Carter, et al., eds. *Historical Statistics of the United States, Earliest Times to the Present: Millennial Edition* (New York: Cambridge University Press, 2006), Volume I, Part A, 75–76, 685–686. Howard P. Chudacoff, in *The Age of the Bachelor: Creating an American Subculture* (Princeton: Princeton University Press, 1999), 258–259, notes that the proportion of Americans age 25 to 34 living alone increased from 5.1 percent to 29.1 percent between 1950 and 1976, an increase of 500 percent.

36. Larry R. Ford, *Cities and Buildings: Skyscrapers, Skid Rows, and Suburbs* (Baltimore: Johns Hopkins University Press, 1994), 219; Marina Management Corporation, *A City within a City* [Marina Towers Prospectus, 1961], CHM; Richard Atcheson, "Marina City: Chicago's Pies in the Sky," *Holiday*, December 1965, 28, 32; Sam Weller, *Secret Chicago: The Unique Guidebook to Chicago's Hidden Sites, Sounds, and Tastes* (Toronto, Ontario: ECW Press, 2002), 24.

37. Clarence Petersen, "The Firm That Rents Fantasies," CT, 17 July 1974, 18; Ford, *Cities and Buildings*, 219; Robert Cross, "Playgrounds for Rent," CT, 16 February 1975, G18.

38. Halberstam, "Love, Life, and Selling Out in Poland," 89.

39. The Port Huron Statement is found in James Miller, *Democracy Is in the Streets: From Port Huron to the Siege of Chicago* (Cambridge: Harvard University Press, 1994), 329. For overviews of the period, see William Chafe, *The Unfinished Journey: America since World War II*, 5th ed. (New York: Oxford University Press, 2003); Barbara L. Tischler, ed., *Sights on the Sixties* (New Brunswick, NJ: Rutgers University Press, 1992), and Farber, *Age of Great Dreams* and *The Sixties*. For the antiwar movement, see Charles DeBenedetti with Charles Chatfield, *An American Ordeal* (Syracuse: Syracuse University Press, 1990); Melvin Small, *Johnson, Nixon and the Doves* (New Brunswick, NJ: Rutgers University Press, 1988); Kenneth J. Heineman, *Campus Wars: The Peace Movement at American State Universities in the Vietnam Era* (New York: New York University Press, 1993); Melvin Small and William D. Hoover, eds., *Give Peace a Chance: Exploring the Vietnam Antiwar Movement* (Syracuse: Syracuse University Press, 1992); for the New Left and the era's social and political divides, Todd Gitlin, *The Sixties: Years of Hope, Days of Rage* (New York: Bantam, 1987); Miller, *Democracy Is in the Streets;* Douglas C. Rossinow, *Politics of Authenticity: Liberalism, Christianity, and the New Left in America* (New York: Columbia University Press, 1998); David Farber, *Chicago '68* (Chicago: University of Chicago Press, 1988); and W. J. Rorabaugh, *Berkeley at War, the 1960s* (New York: Oxford University Press, 1989).

40. Theodore Roszak, *The Making of a Counter Culture: Reflections on the Technocratic Society and Its Youthful Opposition* (Garden City, NY: Anchor, 1969) offers a contemporaneous, sympathetic account of the counterculture. Thomas Frank's *The Conquest of Cool: Business Culture, Counterculture, and the Rise of Hip Consumerism* (Chicago: University of Chicago Press, 1997) views the counterculture as deeply enmeshed in the consumer society. For further discussion of countercultural ambitions, see Farber, *Chicago '68* and *Age of Great Dreams*, 167–189; Peter Braunstein and Michael William Doyle, eds., *Imagine Nation: The American Counterculture of the 1960s and '70s* (New York: Routledge, 2002); and Andrew G. Kirk, *Counterculture Green: The*

Whole Earth Catalog and American Environmentalism (Lawrence: University Press of Kansas, 2007).

41. "Playmate First Class: Jo Collins in Vietnam," *Playboy,* May 1966, 145; Eric Bentley, "Conscience versus Conformity," *Playboy,* January 1967, 150; John Kenneth Galbraith, "Resolving Our Vietnam Predicament," *Playboy,* December 1967, 139; David Halberstam, "The Americanization of Vietnam," *Playboy,* January 1970, 105; Nat Hentoff, "Youth—The Oppressed Majority," *Playboy,* September 1967, 136; Herbert Gold, "The Wave Makers," *Playboy,* October 1967, 128; Harvey Cox, "God and the Hippies," *Playboy,* January 1968, 93; "The Playboy Panel: Student Revolt," *Playboy,* September 1969, 89; "Sex in Academe," *Playboy,* September 1969, 193; Jacob Brackman, "The Underground Press," *Playboy,* August 1967, 83; R. E. L. Masters, "Sex, Ecstasy, and the Psychedelic Drugs," *Playboy,* November 1967, 94; "Playboy Plans a Duplex Penthouse," *Playboy,* January 1970, 235. The magazine's interest in jazz led to its earliest coverage of drugs, a 1960 Playboy Panel on "Narcotics and the Jazz Musician." In 1962, Dan Wakefield's "The Prodigal Powers of Pot," *Playboy,* August 1962, 51, provided an in-depth look at the history and use of marijuana.

42. Roszak, *Making of a Counter Culture,* 5–6. Roszak drew upon the concept of repressive desublimation articulated by Herbert Marcuse in *One Dimensional Man: Studies in the Ideology of Advanced Industrial Society* (Boston: Beacon, 1964).

43. As Thomas Frank has demonstrated in *The Conquest of Cool,* 229, in the 1960s the construction of an endless cycle of "hip versus square" consumption meant that countercultural style as a mark of rebellion became incorporated into the same system against which one rebelled. From this perspective, the counterculture represents another form of self-indulgent, middle-class lifestyle. For further discussion of the counterculture's hedonism and its appeal to mainstream, middle-class audiences, see Barbara Ehrenreich, *Hearts of Men: American Dreams and the Flight from Commitment* (New York: Anchor, 1983), 106–116, and Bill Osgerby, *Playboys in Paradise,* 182–192.

44. For an early critique of this viewpoint, which argued that the counterculture played into the hands of capitalists by mistakenly thinking they "possessed" a culture that capitalists could "steal," see Craig Karpel, "Das Hip Kapital," *Esquire,* December 1970, 84.

45. "Playboy and the Grass Market," *Great Speckled Bird,* 29 May 1972, 19. Variations also appeared as "Playboy Eyes Grass Market," *Fifth Estate,* 6 May 1972, n.p., and "A Pipe Dream," *Win Magazine,* 1 June 1972, 18; *Kaleidoscope,* 20 October 1971, n.p.; "Playboy Forum," *Playboy,* October 1970, 208. On the Diggers, see Farber, *Age of Great Dreams,* 169–171, 186–187.

Chapter 6

1. J. Anthony Lukas, "The 'Alternative Life-Style' of Playboys and Playmates," NYT Magazine, 11 June 1972, 14.

2. "The Lake Geneva Playboy Club-Hotel," *Playboy,* May 1969, 144; "Millionaires. Playboy Goes Public," *Time,* 27 September 1971, 88; "Viewpoints: What Do You Think of *Playboy?*" *Medical Aspects of Human Sexuality* 5 (July 1971): 11–21; "What's New,"

VIP, Winter 1973, 15; "Bunny of the Year Pageant: On the Air," *VIP,* Summer 1974, 16–17. For falling share prices, see F. C. Klein and J. R. Laing, "Playboy's Slide," *Wall Street Journal,* 13 April 1976, 1. Throughout the chapter, I use "Playboy" when writing about the corporate entity, Playboy Enterprises, Inc. (PEI), responsible for the magazine, nightclubs, television programs, and other products and services. *Playboy* refers specifically to the magazine, and "playboy" references the urban, man-about-town depicted in its pages.

3. For this viewpoint, see Anselma Dell'Olio, "The Sexual Revolution Wasn't Our War," *Ms.,* Spring 1972, 104; Linda Phelps, "Death in the Spectacle," *Liberation,* May 1971, reprinted in Rosalyn Baxandall and Linda Gordon, eds., *Dear Sisters: Dispatches from the Women's Liberation Movement* (New York: Basic, 2000), 175–179. On exploitive aspects of the sexual revolution and the counterculture, see Beth Bailey, "Sex as a Weapon: Underground Comix and the Paradox of Liberation," in *Imagine Nation: The American Counterculture of the 1960s and '70s,* ed. Peter Braunstein and Michael William Doyle (New York: Routledge, 2002), 305–326.

4. John D'Emilio and Estelle Freedman use the term "sexualized society" to describe how sex came to permeate American culture after the mid-1960s in *Intimate Matters: A History of Sexuality in America* (New York: Harper & Row, 1988), 326–343. "Playboy Puts a Glint in the Admen's Eyes," *Business Week,* 28 June 1969, 142, 144.

5. HMH to ACS, 9 January 1967 (no other location), HP; HMH to ACS, Jack Kessie, Vince Tajiri, and Art Paul, 9 December 1968, Folder 6, Box 46, SP; Victor Lownes to Bob Preuss, 16 September 1968, Folder 14, Box 46, SP.

6. *Penthouse* advertisement in CT, 19 September 1969, 16; Guccione quoted in Russell Miller, *Bunny: The Real Story of Playboy* (New York: Holt, Rinehart and Winston, 1984), 179; HMH to Vince Tajiri and Art Paul, 8 June 1970, Folder 4, Box 61, SP. On the success of *Penthouse,* see "Bring on the Girls," *Forbes,* 7 August 1978, 75. On circulation battles, see Philip H. Doughtery, "Advertising: Those Illustrated Magazines," NYT, 5 January 1972, 59; Philip H. Doughtery, "Advertising: Risque Magazines," NYT, 12 March 1973, 50; "40-Million Lawsuit Filed by Penthouse against Playboy," NYT, 25 May 1974, 37; Audit Bureau of Circulations, *Magazine Trend Report* (Schaumburg, IL) for 1973 and 1974; Miller, *Bunny,* 187–189.

7. Advertisement for OUI in *VIP,* Winter 1973, 50; Philip H. Doughtery, "Advertising: Fall Debut for Oui," NYT, 15 May 1972, 56.

8. Philip H. Doughtery, "Advertising: Playboy Sales Lag," NYT, 6 March 1974, 55. On imitators and availability of sexually explicit material, see J. Madeleine Nash, "After the Bunny, a Deluge," CT, 9 September 1973, 33–46, and William Serrin, "Sex Is a Growing Multibillion Business," NYT, 9 February 1981, B1. Nancy Friday, *My Secret Garden: Women's Sexual Fantasies* (New York: Pocket Books, 1973); Shere Hite, *The Hite Report: A Nationwide Study of Female Sexuality* (New York: Dell, 1976); Erica Jong, *Fear of Flying* (New York: Holt, Rinehart and Winston, 1973); and foreword to Trudy Baker and Rachel Jones, *The Coffee Tea or Me Girls Lay It on the Line* (New York: Grosset & Dunlop, 1972).

9. Morton Hunt, *Sexual Behavior in the 1970s* (Chicago: Playboy Press, 1974), and "Sex Goes Public," *Playboy,* July 1977, 99. For examples of photography and editorial content,

see "Bunnies of '76," *Playboy*, October 1976, 135; "Who's Been Sleeping in My Dorm?" *Playboy*, October 1975, 94; "Playboy's Guide to the Rites of Spring," *Playboy*, March 1976, 88; "What's Really Happening on Campus," *Playboy*, October 1976, 128; Peter Ross Range, "Sex in America: Miami," *Playboy*, December 1978, 144; Walter L. Lowe, "Sex in Chicago," *Playboy*, April 1979, 123; Barry Farrell and Penelope McMillan, "Los Angeles," and James Wohl, "Hollywood," *Playboy*, December 1979, 181; Peter Ross Range, "Sex in America: New Orleans," *Playboy*, September 1979, 115; and Ken Bode, "Sex in America: Boston," *Playboy*, May 1980, 133.

10. The phrase comes from "The Me Decade and the Third Great Awakening," in Tom Wolfe, *Mauve Gloves and Madmen, Clutter & Vine* (New York: Farrar, Straus & Giroux, 1976). For more on the campaign and *Playboy*'s editorial direction in the 1970s, see Steven Watts, *Mr. Playboy: Hugh Hefner and the American Dream* (New York: Wiley, 2008), 309–316. On therapeutic culture, see Jackson Lears, "From Salvation to Self-Realization: Advertising and the Therapeutic Roots of the Consumer Culture, 1900–1930," in *The Culture of Consumption: Critical Essays in American History, 1880–1980*, ed. Richard Wightman Fox and T. J. Jackson Lears (New York: Pantheon, 1983), 3–38. For therapeutic ethos in the 1970s, see Christopher Lasch, *Culture of Narcissism: American Life in an Age of Diminishing Expectations* (New York: Norton, 1979).

11. Surrey Marshe with Robert A. Liston, *The Girl in the Centerfold: The Uninhibited Memoirs of Miss January* (New York: Delacorte, 1969), 42. On licensing hearings and Bunny costume, see Kathryn Lee Scott, *The Bunny Years* (Los Angeles: Pomegranate, 1998), 126–130.

12. "What's New," *VIP*, Fall 1974, 7; "What's New," *VIP*, Winter 1974, 11; "Hutch Hopping with Hef," *VIP*, Spring 1975, 12–15, 34; "The Good Life," advertisement, *Playboy*, October 1976, 33; Terry Atlas, "Highs and Lows in 'Bunnyland,'" *CT*, 5 March 1978, 38; "Drinks on Hefner," *Newsweek*, 19 August 1968, 66. Former executive Victor Lownes provided an account of Playboy's British operations in *The Day the Bunny Died* (Secaucus, NJ: Lyle Stuart Inc., 1982).

13. F. C. Klein and J. R. Laing, "Playboy's Slide: Hotel Losses, Decline in Circulation Weaken Hugh Hefner's Empire," *Wall Street Journal*, 13 April 1976, 1; Ads for Gift Merchandise and Playboy Club's Holiday Gift Key Package, *VIP*, Fall 1973, 8–9, 41; "Mail," *Oui*, March 1973, 10; "Who Says Men Have All the Fun?" *VIP*, Summer 1975, 33–36; Miller, *Bunny*, 274.

14. Bob Greene, "Beyond the Sexual Revolution," *Newsweek*, 29 September 1975, 13. The married Greene later resigned his longtime post at the CT after an earlier sexual encounter with a teenage girl came to light.

15. John Clellon Holmes, "The New Girl," *Playboy*, January 1968, 182, 214.

16. Holmes, "The New Girl," 181–182, 214–216. On the origins of women's liberation movement and Miss America protest, see Sara M. Evans, *Personal Politics: The Roots of Women's Liberation in the Civil Rights Movement and the New Left* (New York: Knopf, 1979); Susan Brownmiller, *In Our Time: Memoir of a Revolution* (New York: Random House, 1999), 13–23, 35–41; Megan Boler et al., "We Sisters Join Together…," in *Take Back the Night: Women on Pornography*, ed. Laura Lederer (New York: William Morrow & Company, 1980), 261–266.

17. Evans, *Personal Politics*; Brownmiller, *In Our Time*; Betty Friedan, *The Feminine Mystique* (New York: Norton, 1963). On women's liberation see Sheila Tobias, *Faces of Feminism: An Activist's Reflections on the Women's Movement* (Boulder, CO: Westview, 1997); Alice Echols, *Daring to Be Bad: Radical Feminism in America, 1967–1975* (Minneapolis: University of Minnesota Press, 1989); and "Nothing Distant about It: Women's Liberation and Sixties Radicalism," in *The Sixties*, ed. David Farber (Chapel Hill: University of North Carolina Press, 1994), 149–174; Robin Morgan, ed., *Sisterhood Is Powerful: An Anthology of Writings from the Women's Liberation Movement* (New York: Random House, 1970); Kathleen C. Berkeley, *The Women's Liberation Movement in America* (Westport, CT: Greenwood, 1999); Baxandall and Gordon, eds., *Dear Sisters*.

18. Gloria Steinem, "A Bunny's Tale," *Show*, May 1963, 90; Diana Lurie, "An Empire Built on Sex," *Life*, 29 October 1965, 70. Others criticizing Hefner for presenting women as accessories to the playboy lifestyle included Harvey Cox, "*Playboy*'s Doctrine of the Male," *Christianity and Crisis*, May 1961, 56–60; Marie Torre, "A Woman Looks at the Girly Girly Magazines," *Cosmopolitan*, May 1963, 42–47; and Gregor Roy, "Plato, the Penthouse, and the Girl Who Hesitates," *Mademoiselle*, March 1965, 199.

19. See for example Hugh M. Hefner, "The Playboy Philosophy," *Playboy*, December 1964, 218, and "The Playboy Panel: Religion and the New Morality," *Playboy*, June 1967, 156.

20. Charlene Ventura, "Impact of Women's Liberation Movement on Advertising Trends," unpublished paper, 1974, "Advertising Papers," WEF; Women against Violence in Pornography and Media, *Write Back, Fight Back! Media Protest Packet* (San Francisco: Women's Press Project, 1981), WEF; Brownmiller, *In Our Time*, 83–93. Ironically, the students were arrested and charged with indecency; the Playboy Foundation reportedly aided in their defense. Robin Lake, "The Playboy and Miss America Protests," *Women against Violence in Pornography & Media Newspage* 3, no. 8 [1979], n.p.; "Playboy' Strippers Convicted," *Distant Drummer*, 2 July 1969; "The Playboy Foundation," *Playboy*, January 1979, 84.

21. For a conservative assessment of the links between the playboy philosophy and the women's movement and the challenge both posed to family values, see George Gilder, "Suicide of the Sexes," *Harper's*, July 1973, 42–54. For Hefner's surprise over the women's movement, see Gloria Steinem, "What *Playboy* Doesn't Know about Women Could Fill a Book," *McCall's*, October 1970, 76. For further discussion of *Playboy* and the women's movement, see Carrie Pitzulo, "The Battle in Every Man's Bed: *Playboy* and the Fiery Feminists," *Journal of the History of Sexuality* 17 (May 2008): 259–289.

22. HMH to ACS, 17 July 1969, and ACS to Dick Rosenzweig, 15 December [1969], both in Folder 3, Box 61, SP.

23. For staff memos, see Folder 3, Box 61, SP; HMH to ACS, 6 January 1970, Folder 3, Box 61, SP; Susan Braudy, "The Article I Wrote on Women That *Playboy* Wouldn't Print," *Glamour*, May 1971, 202.

24. Morton Hunt, "Up against the Wall, Male Chauvinist Pig!" *Playboy*, May 1970, 95. Hunt was referencing Anne Koedt's widely known essay, "The Myth of the Vaginal Orgasm," published in *Notes from the Second Year* (New York: New York Radical Women, 1969), reprinted in Baxandall and Gordon, eds., *Dear Sisters*.

25. Presumably, the phrase "as men" in this statement was misplaced. Hefner meant women should be allowed the same opportunity as men to establish their own personal lifestyles. HMH to Nat Lehrman, Mary Ann Stuart, 23 June 1970, Folder 4, Box 61, SP. Hunt's subsequent article on "The Future of Marriage," *Playboy*, August 1971, examined divorce, cohabitation, spouse-swapping, marital infidelity, and communal living, claiming these represented not rebellions against traditional marriage but attempts to adapt marriage to modern life. Here, Hunt suggested husbands could pick up some of the slack in household chores to help out working mothers, but again affirmed that child-rearing was primarily a woman's responsibility.

26. Patricia Bradley, *Mass Media and the Shaping of American Feminism* (Jackson: University Press of Mississippi, 2003).

27. Brownmiller, *In Our Time*, 94; and Thomas Weyr, *Reaching for Paradise: The Playboy Vision of America* (New York: Times Books, 1978), 239.

28. "Mindless Sex Objects," *Chicago Seed* 5, no. 3 [1970], 5; Ruth Dear, "Women Shake Up Peace Establishment," *Hyde-Park-Kenwood Voices*, May 1970, 2, Folder 12, Box 27, CWLU; "Playboy Action" *CWLU News*, [spring 1970], 1, Folder: "CWLU Newsletters, CWLU News—1969–1970," Box 19, CWLU; "Storm the Winter Palace," *Chicago Seed* 5, no. 3 [1970]; "The Playboy Mansion Besieged," *Playboy*, July 1970, 43. For discussion of links between racism, sexism, and the Vietnam War, see Gerald Gill, "From Maternal Pacifism to Revolutionary Solidarity: African American Women's Opposition to the Vietnam War," in *Sights on the Sixties*, ed. Barbara L. Tischler (New Brunswick, NJ: Rutgers University Press, 1992), 177–195.

29. On the leaked memo, see Don Rose, "New Feminists Are the 'Natural Enemy'—Hefner," *Hyde Park-Kenwood Voices*, May 1970; and Paul Galloway, "Liberation Sisters Unite," *Chicago Sun Times*, 24 April 1970, Folder 12, Box 27, CWLU; Ventura, "Women's Liberation Movement," 7; "Mr. Hefner's Other Playmates," CT, 17 April 1970, 18; "Women's Liberation Adherents Go to War with Playboy Again," CT, 24 April 1970, 23; "The Playboy and Miss America Protests: First Targets of Feminist Revolt," *WAVPM Newspage* 3, no. 8 [1979]; Braudy, "The Article I Wrote on Women," 202; Steinem, "What *Playboy* Doesn't Know about Women," 79; "Male and Female," *Newsweek*, 18 May 1970, 74; Boler, "We Sisters Join Together," 263–265.

30. For protests against workplace discrimination, see Judith Ann, "The Secretarial Proletariat," in *Sisterhood Is Powerful*, ed. Robin Morgan (New York: Vintage, 1970), 86–100; "Shut Up and Type," *The Old Mole*, 6–19 March 1970, 9; "Wanna Type for a Living?" *Kaleidoscope*, 20 October 1971, 14–15. For anti-*Playboy* protests, see "Women Militants Disrupt Cavett Show with Hefner," NYT, 27 May 1970, 95; "Houston Offs Hugh," *Off Our Backs*, 21 January 1975, 5; "Playboy" and "Press Release," 13 July 1971, both in Folder 10, Box 26, CWLU; Liberation News Service, "Short Bursts," *guerrilla*, 24 November 1971, 3.

31. This paragraph draws on the insights of David Farber's "The Intoxicated State/Illegal Nation: Drugs in the Sixties Counterculture," in Braunstein and Doyle, eds., *Imagine Nation*, 17–40, and Debra Michals's "From 'Consciousness Expansion' to 'Consciousness Raising': Feminism and the Countercultural Politics of the Self," in *Imagine Nation*, 41–68. Michals argues that CR eventually devolved into "encounter

groups," which blunted their political edge. For more on countercultural aspirations, see David Farber, *Age of Great Dreams: America in the 1960s* (New York: Hill and Wang, 1994), 167–189.

32. [Tuesday night group], "Consumer and Media Exploitation of Women," unpublished paper in "Advertising Papers," WEF, and "An Interview with Active WAVPM Members," *WA VPM Newspage*, April 1979, n.p.

33. "Men against the Boy," *Chicago Seed* 5, no. 7 [1970], 6; "M.A.C." *Kaleidoscope*, 24 July 1970, 4; untitled, *Rat*, 23 August 1970, 12. For events at Stonewall Inn, see Martin Duberman, *Stonewall* (New York: Dutton, 1993).

34. Warren Farrell, "Masculine Mystique Plan for Chapter Task Forces," [1972], Folder 3, Box 48, NOW.

35. "First Men's Liberation Conference Planned," typed press release [1974], Folder 3, Box 48, NOW; Lisa Hammel, "Men's Lib: An Unorganized but Significant Movement," NYT, 11 June 1974, 46; "The Masculine Mistake," *Majority Report*, 11 July 1974, 10.

36. "Detroit Men Protest Playboy Club Opening; 'We're Not Playboys, We're Men,'" *Win*, 23 January 1975.

37. Marshe, *Girl in the Centerfold*, 7, 47.

38. "Masturbation," *Brother*, Summer 1971, 5, 18.

39. "Stop Playboying," *Brother*, Summer 1971, 1.

40. "Sour Grapes," *Chicago Seed*, 2 May 1971, 14.

41. Peter Toole, "My Days with Playboy: The Ideal Lover," *Everywoman*, 18 June 1971, 12.

42. "The Masculine Mistake," 10.

43. The cartoons appeared in *Playboy*, March 1971, 195; July 1976, 166; and June 1972, 229. Men are also the objects of female aggression in Adam Erikson's cartoons, "The Aggressive Chick," *Playboy*, November 1974, 162–165. Germaine Greer, "Seduction Is a Four-Letter Word," *Playboy*, January 1973, 80; Richard Woodley, "We Have Met the Enemy and He Is Us," *Playboy*, September 1974, 212. For response to Greer, see "Dear Playboy," *Playboy*, April 1973, 11.

44. "Woman's Work," *Playboy*, June 1973, 99–103, and "Caution: Women at Work," *Playboy*, June 1976, 93–96. This nude pictorial promised that "even if women do take over the country's pneumatic drills, some of them will still get pissed when they break a nail." "Women of the Armed Forces," *Playboy*, April 1980, 168; "Beauty and Bureaucracy," *Playboy*, November 1980, 126. On Title VII, see Tobias, *Faces of Feminism*, 80–85, 97; and Dorothy Sue Cobble, *The Other Women's Movement: Workplace Justice and Social Rights in Modern America* (Princeton: Princeton University Press, 2004).

45. "Bunnies of 1975," *Playboy*, November 1975, 88–89; "Hefner Comes out for 'Real Bunny Lib,'" CT, 23 June 1975, 1; "Notes on People," NYT, 24 June 1975, 39. In response to Hefner's patronizing concessions, *Ms.* magazine, the feminist publication founded in 1971, gave him a "Fascinating Manhood Award—for outstanding achievement by men in the performance of their stereotypes" in the category of "Father of the Year." *Ms.*, October 1975, 62.

46. Suellen Mayfield, "Put Playboy out of Business," *Guardian*, 14 March 1979, 9; and Heather Eisenstein, "Playboy Magazine Mocks Feminism," *Guardian*, 5 September 1979,

20. See also Gail Shister, "Harvard Crimson Says Playboy Is in Wrong League," *Boston Globe*, 5 December 1978; "Playing Hard to Get," *Harvard Independent* 7–13 December 1978; and "Playboy," *Harvard Crimson*, 6 December 1978, all in Subject: "Pornography," SLVFWS.

47. Ellen Goodman, "Pinups and Privilege," *Los Angeles Times*, 15 August 1979, E7; and James Barron, "Campuses Astir over Playboy's Ivy Issue," NYT, 4 August 1979, 8.

48. Paulette Hackman, "Playboy Joins the Class War?" *Mother Jones*, September/October 1979, 16.

49. "Executive Privilege," *Playboy*, October 1976, 146–147; and Michael Korda, "Sexual Office Politics: A Guide for the Eighties," *Playboy*, January 1981, 156, 278–282.

50. "The Women of Playboy," *Playboy*, December 1982, 133–145, 292; Conan Putnam, "Why Would a Smart Woman Work for Playboy?" *Working Woman*, January 1991, 76–79, 102.

51. "The Girls/Women of the Ivy League," *Playboy*, September 1979, 159, and "The Women of Mensa," *Playboy*, November 1985, 73.

52. Press Release, 26 August 1974, Folder 52, Box 29, NOW; "Playboy Forum: Misdirected Anger," *Playboy*, January 1975, 60.

53. "Equality Day Set at Playboy Mansion," *Los Angeles Times*, 20 August 1978, G24; Pat Stahl, "Christie Hefner, Soft-Core Feminist," *Majority Report*, 14 October 1978, 1; "The World of Playboy," *Playboy*, January 1979, 16.

54. Georgia Dullea, "In Feminists' Antipornography Drive, 42nd Street Is the Target," NYT, 6 July 1979, 12; Leslie Bennetts, "Conference Examines Pornography as a Feminist Issue," NYT, 17 September 1979, 10; Paul Montgomery, "'Adult Films Are Assailed by Picketers," NYT, 7 March 1982, 34. For early concern for the need to "clarify NOW's position" on the First Amendment and obscenity, see memo from Whitney Adams to All Task Force Coordinators, 28 March 1975, Folder 3, Box 42, NOW. For NOW's attempt to establish a position on pornography, see Kathleen Fojtik to Jane Wells-Schooley, 11 September 1980, Folder 73, Box 50, NOW. For perspective on pornography as a separate issue from violence against women see memorandum from Kathleen Fojtik to NOW Violence against Women Committee Members, 12 September 1980, Folder 73, Box 50, NOW. Susan Brownmiller's chapter, "The Pornography Wars," in *In Our Time*, 295–325; and John D'Emilio, "Women against Pornography: Feminist Frontier or Social Purity Crusade?" in *Making Trouble: Essays on Gay History, Politics, and the University* (New York: Routledge, 1992), 202–214, provide accounts of the philosophical differences over pornography and this issue's fractious effect on the women's movement.

55. Stahl, "Christie Hefner, Soft-Core Feminist," 1.

56. Frances Chapman, "Can Playboy Buy Women's Lib?" *Majority Report*, 22 July–4 August 1978, 5; "Feminists and Playboy Funding," *WAVPM*, February 1980, n.p., WEF; Catharine A. Mackinnon, "'More Than Simply a Magazine,': Playboy's Money (1982)," in *Feminism Unmodified: Discourses on Life and Law* (Cambridge: Harvard University Press, 1987), 137; minutes of NOW National Board Meeting, 5–6 May 1984, Folder 48, Box 5, NOW; "National Board Report: South Central 5–6 May 1984, St. Louis, Missouri," Folder 50, Box 5, NOW; Bobbe Ross, "All Feminists Pay the Price When Our Purse Strings Are Pulled by Playboy," *Big Mama Rag*, February 1982, 13. A resolution that

member organizations of the National Coalition against Sexual Assault had to refuse Playboy Foundation funding was defeated. See Nan D. Hunter, "The Pornography Debate in Context: A Chronology of Sexuality, Media and Violence Issues in Feminism," in F.A.C.T., *Caught Looking: Feminism, Pornography and Censorship* (1986; Seattle: Real Comet Press, 1988), 26–29.

57. U.S. Commission on Obscenity and Pornography, *Report of the Commission on Obscenity and Pornography* (Washington, D.C.: U.S. Government Printing Office, 1970). On the commission and its findings see "Pornography Goes Public," *Newsweek*, 21 December 1970, 26; and Walter Kendrick, *The Secret Museum: Pornography in Modern Culture* (Berkeley: University of California Press, 1996), 213–219, 234–235. For conservative impulses, see David Farber, "The Silent Majority and Talk about Revolution," in *The Sixties*, 291–310; Bruce J. Schulman, *The Seventies: The Great Shift in American Culture, Society, and Politics* (New York: Free Press, 2001), 193–217, and Gil Troy, *Morning in America: How Ronald Reagan Invented the 1980s* (Princeton: Princeton University Press, 2005).

58. Sponsored by the conservative National Heritage Foundation, the statement appeared in an anti-Playboy advertisement in the CT, 19 October 1980, urging supporters to participate in a silent protest outside Playboy's offices later that month. For the federal drug probe that ensnared Hefner's personal secretary Bobbie Arnstein and prompted her suicide, see Miller, *Bunny*, 211–231 and Watts, *Mr. Playboy*, 258–270.

59. For the feminist antiporn position, see the essays in Laura Lederer, ed., *Take Back the Night: Women on Pornography* (New York: Morrow, 1980); Andrea Dworkin, *Pornography: Men Possessing Women* (New York: Putnam, 1981); Catherine MacKinnon and Andrea Dworkin, eds., *In Harm's Way: The Pornography Civil Rights Hearings* (Cambridge: Harvard University Press, 1997). For opposing feminist viewpoints, see F.A.C.T., "Feminism and Pornograhy: More Than One View," in Subject: "Pornography," SLVFWS; the essays in F.A.C.T., *Caught Looking*, and Nadine Strassen, *Defending Pornography: Free Speech, Sex, and the Fight for Women's Rights* (New York: Scribner, 1995).

60. Robert Shea, "Women at War," *Playboy*, February 1980, 87.

61. "The New Puritans," *Playboy*, November 1980, 20.

62. Nat Lehrman quoted in Shea, "Women at War," 92; "Playboy in the News" *Playboy*, March 1981, 26. Lehrman's statements were in line with those of Art Director Art Paul, who nearly two decades earlier claimed, "I've never put anything pornographic in the book. I know what pornography is and I have never printed it." Paul, quoted in Hal Higdon, "Playboying around the Clock with Hugh Hefner," *Climax*, February 1962, 13.

63. Shea, "Women at War," 184.

64. Christie Hefner, "By Sex Possessed," *Playboy*, August 1981, 21; Arthur Kretchmer to "Dear Editor" [June 1981], Folder 73, Box 50, NOW.

65. Linda Drucker, "Award Winner Exercises Freedom of Expression," *Los Angeles Times*, 27 June 1980, B3; "Judges Jilt Playboy Awards Ceremony; Feminists Humiliate Hefner," *Women against Pornography Newsreport*, Spring 1982, 4. For Playboy's press release affirming protestors' right to express their views, see Pat Quigley to Don Parker, 25 June 1980 in Volume 474, HS.

66. "Nazism and Pornography: Toward a Comparative Analysis," in NOW Hearings on Pornography: Materials on the Personal Testimony of NOW Activists on Pornography

[March 1968], Folder 7, Box 95, NOW; Laura Jean Linn to [NOW] National Board Members, 11 August 1986, Folder 5, Box 95, NOW. For "coffee table pornography" see the untitled 6 August 1984 missive in Folder 4, Box 95, NOW. Boler, "We Sisters Join Together...," 266. *Playboy*'s April 1976 cover, which featured a very young-looking woman clad only in tights and crinoline and surrounded by stuffed animals, was an oft-cited example of sexualized youth. A female photo editor and female photographer received credit for the image.

67. See the following in F.A.C.T., *Caught Looking*: Kate Ellis, Barbara O'Dair, and Abby Tallmer, "Introduction," 5–8; Pat Califia, "Among Us, against Us: The New Puritans," 20–25; Lisa Duggan, "Censorship in the Name of Feminism," 62–71. The Minneapolis ordinance defined pornography as "the sexually explicit subordination of women, graphically depicted, whether in pictures or words." Lisa Duggan, Nan D. Hunter, and Carole S. Vance, "False Promises: Feminist Antipornography Legislation," 72–75.

68. For anticensorship position, see "Censorship Is No One's Civil Right," NYT, 27 May 1984, E16; Judy Klemesrud, "Bill on Pornography Opposed," NYT, 14 June 1985, 18; Daniel L. Feldman, "What New York Pornography Bill Does," NYT, 1 July 1985, 14; Robert Guccione, "When Foes of Pornography Are Censors," NYT, 11 July 1985, 22. A previous ordinance passed in Minneapolis was twice vetoed by the mayor, who cited the expense the city would face trying to uphold the constitutionality of the law in court. Brownmiller, *In Our Time*, 316–322; Tobias, *Faces of Feminism*, 182–185. On the Indianapolis ordinance, see *American Booksellers Association, Inc. vs. Hudnut*, 771 F.2d 323 (7th Cir. 1985), and Leslie Friedman Goldstein, *Contemporary Cases in Women's Rights* (Madison: University of Wisconsin Press, 1994), 289–292.

69. U.S. Commission on Obscenity and Pornography, *Report of the Commission on Obscenity and Pornography* (Washington, DC: U.S. Government Printing Office, 1970). On the commission and its findings see "Pornography Goes Public," *Newsweek*, 21 December 1970, 26, and Kendrick, *Secret Museum*, 213–219, 234–235.

70. *Report of the Select Committee on Current Pornographic Materials* (Washington, DC: U.S. Government Printing Office, 1952), 12; Attorney General's Commission on Pornography, *Final Report* (Washington, DC: U.S. Government Printing Office, 1986); Susie Bright, *Susie Bright's Sexual State of the Union* (New York: Simon & Schuster, 1997), 77.

71. Attorney General's Commission, *Final Report*, 775, 284, 1401.

72. John Tebbel and Mary Ellen Zuckerman, *The Magazine in America: 1741–1990* (New York: Oxford University Press, 1991), 285–286; James R. Petersen, *The Century of Sex: Playboy's History of the Sexual Revolution, 1900–1999* (New York: Grove, 1999), 412; Playboy Enterprises, Inc., *Annual Report* (1986), 4–5; David L. Kirp, "Questions the Porn Panel Forgot to Ask," *Los Angeles Herald Examiner*, PVF, KIL. Charles Storch, "Playboy, at 35, Lining up New Pad," CT, 10 April 1988, 2, reported the number of lost retail outlets as 20,000. Hugh M. Hefner, "The Blacklist," *Playboy*, July 1986, 3. "The Women of 7-Eleven," *Playboy*, December 1986, 112, 121.

73. Brownmiller, *In Our Time*, 322, 325; "7–11 Workers Fight Back!," *WAVPM Newspage*, February 1981, 2–3; Ellen Goodman, "Pinups and Privilege," *Los Angeles Times*, 15 August 1979, E7.

74. Emma Stevens and Stephen Holmes, "Cohabitation: The Tender Trap," *Playboy*, August 1977, 115; "Man and Woman," *Playboy*, November 1978, 211; Asa Baber, "Who Gets

Screwed in a Divorce? I Do," *Playboy*, December 1978, 215; Craig Vetter, "Frigid Men," *Playboy*, September 1984, 89; John Gordon, "What *Else* Do Women Want?" *Playboy*, March 1985, 67.

75. "The World of Playboy," *Playboy*, March 1986, 11; Charles Storch, "3 Playboy Clubs to Close," CT, 2 May 1986, 1; Tom Hundley, "Playboy's Bunnies Are Hopping into History," CT, 24 July 1988.

Epilogue

1. "Aging Playboy," *Newsweek*, 4 August 1986, 50.

2. Richard Rhodes's "Dorothy Stratten: Her Story," *Playboy*, May 1981, 146, documented Stratten's life and tragic end. Peter Bogdanovich leveled his allegations in *The Killing of the Unicorn: Dorothy Stratten, 1960–1980* (New York: Morrow, 1984). Stratten's murder was also portrayed in Bob Fosse, director, *Star 80* (A Ladd Company Release thru Warner Brothers, 1983). For further discussion see "Aging Playboy," 54–56; Hillary Johnson, "Blows against the Empire," *Rolling Stone*, 27 March 1986, 70, and Steven Watts, *Mr. Playboy: Hugh Hefner and the American Dream* (New York: Wiley, 2008), 381–387.

3. Bruce J. Schulman, *The Seventies: The Great Shift in American Culture, Society, and Politics* (New York: Free Press, 2001), 185–189, 241–246; Gil Troy, *Morning in America: How Ronald Reagan Invented the 1980s* (Princeton: Princeton University Press, 2005), 118–124, 198–203, 215–222. *Playboy's* attention to AIDS and the alarmist coverage it received in mainstream media included Craig Vetter, "The Desexing of America," *Playboy*, December 1983, 108; "AIDS Update: Myths and Realities," *Playboy*, June 1986, 52; and Arthur Kretchmer, "Can Sex Survive AIDS?" *Playboy*, February 1986, 48. For Hefner's marriage, see Kim Masters, "To Hef and to Hold: Playboy Founder Weds His Playmate," *Washington Post*, 3 July 1989, C1; Lisa Anderson, "Cinderella and the Playboy," CT, 4 May 1989, 1; "This Playmate of the Year Is a Playmate for a Lifetime," *Playboy*, June 1989, 128; Cheryl Lavin, "The Happy Hefners," CT, 28 March 1990, 1; Alex Witchell, "Father Rabbit," NYT, 22 November 1992, A1.

4. For example, Dan Greenburg, "Adventures in Safe Sex," *Playboy*, July 1992, 74; Roger Simon, "The Politics of Everything," *Playboy*, January 1992, 112; Joe Queenan, "Wake Up and Smell the Nineties," *Playboy*, January 1992, 109. For PEI's finances, see Bernard Weinraub, "Reviving an Aging Playboy is a Fathe-Daughter Project," NYT, 4 February 2002, C1 and Tim Jones, "Playboy Finds Looks NOT Enough," CT, 6 August 2000, C1.

5. Weinraub, "Reviving an Aging Playboy"; Rick Kogan, "Citizen Hef," *Chicago Tribune Magazine*, 12 December 1999, 14; Rick Marin, "More Boogie Nights," NYT, 21 February 1999, 9.1; Sharon Waxman, "The Playboy After Dark," *Washington Post*, 10 October 1999, F.01.

6. Stevenson Swanson, "Hefner, Steinem Have Something in Common Now," CT, 30 April 1998, 1. On *Ms.* see Mary Thom, *Inside Ms.: 25 Years of the Magazine and the Feminist Movement* (New York: Henry Holt, 1997).

7. Gloria Steinem, "What *Playboy* Doesn't Know about Women Could Fill a Book," *McCall's*, October 1970, 139; Emilie Ostrander, "Call Them Anything (but Playmates)," CT, 2 July 2003, sec. 8, 1.

8. Heidi Siegmund Cuda, "Hef Swings Deep into the Night," *Los Angeles Times*, 15 November 2001, F47; "Hef Pals Give Him His 'Way' Chicago Style," CT, 12 April 2000, 1; Steve Friess, "Vegas Primed for the Rebirth of Playboy Cool," *USA Today*, 29 September 2006, D1; Arnold M. Knightly, "Tails Turn Some Heads," *Las Vegas Review Journal*, 10 October 2007, D1; Susan Emerling, "The Playboy Mind," *Los Angeles Times*, 14 December 2003, E4; George F. Will, "Fifty Years of Playboy," *Washington Post*, 29 May 2003, 25.

9. Hugh Hefner, interview with author, Los Angeles, California, 14 January 2009.

10. Hugh Hefner, author interview, 14 January 2009.

11. Hugh Heifner author Interview, 14 January 2009; Weinraub, "Reviving an Aging Playboy"; Mark Scheffler, "Is Hef a Turn-off to Young Readers?" *Crain's Chicago Business*, 3 May 2004, 1.

12. Greg Burns, "Adventures in the Skin Trade," CT, 16 October 2005, 12; Greg Burns, "Playboy Losing a Hefner," CT, 9 December 2008, 20; Greg Burns, "Playboy's Talk of Sale Perks Ears," CT, 19 February 2009, 12; "Playboy.com Launches Completely New Digital Experience," Playboy press release, 6 April 2009, playboyenterprises.com.

13. Quoted in Wyl S. Hilton, "Hugh Hefner," *Esquire*, June 2002, 100.

14. Author interview, 14 January 2009.

15. Steinem, "What *Playboy* Doesn't Know About Women," 139.

16. Hugh Hefner, author interview, 14 January 2009.

17. Hefner quoted in "Playboy Club Mates Old and New," *USA Today*, 20 September 2006, 11D.

18. Paula Kamen, *Her Way: Young Women Remake the Sexual Revolution* (New York: New York University Press, 2000).

19. Following publication of *The Liberated Man: Beyond Masculinity; Freeing Men and Their Relationships with Women* (New York: Random House, 1974), Warren Farrell's works, including *Why Men Are the Way They Are* (New York: McGraw-Hill, 1986) and *The Myth of Male Power: Why Men are the Disposable Sex* (New York: Simon & Schuster, 1993), focused on the difference between the sexes and asserting men's rights. On gender anxiety and the men's movement, see Susan Faludi, *Stiffed: The Betrayal of the American Man* (New York: William Morrow, 1999); Michael S. Kimmel, *Manhood in America: A Cultural History* (New York: Free Press, 1996), 315–322; Michelle Conlin, "The New Gender Gap: From Kindergarten to Grad School, Boys are Becoming the Second Sex," *Business Week*, 26 May 2003, 75–84; Kay Leigh Hagan, ed. *Women Respond to the Men's Movement: A Feminist Collection* (San Francisco: HarperSanFrancisco, 1992); Judith Newton, *From Panthers to Promise Keepers* (New York: Rowman & Littlefield, 2005). Amanda Goldrick-Jones, *Men Who Believe in Feminism* (Westport, CT: Praeger, 1992) discusses the shift from a profeminist stance to a men's rights agenda.

20. Author interview, 14 January 2009. On the video series, see Ariel Levy, *Female Chauvinist Pigs: Women and the Rise of Raunch Culture* (New York: Free Press, 2005), 7–17 and Claire Hoffman, "'Baby Give Me a Kiss': The Man Behind the 'Girls Gone Wild' Soft-Porn Empire Lets Claire Hoffman into His World, for Better or Worse," *Los Angeles Times*, 6 August 2006, I14.

21. Levy, *Female Chauvinist Pigs,* 184. For young women's striving to attain ideals of appearance and sexuality, see Joan Jacobs Brumberg, *The Body Project: An Intimate History of American Girls* (New York: Vintage Books, 1997).

22. Susan B. Carter et al., eds. *Historical Statistics of the United States, Earliest Times to the Present, Millenial Edition* (New York: Cambridge University Press, 2006), Volume I, Part A, 685–686; Andrew Herrmann, "You Know You're a Grown-up When You Grumble at This," *Chicago Sun Times,* 9 May 2003; Tom W. Smith, "Coming of Age in 21st Century America: Public Attitudes toward the Importance and Timing of Transitions to Adulthood," *GSS Topical Report No. 35* (Chicago: NORC, May 2003).

23. Hugh Hefner, author interview, 14 January 2009.

SELECTED BIBLIOGRAPHY

Abbott, Carl. "The Light on the Horizon: Imagining the Death of American Cities." *Journal of Urban History* 32 (January 2006): 175–196.

Abbott, Carl. *The Metropolitan Frontier: Cities in the Modern American West.* Tucson: University of Arizona Press, 1993.

Adams, Michael C. C. *The Best War Ever: America and World War II.* Baltimore: Johns Hopkins University Press, 1994.

Agnew, Jean-Christophe. "Coming up for Air: Consumer Culture in Historical Perspective." *Intellectual History Newsletter* 12 (1990): 3–21.

Aker, John B., and Dan Maust. "An Examination and Refutation of the Playboy Philosophy." M.Div. Thesis, Trinity Evangelical Divinity School, 1970.

Allen, Robert C. *Horrible Prettiness: Burlesque and American Culture:* Chapel Hill: University of North Carolina Press, 1991.

Alston, Jon P., and Frances Tucker. "The Myth of Sexual Permissiveness." *Journal of Sex Research* 9 (February 1973): 33–40.

Anderson, Karen. *Wartime Women: Sex Roles, Family Relations, and the Status of Women during World War II.* Westport, CT: Greenwood, 1981.

Andrew, John A. *The Other Side of the Sixties.* New Brunswick, NJ: Rutgers University Press, 1997.

Armstrong, Elizabeth. *Birth of the Cool: California Art, Design, and Culture at Midcentury.* New York: Prestel Publishing, 2007.

Armstrong, Richard. *Billy Wilder: American Film Realist.* Jefferson, NC: McFarland, 2000.

Aron, Cindy S. *Working at Play: A History of Vacations in the United States.* New York: Oxford University Press, 1999.

Attorney General's Commission on Pornography. *Final Report.* Washington, DC: U.S. Government Printing Office, 1986.

Avila, Eric. *Popular Culture in the Age of White Flight: Fear and Fantasy in Suburban Los Angeles.* Berkeley: University of California Press, 2004.

Avila, Eric. "Popular Culture in the Age of White Flight: Film Noir, Disneyland, and the Cold War (Sub)Urban Imaginary." *Journal of Urban History* 31 (November 2004): 3–22.

Babington, Bruce, and Peter William Evans. *Affairs to Remember: The Hollywood Comedy of the Sexes*. Manchester: Manchester University Press, 1989.

Bailey, Beth L. *From Front Porch to Back Seat: Courtship in Twentieth Century America*. Baltimore: Johns Hopkins University Press, 1988.

Bailey, Beth. "Rebels without a Cause? Teenagers in the 1950s." *History Today* 40 (February 1990): 25–31.

Bailey, Beth. "Sex as a Weapon: Underground Comix and the Paradox of Liberation." In *Imagine Nation: The American Counterculture of the 1960s and '70s*, edited by Peter Braunstein and Michael William Doyle, 305–326. New York: Routledge, 2002.

Bailey, Beth. *Sex in the Heartland*. Cambridge: Harvard University Press, 1999.

Bailey, Beth. "Sexual Revolution(s)." In *The Sixties: From Memory to History*, edited by David Farber, 235–262. Chapel Hill: University of North Carolina Press, 1994.

Baker, Paula. "The Domestication of Politics: Women and American Political Society, 1780–1920." *American Historical Review* 88 (June 1984): 620–647.

Baker, Trudy, and Rachel Jones. *The Coffee Tea or Me Girls Lay It on the Line*. New York: Grosset & Dunlop, 1972.

Ball, Terence. "The Politics of Social Science in Postwar America." In *Recasting America: Culture and Politics in the Age of Cold War*, edited by Lary May, 76–92. Chicago, University of Chicago Press, 1989.

Ballard, Jack S. *The Shock of Peace: Military and Economic Demobilization after World War II*. Washington, DC: University Press of America, 1983.

Banner, Lois. *American Beauty*. Chicago: University of Chicago Press, 1983.

Baranowski, Shelley, and Ellen Furlough, eds. *Being Elsewhere: Tourism, Consumer Culture, and Identity in Modern Europe and North America*. Ann Arbor: University of Michigan Press, 2001.

Barnouw, Eric. *Tube of Plenty: The Evolution of American Television*. New York: Oxford University Press, 1975.

Baxandall, Rosalyn, and Linda Gordon, eds. *Dear Sisters: Dispatches from the Women's Liberation Movement*. New York: Basic, 2000.

Beauregard, Robert A. *Voices of Decline: The Postwar Fate of U.S. Cities*. Cambridge, MA: Blackwell, 1993.

Bederman, Gail. *Manliness and Civilization: A Cultural History of Gender and Race in the United States, 1880–1917*. Chicago: University of Chicago Press, 1995.

Beggan, James K., and Scott T. Allison. "'What Sort of Man Reads Playboy?' The Self-Reported Influence of Playboy on the Construction of Masculinity." *Journal of Men's Studies* 11 (Winter 2003): 189.

Bell, Daniel. *The Cultural Contradictions of Capitalism*. New York: Basic, 1976.

Bell, Daniel. *The End of Ideology: On the Exhaustion of Political Ideas in the Fifties*. New York: Free Press, 1965.

Benn Management Corporation. *Male College Student Survey: Conducted for Playboy Magazine*. Chicago: 1963.

Bennett, Tony, and Janet Woollacott. *Bond and Beyond: The Political Career of a Popular Hero*. New York: Methuen, 1987.

Benson, Susan Porter. *Counter Cultures: Saleswomen, Managers, and Customers in American Department Stores, 1890–1940*. Urbana: University of Illinois Press, 1986.

Berdie, Ralph F. "A Femininity Adjective Checklist." *Journal of Applied Psychology* 43, no. 5 (1959): 327–333.

Berebitsky, Julie. "The Joy of Work: Helen Gurley Brown, Gender, and Sexuality in the White-Collar Office." *Journal of the History of Sexuality* 15 (January 2006): 89–127.

Berger, David G., and Morton G. Wenger. "The Ideology of Virginity." *Journal of Marriage and the Family* 35 (November 1973): 666–676.

Berkeley, Kathleen C. *The Women's Liberation Movement in America*. Westport, CT: Greenwood, 1999.

Berkowitz, Edward D. *Something Happened: A Political and Cultural Overview of the Seventies*. New York: Columbia University Press, 2006.

Berrett, Jesse Isaac. "The Secret Lives of Consumer Culture: Masculinity and Consumption in Postwar America." Ph.D. diss., University of California, Berkeley, 1996.

Bertrand, Michael T. *Race, Rock, and Elvis*. Chicago: University of Illinois Press, 2000.

Berube, Alan. *Coming out Under Fire: The History of Gay Men and Women in World War Two*. New York: Free Press, 1990.

Birenbaum, Arnold. "Revolution without the Revolution: Sex in Contemporary America." *Journal of Sex Research* 6 (November 1970): 257–267.

Black, Gregory D. *Hollywood Censored: Morality Codes, Catholics, and the Movies*. New York: Cambridge University Press, 1994.

Bogaert, Anthony F., Deborah A. Turkovich, and Carolyn L. Hafer. "A Content Analysis of *Playboy* Centerfolds from 1953 through 1990: Changes in Explicitness, Objectification, and Model's Age." *Journal of Sex Research* 30 (May 1993): 135–139.

Borstelmann, Thomas. *The Cold War and the Color Line: American Race Relations in the Global Arena*. Cambridge: Harvard University Press, 2002.

Bourdieu, Pierre. *Distinction: A Social Critique of the Judgement of Taste*, trans. Richard Nice. Cambridge: Harvard University Press, 1984.

Boyd, Malcolm. *My Fellow Americans*. New York: Holt, Rinehart & Winston, 1970.

Boyer, Paul. *By the Bomb's Early Light: American Thought and Culture at the Dawn of the Atomic Age*. Chapel Hill: University of North Carolina Press, 1994.

Boyer, Paul S. *Purity in Print: Book Censorship in America from the Gilded Age to the Computer Age*, 2d ed. Madison: University of Wisconsin Press, 2002.

Bradley, Patricia. *Mass Media and the Shaping of American Feminism*. Jackson: University Press of Mississippi, 2003.

Brady, Frank. *Hefner*. New York: Macmillan, 1974.

Braunstein, Peter, and Michael William Doyle, eds. *Imagine Nation: The American Counterculture of the 1960s and '70s*. New York: Routledge, 2002.

Breazeale, Kenon. "In Spite of Women: *Esquire* Magazine and the Construction of the Male Consumer." *Signs* 20 (August 1994): 1–22.

Breines, Wini. *Young, White, and Miserable: Growing up Female in the Fifties*. Boston: Beacon, 1992.

Brennan, Mary. *Turning Right in the Sixties*. Chapel Hill: University of North Carolina Press, 1995.

Brenton, Myron. *The American Male*. New York: Coward-McCann, 1966.

Brissett, Dennis, and Lionel S. Lewis. "Guidelines for Marital Sex: An Analysis of Fifteen Popular Marriage Manuals." *Family Coordinator* (January 1970): 41–48.

Brod, Harry, and Michael Kaufman, eds. *Theorizing Masculinities*. Newbury Park, CA: Sage, 1994.

Brown, Helen Gurley. *Sex and the Office*. New York: Bernard Geis Associates, 1964.

Brown, Helen Gurley. *Sex and the Single Girl*. New York: Bernard Geis Associates, 1962.

Brownmiller, Susan. *In Our Time: Memoir of a Revolution*. New York: Random House, 1999.

Burger, Chester. *Survival in the Executive Jungle*. New York: Collier, 1964.

Bushman, Richard. *Refinement of America: Persons, Houses, Cities*. New York: Knopf, 1992.

Buszek, Maria. *Pin-Up Grrrls: Feminism, Sexuality, Popular Culture*. Durham, NC: Duke University Press, 2006.

Butler, Judith. *Gender Trouble: Feminism and the Subversion of Identity*. New York: Routledge, 1999.

Byer, Stephen. *Hefner's Gonna Kill Me When He Reads This*. Chicago: Allen/Bennett, 1972.

Byers, Jackie. *All that Hollywood Allows: Re-reading Gender in 1950s Melodrama*. Chapel Hill: University of North Carolina Press, 1991.

Calder, Lendol. *Financing the American Dream: A Cultural History of Consumer Credit*. Princeton: Princeton University Press, 1999.

Campbell, Colin. *The Romantic Ethic and the Spirit of Modern Consumerism*. Oxford: Basil Blackwell, 1987.

Cantor, Muriel G. "Prime-Time Fathers: A Study in Continuity and Change." *Critical Studies in Mass Communication* 7 (September 1990): 275–285.

Carnes, Mark C. *Secret Ritual and Manhood in Victorian America*. New Haven: Yale University Press, 1989.

Carnes, Mark C., and Clyde Griffen, eds. *Meanings for Manhood: Constructions of Masculinity in Victorian America*. Chicago: University of Chicago Press, 1990.

Carter, Susan B., et al., eds. *Historical Statistics of the United States, Earliest Times to the Present: Millennial Edition*. New York: Cambridge University Press, 2006.

Cawelti, John. *Apostles of the Self-Made Man*. Chicago: University of Chicago Press, 1965.

Chafe, William. *The Paradox of Change: American Women in the 20th Century*. New York: Oxford University Press, 1991.

Chafe, William. *The Unfinished Journey: America since World War II*. 5th ed. New York: Oxford University Press, 2003.

Chapman, James. *License to Thrill: A Cultural History of the James Bond Films*. New York: Columbia University Press, 2000.

Chauncey, George. *Gay New York: Gender, Urban Culture, and the Making of a Gay Male World, 1890–1940*. New York: Basic, 1994.

Chudacoff, Howard. *The Age of the Bachelor: Creating an American Subculture*. Princeton: Princeton University Press, 1999.

Clark, Jr., Clifford Edward. *The American Family Home, 1800–1960*. Chapel Hill: University of North Carolina Press, 1986.

Cobble, Dorothy Sue. *The Other Women's Movement: Workplace Justice and Social Rights in Modern America*. Princeton: Princeton University Press, 2004.

Cohan, Steven. *Masked Men: Masculinity and the Movies in the Fifties*. Bloomington: Indiana University Press, 1997.

Cohan, Steven. "So Functional for Its Purposes: The Bachelor Apartment in Pillow Talk." In *STUD: Architectures of Masculinity*, edited by Joel Sanders, 28–41. New York: Princeton Architectural Press, 1996.

Cohen, Lizabeth. *A Consumers' Republic: The Politics of Mass Consumption in Postwar America*. New York: Knopf, 2003.

Collins, Robert M. *More: The Politics of Economic Growth in Postwar America*. New York: Oxford University Press, 2000.

Colomina, Beatrize, et al., eds. *Cold War Hot Houses: Inventing Postwar Culture, from Cockpit to Playboy*. New York: Princeton Architectural Press, 2004.

Cook, David A. *A History of Narrative Film*. 4th ed. New York: Norton, 2004.

Coontz, Stephanie. *The Way We Never Were: American Families and the Nostalgia Trap*. New York: Basic, 1992.

Corber, Richard J. *In the Name of National Security: Hitchcock, Homophobia, and the Political Construction of Gender in Postwar America*. Durham, NC: Duke University Press, 1993.

Costigliola, Frank. "'Unceasing Pressure for Penetration': Gender, Pathology, and Emotion in George Kennan's Formation of the Cold War." *Journal of American History* 83 (March 1997): 1309–1339.

Cox, Harvey. "*Playboy*'s Doctrine of the Male." *Christianity and Crisis* (May 1961): 56–60.

Cross, Gary. *An All-Consuming Century: Why Commercialism Won in Modern America*. New York: Columbia University Press, 2000.

Cuordileone, K. A. *Manhood and American Political Culture in the Cold War*. New York: Routledge, 2005.

Damon-Moore, Helen. *Magazines for the Millions: Gender and Commerce in the* Ladies Home Journal *and the* Saturday Evening Post, *1880–1910*. Albany: State University of New York Press, 1994.

Daniel Starch and Staff. *Male vs. Female: Influence on the Purchase of Selected Products as Revealed by an Exploratory Depth Interview Study with Husbands and Wives*. New York: True—The Man's Magazine, 1958.

Davies, Marjorie. *Woman's Place Is at the Typewriter: Office Work and Office Workers, 1870–1930*. Philadelphia: Temple University Press, 1982.

Davis, Flora. *Moving the Mountain: The Women's Movement in America since 1960*. Urbana: University of Illinois Press, 1999.

Davis, Susan G. "Time Out: Leisure and Tourism." In *A Companion to Post-1945 America,* edited by Jean-Christophe Agnew and Roy Rosenzweig, 64–77. Malden, MA: Blackwell, 2002.

Davisson, Allan. "An Analysis of the Sexual Ethic of Hugh Hefner as Representative of the 'New Morality' in American Culture." B.Div. Thesis, Concordia Theological Seminary, 1966.

Dean, Robert. *Imperial Brotherhood: Gender and the Making of Cold War Foreign Policy.* Amherst: University of Massachusetts Press, 2001.

DeBenedetti, Charles, with Charles Chatfield. *An American Ordeal.* Syracuse, NY: Syracuse University Press, 1990.

DeGrazia, Victoria, with Ellen Furlough, eds. *The Sex of Things: Gender and Consumption in Historical Perspective.* Berkeley: University of California Press, 1996.

D'Emilio, John. *Making Trouble: Essays on Gay History, Politics, and the University.* New York: Routledge, 1992.

D'Emilio, John, and Estelle Freedman. *Intimate Matters: A History of Sexuality in America.* New York: Harper & Row, 1988.

DeMott, Benjamin. "Anatomy of 'Playboy.'" *Commentary* 34 (August 1962): 111–119.

Denning, Michael. *Cover Stories: Narrative and Ideology in the British Spy Thriller.* London: Routledge, 1987.

Denning, Michael. *The Cultural Front: The Laboring of American Culture in the Twentieth Century.* New York: Verso, 1997.

Deutsch, Sarah. *Women and the City: Gender, Space, and Power in Boston, 1870–1940.* New York: Oxford University Press, 2000.

Dichter, Ernest. *The Strategy of Desire.* Garden City, NY: Doubleday, 1960.

Dines, Gail. *Pornography: The Production and Consumption of Inequality.* New York: Routledge, 1998.

Dines, Gail, and Jean M. Humez, eds. *Gender, Race and Class in Media: A Text-Reader.* London: Sage, 1995.

Dines-Levy, Gail, and Gregory W. H. Smith. "Representations of Women and Men in *Playboy* Sex Cartoons." In *Humour and Society,* edited by Chris Powell and George E. C. Paton, 234–259. New York: St. Martin's, 1988.

Doherty, Thomas. *Pre-code Hollywood: Sex, Immorality, and Insurrection in American Cinema, 1930–1934.* New York: Columbia University Press, 1999.

Douglass, Ann. *Terrible Honesty: Mongrel Manhattan in the 1920s.* New York: Farrar, Straus and Giroux, 1995.

Dow, Bonnie J. "Hegemony, Feminist Criticism and *The Mary Tyler Moore Show.*" *Critical Studies in Mass Communications* 7, no. 3 (1990): 261–274.

Duberman, Martin. *Stonewall.* New York: Dutton, 1993.

Dubinsky, Karen. "'Everybody Likes Canadians': Canadians, Americans and the Post-World War II Travel Boom." In *Being Elsewhere: Tourism, Consumer Culture, and Identity in Modern Europe and North America,* edited by Shelley Baranowski and Ellen Furlough, 320–347. Ann Arbor: University of Michigan Press, 2001.

Dudziak, Mary L. *Cold War Civil Rights: Race and the Image of American Democracy*. Princeton: Princeton University Press, 2002.

Dworkin, Andrea. *Pornography: Men Possessing Women*. New York: Putnam, 1981.

Echols, Alice. *Daring to Be Bad: Radical Feminism in America, 1967–1975*. Minneapolis: University of Minnesota Press, 1989.

Echols, Alice. "Nothing Distant about It: Women's Liberation and Sixties Radicalism." In *The Sixties: From Memory to History*, edited by David Farber, 149–174. Chapel Hill: University of North Carolina Press, 1994.

Edgren, Gretchen. *Inside the Playboy Mansion: If You Don't Swing, Don't Ring*. With an introduction by Hugh M. Hefner. Santa Monica, CA: General Publishing Group, 1998.

Edgren, Gretchen. *The Playboy Book: Forty Years*. With an introduction by Hugh M. Hefner. Los Angeles: General Publishing Group, 1994.

Edgren, Gretchen. *The Playmate Book: Five Decades of Centerfolds*. With an introduction by Hugh M. Hefner. Santa Monica, CA: General Publishing Group, 1996.

Ehrenreich, Barbara. *Fear of Falling: The Inner Life of the Middle Class*. New York: Harper, 1990.

Ehrenreich, Barbara. *The Hearts of Men: American Dreams and the Flight from Commitment*. New York: Anchor, 1983.

Ellis, Albert. *If This Be Sexual Heresy*. New York: Lyle, Stuart, 1963.

Ellis, Albert. *The Intelligent Woman's Guide to Man-Hunting*. New York: Lyle, Stuart, 1963.

Ellis, Albert. *Sex and the Single Man*. New York: Lyle, Stuart, 1963.

Ellis, Albert. *Sex without Guilt*. New York: Lyle, Stuart, 1958.

Endy, Christopher. *Cold War Holidays: American Tourism in France*. Chapel Hill: University of North Carolina Press, 2004.

Engelhardt, Tom. *The End of Victory Culture: Cold War America and the Disillusioning of a Generation*. Amherst: University of Massachusetts Press, 2007.

Erenberg, Lewis A. *Steppin' Out: New York Nightlife and the Transformation of American Culture, 1890–1930*. Chicago: University of Chicago Press, 1981.

Erenberg, Lewis A. *Swingin' the Dream: Big Band Jazz and the Rebirth of American Culture*. Chicago: University of Chicago Press, 1998.

Erenberg, Lewis A., and Susan E. Hirsch, eds. *The War in American Culture: Society and Consciousness during World War II*. Chicago: University of Chicago Press, 1996.

Esquire's Handbook for Hosts. New York: Grosset & Dunlap, 1949.

Evans, Sara M. *Personal Politics: The Roots of Women's Liberation in the Civil Rights Movement and the New Left*. New York: Knopf, 1979.

Ewen, Elizabeth. *Immigrant Women in the Land of Dollars: Life and Culture on the Lower East Side, 1890–1925*. New York: Monthly Review Press, 1985.

Ewen, Stuart. *Captains of Consciousness: Advertising and the Social Roots of the Consumer Culture*. New York: McGraw Hill, 1976.

F.A.C.T. *Caught Looking: Feminism, Pornography and Censorship*. 1986; Seattle: Real Comet Press, 1988.

Faderman, Lillian. *Odd Girls and Twilight Lovers: A History of Lesbian Life in Twentieth Century America*. New York: Columbia University Press, 1991.

Fallaci, Oriana. *The Egoists: Sixteen Surprising Interviews*. Chicago: Henry Regnery Company, 1963.

Faludi, Susan. *Stiffed: The Betrayal of the American Man*. New York: Morrow, 1999.

Farber, David. *The Age of Great Dreams: America in the 1960s*. New York: Hill and Wang, 1994.

Farber, David. *Chicago '68*. Chicago: University of Chicago Press, 1988.

Farber, David, ed. *The Sixties: From Memory to History*. Chapel Hill: University of North Carolina Press, 1994.

Farber, David and Beth Bailey. *The Columbia Guide to America in the 1960s*. New York: Columbia University Press, 2001.

Farrell, Warren. *The Liberated Man*. New York: Random House, 1974.

Farrell, Warren. *The Myth of Male Power: Why Men are the Disposable Sex*. New York: Simon & Schuster, 1993.

Farrell, Warren. *Why Men Are the Way They Are*. New York: McGraw-Hill, 1986.

Farrell-Beck, Jane, and Colleen Gau. *Uplift: The Bra in America*. Philadelphia: University of Pennsylvania Press, 2002.

Fass, Paula S. *The Damned and the Beautiful: American Youth in the 1920s*. New York: Oxford University Press, 1977.

Featherstone, Mike. "The Body in Consumer Culture." In *The Body: Social Process and Cultural Theory,* edited by Mike Featherstone, Mike Hepworth, and Bryan S. Turner, 170–196. London: Sage, 1991.

Fesler, Ann. *The Girls Who Went Away*. New York: Penguin, 2006.

Findlay, John M. *Magic Lands: Western Cityscapes and American Culture after 1940*. Berkeley: University of California Press, 1992.

Fine, Lisa. *The Souls of the Skyscraper: Female Clerical Workers in Chicago, 1870–1930*. Philadelphia: Temple University Press, 1990.

Fishman, Robert. *Bourgeois Utopias: The Rise and Fall of Suburbia*. New York: Basic, 1987.

Fishman, Robert. "Urbanity and Suburbanity: Rethinking the 'Burbs." *American Quarterly* 46 (March 1994): 35–39.

Fleming, Ian. "How to Write a Thriller." *Books and Bookmen* (May 1963): 13–19.

Fogelson, Robert M. *Downtown: Its Rise and Fall, 1880–1950*. New Haven: Yale University Press, 2001.

Ford, Corey. *The Office Party*. Garden City, NY: Doubleday, 1951.

Ford, Larry R. *Cities and Buildings: Skyscrapers, Skid Rows, and Suburbs*. Baltimore: Johns Hopkins University Press, 1994.

Foreman, Joel, ed. *The Other Fifties: Interrogating Midcentury American Icons*. Chicago: University of Chicago Press, 1997.

Foucault, Michel. *The History of Sexuality,* trans. Robert Hurley. New York: Vintage, 1990.

Fox, Stephen. *The Mirror Makers: A History of American Advertising and Its Creators*. Urbana: University of Illinois Press, 1997.

Foy, Jessica H., and Thomas J. Schlereth, eds. *American Home Life, 1880–1930: A Social History of Spaces and Services*. Knoxville: University of Tennessee, 1992.

Frank, Thomas. *The Conquest of Cool: Business Culture, Counterculture, and the Rise of Hip Consumerism*. Chicago: University of Chicago Press, 1997.

Frankl, George. *The Failure of the Sexual Revolution*. London: Kahn & Averill, 1974.

Fraterrigo, Elizabeth. "'Entertainment for Men': *Playboy,* Masculinity, and Postwar American Culture." PhD diss., Loyola University Chicago, 2004.

Freeman, Joshua B. "Hardhats: Construction Workers, Manliness, and the 1970 Pro-War Demonstrations." *Social History* 26 (Summer 1993): 725–744.

Friday, Nancy. *My Secret Garden: Women's Sexual Fantasies*. New York: Pocket Books, 1973.

Friedan, Betty. *The Feminine Mystique*. New York: Norton, 1963.

Galbraith, John Kenneth. *The Affluent Society*. Boston: Houghton Mifflin, 1958.

Gallo, Marcia. *Different Daughters: A History of the Daughters of Bilitis and the Rise of the Lesbian Rights Movement*. New York: Carroll & Graf, 2006.

Gehman, Richard. *Sinatra and His Rat Pack*. New York: Belmont, 1961.

Gelber, Steven. "Do-It-Yourself: Constructing, Repairing, and Maintaining Domestic Masculinity." *American Quarterly* 49 (March 1997): 66–112.

Gennari, John. *Blowin' Hot and Cool: Jazz and Its Critics*. Chicago: University of Chicago Press, 2006.

Gertzman, Jay A. *Bookleggers and Smuthounds: The Trade in Erotica, 1920–1940*. Philadelphia: University of Pennsylvania Press, 1999.

Gilbert, James. *A Cycle of Outrage: America's Reaction to the Juvenile Delinquent in the 1950s*. New York: Oxford University Press, 1986.

Gilbert, James. *Men in the Middle: Searching for Masculinity in the 1950s*. Chicago: University of Chicago Press, 2005.

Gilbert, Roger. "The Swinger and the Loser: Sinatra, Masculinity, and Fifties Culture." In *Frank Sinatra and Popular Culture: Essays on an American Icon,* edited by Leonard Mustazza, 38–49. Westport, CT: Praeger, 1998.

Gilfoyle, Timothy J. *City of Eros: New York City, Prostitution, and the Commercialization of Sex, 1790–1920*. New York: Norton, 1992.

Gitlin, Todd. *The Sixties: Years of Hope, Days of Rage*. New York: Bantam, 1987.

Glenn, Susan A. *Daughters of the Shtetl: Life and Labor in the Immigrant Generation*. Ithaca, NY: Cornell University Press, 1990.

Gluck, Sherna Berger. *Rosie the Riveter Revisited: Women, the War, and Social Change*. Boston: Twayne, 1987.

Goldin, Claudia. *Understanding the Gender Gap: An Economic History of American Women*. New York: Oxford University Press, 1990.

Goldrick-Jones, Amanda. *Men Who Believe in Feminism*. Westport, CT: Praeger, 1992.

Gordon, Michael. "From an Unfortunate Necessity to a Cult of Mutual Orgasm: Sex in American Marital Education Literature, 1830–1940." In *The Sociology of Sex: An Introductory Reader,* edited by James M. Henslin and Edward Sagarin, 59–84. New York: Schocken, 1978.

Gordon, Richard E., Katherine K. Gordon, and Max Gunther. *The Split-Level Trap*. New York: Bernard Geis Associates, 1960.

Gorn, Elliot. *The Manly Art: Bare Knuckle Prize Fighting in America*. Urbana: University of Illinois Press, 1986.

Gosse, Van, and Richard Moser, *The World the Sixties Made: Politics and Culture since the 1960s*. Philadelphia: Temple University Press, 2003.

Gould, Robert E. "Measuring Masculinity by the Size of a Paycheck." In *Men and Masculinity*, edited by Joseph H. Pleck and Jack Sawyer, 96–100. Englewood Cliffs, NJ: Prentice-Hall, 1974.

Goulden, Joseph. C. *The Best Years: 1945–1950*. New York: Atheneum, 1978.

Griffith, R. Marie. "The Religious Encounters of Alfred C. Kinsey." *Journal of American History* 95 (September 2008): 349–377.

Haddow, Robert H. *Pavilions of Plenty: Exhibiting American Culture Abroad in the 1950s*. Washington, DC: Smithsonian Institution Press, 1997.

Hagan, Kay Leigh, ed. *Women Respond to the Men's Movement: A Feminist Collection*. HarperSanFrancisco, 1992.

Halberstam, David. *The Fifties*. New York: Villard, 1993.

Hanchett, Thomas W. "Financing Suburbia: Prudential Insurance and the Post-World War II Transformation of the American City." *Journal of Urban History* 26 (March 2000): 312–328.

Handlin, David. *The American Home: Architecture and Society, 1815–1915*. Boston: Little, Brown, 1978.

Hans, Marcie, Dennis Altman, and Martin A. Cohen. *The Executive Coloring Book*. Chicago: Funny Products Company, 1961.

Hardwick, M. Jeffrey. *Mall Maker: Victor Gruen, Architect of an American Dream*. Philadelphia: University of Pennsylvania Press, 2004.

Harrington, Michael. *The Other America: Poverty in the United States*. New York: Macmillan, 1962.

Hartman, Susan. *The Homefront and Beyond: American Women in the 1940s*. Boston: Twayne, 1982.

Hartman, Susan M. "Prescriptions for Penelope: Literature on Women's Obligations to Returning World War II Veterans." *Women's Studies* 5 (1978): 223–239.

Hartmann, Susan M. "Women's Employment and the Domestic Ideal." In *Not June Cleaver: Women and Gender in Postwar America*, edited by Joanne Meyerowitz, 84–100. Philadelphia: Temple University Press, 1994.

Harvey, Brett. *The Fifties: A Woman's Oral History*. New York: HarperCollins, 1993.

Hatch, Mary G., and David L. Hatch. "Problems of Married Working Women as Presented by Three Popular Working Women's Magazines." *Social Forces* 37 (December 1958): 148–153.

Hefner, Hugh M. *That Toddlin' Town: A Rowdy Burlesque of Chicago Manners and Morals*. Chicago: Chi Publishers, 1951.

Hefner, Hugh M., and Bill Zehme. *Hef's Little Black Book*. New York: HarperCollins, 2004.

Heilbronn, Lisa. "Breadwinners and Loafers: Images of Masculinity in 1950s Situation Comedy." *masculinities* 2 (Fall 1994): 60–70.

Heineman, Kenneth J. *Campus Wars: The Peace Movement at American State Universities in the Vietnam Era*. New York: New York University Press, 1993.

Heinze, Andrew R. "*Schizophrenia Americana:* Aliens, Alienists and the 'Personality Shift' of Twentieth-Century Culture." *American Quarterly* 55 (June 2003): 227–256.

Hine, Thomas. *Populuxe.* New York: Knopf, 1986.

Hirsch, Arnold. *Making the Second Ghetto: Race and Housing in Chicago, 1940–1960.* New York: Cambridge University Press, 1983.

Hirsch, Susan E. "No Victory at the Workplace: Women and Minorities at Pullman during World War II." In *The War in American Culture: Society and Consciousness during World War II,* edited by Lewis A. Erenberg and Susan E. Hirsch, 241–262. Chicago: University of Chicago Press, 1996.

Hite, Shere. *The Hite Report: A Nationwide Study of Female Sexuality.* New York: Dell, 1976.

Hoganson, Kristin L. *Fighting for American Manhood: How Gender Politics Provoked the Spanish-American and Philippine-American Wars.* New Haven: Yale University Press, 1998.

Hohman, Leslie B. "The Sex Lives of Unmarried Men." *American Journal of Sociology* 52 (May 1947): 501–507.

Holland, Hilda, ed. *Why Are You Single?* New York: Farrar Straus & Co., 1949.

Holliday, Don. *Bachelor Apartment.* New York: Nightstand Books, 1961.

Hollows, Joanne. "The Bachelor Dinner: Masculinity, Class and Cooking in Playboy, 1953–1961." *Continuum: Journal of Media & Cultural Studies* 16, no. 2 (2002): 143–155.

Honey, Maureen. *Creating Rosie the Riveter: Class, Gender and Propaganda during World War II.* Amherst: University of Massachusetts Press, 1984.

Horn, Patrice D., and Jack C. Horn. *Sex in the Office.* Reading, MA: Addison-Wesley, 1982.

Horowitz, Daniel. *Anxieties of Affluence: Critiques of American Consumer Culture, 1939–1979.* Amherst: University of Massachusetts Press, 2004.

Horowitz, Daniel. *Betty Friedan and the Making of the 'The Feminine Mystique': The American Left, the Cold War, and Modern Feminism.* Amherst: University of Massachusetts Press, 1998.

Horowitz, Daniel. *The Morality of Spending: Attitudes toward the Consumer Society in America, 1875–1940.* Baltimore: Johns Hopkins University Press, 1985.

Horton, Robert. *Billy Wilder: Interviews.* Jackson: University Press of Mississippi, 2001.

Hunt, Morton. *Sexual Behavior in the 1970s.* Chicago: Playboy Press, 1974.

Hunt, Morton. *The World of the Formerly Married.* New York: McGraw-Hill, 1966.

Hurley, Andrew. *Diners, Bowling Alleys, and Trailer Parks: Chasing the America Dream in the Postwar Consumer Culture.* New York: Basic, 2001.

Hutchins, Ken. "Sinatra's Fans: Discussions in Three Tenses: The Past, the Present, and the Future." In *Frank Sinatra and Popular Culture: Essays on an American Icon,* edited by Leonard Mustazza, 83–93. Westport, CT: Praeger, 1998.

Isenberg, Alison. *Downtown America: A History of the Place and the People Who Made It.* Chicago: University of Chicago Press, 2004.

Isserman, Maurice, and Michael Kazin. *America Divided: The Civil War of the 1960s.* New York: Oxford University Press, 2000.

Jackson, Kenneth T. *Crabgrass Frontier: The Suburbanization of the United States.* New York: Oxford University Press, 1985.

Jackson, Lesley. *Contemporary: Architecture and Interiors of the 1950s*. London: Phaidon, 1994.

Jackson, Lesley. *The New Look: Design in the Fifties*. New York: Thames and Hudson, 1991.

Jackson, Peter, and Kate Brooks. "Making Sense of Men's Lifestyle Magazines." *Environment and Planning D: Society and Space* 17 (1999): 353–368.

Jarvis, Christina S. *The Male Body at War: American Masculinity during World War II*. DeKalb: Northern Illinois University Press, 2004.

Johns, Michael. *Moment of Grace: The American City in the 1950s*. Berkeley: University of California Press, 2003.

Johnson, David K. *The Lavender Scare: The Cold War Persecution of Gays and Lesbians in the Federal Government*. Chicago: University of Chicago Press, 2004.

Jong, Erica. *Fear of Flying*. New York: Holt, Rinehart and Winston, 1973.

Kamen, Paula. *Her Way: Young Women Remake the Sexual Revolution*. New York: New York University Press, 2000.

Kasson, John. *Amusing the Million: Coney Island at the Turn of the Century*. New York: Hill and Wang, 1978.

Keats, John. *The Crack in the Picture Window*. Boston: Houghton Mifflin, 1956.

Kelly, Barbara M. *Expanding the American Dream: Building and Rebuilding Levittown*. Albany: State University of New York Press, 1993.

Kendrick, Walter. *The Secret Museum: Pornography in American Culture*. Berkeley: University of California Press, 1987.

Kesselman, Amy. *Fleeting Opportunities: Women Shipyard Workers in Portland and Vancouver during World War II and Reconversion*. Albany: State University of New York Press, 1990.

Kimmel, Michael. *Manhood in America: A Cultural History*. New York: The Free Press, 1996.

Kimmel, Michael. "Men's Responses to Feminism at the Turn of the Century." *Gender and Society* 1 (September 1987): 261–283.

Kinsey, Alfred C. *Sexual Behavior in the Human Female*. Philadelphia: Saunders, 1953.

Kinsey, Alfred C., Wardell B. Pomeroy, and Clyde E. Martin. *Sexual Behavior in the Human Male*. Philadelphia: Saunders, 1948.

Kirk, Andrew G. *Counterculture Green: The Whole Earth Catalog and American Environmentalism*. Lawrence: University Press of Kansas, 2007.

Klassen, Michael L., Cynthia R. Jasper, and Anne M. Schwartz. "Men and Women: Images of Their Relationships in Magazine Advertisements." *Journal of Advertising Research* (March/April 1993): 30–39.

Klein, Christina. *Cold War Orientalism: Asia in the Middlebrow Imagination, 1945–1961*. Berkeley: University of California Press, 2003.

Knupfer, Genevieve. "The Mental Health of the Unmarried." *American Journal of Psychiatry* 122 (February 1966): 841–851.

Komarovsky, Mirra. "Cultural Contradictions and Sex Roles." *American Journal of Sociology* 52 (November 1946): 184–189.

Komarovsky, Mirra. "Cultural Contradictions and Sex Roles: The Masculine Case." *American Journal of Sociology* 78 (January 1973): 873–884.

Koppes, Clayton R., and Gregory D. Black. *Hollywood Goes to War: How Politics, Profits, and Propaganda Shaped World War II Movies*. New York: Free Press, 1987.

Kozol, Wendy. *Life's America: Family and Nation in Postwar Photojournalism*. Philadelphia: Temple University Press, 1994.

Kuznick, Peter J., and James Gilbert, eds. *Rethinking Cold War Culture*. Washington, DC: Smithsonian Institution Press, 2001.

Kwolleck-Folland, Angel. *Engendering Business: Men and Women in the Corporate Office, 1870–1930*. Baltimore: Johns Hopkins University Press, 1994.

Lait, Jack, and Lee Mortimer. *Chicago Confidential!* New York: Crown, 1950.

Larson, Roy. "The Lowdown on the Upbeats." *Motive* (April 1960): 38–41.

Lasch, Christopher. *The Culture of Narcissism: American Life in an Age of Diminishing Expectations*. New York: Norton, 1979.

Lasch, Christopher. *Haven in a Heartless World: The Family Besieged*. New York: Basic, 1977.

Leach, William. *Land of Desire: Merchants, Power, and the Rise of a New American Culture*. New York: Vintage, 1993.

Lears, Jackson. *Fables of Abundance: A Cultural History of Advertising in America*. New York: Basic, 1994.

Lears, Jackson. "A Matter of Taste: Corporate Cultural Hegemony in a Mass-Consumption Society." In *Recasting America: Culture and Politics in the Age of Cold War*, edited by Lary May, 38–57. Chicago: University of Chicago Press, 1989.

Lears, T. J. Jackson. "From Salvation to Self-Realization: Advertising and the Therapeutic Roots of the Consumer Culture, 1900–1930." In *The Culture of Consumption: Critical Essays in American History, 1880–1980*, edited by Richard Wightman Fox and T. J. Jackson Lears, 3–38. New York: Pantheon, 1983.

Lears, T. J. Jackson. *No Place of Grace: Antimodernism and the Transformation of American Culture, 1880–1920*. New York: Pantheon, 1981.

Lebensburger, Myron M. *Selling Men's Apparel through Advertising*. New York: McGraw-Hill, 1939.

Lederer, Laura, ed. *Take Back the Night: Women on Pornography*. New York: Morrow, 1980.

Leslie B. Hohman, and Bertram Schaffner. "The Sex Lives of Unmarried Men." *American Journal of Sociology* 52 (May 1947): 501–507.

Levenstein, Harvey. *People of Plenty: A Social History of Eating in Modern America*. New York: Oxford University Press, 1993.

Levine, Lawrence W. "The Folklore of Industrial Society: Popular Culture and Its Audiences." *American Historical Review* 97 (December 1992): 1369–1399.

Levy, Ariel. *Female Chauvinist Pigs: Women and the Rise of Raunch Culture*. New York: Free Press, 2005.

Levy, Shawn. *Rat Pack Confidential: Frank, Dean, Sammy, Peter, Joey, and the Last Great Showbiz Party*. New York: Doubleday, 1998.

Lhamon, W. T., Jr. *Deliberate Speed: The Origins of a Culture Style in the American 1950s*. Washington, DC: Smithsonian Institution Press, 1990.

Lipsitz, George. *Rainbow at Midnight: Labor and Culture in the 1940s*. Urbana: University of Illinois Press, 1994.

Livingston, James. *Pragmatism and the Political Economy of Cultural Revolution*. Chapel Hill: University of North Carolina Press, 1994.

Lotchin, Roger W., ed. *The Way We Really Were: The Golden State in the Second Great War*. Urbana: University of Illinois Press, 2000.

Louis Harris and Associates. *The Playboy Report on American Men*. Playboy Enterprises, 1979.

Lownes, Victor. *The Day the Bunny Died*. Secaucus, NJ: Lyle Stuart, Inc., 1983.

Luckett, Moya. "Sensuous Women and Single Girls: Reclaiming the Female Body on 1960s Television." In *Swinging Single: Representing Sexuality in the 1960s*, edited by Hilary Radner and Moya Luckett, 277–298. Minneapolis: University of Minnesota Press, 1999.

Lundberg, Ferdinand, and Marynia F. Farnham. *Modern Woman: The Lost Sex*. New York: Grosset & Dunlap, 1947.

Lupton, Ellen. "Power Tool for the Dining Room: The Electric Carving Knife." In *STUD: Architectures of Masculinity*, edited by Joel Sanders, 42–53. New York: Princeton Architectural Press, 1996.

Lynes, Russell. *The Tastemakers*. New York: Grosset & Dunlap, 1949.

MacCannell, Dean. *The Tourist: A New Theory of the Leisure Class*. New York: Schocken, 1976.

MacKinnon, Catharine A. *Feminism Unmodified: Discourses on Life and Law*. Cambridge: Harvard University Press, 1987.

Mailer, Norman. *The Prisoner of Sex*. Boston: Little, Brown, 1971.

Malamuth, Neil M., and Robert D. McIlwraith. "Fantasies and Exposure to Sexually Explicit Magazines." *Communication Research* 15 (December 1988): 753–771.

Marc, David. *Comic Visions: Television Comedy and American Culture*. 2nd ed. Malden, MA: Blackwell, 1998.

Marchand, Roland. *Advertising the American Dream: Making Way for Modernity, 1920–1940*. Berkeley: University of California Press, 1985.

Marchand, Roland. "Visions of Classlessness, Quests for Dominion: American Popular Culture, 1945–1960." In *Reshaping America: Society and Institutions 1945–1960*, edited by Robert H. Bremner and Gary W. Reichard, 163–182. Columbus: Ohio State University Press, 1982.

Marcuse, Herbert. *One Dimensional Man: Studies in the Ideology of Advanced Industrial Society*. Boston: Beacon, 1964.

Marling, Karal Ann. *As Seen on TV: The Visual Culture of Everyday Life in the 1950s*. Cambridge: Harvard University Press, 1994.

Marsh, Margaret. *Suburban Lives*. New Brunswick, NJ: Rutgers University Press, 1990.

Marsh, Margaret. "Suburban Men and Masculine Domesticity, 1870–1915." *American Quarterly* 40 (June 1988): 165–86.

Marshe, Surrey, with Robert A. Liston. *The Girl in the Centerfold: The Uninhibited Memoirs of Miss January*. New York: Delacorte, 1969.

Martin, Kay. *The Bachelor Girl*. New York: Macfadden, 1962.

Matacin, Mala L., and Jerry M. Burger. "A Content Analysis of Sexual Themes in *Playboy* Cartoons." *Sex Roles* 17, nos. 3/4 (1987): 179–187.

Matthaei, Julie A. *An Economic History of Women in America*. New York: Schocken, 1982.

Matthews, Glenna. *"Just a Housewife": The Rise and Fall of Domesticity in America*. New York: Oxford University Press, 1987.

May, Elaine Tyler. *Barren in the Promised Land: Childless Americans and the Pursuit of Happiness*. New York: Basic, 1995.

May, Elaine Tyler. *Homeward Bound: American Families in the Cold War Era*. New York: Basic, 1988.

May, Lary. *The Big Tomorrow: Hollywood and the Politics of the American Way*. Chicago: University of Chicago Press, 2000.

May, Lary, ed. *Recasting America: Culture and Politics in the Age of Cold War*. Chicago: University of Chicago Press, 1989.

May, Lary. *Screening out the Past: The Birth of Mass Culture and the Motion Picture Industry*. New York: Oxford University Press, 1980.

McEnaney, Laura. "Nightmares on Elm Street: Demobilizing in Chicago, 1945–1953." *Journal of American History* 92 (March 2006): 1265–1291.

McGirr, Lisa. *Suburban Warriors: The Origins of the New American Right*. Princeton: Princeton University Press, 2002.

McGovern, Charles F. *Sold American: Consumption and Citizenship, 1890–1945*. Chapel Hill: University of North Carolina Press, 2006.

MacKinnon, Catharine, and Andrea Dworkin. *In Harm's Way: The Pornography Civil Rights Hearings*. Cambridge: Harvard University Press, 1997.

McNeil, Alex. *Total Television: The Comprehensive Guide to Programming from 1948 to the Present*. New York: Penguin, 1996.

McPartland, John. *No Down Payment*. New York: Simon & Schuster, 1957.

Merck, Mandy, and Barbara Creed, eds. *The Sexual Subject: A Screen Reader in Sexuality*. London: Routledge, 1992.

Merrill, Hugh. *Esky: The Early Years at Esquire*. New Brunswick, NJ: Rutgers University Press, 1995.

Meyer, Donald. *The Positive Thinkers: A Study of the American Quest for Health, Wealth and Personal Power from Mary Baker Eddy to Norman Vincent Peale*. Garden City, NY: Doubleday, 1965.

Meyer, Richard. "Rock Hudson's Body." In *Inside/Out: Lesbian Theories, Gay Theories*, edited by Diana Fuss, 259–288. New York: Routledge, 1991.

Meyerowitz, Joanne, ed. *Not June Cleaver: Women and Gender in Postwar America*. Philadelphia: Temple University Press, 1994.

Meyerowitz, Joanne J. *Women Adrift: Independent Wage Earners in Chicago, 1880–1930*. Chicago: University of Chicago Press, 1988.

Meyerowitz, Joanne. "Women, Cheesecake, and Borderline Material: Responses to Girlie Pictures in the Mid-Twentieth-Century U.S." *Women's History* 8 (Fall 1996): 9–35.

Michals, Debra. "From 'Consciousness Expansion' to 'Consciousness Raising': Feminism and the Countercultural Politics of the Self." In *Imagine Nation: The American Counterculture of the 1960s and '70s*, edited by Peter Braunstein and Michael William Doyle, 41–68. New York: Routledge, 2002.

Miles, Mildred Lynn. *Index to Playboy: Belles-Lettres, Articles, and Humor, Dec. 1953–Dec. 1969*. Metuchen, NJ: Scarecrow Press, 1970.

Milkman, Ruth. *Gender at Work: The Dynamics of Job Segregation by Sex during World War II*. Urbana: University of Illinois Press, 1987.

Miller, D. A. "Anal *Rope*." In *Inside/Out: Lesbian Theories, Gay Theories*, edited by Diana Fuss, 119–141. New York: Routledge, 1991.

Miller, James. *Democracy Is in the Streets: From Port Huron to the Siege of Chicago*. Cambridge: Harvard University Press, 1994.

Miller, Russell. *Bunny: The Real Story of Playboy*. New York: Holt, Rinehart and Winston, 1984.

Mills, C. Wright. *White Collar: The American Middle Classes*. New York: Oxford University Press, 1951.

Mintz, Steven, and Susan Kellogg. *Domestic Revolutions: A Social History of American Family Life*. New York: Free Press, 1988.

Moehring, Eugene P. *Resort City in the Sunbelt: Las Vegas, 1930–2000*. Reno: University of Nevada Press, 2000.

Mohl, Raymond A., ed. *Searching for the Sunbelt: Historical Perspectives on a Region*. Knoxville: University of Tennessee Press, 1990.

Morawski, J. G. "The Measurement of Masculinity and Femininity: Engendering Categorical Realities." *Journal of Personality* 53 (June 1985): 196–223.

Morgan, Robin, ed. *Sisterhood Is Powerful: An Anthology of Writings from the Women's Liberation Movement*. New York: Random House, 1970.

Moskowitz, Eva. "'It's Good to Blow Your Top': Women's Magazines and a Discourse of Discontent, 1945–1965." *Journal of Women's History* 8 (Fall 1996): 66–98.

Mulvey, Laura. "Visual Pleasure and Narrative Cinema." In *Visual and Other Pleasures*. Bloomington: Indiana University Press, 1989.

Mustazza, Leonard, ed. *Frank Sinatra and Popular Culture: Essays on an American Icon*. Westport, CT: Praeger, 1998.

Nadel, Alan. *Containment Culture: American Narratives, Postmodernism, and the Atomic Age*. Durham, NC: Duke University Press, 1995.

Neuhaus, Jessamyn. *Manly Meals and Mom's Home Cooking: Cookbooks and Gender in Modern America*. Baltimore: Johns Hopkins University Press, 2003.

Newton, Judith. *From Panthers to Promise Keepers*. Rowman & Littlefield, 2005.

Orben, Bob, ed. *Dick Gregory: From the Back of the Bus*. New York: Dutton, 1962.

Osgerby, Bill. "The Bachelor Pad as Cultural Icon: Masculinity, Consumption, and Interior Design in American Men's Magazines, 1930–1965." *Journal of Design History* 18, no. 1 (2005): 99–113.

Osgerby, Bill. *Playboys in Paradise: Masculinity, Youth and Leisure-style in Modern America*. Oxford: Berg, 2001.

Ouellette, Laurie. "Inventing the Cosmo Girl: Class Identity and Girl-Style American Dreams." *Media, Culture & Society* 21, no. 3 (1999): 359–383.

Packard, Vance. *The Hidden Persuaders*. New York: David McKay Company, Inc, 1957.

Packard, Vance. *The Status Seekers: An Exploration of Class Behavior in America and the Hidden Barriers That Affect You, Your Community, Your Future*. New York: David McKay Company, Inc., 1959.

Panish, Jon. *The Color of Jazz: Race and Representation in Postwar American Culture.* Jackson: University Press of Mississippi, 1997.

Patterson, James T. *Grand Expectations: The United States, 1945–1974.* New York: Oxford University Press, 1996.

Peck, Abe. *Uncovering the Sixties: The Life & Times of the Underground Press.* New York: Pantheon, 1985.

Peiss, Kathy. *Cheap Amusements: Working Women and Leisure in Turn of the Century New York.* Philadelphia: Temple University Press, 1986.

Peiss, Kathy. *Hope in a Jar: The Making of America's Beauty Culture.* New York: Metropolitan, 1998.

Pells, Richard. *The Liberal Mind in a Conservative Age: American Intellectuals in the 1940s and 1950s.* New York: Harper and Row, 1985.

Pendergast, Thomas David. "Consuming Men: Masculinity, Race, and American Magazines, 1900–1950." PhD diss., Purdue University, 1998.

Pendergast, Tom. *Creating the Modern Man: American Magazines and Consumer Culture, 1900–1950.* Columbia: University of Missouri Press, 2000.

Petersen, James R. *The Century of Sex: Playboy's History of the Sexual Revolution, 1900–1999.* New York: Grove, 1999.

Peterson, Theodore. *Magazines in the Twentieth Century.* Urbana: University of Illinois Press, 1964.

Peterson, Theodore. "Playboy and the Preachers." *Columbia Journalism Review* 6 (Spring 1966): 32–35.

Petkov, Steven, and Leonard Mustazza, eds. *The Frank Sinatra Reader.* New York: Oxford University Press, 1995.

Pitzulo, Carrie. "The Battle in Every Man's Bed: *Playboy* and the Fiery Feminists." *Journal of the History of Sexuality* 17 (May 2008): 259–289.

Polsky, Ned. *Hustlers, Beats, and Others.* Chicago: University of Chicago Press, 1967.

Popenoe, Paul Bowman. *Can This Marriage Be Saved?* New York: Macmillan, 1960.

Potter, David Morris. *People of Plenty: Economic Abundance and the American Character.* Chicago: University of Chicago, 1954.

Quirk, Lawrence J., and William Schoell. *The Rat Pack: Neon Nights with the Kings of Cool.* New York: Avon, 1998.

Radner, Hilary. "Introduction: Queering the Girl." In *Swinging Single: Representing Sexuality in the 1960s,* edited by Hilary Radner and Moya Luckett, 1–35. Minneapolis: University of Minnesota Press, 1999.

Radner, Hilary, and Moya Luckett, eds. *Swinging Single: Representing Sexuality in the 1960s.* Minneapolis: University of Minnesota Press, 1999.

Radway, Janice A. *Reading the Romance: Women, Patriarchy, and Popular Literature.* Chapel Hill: University of North Carolina Press, 1984.

Reagan, Leslie J. *When Abortion Was a Crime: Women, Medicine, and Law in the United States, 1867–1973.* Berkeley: University of California Press, 1997.

Reel, Guy. *The National Police Gazette and the Making of the Modern American Man, 1879–1906.* New York: Palgrave, 2006.

Reisman, Judith A. *Images of Children, Crime, and Violence in Playboy, Penthouse, and Hustler*. Arlington, VA: Institute for Media Education, 1989.

Rendell, Jane, Barbara Penner, and Lain Borden, eds. *Gender Space Architecture: An Interdisciplinary Introduction*. London: Routledge, 2000.

Report of the Select Committee on Current Pornographic Materials. Washington, DC: U.S. Government Printing Office, 1952.

Ries, Estelle H. *The Lonely Sex*. New York: Belmont, 1962.

Riesman, David. *The Lonely Crowd: A Study of the Changing American Character*. New Haven: Yale University Press, 1950, New Haven: Yale University Press, 1969.

Roberts, Mary Louise. "Gender, Consumption, and Commodity Culture." *American Historical Review* 103 (June 1998): 817–844.

Roeder, George. *The Censored War: American Visual Experience during World War II*. New Haven: Yale University Press, 1993.

Rogers, Kate Ellen. *The Modern House, U.S.A.: Its Design and Decoration*. New York: Harper & Row, 1962.

Rorabaugh, W. J. *Berkeley at War, the 1960s*. New York: Oxford University Press, 1989.

Rose, Lisle A. *The Cold War Comes to Main Street: America in 1950*. Lawrence: University of Kansas Press, 1999.

Rosen, Ruth. *The World Split Open: How the Modern Women's Movement Changed America*. New York: Penguin Books, 2000.

Rossinow, Douglas C. *Politics of Authenticity: Liberalism, Christianity, and the New Left in America*. New York: Columbia University Press, 1998.

Roszak, Theodore. *The Making of a Counter Culture: Reflections on the Technocratic Society and Its Youthful Opposition*. Garden City, NY: Anchor, 1969.

Rotundo, E. Anthony. *American Manhood: Transformations in Masculinity from the Revolution to the Modern Era*. New York: Basic, 1993.

Rubin, Joan Shelley. "Salvation as Self-Realization." *Reviews in American History* 20 (December 1992): 505–511.

Rupp, Leila. "The Survival of American Feminism: The Women's Movement in the Postwar Period." In *Reshaping America: Society and Institutions*, edited by Robert H. Bremner. Columbus: Ohio State University Press, 1982.

Ryan, Martin. "Portrait of Playboy." *Studies in Public Communication* 1 (1957): 11–21.

Saegert, Susan. "Masculine Cities and Feminine Suburbs: Polarized Ideas, Contradictory Realities." *Signs* 5 (Spring 1980): S96–S111.

Sale, Kirkpatrick. *SDS*. New York: Random House, 1973.

Saul, Scott. *Freedom Is, Freedom Ain't: Jazz and the Making of the Sixties*. Cambridge: Harvard University Press, 2003.

Scanlon, Jennifer. *Bad Girls Go Everywhere: The Life of Helen Gurley Brown*. New York: Oxford University Press, 2009.

Schneirov, Matthew. *The Dream of a New Social Order: Popular Magazines in America, 1893–1914*. New York: Columbia University Press, 1994.

Schulman, Bruce J. *The Seventies: The Great Shift in American Culture, Society, and Politics*. New York: Free Press, 2001.

Schuyler, David. *The New Urban Landscape: The Redefinition of Urban Form in Nine-teenth-Century America*. Baltimore: Johns Hopkins University Press, 1986.

Sconce, Jeffrey. "XXX: Love and Kisses from Charlie." In *Swinging Single: Representing Sexuality in the 1960s*, edited by Hilary Radner and Moya Luckett, 207–223. Minne-apolis: University of Minnesota Press, 1999.

Scott, Joan Wallach. *Gender and the Politics of History*. New York: Columbia University Press, 1988.

Scott, Joseph E., and Steven J. Cuvelier. "Sexual Violence in Playboy Magazine: A Longi-tudinal Content Analysis." *Journal of Sex Research* 23 (June 1986): 534–539.

Scott, Kathryn Lee. *The Bunny Years*. Los Angeles: Pomegranate, 1998.

Sedgwick, Eve Kosofsky. *Epistemology of the Closet*. London: Penguin, 1994.

Sexology Corporation. *Sex and the Unmarried Woman*. New York: Award, 1964.

Sharpe, William, and Leonard Wallock. "Bold New City or Built-Up 'Burb? Redefining Contemporary Suburbia." *American Quarterly* 46 (March 1994): 1–30.

Sies, Mary Corbin. "North American Suburbs, 1880–1950: Cultural and Social Reconsid-erations." *Journal of Urban History* 27 (March 2001): 318–319.

Sitkoff, Harvard. *The Struggle for Black Equality*. New York: Hill and Wang, 1993.

Small, Melvin. *Johnson, Nixon and the Doves*. New Brunswick, NJ: Rutgers University Press, 1988.

Small, Melvin, and William D. Hoover, eds. *Give Peace a Chance: Exploring the Vietnam Antiwar Movement*. Syracuse, NY: Syracuse University Press, 1992.

Smigel, Erwin O. "The Decline and Fall of the Double Standard." *Annals of the American Academy of Political and Social Science* 376 (March 1968): 6–17.

Smith, James F. "Bobby Sox and Blue Suede Shoes: Frank Sinatra and Elvis Presley as Teen Idols." In *Frank Sinatra and Popular Culture: Essays on an American Icon*, edited by Leonard Mustazza, 50–68. Westport, CT: Praeger, 1998.

Smith, Neil. "New City, New Frontier: The Lower East Side as Wild, Wild West." In *Varia-tions on a Theme Park: The New American City and the End of Public Space*, edited by Michael Sorkin, 61–83. New York: Hill and Wang, 1992.

Smith, Tom W. "Coming of Age in 21st Century America: Public Attitudes towards the Importance and Timing of Transitions to Adulthood." *GSS Topical Report No. 35*. Chicago: NORC, May 2003.

Solinger, Rickie. *Wake up Little Susie: Single Pregnancy and Race before Roe v. Wade*. New York: Routledge, 1992.

Sommers, Christina Hoff. *Who Stole Feminism? How Women Have Betrayed Women*. New York: Simon & Schuster, 1994.

Sorokin, Pitirim A. *The American Sex Revolution*. Boston: Porter Sargent, 1956.

Spain, Daphne. *Gendered Spaces*. Chapel Hill: University of North Carolina Press, 1992.

Spectorsky, A. C. *The Exurbanites*. Philadelphia: Lippincott, 1955.

Spigel, Lynn. *Make Room for TV: Television and the Family Ideal in Postwar America*. Chicago: University of Chicago Press, 1992.

Spigel, Lynn, and Denise Mann, eds. *Private Screenings: Television and the Female Con-sumer*. Minneapolis: University of Minnesota Press, 1992.

Steinem, Gloria. "The Myth of Masculine Mystique." In *Men and Masculinity*, edited by Joseph H. Pleck and Jack Sawyer, 134–139. Englewood Cliffs, NJ: Prentice-Hall, Inc., 1974.

Steinmann, Anne, and David J. Fox. *The Male Dilemma: How to Survive the Sexual Revolution*. New York: Jason Aronson, 1974.

Stilgoe, John. *Borderland: Origins of the American Suburb, 1820–1939*. New Haven: Yale University Press, 1988.

Strassen, Nadine. *Defending Pornography: Free Speech, Sex, and the Fight for Women's Rights*. New York: Scribner, 1995.

Strasser, Susan, Charles McGovern, and Matthias Judt, eds. *Getting and Spending: European and American Consumer Societies in the Twentieth Century*. Washington, DC: German Historical Institute, Cambridge University Press, 1998.

Strom, Sharon Hartman. *Beyond the Typewriter: Gender, Class and the Origins of Modern American Office Work, 1900–1930*. Urbana: University of Illinois Press, 1992.

Sugrue, Thomas J. *Origins of the Urban Crisis: Race and Inequality in Postwar Detroit*. Princeton: Princeton University Press, 1996.

Summers, Martin. *Manliness and Its Discontents: The Black Middle Class and the Transformation of Masculinity, 1900–1930*. Chapel Hill: University of North Carolina Press, 2004.

Susman, Warren. *Culture as History: The Transformation of American Society in the Twentieth Century*. Washington, DC: Smithsonian Institution Press, 2003.

Susman, Warren, with the assistance of Edward Griffen. "Did Success Spoil the United States?" In *Recasting America: Culture and Politics in the Age of Cold War*, edited by Lary May, 19–37. Chicago: University of Chicago, 1989.

Talese, Gay. *Thy Neighbor's Wife*. Garden City, NY: Doubleday, 1980.

Taylor, Ella. *Prime Time Families: Television and Culture in Postwar America*. Berkeley: University of California Press, 1989.

Tebbel, John, and Mary Ellen Zuckerman. *The Magazine in America, 1741–1990*. New York: Oxford University Press, 1991.

Tester, Keith. *The Flâneur*. London: Routledge, 1994.

The Sixth New Year: A Resolution. Chicago: Esquire, 1939.

The Third New Year: An Etude in the Key of Frankness. Chicago: Esquire, 1935.

Thom, Mary. *Inside Ms.: 25 Years of the Magazine and the Feminist Movement*. New York: Henry Holt, 1997.

Tichi, Cecelia. *Electronic Hearth: Creating an American Television Culture*. New York: Oxford University Press, 1991.

Tischler, Barbara L., ed. *Sights on the Sixties*. New Brunswick, NJ: Rutgers University Press, 1992.

Tobias, Sheila. *Faces of Feminism: An Activist's Reflections on the Women's Movement*. Boulder, CO: Westview, 1997.

Toossi, Mitra. "A Century of Change: The U.S. Labor Force, 1950–2050." *Monthly Labor Review* (May 2002): 18–24.

Trachtenberg, Alan. *The Incorporation of America: Culture and Society in the Gilded Age.* New York: Hill and Wang, 1982.

Traister, Bryce. "Academic Viagra: The Rise of American Masculinity Studies." *American Quarterly* 52 (June 2000): 274–304.

Troy, Gil. *Morning in America: How Ronald Reagan Invented the 1980s.* Princeton: Princeton University Press, 2005.

Turbin, Carole. "Fashioning the American Man: The Arrow Collar Man, 1907–1931." *Gender and History* 14 (November 2002): 470–491.

Tuttle, William M., Jr. *"Daddy's Gone to War": The Second World War in the Lives of America's Children.* New York: Oxford University Press, 1993.

Ullman, Sharon R. *Sex Seen: The Emergence of Modern Sexuality in America.* Berkeley: University of California Press, 1997.

U.S. Commission on Obscenity and Pornography. *Report of the Commission on Obscenity and Pornography.* Washington, DC: U.S. Government Printing Office, 1970.

U.S. Department of Commerce, Bureau of the Census. *Historical Statistics of the United States, Colonial Times to 1970.* Washington, DC: U.S. Government Printing Office, 1975.

Urry, John. *The Tourist Gaze: Leisure and Travel in Contemporary Societies.* London: Sage, 1990.

Van Deburg, William L. *New Day in Babylon: The Black Power Movement and American Culture, 1965–1975.* Chicago: University of Chicago Press, 1992.

Van Evera, Jean. *How to Be Happy while Single.* Philadelphia: Lippincott, 1949.

"Viewpoints: What Do You Think of *Playboy?*" *Medical Aspects of Human Sexuality* 5 (July 1971): 11–21.

Votolato, Gregory. *American Design in the Twentieth Century: Personality and Performance.* Manchester: Manchester University Press, 1998.

Wagner, George. "The Lair of the Bachelor." In *Architecture and Feminism,* edited by Debra Coleman, Elizabeth Danze, and Carol Henderson, 183–219. New York: Princeton Architectural Press, 1996.

Walsh, Frank. *Sin and Censorship: The Catholic Church and the Motion Picture Industry.* New Haven: Yale University Press, 1996.

Walters, Lee. *Bachelor Husband.* Fresno, CA: Saber, 1960.

Watts, Steven. *Mr. Playboy: Hugh Hefner and the American Dream.* New York: Wiley, 2008.

Weisbrot, Robert. *Freedom Bound: A History of the American Civil Rights Movement.* New York: Norton, 1990.

Weiss, Jessica. *To Have and to Hold: Marriage, the Baby Boom, and Social Change.* Chicago: University of Chicago Press, 2000.

Weiss, Nancy P. "Mother, the Invention of Necessity: Dr. Benjamin Spock's *Baby and Childcare.*" *American Quarterly* 29 (Winter 1977): 519–546.

Weyr, Thomas. *Reaching for Paradise: The Playboy Vision of America.* New York: Times Books, 1978.

Wharton, Annabel Jane. *Building the Cold War: Hilton International Hotels and Modern Architecture.* Chicago: University of Chicago Press, 2001.

White, Kevin. *The First Sexual Revolution: The Emergence of Male Heterosexuality in Modern America.* New York: New York University Press, 1993.

Whitfield, Stephen J. *The Culture of the Cold War.* Baltimore: Johns Hopkins University Press, 1996.

Whitfield, Stephen J. *A Death in the Delta: The Story of Emmett Till.* Baltimore: Johns Hopkins University Press, 1991.

Whyte, William H., Jr. *The Organization Man.* New York: Simon & Schuster, 1956.

Wilson, Sloan. *The Man in the Gray Flannel Suit.* New York: Pocket Books, 1955; reprint, New York: Four Walls Eight Windows, 2002.

Winch, Robert F. "Courtship in College Women." *American Journal of Sociology* 55 (November 1949): 269–278.

Winick, Charles. "The Beige Epoch: Depolarization of Sex Roles in America." *Annals of the American Academy of Political and Social Science* 376 (March 1968): 18–24.

Wolfe, Tom. "King of the Status Dropouts." In *The Pump-House Gang.* New York: Farrar, Straus & Giroux, 1968.

Wolfe, Tom. *Mauve Gloves and Madmen, Clutter & Vine.* New York: Farrar, Straus & Giroux, 1976.

Wolfenstein, Martha. "Fun Morality: An Analysis of Recent American Child-Training Literature." In *Childhood in Contemporary Cultures,* edited by Margaret Mead and Martha Wolfenstein, 168–178. Chicago: University of Chicago Press, 1955.

Wright, Gwendolyn. *Building the Dream: A Social History of Housing in America.* New York: Pantheon, 1981.

Wylie, Philip. *Generation of Vipers.* New York: Farrar & Rinehart, 1942.

Wylie, Philip. *Sons and Daughters of Mom.* Garden City, NY: Doubleday, 1971.

Yates, Richard. *Revolutionary Road.* Boston: Little, Brown, 1961; reprint, Westport, CT: Greenwood, 1971.

Zarlengo, Kristina. "Civilian Threat, the Suburban Citadel, and Atomic Age American Women." *Signs* 24 (Summer 1999): 925–958.

Zuckerman, Michael. "Dr. Spock: The Confidence Man." In *The Family in History,* edited by Charles E. Rosenberg, 179–207. Philadelphia: University of Pennsylvania, 1975.

Zunz, Olivier. *Making America Corporate, 1870–1920.* Chicago: University of Chicago Press, 1990.

INDEX